Assessment
The Special Educator's Role

Cheri Hoy Cheri Hoy is head of the Department of Special Education at the University of Georgia. She has also directed the department's Child and Adolescent Diagnostic Clinic. She teaches courses in assessment, learning disabilities, and working with families. Her research in assessment and in adults with learning disabilities has been published in many journals. Prior to moving into university teaching and research, she was employed as a public school teacher for a number of years. Dr. Hoy received her bachelor of science degree from Illinois State University, her master's degree in education from the University of Illinois and her Ph.D. from Northwestern University.

Noel Gregg Noel Gregg is director of The University of Georgia Learning Disabilities Center and a professor in the Department of Special Education. She has published numerous refereed articles from her empirical research as well as instructional articles pertaining to the assessment and characteristics of individuals with learning disabilities. In addition, she has a book in press that provides an integration of neurolinguistic and social linguistic theory in better understanding written language disorders. Dr. Gregg received her bachelor of science from James Madison University, her master's degree in education from the University of Virginia and her Ph.D. from Northwestern University.

Assessment
The Special Educator's Role

Cheri Hoy
University of Georgia

Noel Gregg
University of Georgia

Brooks/Cole Publishing Company
Pacific Grove, California

To all the individuals with disabilities with whom we have worked over the years. They have taught us the importance of looking past scores to see the potential of the individual. Their continued request to maintain functional and ecologically sound assessment that can have a meaningful impact on their lives has directed our professional development.

I(T)P ™
The trademark ITP is used under license.

Brooks/Cole Publishing Company
A Division of Wadsworth, Inc.
© 1994 by Wadsworth, Inc., Belmont, California 94002. All rights reserved. No part of this book may be reproduced, stored in a retrieval system, or transcribed, in any form or by any means—electronic, mechanical, photocopying, recording, or otherwise—without the prior written permission of the publisher, Brooks/Cole Publishing Company, Pacific Grove, California 93950, a division of Wadsworth, Inc.

Printed in the United States of America
10 9 8 7 6 5 4 3 2 1

Library of Congress Cataloging-in-Publication Data
Hoy, Cheri, [date]
    Assessment : the special educator's role / Cheri Hoy, Noel Gregg.
        p.   cm.
    Includes bibliographical references (p.) and index.
    ISBN 0-534-21132-1
    1. Educational tests and measurements—United States.   2. Special
education—United States.   I. Gregg, Noel.   II. Title.
    LB3051.H847   1993
    371.2'6—dc20   93-22949
                                                                  CIP

Sponsoring Editor: *Vicki Knight*
Marketing Representative: *Susan Windsor*
Editorial Assistant: *Lauri Banks-Wothe*
Production Editor: *Nancy L. Shammas*
Manuscript Editor: *Kay Mikel*
Permissions Editor: *Lillian Campobasso*
Production Assistant: *Chelsea Haga*
Indexer: *Do Mi Stauber*
Cover and Interior Design: *Katherine Minerva*
Cover Illustration: *Katherine Minerva*
Photo Coordinator: *Diana Mara Henry*
Art Coordinator: *Lisa Torri*
Interior Illustration: *Diphrent Strokes*
Typesetting: *Weimer Graphics*
Printing and Binding: *Arcata Graphics*

Excerpts reprinted by permission of Christopher M. Lee and Rosemary F. Jackson:
Faking It: A Look into the Mind of a Creative Learner (Boynton/Cook Publishers, Inc., Portsmouth, NH, 1992).

P R E F A C E

Educational assessment is a dynamic process grounded in theory and inseparable from instruction. Formal and informal classroom-based assessment is the foundation on which individualized assessment is built. Professionals conducting educational assessments must understand how classroom-based and individualized assessments are linked to theory and instruction. They must understand how theory, assessment, and instruction inform each other. This text is an introduction to those linkages.

Assessment: The Special Educator's Role is intended for use in a first course on the assessment process. It is written with the assumption that the user has not yet had experience in a classroom setting. Themes that cut across the chapters include the interrelationship between theory, assessment, and instruction; the need to be systematic in data gathering and record keeping; and the need to have multiple sources of verification of specific strengths and weaknesses that are manifested in actual classroom settings.

The chapters are organized into four parts. Part One, Overview, provides an introduction to the various purposes of assessment, where to obtain information and how to minimize the bias and error inherently present in the assessment process. Part Two, Assessing Foundations, provides the student with an introduction to basic cognitive and affective components of learning and how these are assessed. This section also addresses sensory, health, and addictive disorders that may be the primary disability or may co-occur with other conditions. Part Three, Assessing Skills, focuses on adaptive behavior, oral language, reading, written language, mathematics, and issues of transition. Each chapter in this section includes a brief introduction to the area, a discussion of the developmental progression of the skill area, concerns expressed by classroom teachers, types of assessment tools specific to the area, cultural issues that apply to the area, and steps in the assessment process. Part Four, Using Results, provides information on how the special educator can use assessment data to make decisions on program planning. Appendixes at the end of the text include addresses of test publishers, a test review form, two background information forms, and two case studies.

Each chapter begins with a list of key terms to alert the reader to important concepts. The chapters close with a list of the most important points from each section. The purpose of this format is to provide a structure to help the reader preview and review key concepts. We felt this was especially important in an introductory text. The purpose of this text is to highlight the process of assessment rather than to provide a critique of individual standardized assessment tools. The focus is on the integration of dynamic, curriculum-based and norm-referenced data for diagnostic decisions and program planning.

Acknowledgments

We would like to express our appreciation to the many individuals who have supported the development of this text. Reviewers of the manuscript who offered helpful advice included: Mary T. Brownell, University of Florida, Gainesville; J'Anne D. Ellsworth, Northern Arizona University; Nancy Glomb, Southern Utah University; Mary Ross Moran, the University of Kansas Medical Center; William R. Reid, University of Florida, Gainesville; Regina Sapona, University of Cincinnati; and Gregory J. Williams, Pacific Lutheran University. We thank each of them. We also appreciate the time and attention of Vicki Knight, our editor, Nancy Shammas, our production editor, and Carline Haga and Lillian Campobasso, who helped obtain the necessary permissions to reprint material. Their patience and positive support throughout the development of this text was invaluable. We would also like to thank the many publishers, agencies, and individuals who permitted us to reprint their work.

Our thanks also go to Angela Callaway and Denise Ruggiere. Each was a calming influence in our attempts to meet deadlines. They typed and retyped chapters and charts with good humor and encouragement.

The following graduate students helped with references and initial feedback on the chapters and deserve special recognition: Patti Davidson, Kate Finch, Susan Galis, JoAnn Grayson, Margo Habiger, Sue Koscinski, Judy Marchese, Jane Mitchell, and Betty Jane Pollock. Particular thanks go to Margo Habiger for her input in development of the oral language chapter.

We would also like to specifically thank Rosemary Jackson and Chris Lee for use of their poignant quotes. In addition, we would like to thank Rosemary for her input in the transition chapter.

Cheri Hoy
Noel Gregg

BRIEF CONTENTS

C O N T E N T S

PART THREE   Assessing Skills   235

8   *Assessing Adaptive Behavior   236*

9   *Assessing Oral Language   260*

P A R T   O N E

Overview

C H A P T E R

Defining Assessment

Key Terms

Assessment
Collaborative consultation
Due process
Eligibility
Individualized educational
   program (IEP)

Legislation
Litigation
Modification
Performance range

Placement
Portfolio assessment
Zone of proximal develop-
   ment (ZPD)

Every individual participates in some type of assessment each day, be it formal or informal. The process is identical despite the purpose of the evaluation. This process involves the systematic collection, analysis, and integration of information. Whether the decision revolves around the fact that your car needs a new battery or a student requires specific reading instruction, the process remains the same. The main goal of the educational assessment process is to interpret the learning patterns of students. Variations in how individuals learn should not be judged as strong or weak, but different. Identifying these differences in learning patterns can facilitate development of effective instructional strategies. The special educator must be cognizant of a student's most efficient means of taking in information and the most efficacious means of displaying knowledge. This information can then be used for instructional planning. Teachers not taking the time to carefully assess the variation within a student's profile of learning present haphazard instructional goals leading to inappropriate if not inaccurate teaching objectives. Assessment for instructional planning helps teachers focus on more precise and efficient teaching strategies. A systematic approach is critical to the ongoing assessment process. Such a methodical approach ensures that important information is not overlooked.

Assessment is often viewed as a set of formal tasks administered before instruction is begun. Such a view is very narrow and creates a mind-set that encourages a teacher to ignore many valuable clues useful for instructional planning. A more productive approach is to view assessment as an ongoing process that continually adds new information about the variation within a student's profile of learning. This new information is necessary to enable modification of teaching strategies to enhance learning. This view of assessment as an ongoing process is more flexible and fluid than the more traditional, lockstep approach of test–placement–teach. Using the perspective that assessment is an ongoing process makes many additional sources of information available to the special educator. The kinds of difficulties faced by the student require a teacher to use many different formal and informal measures throughout instruction, and then to supplement these with observation and interview information. *Assessment* is a way of thinking about the processes of learning. It is not a stage that occurs prior to instruction but rather is an ongoing analysis of information that enhances the effectiveness of teaching.

Table 1-1 Purposes of assessment

Purpose of Assessment	Large Group	Small Group	Individual
Placement			
Norm-Referenced	*	*	*
Curriculum-Based			
Criterion-Referenced		*	*
Dynamic			*
Instruction			
Norm-Referenced	*	*	*
Curriculum-Based		*	*
Criterion-Referenced	*	*	*
Dynamic			*
Communication/Reporting			
Norm-Referenced	*	*	*
Curriculum-Based		*	*
Criterion-Referenced	*	*	*
Dynamic			*

Purposes of Assessment

Assessment of students with special needs has traditionally been used to identify student characteristics, determine appropriate placement of students, evaluate student progress, and predict future academic and nonacademic needs of student populations. Information gathered during this assessment process has been used primarily for the purposes of placement, instruction, and reporting. Although the same data can be used for different purposes, the intended use often influences measurement choice and evaluation strategies. In addition, the assessment tools used for placement or instruction of large numbers of students (that is, the entire seventh grade) are very different from those chosen for deciding upon eligibility of a student for special education (see Table 1-1). Unfortunately, the purpose of the assessment has often led evaluators to ignore the other uses of this data. Quite often information gathered for the purpose of a student's eligibility for special education has been primarily norm-referenced data with very little application to direct classroom instruction. Special educators working with students in the classroom have often collected curriculum-based or criterion-referenced data that could not be used when comparing a student's functional level to that of other individuals for the purpose of identification and placement. The assessment process can be integrated to incorporate norm-referenced, curriculum-based, criterion-referenced, and dynamic strategies when assessment is identified as an ongoing process where placement, instruction, and reporting are all seen as integral to accurate planning for students.

Placement

Placement is a term that is used very differently in special education from its use in regular education. In regular education, *placement* refers to the means by which a student is identified for a particular class (seventh grade) or instruction (reading)

Decisions about placing a student in special education are made by a team of educators, psychologists, and parents. The decision is based on all assessment data including attempted modifications.   *Source:* © Gail Meese/Meese Photo Research

group. Group achievement measures are the typical assessment measurement used for making such decisions. In special education, the term *placement* is used very differently. Legislation (PL 101–476) influences the placement decisions in special education by mandating free appropriate education in the least restrictive environment, an individualized program of instruction, and the use of nondiscriminatory assessment in the placement of a student in a special education program. Placement in a special education program could mean the change of a student's current placement (regular education), resulting in possible separation from an individual's peers. Such decisions for special education placement are based on diagnostic information gathered during an assessment of a student using measurement tools designed for the diagnosis of individual patterns rather than group performance.

The primary considerations in placement decisions, be they regular or special education, focus on the most effective means of meeting student(s') needs. Problems arise when preset and narrow sets of solutions are used as the guide for decision making. Assessment measures should be varied and broad enough not to oversimplify or overidentify problems. For instance, if the intelligence test is used as the *primary means* of measuring potential, many students with special needs could be discriminated against due to specific processing or language deficits (see chapters 6 and 9). Intelligence measures can also bias thinking of culturally different students (see chapter 5). Appropriate assessment should include interpretation of broad cognitive, oral language, and basic learning abilities, as well as social/emotional, achievement, and interest/style measures prior to any placement decision.

Instructional options appropriate for the learning profile of a student are part of the placement decision. Data gathered during an assessment incorporate both long- and short-term educational needs. Placement decisions are not limited to the availability of instructional programs within a school district; the needs of the individual direct placement decisions. Assessment strategies that incorporate norm-referenced, criterion-referenced, curriculum-based, and dynamic assessment help professionals identify creative *modifications* of existing placements or select alternative placements (self-contained classrooms or special schools). The radical decision to completely change a student's placement is made only after modifications of the current program are attempted and have failed. Types of modifications that could be tried in the classroom before any placement change include such activities as untimed tests, diverse test formats, use of a computer to write, or structuring the classroom environment to downplay distracting factors. Information gathered during an assessment should help the special educator select instructional interventions.

Instruction

Assessment of students for instructional purposes is a concern of most teachers. Instructional assessment is incorporated into curricula across grade levels and ability groupings. Teachers recognize that assessment helps make their teaching more focused and thus more likely to succeed. The goal of assessment for instruction is the teaching activity. Therefore, the assessment activities must be quick, focused, and easy to interpret. Success of assessment for instruction rests on more than a teacher's knowledge of tests. While it is important for a teacher to have an excellent knowledge of the strengths and weaknesses of particular test measures and techniques, it is equally important that the teacher have a clear plan on how to collect the specific data needed, understand how to interpret this data, have a systematic means of recording the information, and continue to update the evaluation process on an ongoing basis. Unfortunately, it is not uncommon for placement data or out-dated instructional assessments to be used in current decision making for a student.

Assessment cannot be separated from teaching itself. Monitoring the effectiveness of a skill, technique, or format should parallel every step of instruction. This is often done by daily quizzes, workbook summary activities, criterion-based pre- and post-tests, and observation of student performance. Curriculum-based, criterion-referenced, and dynamic assessment techniques have particular strengths in helping professionals monitor the effectiveness of teaching. These different types of assessment will be described in detail in chapter 2.

The special educator must be very careful not to fall into the trap of using limited assessment data to answer the "why" of a student's poor performance rather than "how" they performed on a task. The "why" of the problems encountered by many students with special needs requires extensive diagnostic assessment and interpretation by a team of professionals, each bringing a different perspective to the decision. Unfortunately, professionals are often quick to respond to a student's poor performance on a task with a "why" based on a limited amount of data that is not directly translated to instruction. For instance, a student's poor performance on an intelligence measure might be interpreted as low cognitive ability when in reality a significant language deficit or cultural difference could be the problem. A student's poor performance in a science class might be attributed to a reading problem when the difficulty could be interest, motivation, or the time of day. Focusing on the "how" is usually more important to the teacher unless a "why" solution can make a difference in student performance.

A special educator who focuses only on the "why" can limit a student's potential if a clear assessment of the current needs of the student are not considered during instructional planning. For instance, a middle school student with significant reading or

A teacher and student review the progress reflected in the student's portfolio with his father.
Source: © Jeffrey Dunn Studios

writing problems might be having difficulty in a history class. If the special educator goes back to the "why" of the student's problem, remediation of reading and writing would be the primary emphasis of the instructional program. Such a student, however, might be better helped by identifying strategies to circumvent problem areas in history, allowing the student to continue to receive the content information in the regular class. In this case the student might be helped by having his books on tape, being allowed extended time during test taking, having a note taker, and using a computer for assignments and evaluations. Remedial help in reading and writing strategies might be long-term goals that could be incorporated in the student's English class. Such decisions should be made as the result of careful assessment of a student's current and long-term needs for obtaining his or her true potential.

Communication

Assessment also has the purpose of communicating information to students, parents, teachers, and other professionals. The special educator must give careful consideration to the specific information provided and the format of presenting the diagnostic information. Far too much diagnostic information is conveyed to students, parents, and regular educators using jargon and vague interpretations that result in development of a mystique around the diagnostic process. Such an approach leads to a lack of understanding and, more harmful, a lack of trust in the professionals attempting to help the student.

Norm-referenced tests help compare a student's profile to that of his or her peers. Measures are often reported in terms of standard scores (see chapter 3). It is helpful to describe what standard scores are and to provide a visual explanation of the variation across a student's profile. Curriculum-based and criterion-referenced skill levels can also be charted for others interested in the student's performance. Work samples, classroom tests, and observations help support test findings and are often more understandable to the layperson. Information can be conveyed by a written report or by conferences.

The student being tested should be the recipient of the assessment findings. Feedback during classroom instruction by grades, a smile, or any type of reinforcement is a common means of communicating a student's success in the classroom. Many students with special needs are placed in special education with little understanding of the assessment data that supports that placement. It is the responsibility of the special educator to help communicate placement and instructional assessment in terms that the student with special needs can understand. In addition, an important component of the assessment process for both placement and instructional purposes should be incorporation of a student's own evaluation of his or her ability, interests, feelings, and aspirations. Such self-exploration is useful in encouraging a student to take responsibility for his or her own decisions.

Information from assessment is also shared with other professionals for the purpose of placement decisions and instructional changes. Precise, clear, and objective observations as well as formal and informal data can be shared during decision-making meetings. Again, information should be presented to professionals in the vocabulary they understand and should be followed by clear examples. It is the responsibility of the special educator to be prepared and well organized, to provide clear and accurate records, and to be current about assessment and curriculum issues surrounding students with special needs.

The presentation of a portfolio containing information pertaining to a student's performance is an extremely effective communication tool. This is called portfolio assessment. Educational Testing Service and Harvard University are working jointly on a project using portfolios for large-scale group assessment in the arts and humanities (Wolf, 1989). The special educator can also use portfolios as an effective communication tool for demonstrating student progress.

Portfolio assessment is an extension of the old work folder concept popular with many special educators. Unlike the work folder concept, which mainly becomes a storage folder, the portfolio becomes the assessment measure. By preselecting student performance, both quantitative and qualitative, and providing an analysis of this information, the portfolio summarizes student progress over a period of time and tasks. Portfolio assessment allows for the use of items such as audio/video cassettes, journals, art work, and other creative products that might demonstrate a student's understanding of a concept, and safeguard that reading, writing, and timed measures are not the only way to measure competency. As Valencia (1990) stated, portfolio assessment "is an expanded definition of assessment in which a wide variety of indicators of learning are gathered across many situations before, during, and after instruction" (p. 340). One of the most beneficial aspects of portfolio assessment is the opportunity it provides the special educator in helping guide the student with special needs toward self-assessment (Irwin, 1991). The portfolio should be open and available to the student so that the student can evaluate his or her own progress as well as provide additional data that will help evaluate the student's competencies.

Principles of the Assessment Process

All teachers assess student performance on a daily basis through administration of formal and informal measures. The important component is not the test measures but the systematic collection, recording, and translating of student performance. Unfortunately, many teachers do not know what information to collect, how to integrate the vast amount of formal and informal information on a student, or how to translate that information into instructional programming. Assessment information is of little use if it cannot contribute to effective instruction whether that be regular or special education. Five components are necessary to the assessment process: (1) systematic observation; (2) systematic record keeping; (3) task and student performance analysis; (4) performance range identification; and (5) instructional objectives.

Systematic Observation

The first step in the assessment process is identification of the behavior that requires measurement. Achievement behavior is measured consistently in regular education to monitor student progress. If a student does not make progress commensurate with his peers, the regular education teacher will reassess that student using more exacting measures and often will reteach or provide more experiences for the student who appears to have difficulty grasping a particular concept. When a discrepancy in either learning or behavior varies significantly from that of their peers, or when there is a sudden change in a student's learning behavior, more extensive diagnostic assessment might be advocated. It is important for the special education teacher to keep in mind that variation in learning and behavior exists among normally achieving students. A student's difficulty may be linked to poor instruction (that is, unclear directions or inconsistent routines of the teacher); a mismatch between learner style and curricula (for example, a student who is strong visually and has difficulty with phonics-based reading series); or a lack of teacher tolerance for specific behaviors (for example, a very active learner who is placed with a teacher who has strict and inflexible rules for "proper-in-seat" or "on-task" behavior). A student's learning difficulties may not always be inherent in the student. Learning difficulties can be exacerbated by the monitored considerations. Further investigation is needed for problems in learning or behavior that are persistent, chronic, or that have long-term implications. The special educator should keep three points in mind when determining the seriousness of an observable problem demonstrated by a student.

1. **Observable behavior is often not the underlying cause of a problem.** Problems are often manifested in secondary behaviors. For instance, a student underachieving in an achievement area might deal with the frustration of failing by

developing behavorial problems in the classroom. If the behavior problems are the only focus of the evaluation, the real issue will not be addressed. An appropriate evaluation of a student includes an investigation of cognitive, language, social/emotional, and achievement functioning to identify the cause of the problem.

2. **The longer an observable behavior has gone unaided, the more difficult it is to have a positive impact on the problem.** A problem that has not received attention is much more difficult to treat in a positive manner than problems that are just beginning to emerge. For instance, a student who demonstrates significant underachievement in reading and who has not received special attention has developed some ineffective learning strategies and more than likely has significant negative attitudes toward the process of reading. Such a student has probably received repeated use of reading materials and strategies that have proved unsuccessful. Taking a risk and trying new strategies or techniques to circumvent reading problems is very difficult for many of these students.

3. **Corrective techniques should be attempted prior to identifying an observable behavior as a problem.** A student demonstrating significant underachievement might be aided by special attention or reteaching a concept. Prior to any referral for additional diagnostic assessment, the teacher should attempt corrective methods available in the regular classroom. For instance, a student having difficulty learning rational numbers might be aided by hands-on visual aids rather than workbook sheets. Given a little longer to learn the concept, such a student can easily catch up with the rest of his or her peers. Chapter 2 lists different management and instructional modifications the classroom teacher might consider prior to referring a student for a psychological assessment.

The special educator needs to systematically observe any behaviors identified as problems needing extensive investigation. Observation of behaviors must be carried out in a systematic and concise manner. Chapter 2 discusses techniques for collecting observable behavior. Accurate collection of observable behavior focuses the diagnostic assessment and quickly pinpoints problem areas. Time is always a problem in the assessment process. Rather than waste a student's time by unnecessary evaluation, the special educator's data collection should be the foundation for the assessment plan.

Systematic Record Keeping

A very important part of the assessment process is recording qualitative and quantitative information on a student's performance. Unfortunately, a significant amount of information collected from parents and the classroom teacher is not used adequately for either assessment or instructional purposes. This information is often neglected because the data is not organized in a manner that can be interpreted easily and used for decision making. Classroom or home observations are often more ecologically sound than a formal assessment done on a one-to-one basis. It is not uncommon for the regular educator to complain that the psychologist or special educator who took the student out of the regular education classroom for an assessment did not see the student's true behavior. The dynamics of the classroom or home environment certainly place very different demands on the student from those of sitting in a small testing room with only one person and few distractions. It is very important for the special educator to design record-keeping systems that can effectively present data collected at home or in the classroom. Systematic recorded data, both qualitative and quantitative, presented in a professional manner during a staffing can have a significant impact on the decisions made for the student.

Sources of data to be recorded.   The special educator should collect data from many different sources and record this information in a manner that is quickly understandable to other professionals. One of the first pieces of information that should be collected and coded are interviews with the parents, regular educators, and the student. The special educator might want to develop a form that can be used consistently across different individuals. Interviews provide information about an individual's performance from different perspectives (that is, student, parent, and regular educator). Often, information collected during interviews is not used during staffings because professionals do not have the information recorded in an effective manner. Chapter 2 provides some examples of interview record sheets that the special educator can use while questioning students, parents, and regular educators.

The special educator should always review and code the data included in a student's cumulative record so relevant patterns that might have a significant impact on a student's behavior or academic success can be identified. One of the first pieces of information the cumulative record should include is attendance records. The special educator will want to look for a student's attendance pattern over time and within school years. In addition, the number of transfers or school changes a student has made should be recorded. It is also vital for the special educator to review all norm-referenced group test scores included in the cumulative record to identify any historical patterns that can add support to the evaluation findings. In addition to recording norm-referenced scores, the special educator should analyze the results of any criterion-referenced tests a school system might have administered to all students. Such information can provide corroboration of learning patterns over time.

The special educator also needs to analyze the grade patterns recorded in the cumulative record. It is important to analyze a student's performance within and between school years. Do grades remain consistent within particular instructional areas? All these variables need to be considered relative to significant grade changes. The cumulative record also provides the special educator with some social and conduct evaluations that could be critical for additional documentation of consistent behaviors noted during a formal evaluation. Any relevant medical information pertaining to a student is also recorded in the cumulative record. Some of the most important information needed to better understand a student's performance can be found in the cumulative record. The special educator needs to select the information from the cumulative record and record it in a manner that can be easily interpreted during a staffing. Specific suggestions for reviewing the cumulative record appear in chapter 2.

Observations of a student should also be systematically recorded for use during staffing decisions. The record keeping should clearly display the frequency and intensity of the problem within the regular classroom environment or home to

Table 1-2 Matrix of sociometric information

Class	Individuals Chosen				
	Mary	*Bill*	*Sue*	*Ted*	*Harry*
Mary		*			
Bill			*		
Sue		*			
Ted			*		
Harry			*		
Totals	0	2	3	0	0

establish the critical variables according to task and situation. One of the observations recorded should take place in the area where the referral problem is occurring. The record should document the teacher/pupil ratio in the class observed, contain a brief description of the task (mode of presentation and elicited responses) observed, and describe the classroom setting (the specific activities and the classroom arrangement). Specific observations of learning and behavioral variables relative to task or domain are additional factors that should be clearly indicated on the record. Chapter 2 provides an in-depth discussion of observational techniques.

Samples of a student's regular classroom work provide a significant amount of information that can be analyzed and recorded for use during a staffing. Forms should be developed by the special educator to record any textbook, teacher-made, or standardized test scores, or samples of work sheets and classroom projects that might clearly demonstrate a referral problem. As an example, the regular or special educator might administer a sociometric task to analyze the social interactions occurring in the classroom. The students in the classroom would be asked the question, "If you have a project to do and you can choose another person in this group to work with you, who would it be?" After this question is completed, students are then asked, "If the person you chose could not join you, who would you now pick to work with you?" A record matrix of this information is demonstrated in Table 1-2.

Any past individual assessment that a student might have been given should also be discussed during the staffing. This would include any cognitive, language, social/emotional, or achievement evaluation information. Past psychological reports often have background information about the family that might be helpful for decision making. It is also important to review past psychological data to note if any significant changes have been observed regarding a student's performance. For instance, if a student's overall cognitive ability suddenly dropped significantly, this might indicate some health or emotional problems that need to be explored further.

The type of data collected dictates the approach to recording information. Quantitative information is the easiest type of data to record. Such data includes frequency counts, error counts, tabulations, descriptive statistics, and curriculum or criterion objectives. Table 1-3 provides examples of frequency and error count record forms, while Table 1-4 illustrates a descriptive psychometric record form. Qualitative informa-

Table 1-3 Two samples of quantitative record keeping

Frequency record

Tally of Frequency Behaviors					
Student: Peter					
Time of Day	*Behaviors*				
9:00–9:05	IIII	IIII	III	II	I
9:06–9:14	II	IIII II	IIII IIII	II	II
9:12–9:17	II	IIII IIII	IIII	II	I
9:17–9:22	I	IIII IIII I	IIII IIII II	I	I
9:22–9:30	I	IIII IIII	IIII IIII	I	I
Total	10	43	39	8	6
✕	2	8.3	7.4	1.3	1.1

Error content

Words Spelled Correctly over Five Days					
Words Spelled Correctly	*1*	*2*	*3*	*4*	*5*
10					
9					
8					*
7					
6					
5				*	
4			*		
3					
2					
1	*				
0		*			

tion requires the special educator to develop forms that can highlight the important information necessary for decision making. Such data includes interviews, cumulative record information, classroom observations, work samples, and informal error analysis. Verbal data, such as interviews, can be recorded in such a manner that narrative data can be easily interpreted (see Table 1-5 on page 16).

Record-keeping guidelines. The purpose of record keeping is to reduce the volume of data so that it is easier to assimilate when it is needed. Using standard

Table 1-4 Psychometric summary

Age: 12 years old	*Race:* White
Sex: Female	*Sel:* Middle Class

Acuity
> Visual Acuity–Average
> Auditory Acuity–Average

Social/Emotional Functioning–No problems noted

Cognitive Functioning
> Wechsler intelligence Scale for Children–III
> (Mean score = 100; SD = 15)
> Full Scale Score = 105 (SS); 63rd percentile
> Verbal Scale Score = 102 (SS); 55th percentile
> Performance Scale Score = 106 (SS); 66th percentile

Oral Language Functioning
> Peabody Picture Vocabulary Test–Revised
> (Mean score = 100; standard deviation = 15)
>> standard score = 105; 63%

Oral Language Sample: Poor syntax (word order confused), difficulty with multisyllabic words and substitutes similar sounding words. Omits endings of words and appears to have difficulty discriminating sounds.

Academics
> Stanford Diagnostic Reading Test–Brown Level
>> (Mean = 100 (SS); 50 percentile; SD = 15)
>> (Subtest have scaled scores with average performance of 10)
> Decoding: Auditory Discrimination–4
>> Phonetic Analysis–2
>
> Vocabulary: Auditory Vocabulary–8
> Comprehension: Word Recognition–5
>> Reading Comprehension–9
>
> Gray Oral Reading Test
> (Oral reading quotient–mean score = 100 (SS); 25 percentile–75 percentile; SD = 15)
>> Standard score = 72; 3rd percentile

Test of Written Language–2
> (Mean score = 100; SD = 15)
> Total score = 75

Wide Range Achievement Test–Revised
> (Mean score = 100; standard deviation = 15)
> Reading (Decoding) = 65 (SS)
> Spelling (Recall) = 68 (SS)
> Arithmetic (Calculation) = 102 (SS); 55 (percentile)

Key Math–Revised
> (Mean score = 100; standard deviation = 15 for total test standard scores and areas standard scores)
>> Total Test–95 (SS); 37 percentile
>> Basic Concepts–100 (SS); 50 percentile
>> Operations–93 (SS); 32 percentile
>> Applications–93 (SS); 32 percentile

forms for quantifying information helps speed up recording and reporting information. If information is easier to interpret, the chances that the data will be used for decision making increase. A few simple guidelines can help the special educator

Table 1-5 Summary record of verbal data parent interview

Student: _____   Parents Interviewed: _____

Interviewer: _____   _____

Date: _____

Student Behaviors

Strengths of Student Identified by Interviewer			Weaknesses of Student Identified by Interviewer			Strengths of Student Identified by Parent(s)			Weaknesses of Student Identified by Parent(s)		
	Agreement			Agreement			Agreement			Agreement	
	p^1	p^2		p^1	p^2		I	P^*		I	P^*

*Parent must be identified either as p^1 (mother) or p^2 (father).

develop new records. First, simple recording systems tend to be used more often by teachers. Time is always a problem for the practitioner, and the special educator is no exception to this fact. Second, the recording format will determine the information perceived by the observer. Therefore, the items to be evaluated need to be clearly identified, labeled, and described. Categories or items to be observed should be written in behavioral terms so no confusion occurs when the form is interpreted by other professionals. Third, always leave space on the record sheet for observational comments. These qualitative statements often help clarify a student's particular performance and explain behavior that might not seem to fit with other information collected on the individual.

Task and Student Performance Analysis

The special educator involved in an assessment is required to constantly analyze the tasks presented to the student as well as the student's performance on the task. Analyzing the data often results in the special educator manipulating task variables in a way that produces a good match to the student's needs. Chapter 7 discusses the model we advocate to provide teachers with a framework by which to analyze tasks and student performance regardless of the disability or type of task (academic or social). We provide information on how to identify the skill, stage of learning, cues/ prompts, response types, modality, and basic learning abilities required of an individual completing a particular activity. The information that requires task and student analyses comes from norm-referenced, criterion-based, curriculum-based, and dynamic assessment methods. No one type of assessment provides the special educator with enough information to make a professional judgment of the why and how of a student's performance.

The main goal of the ongoing assessment process is interpretation of the student's patterns of learning. Identifying these preferred learning patterns will facilitate development of instructional strategies.

Performance Range Identification

Designing effective assessment for students with special needs has often neglected the dialogic nature of effective problem solving (Stone, 1989). Traditionally, most diagnostic procedures have been static, dictated by single scores or criterion levels. Recently, the concept of process or dynamic assessment has led clinicians to reevaluate diagnostic models. The work of Vygotsky (1962, 1978a,b), Feuerstein (1979 a,b), and Brown and Campione (1981) have provided the theoretical and empirical base for restructuring the purpose and means of assessment in special education.

Vygotsky (1962) advocated the importance of measuring a student's assisted performance. Assisted performance is defined by Vygotsky as what an individual can do with help from the environment, others, and the self. An individual's performance from assisted to nonassisted behaviors constitutes what Vygotsky (1962) called the *zone of proximal development* (ZPD). It is imperative for the special educator to assess beyond the developmental level of an individual (unassisted performance) to also measure the proximal zone (assisted performance) for both assessment and instructional purposes. The majority of evaluations currently used to identify a student's ability levels only investigate unassisted performance. Any norm-referenced, criterion-referenced, or curriculum-based assessment measures unassisted performance. But according to Vygotsky (1956) the proximal zone is where instruction can be defined in terms of developmental levels for good teaching, which "awakens and rouses to life those functions which are in a stage of maturing, which lie in the zone of proximal development" (Vygotsky, 1956,: quoted in Wertsch and Stone, 1985).

Assessment that identifies a student's zone of proximal development is sensitive to the degree of structure, response modes, and input/output demands on a student's *performance range* (see chapter 9 for additional information). Diagnostic interpretation of test information should go beyond a simple error rate or standard score. Unfortunately, the majority of assessments used to predict a student's success in school or work are simply static records of performance. Attention to the dialogic dynamics of the learning experience and sensitivity to the role of the learner's characteristics as mediators to problem solving should become the focus of the evaluation process. For instance, it might be hypothesized that a student with mild learning disabilities needs fewer prompts or cues from an evaluator to learn how to generalize a problem solving technique than does a student with moderate intellectual deficits. In addition, students from minority cultures might not have experience with a task (for example, picture puzzles), but given a few cues they could do the task without difficulty. If the examiner took the score on the child's first unassisted attempt, the conclusion would be that the student was "deficient" in a particular area (for example, visual spatial skills). The number of cues or guided assistance required provides the examiner with important information about the differences due to experience rather than to underlying disabilities.

Classroom teachers need to know what students are capable of doing with assistance and without assistance. This is the old concept of independent and guided instruction. The special educator is able to identify such instructional levels (ZPD) if dynamic assessment is part of every evaluation. As we will discuss further, dynamic assessment is only one type of assessment that is necessary to identify students with special needs.

Behavioral Objectives

Behavioral objectives are as important in the assessment process as they are in the instruction of students with special needs. Not only are appropriately written behavioral objectives in fulfillment of individualized educational program (IEP) requirements for the inclusion of short-term objectives to guide students' individualized programs, they demonstrate accountability to students, teachers, parents, and administrators. In addition, they provide a checklist for maintaining effective record keeping. Depending upon a student's performance on a particular objective, special educators can continue appropriate instruction. Research has demonstrated that properly written behavioral objectives positively correlate with improved quality of instruction and rate of student growth (Fuchs, Fuchs and Deno, 1985; Hartley and Davies, 1976).

Mager (1975) defined behavioral objectives as descriptions of the performances learners must exhibit before they are considered competent. Behavioral objectives should contain three components: a description of the student's *behavior* in measurable terms, *conditions* under which the student demonstrates this behavior, and the *criteria* used to evaluate the behavior. Meyen (1981) reinforces the point that behavioral objectives should clearly describe the student's age level and relevant prerequisite skills. When writing behavioral objectives, the special educator should describe a student's behavior using action verbs (that is: to state, to read, to mark) that can be clearly observed. According to Mager (1975), the special educator might want to state a student's "overt" as well as "covert" behaviors by giving the suggestion that "behavioral indicators" should accompany objectives. The following objective illustrates an example of a behavioral indicator: "John will divide (write solutions to) _____." The word "divide" is a covert behavior since the special educator cannot see John divide the problem. The behavioral indicator, the words in parentheses, are the overt or observable answers.

The special educator should evaluate clearly specified behavioral objectives. Criterion-referenced assessment tools provide the teacher with objectives for items used on curriculum-based or norm-referenced measurement tools. Objectives help limit the generalizability of a student's score to all areas of the curriculum. For instance, if a teacher has assessed a student's ability as average in orally decoding (reading out loud) fifteen high-frequency words, it should not be stated that the student can decode all high- or low-frequency words. The special educator can only state that when asked to read fifteen high-frequency words from a given stimulus (flashcards) on a one-to-one administration, the student performed in the average range. As we will discuss in chapter 6, the degree of structure, task response, and

Table 1-6 Collaborative consultation team functions

Team Member	Primary Expertise and Data Source
Student	Perspective of the situation from the person being evaluated.
Parent	Perspective of the student's functional levels in an environment other than school.
Regular Educator	Perspective of the student's functional level compared to other peers in regular classroom setting.
Special Educator	Provide diagnostic assessment.
	Provide expertise regarding characteristics and instructional needs of students with special needs.
Psychologist	Provide cognitive and social/emotional functional levels.
Speech/Language Clinician	Provide oral language functioning.
Medical Personnel	Provide medical information pertaining to student.
Social Worker/Counselor	Provide information pertaining to family dynamics and student's social/emotional functioning.
Vocational/Rehabilitation Counselor	Provide vocational readiness/functional needs.
Administrator	Building or special education supervisor provides information pertaining to school or state policy, due process, and so forth.
Others	Could include adaptive physical education teacher, physical therapist, occupational therapist.

modality can all have an impact on a student's performance level. Behavioral objectives help teachers state clearly what they have measured and limit generalization beyond the purpose of specific assessment tools.

Collaborative Consultation: Key to Decision Making

Assessing students with special needs involves a team of individuals, each person bringing a particular area of expertise to help solve a problem. When the team of professionals meets to discuss a student's performance, we call this a staffing. A staffing team consists of parents, regular educators, administrators, special educators, psychologists/counselors, medical personnel, and social workers. Each individual on the team shares information about the student from his or her perspective and professional judgment. Staffing teams that consist of professionals representing different disciplines (that is, psychology, special education, regular education) are called multidisciplinary teams. See Table 1-6 for a summary of typical team members and the information they provide in the decision-making process. The contribution of each team member has equal impact on the decision-making process. There has been growing recognition among professionals that the number of students who can benefit from the expertise of multidisciplinary teams is increasing (AASA, 1988; Knitzer, 1982). No one discipline has the expertise to solve the multifaceted problems students with special needs can present to school systems.

Collaboration and consultation are the current rhetoric used to advocate for the importance of shared responsibility (Will, 1986) during decision making. *Collaborative consultation* grew out of a recognition of the need to pool professional expertise to solve the increasingly complex problems students with special needs present to school systems. While multidisciplinary teams have been in operation in school systems since 1977, with passage of Public Law 94–142 the modus operandi has been that a single professional, quite often the psychologist or special education coordinator, controls the decision making during the staffing. Such an approach results in other members of the team feeling little ownership for making and carrying out decisions. As Margolis and McGettigan (1988) state: "People commonly withdraw from participation in decision-making groups when they think their knowledge is less than that of other members. Active participation in a group in which one feels respected and understood increases ownership of the group's ideas" (p. 9). Collaborative consultation models encourage all members of a team to share the responsibility and concern for the student's evaluation; thus, each person is responsible for solving the problem. Therefore, each team member is accountable and should be recognized in the resolution of the decision-making process. Underlying such a model is the belief that pooling expertise is the key to solving problems and implementing solutions. Specialists, such as special educators or psychologists, should not be given more or less input or power during the assessment process. The parent or regular educator's view are equally important and valued. Current literature on empowerment and leadership supports the concept that when participants in a group are able to have a dialogue about their own expertise and impact, increased effectiveness and a greater sense of professionalism will result (Lieberman and Miller, 1986). The special educator plays a key role in helping facilitate collaborative sharing of expertise during multidisciplinary staffings.

Public Law and Litigation Pertaining to Assessment of Special Needs Students

A number of public laws (*legislation*) and *litigation* (court cases) protect the rights of students with special needs. The official standards of different professional organizations are incorporated in many of the laws currently protecting the rights of individuals undergoing assessments in public and private settings. The "Ethical Principles of Psychologists and Code of Conduct" (American Psychological Association, 1992) has just been revised and provides a set of criteria that the special educator involved in testing students should strictly use as a guide to their assessment performance. See Table 1-7 for a listing of American Psychological Association (APA) standards that apply specifically to the assessment process. It is very important that special educators be cognizant of the serious ethical responsibilities associated with the assessment process. An administrative error or ethical mistake can have a direct impact on a student's potential for success. It is inappropriate for the special educator to discuss referral or diagnostic information pertaining to any student with anyone outside the staffing with the exception of the parent/guardian or the student. Mentioning individuals on a referral list, discussing test performance, or providing family background information outside of staffing, even to other special educators, is unethical. The special educator is trusted with confidential information that is clearly protected information. Professional ethical standards protect the rights of any individual participating in the assessment process.

Table 1-7 Ethical principles of psychologists related to evaluation assessment or intervention

2.01 Evaluation, Diagnosis, and Intervention in Professional Context

(a) Psychologists perform evaluations, diagnostic services, or interventions only within the context of a defined professional relationship. (See also Standard 1.03, Professional and Scientific Relationship.)

(b) Psychologists' assessments, recommendations, reports, and psychological diagnostic or evaluative statements are based on information and techniques (including personal interviews of the individual when appropriate) sufficient to provide appropriate substantiation for their findings. (See also Standard 7.02, Forensic Assessments.)

2.02 Competence and Appropriate Use of Assessments and Interventions

(a) Psychologists who develop, administer, score, interpret, or use psychological assessment techniques, interviews, tests, or instruments do so in a manner and for purposes that are appropriate in light of the research on or the evidence of the usefulness and proper application of the techniques.

(b) Psychologists refrain from misuse of assessment techniques, interventions, results, and interpretations and take reasonable steps to prevent others from misusing the information these techniques provide. This includes refraining from releasing raw test results or raw data to persons, other than to patients or clients as appropriate, who are not qualified to use such information. (See also Standards 1.02, Relationship of Ethics and Law, and 1.04, Boundaries of Competence.)

2.03 Test Construction

Psychologists who develop and conduct research with tests and other assessment techniques use scientific procedures and current professional knowledge for test design, standardization, validation, reduction or elimination of bias, and recommendations for use.

2.04 Use of Assessment in General and with Special Populations

(a) Psychologists who perform interventions or administer, score, interpret, or use assessment techniques are familiar with the reliability, validation, and related standardization or outcome studies of, and proper applications and uses of, the techniques they use.

(b) Psychologists recognize limits to the certainty with which diagnoses, judgments, or predictions can be made about individuals.

(c) Psychologists attempt to identify situations in which particular interventions or assessment techniques or norms may not be applicable or may require adjustment in administration or interpretation because of factors such as individuals' gender, age, race, ethnicity, national origin, religion, sexual orientation, disability, language, or socioeconomic status.

2.05 Interpreting Assessment Results

When interpreting assessment results, including automated interpretations, psychologists take into account the various test factors and characteristics of the person being assessed that might affect psychologists' judgments or reduce the accuracy of their interpretations. They indicate any significant reservations they have about the accuracy or limitations of their interpretations.

2.06 Unqualified Persons

Psychologists do not promote the use of psychological assessment techniques by unqualified persons. (See also Standard 1.22, Delegation to and Supervision of Subordinates.)

2.07 Obsolete Tests and Outdated Test Results

(a) Psychologists do not base their assessment or intervention decisions or recommendations on data or test results that are outdated for the current purpose.

(b) Similarly, psychologists do not base such decisions or recommendations on tests and measures that are obsolete and not useful for the current purpose.

2.08 Test Scoring and Interpretation Services

(a) Psychologists who offer assessment or scoring procedures to other professionals accurately describe the purpose, norms, validity, and applications of the procedures and any special qualifications applicable to their use.

(b) Psychologists select scoring and interpretation services (including automated services) on the basis of evidence of the validity of the program and procedures as well as on other appropriate considerations.

(c) Psychologists retain appropriate responsibility for the appropriate application, interpretation, and use of assessment instruments, whether they score and interpret such tests themselves or use automated or other services.

(continued)

Table 1-7 Ethical principles of psychologists related to evaluation assessment or intervention *(continued)*

2.09 Explaining Assessment Results

Unless the nature of the relationship is clearly explained to the person being assessed in advance and precludes provision of an explanation of results (such as in some organizational consulting, preemployment or security screenings, and forensic evaluations), psychologists ensure that an explanation of the results is provided using language that is reasonably understandable to the person assessed or to another legally authorized person on behalf of the client. Regardless of whether the scoring and interpretation are done by the psychologist, by assistants, or by automated or other outside services, psychologists take reasonable steps to ensure that appropriate explanations of results are given.

2.10 Maintaining Test Security

Psychologists make reasonable efforts to maintain the integrity and security of tests and other assessment techniques consistent with law, contractual obligations, and in a manner that permits compliance with the requirements of this Ethics Code. (See also Standard 1.02, Relationship of Ethics and Law.)

Source: From "Ethical Principles of Psychologists and Code of Conduct." Copyright 1992 by the American Psychological Association. Reprinted by permission.

Legislation

Public Law 94–142, the Education for All Handicapped Children Act of 1975, is the legislation that has had the most far-reaching implications for assessment of school-age children. The law specifically established safeguards for evaluation and placement of students with special needs that are applicable to private as well as public schools. Public Law 94–142 was reauthorized by congressional action in 1986. The reauthorization (PL 99–457) extends the original law to preschool services, which has significance for assessment. This legislation provides financial assistance to states for early intervention (birth to age 2) and provides free appropriate public education to students with disabilities ages 3 to 5 years. Appropriate assessment tools and measures for preschool children with disabilities are lacking, as is the research to support diagnostic decision making. On October 30, 1990, further amendments were made to 94–142. These amendments are known as Public Law 101–476. The title of the law was changed from the Education for All Handicapped Children Act to Individuals with Disabilities Education Act (IDEA). The amendments focus on the person, not the disability. Within the new legislation, all references to "handicapped children" were changed to "children with disabilities." In addition, autism and traumatic brain injury were added as categories of disabilities. Rehabilitation and social work services are new related services provided to individuals with disabilities. These amendments also state that needed transition services for a student's school to post school activities must be added to the IEP by age 16.

Tests and test administration.   Public Law 94–142 and Public Law 101–476 require that state and local educational agencies adhere to the following guidelines pertaining to tests and test administration.

1. Tests and other evaluation materials are provided and administered in the individual's native language or other mode of communication, unless it is clearly not feasible to do so;
2. Tests and other evaluation materials have been validated for the specific purpose for which they are used;

3. Tests and other evaluation materials are administered by trained personnel in conformance with the instructions provided by their producer.
4. Tests and other evaluation materials include those tailored to assess specific areas of educational need and not merely those which are designed to provide a single general intelligence quotient;
5. Tests are selected and administered so as best to ensure that when a test is administered to an individual with impaired sensory, manual, or speaking skills, the test results accurately reflect the child's aptitude or achievement level or whatever other factors the test purports to measure, rather than reflecting the individual's impaired sensory, manual, or speaking skills (except where those skills are the factors which the test purports to measure);
6. No single procedure is used as the sole criterion for determining an appropriate educational program for an individual; and
7. The evaluation is made by a multidisciplinary team or group of persons, including at least one teacher or other specialist with knowledge in the area of suspected disability.
8. The individual is assessed in all areas related to the suspected disability, including, where appropriate, health, vision, hearing, social and emotional status, general intelligence, academic performance, communicative status, and motor abilities.
9. Testing and evaluation materials and procedures used for the purposes of evaluation and placement of individuals with disabilities must be selected and administered so as not to be racially or culturally discriminatory.

Source: Federal Register, August 23, 1977, Vol. 42, No. 163, pp. 42496–42497, 121a.532 and 121a.530.

Individualized educational program (IEP).   Public Law 94–142 and later Public Law 101–476 mandates that for any individual demonstrating a disability, an *individualized educational program* (IEP) must be developed for their specific needs. The IEP is a document that specifies the expectations the professionals involved in the diagnostic assessment have for students with special needs. In chapter 15 we will discuss in detail the safeguards and the development of the IEP.

Due process.   Public Law 94–142 and Public Law 101–476 also mandate *due process,* safeguards that are considered essential to achieving individual justice (Friendly, 1975). Parents or guardians have the right:

• to receive adequate notice of any meetings pertaining to their child with special needs prior to or after the assessment process has begun,
• to be notified of when and where any part of the evaluation will be conducted,
• to examine school records,
• to be represented at any meeting pertaining to their child being evaluated or reconsidered for services,
• to be represented by an advocate at any meeting, and
• to appeal any decision made regarding their child to a hearing officer.

Some of the key due process mandates that have an impact on the assessment process include:

1. *Right to an Independent Educational Evaluation.* If a parent or guardian disagrees with the decision of the school system, they have the right to obtain an

independent educational evaluation. The parent or guardian will only be compensated and the school system required to comply with an outside evaluation if the outside evaluation was required by a hearing officer.

2. *Periodic Evaluations.* Any individual receiving special education services must be reevaluated at least every three years and more often if conditions require it. The purposes of reevaluations are (1) to review efficacy of placement in special education, (2) to monitor progress made in special education, and (3) to identify new areas of need for the student.

3. *Right to Examine Records.* A parent or guardian has a right to inspect any information in their child's record. Special educators must always keep this in mind when they jot notes on protocols or work sheets that will be filed in a student's record. The question of whether a parent has the right to copy a protocol has been answered best by the Division of School Psychology (Division 16) of the American Psychological Association.

> Some of the legal constraints impinging on this issue are discussed in a policy letter (dated Jan. 9, 1979) from the Bureau for Education of the Handicapped (BEH). This policy letter was in response to a question raised by a school district regarding parents' right to assessment information as outlined in PL 94–12. The BEH response made several important points.
>
> (1) The provisions for parents' rights to information outlined in part B of PL 94–142 are essentially identical to regulations from the Family Education Rights and Privacy Act. This act considers test protocols to be educational records, and states that they must be accessible to parents.
>
> (2) This mandate is met if the school district allows parents to examine and discuss the protocols under school supervision.
>
> (3) If this procedure were followed, schools and other agencies would not be required to provide copies of protocols to parents.
>
> (4) However, an agency must give test protocols to parents if (a) the parents cannot come to school during a 45-day period after a request has been made to review the record if the reasons for not coming during this period are serious illness, extended travel, or related reasons, and if parents request copies of their child's protocol, or (b) if the parents or agency request a due process hearing in which the test protocols will be introduced by either party as evidence at the hearing.
>
> APA Division 16 Ethics Committee suggest the following procedure for situations other than those that legally require that copies be sent to parents. The procedure is designed to meet the applicable ethical standards when parental requests for test protocols are made.
>
> (1) Parents should be made aware of their rights to all information in their child's educational records including information included on test protocols.
>
> (2) Parents should be given the right to inspect test protocols. This might include discussion of examples of test items and responses to these items. This inspection should be done under the supervision of the school psychologist, or other responsible, appropriately trained personnel.
>
> (3) Parents should not be given photocopies of completed protocols or copies of blank protocols, nor should they be allowed to copy word-for-word extended portions of test protocols.

(4) If parents request copies of protocols, they should be made aware of the ethical obligation of the psychologist to maintain test security. (Martin, 1985:9)

4. *Right to a Hearing.* Public Law 94–142 and Public Law 101–476 both mandate due process hearings in special education disputes to ensure parental involvement in educational decision making. Goldberg and Kuriloff (1987) discuss the problems with due process hearings for both the school system and the parents. According to Goldberg and Kuriloff, neither party feels positive about the experience. Such evidence leads to the need for greater use of mediation and negotiation before parents or schools proceed into due process hearings.

Eligibility.   After the multidisciplinary team has completed its assessment and staffed a student, a decision must be made as to whether the student is eligible for special education services. Each state has specific legal criteria to determine whether a student's performance is different enough for the student to be eligible for special services. The criteria for eligibility for services in special education vary across states. A student might meet the criteria for learning disability services in one state and not in another. In addition, an outside evaluator might diagnose a student as disabled, but the student still may not meet the state regulations for placement in special education. The guidelines used by a state can include formulas or cutoffs to measure the degree of impairment. Table 1-8 provides some sample criteria used to determine *eligibility* for services under the categories of learning disabilities, mild/moderate/severe intellectual deficit, and behavioral disorders. Standardized assessment provides the primary documentation for mild to moderate disabilities. This does not discount the need for clinical judgment to override test scores in some individual cases.

Procedural Steps in the Assessment Process

Public Law 94–142 and Public Law 101–476 outline specific steps in the assessment process that state and local districts must follow. While these steps are somewhat general, allowing for a fair degree of variability between states, the process is the same. The steps include:

1. *Screening.* The law is very clear that state agencies are responsible for identifying, locating, and evaluating all students with disabilities. Screening can be identified as providing information about disabilities to the public by different types of media (for example, print or video). Regular education teachers are usually the key participants in the screening step. They are often asked to fill out checklists or rating forms on high-risk students. Classroom observation and standardized group assessment tools help identify students with possible special needs. Once high-risk students are identified, the regular education teacher is expected to modify instructional and environmental demands to try to solve problems within the regular setting. When a teacher has modified her behavior, attempted modification of the curriculum or environment, and a student is still demonstrating problems in the classroom setting, the student is referred for further assessment. The law also provides the option for a parent, tutor, physician, or anyone else to refer a student for further assessment.

Table 1-8 A sample of state eligibility criteria
Documentation Needed

Mildly intellectually disabled
1. Significant education deficits
2. Subaverage intelligence (IQ = 70–55)
3. Significant deficits in adaptive behavior

Moderately intellectually disabled
1. Significant educational deficits
2. Subaverage intelligence (IQ = 55–40)
3. Significant deficits in adaptive behavior

Severely intellectually disabled
1. Significant educational deficits
2. Subaverage intelligence (IQ = 40–25)
3. Significant deficits in adaptive behavior

Profoundly intellectually disabled
1. Significant educational deficits
2. Subaverage intelligence (IQ = 25 or less)
3. Significant deficits in adaptive behavior

Specific learning disabilities
1. Alternative approaches were attempted prior to referral
2. Psychological information
   a. link between processes, severe discrepancy, and academics
   b. cognitive ability level
   c. strengths commensurate with cognitive ability
   d. conclusions important in program planning
3. Educational information
   a. statement of status
   b. deficits confirmed by a minimum of two assessments in each area (one may be informal)
4. Supportive information
   a. work samples
   b. classroom observation
5. Discrepant performance not primarily due to other factors

Behavioral disorders
1. Duration, frequency, and intensity of one or more of the following:
   a. inability building and maintaining satisfactory interpersonal relationships
   b. inability to learn not explained by other factors
   c. chronic inappropriate behavior or feelings
   d. pervasive unhappiness or depression
   e. tendency to develop physical symptoms associated with problems
2. Exhibits characteristics after regular assistance
3. Characteristics significantly interfere with educational performance
4. Difficulty not explained by other factors

---

2. *Referral.* School systems usually have an individual or team that receives refer-rals for special education assessment. The first job to be completed by the referral team is notifying the parents in writing of the need to evaluate the student so that the parents can give permission and receive an explanation of the process. When given permission

by the parent to begin the assessment, the referral team develops an individualized assessment plan. This plan identifies the areas needing specific attention in the testing procedures in addition to a general evaluation of cognitive, language, social/emotional, and achievement skills.

3. *Assessment.* Appropriate assessment of students with special needs is the focus of this book. The following chapters provide information for special educators pertaining to effective formal and informal assessment tools used to identify a student's patterns of learning. It is imperative that the special educator always keeps in mind that no one assessment tool or measure should be used exclusively to determine functioning level in any area.

4. *Eligibility.* After the assessment process has been completed and all tests have been scored and interpreted, the staffing team meets to determine if a student is eligible for services by special education. The legal criteria are established by the individual states (see Table 1-8).

5. *Individualized Educational Program.* Once a student is determined to be eligible for special education, an individualized educational program (IEP) must be developed. Chapter 15 discusses the components of an IEP in detail.

Litigation

Litigation pertains to court cases used to interpret the legislation mandated by law. According to Sattler (1988), the litigation investigating the appropriateness of laws used to place individuals in special education have focused primarily on (1) the rights of individuals to a free and appropriate education and (2) the overrepresentation of ethnic minority individuals in classes for the intellectually deficient. Table 1-9 provides a list of the major cases that have had a significant impact on assessment and placement of students in special education.

Summary

Introduction

1. Assessment requires the systematic collection, analysis, and integration of information.
2. The main goal of the educational assessment process is to interpret the differences in learning patterns of students.
3. Assessment helps teachers focus on more precise and efficient teaching strategies.
4. Assessment is an ongoing process.

Purpose of Assessment

1. In special education, legislation influences placement decisions by mandating free appropriate education in the least restrictive environment, an individualized program of instruction, and the use of nondiscriminatory assessment in placing a student in a special education program.

Table 1-9 Landmark litigation for assessment of special needs students

Case	Impact on Assessment
Diana v. California State Board of Education c-70 37RFT (N.D. Cal. 1970)	1. Linguistically different students (Mexican-American) would be tested in their primary language. 2. Nonverbal measure used for measure of cognitive functioning. 3. Interpreter would be used if a bilingual examiner could not be found.
Guadalupe v. Tempe Elementary School District—Stipulation Order (January 24, 1972)	1. Diagnosis of mental retardation required a student scoring at least 2 standard deviations below the population mean on an approved IQ test administered in the child's own language. 2. Additional assessment to IQ required.
Mattic T. v. Holladay—No. DC-75-31-5 (1979)	1. Remedy required to solve the problem of a larger number of black children in classes for mentally retarded. 2. All misclassified children to be identified and given compensatory education.
Larry P. v. Riles—No. C-71-2270RFP (1979) and No. 80-4027DC No. C1-71-2270 in the United States Court of Appeals for the Ninth Circuit (1984)	1. District court in California ruled that standardized intelligence tests are culturally biased and cannot be used in the assessment of black children for possible placement in classes for the educable mentally retarded.
Parents in Action on Special Education v. Joseph P. Hannon—No. 74 C 3586 (N.D. III. 1980)	1. District court in Illinois ruled that the WISC, WISC-R, and Stanford-Binet are not racially or culturally biased.
Georgia State Conference of Branches of NAACP v. State of Georgia Eleventh Court of Appeals, No. 84-8771 (Oct. 29, 1985) and *Marshall v. Georgia,* U.S. District Court for the Southern District of GA CV 482-233, June 28, 1984; Amended Aug. 24, 1984	1. District court ruled that Georgia did not discriminate against black children by using standardized assessment procedures for the evaluation and placement of black children in special education programs for the educable mentally retarded.

2. The primary consideration in placement decisions focuses on the most effective means of meeting the student's needs.
3. Assessment measures should be varied and broad enough not to oversimplify or overidentify a problem.
4. Data gathered during an assessment incorporates both long- and short-term needs.
5. The placement decision is not limited to the availability of instructional programs within a school district.
6. The radical decision to completely change a student's placement is made only after modifications of the current program are attempted and have failed.
7. The goal of assessment for instruction is the teaching activity.
8. Assessment cannot be separated from teaching itself.
9. The special educator must be very careful not to fall into the trap of using limited assessment data to answer the "why" of a student's poor performance rather than the "how" of that performance.

10. Assessment also has the purpose of communicating information to students, parents, teachers, and other professionals.
11. Portfolio assessment is the summary of a student's performance over time and on different tasks collected together in one folder.

Principles in the Assessment Process

1. Professionals must include five components in the assessment process: (1) systematic observation, (2) systematic record keeping, (3) task and student performance analysis, (4) performance range identification, and (5) instructional objectives.
2. Observable behavior is often not the underlying cause of a problem.
3. The longer an observable behavior has gone unaided, the more difficult it is to have a positive impact on the problem.
4. Corrective techniques should be attempted prior to identifying an observable behavior as a problem.
5. Systematic recording of data, both qualitative and quantitative, presented in a professional manner during a staffing can make a significant impact on the decisions made for a student.
6. The special educator should collect data from many different sources and record this information in a manner that is quickly understandable to other professionals.
7. The purpose of record keeping is to reduce the volume of data so that it is easier to assimilate when it is needed.
8. If information is easier to interpret, it increases the chances that the data will be used for decision making.
9. The special educator involved in an assessment is required to constantly analyze the task presented to the student as well as the student's performance on the task.
10. The special educator needs to investigate beyond the developmental level of an individual (unassisted performance) to also measure the proximal zone (assisted performance) for both assessment and instructional purposes.
11. An individual's performance from assisted to unassisted behaviors constitutes what Vygotsky (1962) called the zone of proximal development (ZPD).
12. Behavioral objectives are as important in the assessment process as they are in the instruction of students with special needs.

Collaborative Consultation: Key to Decision Making

1. The assessment of students with special needs involves a team of individuals, each using his or her area of expertise to help solve the problem.
2. When a team of professionals meet to discuss a particular student's performance, it is called a staffing.
3. Staffing teams that consist of professionals representing different disciplines (that is, psychology, special education, regular education) are called multidisciplinary staffing teams.
4. The contribution of each team member has equal impact on decision making.

5. Collaborative consultation refers to the importance of shared responsibility during decision making.
6. Current literature on empowerment and leadership supports the concept that when participants in a group are able to have a dialogue about their own expertise and impact, increased effectiveness and a greater sense of professionalism will result.
7. The special educator plays a key role in helping facilitate collaborative sharing of expertise during multidisciplinary staffings.

Public Law and Litigation Pertaining to Assessment of Special Needs Students

1. Legislation pertains to the public laws enacted to protect the rights of individuals.
2. Litigation pertains to the court cases that result from the attempt to interpret legislation.
3. Public Law 94–142 and Public Law 101–476 require that state and local educational agencies adhere to specific guidelines pertaining to tests and test administration.
4. The individualized educational program (IEP) is a document that specifies the expectations professionals involved in the diagnostic assessment have for students with special needs.
5. Due process safeguards rights that are considered essential to achieving individual justice.
6. Eligibility refers to specific legal criteria established at the state level that determine whether an individual meets the requirements to be served by special education in that state.

Sources of Information

Key Terms

Antecedent-consequence anec-
dotal record
Assistance/support team
Continuous recording
Criterion-referenced
Diagnostic test
Discrete behavior
Dynamic procedures

Evaluation team
Event recording
Interval recording
Latency
Nondiscrete behavior
Norm-referenced
Outcome recording
Permanent product analysis

Portfolio assessment
Real-time recording
Record of discriminated oper-
ants
Screening test
Sequence analysis
Time sampling

The realization that learning is largely dependent on events in the environment with which the individual interacts makes it possible to view learning as an occurrence that can be examined more closely and understood more profoundly. Learning is not simply an event that happens naturally; it is also an event that happens under certain observable conditions.

Gagné, 1965, p. 4

Regular classroom teachers gather data on students every day. Students are called on to read out loud or to answer oral questions during class discussions as a way of determining if the lesson objectives are being met. Daily assignments are evaluated for progress on learning new material or developing mastery of a skill. Periodic tests are used to examine how well a student has learned and can apply a larger body of material. This is the ongoing assessment process teachers use to identify students who are at risk for academic difficulty. Teachers use the data they gather to assign grades as a way of communicating progress or academic difficulty to parents. When these data suggest that a student is experiencing more than the usual amount of difficulty learning, the assessment process expands beyond the classroom, involving other people and becoming more formalized. However, it remains a process. Just as a classroom teacher does not assign a term grade based on one assignment, the process of assessment involves gathering data from several sources rather than relying on one test score. The different sources are then examined in an attempt to find a pattern of performance indicating strengths and weaknesses that can be used to develop instructional goals and objectives. In this chapter, we discuss the sources for these data.

School Records

The regular classroom teacher may examine the records of a student experiencing difficulty even before making a formal referral for help. These records can provide enormous amounts of information related to school changes, attendance, previous academic performance, and previous test performance.

School Changes

One of the first questions that can be answered from the school records is, "How many schools has the student been enrolled in?" Students who move every two or three years, or more often, may be at risk. Different schools use different curricula, so skills may have been missed if there were frequent moves. For some students, moving to another school can be very upsetting. During the transition period of adjusting to a new school, such a student may not be as available to learning experiences and may, therefore, miss critical information.

When a pattern of frequent moves is present, the teacher should check with the student's primary caregiver about the reasons for the moves. When one or both parents are in the military, frequent moves are common. However, these students are typically in geographical areas where other students share this experience. The family expects to move and may be able to adjust better than families for whom a move is unexpected. Another student may have a record of frequent moves because of family stresses such as divorce, unemployment, taking care of aging relatives, or foster home placement. When stress prompts a move, the student may experience a longer adjustment period during which learning may be more difficult. Finally, a student may have lived in the same town but may have moved between schools. The student may live with different relatives for a variety of reasons. Another possibility is that the parents may have shifted the student between various private and public schools or may have tried schooling the student at home. Perhaps the parents are in disagreement about the best type of education, or they may be dissatisfied with how a school is run. It is important to work closely with these families to provide a more stable educational experience.

Attendance

Regularity of school attendance is another important piece of information that can be obtained from school records. The classroom teacher will already have a sense of student attendance for the current academic year; however, regularity of attendance can fluctuate from year to year, or from season to season. Students with respiratory problems or allergies may have poor attendance during specific times of the year. A student may have a health crisis one year but have relatively good attendance during other years. A student may have had excellent attendance in the early grades but be developing a pattern of more absences each year the student is in school. Such a pattern could signal that the student's motivation is declining and he or she is at risk of dropping out, or a serious health problem may be undiagnosed yet emerging.

A decline in attendance may reflect a family change. If a caregiver starts working after a period at home or changes work schedules, the student may experiment with some newfound freedom by cutting classes. A student who is frequently absent on Mondays or who is often tardy may be trying to help an alcoholic or drug dependent caregiver manage the morning routine. Frequent tardiness may also signal a positive family change. A new baby in the family will create a period of adjustment during which a student might be late. These patterns or changes in patterns need to be explored with the student and with the student's caregivers.

Grades

The classroom teacher will know the grades the student is earning in his or her class but may wonder if the current performance is typical of the student's past performance. The student's records should contain all previous report card grades. These grades will help clarify whether a particular subject has always been difficult for a student or if the present difficulty is new. Some students have problems making the

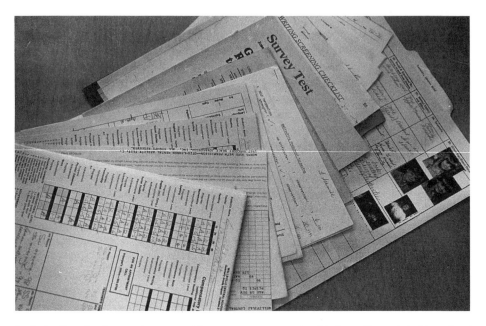

A student's school record can provide enormous amounts of information related to school changes, attendance, previous academic performance, and previous test performance. *Source:* © Barrie Fanton/Omni Photo Communications, Inc.

transition back to school following summer vacation. For these students, the teacher may find a pattern of poor grades for the first term with gradual improvement during subsequent terms. Other students may do well during the first term when the curriculum provides a review of previous material. These students may experience more difficulty after Christmas break when the pace of new material accelerates.

Certain types of academic problems can be reflected in the pattern of a student's grades. For example, a student with adequate word attack skills but poor reading comprehension may have poor grades in reading but relatively good grades in other subjects through the primary years. When reading is required to learn content, typically beginning around fourth grade, the student's grades in other courses may decline. Similarly, students are required to accept more responsibility for long-term projects as they move into middle school. A student with organization problems may experience a decline in grades because of this demand.

The list of marks earned in each grade also indicates whether the student has been retained in one or more grades. If a retention occurred, did the student's earned marks improve during the second year in that grade? If not, the student may have been socially promoted.

Test Scores

Another piece of valuable information that can be obtained from the student's records is past performance on standardized tests. The results recorded in a student's records generally come from group administered achievement and ability tests. The classroom teacher should compare the student's current class performance with performance on past group tests. A discrepancy may suggest a personal or environmental change that is affecting the student and that needs to be explored more fully. The pattern of test scores may also suggest that a particular skill area has always been difficult. In this situation, the current problems the student is experiencing indicate that the classroom demands have reached a point that the student requires more support to be successful.

Organizing Information from School Records

Information from school records is most useful if it is organized in a way that facilitates discovery of important patterns. The information on each student exists but is often not used until the student experiences difficulty. When that information is summarized in a systematic manner, important patterns may become apparent. Summaries of school records also help in communicating the information to other professionals engaged in the assessment process for a given student. Table 2-1 provides one suggestion for organizing the information from school records.

Work Samples and Portfolio Assessment

Analyzing work samples and conducting portfolio assessments are two related ways of examining a student's current classroom performance. Many professional educators analyze work samples or develop work portfolios for their students. Some teachers, however, wait to engage in these tasks until a student begins to experience difficulty. The suggestions listed below will help in working with these teachers.

Work Samples

Analyzing work samples has also been called *permanent product analysis* or *outcome recording* (Alberto and Troutman, 1986; Cooper, 1981). It is a way of systematically observing the work that a student attempts in the classroom. Typically, work sample analysis is used to examine academic skills. During the assessment process, the classroom teacher collects work samples from the subject areas in which the student experiences the most difficulty. These samples are often attached to the referral form when an individual comprehensive evaluation is requested. This material then becomes part of the documentation for the need for special services.

Collecting the samples is only one part of the process. For the samples to be useful, it is important to have a systematic approach to examining each piece of work and summarizing the key data. A form can be attached to each work sample that facilitates the process of looking at the directions for the assignment, the completion time, the general appearance of the work, the patterns of errors, and the patterns of correct responses. Table 2-2 illustrates one possible form that could be attached to each work sample. Discussions of error patterns for specific subjects appear in later chapters.

Table 2-1 Organizational system for data from school records

Name _____ Date _____
Birth _____ Current Grade Placement _____

School Changes
How many school changes have occurred? _____
Grade level when changes occurred? _____
Reasons for each school change: _____
Describe any fluctuations of grades following each change: _____
_____
_____

Attendance
Seasonal attendance problems during _____ fall, _____ winter, _____ spring
Grade levels when attendance was problematic _____
Reasons for problematic attendance: _____
Attendance is becoming a problem but was not a problem before
_____ yes _____ no   Tardiness _____ is a problem now
                                 _____ has been a problem in the past
                                 _____ has never and is not now a problem
Reasons for tardiness: _____

Grades and Retention
Was this student ever retained? _____ yes _____ no
If so, what grade level(s)? _____
In what subjects are the poorest grades earned? (list subject and grades) _____
_____
When were poor grades first earned in these subjects? _____
Describe any annual pattern of grade fluctuations: _____
_____

Group Administered Test Scores

Test Name	General Ability (Date Given)	Score (Standard Score or Percentile)

Achievement Percentile Rank

Test Name & Date	Word Attack	Comprehension	Calculation	Problem Solving	Grammar/ Spelling

Other Important Observations from School Records

_____
_____
_____

Table 2-2 Description of work sample

Work Sample for (Name) _____ Subject _____

Directions were: given orally _____ read by the student _____ other (describe) _____

Completion time for this student: _____

Estimated average completion time for majority of classmates: _____

Appearance (yes–y, no–n)

Letters/numbers formed correctly _____

Letters/numbers adequately spaced _____

Legible _____

Writing either too dark or too light _____

Writing uniform size _____

Reversals _____ Inversions _____ Transpositions _____

Task completed _____

Quality of work deteriorates with length of task _____

Task completed _____

Concept Required or Objective of Task:

Describe Error Patterns:

Describe Strengths or Patterns of Correct Responses:

Portfolio Assessment

Portfolio assessment, introduced in chapter 1, is an expansion of the work folder concept that has been popular with teachers for many years. Teachers often collected samples of students' work in individually labeled folders. Periodically, these folders were sent home for the parents to review, sign, and return, or the folder was shown during regularly scheduled parent conferences as an illustration of why specific grades were earned. The work folder concept emerges as a portfolio assessment when it becomes a systematic source of planning and communication with the student as well as the parents.

Suggestions for using portfolio assessments can be found in the work of several authors (Choate, Enright, Miller, Poteet, and Rakes, 1992; Fields, Spangler, and Lee, 1991; Irwin, 1991; Paulson, Paulson, and Meyer, 1991; Valencia, 1990). Portfolios should be developed in a systematic manner by collecting assignments over predetermined intervals. The collected assignments should also reflect the student's various stages of learning a new concept or skill. The teacher should analyze the samples collected using a form like the one in Table 2-2. However, the portfolio should also serve as a focus of teacher/student problem solving discussions. The teacher can assist the student in some self-evaluation of selected samples. Together the teacher and the student can discuss reasons for difficulty or success with particular assignments. The teacher may modify how instruction is presented or the student may modify an approach to tasks based on these discussions. Notes about the discussions, the decided modifications, and samples of future assignments are included in the portfolio and provide invaluable data about attempted strategies. This information can also be shared with the student's parents or members of the assessment team.

Special education teachers should develop portfolios for students with whom they work and for each area requiring special instruction. Special education teachers can work with regular classroom teachers on the development of portfolios for students not currently served in the special education classroom. For example, the regular teacher can be encouraged to keep reading, written language, or mathematics portfolios on all students. Tape recordings of oral reading, successive drafts of written compositions, or math practice work sheets can be included in the portfolios. The regular classroom teacher can use these as vehicles to teach self-monitoring in problem solving discussions with students. Samples of exemplary products as well as substandard products provide important balance for these discussions. If the classroom teacher and the student reach an impasse in terms of knowing how to proceed with instruction on a skill or concept, the portfolio can be used as a point of consultation with other teachers. This preferral consultation may result in suggestions for further modifications that can be attempted in the regular classroom. Should these modifications not result in success, the time for referral has been reached. But the teacher already has systematically collected and analyzed data that can help the assessment team develop more precise evaluation questions.

Attempted Modifications

Dedicated classroom teachers frequently adjust or modify instruction to meet the needs of students. Sometimes these modifications are made because the whole class experienced more difficulty on an assignment than was expected. That is a signal to the teacher that reteaching the material or using a different approach to teaching the material is needed. At other times, a teacher works one-to-one with a particular student because that student is experiencing more difficulty than classmates are on a task. During these sessions, the teacher may ask the student more questions than was possible in the group instruction to learn how the student is thinking about the material. The teacher can then demonstrate or explain in a different way the material the student does not understand. This type of modification of instruction is such a natural part of good teaching that some teachers may not even be aware they are doing it.

There are times when even a highly experienced teacher has trouble thinking of a different way to present a concept or meet the instructional needs of a student. Frequently, this happens because the teacher and the student are too close to the situation to see solutions that might be more apparent to someone else, or the student has a unique learning need that is unfamiliar to the classroom teacher. When confronted with either of these situations, experienced and confident teachers seek the advice of another teacher. Such experienced teachers are not threatened profes-

Table 2-3 Instructional modifications

Teacher Modifications
1. Adjust language structures and speed to the needs of the student.
2. Provide a model of organization by using advanced organizers.
3. Provide a consistent means of rewarding the student's behaviors.
4. Give feedback more often and closer to the student's responses.
5. Make full use of resource personnel.
6. Train student helpers.
7. Involve students in the decision making pertaining to their own work assignments and reward systems.
8. Guide students to chart progress.
9. Provide extra repetition or practice.
10. Provide a visual stimulus with oral instruction.
11. Slow the pace of instruction.

Student Instructional Modifications
1. Provide untimed test or assignment completion time.
2. Rephrase instructions.
3. Supplement instruction with study guides or concept previews.
4. Adjust length of activity (section off pages; reduce number of items).
5. Change response mode (cross-out, oral, computer).
6. Highlight key words/letters in color.
7. Accompany verbal concepts with concrete examples.
8. Use aids such as a calculator or word processor with spell check.

Environmental Modifications
1. Establish clearly posted rules for behavior.
2. Establish clearly posted rules and place for turning in assignments.
3. Provide a visual display of a sample lesson format.
4. Provide a carrel to isolate the student from the distractions of the classroom.
5. Change the student's location in the room.
6. Mark clearly all centers in the classroom.
7. Arrange furniture in the classroom to avoid congestion and to provide distraction-free work areas.

sionally by the need to ask for help in solving an instructional problem. There are teachers, however, who feel that asking for help is like admitting they are not capable teachers. Unfortunately, this attitude can interfere with collegial consultations that would help everyone feel more able.

Since some teachers may be hesitant about asking for assistance in solving an instructional or behavioral problem, many school districts have prereferral procedures that require that consultation take place before a student is referred for an individualized evaluation. These prereferral procedures are often coordinated by small groups of teachers called student support teams, *assistance/support teams,* or teacher/student assistance teams. The purpose of the team is to try to solve the problem within the regular classroom and without putting a student through an individualized evaluation. These teams recognize that the problem may be rooted in environmental variables, teacher variables, learner variables, or some interaction of these variables. Some of the suggestions that an assistance team might make are listed in Table 2-3.

Assistance teams are different from evaluation teams. Assistance teams are often composed of regular classroom teachers. These teachers understand what would be reasonable modifications within the context of regular classrooms. Sometimes a special education teacher, school psychologist, school social worker, or principal is invited to participate, depending on the nature of the problem, but these specialists typically are not regular members of the team. The assistance team asks that the regular classroom teacher provide a description of the problem and some work samples if the problem is academic rather than behavioral. The assistance team talks with the teacher, and at times with the student, about attempts to solve the problem. The assistance team may then suggest possible modifications that have not been tried, or they will assure the teacher that what has been done is all that can reasonably be done in the regular classroom and suggest that the student be referred for an individualized evaluation. Some school districts impose a guideline for how long modifications should be attempted before a referral is made. Some assistance teams meet with a teacher across several sessions to fine-tune modifications based on the outcome of the first attempts to implement suggested changes. The assistance team uses the data from school records, work samples, and portfolios assembled from the regular classroom. A team member may interview the student or observe in the classroom. However, assistance team members should not administer any screening or diagnostic tests individually. If the assistance team feels everything has been tried and additional individual test data is needed, a formal referral of the student is made. At this time, the parents must give written permission for individual assessment procedures to be used. Then an *evaluation team* becomes involved. While the evaluation team may include a classroom teacher, this team more typically is made up of a school nurse, a school social worker, a school psychologist, a special educator, a speech/language therapist, and an occupational or physical therapist.

Interviews

Regular classroom teachers have frequent conversations with students and their parents about academic and behavioral progress. These conversations are not interviews, but they do provide important information that should be shared with the assistance team and with the evaluation team. Members of either the assistance team or the evaluation team may conduct more formal interviews of the classroom teacher, the student, or the student's parents to help shape hypotheses that will be examined during modifications or assessment.

According to Barnett and Zucker (1990), interviews have four specialized functions: a formal diagnostic technique, a method to study private experiences, a data-gathering technique, and an educational technique. These four functions are discussed in more detail in chapter 7. Interviews used as a formal diagnostic technique or method to study private experiences require specialized training and experience to conduct. However, teachers serving on an assistance team or an evaluation team may be in the position of conducting an interview to gather data. Ideas about preparing for, conducting, and reporting on data-gathering interviews are discussed in this chapter.

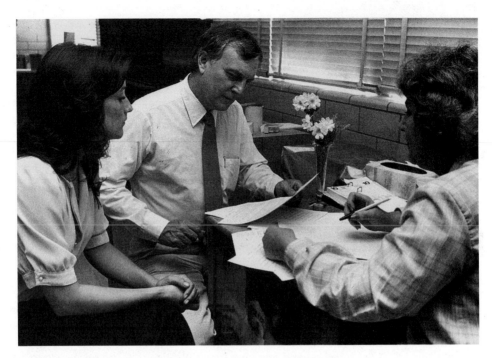

Parents review work samples the teacher has gathered for a planned interview. *Source:* Meri Houtchens-Kitchens/The Picture Cube

Preparing for the Interview

Interviewing is a planned, purposeful activity, not a quick question in the hall or lunchroom. The quality of the information collected often depends on careful preparation. Data-gathering interviews seek information on the perceptions of people involved with a student at risk for academic or behavioral problems. It is important to learn about the student's, teacher's, and parents' views of why the learning or behavior problem exists, what has been done to improve the situation, what could be done that has not been tried, and the motivation of all involved to participate in changes to solve the problem.

Several steps are taken during the preparation of a data-gathering interview. The first step is a careful review of existing school records and work samples as described earlier in this chapter. If this information was organized several days before the actual interview, the interviewer should spend some time scanning it just before beginning the interview. This preparation will convey a message of caring and concern to the person being interviewed.

Another important step in preparing for an interview is making decisions about who will be interviewed and why. All key participants should be interviewed—the student, the parents, and current teachers. Sometimes it is helpful to interview past teachers. Students may live with relatives even though parents have custody. In these situations it is important to interview the relatives with whom the student lives.

Each person interviewed will have a unique perspective on the student and the problem situation. Discovering these diverse viewpoints is the reason each person is picked for an interview. The next step in preparation for the interview is developing questions that need to be explored. Some of the same questions may be asked of all individuals interviewed. These questions might explore perceptions of specific strengths, specific weaknesses, the source of the problem, and possible solutions. Questions about classroom performance are directed to current teachers, while parents can answer questions about developmental history, homework routines, and responsibilities for chores and self-care. Both teachers and parents can be asked about effective management techniques and their perceptions of possible solutions. If there is a discrepancy in viewpoint between the parents and the teachers, between teachers, or between parents, the reasons for those discrepancies can be probed during an interview. Most of these questions should also be addressed to the student if the student has the language and cognitive skills to respond. All persons interviewed should be asked if they know of information important to the solution of the academic or behavior problem that was not covered during the interview. Using this last open-ended question again conveys an attitude of care and concern about the person's perspective.

The fourth step in preparing for the interview is to schedule a time and place for conducting the interview. The length of time needed will depend on how many questions need to be explored. The interview time should be long enough to probe responses to questions so the interview has the feel of a dialogue rather than a rapid-fire question and answer session. While it may be necessary to structure the time so the interview does not go on for hours, it is important that the available interview time be unhurried. If an important piece of information has to be explored in greater depth, it would be better to schedule a follow-up interview than to try to rush. When scheduling the interview, it is also important to conduct it in a place that is convenient to as many of the participants as possible. Many times that will be the centrally located school. However, if students are bused long distances or parents do not have transportation, another location—the student's home, the local church, or the local community hall—may be preferred. Flexibility in scheduling the time and location of the interview is another way to express genuine interest in the person's point of view.

The final step in preparing for the interview is arranging the physical environment just before the beginning of the interview. Simpson (1990) urges that interviewers ensure that the environment is professional and private and that appropriate furniture is available. Privacy conveys a sense of importance and concern. It also helps the person being interviewed be more open about embarrassing or difficult subjects. Adult-size furniture should be provided for all adults. If a child is being interviewed, the child should have a comfortable chair that allows his or her feet to touch the floor. An adult folded into a too small chair or a child whose feet dangle in mid-air will become uncomfortable and restless. Answers and comments may be cut short to escape the uncomfortable physical environment. Finally, the furniture should be arranged in a small group without barriers between participants. If a table is needed to review work samples, a small round table should be used. It is preferable, however, to avoid the use of tables or desks as they may create the sense of barriers.

Conducting the Interview

An interviewer who is well prepared will be able to enter the interview in a more relaxed manner. When the interviewer is well prepared, attention can be directed to body language, eye contact, and active listening. This is critical in establishing an open and caring tone that will facilitate the information exchange. As the interviewer begins the interview, it is helpful to think of the available time period as divided into stages. Friend and Cook (1992) divide the interview into three stages, the introduction, the body of the interview, and the close. During the introduction stage, the interviewer helps set a relaxed and open tone. Introductions of all participants are made and some time is spent in casual conversation. The purpose of and the available time for the interview are also stated explicitly. The final item covered during the introduction is how the material will be recorded and used. Most interviewers need to take notes during the interview so important information is not forgotten and can be shared with other team members later. This should be explained during the introduction phase of the interview. Tape recording is generally not a good idea. Taping makes people nervous and could arouse suspicion, which may interfere with the quality of information obtained. Taping is also time consuming. Once the tape is made, the only way to summarize the information is to listen to the interview again. If notes are made during the interview, time is saved. Finally, mechanical difficulties can occur. Batteries can run down or the tape may fail to record. If the interviewer is relying on the tape in this situation the material is lost.

The body of the interview occurs after the introductions and contains the most substance. Several authors have offered suggestions on this stage of the interview (Brinkley, 1989; Friend and Cook, 1992; Gargiulo, 1985; Gazda, Asbury, Balzer, Childers, and Walters, 1991; Simpson, 1990). The interviewer needs to actively listen in a nonjudgmental fashion. The interviewer should use open-ended questions rather than yes/no questions or single-word response questions. Asking parents to describe the morning or homework routine of a student or to discuss management strategies that have worked for them are ways of encouraging parents to share information freely. Asking the teacher what modifications have been tried already and the success of each is a focused way of encouraging a teacher to share. If the teacher or parent pauses to gather their thoughts, the interviewer should allow the needed silence rather than pose another question too quickly. If the interviewer does not fully understand what the person is explaining, the interviewer should press for clarification. It is also important to listen to the feelings of the person being interviewed and reflect those feeling to the person. Acknowledging that a situation is discouraging or frustrating helps the person feel that the interviewer really hears and understands the feelings behind a situation. Throughout the body of the interview, the interviewer should monitor the time and pace the questions so that all critical material is covered.

The third stage of the interview, the close, provides an opportunity to summarize the main points covered in the interview. The interviewer should remind the person of the purpose of the interview and with whom the information will be shared. Next the interviewer should summarize the main points that will be shared. The close of the interview is a good opportunity to ask if any important information has not been

Table 2-4 Organizational form for summarizing interview data

Informant	Primary Problem	Perceived Cause	Attempts to Solve	Recent Changes in Severity	Causes of Recent Changes	Alternative Solutions	Student Strengths	Student Weaknesses
Student Mother/Guardian Father/Guardian Teacher 1 subject Teacher 2 subject Other (Specify)								

covered. This permits the person being interviewed to add comments or topics the interviewer may not have considered. The interviewer should also explain the next step in the process and when the next opportunity for information exchange will occur. Finally, the interviewer should thank the person for his or her time and effort in sharing information.

Reporting Interview Results

Interview information is invaluable, but it must be summarized in some fashion so it can be efficiently communicated to other team members. It is too time consuming to repeat all the details of the interview during a team meeting. It is best if the interviewer can summarize the perceptions of each person interviewed in a way that conveys similarities and differences in viewpoints. An organizational form like the one shown in Table 2-4 is one way to summarize pages of interview notes from several different interviews.

Observations

Interviews are indirect methods of gathering data. Just because the person being interviewed reports that a behavior or skill occurs does not mean that it actually occurs or that it occurs with the frequency or intensity reported. Observations provide a means for verifying reports gathered during interviews. Methods for conducting and recording observational data vary depending on whether the observation is a preliminary one or a follow-up.

Preliminary Observations

Preliminary observations are conducted by a member of either the assistance team or the evaluation team. Typically, the team member has interviewed the parent or the classroom teacher and has a general idea of the behaviors or skills that are of particular concern. The team member has not yet interviewed the student and will not do so until after the observation has been made. This allows the observation to

Table 2-5 Continuous record observational form

Student Minnie	Date April 3, 1993
Observer Ms. Brown	
Classroom Activity Independent seat work	

Reason for Observation: Minnie seems to be out of her seat constantly when she should be at her seat working on her work sheet.

Time	Event
11:00–11:02	Minnie comes in from playground, goes directly to her desk, and sits
11:02–11:05	Minnie sits while teacher hands out and explains spelling work sheet
11:05–11:08	Minnie gets pencil from desk, reads work sheet
11:08–11:09	Minnie begins to write, breaks pencil
11:09–11:13	Minnie gets up, walks to pencil sharpener, sharpens pencil, returns to seat
11:14–11:18	Minnie writes on work sheet
11:18–11:20	Minnie drops pencil on floor, gets up, picks up pencil, returns to seat
11:20–11:25	Minnie writes on work sheet
11:25–11:27	Minnie gets up, places work sheet in folder on teacher's desk
11:27–11:28	Minnie returns to seat, puts pencil in desk, looks around room
11:28–11:30	Minnie gets up, walks to teacher's desk, asks teacher if she can get a drink of water, teacher tells Minnie to return to seat
11:30	Minnie begins to return to seat, lunch bell rings

Source: Reprinted with the permission of Merrill, an imprint of Macmillan Publishing Company from ASSESSING SPECIAL STUDENTS, Third Edition by James A. McLoughlin and Rena B. Lewis. Copyright ©1990 by Macmillan Publishing Company. Originally published by Merrill Publishing Company.

take place without the student's awareness of who is being observed. The observer has a better opportunity to see the student's typical behavior if the student is unaware that he or she is the focus of the observation.

Preliminary observational data must be gathered in a way that facilitates communication to other team members. Two approaches are used to conduct and record preliminary observations. One approach is called *continuous recording* or *real-time recording*. In this approach, the recording form lists the student's name, the observer, the class activity, and the reason for the observation. The reason is an observable description of the problematic behavior as reported during interviews. The observer then records the time along the left margin of the form and notes the events occurring opposite each time notation. Table 2-5 provides an illustration of a continuous record observational form.

A second approach to making a preliminary observation is called *sequence analysis* (Sulzer-Azaroff and Mayer, 1977), *antecedent-consequence anecdotal record*, or *record of discriminated operants* (Barlow, Hayes, and Nelson, 1984). In this approach the observer identifies the problematic behavior, such as failure to comply with rules. The observer records the time along the left margin of the observational form, then notes the event that preceded the behavior, the behavior, and the consequence of the behavior. This type of recording is particularly helpful if it is suspected that the environmental response to the behavior is reinforcing or perpetuating the behavior. In this situation the assistance team may be able to make recommenda-

Table 2-6 Antecedent-consequence anecdotal record

Student Becky		Date April 4, 1993	
Observer Ms. Brown			
Class Language Arts–Grade 6		Teacher Mr. Willis	
Reason for Observation: Failure to comply with rules			
Time	Antecedent	Behavior	Consequence
10:05	B. raises hand but is not recognized by teacher	B. leaves seat and goes to pencil sharpener	Teacher reminds B. of rule not to leave seat without permission
10:10	B. working, throws pencil down	B. whispers to classmate	Teacher reminds B. of no-talking rule
10:20	Teacher asks class a question	B. raises hand	Teacher calls on classmate
10:23	Teacher asks class a question	B. calls out answer	Teacher reminds B. to raise hand

tions for changing the behavior that will resolve the problem and not necessitate an individualized evaluation. Table 2-6 illustrates an antecedent-consequence anecdotal record.

Preliminary observations provide data on the referred student, but the observer needs to consider the possibility that environmental variables or the quality of interactions are promoting the problematic behavior. Chapter 7 contains information about the importance of environmental and interactional factors that should be considered during preliminary observations.

Follow-Up Observations

Preliminary observations help the evaluation team define problems more precisely. In follow-up observations, the observer uses more precise definitions of problem behaviors and attempts to gather data that can be used as a baseline for determining how deviant the student is and the effectiveness of future interventions. As with preliminary observations, there are different approaches to conducting a follow-up observation depending on whether the problematic behavior is discrete or nondiscrete.

Discrete behaviors are observable and have a clear beginning and ending. Examples of discrete behaviors are calculation errors, oral reading errors, hitting, or throwing an object. Some discrete behaviors, like errors, hitting, or throwing objects, are best recorded using an *event recording* system. An observer using this system has a precise definition of the problem behavior and merely records a tally each time the behavior occurs. Since this is such an easy recording system to use, the classroom teacher can use it while teaching, or a paraprofessional can be directed to record the data. Data can be gathered during specific class periods or across several days. Table 2-7 illustrates an event recording system.

Some discrete behaviors can be tallied using an event recording system, but team members may also be interested in the duration of the behavior. Behaviors that fall

Table 2-7 Event recording system

Example 1

Student _____ Lisa _____	Date _____ April 24, 1992 _____
Class/Setting _____ Recess/Playground _____	Observer _____ Ms. Radogno _____
Behavior _____ Hitting another student _____	Grade _____ 3 _____

Day 1	Day 2	Day 3	Day 4	Day 5
II	III	I	IIII	IIIII
Total = 2	Total = 3	Total = 1	Total = 4	Total = 5

Total for 5 days = 15

Example 2

Student _____ Brian _____	Date _____ October 12, 1992 _____
Class _____ Reading _____	Observation Time _____ 8:30–9:00 _____
Grade _____ 3 _____	Observer _____ Ms. Cebula _____
Behavior _____ Oral reading errors _____	

Type of Error	Tally	Total
Substitution	I	1
Mispronunciations	IIIII II	7
Repetition	I	1
Omission	II	2
Hesitation	IIIII	5
Unknown or aided	III	3
Spontaneous self-corrections	IIII	4

---

into this group include sleeping in class, temper tantrums, and being out of the seat inappropriately. These behaviors can be recorded using a combination of an event recording method and a duration method. Table 2-8 provides an example of this combination system.

A dimension of behavior of interest in some situations is *latency*; that is, how long from a request or question until the student responds? A teacher may note that a student requires more time than classmates to formulate answers to oral questions even when the student raises his or her hand suggesting the information is known. Another teacher may observe that a student tends to procrastinate when directions to an assignment are given. Instead of recording the beginning and ending of behaviors, the observer records the time the request or question was posed and the time the student responded. This format provides data on latency.

Nondiscrete behaviors are overt, like discrete behaviors, but may have less distinct beginnings or endings or may occur too rapidly to be recorded using *event* or *duration* recording. Examples of nondiscrete behaviors include working, sitting, making noise, talking with friends, or daydreaming. Recording systems that lend themselves to these behaviors include *time sampling* and *interval recording*. In both systems the observational time is subdivided into small blocks. For example, a fifteen-minute period is subdivided into fifteen-second blocks. With the time sampling method, the observer places a check in the block if the behavior is occurring at the end of each fifteen-second time period. Some observers use an audio cuing

Table 2-8 Event/duration recording

Example 1: During a single class

Student __Christopher__   Date __November 11, 1992__

Class __Math__   Observation Time __11:00–11:30 AM__

Grade __5__   Observer __Ms. Feigh__

Behavior __Inappropriately out of seat during independent work__

Behavior Begins	Behavior Ends	Duration
11:02	11:05	3 minutes
11:08	11:15	7 minutes
11:20	11:22	2 minutes

Total Episodes – 3   Total Time – 12 minutes

Example 2: Across five days

Student __Samantha__

Grade __Kindergarten__

Observer __Ms. Matook__

Behavior __Temper tantrums consisting of throwing self on floor, kicking and crying__

	Day 1	Day 2	Day 3	Day 4	Day 5
	8:15–8:20	—	10:20–10:25	2:15–2:18	11:30–11:40
	11:05–11:08				2:05–2:09
	1:45–1:55				
Total Episodes	3	0	1	1	2
Total Time	18 minutes	0	5 minutes	3 minutes	14 minutes

---

system so attention is directed only at the end of each block. The observer listens to a tape that has a tone every fifteen seconds. When the tone occurs, the observer looks up to determine if the behavior is occurring, then looks down to record and wait for the next tone.

A similar type of recording form is used with interval recording systems. However, the time when the behavior is recorded differs. When the observer is using a whole-interval recording system, a mark is made if the behavior occurred for the entire fifteen-second interval. When the observer is using a partial-interval system, a mark is made if the behavior occurred at least once during the interval.

Recording systems for time sampling and interval recording can be developed that simultaneously provide data on a comparison student. Before beginning the observational period, the observer asks the classroom teacher to identify a student who has behavior typical of that of others in the class. During the observational session, the observer records data for the student who was referred and for the comparison student. Having this comparison data can be invaluable in determining the deviancy of the behavior of the referred student. Two or three behaviors can be observed during the same session. Table 2-9 provides an example of an interval or time sampling recording form in which a comparison student was used.

Time sampling and interval data can be converted to percentages as a way of communicating the data. The number of times the behavior occurred is divided by the number of intervals. Using the data from Table 2-9, for example, Jessica was talking with classmates at the end of six of the fifteen-second segments. This is

Table 2-9 Time sampling or internal recording system

Referred Student (R) _____Jessica_____
Comparison Student (C) _____Michelle_____
Grade __3__ Class __Reading__ Date __January 12, 1993__
Method __✓__ Time Sampling _____ Whole Interval _____ Partial Interval
Start Time _____ Stop Time __11:06__

	15	30	45	60	15	30	45	60	15	30	45	60	15	30	45	60	15	30	45	60	15	30	45	60
R	X	X	O	O	O	X	O	O	X	O	O	X	X	X	O	O	O	X	X	O	O	O	X	X
C	O	O	O	O	O	O	O	O	O	O	X	O	O	O	O	O	O	O	O	O	O	O	O	O
R	O	O	X	X	X	O	O	O	O	O	O	O	O	O	O	O	O	O	O	O	X	X	X	O
C	X	X	O	O	O	O	O	O	O	O	O	O	O	O	O	O	O	O	O	O	O	O	O	O
R	X	X	X	O	O	O	X	X	X	O	O	O	O	O	O	O	O	O	O	O	X	X	X	O
C	O	O	O	O	O	O	O	O	O	O	O	O	O	O	O	X	O	O	O	O	O	O	X	O

X–Behavior Occurring
O–Behavior Not Occurring

Data Summary

Noises: $R - \dfrac{11}{24} \times 100 = 46\%$ $C - \dfrac{1}{24} \times 100 = 4\%$

Talking: $R - \dfrac{6}{24} \times 100 = 25\%$ $C - \dfrac{2}{24} \times 100 = 8\%$

Tapping: $R - \dfrac{9}{24} \times 100 = 38\%$ $C - \dfrac{2}{24} \times 100 = 8\%$

divided by the total number of fifteen-second segments (twenty-four), and multiplied by one hundred, resulting in talking 25 percent of the time. In contrast, Michelle was talking at the end of only two of the fifteen-second segments, or 8 percent of the time.

Observation During Testing

Evaluation team members also have the opportunity to observe the student during the one-to-one testing situation. This opportunity provides data on differences in the student's behavior between the regular classroom setting and the more structured testing setting. However, to make the best use of this opportunity the team member must be very familiar with the testing materials and procedures and have a way of organizing the data to facilitate communicating it to other team members. Familiarity with test materials and procedures frees the examiner to attend to the behaviors and reactions of the student. If the examiner is not proficient with a test, the examiner's tendency is to overfocus on the manual components, manipulating test materials and recording responses. When the examiner is so occupied with these

Table 2-10 Behavioral observations

Name	Date
Chronological Age	Examiner
Assessment Time	Measures Given

Handedness: _____ right _____ left _____ *variable, explain:* _____

Reaction to New Examiner: *(yes–y or no–n)*

_____initially reserved

_____eye contact within first two minutes

_____answers direct questions

_____gradual warming

_____engages in spontaneous conversation

_____nervous or fearful

_____overly friendly

_____asks personal or inappropriate questions

_____resistant

_____other (describe on back)

Reaction to Novel Tasks: *(yes–y or no–n)*

_____reasonably confident

_____frustrated or discouraged

_____other (explain)

_____requires repetition of directions

_____inclined to distrust own ability

Need for Reassurance: *(yes–y or no–n)*

_____seeks feedback on responses

_____needs encouragement to continue

_____other (explain)

_____indifferent to encouragement

_____seems pleased by periodic encouragement

Attention/Activity Level: *(yes–y or no–n)*

_____lethargic

_____attention/activity appropriate

_____constantly moving, agitated

_____frequent off-task comments

_____activity level interferes with work

_____variable depending on task

_____needs frequent redirection

Work Effort: *(yes–y or no–n)*

_____persists until task completed

_____gives up after brief effort

_____complains, resists

_____other (explain)

Work Style: *(yes–y or no–n)*

_____impulsive, begins work before directions completed

_____strategic approach to problem

_____other (explain)

_____random approach to problem solving

_____spontaneously self-monitors

_____reflects before answering

_____no self-monitoring

Inappropriate or Resistant Behavior (Explain):

Other Comments:

things, important student behaviors can be missed. Therefore, it is vital that the examiner review the test and accompanying materials and have practiced giving the test several times before actually working with a student.

Experienced examiners tend to make observational notes on the recording forms while administering tests. After the session is completed, the examiner can review the comments and summarize the behavior observed during testing. Some evaluation teams develop a common form for summarizing these observations during testing. The form helps remind examiners to consider behaviors in several different categories. When several examiners complete the same form, the team can form an impression of how consistent the student's behavior is and how task demands may serve to alter the behavior. Table 2-10 provides a sample of a behavioral observation form that could be completed by each examiner after each testing session.

Noting the examiner, the assessment time, and the measures given helps in determining consistency of behavior and possible reasons for any noted inconsistencies. Some students respond better to examiners of the same sex and race. For other students, the sex or race of the examiner makes little difference. Some students perform better at certain times of the day, such as first thing or immediately after recess. Other times of the day may make it difficult for students to perform their best. Noting the measures given will help the team determine if the student shows a consistent pattern of behaving more appropriately during verbal or nonverbal tasks, tasks with a lot of examiner involvement versus more independent tasks, or tasks requiring specific skills like writing or answering orally.

Students going through an individualized evaluation are often tested by examiners who are unfamiliar to them. The student's reaction to a new, unfamiliar examiner provides some insight to the student's social skills. Many students are somewhat cautious upon meeting a new adult. As the student feels more comfortable, he or she will relax, give better eye contact, and engage in more spontaneous conversation. This gradual warming is fairly typical. When a student remains very nervous, is overly friendly, or asks inappropriate questions, these behaviors suggest social skill difficulties. It is important to determine whether these behaviors are also present in other settings.

The section on the student's reaction to novel tasks provides some information on the ability to make transitions and take risks. Students with low self-esteem may be resistant to novel tasks or require several repetitions of directions before understanding what to do. The student's comments may indicate that he or she feels incapable of completing something that looks different from assignments given in the classroom. Students who have aversive reactions to novel tasks during evaluation sessions sometimes have similar reactions in the regular classroom. The teacher may report that the student complains of an inability to do an assignment until the teacher provides extra, individualized direction and encouragement.

The student's need for reassurance also provides information about how the student responds to adult feedback. Some students will ask frequently if their answers are correct. The examiner must remind the student that feedback on correctness of answers cannot be given. However, the examiner can make periodic positive remarks about the student's effort and attention. Some students will appear pleased by such remarks while others may treat the remarks with disdain. Some students will attempt a few items and then give up. These students may need encouragement to keep working. Again, the consistency between observations in the testing sessions and in the regular classroom are important to note.

A student's attention and activity level are often factors prompting a referral. Some students become very distractable in the regular classroom but can maintain better attention in the more structured evaluation sessions. For some students, their activity level indicates task difficulty. On appropriately challenging tasks within their skill level, these students are able to sustain attention. When the task becomes difficult, these students may have an increased activity level and may have more difficulty sustaining their attention. Some students need to move around a lot, but their movement does not interfere with their ability to complete tasks correctly. Finally, some students may seem underactive compared to age-mates. Lethargy is as important to note as hyperactivity.

Work effort can suggest motivational level of self-esteem. Students who give up after attempting only a few items may feel unable to complete the task or may feel the task is unimportant. Whatever the underlying reason, this behavior is hard to accept in a regular classroom and, over time, this behavior can influence teacher/student interactions.

Work style relates to the student's typical approach to tasks. Some students will think about questions before attempting to answer them, while others attempt an answer before the examiner finishes the question. Teachers tend to react more positively to reflective than to impulsive answerers. Self-monitoring is another important behavior related to how the student approaches work. Again, teachers tend to respond more favorably to students who spontaneously review the correctness of their work than to students who do not. Work style observations are important because these are behaviors that can be taught and may have a positive influence on teacher/student interactions as well as the quality of the student's work.

A summary sheet of observations made during testing allows comparison of the student's behavior across examiners and tasks. It aids the team in making judgments about the consistency of the student's behavior between examiners and between settings. A summary sheet also helps each examiner organize notes made during testing in a way that facilitates communication of the observational data to others.

Decisions about Tests and Procedures

Any test or procedure used during the assessment process should be selected with a specific question or hypothesis in mind. Initial questions may be fairly broad, but as the process continues more precise questions can be developed. The question or hypothesis being explored will help determine the type of test or procedure that should be used. The evaluation team needs to consider seven dichotomies in selecting types of tests or procedures.

Group versus Individual Data

The assessment data on a student will ultimately contain data from both group and individually administered tests. However, which tests are used will be determined by the stage in the assessment process. Group tests are routinely used in the regular classroom to assess progress on skill development with respect to a specific curriculum or to assess more general achievement. Periodic tests on skills specific to a curriculum are given several times during a grading period and help the teacher adjust instructional procedures for the class. These tests also help identify specific students experiencing atypical difficulty with the skill. Group achievement tests are given in many school districts on an annual or biannual bias. These results compare students to larger populations of students and help track a student's progress over time. Group tests offer the advantage of being able to survey the progress of many students in a relatively brief period of time, making them very cost effective. However, group tests do not allow the close observation of a particular student's approach to the task. Group test data are used by the classroom teacher and the prereferral assistant team members.

Individual tests are not routinely used with the general student population because they are very time consuming to administer when many students must be assessed. However, individually administered tests allow the examiner to make more precise observations of the student's approach to the task. According to PL 94–142, if a student is singled out for an individually administered test, the parents need to be notified and give their permission for the testing to occur, unless all students in a class or group will be tested individually. For this reason, individually administered tests are more typically used by the evaluation team rather than by the prereferral assistance team or the classroom teacher.

Screening versus Diagnostic Data

Another decision that must be made is whether the test or procedure will be used for screening purposes or for diagnostic purposes. A preliminary observation or a test can be used to identify students who may be experiencing more than the usual amount of difficulty. Used in this fashion, the observation or test serves a screening purpose. Salvia and Ysseldyke (1988) recommend that group screening tests have a minimum reliability of .60 while individually administered screening tests have a minimum reliability of .80 (see chapter 3 for a further discussion of test reliability). *Screening tests* survey several areas or a broad range of skills in a particular area. Because a range of areas or skills is examined, there are typically only a few items representing each area or skill level.

Once a student has been identified as having more than the usual amount of difficulty, it is important to pinpoint the nature of the difficulty. *Diagnostic tests* and procedures are used in this situation. Determining the nature of a student's learning patterns allows for more careful instructional planning. If the instructional needs are beyond what can be reasonably addressed in the regular classroom, the student will be placed in special education.

Planning and placement decisions must be based on diagnostic data. Diagnostic tests are typically individually administered. Salvia and Ysseldyke (1988) recommend that individually administered diagnostic tests have a minimum reliability of .90.

Cognitive versus Performance Data

Cognitive data helps determine if a student knows specific information. Performance data helps determine if a student can executive a specific skill. For example, paper and pencil tests or oral questions about the rules of the road in driving, how to dissect a frog in biology, or the steps one would follow to serve a tennis ball illustrate cognitive data. Performance data consists of the behind-the-wheel driving test, actually performing the frog dissection, or serving several tennis balls effectively. When assessing students with disabilities, it is important to have performance data on adaptive behavior, social skills, and oral language.

Norm-Referenced versus Criterion-Referenced Data

Norm-referenced tests are published assessment tools that compare an individual to others who have similar characteristics. The quality of the data depends on the technical adequacy of the measure (see chapter 3 for a further discussion of technical adequacy) and on selecting measures where the norming sample includes students with similar age, ability, racial, economic, and geographic characteristics. Norm-referenced tests contain standardized directions for administering and scoring the measure. If these directions are not followed, the data should not be interpreted. If the directions are not followed, the obtained performance is not comparable to data from an administration where the directions were followed. Because norm-referenced data help make comparisons between individuals, it is necessary for making decisions about the presence of disabilities and the eligibility for special education services. However, examiners must be careful to select measures that were normed on students like the one they are about to test. Many norm-referenced measures do not have adequate representation of culturally diverse students in the norm sample. As new tests are being developed or older tests being renormed, more inclusive norm samples are being used. Many tests remain available, however, in which not enough attention was paid to the diversity of the norm sample.

While norm-referenced data are helpful in making comparisons between students, *criterion-referenced* data help examine skill mastery for a particular student. Between-student comparisons are needed to identify disabilities and determine the need for special education. Data on skill mastery for a student are needed for careful instructional planning. On criterion-referenced measures, the student's performance of a specific skill is evaluated relative to a level of mastery. While some criterion-referenced tests are published, teachers can develop criterion-referenced measures based on the curriculum the student has been using. These curriculum-based, criterion-referenced measures are very helpful in determining which skills in the curriculum the student has mastered and which skills require further instruction. Curriculum-based, criterion-referenced measures are particularly good to use with culturally diverse student populations. Suggestions for developing these measures appear in the chapters on each skill area.

Commercially Produced versus Teacher Developed Measures

Many commercially produced tests exist for group or individual administration, and for screening or diagnostic purposes. Data from commercially produced measures are needed for diagnosis of disabilities and eligibility for special education. Information from these measures is relatively easy to communicate to others. Commercially produced tools are relatively easy to give and save the time needed to develop a measure. A disadvantage of commercially produced tools is that they may not measure the exact content the student has been taught.

Teacher developed measures can be tailored to the instruction the student has had. The qualitative data generated by teacher developed measures are invaluable, but it is sometimes difficult to understand the meaning of any quantitative information and to communicate that data to others. Teachers also have varying skill in development of assessment measures. This can affect the quality of the obtained data.

Objective versus Subjective Data

Some tests are considered objective because there is little qualitative judgment involved in evaluating the responses. Objective tests frequently have a multiple-choice, matching, or true-false format. Objective tests are easy to score and, therefore, place fewer demands on the examiner. However, there are some disadvantages to objective measures. The student is not given an opportunity to elaborate, preventing the examiner from discovering the correct aspects of the student's thinking processes. Objective tests limit the kind of knowledge that can be assessed effectively. It is difficult to assess application, critical evaluation, and written language skills on objective tests.

Subjective data require a qualitative judgment on the part of the examiner or informant as to whether or not the student knows information or can perform a skill. Subjective measures typically require performance of a skill or extended discourse in order to answer. Application, critical evaluation, and problem solving skills can be assessed effectively with subjective measures. The variability in the judgment about the response can be reduced by establishing criteria to evaluate the quality of the answer ahead of time.

Static versus Dynamic Procedures

Static procedures are most commonly used in the assessment process. They help capture what the student knows under given conditions. However, interpretation of static procedures can leave many unanswered questions. Often, the examiner does not know why a student obtained an incorrect answer on a test. The student could have been momentarily distracted and marked the wrong answer inadvertently. The student may have felt rushed or unmotivated and marked random answers without really thinking about the questions. On an individually administered test, the examiner may feel that the student knows the information but because of standardized procedures the examiner is prohibited from probing the student's responses. Most standardized tests are static measures.

Dynamic procedures help identify emerging knowledge and provide insight into the student's thinking processes. Dynamic procedures involve a structured dialogue between the student and the examiner. The examiner may pose a problem and then, if the student has difficulty, may provide some structuring cue or prompt. If this cue or prompt is not enough to help the student answer the problem, another cue or prompt can be provided. The examiner can ask the student to explain his or her thinking processes as the student solves the problem. This allows the examiner to identify parts of that process that are correct; instruction can then build from that point. This allows instruction to address emerging knowledge rather than something too difficult for the student or that the student already knows but carelessly answered incorrectly. Dynamic procedures provide a nonbiased way of assessing the knowledge and skills of students from culturally diverse populations. These procedures are discussed further in the chapters on specific skill areas.

Summary

School Records

1. It is important to determine how many schools the student has been enrolled in and why school changes were made.
2. Regularity of attendance can fluctuate from year to year, from season to season, or may change from a previous pattern.
3. Course grades may signal transition difficulties, the recency of subject-specific difficulties, and the benefit of any previous retentions.
4. Information from school records is most useful if it is organized in a way that facilitates discovery of important patterns.

Work Samples and Portfolio Assessment

1. Analyzing work samples is a systematic way to observe the student's classroom products.
2. Work samples should be analyzed for completion time relative to others in the class, general appearance, patterns of errors, and patterns of correct responses.
3. Portfolio assessment is an expansion of the work folder concept.
4. Using a portfolio for instructional planning and dialogue distinguishes it from the work folder.
5. Portfolios should contain analyzed work samples that illustrate both the student's best performance and substandard work.

Attempted Modifications

1. Dedicated classroom teachers frequently adjust or modify instruction to meet the differing needs of students.
2. Prereferral assistance teams can help brainstorm modifications.
3. When suggestions from the assistance team fail to solve the problem, the student is referred to the evaluation team for a comprehensive individualized assessment.
4. Parents must give their written permission before the evaluation team can work with a student.

Interviews

1. Interviewing is a planned, purposeful activity that is very different from a quick question in the hall or lunchroom.
2. The first step in planning an interview is to review existing school records and work samples.

3. Deciding who will be interviewed and why is another important planning step.
4. Selected questions should be planned in advance of the interview so important information is not overlooked.
5. Scheduling a time and place and setting up the physical environment before the interview begins are also important preparation steps.
6. Interviewers should be conscious of their body language, eye contact, and active listening strategies as a way of establishing a caring tone to facilitate information exchange.
7. During the introduction stage of the interview, the interviewer helps set a relaxed and open tone.
8. During the body of the interview, specific information is obtained.
9. The close of the interview provides an opportunity to summarize the main points covered in the interview and to describe what will happen to the information obtained.
10. Interview information should be summarized in a way that facilitates communicating the similarities and differences of the perceptions of all the people interviewed.

Observations

1. Observations provide a means for verifying reports gathered during interviews.
2. Preliminary observations help the evaluation team define problems more precisely.
3. Continuous recording and sequence analysis are two ways to record preliminary observation data.
4. Follow-up observations provide baseline data on clearly defined problems that can be used to determine deviance and to establish intervention programs.
5. Discrete behaviors that have a clear beginning and ending are best recorded using an event recording system.
6. Recording systems that are useful with nondiscrete behaviors include time sampling and interval recording.
7. Time sampling and interval recording systems can be developed that simultaneously provide data on a comparison student.
8. Time sampling and interval recording data can be converted to percentages as a way of communicating the data.
9. During testing, familiarity with test materials and procedures frees the examiner to attend to the behaviors and reactions of the student.
10. During testing, examiners should note the student's reaction to new examiners, reaction to novel tasks, need for reassurance, attention/activity level, work effort, work style, and any inappropriate or resistant behaviors.

Decisions about Tests and Procedures

1. Group tests are a cost effective way of gathering prereferral data on a large number of students, while individually administered tests allow the examiner to make more precise observations of the student's approach to the task.

2. Screening procedures survey several areas or a broad range of skills, while diagnostic procedures are used to pinpoint the nature of the difficulty.
3. Cognitive data help determine whether a student knows specific information, while performance data determine whether a student can execute a skill.
4. Norm-referenced data facilitate comparisons between individuals, while criterion-referenced data help examine mastery of a concept or skill.
5. Commercially produced measures save test development time but may not measure what has been taught the way teacher developed measures can.
6. Little qualitative judgment is used in evaluating responses on objective tests, but subjective measures are more appropriate for some skills, like application, critical evaluation, and problem solving.
7. Static procedures assess what the student has already learned, but dynamic procedures help tap emerging knowledge and provide insight into the student's thinking processes.

Minimizing Bias and Error in Assessment

Key Terms

Alternate form
Basal
Ceiling rule
Concurrent criterion-related
  validity
Confidence interval
Construct validity
Content validity
Correlation
Correlation coefficient
Criterion-related validity
Derived score
Face validity
Functional exclusion

Internal consistency reliability
Interval data
Likert-type scale
Mean
Median
Mode
Nominal data
Normal or bell curve
Norms
Ordinal data
Percentile rank
Predictive criteria-related
  validity

Protocol
Pure exclusion
Ratio data
Reliability
Split-half reliability
Standard deviation
Standard error of measure-
  ment
Standard score
Stanine
Testing the limits
Test–retest reliability
Validity

Assessment is a complex, multistep process involving several people who gather data from multiple sources. The data has to be organized to facilitate communicating the results to the student, the parents, and the service providers. What is communicated will influence the type of educational program the student receives. At each step in the assessment process it is possible that bias or error could shape the outcome. People have beliefs and perceptions that influence their approach to educational problems and that might be different from those of others involved in the assessment process. Selecting appropriate tools requires judgment on the part of the team and depends on the availability of those tools. Measurement error is always present in assessment tools and needs to be considered. Even statistically good measurement tools can be rendered useless if they are not used correctly or if scoring errors are made. Finally, meaning must be assigned to the data. Error can be introduced during this interpretation stage of the assessment process.

So many opportunities for bias and error are present in the assessment process that it may be tempting to discount the value of the process. However, the assessment process provides a means for solving educational problems that is too important to abandon. For this reason, professionals involved in the assessment process must be aware of how bias and error can be introduced to the process.

PL 94–142 provides a legal mandate that steps be taken to provide a nondiscriminatory assessment by reducing error as much as possible. More important, professionals have an ethical responsibility to ensure that social bias and measurement error do not unduly contaminate assessment outcomes. This important point is reflected in the following statement from Reschly (1979):

> The ultimate criteria that should guide our evaluations of test bias are the implications and outcomes of test use for individuals. . . . [T]est use is fair if the results are more effective interventions leading to improved competencies and opportunities for individuals. Test use is unfair if opportunities are diminished or if individuals are exposed to ineffective interventions as a result of tests. (p. 235)

The purpose of this chapter is to develop an awareness of the opportunities for increasing the amount of bias and error in the assessment process so that these variables can be better controlled.

The Human Factor

All people have beliefs and perceptions that shape their decisions and actions. All people make mistakes. People are intimately involved in every aspect of the assessment process. For all these reasons, people are the most frequent source of bias and error in the assessment process.

Beliefs and Perceptions

Beliefs and perceptions are shaped over time through personal experiences and the influence of significant others in a person's life. Cultural group membership, socio-economic level, and the range of experiences a person has also help form beliefs. The demographics of the student population in American public schools is becoming increasingly diverse (Hodgkinson, 1991), yet educational professionals tend to come from predominately white, middle-class backgrounds. All professionals involved in the assessment process need to be aware that their beliefs and perceptions may not match those of the population they serve. Professionals must be watchful for the contaminating influence of both overt and subtle prejudice. An awareness of the possibility of prejudice is one way to prevent its impact. Another way to prevent cross-cultural misunderstanding from contaminating the assessment process is to develop an understanding of the customs and beliefs of the community served by the school.

Differences in the perceptions and beliefs between the professionals involved can also influence what happens during assessment. Ehrenberg (1992) studied the perceptions of regular and special educators on meeting the needs of students at risk for academic failure. She found that regular educators were influenced by their beliefs in what was good for the group as a whole, while special educators were more concerned with individual needs. Certainly, training differences shape these beliefs, but the beliefs have an impact on who is referred for assessment and how assessment questions are formulated. Using a team approach is the best way to ensure a nonbiased assessment. The team should focus on finding solutions to educational problems rather than affixing blame (that is, on the student, the parent, or the regular teacher), because in most instances the problem results from an interaction of environmental and human variables. Team members need to respect each others' expertise and value the information that can be supplied by all informants.

Due Process and Record Keeping

Prior to the passage of PL 94–142, students with severe disabilities were frequently excluded from public education. Decisions were often made to place students in existing special classes without parent input. These decisions reflected a fear of people with disabilities and low expectations of minority populations, beliefs shaped by inexperience and a lack of understanding of and tolerance for diversity. Gradually, during the 1950s and 1960s, parents and others concerned about this situation began meeting in small groups to provide support and encouragement to each other. Small groups merged and ultimately formed nationwide organizations. These small groups and national organizations began using the courts to test the fairness of practices that excluded or restricted students with disabilities or minority students.

Several landmark class action lawsuits found that unfair practices existed that limited access to education, resulted in inappropriate education, or were based on discriminatory testing procedures. One case often cited in the historical development of PL 94–142, which on first examination may seem to have little to do with the education of students with disabilities, was *Brown* v. *Board of Education* in 1954. In this case, the Supreme Court ruled that racial segregation in public education violated the Fourteenth Amendment. The Court ruled that the equal protection doctrine protected a class of persons in educational placement because of the importance of education to a democratic society. Separate placement did not ensure equal opportunity. In the *Brown* case, the class of persons involved was a racial minority, but in later cases the same equal protection doctrine argument was used on behalf of students with disabilities.

Another significant access to education case was *Pennsylvania Association for Retarded Children (PARC)* v. *Commonwealth of Pennsylvania* (1971). The parents of thirteen children with mental retardation filed this class action suit because the children had been labeled uneducable and had been denied an education. The three issues involved included a violation of due process surrounding the exclusion of these children, a violation of equal protection because the schools lacked a rational basis for saying that the children were uneducable, and finally, charging that the children did not have an equal education to which, under state law, all children were entitled. This case was important because it won access to public school programs, tuition and maintenance costs in approved institutions, and homebound instruction when appropriate.

Brown provided the legal foundation for the decision in *PARC*. *PARC* provided the impetus for two other landmark cases. *Mills* v. *Board of Education of the District of Columbia* cited violations of due process of law surrounding excluding, suspending, expelling, reassigning, and transferring children with disabilities from regular education classes. *Maryland Association for Retarded Children (MARC)* v. *State of Maryland* ruled that when the opportunity for education is made available and the state is providing it, this opportunity must be made available to all on an equal basis regardless of the degree of disabling condition, and at no charge to the family. During the early seventies, approximately two dozen similar access to education suits were filed across the country that dealt with the *pure exclusion* of students with disabilities.

While cases were being filed concerning students eligible for access to education, other cases looked at the appropriateness of education and the issue of *functional exclusion*. One such case was *Lau* v. *Nichols*. This 1974 Supreme Court case was a class action suit brought by non–English speaking Chinese students. The Supreme Court ruled in favor of the students in this suit against the San Francisco Unified School District. In essence, the Supreme Court ruled that despite the same facilities, textbooks, teachers, and curriculum as the other students, these non–English speaking students had been excluded from a meaningful education because of the language difference.

Another case that addressed the issue of appropriate programs was *Fialkowski* v. *Shapp* (1975). The two multihandicapped Fialkowski children were the plaintiffs in this action that charged that their rights to an appropriate education had been violated under the equal protection and due process clauses of the Fourteenth Amendment. The plaintiffs, because of intelligence approximating that of preschoolers, had no chance to benefit from the programs emphasizing reading and writing skills that were offered to them in the Philadelphia schools. The trial brief summarized standards and procedures for an appropriate educational offering.

The issue of nondiscriminatory evaluations and placements was addressed by two cases. *Hobson* v. *Hansen* (1967) challenged the rigid tracking system used by the Washington D.C. public schools. This tracking system seemed to discriminate against black students and poor students. The differentiated curricula resulted in unequal educational opportunity and an inferior education. This case laid the foundation for cases involving the fairness of testing procedures that resulted in disproportionate representation of minority students in special education classes.

The *Larry P.* v. *Riles* class action suit was first filed in 1979 on behalf of six black elementary children alleged to be educable mentally retarded. The plaintiffs' argument contended that the children had been inappropriately classified and placed in special classrooms. The plaintiffs further argued that such misplacement resulted in serious injury to the childrens' educational, social, and future economic status. Statistical evidence suggested that a disproportionate number of black children were enrolled in programs for the mentally retarded. The Court found that many measures for assessing intelligence are culturally biased, that misplacement in special education classes carries irreparable harm, and that the racial imbalance in special classes is suggestive of a suspect classification of black children. Similar issues were considered in *Diana* v. *State Board of Education* (1970), filed on behalf of nine Hispanic children with mild mental retardation.

Cases involving access to education, appropriateness of education, and discriminatory testing and placement procedures helped shape the due process and record-keeping requirements of PL 92–142. These requirements help ensure that prejudicial perceptions and beliefs do not contaminate the assessment, IEP planning, or placement process. Records kept throughout these processes document that all who should be involved were involved, that appropriate tools were used, and that the educational decisions were based on performance data. Periodically school districts are monitored by state education officials to ensure that thorough records are kept and that systematic errors are not introduced. It is critical that thorough and accurate records document how decisions were reached and that procedural safeguards are followed.

Competence

The final human factor that can introduce error and bias in the assessment process is the competence of the professionals involved. All professional training programs rest on theoretical perspectives. Therefore, different professionals have different contributions to make to the assessment process. When one professional is given too much responsibility during the process, important theoretical balance is lost and the chance for error increases. Similarly, when a professional is asked to perform a task for which there has been no prior training or only limited supervised experience, the possibility of error increases. All team members share the ethical responsibility for performing only those tasks for which they are thoroughly trained, for maintaining test security, and for ensuring confidentiality for the student and the family involved. Table 1-7 (chapter 1) contains the ethical standards for psychologists developed by the American Psychological Association. All assessment team members need to recognize the boundaries of their competence and follow these ethical standards.

Test Selection

Competent assessment team members use various concepts and principles to guide them in selection of appropriate tests. Failure to attend to these concepts and principles increases error in the assessment process and could result in biased decisions that prevent students from making gains they might otherwise make. Assessment team members must consider the purpose of the test, the various aspects of technical adequacy, and the efficiency of the instrument in data collection.

Purpose of Tests

All tests are developed for specific purposes. Examiners must select tests and use them only for the purposes for which they were developed. Some measures are intended to broadly survey achievement in several areas. These screening tests are helpful in determining which students may need to have a more in-depth assessment, but they should not be used to diagnose a disability. It is also critical that the examiner consider whether the test is able to provide data that answer important questions. For example, if the team is assessing a student who appears to have moderate levels of retardation, it is important to explore the student's adaptive behavior skills in depth. It would not be as important to document low achievement in social studies, even if a great test was available. Assessment time is better spent examining adaptive behavior.

Examiners also need to consider the nature of the suspected disability and select tests that are not affected by the disability unless the purpose is to document its presence. A student with cerebral palsy may have severe motor problems involving upper limb, fine, and gross motor movement. If the team wants to assess the residual motor skills available to the student, a motor test is appropriate. However, if the team wants to assess the student's general intelligence, it is important to pick a test that does not require motor skills like assembling puzzles or completing mazes. The student's performance on such a test would reflect the student's motor problems and might be very discrepant with the student's general intelligence when motor proficiency is not required.

Norms

Norm-referenced tests help the assessment team make decisions about level of performance compared with other people. This type of information is used to determine eligibility for special education. A critical variable in the quality of this kind of test is the composition of the comparison group and how closely those people match the demographic characteristics of the student being tested. The examiner should check the description of the norming sample, which should appear in the test manual. The examiner will want to know the age, grade placement, and sex of the people in the sample. At each age or grade level, the examiner needs to look at how representative the sample is with respect to race, geographic location in the nation, urban or rural setting, and acculturation or socioeconomic level. A well-developed test should represent these variables in the same proportion as that of the general population. A test developer should state which census data were used and how the proportions of these variables for the norm sample compared to the general population. The year or years the sample data were collected helps the examiner evaluate the recency of the norms. Finally, a description of special characteristics may have been systematically included. For example, were students with disabilities included in the norm sample and, if so, in what proportion and at what age levels? When selecting a norm-referenced test for a specific student, the examiner must be sure that the characteristics of the student are well represented in the norm sample.

The examiner also needs to look at the number of subjects included at each norm level. Salvia and Ysseldyke (1988) recommend a minimum of one hundred subjects at each level for which *norms* exist. Assuming that the array of scores were normally distributed, this ensures that the full range of percentiles can be computed without extrapolation.

Correlations

Correlations are the relationship between two variables. Relationships between variables are computed statistically and expressed as a *correlation coefficient.* Correlation coefficients typically range from plus or minus .00 to plus or minus 1.00. When a correlation coefficient falls near the .00 level, it means there is little or no relationship between the variables. One might expect that if eye color was examined in relationship to whether a person smokes or does not smoke, a low correlation near the .00 level would exist. It would be interpreted that eye color bears no meaningful relationship to smoking preferences. In contrast, if the correlation coefficient falls near the 1.00 level, it means that the two sets of measures vary in perfect unison. The plus or minus indicates the direction of the relationship. A plus denotes that if one set of measures increases then the other set of measures increases, for example, weight increases with calories consumed. This is known as a positive correlation. A minus denotes that as one set of measures increases the other set of measures decreases, for example, the more alcohol one drinks the less coordinated he or she becomes. This is known as a negative correlation. Although it is theoretically possible, it is unusual to have a perfect correlation (± 1.00) between sets of variables. In reality correlation coefficients fall somewhere between .00 and 1.00.

It is important to remember that correlation does not imply causation. If one set of measures has a high correlation with another set, it does not mean that one measure causes the other. It merely means that when one measure varies in a particular direction the other measure is likely to vary in a similar fashion. It is important for examiners to understand this interpretation issue for correlation coefficients because correlation techniques are used to determine test reliability and validity.

Reliability

Reliability is the degree to which a test is consistent in measuring what it purports to measure. This is important because examiners want to generalize a student's performance on tests to other situations. If a test is inconsistent and produces different results each time it is administered, the results cannot be easily generalized.

Different types of reliability are associated with generalizations that might be of interest. When examiners are interested in a test's stability or generalizability over time, *test–retest reliability* is critical. To determine test–retest reliability, the test developer/publisher administers the test to a subgroup of the norming population. After a brief interval, the test is readministered to the same group. The interval between testing sessions should be long enough that specific questions are forgotten but not so long that new learning occurs. Salvia and Ysseldyke (1988) point out that the shorter the interval between sessions the higher the reliability estimate is likely to be. Once the two sets of scores from the same subjects are obtained, correlation techniques are used to determine the relationship of the first set of scores to those of the second set.

When examiners are interested in generalizing test performance to tasks involving similar types of questions, two types of reliability can be examined. Alternate form reliability requires that the test developer construct two equivalent forms of the same test. Then a large subgroup of subjects is divided into two groups. Group A takes one form first and the other form second. Group B also takes both forms but in reverse order. The length of time between administration of the two forms is a factor in alternate form reliability just as it is in test–retest reliability. Then, for each group, correlation techniques are used to examine the relationship between the scores on the first form with the scores on the second form. In some test manuals authors use term-equivalent form reliability in place of alternate form reliability. Another type of reliability that examines generalizability of performance to similar task items is *internal consistency reliability,* also called *split-half reliability.* To obtain internal consistency reliability, the test developer administers the instrument to a subgroup of the population. After the subjects complete the test, their responses are divided into two forms of the test. For example, even numbered items comprise one form while odd numbered items comprise a second form. The relationship between these two created forms is then examined with correlation techniques. This way of determining reliability should only be used with untimed tests. When a test is timed, it is possible that all subjects will not complete all items; this would distort the results of the correlation procedures.

In addition to generalizability over time or between similar items, an examiner may be concerned with reliability between people who count or evaluate a behavior or skill. This type of reliability is important when there is a specific procedure for coding observational data such as time sampling, interval sampling, or event recording (see chapter 2 for a discussion of these procedures). Such reliability is called interrater reliability. Interrater reliability is important for standardized behavior rating scales. The target behaviors on these scales should be described clearly enough that people who have known the student for similar lengths of time in the same setting would rate the behavior in a similar manner. Interrater reliability considers the percentage of observer agreements relative to the total number of observations recorded.

Regardless of the type of reliability of interest to the examiners, a well-constructed measure with good reliability can be made unreliable if standardized procedures are not followed. Therefore, it is extremely important that all standardized directions be given in exactly the same manner they were given to the norming sample. The environmental conditions relative to group or individual administration, group size, noise level, and test materials should also be followed. Specific information about these important variables is contained in the test manual.

Data about the reliability of the measure should also be included in the test manual or an accompanying technical manual. When reviewing this information, the examiner needs to make a judgment about whether to use a measure based on the reliability data. Salvia and Ysseldyke (1988) recommend two standards for determining the acceptability of reliability:

1. Group Data. If test scores are to be used for administrative purposes and are reported for groups, a reliability of .60 should probably be the minimum.
2. Individual Data. If a test score is used to make a decision for one student, a much higher standard of reliability is demanded. When important educational decisions, such as tracking and placement in a special class, are to be made for a student, the minimum standard should be .90. When the decision being made is a screening decision, such as a recommendation that a child receive further assessment, there is still need for high reliability. For screening devices, we recommend a .80 standard. (p. 128–129)

Standard Error of Measurement

Error is present in all psychometric measurement. The score a student obtains on any given test is the sum of the student's theoretical true score and some inherent measurement error (that is, obtained score = true score + error). One way to determine the amount of error is to give the same test over and over again to the same student and examine the standard deviation of the distribution of the student's scores. This is not practical. Instead, a statistic called the *standard error of measurement* helps determine the amount of measurement error in a test.

The test developer uses the reliability coefficient for a test and the standard deviation, a measure of variability of the test, to calculate the standard error of measurement. The formula is:

$$SE_m = \sigma \sqrt{1 - r}$$

where σ represents the test's *standard deviation* and r represents reliability. The standard error of measurement is a function of the technical quality of the test. The higher the reliability of a test, the lower the standard error of measurement.

Knowing the standard error of measurement not only helps determine test quality

Table 3-1 Determining a confidence interval

Step 1.	Student's obtained score is 93
Step 2.	Reliability coefficient for the test is $r = .87$ Standard deviation for the test is $\sigma = 11$
Step 3.	$SE_m = \sigma \sqrt{1 - r}$ $SE_m = 11 \sqrt{1 - .87}$ $SE_m = 11 \sqrt{.13}$ $SE_m = 11 \times .36$ $SE_m = 3.96$ or rounded to 4
Step 4.	Confidence interval of ± 4 $93 + 4 = 97$ $93 - 4 = 89$
Conclusion	68 percent of the time the student's true score falls in the range of 89 to 97

but it also helps determine the range in which the student's true score might fall. This range is called a confidence interval. For example, if a student obtains a score of 93 on a test, it is important to know the range in which the true score falls. This prevents a rigid interpretation of single scores in the decision-making process. In our example, the examiner would look at the standard deviation of the test and the reliability of the test to determine the standard error of measurement. The standard error of measurement is then used to construct a confidence interval around the obtained score. This confidence interval tells the examiner that the student's true score falls within this range 68 percent of the time. Sixty-eight percent is used because that is the portion of the population that falls within one standard deviation of the mean within a normal distribution. Table 3-1 outlines the steps used to calculate the standard error of measure and how that measure is used to determine the confidence interval for our example.

Validity

Reliability and standard error of measurement are two variables that help the examiner judge the technical quality of a test. However, these two variables mean little without information about the validity of the test. *Validity* of a test indicates that the test measures what it claims to measure. For example, suppose a test claimed to measure skill in identifying trees, and the test had good reliability, meaning that over repeated administrations the same student obtained similar scores. The test also had a low standard error of measurement, so the confidence interval was small. However, the items on the test related more to flower identification and had few items about trees. Even if a student received a high score on this test, it would not relate to tree identification skills. For this reason, it is important that the test developer report how the test scores compare to some current skill or some future skill. A test can have good reliability but lack validity.

Validity is the technical aspect of the test that addresses the question of, "Does this test measure what it claims to measure?" Validity is the most important technical attribute of a test. Just as there are different ways to examine reliability depending on the type of generalization you want to make, so too there are different types of validity. *Face validity* is a nonstatistical judgment of the examiner that the test looks like it measures what the title or description states it measures. If a test is reported to be a math test, the examiner can scan the test to see if there are math questions on it. *Content validity* is also nonstatistical but requires a more detailed examination of the test. The examiner looks carefully at the items to determine whether they tap the depth and breadth of the area of interest. In the previous example, the examiner may be satisfied that the test has math problems on it—it has face validity—however, on closer examination it is apparent that the test only assesses addition facts. This test might be appropriate if the only math assessment question relates to knowing addition facts, but if the examiner is interested in a wider range of math skills, such as other calculation skills and solutions of word problems, this test is too restricted. It lacks content validity.

Examiners need to judge face and content validity relative to the assessment questions they are trying to answer. Test developers may report the steps taken to ensure face and content validity by reporting how the items were developed and if experts in the field were used to judge item appropriateness. Since face and content validity are especially important for achievement tests, the test developer may refer to the match of test items to the scope and sequence charts of various curricula, in specific achievement areas.

Criterion-related validity is determined statistically and relates to how closely a test's scores match some criterion of performance. Correlational techniques are used to determine criterion-related validity. There are two types of criterion-related validity, concurrent and predictive. *Concurrent criterion-related validity* indicates the relationship between performance on the test relative to current performance on some test or skill where a standard already exists. For example, when a new achievement test is developed, the test publisher may use correlational techniques to study the relationship of test scores on the new test to current grades in the subject area or to test scores from an existing test that measures the same achievement skills. *Predictive criterion-related validity* indicates the relationship between performance on the test relative to future skill or success level. Predictive criterion-related validity is important when a test score is used as an entry requirement. For example, the Scholastic Aptitude Test (SAT), Graduate Record Exam (GRE), and Miller's Analogy Test (MAT) are published by the Educational Testing Service and are often used to determine entry to undergraduate or graduate programs of study. The thinking behind these tests is that high scorers on these tests have a greater chance of earning adequate grades and completing the program of study. Since the score is used as a predictive indicator of probable success, it is important that the test developer document a strong correlation between the score and the criterion of successful completion of degrees. Whether a test developer is interested in concurrent or predictive validity, it is critical that a valid criterion measure exists to make the comparison. When discussing criterion-related validity, the test developer should state the criterion selected and the validity coefficient (correlation coefficient) between performance on that criterion and the test described in the manual.

Another type of validity is *construct validity*. This relates to how meaningfully a test measures a psychological trait. These constructs may be traits like intelligence, depression, introversion, or anxiety. Construct validity requires that there be a theoretical model of the trait and that a series of studies supports the meaningful existence of the trait. Then studies are conducted to determine how well the test being developed helps group people (that is, clinically depressed versus nondepressed) or classify them along a continuum (that is, how intelligent or severity of depression). Correlational and factor analytic techniques are used to study construct validity.

Locating Information about Tests

School-based professionals involved in the assessment process have many responsibilities; this limits the time they have to research the quality of tests. Limited time, however, does not relieve them of responsibility for conducting a nondiscriminatory assessment using appropriate tools. There are several sources of information on tests that can help professionals use their time efficiently.

One of the best sources of information on tests is the manual that accompanies the test. The manual should contain information on how to administer and score the test accurately. It should also report the characteristics of the norming sample, reliability data, validity data, and the standard error of measurement. Some tests have two manuals: one contains the administration and scoring procedures; a second technical manual contains the other information needed to evaluate technical quality. An important book, *Standards for Educational and Psychological Testing* (American Psychological Association, 1985), developed by a joint committee of representatives from the American Educational Research Association, the American Psychological Association, and the National Council on Measurement in Education, provides guidelines for standards for tests, the manuals that accompany them, and research reports. This helps test users understand what should be in test manuals and standards for test use. It also helps test developers write manuals that contain information needed to make important test selection decisions. Test users need to be aware that all test developers do not follow the guidelines. Some test manuals do not have critical information; when this occurs, it should be considered a weakness of the test.

When professionals do not have access to manuals of tests but wonder whether a test would be useful, several sources of information can be consulted. Test publishers usually have catalogs that contain information about the type and purpose of the test, age or grade appropriateness, administration time needed, type of scores available, and cost. These catalogs alert professionals to newly developed instruments. Once a test is published, descriptive, evaluative, and related research information about it may appear in professional journals. Journals that frequently contain this type of information include the *Journal of Psychoeducational Assessment* and *Diagnostique*. Other journals that often have articles about assessment tools are *Exceptional Children, Journal of Special Education,* and *Remedial and Special Education*. Descriptive and evaluative information about tests is often collated in reference volumes that are published periodically. Examples of these sources include the *Mental Measurement Yearbook* series (Buros, 1938–1978). *A Consumer's Guide to Tests in Print* (Hammill, Brown, and Bryant, 1989), and *Tests in Print III* (Mitchell, 1983).

Using Measures Appropriately

Competent professionals take steps to ensure appropriate and accurate use of assessment measures. While this starts with selection of technically adequate measures that can provide substantive data on important assessment questions, it also includes preparing the environment, preparing the student, and administering the instrument in an efficient, accurate manner. Failure to attend to these important variables increases the chance that human error will be introduced to the assessment process.

Preparing the Environment

Environmental surroundings influence an individual's concentration and performance on any assessment measure. Therefore, it is important that the examiner set up the environment to minimize distractions. Whether the evaluation is given in a group or individual setting, the examiner should ensure that the room temperature is comfortable, the lighting does not produce distracting shadows or glare, and the furniture is the appropriate size for the individuals being tested. The examiner should be sure that extra maintenance work or construction will not be under way in the vicinity during the planned testing time. Such work can produce unusual and distracting noises that interfere with concentration. A "Do Not Disturb" sign should be posted on the door during testing so the session is not interrupted.

The testing session should be scheduled based on the recommendations listed in the test manual. Typically, testing sessions occur when the individual is well rested and alert. The session length should not produce undue fatigue. If a long session must be scheduled, rest, snack, and activity breaks should be planned to help the individual maintain effort and concentration.

An individually administered test must be given in a private setting. Examiners who are also classroom teachers may not have access to a private testing room. If the examiner is using a classroom for the testing session, other students should not be in the room at the time of the assessment. Privacy can be created in a full-sized classroom by setting up a table in a corner away from the door. The student should face the corner while the examiner is seated looking out toward the rest of the room. This arrangement cuts down on the distractions inherently present in a large classroom. See Figure 3-1 for a model of how a large classroom can be arranged to accommodate a private testing corner. If a group administered test were given in this same classroom, the student desks should be separated and spread out to ensure confidentiality of student responses.

Finally, the examiner must be sure that all the materials needed during the testing session are close at hand. The examiner should check that all the pieces of a test kit are present. The test manual, appropriate student response sheets, and examiner's protocol need to be readily accessible. Other materials, such as extra paper, sharpened pencils, pens, erasers, clipboard, stopwatch, or tape recorder, may also be needed. It is a good idea to have a box of tissue close at hand for the comfort and convenience of both the examiner and the student. These materials

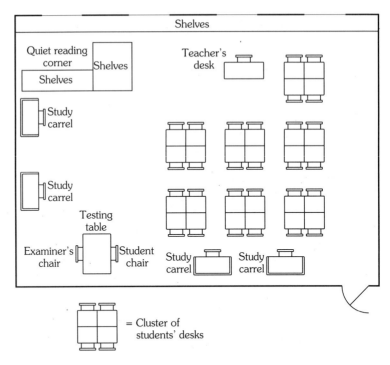

FIGURE 3.1 Testing corner set up in classroom

should be located close to the testing table but out of sight so as not to be distracting. Only those materials that the student is currently using should be on top of the table, and these items should be removed as soon as the student is finished with the task.

Preparing the Student

The physical and psychological state of the student can greatly affect test performance. Therefore, the examiner should take steps to ensure optimal functioning of the student. These steps begin with scheduling the testing session. Sessions need to be scheduled when the student is rested, alert, and not distracted by thoughts of missing a favorite activity. The examiner must coordinate with the classroom teacher to find a good time for the testing. The classroom teacher knows when the student tends to function best and knows the schedule for the student's favorite activities or upcoming special events. A student will not concentrate very well when missing a long-anticipated assembly or special play-off game in physical education. Students with certain health conditions may have variable performances before or after lunch. If a student is on medication, the classroom teacher may have noticed whether performance is affected just before or after taking the medication. All these variables need careful consideration.

On the scheduled day of testing, the examiner should meet the student and spend some time developing a good working relationship. This is called establishing rapport and is critical to optimal performance. The examiner should introduce himself or herself to the student in a friendly, nonthreatening way. If the examiner meets the student at the classroom, the teacher may offer the introduction as a way of smoothly transferring the student from the classroom activities to the testing session. The examiner should also inquire about the student's health on that day. If the student has a cold or other physical complaint, or if the student has experienced a very upsetting event, testing should be postponed until the student feels better. On the way to the testing room, the examiner should offer the student an opportunity to go to the water fountain and restroom. Throughout testing, the examiner should repeat this offer when there is a natural break in testing. Planned breaks are especially important with young children, who may not express their needs to use the restroom even if it is rather urgent that they do so.

The examiner engages the student in conversation to develop a good working relationship. While walking to the testing room, the examiner may inquire about the student's age, favorite sports or play activities, or upcoming social events. Once in the privacy of the testing room, the examiner should encourage conversation about the student's perceptions of strengths and weaknesses. This conversation gives the examiner a view of the student's style of interacting before testing begins.

The examiner should provide an introduction to the testing. After some brief, informal conversation, the examiner should explain to the student that the two of them will be working together to learn more about the best way for the student to learn. Emphasizing this joint working relationship indicates that the activities are serious business, not just games. This can reinforce the message that good effort is needed. Avoid using words like "test" to prevent the anxiety some students have come to associate with testing experiences. Some students need to be reassured that the work done with the examiner will not influence report card grades. Next the examiner should discuss the type of work the student will be doing. Broad information about looking at pictures, reading, talking, and writing helps the student know what to expect. General information about some tasks being relatively easy and some being hard helps the student know that there will be a range of activity difficulty. The student should be encouraged to try to answer all questions, even if they seem hard. The examiner should tell the student at this point that the examiner cannot tell whether an answer is right or wrong. Some students need to be reminded of this throughout testing. The examiner should also explain that the student will be told if an activity has a time limit and needs to be performed quickly. Finally, the examiner should let the student know when the session will end or how long they will be working together. This prevents the student from worrying that recess, lunch, dismissal, or a favorite activity will be missed. During this time, the examiner should also explain that periodic breaks will be taken.

A student may not understand everything the examiner says in the introduction to testing. This will be reflected by questions the student asks during the testing session. The student should be encouraged to ask questions if something is not clear. However, the examiner must be sure to stay within the constraints of the standardized directions when responding to these questions. The guidelines in Table 3-2 provide the help needed to strike a balance between test directions and student questions.

Table 3-2 General guidelines for test administration

Test administration is a skill, and testers must learn how to react to typical student comments and questions. The following general guidelines apply to the majority of standardized tests.

Student Requests for Repetition of Test Items
Students often ask the tester to repeat a question. This is usually permissible as long as the item is repeated verbatim and in its entirety. However, repetition of memory items measuring the student's ability to recall information is not allowed.

Asking Students to Repeat Responses
Sometimes the tester must ask the student to repeat a response. Perhaps the tester did not hear what the student said, or the student's speech is difficult to understand. However, the tester should make every effort to see or hear the student's first answer. The student may refuse to repeat a response or, thinking that the request for repetition means the first response was unsatisfactory, answer differently.

Student Modification of Responses
When students give one response, then change their minds and give a different one, the tester should accept the last response, even if the modification comes after the tester has moved to another item. However, some tests specify that only the first response may be accepted for scoring.

Confirming and Correcting Student Responses
The tester may not in any way—verbal or nonverbal—inform a student whether a response is correct. Correct responses may not be confirmed; wrong responses may not be corrected. This rule is critical for professionals who both teach and test, because their first inclination is to reinforce correct answers.

Reinforcing Student Work Behavior
Although testers cannot praise students for their performance on specific test items, good work behavior can and should be rewarded. Appropriate comments are, ''You're working hard'' and ''I like the way you're trying to answer every question.'' Students should be praised between test items or subtests to ensure that reinforcement is not linked to specific responses.

Encouraging Students to Respond
When students fail to respond to a test item, the tester can encourage them to give an answer. Students sometimes say nothing when presented with a difficult item, or they may comment, ''I don't know'' or ''I can't do that one.'' The tester should repeat the item and say, ''Give it a try'' or ''You can take a guess.'' The aim is to encourage the student to attempt all test items.

Questioning Students
Questioning is permitted on many tests. If in the judgment of the tester the response given by the student is neither correct nor incorrect, the tester repeats the student's answer in a questioning tone and says, ''Tell me more about that.'' This prompts the student to explain so that the response can be scored. However, clearly wrong answers should not be questioned.

Coaching
Coaching differs from encouragement and questioning in that it helps a student arrive at an answer. The tester must never coach the student. Coaching invalidates the student's response; test norms are based on the assumption that students will respond without examiner assistance. Testers must be very careful to avoid coaching.

Administration of Timed Items
Some tests include timed items; the student must reply within a certain period to receive credit. In general, the time period begins when the tester finishes presentation of the item. A watch or clock should be used to time student performance.

Source: Reprinted with the permission of Merrill, an imprint of Macmillan Publishing Company from ASSESSING SPECIAL STUDENTS, Third Edition by James A. McLoughlin and Rena B. Lewis. Copyright © 1990 by Macmillan Publishing Company. Originally published by Merrill Publishing Company.

Efficient, Accurate Administration

Error can be increased in the assessment process if there are distractions in the environment or if the student is ill-prepared to concentrate and put forth effort. Error can also be increased by the examiner, especially by the way the test is administered. The examiner must be very familiar with the assessment instrument being used and should have prior experience using the instrument. This enables the examiner to deliver directions in a smooth, natural manner even when reading verbatim from the manual, and necessary materials can be given to the student without delay. The examiner should review all directions and materials before starting an evaluation session. This is especially important if the examiner has given the measure infrequently or if other examiners may have used the materials and gotten them out of order. If the examiner has never given a test before, it is his or her ethical responsibility to study it thoroughly and do several practice administrations before using it with a student being considered for special education eligibility. When possible, someone more familiar with the instrument should administer it or double check the scoring.

The examiner needs to review the basal and ceiling rules for each test to be given. These rules change from test to test and can be a source of error if not reviewed. The *basal* on a test is a point early in the test where the examiner can assume that the student can answer all earlier items correctly. Typically, test developers state that if a student is a certain age or in a certain grade, testing should begin with a particular item. If the student correctly answers a certain number of consecutive items, a basal has been established. This prevents wasting valuable testing time on items that are too easy for the student. Similarly, a *ceiling rule* indicates when during testing the examiner can assume that all later items will be too difficult and testing should be discontinued. Ceiling rules usually indicate the number of consecutive items that can be missed by the student before testing should be stopped. This prevents frustration, which develops when a student is asked too many questions well beyond his or her ability level. Basal and ceiling rules are usually used with untimed tests. Timed tests generally require that the student begin with the first item and continue working until time is called or until finished, whichever comes first. Test manuals state the basal and ceiling rules for each test. Sometimes these rules are printed in an abbreviated form on the test *protocol* (that is, the examiner's form). Typically, the examiner should follow the basal and ceiling rules strictly. Sometimes two basals or two ceilings will be met. For example, if the examiner starts with item 10 and the student fails to meet the basal rule, the examiner may drop back and administer easier items until a basal is established. Later the student may answer enough consecutive items after item 10 to establish a second basal. Which basal should be used, and should that early missed item be counted as right even though the student answered incorrectly? The test manual should provide a clear answer for these questions. If it does not, the general rule is that the second basal and the first ceiling dictate how the test is scored.

Before administering a test, the examiner should review ways to record the student responses. Some tests require that the examiner only indicate whether the answer is correct or incorrect. In this case, the examiner will want to use the marking system specified in the manual so other professionals looking at the protocol will understand how each item was scored. Other tests require that the examiner write the verbatim response of the student. This type of recording is used when different points are assigned for the quality of the answer. Verbatim recording allows the examiner to make a qualitative judgment later rather than deliberate during the testing session. Verbatim recording is frequently using when assessing oral language skills.

Prior to beginning the testing, the examiner should explain to the student that the student's responses will be written by the examiner. This gives the examiner time to make the verbatim recording without increasing the student's anxiety. However, whether using a marking system or verbatim recording of the student's responses, it is important to conceal the protocol from the student. Some students will try to see if an answer is correct or incorrect. The examiner should remind the student that, as stated before testing started, accuracy information cannot be given. One easy way to conceal the protocol is to put it on a clipboard and set it in the examiner's lap. This is especially effective if the student persists in trying to see how the examiner is recording responses. Another approach is to place the protocol on the table but behind a test easel so the student cannot see it.

Examiners working with unfamiliar measures tend to spend more time looking at the manual and test materials than at the student. When the examiner is very familiar with the test materials and administration procedures, the examiner is free to spend time observing the student during testing. The examiner can make notes in the margin of the test protocol about the student's level of attention, style of responding, and manner of handling frustration. These notes can be summarized and compared to observations of other examiners and to those of the classroom teacher. Chapter 2 provides additional specific information on the types of observations that can be made during a testing session.

Modifying Testing Procedures

Assessment teams need normative data on a student to determine eligibility for special education services. When obtaining this data, it is critically important that all standardized procedures be followed as stated in the manual. This allows interpretation of numerical data. However, sometimes the assessment team is also interested in the student's potential. Examiners may feel that the student would perform better if the administration procedures were altered in some way. This type of information can be extremely valuable clinically, especially in developing suggestions for classroom modifications. In this case, the test data should be interpreted very cautiously and should not be used to determine eligibility.

One way examiners strike a balance between these competing needs for different types of information is called "testing the limits." In these situations, the examiner first administers the test following the exact procedures stated in the manual. Once the examiner obtains this data, the examiner may return to specific questions or sections of the test and change the administration in some way to test a hypothesis about how to enhance the student's performance. For example, an examiner may hypothesize that a student has a particular skill assessed by a timed test but performs so slowly that the score seems too low. The examiner may test this hypothesis by readministering a section of the test or an *alternate form* of the subtest without the time limit. The examiner makes notes about the student's concentration and sustained effort. In this case, the score could not be used for eligibility decisions. However, the information indicates whether the teacher needs to teach the skill, work on automaticity of the skill, develop a student self-monitoring strategy for staying on task, or give extended time on certain classroom assignments. Any test

Table 3-3 Test modifications and selected hypotheses

Modification	Hypothesis
Paraphrase test directions	Language problems interfere with the student understanding what to do. Student probably has the skill.
Ask student to explain how answer was obtained	Student knows part of the information but uses an incorrect procedure to obtain the final answer.
Change the response made	Student performs task but not using the specified response (i.e., can respond orally but has trouble with written responses).
Change presentation made	Student can perform skill if examiner reads question but has difficulty if he or she must read the questions.
Demonstrate how to solve one item	Student capable of using solution strategy if it is made explicit.
Provide aids	Student can perform task if allowed to use paper and pencil (or other aid) but cannot do so mentally or without the aid.
Change examiners	Rapport difficulties.
Have someone else present during testing	Presence of parent or familiar teacher reduces anxiety of testing situation.
Provide cues	Skill is being acquired and a certain cue facilitates performance.
Change testing arrangement	Sitting on the floor rather than at a table helps relax the student.
Provide reinforcement or feedback	Lack of feedback increases self-doubt about performance and decreases accuracy.

modification must be done for a specific reason and must be noted on the protocol. Other types of modifications and selected hypotheses about when to use them appear in Table 3-3.

Modifying test procedures results in scores that should not be used for eligibility and should only be used with a great deal of caution. If a score is obtained using the standardized procedures first and then the examiner tests the limits with some modification, the time needed to complete an evaluation can be extended. For these reasons, testing the limits and modifications in administration are used only when absolutely necessary to obtain critical information for program planning and should be done only by very experienced examiners. An examiner would not test the limits on every test that is being administered. Modifications in the initial use of a test are made only if the student cannot or will not perform under the standard conditions and tend to be made when students are very young or have severe disabilities.

Obtaining Scores

After the assessment measure is given, the examiner needs to be able to communicate the student's level of performance in some meaningful way to other members of the assessment team. Raw score information is oftentimes not very useful. Therefore, the raw data need to be transformed into some usable form. Assessment team members may code and use various types of data, depending on the purpose of the testing. Raw score data may be counted incorrectly. If raw data are transformed in some way, team members need to be aware that error may be introduced at any step in the process.

Types of Data

Data from assessment measures are of four types: nominal, ordinal, ratio, or interval. Each type has strengths and limitations that must be considered. Examiners need to understand when to use each type. *Nominal data* provide identification information or categorical information. For example, a student's case number is nominal data. The number, like the number on a football jersey, helps identify the student but has no relationship to the student. These numbers are used to preserve confidentiality but are never used in mathematical formulas. Nominal data can also be descriptive or categorical. Shading a "1" for male and a "2" for female on a computerized scoring form is another example of nominal data. If the teacher indicates "yes" or "no" on a checklist, indicating that a student exhibits a particular behavior, this is an example of nominal data. Criterion-referenced measures use nominal data to specify whether the student "passed" or "failed" a skill area.

Ordinal data rank order information by using a number to indicate a person's relative standing on a continuum of best to worst, or oldest to youngest. Examples of ordinal data are adjectives (that is, tall, taller, tallest; above grade level, below grade level; very punctual), age and grade ratings, and class standing. Sometimes the ranking gives no clue to the interval between data points. This is true with respect to the use of adjectives or class standing. Other ordinal data imply intervals, such as age or grade ratings, but the distance between the intervals is not consistent. Like nominal data, ordinal data cannot be manipulated mathematically.

Ratio data and *interval data* are similar to ordinal data but the distance between any two adjacent points is equal in these two types of data. Standardized tests rarely use ratio data, but such data is useful in observation. For example, if the observer is interested in how long a behavior occurs within a time period, that data can be expressed as a ratio. Ratio data have an absolute zero. In contrast, interval data do not have an absolute zero but, like ratio data, the distance between any two adjacent points is equal. *Likert-type scales* are assumed to produce interval data because the distance between options appears to be equal intervals. These scales require a person to rate their experience, opinion, or judgment on a numerical continuum. For example, a student may be asked to respond to a statement in terms of how closely it applies, such as, "When I have spare time, I enjoy reading."

1	2	3	4	5
Never	Rarely	Sometimes	Frequently	Always

Other examples of interval data include frequency counts, percentage correct, percentile ranks, standard scores, and stanines. Ratio and interval data can be manipulated mathematically.

Data from Teacher Produced Tests

Teachers need to see how a given student performs on a particular task to determine if additional instruction is needed. Teachers also need to look at the performance of the whole class to determine whether only one student needs additional instruction or whether several students need more practice. To gain a better understanding of what a given score means, the teacher looks at measures of central tendency (that is, mean, median, and mode) and range.

The *mean* is the arithmetic average of all the test scores and is obtained by adding all the scores together and dividing the sum by the number of scores. The *median* is the score that divides a set of scores into two equal groups. If there are seventeen students in the class, the score that divides the class into two groups of eight scores each would be the median. The *mode* is the most frequently obtained score. When a class has a normal distribution of ability and the scores are plotted, a symmetrical curve, *normal curve,* or *"bell" curve* is the result. When a true normal curve is present, 68 percent of the population fall within one standard deviation (σ) of the mean, while 95 percent of the population fall within two standard deviations of the mean. In this case, the mean, median, and mode are about the same. If the assessment was hard for the students, the distribution would reveal more low scores. This is called a positively skewed distribution, with the mode lower than the median, which, in turn, is lower than the mean. If the test was very easy for the students, the distribution would show more high scores. This is called a negatively skewed distribution. In this kind of distribution, the mean is lower than the median, and the median is lower than the mode. Figure 3-2 illustrates these three types of curves.

The classroom teacher also needs to know whether the scores were spread out or clustered close together. This requires that the teacher look at the range of scores. The range is the difference between the highest and lowest score. It tells how much variability there is in a set of scores.

Chronological Age

Different types of scores are available on norm-referenced tests. These include percentile ranks, standard scores, stanines, and age and grade equivalents. To obtain these derived scores, the examiner typically counts the correct responses and uses reference tables that accompany the test to convert the raw score to a different type of score that allows comparison to the norming sample. Reference tables are often organized according to age, which requires that the examiner count correct responses accurately and calculate the student's chronological age correctly. Error is possible in either procedure. Examiners should develop the practice of counting correct responses two times to ensure that simple counting errors are not made. Similarly, double checking the calculation of chronological age is also wise.

Calculating the exact chronological age at the time of testing is very clear cut. The examiner subtracts the student's date of birth from the date of testing. The subtraction problem is set up so the year appears first, then the month, followed by the days. The examiner begins subtracting with the days. When borrowing is required, one year is converted to twelve months and one month is converted to thirty days. These conversions remain the same even if a month has thirty-one days. The final age is expressed in years and months; days are not reported. If the calculation results in more than fifteen days, a month is added to the age. If the calculation results in fifteen days or less, only the year and month are reported; no additional months are added. Table 3-4 provides examples of these different situations.

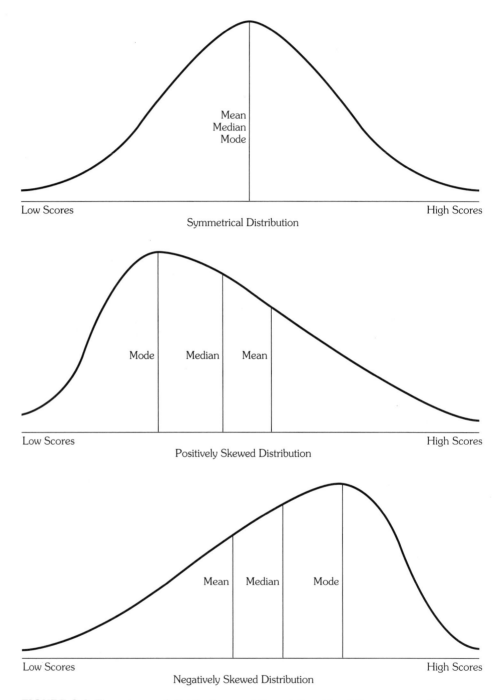

FIGURE 3.2 Three types of distributions and the relationship of the mean, median, and mode in each   *Source:* From Salvia, John and James F. Ysseldyke, *Assessment in Special and Remedial Education,* Fourth Edition. Copyright © 1988 by Houghton Mifflin Company. Used with permission.

Table 3-4 Calculating chronological age

No Renaming Needed

	Year	Months	Days	
	'92	10	28	Date of Test
−	'81	9	10	Date of Birth
	11	1	18	

More than 15 days, expressed as CA = 11–2

Renaming Days

	Year	Months	Days	
	'92	10	33	Date of Test
−	'83	7	12	Date of Birth
	9	3	21	

More than 15 days, expressed as CA = 9–4

Renaming Months

	Year	Months	Days	
	'92	16	18	Date of Test
−	'80	6	9	Date of Birth
	12	10	9	

Less than 15 days, expressed as CA = 12–10

Renaming Days and Months

	Year	Months	Days	
	'92	13	25	Date of Test
−	'78	5	10	Date of Birth
	14	8	15	

15 days, expressed as CA = 14–8

Percentile Ranks

Percentile ranks are a relatively easy way to understand derived score as long as one does not confuse them with percentage correct. Percentage correct is a way to make an absolute comparison. The examiner determines the percentage correct by dividing the number of items answered correctly by the total number of items. This refers to the percentage of test items and shows how close the student came to 100 percent accuracy.

In contrast to percentage correct, percentile ranks help the examiner make a relative comparison. These scores answer the question, "How did this student compare to students in the norming sample who took the test?" The percentile rank indicates the percentage of people in the norming sample who achieved a specific score or a lower one. If a raw score of 33 is equivalent to a percentile rank of 72, that means that 72 percent of the people who took the test originally had a score of 33 or less; 28 percent of the people in the norming sample had better scores. Percentile ranks refer to the percentage of the people in the norming sample rather than to the test items.

To obtain a percentile rank, the examiner first counts the number of correct items. The examiner then refers to tables organized by age level. If the student tested had a chronological age of 11–7, the examiner consults the table for norming subjects of that age, taking care to inspect the appropriate column. This table indicates the percentile rank of norming subjects in that age range who obtained the same raw score. Tables organized by age allow for more precision than if the entire norming sample is considered as one group.

Standard Scores

Standard scores are *derived scores* that have a set mean and standard deviation. Mean is the measure of central tendency that represents the arithmetic average of a set of scores. The mean for a set of standard scores is established in advance; then the raw scores are transformed mathematically so they fit with the established mean. The standard deviation is a measure of variability much like the range. The difference is that the standard deviation is more dependable and fits mathematically with other types of statistics. The standard deviation for standard scores is also established in advance, and the obtained raw score distribution is transformed mathematically. The standard deviation is used to express the difference between scores.

All standard scores are based on the assumption that the distribution of the obtained scores is a normal distribution. Various types of standard scores differ in terms of the identified mean and standard deviation. One type of standard score is the *z* score, which has a mean of 0 and a standard deviation of 1. This type of standard score scale often results in scores containing decimals or negative numbers. These can be difficult to manipulate, so the possibility of error increases when using them. For this reason, most educational and psychological tests use a different type of standard score.

A second type of standard score is known as the *T* score. This standard score has a mean of 50 and a standard deviation of 10. Since decimals and negative numbers are not part of the scale, *T* scores are easier to use. Assessments of oral language often use *T* scores.

Deviation intelligence quotients and scale scores are two other types of standard scores frequently used on educational and psychological tests. Deviation intelligence quotients are also called test standard scores. They have a mean of 100 and a standard deviation of 15. This type of standard score is frequently used as a total test score or a composite score for several subtests. The scale score has a mean of 10 and a standard deviation of 3. This type of standard score is frequently used for subtests. On many educational and psychological tests, both test standard scores and scale scores are used.

If a student took two tests that report performance in terms of different standard scores, examiners use the standard deviation to compare the student's performance on the two tests. For example, suppose a student took a reading achievement test that used the scale of a mean of 100 and a standard deviation of 15, and a language test that used the scale of a mean of 50 and a standard deviation of 10. The student obtained a score of 85 on the reading test and a score of 60 on the language test. The student's score was one standard deviation below the mean on the reading test but one standard deviation above the mean on the language test. In this case, the student seems to have better language skills than reading skills, even if the numbers do not immediately suggest that.

Stanines

Stanines, another type of derived score, are standardized bands or ranges that divide a distribution into nine equal units. Each band contains a percentage of the scores in the distribution. For example, the fifth stanine includes the 20 percent of scores around the mean of the distribution. The bands are .5 standard deviations wide. Information provided by stanines is less precise than other types of derived scores because they describe performance in terms of a range.

Age and Grade Equivalents

Two final types of derived scores available on many tests are age scores and grade scores. These scores are popular with parents and classroom teachers because they appear to be easy to understand. Unfortunately, these are not precise scores and are often misunderstood.

Examining how age and grade scores are determined helps highlight the reasons for possible misunderstanding of these data. If the average child in the norming sample who is 6 years 3 months old obtained a raw score of 39, then any student who obtains a raw score of 39 is assigned an age score of 6–3. The problem is that no real child in the norming sample may have actually obtained a score of 39; some obtained scores that were higher and others obtained scores that were lower. This is the average of all the children age 6. Another problem is that development does not proceed in a smooth curve. Often more growth occurs in particular skills at some ages than at others, but age scores imply that the growth curve is smooth. If two students obtained an age score of 8–5 on a language test, and one student was actually 6–1 and the other was 12–9, there would be a tremendous qualitative difference in the language of the two students, yet the score implies they perform the same. Grade scores are similarly based on averages, estimates, and the assumption of a smooth development curve. Grade scores are expressed as numbers with decimals (for example, 3.2) indicating the grade and the tenth of the school year. However, schools do not present the same information throughout the year, and the norming sample contains students from both good and poor schools. The scores of real third graders are averaged, and the raw score is assigned based on that average. A third grade student who obtained a raw score well above that average might be assigned a grade score of 6.5. This is an estimated score, and it does not mean that the third grade student has the skills of the average student in grade 6.5.

Age and grade scores are ordinal data, so there is not an equal interval between adjacent scores. These scores represent median scores for a particular level. Oftentimes the score is based on estimation (interpolation and extrapolation) rather than on the performance of actual people in the norming sample.

These three problems illustrate that age and grade scores are complicated and open to misinterpretation. Examiners should select tests that offer more precise types of derived scores.

Interpreting the Meaning of Scores

Once the assessment measures have been scored, the evaluation team looks at all the data to understand the meaning of any score. The team compares the student's test performance with performance in the classroom and makes comparisons of performance in different areas. The team looks for consistent patterns of performance across settings and skill areas. Isolated scores mean very little.

Comparing Test Performance and Classroom Functioning

Performance on standardized tests should be compared to the student's performance in a natural setting. In most cases that means comparing classroom performance with performance on standardized measures. If the results indicate a discrepancy in performance between the classroom and a well-structured testing situation, the team must try to sort out why. One hypothesis may be that the structure during individual testing helped the student perform better. In this case, it would be beneficial to add more structure to the classroom to see if the student's performance improves. If it does improve, there is no need to diagnose a disability.

Another hypothesis might be that the way questions were posed and the way the student responded accounts for the difference. Individually administered tests often present questions orally and require the student to give an oral response. However, classroom teachers primarily evaluate students on their written work. If this is the case, the team needs to determine whether the student can perform when written responses are required. If the student cannot or has extreme difficulty, it may be appropriate to diagnose a disability and obtain special services for the student. Comparing the student's test performance with actual functioning is one critical step in determining the meaning of test scores.

Comparing Scores on Different Tests

Another critical step in interpreting the meaning of test scores is comparing scores earned on different tests. This type of comparison helps the team diagnose different types of disabilities. The team is looking for the consistency of the pattern of scores. The profile of a student with learning disabilities is characterized by near average achievement in some areas and significant underachievement in others. In contrast, the student with mental retardation has a pattern of very low achievement, which is consistent with low intelligence and low adaptive behavior. Two critical issues emerge when looking at scores from different tests: consistency and significant discrepancy. For both issues, it is important to look at confidence intervals.

Earlier in this chapter, the discussion of standard error of measurement illustrated that a true score is theoretical. When a student obtains a score on a test, part of the score is true score and part is measurement error. This concept needs to be considered in interpreting test scores. To remind every team member of this concept, it is important to present confidence intervals along with scores. Table 3-1 outlined the steps to obtain an interval when the confidence level was 68 percent. Oftentimes team members want to make decisions on scores when the confidence level is higher. This is accomplished by using a z score associated with the confidence level. This score is based on the normal curve and is available in many statistics books. The other information needed is the standard error of measurement, which can be found in the test manual. Table 3-1 demonstrated that .68 confidence level resulted in a range of 89 to 97 for an obtained score of 93 when the

Table 3-5 Determining different levels of confidence

Confidence Interval = Obtained Score $\pm$ z (S_{EM})

Obtained Score = 93 S_{EM} = 4

68% level	z = 1.00		
85% level	z = 1.44		
90% level	z = 1.65		
95% level	z = 1.96		
99% level	z = 2.58		

	85% Level		*90% Level*
	93 $\pm$ 1.44(4)		93 $\pm$ 1.65(4)
	93 $\pm$ 5.76		93 $\pm$ 6.6
True Score Range	87.24 to 98.76	True Score Range	86.4 to 99.6
	95% Level		*99% Level*
	93 $\pm$ 1.96(4)		93 $\pm$ 2.58(4)
	93 $\pm$ 7.84		93 $\pm$ 10.32
True Score Range	85.16 to 100.84	True Score Range	82.68 to 103.32

standard error of measurement was 4. Table 3-5 illustrates how to obtain higher confidence intervals for the same obtained score.

Consistency within an area is important when making eligibility decisions. If the team is considering that mental retardation may account for the achievement problems a student is experiencing, team members should verify the level of intelligence on two measures. In most cases, the scores on each measure will be slightly different. But they should be close to each other, and there should be considerable overlap in the confidence intervals for the two measures. Once consistency is established with respect to intelligence, the team can look at the consistency between IQ and adaptive behavior. If consistency is found between these two areas, the team can compare the test data with actual classroom functioning. If consistency is not found, the team needs to look for data explaining this.

Consistency is important in the diagnosis of any disability. However, some disabilities are based on significant discrepancies. Learning disabilities is one such condition. The team still needs data to demonstrate that performance within an area is consistent. For example, two sources may indicate average mental ability while two or more sources may document consistent problems in math reasoning. When consistent patterns are found within an area, the team should document differences between areas that are significant and represent a manifestation of the disability.

This opens the question, "How much discrepancy is significant?" Part of the answer rests with the reliability of the tests involved. When a "difference" score is obtained, the reliability of that score is lower than the reliability of the two test scores on which it is based. Therefore, it is critically important that tests used to determine a "difference" score have good reliability. Also, the test scores must be expressed in the same scale, and the scale should have an underlying foundation of a normal curve. For all these reasons, standard scores are generally used to determine "difference" scores.

Calculating the reliability of a "difference" score involves the reliability coefficient of each test and the correlation between the two tests. Examiners vary in their skill in obtaining this information and making this calculation accurately. Therefore, many states establish guidelines for determining whether a difference between intelligence and achievement is significant. Evaluation teams must understand that these guidelines are used in conjunction with professional judgment. That judgment includes the consistency of the obtained information, how it relates to classroom functioning, and how confidence intervals may add to the interpretation of the data.

Issues Surrounding Nonbiased Assessment

In this chapter we have discussed ways statistical error and human error can introduce bias in the assessment process. All these problems exist for all students who are assessed. However, when a student has characteristics that deviate from those of mainstream society, other opportunities for bias emerge. These characteristics may include the presence of a disability, low socioeconomic status, ethnic or cultural differences, and a primary language other than English. Evaluation teams have tried several strategies to address these problems.

One important strategy is to use technically adequate tests with a diverse norming sample. Comparing the characteristics of the target student with the characteristics of the norming sample is critical. There will be cases for which tests that have samples that represent all characteristics are not available. Sometimes data from these tests can still be used on an informal or cautious basis in conjunction with data on how the student functions in everyday settings.

Another strategy is to use tests in the student's primary language, but it is important to keep in mind that the other norming variables still need to be considered. More and more tests are now available in Spanish, but a Spanish version of a test normed only on students in the Southwest may not be appropriate for a student in New York. Also, dialects of Spanish can vary, so the fact that the student speaks Spanish and takes a test in Spanish is no guarantee that bias will not be present. Finally, while there are Spanish versions of many tests, there are students who speak languages other than English or Spanish. Tests may not be available in the student's native language.

Lack of access to tests in the student's native language raises the question of having a native speaker interpret during test administration. This is not recommended. It modifies the test, accuracy in translation is an issue, and the norms cannot be used in this situation. However, there are times when the assessment team has few other options. When translators must be used, the results have to be considered cautiously and only in conjunction with the student's actual functioning in everyday settings.

Another possibility in working with students from linguistically diverse backgrounds is to use nonverbal or criterion-referenced tests. Examiners cannot assume that these tests are automatically unbiased. Even though criterion-referenced tests only compare the student to a level of mastery, McLoughlin and Lewis (1990) point out that the information may be subjective and can be interpreted in a biased manner. Similarly, there is no guarantee that a nonverbal test is unbiased. These tests are often norm-referenced, so characteristics of the norming sample must be considered. There must be data indicating that there are no cross-cultural differences with respect to the development of the assessed ability. These data are rarely available. Therefore, these data must be used cautiously and only in conjunction with the student's actual functioning.

Culture specific tests and separate norms for minority populations are two other options available to evaluation teams. However, these options are not available for all cultures or all minority groups. Another factor that limits their usefulness is the generalizability of the results. Culture specific tests provide little predictive information (Duffey, Salvia, Tucker, and Ysseldyke, 1981). Adequate performance on such tests indicates that the student has information and sensitivity to a particular culture, but this does not necessarily generalize to how the student will perform in a school setting. Similarly, special norms are available for some minority groups, but these norms are often specific to the region of the country where they were collected and should not be used in other regions. Some research indicates that norms based on socioeconomic status are more revealing than norms based on minority group membership (Yando, Seitz, and Zigler, 1979). This should be considered if the team decides to use separate norms. When separate norms and culture specific tests are available, they can provide information that may counteract the covert prejudice team members may have toward particular minority groups. This information is helpful from an awareness standpoint. However, the information may not contribute substantially to program planning and may serve to maintain a separateness view of diverse groups (Alley and Foster, 1978). This may be counterproductive in educational settings in which grouping for instructional purposes is fiscally necessary.

There are no easy answers for the many problems and issues surrounding the assessment of students from diverse cultural, linguistic, and socioeconomic backgrounds. However, abandoning the assessment process is not the best response either; such a policy may inadvertently limit access to needed modifications and special instruction. Sattler (1988) states that "tests allow for accountability, for measurement of change, and for program effectiveness" (p. 6). Evaluation teams must be aware of their ethical responsibility to use data to help students increase their opportunities for success rather than limit them. Team members must be cognizant of the numerous opportunities for bias to enter the assessment process and take steps to control that bias as much as possible. Team members must also be aware that the team process and the professional training of various team members provides an important check so appropriate professional judgment will be used in interpreting assessment data in a nonbiased fashion.

Summary

The Human Factor

1. Professionals involved in the assessment process need to be aware that their beliefs and perceptions may not match those of the population they serve.
2. Differences in training help shape the expertise of various team members and provide important balance on the team.

3. Due process regulations are necessary to protect the rights of students and to ensure that all have equal educational opportunities.
4. Careful record keeping during the assessment process helps document that all who should be involved were involved, that appropriate tools were used, and that the educational decisions were based on performance data.
5. Trained professionals can introduce error into the assessment process when given too much authority for what should be a team effort or when asked to perform a task for which there has been limited training and supervised experience.

Test Selection

1. Examiners must select tests that have the potential for answering important questions and use them only for the purposes for which they were developed.
2. A critical variable in the quality of a test is who made up the group norm and how closely those people match the demographic characteristics of the student being tested.
3. A correlation is the relationship between two variables.
4. Reliability is the degree to which a test is consistent in measuring what it purports to measure.
5. Different types of reliability are associated with the kinds of generalizations that can be made.
6. Even a very reliable test can be made unreliable if the standardized procedures are not followed.
7. The statistic called the standard error of measurement helps determine the amount of measurement error in a test.
8. Validity of a test indicates how well the test measures what it claims to measure.
9. While reference books and professional journals can provide information about tests, the best source of information about any one test is the test manual.

Using Measures Appropriately

1. Before administering any test, the examiner should prepare a distraction-free, quiet environment that will facilitate concentration.
2. It is important that the student has no unusual physical discomfort and is prepared psychologically before beginning any testing.
3. Error is reduced when the examiner is prepared enough to ensure efficient, accurate administration of the test.
4. Under some circumstances, modifying the testing procedures may be necessary, but in those cases the modifications must be recorded and the data used with extreme caution.

Obtaining Scores

1. Nominal, ordinal, ratio, and interval data are used for different purposes.
2. Measures of central tendency and range help teachers interpret results from teacher produced tests.

3. Calculating the student's exact chronological age is one of the first steps in converting raw scores for a test to a derived score that is more useful in interpretation.
4. Percentile ranks are easy-to-use derived scores that help the examiner make a relative comparison.
5. Standard scores are derived scores based on a predetermined mean and standard deviation.
6. Stanines, another type of derived score, are less precise than percentile ranks and standard scores because they describe performance in terms of ranges.
7. Age and grade equivalents are imprecise derived scores that are often misunderstood and, therefore, should not be used.

Interpreting the Meaning of Scores

1. Individual test scores should not be interpreted in isolation.
2. Test performance should be compared to functioning in the classroom.
3. Scores from different tests assessing the same area should be compared for consistency.
4. Test performance in one area should be compared to performance in other areas.
5. Differences between test scores need to be interpreted cautiously and in light of confidence intervals and classroom performance.

Issues Surrounding Nonbiased Assessment

1. Availability of technically adequate measures is one problem examiners face when working with minority students.
2. Translated tests are available in Spanish, but other demographic characteristics of a norming sample may require that the test be used cautiously.
3. While using a native speaker to translate during testing is not recommended, it is sometimes one of the few available options.
4. Criterion-referenced measures and nonverbal tests do not guarantee a nonbiased assessment of linguistically diverse students.
5. Culture specific tests and separate minority norms provide little usable predictive information.
6. Despite the numerous criticisms of tests, they can provide important information.

P A R T   T W O

Assessing Foundations

C H A P T E R

Sensory, Health, and Addictive Disorders

Key Terms

AIDS
Alcohol addiction
Allergy
Anorexia nervosa
Asthma
Audiologist
Bone, muscle and joint
    problems
Bulimia nervosa
Central nervous system

Cerebral palsy
Color blindness
Compulsive overeating
Depressants
Diabetes
Dual diagnosis
Epilepsy
Hallucinogens
Hearing acuity

Muscle balance
Narcotic
Ophthalmologist
Peripheral nervous system
Restricted vision
Spina bifida
Stimulants
Thyroid problems
Visual acuity

Students with sensory impairments or health problems are no longer segregated from the mainstream school setting. Rather, these students are integrated in regular and special education classes as early as preschool. Special educators play a significant role in the multidisciplinary team that helps assess such students' potential and develops appropriate instructional objectives. It is imperative that professionals understand the impact of sensory and health-related disorders on the cognitive, affective, and academic performance of students. Assessment tools should be selected that allow students to respond at their optimal level. This often requires that the examiner modify or substitute standardized procedures for the student. Special educators must be sensitive to a student's disability and not allow bias in their perception of that student's optimal performance, nor overlook behaviors that do not fit with teacher perceptions. In particular, the special educator should keep in mind that the disability is only one of many influences that have an impact on the life of the student.

Special education classes, both resource and self-contained, are receiving more and more students with a *dual diagnosis*. This term refers to students who demonstrate two or more disabilities, for example, learning disabled and hearing impaired, behaviorally disordered and physically disabled, or deaf and blind. Understanding the impact of these disabilities on the assessment process helps alleviate test bias and leads to effective instructional objectives. In addition, an alarming number of elementary, secondary, and postsecondary students with special needs have problems with addictive behaviors (for example, alcohol, drugs, eating disorders). Special educators must have the expertise to provide evidence to the multidisciplinary assessment team to identify behaviors that are the result of addictive disorders so appropriate psychological or academic therapy can be provided.

In this chapter, we will introduce a select number of sensory, health-related, and addictive disorders commonly seen in school settings that can have an impact on the assessment process, requiring special attention and possibly testing modifications. Suggestions provided to deal with these disorders can be generalized to other similar impairments not discussed here. The disabilities have been organized in five major categories: (1) sensory impairments; (2) central nervous system impairments; (3) bone, joint, and muscle problems; (4) health-related problems; and (5) addictive disorders.

Sensory Impairments

When a student is having trouble in school, one of the first areas to assess is sensory functioning. Is the individual receiving information from the environment? Our senses provide us with the ability to see, hear, smell, taste, and feel. Impairment of any of these abilities can have a significant impact on educational, vocational, and social functioning. For example, a student might be referred for assessment for refusing to follow the teacher's directions as well as for lack of attention in the classroom. Upon further testing, it may be discovered that the student has a mild to moderate hearing impairment. If only the overt behaviors of the student are assessed, it would be easy to diagnose an affective problem rather than a hearing impairment. Another student might have significant difficulty reading textbooks and be referred for possible learning disabilities. The special educator may discover that this child has some mild visual or hearing impairments. With appropriate modifications and aides, such a child would be able to learn the skills required to read. Usually, only vision and hearing are screened in the schools, but the senses of taste, touch, and smell may also be impaired. Although no specific standardized tests are available to the special educator attempting to evaluate these other senses, it is important to determine if these senses are intact. Many instructional and safety skills are dependent on the ability to touch, taste, or smell. Assessment of the ability to touch (sizes, relationships between objects, temperature changes), taste, or smell (awareness of, discrimination between, localization of) can be accomplished through informal evaluation. The special educator working with adolescents or adults should not ignore the evaluation of sensory acuity. Many of these older students did not received adequate sensory acuity assessment, and instructional or social skills problems have been blamed totally on cognitive or behavior disorders without a careful examination of the student's sensory acuities.

Visual Impairments

Visual impairment problems can be considered mild, moderate, or severe. Mild impairments are typically correctable with glasses or contact lenses. Students with moderate impairments learn mainly through sight but also need some modification of instructional materials, such as larger print or books on tape. Students with severe visual impairments are not always blind but must use senses other than vision, such as auditory or tactile cues, in the instructional process (Bradley-Johnson, 1986).

Symptoms.   The special educator should work with the classroom teacher to identify students at risk for visual impairment problems. Identifying characteristic behaviors include frequent blinking, squinting, rubbing the eyes, abnormal tilt of the head, inattention to board lessons, poor alignment of written work, loss of place while reading, avoiding close visual work, difficulty judging distances, crossed eyes, red-rimmed, encrusted or swollen eyes, watery eyes, or recurring sties. Such students may complain of frequent headaches, dizziness, blurred or double vision, or

look for signals

Table 4-1 Common visual disorders and their treatment

Disorder	Primary Symptoms	Usual Treatment
Astigmatism	Uneven cornea produces distorted vision.	Corrective lenses.
Amblyopia	Loss of vision due to disuse of eye; often due to strabismus.	Patching of good eye to force use of weak eye.
Cataract	Opaque or cloudy lens.	Reading lenses or telescopic devices. Surgery and special cataract eyeglasses.
Hyperopia	Farsightedness; near vision is poor.	Corrective eyeglasses or contact lenses.
Myopia	Nearsightedness; distance vision is poor.	Corrective eyeglasses or contact lenses.
Nystagmus	Uncontrolled rapid movement of the eyeball.	Correct the eye disease or muscular defect causing nystagmus.
Strabismus	Eye deviates upward, downward, or inward.	Patch the good eye. Corrective eyeglasses. Muscle surgery. Eye exercises.

Source: From *Medical Problems of Students with Special Needs: A Guide for Educators,* by J. Holvoet and E. Helmstetter p. 38. Copyright © 1989 by PRO-ED, Inc. Reprinted by permission.

sensitivity to light. The special educator should be aware that a lack of these signs does not mean visual acuity problems do not exist. Slight astigmatisms or binocular visual defects can have an impact on reading even though no overt symptoms are observed.

Types.   According to Bradley-Johnson (1986), 5 to 33 percent of school-age children have vision problems. The most common types of visual impairments confronting the special educator include visual acuity, restricted vision, color blindness, and muscle balance. Table 4.1 lists the different types of visual impairments as well as a description of the characteristics of and treatment for each type.

Visual acuity refers to the clarity with which a person sees. A person with 20/20 vision has normal vision and can see at 20 feet what most people see at 20 feet; 20/40 vision means a person can see at 20 feet what is typically seen at 40 feet. A person with 20/200 vision is considered legally blind, seeing at 20 feet what is normally seen 200 feet away. Legal blindness is determined when a person's corrected central vision acuity is not more than 20/200 in the better eye or when the field of vision is no more than 20 degrees. This does not mean, however, that the person is totally blind; more than 75 percent of legally blind people in the United States have some usable vision (Bradley-Johnson, 1986). Therefore, the special educator is confronted with assessing very few students who demonstrate no usable vision. Many students with visual impairments are able to read large or even regular print. It may take these students longer to read since they may use some type of magnifying lens or special light to aid the reading process. Rate of reading should be considered when evaluating such a student's test scores. For this student, it is discriminatory to evaluate performance on a measure for which time to complete the task was the factor that produced a lower score rather than a lack of understanding of the content. The special educator should formally assess the student's use of vision in and outside the classroom and review available data from the physician and guardians before beginning an educa-

A young child has her vision checked at school by a visiting nurse.   *Source:* © Jon Meyer/ Custom Medical Stock

tional evaluation. Common types of acuity problems include astigmatism, cataract, hyperopia, and myopia (see Table 4-1).

Restricted vision refers to a visual impairment in which the visual field is restricted, such as in tunnel vision, where the person can see only what is straight ahead. Another form of restricted vision is when a black spot blocks a portion of a person's field of vision. The person is able to see only those images on the perimeter of the black spot.

Color blindness is the impairment of color vision. The color-blind person sees the same images that others see, but some hues appear different. Color blindness is of two kinds: protanopia, or red blindness, and deuteranopia, or green blindness. These differences are caused by two different recessive sex-linked genes (Guyton, 1977). While color blindness does not qualify as a disability, it has a significant impact on instruction at school, social functioning, and safety. In fact, many test items require the use of color identification to successfully complete problems. A student who cannot differentiate the green blocks from the black blocks on a block design task would score lower on visual spatial competency because of his or her color blindness. Unfortunately, tools assessing color blindness are not very reliable, so at least two measures should be used (Salvia and Ysseldyke, 1988).

Muscle balance refers to the muscles that control eye movement. Vision requires not only the sensory elements (acuity) but also a series of precisely coordinated eye movements (Berthoz and Jones, 1985). In addition to the flicking movements required for a stable visual image, there are four motor systems involved in sight: saccadic, pursuit, vergence, and vestibular. Westman (1990) uses the following anecdote from Goldberg and Schiffman (1983) to depict all the motor aspects the muscles of the eye control.

> A man is hunting ducks, when he hears sounds, his eyes make a rapid saccadic motion to fix on a flying duck and then follow the moving target with a pursuit movement. As he aims his rifle, the hunter's eyes converge in a vergence movement on the rifle sight. After he shoots, the boat begins to rock and his vestibular system coordinates his resulting eye and head movements. In addition, as the duck flies away, optokinetic nystagmus is produced by the hunter's repeated fixations on the duck. (p. 120)

Eye movement has been of significant interest to researchers investigating reading disorders (Pavlidis, 1987). In addition, the diagnostic usefulness of eye movements has been documented in such conditions as comas (Coahley and Thomas, 1977), schizophrenia, attentional disorders (Holzman, Levy, and Procotor, 1976), and hyperactivity (Bala, Cohen, Morris, Atkin, Gittelman, and Kates, 1981). While it is apparent that eye movement has an impact on learning certain types of skills (for example, reading), the significance of particular eye movement problems has received little attention in the literature, and the connection between muscle balance problems and academic disorders is not clear. The ophthalmologist, a specialist equipped to evaluate eye movement, can help the special educator interpret findings for a specific student's eye movement performance. It is important for the special educator to keep in mind that muscle balance differences do not always lead to academic underachievement.

Assessment.   The special educator involved in assessing a student with a visual impairment should review all background data prior to beginning the evaluation. It is important to remember that the student might be referred because of additional cognitive, affective, or academic problems that are unrelated to the visual impairment. A student with visual acuity problems may also demonstrate specific learning disabilities. It is important for the special educator to be sure that any additional disabilities diagnosed are not a bias of the instruments or of the administrator's perceptions. In other words, it would be easy to say a student with certain types of acuity problems cannot stay on the line when they read due totally to a visual acuity problem. The special educator needs to determine whether the inability to read is a problem related to acuity or is also resulting from cognitive processing deficits (see chapter 5) that are the result of a learning disability. A student with visual impairments and learning disabilities (VI/LD) requires instruction individualized to both disabilities.

Data should be collected from multiple sources. Parents' and classroom teachers' observations should be part of the assessment process. The special educator should also observe the student at home and in the classroom to record functional skills across settings. For a sample observation form, see Table 4-2. In addition, visual screening tests are used in most schools; these data might provide additional information for the special educator. The Snellen Wall Chart and the Snellen E Test are commonly used to assess visual acuity in the schools. The Flash Card Vision

Table 4-2 Teacher interview/classroom observation checklist for visually impaired and blind students

Does student:	*Yes*	*No*
1. Request help when needed?	_____	_____
2. Accept help courteously?	_____	_____
3. Refuse help courteously?	_____	_____
4. Display an appropriate degree of independence?	_____	_____
5. Listen well to instructions?	_____	_____
6. Move freely about the classroom?	_____	_____
7. Avoid hazards as much as possible?	_____	_____
8. Have desk well organized and free of unnecessary materials?	_____	_____
9. Put materials back in appropriate places so they can be easily located?	_____	_____
10. Interact with peers about as often as other students?	_____	_____
11. Interact in a positive way with peers?	_____	_____
12. Handle difficult or frustrating tasks without becoming overly upset?	_____	_____
13. Respond to corrective feedback appropriately?	_____	_____
14. Seem to appreciate praise from the teacher? Examples of effective praise statements:	_____	_____

15. What type of instructional materials are used?

    _____braille   _____talking books   _____large print

    _____Optacon   _____cassettes   _____material read to student

    _____computer

    other_____

16. What low-vision aids are used? _____

17. What special writing materials are used?

    _____braillewriter   _____slate and stylus   other_____

    _____typewriter   _____special paper
                                   (embossed or bold line)

18. What special arithmetic aids are used?

    _____abacus   _____computer aids

    _____talking calculator   _____braille ruler

    _____special paper   _____special clock
    (embossed or bold line)
    (braille or raised numbers)

19. How frequently does student need breaks due to fatigue?_____

20. Approximately how much extra time does student require to complete assignments?

    _____

21. What, if any, special lighting is required for reading?_____

22. About how far are materials held from eyes for reading?_____

    _____

Source: From *Psychoeducational Assessment of Visually Impaired and Blind Students,* by S. Bradley-Johnson p. 9. Copyright © 1986 by PRO-ED, Inc. Reprinted by permission.

Test for Children (N.Y. Association for the Blind, 1966) is an acuity test that is an adaptation of the Snellen for preschool children, non–English speaking students, and individuals with significant cognitive, language, or physical impairments. It requires that students identify pictures (apple, house, umbrella) rather than letters. Beside its use with severely disabled students, this acuity test is also helpful in visual assessment of students with learning disabilities for whom letter recognition and recall is often difficult. The ability to identify pictures is easier than identifying letters for some students. Other tests used by many schools that screen for near point, far point, and muscle balance include the Titmus Vision Tester and the Keystone Telebinocular.

Students who fail vision screening are referred to a vision specialist for more thorough assessment. The *ophthalmologist,* a medical doctor, uses more complicated instruments. Examination with an ophthalmoscope that allows the doctor to look in the eye shows any gross irregularities in the eye, cataracts, abnormalities in the way the pupil reacts, and abnormalities in the retina or the blood vessels that nourish the eye. Ophthalometers are used to diagnose astigmatism and to prescribe corrective lenses. Ultraviolet light can detect wounds on the cornea. Tests of fixation assess the muscles that control the eye. Visual acuity tests more sensitive than those administered in the schools measure the eye's ability to recognize details. A report from the ophthalmologist should tell the special educator what types of tests were administered, what the results mean in terms of appropriate size and placement of reading materials, what types of therapy (glasses, contact lenses, eye exercises, surgery) were prescribed, and what the therapy is supposed to accomplish (Holvoet and Helmstetter, 1989).

The special educator evaluating a student with a visual impairment will often need to administer norm-referenced tests for eligibility and placement purposes. Therefore, the correct tests for students with visual impairments must be decided upon. In some instances tests that have been standardized on the typical peers population can be used, particularly if there is not a strong visual component to the instrument. Sometimes only those standardized on the blind or visually disabled are appropriate. According to Bradley-Johnson (1986), criterion-referenced tests have an advantage over norm-referenced tests when assessing the visually impaired because adapted materials and flexible administration procedures can be used. In addition, dynamic approaches to assessment provide an ideal means for evaluating true learning potential of a student with a visual impairment since the evaluator explores the student's process of learning rather than being dependent on a state score.

Sometimes special materials or equipment to aid in reading and writing should be used during testing. These include large print and braille materials; the Optacon, a device that converts print to braille; closed circuit TV that magnifies print on the screen; hand-held magnifiers, stand magnifiers, or magnifying spectacles; bookstands; a braillewriter, typewriter, or braille slate and stylus; and paper with bold or raised lines (Bradley-Johnson, 1986). If the special educator is unfamiliar with this special visual equipment, a vision specialist should be consulted prior to the evaluation.

The special educator working with a visually impaired student during assessment can help reduce the student's anxiety by constantly verbalizing everything that is happening during the evaluation process. For example, the special educator could explain that prior to asking the student to complete a task, the examiner needs to take test materials out of a box on the table in front of the student. When evaluating a visually impaired student the special educator should:

1. Place the student's hand on the object rather than simply hand the object to the person.
2. Explain everything going on during the assessment.
3. Provide verbal rather than physical guidance.

4. Give specific directions, such as "to your left" rather than "over there."
5. Make a conscious effort to convey approval through what is said and through voice tone.
6. Use untimed tests whenever possible, because braille takes longer to read.
7. Test over several sessions rather than one long session.
8. Give credit for correct responses given in any form of communication (for example, braille).
9. Provide adaptive equipment made or bought for that specific student with visual impairment.
10. Understand that "reading" a test or other material to a student requires different cognitive processes than if that student could read the information for himself or herself. It requires a significant amount of attention and memory skills not required of reading with print material. Reading a test to a student takes significantly longer, and students who might have just lost visual acuity have to learn how to respond to material read out loud to them.
11. Ask the student directly if he or she needs help.
12. Do not shout at the student with visual impairments, the problem is visual not auditory.
13. Do not be afraid to use common expressions such as "see" in talking with the student. Students with visual impairments commonly use the term "see" in reference to themselves.
14. Ask the student how you can help provide a comfortable evaluation setting. Many students have learned strategies that could make the evaluation process easier for everyone involved.

Special educators play an important role in assigning students with visual impairments. Understanding the impact of visual impairments on assessment tasks will help distinguish between these and other disabilities the student might demonstrate as well as allow for development of effective instruction and programs geared to the individual needs of the student.

Hearing Impairments

As with visual impairments, hearing impairments can be considered mild, moderate, or severe. An individual with a mild hearing loss can usually cope with spoken language but may have language and learning problems. The person with a moderate hearing loss will not be able to hear or understand speech in noisy places. The person with a severe hearing loss will not be able to depend on spoken communication alone for understanding, not even with a hearing aid. The person with a profound hearing loss is considered "deaf" (Lazrus and Strichart, 1986).

Symptoms. Individuals with hearing problems characteristically fail to pay attention, give wrong answers to simple questions, hear better when watching the speaker's face, and frequently ask to have things repeated. Also, they often function below their educational potential, are withdrawn, or demonstrate behavior problems. Students with hearing impairments often do not articulate clearly or

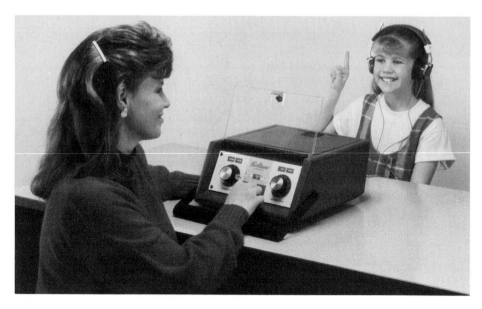

An audiologist screens a student's hearing with an audiometer.   *Source:* © Beltone Electronics Corp. 1992

they demonstrate other speech and language problems. Those individuals with moderate to severe hearing loss often use verbal utterances that are unintelligible to the untrained ear. Before diagnosis of a hearing loss is made, the behaviors of a student may be misunderstood. Many students with hearing impairments are mis-diagnosed as unintelligent, autistic-like, having learning disabilities, or having behavior problems. Since at least 20 percent of all students suffer from some hearing loss, to circumvent inappropriate diagnosis the special educator needs to be aware of characteristics that might indicate hearing impairment (Campbell and Baldwin, 1988).

1 in every 5 students some level of H.I

also mixed + central

Types.   Hearing impairments are of two types: conductive and sensorineural. A conductive hearing loss, where sounds are muffled but not distorted, is caused by damage to the bones, eardrum, or membranes that carry sound from the outer to the inner ear (*Better hearing*, 1985). Damage can also result from ear infections or by earwax. Conductive hearing loss is sometimes treated with tubes to drain fluid from the middle ear. A sensorineural hearing loss, where sounds are distorted, is caused by deterioration of the inner ear (cochlea, auditory nerve, associated brain cells). Sometimes it results from childhood disease, certain medications, head injury, repeated trauma, or exposure to extremely loud sounds (Hovoet and Helmstetter, 1989). It can also be genetic (Lazrus and Strichart, 1986) or from malformation during fetal development (Gillham, 1986). Sensorineural loss is almost always untreatable (Holvoet and Helmstetter, 1989). Hearing loss is classified by how well a person can hear certain frequencies. Table 4-3 provides the most common classification of hearing impairments used by professionals.

Table 4-3 Handicapping effects of hearing loss in children

Average Hearing Level 500–2000 Hz	Description	Possible Condition	What Can Be Heard without Amplification	Handicapping Effects (if not treated in first year of life)	Probable Needs
0–15 dB	Normal range	Conductive hearing losses	All speech sounds	None	None
15–25 dB	Slight hearing loss	Conductive hearing losses, some sensorineural hearing losses	Vowel sounds heard clearly; may miss unvoiced consonant sounds	Mild auditory dysfunction in language learning	Consideration of need for hearing aid, speech-reading, auditory training, speech therapy, preferential seating
25–30 dB	Mild hearing loss	Conductive or sensorineural hearing loss	Only some of the speech sounds, the louder voiced sounds	Auditory learning dysfunction, mild language retardation, mild speech problems, inattention	Hearing aid, speech reading, auditory training, speech therapy
30–50 dB	Moderate hearing loss	Conductive hearing loss from chronic middle ear disorders; sensorineural hearing losses	Almost no speech sounds at normal conversational level	Speech problems, language retardation, learning dysfunction, inattention	All of the above, plus consideration of special classroom situation
50–70 dB	Severe hearing loss	Sensorineural or mixed losses due to a combination of middle ear disease and sensorineural involvement	No speech sounds at normal conversational level	Severe speech problems, language retardation, learning dysfunction, inattention	All of the above, probable assignment to special classes
70 + dB	Profound hearing loss	Sensorineural or mixed losses due to a combination of middle ear disease and sensorineural involvement	No speech or other sounds	Severe speech problems, language retardation, learning dysfunction, inattention	All of the above, probable assignment to special classes

Source: From *Hearing in Children,* 4th Edition, by J. L. Northern and M. P. Downs. Copyright © 1991 Williams & Wilkens p. 14. Reprinted by permission.

Assessment. Hearing acuity is usually first screened with an instrument called an audiometer. A pure-tone audiometer is usually used in the schools by a trained professional (*audiologist*). It is important that the special educator have some understanding of the information provided by the audiometer, since it will often be in the records of students with special needs and provides significant information for a student's instructional needs. The audiometer measures pitch in frequencies and

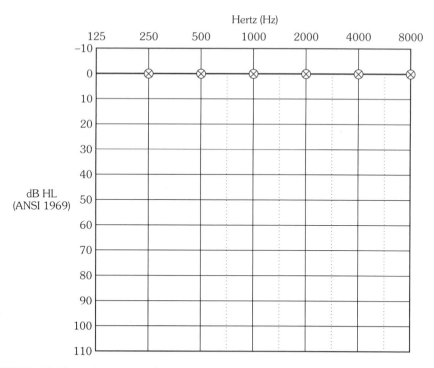

FIGURE 4-1 Normal sample audiogram (pure tone audiometry)

loudness in decibels. The student who fails an audiometric screening is then administered what is called a pure-tone threshold test, which determines the level at which the
person barely hears the sound. The results of this test are plotted on an audiogram.
An audiogram portrays the degree and nature of the hearing loss in precise measurements of decibels (loudness) and frequencies (pitch). The audiogram is a graph with
the person's profile mapped on it. Figure 4-1 illustrates a normal sample audiogram
(0–15 dB), and Figure 4-2 illustrates a severe hearing loss audiogram (50–70 dB).

Hearing aids are sometimes used to correct hearing problems. There are many
types, but all of them have a microphone, an amplifier, an earphone, an earmold, a
battery, and a volume control. Sometimes students have trouble using or maintaining their hearing aids. Special educators involved in assessing students with hearing
impairments should have some knowledge of the types of problems that frequently
occur when students wear hearing aids. A description of frequent hearing aid
problems and what to do when the problem occurs is listed in Table 4-4. This
information should also be communicated to the regular or special education teachers working with such students.

Students with hearing impairments often communicate with oral language. However, the most severely impaired can only communicate with sign. Only a specially
trained professional should attempt educational evaluation of students who require
the use of sign to communicate.

The special educator not trained in the use of sign can, however, help assess
students with hearing impairments who use oral communication. Many students

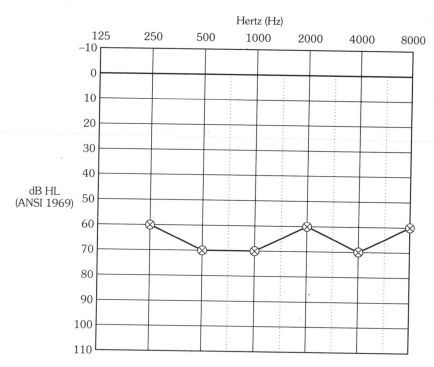

FIGURE 4-2 Severe hearing loss sample audiogram (pure tone audiometry)

with hearing impairments are high risk for other types of disabilities, particularly learning disabilities and behavior problems. Therefore, more than the assessment of hearing acuity is needed to provide documentation for eligibility. The special educator involved in assessing students with hearing impairments should consider:

1. using nonverbal assessment tools;
2. using tests, as available, that were normed on the hearing impaired;
3. assessing over several short sessions rather than one long session;
4. using untimed tests when verbal input or output is required;
5. facing the student at all times to be sure the student can read your lips (speak clearly without exaggerating lip movements);
6. using gestures (nods, smiles, and so forth) to help convey meaning;
7. giving credit for correct responses given in any form of communication (sign, finger spelling, teletouch);
8. maintaining visual contact with the student during the assessment session;
9. using only words or directions the student understands;
10. waiting and listening for the student to speak (do not provide words or try to outguess a student who is slow responding to questions);
11. using pantomime, demonstration, and manual communication to help the student understand what you are trying to have them do; and
12. maximizing assessment information by testing the limits, reinforcing responses, practicing test-type items, and demonstrating task strategies (dynamic assessment).

Table 4-4 Hearing aid problems and what to do about them

Type of Problem	Possible Causes	What to Do
Sound goes on and off	Battery needs charging or replacement Corroded battery Breaking cord	Charge or replace batteries Remove corrosion with pencil eraser Replace cord or tell parents
No Sound	Not turned on Dead battery Battery in upside down Earmold or tubing plugged with wax or water Broken cord, switch, etcetera Earmold is not inserted correctly in ear	Turn it on or turn volume up Replace battery Check polarity Clean earmold and tubing Tell parents Insert earmold correctly
Whistling/squealing	Earmold is plugged Earmold is too small Tubing disconnected from receiver Broken tubing, receiver button, etcetera Battery is low	Clean the earmold Tell parents Reconnect tubing Tell parents Change or charge batteries
Putt-putt sound	Wrong battery Dirty battery or contacts Broken contacts	Charge batteries Clean batteries and contacts Replace cord or tell parents

Source: From *Medical Problems of Students with Special Needs: A Guide for Educators,* by J. Holvoet and E. Helmstetter p. 52. Copyright © 1989 by PRO-ED, Inc. Reprinted by permission.

Learning disabled/hearing impaired. Students with severe/profound hearing losses who also demonstrate additional disabilities are increasingly being identified in school settings. These disabilities are often the result of meningitis, premature birth, birth trauma, maternal rubella, infections, febrile episodes, Rh incompatibility, and cytomegalovirus resulting in additional disabilities beyond hearing impairment alone. The rubella epidemic of the 1960s has been replaced by meningitis, prematurity, birth injury, and newer etiologies (AIDS/crack babies) as contributors to hearing impairment with additional disabling conditions. The needs of students with such multidisabilities, referred to in the literature as learning disabled/hearing impaired (LD/HI), bring challenges to teachers of hearing impaired students and speech-language pathologists, and demand the expertise of learning disabilities specialists to provide comprehensive evaluations. At times the impacts of the disabilities are so severe that the student is actually functioning in the mild/moderate intellectual deficit range. Evaluation of such students requires special educators to use more curriculum, criterion, and dynamic assessment approaches, since norm-referenced tools do not usually include such samples in their norming procedures. In addition, criterion and dynamic assessment procedures have direct application for instruction.

Central Nervous System Problems

The *central nervous system* is made up of the brain and spinal cord, while the nerves outside this network, both sensory and motor, constitute the *peripheral nervous system.* The visual and auditory impairments discussed here are the result of breakdowns in the

A special education teacher uses sign language while teaching students with severe hearing impairments.   *Source:* © Will/Deni McIntyre/Photo Researchers, Inc.

peripheral nervous system. In addition to such disabilities, the special educator will often be involved in assessing students with specific central nervous system (CNS) problems that can co-occur with other disabilities. CNS disorders most often encountered by special educators in school settings and that require specific test modification include epilepsy, spina bifida, and cerebral palsy. The special educator, while not assessing these CNS disorders directly, must understand the implications of such disorders on a student's cognitive, affective, motor, and academic functioning. Appropriate modification is necessary to guard against discriminatory and biased assessment procedures.

Epilepsy

Epilepsy is defined as two or more seizures or convulsions that occur in the absence of disease, fever, or injury to the brain (Holvoet and Helmstetter, 1989). Epileptic seizures are caused by a temporary malfunction of the central nervous system. Even though most special and regular education teachers have heard about epilepsy, some remain insensitive and ignorant of its nature, as well as how to handle it during assessment or instruction. Some professionals misinterpret the behavior of students with epilepsy, thinking it results from mental retardation or some form of emotional disturbance. Such a perception of epilepsy can only serve to further alienate a student in the school environment, encourage emotional problems, and aggravate all forms of learning.

   Types.   There are four types of epileptic seizures: grand mal or convulsive seizures, focal seizures, petit mal seizures or absences, and psychomotor seizures. All except convulsive seizures occur without loss of consciousness and often go undiagnosed.

Table 4-5 Health and learning side effects of drugs commonly used for seizure control

Drugs	Health Side Effects	Learning Side Effects
Carbamazephine (Tegretol)	Rash, blood abnormalities, frequent urination, loss of appetite, changes in blood pressure, impaired liver function	Confusion, poor coordination, speech disturbances
Diazepan (Valium)	Weight gain, constipation	Drowsiness, fatigue, lethargy, difficulty with coordination, depression
Ethosuximide (Zarontin)	Gastric irritation, dizziness, insomnia, blood abnormalities, rash, loss of hair, vaginal bleeding	Drowsiness, difficulty with coordination, irritability, hyperactivity, inability to concentrate, blurred vision
Mephobarbital (Mebaral)	Dizziness, nausea, diarrhea, blood abnormalities, rash	Lethargy, irritability
Phenobarbital (Lunimal)	Dizziness, rash, nausea, diarrhea, blood abnormalities, loss of calcium, bone weakness	Hyperactivity, sedation, general learning impairment
Phenytoin (Bilantin)	Overgrowth of gums, coarsening of facial features, drowsiness, loss of calcium, bone weakness, nausea, vomiting, diarrhea, difficulty swallowing, rash, increased facial and body hair, joint pain, liver damage, blood abnormalities	Impaired coordination, slurred speech
Valproic acid (Depattiene)	Nausea, vomiting, indigestion, liver damage, dizziness, tremor, loss of hair, weakness	Lethargy, eye damage, impaired coordination, hyperactivity, aggression

Symptoms.   Focal seizures cause twitching movements, usually involving one side of the face, the thumb and fingers of one hand, or one entire side of the body. Psychomotor seizures cause the person to move in a trancelike state, making movements that appear purposeful but are irrelevant to the situation. For example, students might smack their lips, make chewing motions, speak phrases, or walk around the room—all activities divorced from the main activity of the classroom at that time. After a psychomotor seizure, the student appears confused or has no memory of the occurrence of inappropriate behavior. Petit mal seizures or absences are characterized by momentary staring spells. The student may have a blank stare or blink rapidly. Sometimes hands, legs, or facial muscles twitch (Wagman, 1982). The student will not speak or respond but will soon resume activity without being aware that anything has happened. These absences can occur ten to twenty times a day, or more (Gillham, 1986). A student who suffers from these milder types of seizure, such as petit mal, may be considered by professionals insensitive to epileptic behaviors to be a daydreamer, a poor listener, preoccupied, inattentive, uncooperative, negative, or deviant. Unfortunately, many medications prescribed for seizure control cause side effects that can seriously affect behavior and learning. Table 4-5 lists some of the drugs commonly administered for seizure control and the physical and learning problems that are side effects of their use. The special educator needs to be aware of the side effects of medication used for convulsive behavior to accurately interpret assessment results.

Assessment.   The special educator involved in assessing a student with a history of any type of convulsive behavior or for whom the special educator suspects possible seizure activity, should consider the following items.

1. Students for whom there is any question of convulsive behavior should be referred immediately to a neurologist for further evaluation.
2. Special educators should be tactful and kind when discussing convulsive behavior, for such a problem is often embarrassing and scary to the student or family.
3. Special educators need to be aware that a student having a grand mal attack may fall to the ground, become stiff, and begin to jerk or thrash. The special educator should take the following action with a student having a grand mal seizure:
   a. Remain calm and reassure any other students or staff that might be present when the student begins the seizure.
   b. Ease the student to the floor on his or her back with their head to the side.
   c. Clear the area of any furniture or objects that could injure the student.
   d. Place a soft object under the student's head.
   e. Loosen any clothing around the student's neck.
   f. Allow the seizure to run its full course.
   g. Allow the student to rest after the seizure. If testing was going on prior to the seizure, discontinue the assessment until another day.
   h. Notify administrative personnel of the incident so parents or guardians can be contacted.
   i. Reassure the student that he or she is going to be fine. Be sensitive to how scary this must be for the student and help the student understand that you do not think less of him or her because of the seizure.
4. Special educators need to be aware that with petit mal seizures it is important to be a keen observer for the behavior may last only a few seconds. Petit mal seizures may appear as a sudden jerk or a frozen posture. A student may drop something for no observable reason. Another sign of petit mal seizures is rapid eye blinking.

Spina Bifida

Spina bifida is a general term used to describe any incomplete development of the spinal column or spinal cord. It is the most prevalent birth defect, causing paralysis of the lower half of the body (Holvoet and Helmstetter, 1989). Because of medical advances, many students with spina bifida are now able to attend regular classes; however, many of these students are placed in special education classes for at least a part of their day. Although some spina bifida children are of superior intelligence, most are below average, and a sizeable minority are mentally handicapped (Gillham, 1986). Recently, it has been recognized that a significant portion of students with spina bifida who are functioning in the average range of intelligence also demonstrate specific learning disabilities, particularly in the area of visual perceptual skills. The special educator will more than likely be involved in assessing students with spina bifida to determine whether they need the special services of teachers working with the gifted, learning disabled, or mentally handicapped.

Types.   There are three types of spina bifida. In spina bifida occulta, the spinal cord is not damaged and neurological functioning is usually normal. In meningocele, the spinal cord bulges out from an opening in the spine and forms a small sac filled with cerebrospinal fluid. The person with meningocele is sometimes wheelchair

Students with certain types of physical disabilities fatigue easily and need shorter work periods.   *Source:* David S. Strickler/The Picture Cube

bound and always suffers some paralysis. In the most serious form of spina bifida, myelomeningocele, the spina cord and its covering, the meninges, protrude from the spine, forming a sac that contains part of the spinal cord, meninges, and cerebrospinal fluid (Williamson, 1987). The spinal nerves above and below this sac are damaged, and the person is always wheelchair bound. Surgery, performed soon after birth, places the spinal cord and meninges back into the spine and covers the area with skin and muscle. This keeps out germs and seals in the cerebrospinal fluid. Surgery does not, however, improve functioning of the damaged nerves. Figure 4-3 provides an illustration of the three types of spina bifida.

Assessment.   The special educator evaluating a student with spina bifida should consider the following items to ensure that a nonbiased assessment is provided for the individual.

1. Schedule shorter test sessions spaced over several days to counter the problem of fatigue.
2. Position the student with spina bifida in the way most preferred by the individual.
3. Speak directly to the student. Do not converse with an aid or attendant as if the student does not exist.
4. Be attentive to the student's need for a regular schedule for food, exercise, and toileting.
5. Monitor the temperature of the evaluation room throughout the assessment to avoid exposing the student to extreme temperatures.

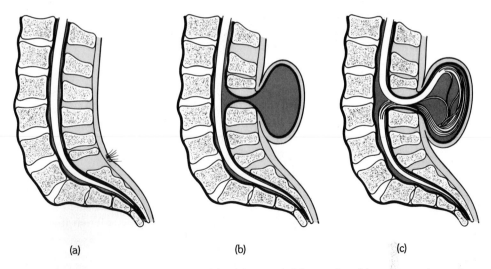

(a)   (b)   (c)

FIGURE 4-3 Three types of spina bifida: (a) spina bifida occulta, (b) meningocele, and (c) myelomeningocele.   *Source:* From *Children with Spina Bifida: Early Intervention and Preschool Programming,* edited by G. G. Williamson p. 2. Copyright © 1987 by Paul H. Brookes Publishing Company. Reprinted by permission.

6. Help the student reposition his or her body frequently. Ask how they would like you to help.
7. Be sure an attendant is available to help the student change wet and soiled diapers as soon as possible.
8. Have an evaluation room and bathroom available that are barrier free for the student.

Cerebral Palsy

Cerebral palsy (CP) is a label that represents a problem in locomotion and refers to nonprogressive abnormalities of the brain that occurred early in life stemming from many different etiologies (Wagman, 1982). Special educators assess students demonstrating CP often, since several disabilities can co-occur with CP. About half the student population that demonstrate CP also exhibit significant speech disorders, 20 percent have some type of visual or auditory impairment, and about 25 percent have epilepsy. Often, the cognitive functioning abilities of these students are affected. Specific learning disabilities are common and are probably related to the site of the brain lesion. The cognitive functioning levels of students with CP range from the gifted to the retarded (Gillham, 1986).

Symptoms.   The prominent characteristics of CP help to define this disability. These features include the following:

1. CP is a condition, not a disease;
2. CP originates from a brain trauma;

3. CP occurs during childhood; and
4. damage to the central nervous system results in motor handicaps often characterized by impaired movement, poor coordination, and paralysis.

In addition, CP often co-occurs with other sensory, psychological, language, and cognitive disabilities, all in varying degrees (Lazrus and Strichart, 1986). There are many causes of CP, including prematurity or infectious diseases during pregnancy; Rh incompatibility, fetal anoxia, metabolic disorders and inherited conditions; birth injuries such as trauma and asphyxia; and postnatal head injury, infectious diseases, clots, hemorrhages, and tumors of the brain.

Types.   The severity of CP varies. Sometimes CP goes undetected for years, especially when only one side of the body is affected (hemiplegia). A very mild condition may not be detected until school age when the child appears clumsy for his/her age or cannot control his/her hand to write. In some cases both lower limbs or all four limbs are involved. Spastic CP is more obvious due to the exaggerated or involuntary movements of the body. With athetosis CP there are facial contortions and writhing movements of the limbs. Ataxia CP is characterized by uncoordinated head movement and tremor.

Assessment.   The special educator working with a student demonstrating CP should keep in mind that the learning problems vary widely, as do learning styles and abilities. While many of the factors relevant to assessing students with spina bifida also apply to students with CP—speaking directly to the student, keeping testing sessions short to prevent fatigue, helping the student reposition his or her body frequently, and providing a barrier-free evaluation room and restroom for the student—it is also important to keep the following factors in mind. Students with CP:

1. often have poor self-concepts, even withdrawing to the point of nonresponse;
2. may have a limited field of vision and a limited scanning ability;
3. may have visual perception problems that could affect their interpretation of visual tasks;
4. have a high prevalence of oral language disorders; and
5. have significant motor impairments that can bias the results of timed task tests.

The choice of test instruments and assessment approaches (for example, standardized or dynamic) for use with such individuals must be guided by these constraints. Visual stimuli should always be presented where the student can easily see them. Test tasks should not require verbal responses only but must be adaptable to alternate response modes (see chapter 9 on oral language) such as finger pointing, head nodding, or a word that can be understood as a consistent communication response between the examiner and the student. Dynamic assessment approaches may allow more accurate measurement of the learning potential of students with CP; results of timed task tests can be extremely biased for students with significant motor impairments. And above all, the special educator should remember to interact with the student as a person, not as their disability.

Bone, Joint, and Muscle Problems

The special educator is very likely to be involved in assessing students with some types of *bone, joint, or muscle problems*. Common disorders of these types encountered in school settings include juvenile rheumatoid arthritis, muscular dystrophy, brittle bone disease (osteogenesis imperfecta), or curvature of the spine (scoliosis). As with other sensory and health disorders discussed throughout this chapter, the special educator is involved in an educational assessment of such students because they have been referred by teachers due to additional learning problems. The special educator should begin the assessment process by collecting extensive developmental and medical histories on such students. In addition, experts (teachers, physicians) should be contacted so information concerning the primary problem can be collected. Prior to testing, the special educator should have a thorough knowledge of the medications the student is taking and their side effects. Some additional factors to consider for students with bone, joint, or muscle problems are included in the following list.

1. Students with these disorders fatigue easily; short assessment sessions should be planned.

2. Students must avoid severe twisting or jarring that can exacerbate or restart inflammation.

3. Many of these students are depressed and often are angry. Unfortunately, they are also usually inhibited, shy, and introverted, so their emotions are not generally released. Repressed emotions surface on occasion, and these students then demonstrate acting out behavior. During an assessment, it may be important for the special educator to stop testing and simply talk to the student about how he or she is feeling. In addition, it is important to include a thorough social/emotional evaluation of these individuals (see chapter 7).

4. Many of these students suffer severe bouts of pain that leave them fatigued, irritable, and able to demonstrate only the lower end of their potential. The impact of pain on current functioning must always be considered. Older students often complain that people do not seem to believe or understand that they are experiencing pain, a complaint often traced to the demands of teachers or therapists for consistent behavior.

5. Students with arthritis and other forms of muscle or joint disorders often demonstrate "gelling," which is stiffening in the joints and muscles. This problem leads to "morning stiffness" and an inability to move the joints freely after a student has been in one position for a long time. Therefore, opportunity for frequent movement must be available during the assessment. When choosing assessment instruments, consideration of the impact of such disorders on fine and gross motor activities must be made.

6. Students taking high doses of aspirin may experience a high-tone hearing loss. This deafness disappears when the aspirin treatment is stopped. The special educator should request that the student have a full audiological evaluation to be certain other auditory processes are not involved, but this temporary loss must be considered during the assessment process.

7. Careful observation and assessment of these students in the classroom setting, alone and with other peers, at different times of the day, and at varying levels of fatigue help inform the special educator of the students' capabilities.

8. Parents or guardians should be questioned about activities performed outside of school, how tired the student is on returning from school, how much sleep the student needs, and what special adjustments are made in the home.

9. Many students with muscular dystrophy require constant repositioning. The special educator should help the student reposition an arm, leg, or torso. The teacher should ask the student directly if he or she can be provided with a more comfortable situation.

10. The special educator should talk directly to the student and not to an aid or attendant.

11. The special educator should be sure that a barrier-free assessment room is used and that a barrier-free restroom is very close.

Health-Related Problems

The special educator is often involved in assessing students with special needs who have specific health-related conditions that have an impact on learning, teaching, and the evaluation process. In such cases, the special educator should be aware of these conditions so decisions can be made regarding medical advice or intervention before the assessment begins. Some of the most common health-related problems encountered by special educators include:

1. allergies;
2. blood problems: anemia (sickle cell) and hemophilia;
3. endocrine problems: diabetes and thyroid;
4. respiratory problems: asthma and cystic fibrosis;
5. cardiovascular problems: congenital heart defects and rheumatic heart condition;
6. kidney problems: nephritis and nephrosis;
7. neoplastic diseases: childhood leukemias and solid tumors; and
8. infectious diseases: AIDS and other infectious diseases.

The health problems and diseases most often encountered by special educators will be discussed in the remaining pages of this chapter. Whenever, a special educator is involved with assessment of a student with a significant health record, contact with the student's family is imperative. Permission to discuss the student's health record with the physician treating the child should be obtained from the family or guardian prior to any assessment. The special educator needs to understand any modifications or substitutions required for the assessment process due to the health-related problem. In addition, this detailed health information should be available to all professionals working with the student so effective and nonbiased assessment and instruction can be developed and administered throughout the student's curriculum.

Allergies

An *allergy* is an abnormal reaction or increased sensitivity to certain substances that in similar amounts are harmless to others. The substances that trigger an allergic reaction are called allergens. The system of an allergic person reacts to these allergens as if they were germs, producing antibodies to neutralize the allergens. The reaction between allergens and antibodies causes the release of various chemicals, especially histamines, which produce the allergic symptoms. A significantly high proportion of students with learning disabilities and attentional deficit disorders have histories of allergies.

Symptoms. The symptoms of allergies are many. Grass and dust allergens often cause sneezing, itching eyes, itchiness of the throat and palate, rhinitis (inflammation of the mucous membranes of the nose), and nasal discharge. The symptoms of food allergies are varied. They range from digestive tract upsets to eczema and hives to asthmatic attacks. But food allergies can also be more obscure. Symptoms can include nasal speech, dark circles under the eyes, fatigue, hyperactivity, headache, ear and hearing problems, blurred vision, irritability, or general malaise.

It is commonly thought that an allergen will cause a reaction immediately upon contact. This is true much of the time, however, food allergies sometimes have delayed reactions. Symptoms may occur hours or days after ingestion. Often, the most desired daily food is the allergen. "Problems arising from food allergy may be intermittent or cyclic even though the food is eaten daily. Virtually every organ and system can be involved with a puzzling array of symptoms or dysfunctions" (*Phadebas*, 1982, p. 6).

Types. The most common allergens are pollen, animal dander, house dust, mites, molds, drugs, food, and bee and wasp stings (*You and your allergy*, 1990). Common allergies include hay fever, conjunctivitis (itching, tearing eyes), asthma, nettle rash (urticaria, hives), contact eczema (dermatitis), insect allergy, and food allergy.

Assessment. Many different factors can trigger an allergy attack; foods, inhaled allergens, drugs, and direct contact with the skin. Stress and sometimes exercise can trigger an attack. A new school, oral reports, tests, or being singled out from classmates is extremely stressful for some students. Such situations can easily trigger an allergy reaction. The special educator assessing a student with special needs should be aware of possible allergies for several reasons. First, the performance of the student might not be optimal due to the fact that he or she is suffering an allergic reaction. Second, allergies often appear disguised as school-related problems. Common characteristics of allergies include: blurred vision, dizziness, drowsiness, headache, hyperactive behavior, and nervousness. If dealt with only on the surface, these behaviors could be attributed to visual acuity problems, behavior problems, or learning disabilities. Medications students take to control their allergies also have side effects that the special educator needs to be aware of before drawing conclusions regarding an assessment. Table 4-6 lists some

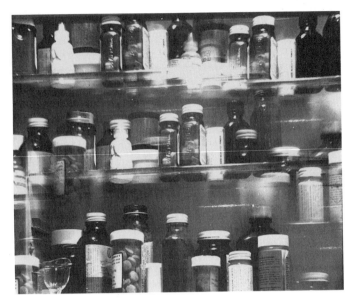

Medications that many students take to control their allergies have side effects that need to be considered during the assessment process. *Source:* © Kenneth Karp/Omni Photo Communications, Inc.

prescription and nonprescription drugs used to treat allergies and the side effects of these drugs.

Asthma

Asthma is a chronic respiratory disorder characterized by recurrent coughing caused by spasms of the bronchi or the diaphragm. Asthma may be nonallergic, or it may be an allergic reaction triggered when allergens are inhaled or ingested. Asthmatics suffer from these attacks, which obstruct the flow of air to the lungs and make breathing difficult. Sometimes forced breathing becomes necessary. Wheezing occurs, due to the rush of air through narrow airways, followed by coughing.

Many different factors can trigger an asthma attack. In children an attack is most often triggered by allergens or by emotional stress (Wagman, 1982). An asthma attack is usually very frightening for the individual having the attack and for the person with them. The wheezing sounds and labored breathing characteristic of asthma make the person having the attack seem to be suffocating.

Assessment. The special educator evaluating a student with special needs might easily be with a student when an asthma attack occurs, since emotional stress, such as an assessment, could trigger an attack. Parents, guardians, and the student's physician should always be contacted promptly. Sometimes the individual has prescribed medicine to take when an attack begins. As with allergy medications, many students demonstrate side effects from these prescriptions. Table 4-7 lists some of

Table 4-6 Side effects of allergy medications

Drug	Side Effects
Nonprescription	
Actifed	Drowsiness, nervousness, dizziness, excitability
Allrest	Drowsiness, excitability
Benadryl	Drowsiness, excitability
Benadryl Decongestant	Drowsiness, nervousness, dizziness, excitability
Chlor-Trimeton	Drowsiness, excitability
Chlor-Trimeton decongestant allergy medication	Drowsiness, nervousness, dizziness, excitability
Comtrex AS	Drowsiness, excitability
Dimetapp Extentabs	Drowsiness, nervousness, dizziness, excitability
Drixoral	Drowsiness, nervousness, dizziness, excitability
Sinutab	Drowsiness, nervousness, dizziness, excitability
Sudafed	Drowsiness, nervousness, dizziness, excitability
Prescription	
Actifed C	Blurred vision, dizziness, drowsiness, headache, nervousness, restlessness
Ambenyl	Blurred vision, dizziness, drowsiness, headache, nervousness, restlessness
Atarax	Drowsiness
Dimetane	Blurred vision, dizziness, drowsiness, headache, nervousness, restlessness
Naldecan	Blurred vision, dizziness, drowsiness, headache, nervousness, restlessness
Ornade Spansule	Blurred vision, dizziness, drowsiness, headache, nervousness, restlessness
Periactin	Blurred vision, dizziness, drowsiness, headache, nervousness, restlessness

the commonly used asthma medications and the possible side effects of such drugs. The special educator needs to carefully consider the impact of drug side effects on the assessment process. Immediate relief can be given by placing the individual in a moist environment, such as in the bathroom with all the faucets turned on (but not in the shower or tub). Before any assessment, the special educator should check the student's medical history to be aware of any potential asthmatic condition.

Diabetes Mellitus

The special educator involved in assessing students with special needs will at some time or another be involved with students who have diabetes or diabetic characteristics. Diabetes can be fatal, and requires careful attention by school professionals. Diabetes prevents the body from properly converting carbohydrates (sugar and starch) into the energy needed for normal activity. After the body digests and absorbs the carbohydrates, they are burned for energy or stored in the form of glycogen for later use. Insulin, a protein hormone secreted by the pancreas, is necessary for both storage and reconversion of glycogen. In the diabetic, production of insulin is insufficient and an abnormal amount of sugar accumulates in the bloodstream.

Diabetes is treated with insulin injections, by oral drugs, or by controlling the diet. Insulin reaction, also called hypoglycemia, occurs when the blood sugar level drops so low that it causes problems in body metabolism. Hypoglycemia is a suddenly

Table 4-7 Side effects of asthma medications

Drug	Side Effects
Aminophylline bronchodilator	Drowsiness, headache, nervousness, restlessness
Brethine bronchodilator	Dizziness, headache, nervousness
Choledyl bronchodilator	Headache, nervousness
Medrol	Dizziness, headache, restlessness
Prednisone steroid	Dizziness, headache, nervousness, restlessness
Quibron	Headache, restlessness
Slo-Phyllin bronchodilator	Dizziness, headache, nervousness
Theo-dur bronchodilator	Dizziness, headache, nervousness
Ventolin bronchodilator	No known side effects

occurring, emergency situation. The symptoms of hypoglycemia include shaking, pounding of the heart, excessive sweating, faintness, paleness around the mouth or nose, difficulty carrying on a conversation, nervousness, irritability, headache, nausea, fatigue, laziness, and yawning (Holvoet and Helmstetter, 1989). If the episode continues without treatment, the student will lose consciousness and may have a seizure. Most insulin users carry lumps of sugar or hard candies with them to forestall an oncoming insulin reaction. This raises the blood sugar level rapidly.

Another emergency situation for the diabetic is hyperglycemia. This occurs when the blood sugar level becomes very high. Onset of hyperglycemia is gradual and usually happens only when the person neglects his or her diet, forgets to take prescribed medication, or has an infection or other illness. Symptoms include increased thirst, increased urination, increased appetite, weakness, itching, dry skin, weight loss, blurred vision, and sugar in the urine (Holvoet and Helmstetter, 1989). If hyperglycemia is suspected by the special educator, a doctor should be contacted at once. Insulin must be given, but the amount must be calculated by a medical professional. The special educator should never undertake any treatment for diabetes.

Thyroid Problems

The thyroid gland is an important organ of the endocrine system. Three hormones, thyroxine (t4), triiodothyronine (t3), and calcitonin are produced by the thyroid glands. Insufficient thyroid hormone production is known as hypothyroidism. Students demonstrating this problem show symptoms that include tiredness, dry skin, hair loss, weight gain, constipation, and sensitivity to cold. In childhood, deficiency often causes significant growth retardation. Overproduction of thyroid hormones (hyperthyroidism) causes symptoms including fatigue, anxiety, palpitations, sweating, weight loss, diarrhea, and intolerance of heat. A student's fatigue and anxiety are often seen as emotional rather than physical problems, but the special educator should check the student's medical record to note whether a history of *thyroid problems* exists in the student's developmental background or in the family background. If there is any concern that a thyroid problem exists, the student should be referred to a physician. Thyroid problems often co-occur with affective (depression, anxiety) disorders (see chapter 7).

Infectious Diseases (AIDS)

Acquired Immune Deficiency Syndrome (*AIDS*) is an infectious disease that results in a defect in cell-mediated immunity, occurring with no known cause and producing diminished resistance to disease (Falloon, Eddy, Roper, and Pizzo, 1988). Students can receive AIDS from many sources: blood transfusions, poor prenatal care, sexual abuse, intravenous drug use, and sexual activity. Sixty percent of children who test positive for this virus eventually die (Falloon, Eddy, Roper, and Pizzo, 1988). Currently, there is no known cure for AIDS.

Students who have developed AIDS should be treated with dignity and compassion. It is important that the special educator recognize that shaking hands, testing, or interacting with such students in normal school activities do not place anyone at risk for catching AIDS. There is only a risk if there is an exchange of bodily fluids such as semen or blood.

Special educators will very likely be involved with assessment of students with AIDS on an increasing basis in future years. The pediatric neurological findings, scant as they are, indicate that infants with AIDS are at high risk for developmental delays, seizures, abnormal CAT scans, and motor dysfunctions (Bell, 1990). In addition, there are definite linkages between drug abuse and the birth of infants with AIDS. Babies exposed to crack during their mothers' pregnancies are more likely to be premature, demonstrate poor impulse control, be distractable, and have expressive language problems and personality disorders (Gittler, 1990). Such children will very likely receive dual diagnosis and be placed in special education classes.

Addictive Disorders

Addictive disorders are a significant problem for many students in elementary, secondary, and postsecondary education. Students with addictive disorders often bring the effects of their problems to school. The special educator needs to be informed about signs of addictive disorders to identify and refer such students to appropriate medical and legal authorities. During an assessment process, the special educator might begin to document behaviors that indicate possible addictive disorders. Information collected in interviews with students, classroom teachers, and parents or guardians, as well as case history information, provides additional documentation of physical or personality changes that might be the result of an addictive disorder.

Alcohol Addiction

The National Institute on Alcohol Abuse and Alcoholism (NIAAA) estimates that 1.3 million students between the ages of twelve and seventeen have a serious drinking problem. Alcohol consumption has increased more than 300 percent among youth in the last decade (Cartwright, Cartwright, and Ward, 1984). If a special education teacher feels that a student might have problems with alcohol, referral to the school psychologist or social worker is appropriate. Any testing that might have been done with that student should be reevaluated in light of the findings of the clinical interview by the psychologist or social worker. The following behaviors are red flags for *alcohol addiction* that the special educator should always be alert for during an assessment.

1. Drowsiness
2. Slurred speech
3. Dizziness
4. Nausea
5. Poor coordination
6. Uninhibited behavior
7. Impaired reactions and judgment
8. Aggressive behaviors
9. Blackouts
10. Denial of drinking as a problem despite frequent difficulties due to drinking (school suspension, DUIs)
11. Personality changes

Observations of the student in the classroom, with peers, and outside the classroom setting should also be collected to document behaviors across time periods, settings, and individuals.

The special educator may also assess students who were born with fetal alcohol syndrome (FAS). Quite often students with FAS demonstrate mental retardation, growth deficiencies in both height and weight, unusual facial features, and cardiac problems.

Drug Addictions

Cartwright, Cartwright, and Ward (1984) discuss four categories of drugs that have potential abusive risks for students. Each of these drugs has a different impact on an individual's senses and behavior. These four categories of drugs are described below.

1. *Stimulants.* Drugs in this category increase alertness, reduce hunger, produce a feeling of well being, and reduce fatigue. Table 4-8 lists types of stimulants often used by drug abusers and behaviors for a teacher to observe when suspecting abuse of stimulants.

2. *Depressants.* Depressants are sedatives that reduce brain and muscle activity. Alcohol is one type of depressant abused by many students. In addition, Table 4-8 lists common drugs that are depressants that could be abused by students.

3. *Hallucinogens.* Drugs in this category produce alterations in the senses of time, color, space, and sound. LSD, STP, and peyote are examples of drugs in this category. Table 4-8 lists additional hallucinogens and behaviors for a teacher to observe when suspecting drug use.

4. *Narcotics.* Drugs in this category relieve pain and blunt the senses. Table 4-8 lists commonly used narcotics.

The special education teacher involved in assessing children and young adults will often come face-to-face with individuals they suspect are abusing drugs. Students with special needs are often at high risk for becoming addicted to drugs. Lowered self-

Table 4-8 Selected list of common abusable drugs

Drug	Classification	Slang Names	Behaviors to Observe
Amphetamines Benzedrine Dextroamphetamine Methamphetamine	Stimulant	Benzedrine–bennies, pep pills Dextroamphetamine–Dexedrine, dexies Methamphetamine–meth, speed crystal General names–uppers, purple hearts, jolly beans, co-pilots, wake-ups, lid-poppers, ups, footballs	Incessant talking, irritability, restlessness, malnutrition, weight loss, paranoia
Cocaine		Cocaine–snow, coke, stardust	Impaired nasal membrane
Barbiturates Pentobarbital sodium Amobarbital sodium Phenobarbital seconal	Depressant	Pentobarbital sodium–yellow jackets Amobarbital sodium–blue, blue devils, blue birds, blue heaven Phenobarbital seconal–downers, rainbow, candy peanuts	Sleepiness, slurred speech, lack of coordination, confused thinking, dulled reaction, impaired memory
Tranquilizers Miltown Placidyl Valium Librium	Depressant	Downers	Sleepiness, slurred speech, lack of coordination, confused thinking, dulled reaction, impaired memory
Heroin	Narcotic (Opiates)	Smack, skag, lemonade, horse, hard stuff, H, dynamite or dolly, scat, junk, snow, stuff, Harry, Joy	Tranquil, euphoric feeling, dizziness, nausea, itchiness, sweating, constipation, loss of appetite, loss of physical energy, very small pupils, disassociation, sluggishness, drowsiness, slurred speech, weight loss
Cannabis Marijuana Hashish THC	Hallucinogens	Weed, stick, roach, reefer, joint, pot, hash, hay, grass, gage, tea, MaryJane, locoweed	Reddened eyes; intensification of mood, feelings, and senses; lessening of inhibitions; increased appetite (particularly for sweets); distortion of time and space; irritability; paranoia
Inhalants Aerosol Airplane glue	Inhalant	Flasher, glue, gas, kidstuff, spray	Reddened eyes, slurred speech, impaired reaction and judgment, mild euphoria, lack of coordination, hallucinations

Source: Hensing, 1972; Green, 1977; Schuckitt, 1984; Talbott and Cooney, 1982.

esteem, peer pressure, and living in a dysfunctional family have been linked to drug and alcohol abuse. It is important to keep in mind, however, that even in the best of families, students can become addicted to drugs. Table 4-8 lists some of the slang names used by drug users to refer to specific types of drugs, as well as behaviors that might lead you to suspect drug use. The special educator who suspects any drug use should contact the school psychologist or social worker to explore the issue further with the student. Results of any assessment completed with such a student should be considered in light of the findings of the psychologist or social worker.

Eating Disorders

The third addictive behavior that is increasing among young adults is eating disorders. Such disorders are characterized by gross disturbances in eating behaviors

Many students with addictive disorders bring the effects of such problems to school. *Source:* © Richard B. Levine

(American Psychiatric Association, 1987). Three types of eating disorders that the special educator will more commonly observe include anorexia nervosa, bulimia nervosa, and compulsive overeating.

1. *Anorexia nervosa.* The characteristics of this addictive disorder include refusal to maintain body weight, an intense fear of becoming overweight, a distorted body image, and amenorrhea in females (DSM-III-R, 1987).

2. *Bulimia nervosa.* The characteristics of this addictive disorder include episodes of binge eating, feelings of lack of control over eating binges, self-induced vomiting, use of laxatives or diuretics, strict dieting, vigorous exercise to prevent weight gain, and overconcern with body image (DSM-III-R, 1987).

3. *Compulsive overeating.* The characteristics of this addictive behavior include episodes of binge eating, hording food, unusual eating habits, anxiety reduced by the eating process, eating when not hungry, and an obsession with food.

All three types of psychological disorders are the result of dealing with feelings through inappropriate eating habits. The special educator suspecting eating problems should quickly contact the school psychologist or social worker to explore the concern and to provide help for the student. Eating disorders can be fatal to a student if carried to an extreme, and in milder forms they signal significant emotional distress that will have an impact on the student's performance in academic and social domains.

The special educator will often be called upon to assess students demonstrating more than one disability. Some of these disabilities are physical (spina bifida) while some are more behavioral (drug or alcohol abuse). It is imperative that the special educator be aware of the characteristics and the impact of these disabilities on the cognitive, affective, and academic functioning of students to ensure that nonbiased assessment is provided to all individuals.

Summary

Sensory Impairments

1. Dual diagnosis refers to students who demonstrate two or more disabilities, for example, learning disabled and hearing impaired.
2. Mild visual impairments are typically correctable with prescription lenses; students with moderate or severe visual impairments will need instructional modifications.
3. The most common types of visual impairments include problems with visual acuity, restricted vision, color blindness, and muscle balance.
4. A student with visual impairments may be referred because of additional cognitive, affective, or academic problems that are unrelated to the visual impairment.
5. Students who fail vision screening are referred to a vision specialist for more thorough assessment.
6. Hearing impairments may be mild, moderate, or severe.
7. Three types of hearing impairment are conductive, sensorineural, and a combination of conductive and sensorineural termed a *mixed loss*.
8. An audiometer is used to assess hearing acuity.
9. Special educators may be asked to assist in assessing a student with vision or hearing impairments and can take steps to ensure a valid evaluation.

Central Nervous System Problems

1. The central nervous system is made up of the brain and spinal cord, while the sensory and motor nerves outside this network constitute the peripheral nervous system.
2. Special educators will often be involved in assessing students with CNS disorders such as epilepsy, spina bifida and cerebral palsy, which may require test modifications.
3. Important factors in assessing students with CNS disorders include speaking directly to the student, keeping testing sessions short, helping the student reposition as necessary, providing a barrier-free environment, and considering motor and language problems when selecting appropriate test instruments.

Bone, Joint, and Muscle Problems

1. Common bone, joint, or muscle problems encountered by special educators include juvenile rheumatoid arthritis, muscular dystrophy, osteogenesis imperfecta, and scoliosis.
2. Students with these problems may be referred for assessment because of other cognitive, affective, or academic problems.

3. Special educators involved in the assessment process can take steps to ensure a valid assessment and make the student as comfortable as possible.

Health-Related Problems

1. Common health-related problems encountered by special educators stem from difficulties with allergies, blood, kidneys, the endocrine system, the respiratory system and the cardiovascular system, neoplastic diseases, and infectious diseases.
2. The special educator working with a student who has a health problem should know about the problem, understand the potential side effects of medications the student takes, and consult with the student's doctor or parents about health considerations during assessment.
3. All students with health-related problems should be treated with dignity and compassion.
4. Special educators need to recognize that shaking hands, testing, or interacting with students in normal school activities do not place anyone at risk for catching AIDS.

Addictive Disorders

1. Students with special needs are often at high risk for addictive disorders so it is important that special educators be aware of behaviors suggesting addiction.
2. The most common types of addiction observed in the school setting involve alcohol, drugs, and food.
3. The special educator who suspects a student has any addictive disorder should contact the school psychologist or social worker.

Assessing Cognitive Development

Key Terms

Cognitive development
Dynamic assessment
Factor analytic theory
Global theory
Graduated prompting
Information processing
   models

Mediation
Method clinique
Nonbiased assessment
Nonverbal measures of cognitive development

Piagetian theory
Psychometric approach
Testing the limits
Zone of proximal development

Cognition, thinking, or intelligence are all terms that define an individual's ability to problem solve. Although not a term universally accepted among researchers, problem solving is a useful way to describe cognitive development. The term *problem solving* stresses the active nature of intelligence rather than focusing on intelligence as passive mental entities (for example, memory, percepts). Such a view of cognitive development focuses on the processes rather than the products of development. Distinctions between cognition, affective relations and social processes become more difficult to make if cognitive development is defined as the means to reach goals. "The thinking organism is active in participating in an event, exploring a situation, directing attention, attempting solutions" (Rogoff, 1990, p. 31).

In recent years the study of *cognitive development* has focused on the individual's ability to construct or make sense of reality. Researchers are beginning to recognize the impact of social context on individual achievement and to develop methods to investigate cognitive development in real-world settings rather than by defining "intelligent" behavior as a totally innate capacity.

The special educator has an important role to play in documenting cognitive development, particularly since more emphasis is being placed on the influence of guided learning or social interaction as the key to understanding an individual's true potential. No longer is intelligence assessment seen as the domain of psychologists only. The special educator who interacts on a daily basis with students with special needs has an excellent opportunity to observe maximum performance, particularly when content and strategies are familiar to the student. The special educator provides expertise in observing students' processes of learning rather than only the products (IQ scores) of learning.

Cognitive development has also been recognized as specific to the domain of thinking and the task context. A generic approach to cognitive performance is being replaced by a more central position that defines cognitive development in terms of the interaction of the individual and the domain of the problem. The goal of the activity and the interpersonal and sociocultural context are as important to defining cognition as are the individual's neurological assets.

Although this chapter will focus on the cognitive aspects of problem solving (for example, reasoning, planning, remembering), development of affective and social relations are not separate from cognitive development.

Assumptions about Cognition

The term *intelligence* is used quite frequently in everyday conversation, often in relation to an individual's performance on a specific task. While intelligence is a common term, many different theories exist to explain the natural laws that govern it. Developers of psychometric measures that assess cognitive development all subscribe to one of three differing views of intelligence.

The *global theory* proposes that intelligence is the ability to think abstractly. An author using this theoretical perspective to develop an intelligence test is concerned with how individual test items relate to the total test score rather than to each other or to subtest test scores. The author strives to develop test items that have the strongest correlation with the overall score rather than strong correlations with other test items. The 1960 Stanford–Binet (Terman and Merrill, 1960) is an example of an intelligence test based on this model. Statistically, only one factor emerged from the 1972 Stanford–Binet; it was referred to as the G–Factor and was presumed to represent general intelligence. From a developmental standpoint, the amount of "G" possessed by an individual increases with age, so scores were expressed in terms of mental age or mental level.

The new revised Stanford–Binet, Fourth Edition (Thorndike, Hagen, and Sattler, 1986) is based on a factor analytic model and provides composites for Verbal Reasoning, Abstract-Visual Reasoning, Quantitative Reasoning, Short-Term Memory, and a Total test score.

The *factor analytic theory* has significantly influenced the assessment of intelligence in the United States over the last century. The two-factor theory, as hypothesized by Spearman (1927), posited an underlying G–Factor that influences all performance, plus multiple S–Factors specific to given tasks. The Wechsler (1974, 1991) tests, the most common intelligence tests used to assess students with special needs, conform more to this orientation. Wechsler groups S–Factors into verbal and performance functions. Scores are derived in terms of an overall IQ that represents an index of general mental ability. However, Wechsler's concern with the global nature of intelligence influenced the construction of his tests despite the factor analytic orientation of the measures. Wechsler advocates that subtests be seen as contributing to the total intelligence of an individual and not as isolated skills.

Multifactor theories have been described by a variety of researchers (Thorndike, 1927; Thurstone, 1938; Guilford, 1967; Cattell, 1963). Thorndike and Thurstone's theories resemble Spearman's notions in that they postulate an underlying G–Factor. Thorndike (1927) offered three additional primary factors: abstract ability, mechanical ability, and social ability. Thurstone (1938) identified seven primary mental abilities: word fluency, memory, reasoning, perception, verbal, number, and spatial skills. Guilford (1967) systematized his approach by identifying three facets of intelligence—content, operations, and functions—each with a set of subfactors. Gustafsson (1984) offers one of the newest factor analytic models of intelligence.

His "G" consists of crystallized intelligence (verbal information), fluid intelligence (adaptive nonverbal abilities), and general visualization (figural information). Each of these factor analytic approaches to intelligence stresses tapping into "G" or into "primary mental abilities" of intelligence with a sample of independent tasks.

Information processing models of intelligence have been significantly influenced by Soviet psychology. Vygotsky (1962), a Russian psychologist, and Luria (1961), a Russian neurologist, laid the foundation for many of the current information processing models of intelligence used by professionals interested in cognitive development. Vygotsky proposed that the principle mental functions of complex perception, memory, voluntary attention, and conceptualization are neither inherited genetically nor developed independently but are a product of an individual's organization of activities with objects and interactions with adults.

Soviet psychology stresses the role of the adult in guiding the child's development. The mother directs the child's perceptions, making some objects more powerful stimuli and attaching to those objects a new "signaling sense." The child approaches the mother's guidance independently, thereby organizing individual perceptions. Thus, intelligence develops in a social manner: functions previously divided between two people become internal psychological organizers for the child. Cognitive ability develops through internalization of social experience.

Soviet psychology introduced a new concept to the study of intelligence: the proximal zone of development. The proximal zone is "the distance between the actual developmental level as determined by independent problem solving, and the level of potential development as determined through problem solving under adult guidance or in collaboration with more capable peers" (Vygotsky, 1978a, p. 86). This concept characterizes prospective development, including concepts currently in the process of being integrated by an individual. The Soviets take a dialectical approach to the development of intelligence; the process of intellectual growth has no terminal point of equilibrium but continues throughout life. Campione and Brown (1984), Borkowski (1985), Sternberg (1986), and Das, Kirby, and Jarman (1975) have all based their models of intelligence on an information processing approach that describes cognitive development.

Other approaches to cognitive development that have influenced the measurement of intelligence include the work of Jensen (1980), Gardner (1983), and Piaget (1971). Piaget attempted to trace the evolution of abstraction from its sensori-motor beginning to its logico-deductive conclusion. Opposing the purely maturational approach, he felt that intelligence does not develop linearly but is constructed by successive stages of development; each stage reconstructs the previous one at a higher level of abstraction (Piaget, 1971). According to Piaget, each stage is characterized by a particular view of the world and the child's relationship to it. During the *sensorimotor stage* (approximately birth to 24 months) the child comes to grips with the permanence of objects and the difference between objects and self. In this stage the child is limited to what is present and really does not have the ability to engage in pretend play. In the *preoperational stage* (approximately 24 months to 7 years), the child begins to represent things to himself and to understand cause and effect relationships. In this stage the child can pretend but reasoning is limited to things the child can see and manipulate. For example, a child in the preoperational stage may demand more cookies and be satisfied if the cookies are broken into two pieces. Although the adult knows the amount does not change, the child is distracted by the perception of quantity. During the stage of *concrete operations* (approximately 7 to 11 years), the child develops the ability to think independent of perceptions or how things look. This child is no longer satisfied that a broken cookie is more and can mentally reconstruct the cookie (reversibility of operations) and know that the amount remains the same (conservation). In the final stage, *formal operations*, the ability to reason logically develops even when more than two variables must be considered. The young person can form hypotheses and explore them in a systematic manner, drawing conclusions after considering several points of view. Formal operational thinking allows an individual to understand and use more abstract reasoning, such as inference, figurative language, and ambiguity.

From a Piagetian perspective, each stage of development is discrete. Transfer from one stage to the next results when the child reorganizes old schemata, coordinating some elements that were previously independent and differentiating some that were previously combined. The child's goal in activity is adaptation, which is accomplished through assimilation and accommodation. Assimilation involves changing reality to suit existing structures (for example, symbolic play). Accommodation entails changing existing structures to adjust to reality. Assimilation and accommodation operate in a closed system; changes in assimilation effect changes in accommodation. Equilibrium is not reached until the final stage. The imbalance between assimilation and accommodation is the innate, driving force behind cognitive development (Woodward, 1963).

Jensen (1980) proposes a model that divides intelligence into two levels, Level I, Associative Ability, and Level II, Cognitive Ability. Associative abilities involve rote and short-term memory skills; cognitive abilities require reasoning and problem solving. Most current assessments of cognitive development tap into both Levels I and II of Jensen's model.

In contrast to levels of intelligence, Gardner (1983) proposes six intellectual competencies or multiple intelligences that exist rather autonomously. These intellectual competencies include linguistic intelligence, musical intelligence, logical–mathematical intelligence, spatial intelligence, bodily–kinesthetic intelligence, and personal intelligence.

Defining intelligence or cognitive development is not an easy matter. Table 5-1 lists several definitions of intelligence that are each based on very different theoretical orientations. Part of the confusion concerning definitions of cognitive development and ways of measuring intelligence results from the failure to understand (a) that intelligence is an attribute, not an entity, and (b) that intelligence is the summation of the social learning experiences of the individual. As Rose (1989) said, "What we define as intelligence, what we set out to measure and identify with a number, is both in us and out of us. We have been socialized to think of intelligence as internal, fixed, genetically coded. There is, of course, a neurophysiology to intelligence, but there's a feeling to it as well, and a culture" (p. 241). It must be recognized that affective and cultural influences will have an impact on a student's performance during the assessment of intelligence, particularly in relation to decisions pertaining to true potential. In view of this, the

Table 5-1 Definitions of cognitive development

Theorist	Definition
Binet and Simon (1976)	"Judgment otherwise called good sense, initiative, the faculty of adapting one's self to circumstances. To judge well, to comprehend well, to reason well, these are the essential activities of intelligence" (p. 42–43).
Spearman (1923)	"Everything intellectual can be reduced to some special case . . . of educating either relations or correlates: Education of relations—'The mentally presenting of any two or more characters . . . tends to evoke immediately a knowing of relation between them' Education of correlates—'The presenting of any character together with any relation tends to evoke immediately a knowing of the correlative character'" (p. 91).
Wechsler (1958)	"The aggregate or global capacity of the individual to act purposefully, to think rationally and to deal effectively with his environment" (p. 7).
Das (1973)	"The ability to plan and structure one's behavior and an end in view" (p. 27).
Vygotsky (1987)	"Thought is not born of other thoughts. Thought has its origins in the motivating sphere of consciousness, a sphere that includes our indignations and needs, our interests and impulses, and our affect and emotion. The affective and volitional tendency stands behind thought. Only here do we find the answers to the final 'why' in the analysis of thinking" (p. 282).
Rogoff (1990)	"I assume that thinking is functional, active, and interpersonal in practical goals, addressed deliberately (not necessarily consciously or rationally). It is purposeful, involving flexible improvisation toward goals as diverse as planning a meal, writing an essay, conniving or entertaining others, exploring the problems of an idea or unfamiliar terrain of objects, or remembering or inferring the location of one's keys" (p. 7).
Rose (1989)	"What we define as intelligence, what we set out to measure and identify with a number, is both in us and out of us. We have been socialized to think of intelligence as internal, fixed, genetically coded. There is, of course, a neurophysiology to intelligence, but there's a feeling to it as well, and a culture" (p. 241).

concept of intelligence is subject to change as our understanding of human intelligence and affective and cultural influences increases.

Approaches to the Assessment of Cognitive Development

Psychometric, Piagetian, and Soviet-based assessment techniques used in the investigation of cognitive development differ in terms of question format, item selection, scoring criteria, and clinical interpretation. These differences stem directly from the theoretical underpinnings upon which the measure is based. Individuals without disabilities normally perform equally well on psychometric, Piagetian, and Soviet measures of cognitive development. However, you should not interpret this to mean that these various measures are tapping the same abilities; rather, it indicates that among normally achieving persons different abilities are correlated. Special educators working with individuals demonstrating diverse learning patterns find that these students tend to score differently depending on the test administered. Since diagnostic categories and programming decisions depend on test scores, essential differences between assessment philosophies should be carefully considered by the professionals working with students who have special needs.

Psychometric Approach

The *psychometric approach* emphasizes adherence to standardized procedures in test administration. Standard presentation of test items across subjects is crucial for comparing results to those obtained by the standardization sample. When standardization is violated, the subject has been given a different test than that given to the normative population; therefore, performance is not comparable to the norm. Adherence to standardization requires that the administrator read questions, record answers, and refrain from discussing success or failure of the items with the individual being tested. The assessment becomes very focused on the subject's product scores rather than on the processes or strategies used to obtain the answer to a problem. The examiner's inability to give feedback may also threaten an anxious subject, lessening rapport, increasing anxiety, and reducing performance. This criticism is particularly important when evaluating emotionally labile, severely disabled, minority, or low socioeconomic status (SES) individuals intimidated by the tester and the situation from the start.

Psychometric measures of cognitive development consist of items selected on statistical criteria. Correlation with a total test score is crucial to item selection on tests constructed according to a unifactor theory. For tests derived from a two-factor or multifactor theory, items must correlate either with "G" or with predominate item clusters. Subsequently, each cluster is labeled as measuring a given trait (for example, memory, fluency, verbal comprehension). It should be clear that factors, including "G," are merely statistical clusters of items that have been described according to the theoretical orientation of test constructors or analyzers.

Scoring criteria differ for power and speed subtests on psychometric measures of cognitive development. For some items, speed and accuracy are emphasized, while for others only accuracy is important. In both cases, the student receives a number quantifying performance; analysis of wrong answers does not affect final scoring. Extreme scores on individual subtests can significantly influence total test scores, resulting in unrepresentative final IQs. Figure 5-1 illustrates an example of an adolescent with a severe language disability. Jeff's WISC–III scores are significantly discrepant between the verbal and performance components of this IQ measure. The verbal scale scores focus on oral language processes, whereas the performance scale scores focus on visual and nonverbal processes. When Jeff's two discrepant scores are averaged together into a full scale score, he functions within the below average range. This is not an accurate representation of his cognitive potential, since the language deficits pull down the full scale score. In such a case, a professional should recommend the use of intelligence measures that are not so dependent on verbal expression or use the performance scale of the WISC–III as a better indicator of potential.

Many students with special needs demonstrate significant scatter across the individual subtests of IQ measures. This scatter, as illustrated in Figure 5-1, can be between cluster areas (verbal or performance) as well as within an area (verbal). Scatter, an uneven performance, has implications for the interpretation of a total scale score. The special educator must be careful to examine performance within and between subtest scores.

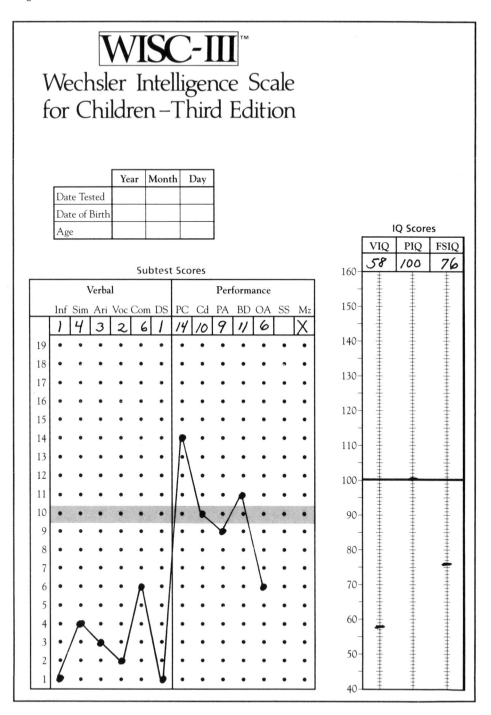

FIGURE 5-1 WISC–III profile for a 15-year-old student with learning disabilities

Clinicians who wish to draw a profile should first transfer the child's scaled scores to the row of boxes below. Then mark an X on the dot corresponding to the scaled score for each test; and then draw a line connecting the Xs.

Interpretation of test scores is primarily quantitative, with verbal labels attached to numerical results. The final score (IQ or MA) reflects the sum of all the subject's tests, although various tests provide different types of intermediate scores (verbal, performance, factor, cluster). The sum of the subject's scores is converted to IQ or broad cognitive scores based on the distribution of scores obtained by the standardization sample. In this way, each individual is given a number that designates his relative standing as compared to the general population. Since inadequate standardization samples wreak havoc with the relative standing of underrepresented groups, testers must take great pains to obtain information regarding their composition. Professionals should carefully examine the manuals of psychometric assessment tools and critically evaluate the information provided on sample populations used for test construction.

Commonly Used Psychometric Assessment Tasks

A variety of tasks are used to assess intelligence; in most cases, the kinds of tasks used reflect a test author's conception of intelligence. A description of commonly used tasks found on standardized intelligence tests follows.

Discrimination. Intelligence test tasks that sample skill in discrimination usually present a variety of stimuli, either visual or auditory, and ask the student to identify the one that is different from all others. Pictures, numbers, letters, words, and sentences are common types of stimuli presented to the student.

Generalization. Generalization tasks range from asking students to simply match stimuli to more difficult types of classification groupings. Again, the stimuli can be pictures, numbers, letters, words, sentences, or paragraphs, depending on the age and ability level of the individual.

Motor behavior. Many tasks on intelligence tests require a motor response. The tasks for young children include throwing objects, walking, building blocks towers, and so forth. Most motor tasks at higher age levels are actually visual–motor tasks. The student may be required to copy geometric designs, trace paths through a maze, or reconstruct designs from memory. Since motor responses can be required for tasks assessing understanding and conceptualization, many tasks assess motor skills at the same time that they assess other skills.

General information. Students are sometimes required to answer specific factual questions on intelligence tests, such as: "In what direction would you travel if you were to go from Poland to Argentina?" and "What is the cube root of 8?" These types of questions primarily assess what has been learned.

Vocabulary. Many different types of tasks are used to assess vocabulary. In some cases, students must point to objects in response to words read by the examiner and in others must name pictures. Some vocabulary tasks require the student to give oral definitions of words, while others call for reading definitions and selecting one of several words to match the definition. Some tests score a student's definition of a word as simply pass or fail, while others use a weighted scoring system to reflect the degree of abstraction used in defining words.

Comprehension. In assessing comprehension, the student is asked to give evidence of comprehension of directions, printed material, or societal customs and mores. The examiner presents a specific situation and asks what actions the student would take, for example "What is the thing to do if you have a bloody nose?" In other cases, the examiner reads paragraphs to a student and then asks specific questions about the content of the paragraphs. In still other instances, the student is asked specific questions like, "What are some reasons we need an army?"

Sequencing. Tasks assessing sequencing consist of a series of stimuli that have a progressive relationship between them. The student is asked to organize the stimuli to show that relationship. Pictures, numbers, letters, words, or sentences are often used as the stimuli, depending on the age and ability level of the student.

Analogies. "A is to B as C is to _____" is the usual form for analogy tasks. Element A is related to element B. The student must identify the response that has the same relationship to C as B has to A.

Abstract reasoning. Abstract reasoning is assessed with a variety of tasks. One task, for example, presents absurd verbal statements and pictures and asks the student to identify the absurdity. Another task asks the student to state the meanings of proverbs.

Memory. Several different kinds of tasks assess memory: repetition of sequences of orally presented digits, reproduction of geometric designs from memory, verbatim repetition of sentences, and reconstruction of the essential meaning of paragraphs or stories.

Paired-associate learning. A paired-associate learning task provides a direct measure of learning ability. In this type of task an individual may be required to learn noun pairs or pairs of visually presented objects. For instance, a student might be told, "ball–chair, brick–curtain, plant–tape." The first word of each pair is then repeated and the student must provide the associated word. Typically, the number of trials necessary for the subject to complete the associations is used as the measure of learning. The use of paired-associate learning is based on the assumption that learning new material is a good indication of learning ability.

The IQ obtained from standardized intelligence tests can be extremely helpful for working with individuals with disabilities. Because IQ is the best available long-range predictor of academic achievement and adjustment, it provides teachers and parents with a helpful timetable for planning an individual's progress (Sattler, 1988). Since intelligence tests provide some measure of the individual's developmental limitations or impairments, teachers and parents can develop individualized curricula within these limits. Yet the psychometric approach has significant limitations for special educators working with severely cognitively disabled, physically disabled, multidisabled, and minority/culturally different students.

A central concern at the heart of many criticisms of the psychometric approach is that standardized IQ tests are used to allocate the limited resources of our society (Lewis, 1973). Intelligence test results are used to provide rewards or privileges,

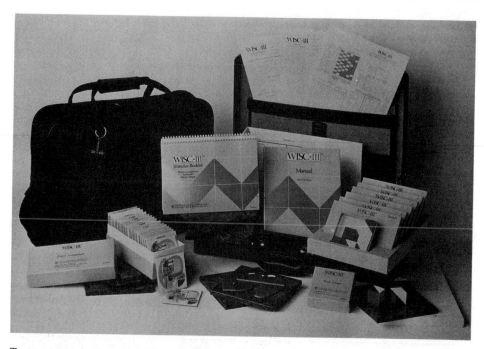

Test materials for the Wechsler Intelligence Scale for Children, third edition. *Source:* Courtesy, The Psychological Corporation

such as special classes for the gifted, admission to college or advanced study, and jobs. Those who do not qualify for these programs may readily direct their anger at the tests because they see the tests as denying them opportunities. Hudson (1972) points out that, for reasons that are still unclear, the IQ has come to be associated not only with an individual's ability to perform certain tasks but with his or her essential worth as well: to have a low IQ is seen as the equivalent of having low caste. This mystique surrounding the IQ is extremely damaging and has no place in our society.

Psychometric instruments measuring intelligence are usually "protected tests." A protected instrument means that the examiner must have a specific credential or certification to be qualified to administer the test. Psychologists are usually the only professionals certified to administer such instruments. The special educator, however, must have an extensive background in the area of assessment to bring meaning to the results provided by psychologists as well as to translate psychological concepts into instructional planning. In addition, the special educator can provide helpful information to a psychologist in choosing an intelligence tool that is most appropriate to the special needs of a specific student.

Assessment tools are based on different perspectives of what it is important to measure when trying to quantify intelligence and whether quantifying intelligence is an appropriate means for investigating cognitive development. Table 5-2 identifies several commonly used intelligence measures that psychologists administer to students with special needs. In addition, the table describes the theory that guided the

Table 5-2 Commonly used psychometric measures of intelligence

| Intelligence Test | Age | | | Theoretical Orientation |
	Preschool	Elementary	Secondary or Postsecondary	
Wechsler Intelligence Scale for Children–3 (Wechsler, 1991)		X		Factor analytic (Spearman)
Wechsler Preschool and Scale of Intelligence– Revised (Wechsler, 1989)	X			Factor analytic (Spearman)
Wechsler Adult Intelligence Scale–Revised (Wechsler, 1981)			X	Factor analytic (Spearman)
Kaufman Assessment Battery for Children (Kaufman and Kaufman, 1983a)	X	X		Information processing simultaneous/successive processing
Stanford–Binet Intelligence Scale, Fourth Edition (Thorndike)	X	X	X	Factor analytic (Cattell, 1963)
Kaufman Assessment Battery for Adolescents/ Adults (Kaufman and Kaufman, 1992)			X	Information processing simultaneous/successive processing

selection of tasks for each of these instruments. A professional's belief about what intelligence means governs his or her selection of an instrument to assess this concept.

Piagetian Approach

Piaget's major interest in cognitive development did not focus on individual differences. Therefore, students of *Piagetian theory* have been the primary force behind these test development projects. The Piagetian format for test administration utilizes the *method clinique*, consisting of a structured interview with the individual that focuses on the task stimuli. See Table 5-3 for a sample interview using Piagetian techniques during a diagnostic assessment. The methodology values qualitative analysis of the individual's reasoning rather than quantitative ranking of his or her ability. Most tasks require verbal explanations of the individual's reasoning process, with attention given to wrong answers as well as to right ones. At some point, however, a decision is made regarding whether the subject passed or failed each item.

Piagetians aim to tap specific mental operations possessing properties of mathematical groups rather than general intelligence. As the developmental nature of Piagetian theory dictates, most tests are constructed according to age levels, rather than using subtests with different levels containing different types of items. Item clusters are intended to tap various aspects of cognition including seriation, conservation, number concepts, spatial concepts, object permanence, deductive logic, inductive logic, classification, and decentration (Modgil and Modgil, 1976). Influ-

Table 5-3 Piagetian interview

Example 1

> **Interviewer:** What are you doing now in school?
> **Butch:** Fractions.
> **Interviewer:** Fractions? Can you show me what you are doing with fractions?
> **Butch:** [writes] 8/16
> **Interviewer:** OK. So what do you do with it?
> **Butch:** 8, 16.
> **Interviewer:** What do you do with it?
> **Butch:** You add it up and put the number up there.
> **Interviewer:** OK. What is the number?
>   23
> **Butch:** [writes] 8/16
> **Interviewer:** How did you do that?
> **Butch:** I went, 16, 17, 18, 19, 20, 21, 22, 23. I added from 16.

Several features of the interview stand out. First, the interviewer gives Butch some freedom to determine the topic for discussion and does not impose on him a preconceived plan of interviewing. The interviewer's aim is to explore the issues that concern the student, to discover the topics that might cause him difficulty. Second, the interviewer tries to get Butch to explain in his own words what he is doing. The questions were designed to be open-ended, like "What do you do with it?" so Butch can answer them in a way that would reveal his thinking or mental strategies. Third, the interviewer's questions are not standardized. They are responsive to or contingent upon the student's answers. The interviewer's questions were not formulated beforehand but depend on what the student said. The aim is to follow-up on interesting responses and to discover how the student thinks. In brief, the flexible interview gives the student some freedom to determine the content of the interview, employs open-ended questions that allow the student to reveal his or her thinking, and uses a contingent method in which the interviewer's questions are determined in part by the student's responses. These basic features of flexible interviewing distinguish it sharply from standardized testing.

Example 2

Hypothesis testing in flexible interviewing may be illustrated by an interview with a third grader named Patty. It began with an addition problem on which Patty used a misalignment strategy. Given the problem 29 − 4, she wrote:

Asked to describe the problem in words she said, "29 plus 4 equals 69." The interviewer then decided to see whether Patty really believed this.

> **Interviewer:** Are you sure that 29 and 4 are 69?
> **Patty:** Altogether?
> **Interviewer:** Yes.
> **Patty:** No.
> **Interviewer:** How much are 29 and 4?
> [Patty then used tallies to calculate the correct result to 33.]
> **Interviewer:** How come this (the written problem) says 69?
> **Patty:** Cause you're not doing it like that (pointing to the tallies).

The interviewer then conceived of two hypotheses to explain the student's behavior. One is that Patty experienced difficulty with written addition problems, misaligning addends with different numbers of digits and yet could solve essentially the same problems when they were presented in concrete form. This hypothesis seemed plausible because many students who fail on written problems nevertheless exhibit skill in informal calculation. A second hypothesis, which seemed less likely is that the source of Patty's difficulty involved the word "plus." When she or the interviewer used this word, Patty misaligned the addends. When the word "altogether" was used, she had no difficulty.

(continued)

Table 5-3 Piagetian interview (continued)

Example 2 (con't)

To decide between the two hypotheses, the interviewer proceeded as follows:

Interviewer: Let's do this. Here are 10 chips, and here's one more. How many do you think there are altogether?

Patty: Altogether, it would be 11.

Interviewer: OK. What about 10 plus 1, not altogether but plus?

Patty: Then you'd have to put 20.

[She apparently said this because she would write:]

Interviewer: Now what if I write down on paper, here's 20, now I write down another 1, and you want to find out how much the 20 and the 1 are altogether?

Patty: It's 21.

Interviewer: Now what would 20 plus 1 be?

Patty: 20 plus 1?

[She wrote:]

$$\begin{array}{r} 20 \\ \times\ 1 \\ \hline 30 \end{array}$$

Note that to decide between the alternative hypotheses, the interviewer deliberately varied certain features of the problem. She began by using two different words—altogether and plus—to ask about the addition of the same concrete objects. Patty solved the "altogether" problem correctly but not the "plus." This seemed to indicate that language was the culprit.

Source: From "Assessment Techniques: Tests, Interviews, and Analytic Teaching," by H. P. Ginsburg. In *Assessing the Abilities and Instructional Needs of Students,* edited by D. D. Hammill, Example 1, p. 444; Example 2, pp. 454–455. Copyright © 1987 by PRO-ED, Inc. Reprinted by permission.

enced by the psychometric tradition, factor analyses have been done on some Piagetian tests (Tuddenham, 1970) with mixed results. Problems encountered finding theoretically consistent items that cluster statistically are ascribed to item selection difficulties rather than theoretical weaknesses.

The primary focus of testing from a Piagetian perspective is to investigate reasoning abilities. Likewise, scoring focuses on the quality of the child's response, without concern for speed. Piagetian researchers have attempted to build reliability into assessment tasks by developing such items as structured response formats (Pinard and Laurendeau, 1964), scores for mental age, chronological age, and quality of error, as well as normative data (Green, Ford, and Flamet, 1971). Tuddenham (1970) attempted to alter traditional Piagetian tasks to permit inference of reasoning abilities from actions rather than from explanation. He built a checklist of the individual's comprehension of terms (for example, more, less, same, different, longer, shorter) into his scale. In each test, although quality as well as accuracy of response is considered, the final conclusion requires classification in an operatory level, thus qualitative analysis merges with a binary classification system of "have" and "have not."

Interpretation as well as administration of Piagetian tests requires mastery of Piagetian theory. It is assumed that the items pertain to actual operational mech-

A special educator can obtain valuable diagnostic information by conducting a structured interview with a younger child interacting on Piagetian tasks.   *Source:* © Mary Kate Denny/ PhotoEdit

anisms that govern behavior; this contrasts starkly with the psychometric approach that deals only in vague, global capacities rather than structures of the intellect. As Piaget (1952) wrote, "it is indisputable that (traditional) tests of mental age have, on the whole, lived up to what was expected of them: a rapid and convenient estimate of an individual's general level. But it is no less obvious that they simply measure a 'yield' without reaching constructive operation themselves" (p. 230). In accordance with this assumption of direct measurement, individuals are classified as sensorimotor, preoperational, concrete operational, or formal operational based on test results. Table 5-4 provides examples of Piagetian tasks.

Piagetian techniques have been used most extensively in assessing preschool children. The special educator with a knowledge of Piagetian theory could certainly obtain valuable diagnostic information by conducting a structured interview with a younger child interacting on Piagetian tasks. Again, a problem with this assessment approach is that the tasks are often divorced from real-world activities and provide very little observation of social interaction skills. Piagetian theory has also been criticized for its assumption that learning develops in a hierarchical progression, particularly whether children do develop cognitively only after the sensorimotor

Table 5-4 Sample Piagetian diagnostic tasks

Conservation of Number
This conservation task measures the child's understanding that variations in the configuration of a row of objects do not affect the number of objects.

Materials: Twenty checkers.

Procedure: Present two rows of 10 checkers in one-to-one correspondence. Say: "Do the two rows contain the same number of checkers?" If the child says "No," help him or her to understand that both rows have the same number of checkers. Then spread apart the row closest to the child. Say: "Do the rows have the same number, or does one row have more? How do you know?"

Age: 5 to 16 years.

Conservation of Continuous Quantity: Solids
This conservation task measures the child's understanding that changes in the shape of a solid do not change the quantity of that solid.

Materials: Two balls of clay identical in size, shape, and weight.

Procedure: Show the two balls of clay to the child. Say: "Do the two balls have the same amount of clay?" If the child says "No" or if there is any doubt about the child's understanding, encourage the child to make them the same. Then say, "Suppose I roll one of the balls into a hot dog. Will there be as much clay in the hot dog as in the ball? Will they both have the same amount of clay?" After the child answers, roll one of the balls into a sausage shape. Say: "Is there as much clay in the hot dog as in the ball? Do they have the same amount of clay?" After the child responds, say, "Why did you say that?"

Age: 6 years.

Conservation of Weight
This conservation task measures the child's understanding that changes in the shape of an object do not cause changes in its weight.

Materials: Two balls of clay, identical in size, shape, and weight.

Procedure: Give the two balls of clay to the child. Say: "Do the two balls weigh the same?" If the child says "No" or if there is any doubt, encourage the child to make them the same. Then say: "Suppose I roll one of the balls into a hot dog. Will the hot dog weigh the same as the ball?" After the child answers, roll one of the balls into a sausage shape. Say: "Do they both weigh the same?" After the child responds, say: "Why is that?"

Age: 6 years.

Seriation: Size
This test of seriation measures the child's understanding that objects can be put in order according to their size.

Materials: Twelve sticks, 10 of which range in length from 9 to 16.2 cm, each being .8 cm longer than the preceding one, one of which is midway between sticks 3 and 4 in length, and one of which is midway between sticks 7 and 8 in length.

Procedure: Place the first 10 sticks before the child in random order, but all in the vertical direction. Say: "Look at these sticks carefully. I want you to put them in order so that the very smallest comes first, and then the next smallest, and then the next smallest, all the way to the biggest. Go ahead."

After the child finishes arranging the set of sticks, give him or her the additional stick that goes between the 7th and 8th stick. Say: "Here's an extra stick. You put it in the right place where it belongs."

After the child inserts the stick remove it, give the child the second stick, and say: "Here's another stick. Put this stick in the right place where it belongs."

Age: 7 years.

Source: From *Assessment of Children,* 3rd Edition, by J. Sattler p. 318. Copyright © 1988 by Jerome Sattler. Reprinted by permission.

period ends. A popular preschool assessment tool based on Piagetian theory is the ordinal scale developed by Uzgiris and Hunt (1975). Characteristics of the six scales are as follows:

Scale 1. **Visual pursuit and performance of objects:** Measures the young child's awareness of existence of hidden objects.

Scale 2. **Means for obtaining desired environmental events:** Measures the young child's actions to achieve a particular event.

Scale 3. **Imitation:** Measures the young child's vocal and gestural imitation.

Scale 4. **Operational causality:** Measures the young child's anticipatory behavior.

Scale 5. **Object relations in space:** Measures the young child's ability to understand three-dimensional space.

Scale 6. **Relation to objects:** Measures the young child's ability to develop schemes to relate to objects.

A recent interest in using Piagetian cognitive theory to design assessment and intervention plans for adolescents and adults with special needs has resurfaced in the special education literature (Moses, Klein, and Altman, 1990). Current constructive theorists are encouraging diagnosticians to utilize Piagetian and Soviet approaches to assessment in an attempt to engage the student in problem solving tasks to facilitate cognitive functioning and reduce the anxiety of being right or wrong. In addition, such facilitative interventions (see Table 5-3) during the assessment process reinforce the student's potential and extinguish the "passive learner" syndrome indicative of many special needs students (Moses and Papish, 1984).

Soviet Approach

Soviet assessment reflects the optimism inherent in Soviet psychology. Although the content of batteries used in diagnosis is equivalent to that of American psychometric tools, the methods and emphasis of testing diverge. A distinction is drawn between actual developmental level, as indicated by performance on a psychometric test, and potential level of development, as determined by the width of the proximal zone. Thus, two children with identical IQs and different proximal zones are not considered to have equal intelligence. For instance, a child with significant cognitive limitations cannot put a puzzle together. Another child from a culturally different background might also have difficulty putting the puzzle together. Each of these children would score low on a standardized assessment measuring perceptual organization and reasoning. The Soviet approach, however, states that this standardized score is only the low end of the child's potential. If provided guided instruction or cues from the teacher, the student with a different cultural background would more than likely require fewer hints on how to develop strategies to complete the task than would the child with severe cognitive limitations. The amount and type of guided instruction should be part of a cognitive assessment. Therefore, the special educator must look at the individual's range from independent learning to mediated or cued help during a problem solving task. This range is what Vygotsky (1962) called the "*zone of proximal development.*" According to this philosophy, such a technique of guided learning is a more accurate measure of true potential than the static tasks on psychometric measures.

Procedures utilized in the Soviet approach involve giving tasks similar to those found in American IQ tests and having the individual solve them independently. If the individual fails, the adult gives progressively more cues to assess how much information (how many cues) the person needs to successfully complete the problem. When the individual reaches a solution, another form of the original task is given to observe transfer to novel stimuli. The width of the proximal zone is indicated by analyzing the number of cues needed to solve the second problem relative to the number of cues needed to complete the first one.

Scoring requires consideration of the original level of development, the number of cues needed to solve, and the degree of transfer. Developmental levels are determined in a fashion equivalent to psychometric techniques. Determination of the number of cues needed relies upon detailed task analysis. Ascertaining the degree of transfer depends on the appropriateness of the transfer task.

The Soviet approach provides an information processing method that yields information regarding how the individual profits from assistance, the individual's speed of learning, and his or her generalization abilities. Students with learning disabilities and those with mild mental handicaps may have similar developmental scores but differ dramatically in the amount of benefit derived from adult assistance or in the amount of transfer to novel stimuli. Research indicates that individuals with learning disabilities require fewer cues and transfer more efficiently than do individuals with mild mental retardation (Brown and French, 1979). Changes in the width of the proximal zone across task constellations was also found to be associated with specific learning disabilities rather than with mental retardation. The Soviet approach to investigating cognitive development provides the special educator with a rich fund of information regarding intra-individual functioning in a variety of situations; however, the results also give some inter-individual comparisons. Soviet approaches to explaining cognitive development (Campione and Brown, 1978) have direct application to instruction. Vygotsky's (1962) description of assessment procedures to investigate problem solving and thinking skills are the basis of the dynamic assessment process advocated throughout this textbook as a useful method for special educators to use in conjunction with standardized, criterion-based, and curriculum-based testing.

Soviet approaches to assessment.   The design of effective assessment and intervention programs for students with special needs has often neglected the dialogic nature of effective problem solving (Stone, 1989). Traditionally, diagnostic procedures have been static, leading only to diagnostic labels and placement decisions. Recently, the concept of process or *dynamic assessment* has led clinicians to reevaluate diagnostic models. Dynamic assessment is based on the following principles:

a. there must be a link between assessment and intervention;
b. assessment must be tied to the environment;
c. assessment must focus on the process as well as the product of behavior; and
d. assessment must involve a means of generating and testing hypotheses (Meyers, 1987, p. 403).

The work of Feuerstein (1979a, b), Campione and Brown (1987), and Vygotsky (1962) have provided the theoretical and empirical base for restructuring the purpose and means of assessment in special education.

Dynamic assessment models advocate that greater attention be given to the dialogic nature of assessment and instruction. Stone and Wertsch (1984) use the term *proleptic instruction* to describe the importance of having students construct an understanding of a concept rather than simply having an adult demonstrate or explain a task. It is the dialogic interaction between the adult and the child that helps the child learn and later transfer that learning. Palinesar and Brown (1984) refer to their procedure as "on-line diagnosis." Ideally, assessment should be an ongoing process that goes hand-in-hand with instruction. According to Vygotsky (1962), dynamic assessment should involve an initial assessment of competence followed by instruction on the target tasks within the individual's zone of proximal development. A measure of this type of gain should possess greater predictive validity than the initial, unaided level of performance. Vygotsky (1962) maintained that with instruction zones of proximal development change rapidly, and it becomes necessary to continually update the diagnosis if instruction is to be aimed at the appropriate level. Thus, according to Lidz (1987a, b), the term *dynamic assessment* refers to "(a) assessment of process, or of the dynamics of change; and (b) the need to continually change and refine the diagnosis of the individual learner, that is, the dynamic, constantly changing nature of assessment itself" (p. 88). Three major dynamic approaches commonly cited in the literature as effective dynamic assessment techniques will be discussed next.

Learning potential assessment strategy (coaching).   Budoff (1987) uses a test–train–retest paradigm to measure an individual's ability to learn. The procedure was developed initially for adolescents who had been classified as mildly mentally disabled. Using nonverbal measures (for example, Raven's Progressive Matrices, Koh's Block Design), Budoff pretests the subject, then coaches the subject on problem solving strategies, and finally posttests the subject over a one-month period. He classifies subjects as high scorers (pretest scores are high—gain little from training), gainers (pretest scores are low—gain from training), or nongainers (pretest scores are low—gain little from training). Budoff supports such a model to identify students who are educationally retarded as opposed to those who are mentally retarded. Such a dynamic assessment technique is really a measure of the magnitude of response to instruction and is more valid in predicting success on specific but similar tasks.

Learning potential assessment device (mediation).   Feuerstein's (1979a) approach, like Budoff's, uses a test–train–retest paradigm. The Learning Potential Assessment Device (LPAD) consists of four nonverbal tasks (including Raven's Progressive Matrices). The training in the LPAD, however, is somewhat different from Budoff's training. Feuerstein encourages the examiner to interact constantly with the student to maximize the probability of solving the problem. This interaction is called *mediation*. The student's answers to questions or problems presented by the examiner (special educator) direct the assessment goals. Table 5-5 provides an example of a mediated learning task. Mediation requires that the examiner analyze the cognitive processes involved in completing a task, that the student understands the instructions of the task, and that constant feedback on performance is provided

Table 5-5 Sample of mediated procedure for a stencil design task

Familiarizing the Child with Materials and Relevant Dimensions
1. Point out cut-outs (I CUT THEM OUT).
2. Label shapes. If there is resistance or difficulty learning labels then tell the child the label, but go quickly to finding shapes that match and say: FIND ALL THE CARDS LIKE THIS. Comment on the lack of labels in a report but do not get bogged down—the matching encourages comparative behaviors while establishing shape as a relevant feature.
3. Point out sounds (NOT CUT OUTS—No Holes). Note all are in bottom row near child.
4. Label colors (see notes for label shapes).
5. Have child COUNT THE SOLIDS. Focus here is not on the ability to count but on the child's conceptualization of "solid" or "not-cut-out." If child counts correctly to 6, then distinction is being made.
* * * WARNING * * *
If child cannot count all the solids, he or she needs more work on the preceding concepts.
6. Compare 2 circles (one small), 2 white squares (straight, crooked), 2 blue cards (solid, cut-out), 2 yellow cards (solid, cut-out), yellow and blue crosses (yellow, blue).
7. At some point, put solid and cut-out back in wrong place—again to gauge whether the discrimination is being made.
* * * WARNING * * *
If child cannot see that you put solid back in wrong place, he or she needs more work on preceding concepts.

Combination Rules
1. Demonstrate what happens when a green circle is placed on a yellow solid. Point out 2 colors, made from 1 = 1.
2. Change solids, showing that the inside color changes by changing solids. Allow child to try 1 or 2 color changes. Emphasize that it is solid that is changing.
* * * WARNING * * *
If child cannot change the color of the solid, he or she needs more work on the preceding concepts.
3. Use white solid with green circle. Change cut-outs (don't reproduce any of the upcoming designs). Show that outside color changes by changing cut-outs.
4. Put solid on top of cut-out and establish necessary order rule and reason. Have child repeat the rule "I put a cut-out on top of a solid and the color of the solid is in the middle."
5. End with the sample design formed into stencils, then introduce the sample design model.

Helping the Child Reproduce the Model
1. Display model while reproduction is still on the table, discussing how a picture was made of it. Point out that there are 2 colors in the picture and 2 colors in the reproduction, but only 1 color on each separate card.
2. Put stencils back in place and request reproduction. Teach search pattern over cut-outs and over solids. Have child say, "Is it this one?"
3. When production is made, encourage checking back to model. Go over what is right and what is wrong about the production.
* * * WARNING * * *
If the child's production is wrong, he or she needs more work on the preceding concepts. Refer to any errors made en route to the correct answer (spontaneous corrections) and discuss why they were wrong. Alternate the correct one and the wrong one. Always end with the correct solution.
4. Repeat Step 3 with each of the remaining training modules.

Source: From "A Comprehensive Approach to Assessing Intellectually Handicapped Children," by N. Vye, J. Burns, V. R. Delcos, and J. D. Bransford. In *Dynamic Assessment: An Interactional Approach to Enhancing Learning Potential,* by C. S. Lidz, (Ed.), pp. 357–358. Copyright © 1987 by Guilford Publications, Inc. Reprinted by permission.

to the student. Feuerstein, Rand, Jensen, Kaniel, and Tzuriel (1987) discuss the following behaviors as important for a mediator (special educator) to be conscious of during the mediation of cognitive development.

1. *Intentionality.* The mediator deliberately assumes the role of teacher by instructing the individual being tested.
2. *Reciprocity.* The student responds to the mediator in the role of learner.

3. *Meaning mediation.* The mediator helps the student make sense of the task by attributing meaning, values, or affect.
4. *Transcendence.* The mediator relates the task to experience and concepts beyond the immediate test situation. If the mediator relates to the student's experience, it is transcendence; if to the mediator's, it is sharing.
5. *Mediation of feelings of competence.* The mediator regulates the task to enable the student's success.
6. *Praise/encouragement.* The mediator encourages the student.
7. *Mediation of control behavior.* The mediator regulates instructions to inhibit impulsivity and promote attention to the task.
8. *Mediation of goal relatedness.* The mediator helps the student think in terms of the goal and plan steps to achieve the goal.
9. *Mediation of psychological differentiation.* The mediator separates from the task, not becoming competitive with the student.
10. *Mediation sharing behavior.* The mediator shares values, ideas, and feelings with the student and encourages the student to do the same.
11. *Mediation of challenging behavior.* The mediator enhances the individual's desire to search for novelty by encouraging the student to strive for higher levels of thinking.

All of these examiner/student behaviors are extremely important. The special educator working with students with special needs must keep alert for and subsequently evaluate these behaviors.

From the Soviet perspective, it is just as important for the examiner to observe and critique his or her own performance during assessment as it is to critique that of the student. According to this model, breakdowns in communication and learning are not all student-centered. By modifying a task, strategy, or technique, a student's performance could change significantly. Feuerstein suggests that results from his measure can be used to identify appropriate teaching strategies as well as to supply information helpful in classifying a student. The mediation procedure focuses on the efficiency of operations of specific cognitive processes (that is, attention, perception, reasoning, and so forth). (See chapter 6 for a thorough discussion of learning behaviors.) Feuerstein's dynamic assessment approach appears to be more useful in promoting a transfer of learning than it is at predicting cognitive success.

Graduated prompting.   Campione and Brown (1987) discuss a *graduated prompting* approach to dynamic assessment. In graduated prompting, a series of behavioral hints are used to teach the rules needed for task completion. Whenever the student cannot complete a task, one prompt or hint is provided. These hints do not evolve from the student's responses, as in mediation, but are generated from a preset script the special educator follows during the assessment process. General prompts are given first, and more explicit prompts follow if the individual needs additional guided assistance. Such a preset script provides a standard format that is reliable and valid for comparison across students. Table 5-6 is an example of one of Campione and Brown's (1987) hint sequences for a rotation problem. The graduated prompting technique assesses the efficiency of cognitive

Table 5-6 Sample of graduated prompting procedure for a stencil design task

1. DO YOU REMEMBER HOW YOU DID IT WITH THE LAST ONE? If not, HOW DID YOU DO IT? If not, point out and label the solid cards and the cut-outs, then explain that a solid and a cut-out are put together to make one that looks just like the model.
2. LOOK AT ALL THESE CARDS (point out each card individually, a pencil is used for this). EVERYTHING YOU NEED TO MAKE THIS ONE IS HERE, SEE IF YOU CAN MAKE ONE THAT LOOKS JUST LIKE THIS ONE.
3. SEE THIS MODEL (point to the model)? DOES ONE OF THESE (point to students) LOOK JUST LIKE THE MODEL? If child responds no, say RIGHT. NONE OF THEM LOOKS JUST LIKE THE MODEL. Then say, YOU SEE IN THE MODEL WE HAVE A (point out and name the color) SOLID AND A (point out and name the color) CUT-OUT. YOU NEED TO PUT SOME OF THESE TOGETHER (point to solids and cut-outs) TO MAKE ONE THAT LOOKS JUST LIKE THE MODEL. SEE IF YOU CAN MAKE ONE THAT LOOKS JUST LIKE THIS MODEL.
4. LET'S LOOK AT THESE AGAIN. THESE ARE THE SOLID COLORS (point). DOES EACH SOLID HAVE ONE COLOR OR TWO COLORS? LOOK AT THIS ONE, FOR EXAMPLE (holds up white solid, #5). If child does not respond correctly, give correct answer.
   THESE ARE THE CUT-OUTS (point). DOES EACH CUT-OUT HAVE ONE COLOR OR TWO COLORS? LOOK AT THIS ONE, FOR EXAMPLE (hold up red-over-white sample model). If child does not respond correctly, give correct answer.
   YOU NEED ONE SOLID AND ONE CUT-OUT TO MAKE ONE THAT LOOKS JUST LIKE THE MODEL (point). SEE IF YOU CAN MAKE ONE THAT LOOKS JUST LIKE THIS MODEL (point to item model).
5. LET'S LOOK AT THE MODEL AGAIN. POINT TO (or NAME THE COLOR OF) THE PART THAT LOOKS LIKE IT COMES FROM A SOLID. Point if the child responds incorrectly. POINT TO (or NAME THE COLOR OF) THE PART THAT LOOKS LIKE A CUT-OUT. Point if the child responds incorrectly. NOW SEE IF YOU CAN MAKE ME ONE THAT LOOKS JUST LIKE THE MODEL.
6. LOOK AT THIS MODEL. (Show red-over-white sample model). LET'S SEE WHAT SOLID I NEED TO MAKE THIS ONE? Explore the cut-outs up to the correct one. LOOK AT WHAT HAPPENS WHEN I TAKE A WHITE SOLID AND I PUT A RED CUT-OUT ON TOP OF IT, PART OF THE WHITE SOLID GETS COVERED UP. THAT IS HOW I MAKE ONE JUST LIKE THIS MODEL. (Point to original model.) If the child uses the correct solid, skip prompt 7 and use prompt 8.
7. LOOK AT THIS MODEL, WHICH SOLID COLOR DO YOU NEED TO MAKE THIS MODEL? If the child does not answer, say SHOW ME ON THE MODEL. Demonstrate if child responds incorrectly. THESE ARE THE SOLID COLORS (point). PICK ONE OF THESE AND SEE IF YOU CAN MAKE ONE THAT LOOKS JUST LIKE THE MODEL.
8. THIS (name the color of the solid) ONE IS PART OF THE MODEL. (Place the correct solid in the center of the board if it is not already there.) LOOK AT THIS PART OF THE MODEL (point to part that looks like a cut-out). FIND A CUT-OUT FROM HERE (point) THAT LOOKS JUST LIKE THIS PART OF THE MODEL. SEE IF YOU CAN MAKE ME ONE THAT LOOKS JUST LIKE THE MODEL.
9. PUT THIS (name color) CUT-OUT ON YOUR SOLID COLOR. SEE, YOURS LOOKS JUST LIKE MINE.

development. However, it requires detailed task analysis of cognitive or academic learning problems. It is more valid as a predictor of classroom success than it is for promoting a transfer of learning (Campione and Brown, 1987). Campione and Brown are developing a reliable method of dynamic assessment for teachers to use in school settings.

Dynamic assessment techniques have been based primarily on either Feuerstein's mediation techniques or Campione and Brown's graduated prompting assessment techniques. But research by Vye, Burns, Delcos, and Bransford (1987) indicates that mediational assessment may be better suited than graduated prompting assessment as a diagnostic–prescriptive device since it has a greater emphasis on contin-

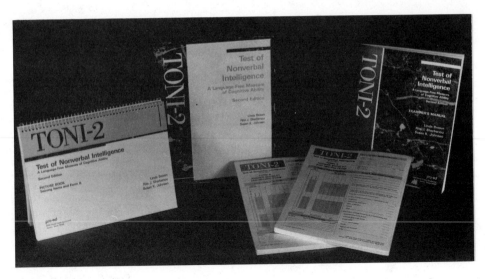

Test materials for the Test of Nonverbal Intelligence, second edition.   *Source:* Courtesy, Pro-Ed.

gency in instruction and the use of metacognitive skills. However, graduated prompting assessment seems more suited for prediction of behavior.

Nonverbal Measures of Cognitive Development

The special educator who is concerned about a student's significant language disability, hearing impairment, or language difference having an impact on the student's performance on popular standardized intelligence measures might encourage that a *nonverbal measure of cognitive development* be chosen to test potential strengths. Nonverbal measures tap a student's reasoning ability without requiring the use of verbal language skills. However, such assessment tools only measure cognition based on figural reasoning. While it can lend support to cognitive strengths, the impact of language on advanced problem solving cannot be discounted. Table 5-7 lists some of the measures of nonverbal cognitive development currently in use.

Modifications for Special Populations

A major issue in assessing students with special needs, particularly those with visual, auditory, motor, or multidisabilities is that the examiner must be sure that the score obtained is a measure of the student's ability and not a measure of the degree of impairment. The special educator has an important role in helping a psychologist choose instruments that are appropriate to specific individuals with special needs.

Unfortunately, the majority of psychometric intelligence measures were not standardized for individuals with disabilities, particularly students with language and severe physical disabilities. Examiners are left with the problem of knowing how to best modify an instrument, recognizing that any modification will have an impact on

Table 5-7 Nonverbal assessment tools

Measure	Facts
Wechsler Intelligence Scale for Children–3 (Wechsler, 1991) Performance Scales Only	Standardized procedures must be followed Speed and accuracy valued Language deficits can still influence performance
Wechsler Intelligence Scale for Adults–Revised (Wechsler, 1981) Performance Scales Only	Standardized procedures must be followed Speed and accuracy valued Language deficits can still influence performance
Leiter International Performance Scale (Leiter, 1948)	Directions very short and clear Norms poor Test materials are colorful and interesting Measures nonverbal, visual discrimination, classification and sequencing
Progressive Matrices (Raven, 1960)	Biased against individuals from non-European backgrounds Susceptible to practice effects Susceptible to educational level Measure of nonverbal reasoning Poor psychometric information in manual
The Columbia Mental Maturity Scale, Third Edition (Burgemeister, Blum, and Lorge, 1972)	Developed for use with individuals afflicted with cerebral palsy Measures classification skills Good for screening, particularly Hispanic students (Wilen and Sweeting, 1986)
Nebraska Test of Learning Aptitude (Hiskey, 1966)	Developed for use with deaf Separate norms for deaf and hearing populations Pantomime and practice items are used Subtests not timed Useful with LEP students
Test of Nonverbal Intelligence–2 (Brown, Sherbenou, and Johnsen, 1990)	Examiner mimics the instructions and does not speak during the entire test 15–20 minutes to administer Measures a limited number of nonverbal abilities
Universal Test of Nonverbal Intelligence (Bracken, in press, Riverside)	Currently being normed

the interpretation of the test scores. Particular care must be given to understanding the limitations of the disability, any medications the individual might be taking that would affect test performance, and the individual's preferred mode of response (see chapter 9).

The special educator must also work with psychologists in understanding that multidisabilities occur frequently with developmentally delayed individuals. For instance, Haeussermann (1952) noted that one of the problems in testing young children with cerebral palsy is that concurrent sensory problems are a frequent issue. If such a child does not have the ability to speak because of paralysis of the speech muscles, deafness may not be suspected and yet the child may not hear.

A significant problem in testing the cognitive development of individuals with disabilities is the lack of tests and the age of those tests that are available to professionals. According to Mulliken and Buckley (1983), many of the current tests have obsolete items that would not be recognized by average children and are definitely

Table 5-8 Special cognitive measures modified for populations with specific disabilities

Measure	Age	Facts
Blind Learning Aptitude Test (Newland, 1971)	6–16	Measures nonverbal cognitive processes in blind children through a series of raised dots
Columbia Mental Maturity Scale (Burgemeister, Blum, and Lorge, 1972)	3–9	Useful for children with motor and language deficits
French's Pictorial Test of Intelligence (French, 1964)	3–8	Requires only pointing response Measures receptive vocabulary through pictures, similarities, recall and comprehension, and visual memory
Perkins–Binet (Perkins School for the Blind, 1980)	4–18, Form N 3–18, Form U	Mental age of 7 years and over required
Hiskey–Nebraska Tests of Learning Aptitude (1966)	3–16	Deaf and hard of hearing norms Norms for normals
Peabody Intellectual Performance Scale–Experimental Edition (Peabody Child Study Center, 1974)	5–53 months	Assessment for young children with significant auditory and visual impairments
Topeka Association for Retarded Children (TARC) Assessment System (TARC, 1975)	No age specified	Short behavioral observation to assess capabilities of children with severe disabilities

not in the experience of individuals with disabilities. In addition, since motivation is an important factor in assessment, obsolete items more than likely do not encourage students to respond to task demands. Table 5-8 lists psychometric tests with special adaptations that are currently used in assessing individuals with special needs. The special educator should carefully examine the copyright date and the technical adequacy of these instruments before selecting them for use.

The special educator should work closely with any psychologist attempting to assess the cognitive development of individuals with language, sensory, or severe disabilities. Careful consideration must be given to the individual's most appropriate mode of response, use of reinforcement to motivate response, and appropriateness of items selected. Many researchers (Holowinsky, 1980; Mulliken and Buckley, 1983; Lidz, 1987a, b) advocate a dynamic assessment approach when assessing individuals with moderate to severe disabilities. Such an approach looks at the cognitive processes an individual utilizes in attempting solutions to problems under independent and guided instruction. The dynamic assessment approach has direct application to placement, individual goals, and teaching strategies to meet those objectives.

Many psychologists have little knowledge or experience working with students with developmental disabilities, particularly disabilities in the moderate to severe range. Therefore, the special educator plays a significant role in helping to ensure that nondiscriminatory practices are followed in assessing individuals with disabilities. Far too many individuals with disabilities have been considered hopeless by professionals (and parents) who depended on psychometric instruments as the predictor of future success and independence. The special educator can help all professionals involved in the cognitive testing of individuals with special needs to structure the assessment so that potential to learn is observed and recorded.

Cross-Cultural Issues and Assessment of Cognitive Development

Researchers have defined the concept of intelligence in a wide variety of ways. Cultural differences also contribute to indigenous concepts of intelligence. For instance, Chinese students value memory, while Australian students consider memory a trivial skill (Chen, Braithwaite, and Huang, 1982). Ugandan villagers consider slow, careful behaviors to be more important than speed, which is very important in Western cultures (Wober, 1972). In addition, members of different social classes in the same culture define intelligent behavior differently. Middle-class groups in the United States differ from other classes in valuing the separation of form from content and in feeling that technical intelligence is distinct from social and emotional skills (Lutz and LeVine, 1982). According to Rogoff (1990), performance on cognitive tasks cannot be separated from "values about appropriate social relationships in such situations" (p. 59).

Cognitive tasks presented to an individual in a socially structured situation will be responded to based on the individual's interpretation and management of social relationships. How a student with special needs approaches a cognitive task is intrinsically related to the tone of the social interaction and to the student's social values and goals. These factors might be very different from the social values of the norming population from which the test instrument was developed. Rose (1989) best summarized this concept when he described the intellectual performance of underprepared and minority writers he worked with in the Los Angeles area:

> We seem to have a need as a society to explain poor performance by reaching deep into the basic stuff of those designated as other: into their souls, or into the deep recesses of their minds, or into the very ligature of their language. It seems harder for us to keep focus on the politics and sociology of intellectual failure, to keep before our eyes the negative power of the unfamiliar, the way information poverty constrains performance, the effect of despair on cognition (p. 222).

Racial Differences and Cognitive Ability

Most studies of racial difference use general intelligence measures and compare black and white group differences. In most studies, the mean for blacks is 10 to 20 IQ points below the mean for whites (Jensen, 1980). As with other group differences, however, the two distributions overlap, and the range of individual differences within one group exceeds the range of differences between groups. In looking at the issue of racial differences in intelligence, it must be pointed out that the heritability estimate for intelligence is based on studies of white persons; consequently it is difficult to know how accurate this estimate is for other racial groups. Valid inferences cannot be drawn about genetic differences among races as long as there are relevant systematic differences in cultural patterns and in psychological environment (Layzer, 1974). Centuries of discrimination against the black population makes direct comparisons of mental ability traits between blacks and whites highly questionable.

Social Class Differences and Cognitive Ability

Social class membership is another characteristic associated with differences in performance on intelligence tests. The values and activities of the home environment vary across different social classes, and it is in the home that students are exposed to occupational models, language models, and personal models, each of which influences the student's behavior and values. The discrepancy between the test developers' values regarding intelligence and the values of a student from a low-income family are even more pronounced when income differences are compounded by culture and race. Students with special needs from low-income families may be at a disadvantage both in the school environment and during the assessment process. Social class differences can be further compounded by language and race. (See chapters 9 and 11 for a discussion of the impact of class, race, and language differences on the development of oral and written language skills.)

Bilingual Differences and Cognitive Ability

Many allegations have been made about the inappropriateness of using tests, and in particular intelligence tests with bilingual individuals. Certainly, an individual with limited English proficiency (LEP) who is being evaluated in a situation in which English is the primary language is at risk for inaccurate assessment of true ability. The identification of mild disabilities among LEP populations is riskier than it is for those with severe developmental delays. The more severe and pronounced a disability is, the easier it is to recognize the underlying problem of poor achievement. LEP students performing within a mild to moderate range of underachievement can easily be diagnosed as having a disability when the problem might be one of language differences rather than disabilities.

Protection for Limiting Bias during Cognitive Evaluation

Holtzman and Wilkinson (1991) discuss several assessment guidelines for limiting bias during cognitive evaluations of LEP students. The special educator is a significant member of the team that gathers the information about LEP students so that legal requirements are followed as well as ensuring that appropriate data are collected. Holtzman and Wilkinson's guidelines are important for the special educator, and these guidelines include the following steps.

1. **Prereferral intervention.** First, ensure that the LEP student has received appropriate instruction and educational interventions of different types in his or her regular environment. The special educator needs to document that instruction in the student's native language has been attempted over a period of time

(Barona and Santos de Barona, 1987). Types of teaching techniques and materials used with a student should be evaluated for appropriateness.

2. **Situational analysis.** Second, ensure that the referral is appropriate. Special educators need to be sure that the referral does not reflect a lack of knowledge or a teacher's prejudice concerning culture, race, or income level differences.

3. **Direct observation.** Third, directly observe LEP students across different settings (see chapter 2). Discrepant behavior in relation to peers and adults across different school, play, or work settings should be documented by the special educator.

4. **Establishing language dominance.** Fourth, carry out formal language assessments in both the native language and in English prior to any assessment. Assessment of both school language and conversational or interpersonal language is necessary.

5. **Dual-language testing.** Fifth, evaluate the LEP student in both the primary and the secondary language. If a student is only tested in his or her primary language, information about knowledge that might have been stored in the secondary language would not be evaluated.

6. **Informed selection of a test battery.** Sixth, testing cognitive development for LEP students should include both psychometric and dynamic approaches. Careful consideration should be given to using instruments and methods of assessment that do not contain inappropriate norms or culturally biased tasks.

7. **Careful test interpretation.** Seven, be aware of linguistic and cultural differences when interpreting the assessment results from LEP students. Unfortunately, linguistic and cultural differences are often ignored during staffings due to lower expectations or prejudice.

Approaches to Encourage Nonbiased Assessment

Public Law 94–142 required that testing for students with disabilities be nondiscriminatory. Following this federal mandate, a significant amount of litigation suggested that IQ tests have a discriminatory impact. While concern for protecting students' rights is a major theme underlying present-day legislation and litigation, "there is little agreement on the concept of non-discriminatory assessment" (Salvia and Ysseldyke, 1978, p. 50). Each of the approaches discussed in this chapter that are used to investigate a student's cognitive development will next be reviewed in relation to their sensitivity to *nonbiased assessment*.

Psychometric approach.   The appropriateness of using psychometric tests with students of different races, income levels, cultures, and primary languages has received both praise and criticism. Cummins (1984) discusses concerns that the norming process biases IQ tests against minority groups. The norm group consists of more people from the dominant culture, thus the items reflect the learning and experiences of the majority. However, some research (Sattler, 1988) suggests that reliability and validity on the WISC-R are not adequate for minority populations. Holtzman and Wilkinson (1991) point out that Hispanics included in the WISC-R norms were not representative of the sample since a disproportionate number came from higher income levels than normally found in the Hispanic population in the United States.

The long-term stability of intelligence tests for populations from different cultures has received very little empirical research. In addition, no IQ test has been normed for widespread use with LEP students. Cultural bias often occurs when tests are translated. The English WISC-R Verbal Scale items are translated to Spanish on the Escala de Inteligencia Wechsler para Ninos-Revisada (EIWN-4, Wechsler, 1982). However, as discussed in chapter 9, the translation of words or ideas across languages is not always possible. And, as mentioned earlier, the value system of a student, which differs across cultures and income levels, can influence the answers the student gives on an intelligence measure. Cummins (1984) feels that of all the IQ tests currently used with LEP students, the Kaufman Assessment Battery for Children (K-ABC) is least culturally biased. The K-ABC has a Spanish translation, however test items must be presented in English if norms are to be used (Kaufman and Kaufman, 1983a, p. 44), limiting its usefulness in testing LEP students.

The psychometric approach has significant limitations when used with students of different races, cultures, and languages. The special educator must be very careful in interpreting psychometric scores from such populations, certainly using the information as only one piece of the entire assessment profile.

Alteration of norms and tasks is one way to modify psychometric practices for students with racial, cultural, or language differences. Another way to provide nonbiased results is to keep the tasks and content of the tests similar but change the interpretation of results in a way that reflects culturally determined differences. Such an attempt was made in the System of Multicultural Pluralistic Assessment (SOMPA) developed by Mercer (1979). The SOMPA is a comprehensive battery of tests designed to evaluate children in a multidimensional manner. The SOMPA has three basic purposes:

1. to reduce overlabeling of non-Anglo students as mentally retarded and underlabeling of non-Anglo students as gifted as a result of assessment that does not take the sociocultural distance between the family and the culture of the school into account in interpreting the student's performance;
2. to provide sufficient information concerning each student's sociocultural background, health history, current performance in nonacademic social systems and estimated learning potential to enable schools to develop educational programs that treat each student as an individual; and
3. to identify the educational needs of children who are being served by present monocultural, monolingual, Anglo-centric programs in public school.

There are three models within SOMPA: medical, social system, and pluralistic. The Estimated Learning Potential (ELP) is a component of the pluralistic model. In this model, scores from the Wechsler Intelligence Scale for Children–Revised are transformed into ELP scores that Mercer states "indicate the position of the student's score relative to others from similar sociocultural backgrounds." The WISC-R IQ is transformed into an ELP using statistical procedures that take into account the sociocultural characteristics of the student. According to Mercer (1979), the ELP is a truer estimate of the student's learning ability than the WISC-R score.

Criticism of the ELP has been significant enough to cause school systems to hesitate in using it for assessing students from different races, cultures, and languages. One of the problems with the ELP is that it was normed on Anglo, black, and English-fluent Hispanic students. In addition, SOMPA requires that the WISC-R be administered in English (Wilen and Sweeting, 1986), thereby limiting its usefulness in assessment of LEP students. The norms for SOMPA were only collected in California, and Buckley and Oakland (1977) suggest that significant differences exist between the regression weights used to predict the ELP across states. The major criticism voiced by Oakland (1983) is that the ELP does not predict school achievement as accurately as the uncorrected WISC-R.

Piagetian approach.   The Piagetian approach to assessment has provided special educators with an innovative approach to measure cognitive development. DeAvila (1977) developed the Cartoon Conservation Scales (CCS) based on the theories of Piaget. Accordingly, the CCS measures eight Piagetian concepts: conservation of number, length, substance, distance, and volume; water level; egocentricity/perspective; and probability. The age range for these scales is kindergarten through eighth grade. The special educator presents a problem to a student in a story illustrated by a cartoon. The test manual provides English and Spanish scripts with suggestions on how to translate the test into other languages. DeAvila and Havassy (1974) found Mexican-Americans often score lower than Anglos on the WISC-R. Since about 60 percent of the subjects included in the CCS norms had Spanish surnames, this appears to be an appropriate measure for Cuban, Puerto Rican, and Mexican-American students. However, Holtzman and Wilkinson (1991) caution that not enough is known about the relation of the CCS to school achievement. In addition, they cite problems with test directions and item content. Presently, the application of the CCS, as well as most Piagetian assessment procedures for the assessment of students with disabilities from different cultural or social backgrounds, is limited for theoretical and psychometric reasons.

Soviet approach.   The major premise underlying the different Soviet approaches to the assessment of cognitive development is that intelligence is a dynamic entity. Feuerstein (1980) argues that the intellectual performance of retarded individuals is modifiable and that the "individual's manifest level of performance at any given point in his development cannot be regarded as fixed or immutable" (p. 2). Dynamic assessment approaches, therefore, advocate that modifiability is central to conceptions of intelligence. Direct measurement of 'learning potential' facilitated by a focused intervention is the means by which dynamic assessment is practiced by professionals.

Feuerstein (1979b, 1980) and Babad and Bashi (1978) provide empirical studies that support the use of a dynamic approach with students from low socioeconomic or minority backgrounds. Use of a dynamic assessment approach to supplement, if not substitute for, the use of the psychometric IQ test with students from different races, cultures, languages, and income levels has been increasing among professionals. Holtzman and Wilkinson (1991) encourage professionals working with LEP students to "test the limits" during assessment. According to these researchers, *testing the limits* is "an informal procedure in which the examiner purposefully violates the standardized administration conditions in some way" (p. 265). Testing the limits is really a dynamic approach to assessment. An example of testing the limits would be for the special educator to substitute simpler syntax and more common vocabulary in the test directions to see if the student's performance changes. Dynamic or testing the limits approaches to assessment of cognitive development consider the relevance of the content to the individual being evaluated, the historical experiences the individual has had with such tasks, and whether cognitive strategies can be taught to the student to improve test performance. The focus of the assessment is more on the instruction and social environment than on the student's abilities. As Sewell (1987) summarized, it is the "social system where social and political ideologies often determine educability as well as retardation" (p. 441).

Role of the Special Educator in Cognitive Assessment

In determining present performance levels of cognitive development, the special educator shares equal duties with the psychologist. In most cases, the psychologist handles administration and scoring of psychometric tests of intelligence. The special educator should be conducting additional cognitive assessment, particularly utilizing a dynamic assessment approach. It is important to keep in mind that cognitive development occurs in socioculturally organized events. The weaving of individual and social resources allow all of us to construct and understand the world we interact with on a daily basis. Effective assessment of cognitive development includes an investigation of all the parameters that can affect a person's problem solving abilities. Such an approach to evaluation includes observing not only the student's individual cognitive functioning but also the interaction of the student and the examiner during a shared problem solving activity.

Summary

Introduction to Cognition

1. Researchers are beginning to recognize the impact of social context on cognitive development.
2. Cognitive development has been recognized as specific to the domain of thinking and the task context.
3. Special educators are equally as important as psychologists in assessing a student's cognitive development.
4. *Cognition, thinking,* or *intelligence* are all terms that define an individual's ability to problem solve.
5. The term *problem solving* stresses the active nature of intelligence rather than focusing on intelligence as passive mental entities.
6. The development of affective and social relations is not separate from cognitive development.

Assumptions about Cognition

1. The global theory of intelligence focuses on factors that contribute to the total intelligence of the individual, suggesting that a single underlying function of intelligence exists.
2. The factor analytic approach to intelligence advocates that intelligence is multidimensional; that is, it is made up of general and specific abilities.
3. Information processing theorists focus on the ways individuals construct and process information rather than on static scores.
4. Piaget felt that intelligence does not develop linearly but is constructed by successive stages of development, each stage reconstructing the previous one at a higher level of abstraction.
5. A professional's belief as to what intelligence means governs that individual's selection of an instrument to assess cognition.
6. The affective and cultural influences that affect a student's performance during the assessment of intelligence must be recognized, particularly in making judgments pertaining to the student's true potential.

Approaches to the Assessment of Cognitive Development

1. The psychometric approach emphasizes adherence to standardized procedures in test administration.
2. Adherence to standardization requires that the administrator read questions, record answers, and refrain from discussing success or failure on specific items with the individual being tested.
3. Extreme scores on individual subtests can significantly influence total test scores.
4. Many students with special needs demonstrate significant scatter across individual subtests of IQ measures.
5. Psychometric instruments measuring intelligence are usually protected tests. A protected instrument means that specific credentials or certification are required of the examiner who administers the test.
6. The Piagetian format for test administration utilizes the method clinique, consisting of a structured interview with the individual.
7. The primary focus of testing from a Piagetian perspective is to investigate a student's reasoning ability.
8. Piagetian techniques have been used more extensively in assessment of preschool children.
9. Soviet approaches to assessment consider the amount and type of guided instruction involved in discovering the solution to a problem.
10. The range between independent and guided instruction is called the zone of proximal development.
11. The Soviet approach provides an information processing method that yields data regarding how the individual profits from assistance, speed of learning, and generalization abilities.
12. Students with learning disabilities and those with mild mental disabilities who have similar developmental scores may differ dramatically in the amount of

benefit they derive from guided assistance or the amount of transfer to a novel situation.

Soviet Approach

1. Traditionally, most diagnostic procedures have been static, leading only to diagnostic labels and placement decisions.
2. Dynamic assessment is based on the following principles: (a) there must be a link between assessment and intervention; (b) assessment must be tied to the environment; (c) assessment must focus on the process as well as the product of behavior; and (d) assessment must involve a means of generating and testing a hypothesis.
3. *Mediation* is a term used to describe the examiner/examinee interaction.
4. In graduated prompting, a series of behavioral hints are used to teach the rules needed for task completion.
5. Dynamic assessment techniques have been based primarily on Feuerstein's mediation techniques of Brown and Campione's graduated prompting assessment techniques.

Nonverbal Measures of Cognitive Assessment

1. Nonverbal measures tap a student's ability to reason without the use of verbal language skills.
2. Students with oral language deficits, hearing impairments, or language differences should be given a test using nonverbal assessments to minimize the potential bias from their disabilities in attempting to determine their true potential.

Modifications for Special Populations

1. A major issue in assessing students with special needs is that the examiner must be sure that the score obtained is a measure of the student's ability and not a measure of the degree of disability of that individual.
2. The special educator must carefully consider a student's most appropriate mode of response, use of reinforcement to motivate response, and the appropriateness of items selected.
3. Many researchers advocate a dynamic approach when assessing individuals with moderate to severe disabilities.

Cross-Cultural Issues and Assessment of Cognitive Development

1. Cultural differences contribute to indigenous concepts of defining intelligence.
2. How a student approaches a cognitive task is intrinsically related to that student's social values and goals.
3. A student's race, social class, and primary language all influence performance on an intelligence test.

4. Public Law 94–142 required that testing for students with disabilities be nondiscriminatory.

5. SOMPA is a comprehensive battery of tests designed to evaluate children in a nondiscriminatory way.

6. Presently, Piagetian assessment procedures for the evaluation of students with disabilities, particularly those from different cultural or language backgrounds, is very limited due to theoretical and psychometric reasons.

7. "Testing the limits" is an informal procedure in which the examiner purposefully violates the standardized administration conditions in some way to determine a student's true learning potential.

8. Dynamic assessment procedures consider the relevance of the content of the task to an individual, the experiences of the individual with such a task, and whether cognitive strategies can be taught to the student to improve test performance.

9. Cognitive development occurs in socioculturally organized events.

10. Effective evaluation includes observing not only the student's individual cognitive functioning but also the interaction of the student and the examiner during a shared problem solving activity.

Assessing Basic Learning Abilities and Learning Strategies

Key Terms

Acquisition
Adaptation
Analysis and synthesis
Attention
Auditory
Automaticity
Basic learning abilities
Basic learning behaviors
Central processes
Closure
Cognitive flexibility
Cognitive processes
Conceptualization/reasoning
Discrimination
Generalization

Haptic
Higher order processes
Learning strategies
Lower order processes
Maintenance
Memory
Modalities
Organization
Perception
Perceptual–motor abilities
Physical prompt
Processing style
Proficiency
Psycholinguistic abilities
Psychological processes

Psychoneurological capacities
Response shaping
Response types
Sequencing
Simultaneous style of
  processing
Specific learning abilities
Speed of processing
Stages of learning
Stimulus fading
Successive style of processing
Symbolization/representation
Time delay
Visual
Visual–motor integration

Instruction begins with the initial state of the learner and proceeds from this point toward the development of competent performance. Thus, it is essential that we have specific knowledge of what a given individual knows and does not know at particular points in his or her learning. Another critical aspect of the initial state of the learner is knowledge of general and specific abilities and strategies that can affect how and how readily an individual learns.

Pellegrino and Goldman, 1990, p. 46

Individuals have repertoires of abilities and strategies they use to learn information and perform skills. Some of these abilities relate to gross and fine motor development. Other abilities and strategies relate to how the individual obtains, integrates, and produces information. All people have some variability in these abilities and strategies. However, individuals with wide variability in their abilities and strategies for learning material, integrating it, and demonstrating what they know are identified as having learning disabilities.

People with learning disabilities are believed to have deficits in basic learning abilities or learning strategies that selectively have an impact on communication, academic, daily living, vocational, and social skills. Knowing about an individual's strengths and weaknesses in basic learning abilities and learning strategies is extremely important in diagnosing learning disabilities and in planning an appropriate educational program. When a student has another type of disability, knowledge about basic learning abilities and strategies can be helpful in planning instruction.

What Are Basic Learning Abilities?

Basic learning abilities are the specific cognitive behaviors an individual uses to collect, sort, store, and retrieve various types of information. The behaviors can have receptive functions entailing perceiving, abstracting, understanding, and retaining, or expressive functions involving retrieving, revisualizing, sequencing, organizing, and producing (Johnson, 1987). The concept of basic learning abilities has been discussed widely in the literature from psychology, particularly in the areas of information processing and cognitive psychology, and in the literature from the field of learning disabilities. Special education teachers are sometimes confused by this literature because many different terms are used to refer to basic learning abilities. Terms that were used as the field of learning disabilities was evolving include *perceptual–motor abilities* (Ayers, 1975; Barsch, 1967; Cratty, 1969; Frostig, Lefever, and Whittlesey, 1966; Kephart, 1960), *psycholinguistic abilities* (Kirk, McCarthy, and Kirk, 1968), and *psychoneurological capacities* (Johnson and Myklebust, 1967). Special education teachers are probably most familiar with the term *basic psychological processes,* which is used in the definition of learning disabilities that appears in PL 94–142. Other terms that are widely used include *cognitive processes, central processes, basic learning behaviors,* and *specific learning abilities.*

Knowing that these terms are used interchangeably will help teachers interpret the literature on basic learning abilities. In all cases the authors who use these terms are addressing issues of how individuals selectively attend to environmental stimuli, gather different sensory information from the stimuli, interpret the sensory information, relate it to existing knowledge, store it, retrieve it, and demonstrate the retrieved information. Although the information is gathered through the senses, basic learning abilities does not mean how well the individual sees or hears. Authors writing about basic learning abilities assume that hearing and vision have been checked and that the individual's difficulties are not due to acuity problems. (See chapter 5 for a discussion of how to check auditory and visual acuity.)

Why Should Teachers Know about Basic Learning Abilities?

Teachers need to know about basic learning abilities for a number of reasons. First, the literature from the field of learning disabilities on the relationship between basic learning abilities, learning strategies, and achievement is still evolving. Early pioneers in the field of learning disabilities devoted considerable time to studying and training perceptual–motor skills, visual–perceptual processes, and auditory–perceptual processes. The belief was that weaknesses in these skills and processes should be identified, teachers should provide practice exercises to strengthen weak skills and processes, and, after sufficient training, improvements in skills and processes would automatically generalize to improved readiness to learn academic skills.

Several pioneers developed tests for assessing processing areas as well as companion training materials for improving processing weaknesses (Frostig and Horne, 1964; Frostig, Lefever, and Whittlesey, 1966; Kirk and Kirk, 1971; Kirk, McCarthy, and Kirk, 1968; Roach and Kephart, 1966). One problem with this approach was that the tests developed often did not have sufficient technical adequacy (Arter and Jenkins, 1979; Coles, 1978; McLoughlin and Lewis, 1990; Salvia and Ysseldyke, 1988).

A second problem with this approach is that empirical research on its effectiveness is inconsistent. During the early seventies, some researchers looked at many of the studies that examined the relationship between processes and academic achievement (Hammill, 1972; Hammill and Larsen, 1974a, 1974b) and concluded that there was not a strong enough educationally significant relationship between selected processes and early reading skills to warrant spending instructional time on processes. Another researcher (Kavale, 1981, 1982) reviewed most of the same literature but drew different conclusions. Kavale's meta-analysis found that there was a significant relationship between auditory- and visual-perceptual skills and reading achievement. Methodological differences between the different researchers can account for only part of this discrepancy.

The heterogeneity of the population with learning disabilities may also account for some of the discrepancy. Research studies in the field of learning disabilities frequently fail to describe the strengths and weaknesses of subjects in enough detail so other researchers can duplicate subject characteristics. Therefore, some studies find processing/achievement relationships and positive training outcomes and others do not. Teachers need to know about basic learning abilities so they can compare studies that purport to use similar subjects but seem to have different results.

Another reason for discrepancies found in the literature on processing and achievement has to do with the focus of the direct instruction. Studies in which training procedures focused on processes and then assessed gains in reading typically found few academic gains. Studies in which training focused on both processes and academics found achievement gains. A study by Wade and Kass (1987) illustrates the importance of developing instructional procedures that consider both basic learning abilities and academics. In their study, Wade and Kass used two groups of students with learning disabilities. One group received three weeks of work on basic learning abilities followed by six weeks of work on specific academic problems. The other group had nine weeks of work on specific academic problems. When the two groups were compared on score improvement on the Stanford Diagnostic Reading Test, the group that worked on both processes and academics gained more than the group that only worked on academics. An important factor to consider from this research is that if processes are considered in developing interventions, they should be matched to student needs. Swanson and Watson (1989) write, "perceptual-training programs do not produce academic gains in subjects who have no perceptual difficulties. Subjects with significant perceptual problems will gain only from instructional programs that use academic content and that also deal with the other aspects of their academic difficulties" (p. 196). Therefore, special education teachers need to plan direct instruction using academic content that considers the student's basic learning abilities.

Besides critically evaluating empirical research and planning academic instruction that considers basic learning abilities, to actively participate in the assessment process, special education teachers need to know about processes. Some special education teachers mistakenly assume that the psychologist will identify processing difficulties based on tests he or she administers. Basic learning ability difficulties should be identified by consistent patterns of performance across settings and tasks. While behavior during testing and performance on psychological tests provide some important information about basic learning abilities, that information must be compared to performance in the regular classroom and to performance on assessment tools used by the special education teacher. A consistent pattern of difficulty with selected basic learning behaviors suggests a learner-specific disability that must be addressed in planning instruction. An inconsistent pattern of difficulty suggests tasks or setting variables that might be resolved with appropriate environmental modifications.

Finally, special education teachers need to know about basic learning abilities and *learning strategies* to be effective consultants to regular classroom teachers and parents. Students with special needs often have files containing reports from various agencies describing strengths and weaknesses. These reports use a variety of techni-cal jargon to describe basic learning abilities and learning strategies. Knowing the jargon and understanding what it means in terms of daily functioning at home and school allows the special education teacher to translate reports for parents and regular classroom teachers in a practical, meaningful way. This promotes a better understanding of the nature of the student's disability, leading to reasonable and appropriate expectations for that individual. Because the special education teacher has more frequent contact with parents and regular classroom teachers, he or she is in a better position to provide this type of consultation than is the school psy-chologist.

A Framework for Thinking about Learners and Tasks

Special education teachers engage in a lot of simultaneous, analytic thinking about the student and the academic content as they plan appropriate instruction. This thinking allows special education teachers to systematically manipulate task vari-ables in a way that produces a good match to the student's needs. Experienced special education teachers become proficient and very automatic in this kind of thinking. Those who are beginning their work in special education find it helpful to have a model that illustrates the different components of this thinking. Figure 6-1 provides such a model for thinking about analyzing learner characteristics regardless of the disabling condition, and task characteristics regardless of the specific content area.

Subskills

The subskills component of the model is important for planning direct instruction and contains two dimensions, the specific skill and the stage of learning. The specific skill refers to the content-specific subskill where the learner requires more instruc-tion. For example, the area of mathematical calculation can be subdivided by type of operation (that is, addition, subtraction, multiplication, division). Addition can be subdivided by type of number (that is, single-digit whole numbers, multidigit whole numbers, decimals, fractions with like denominators, fractions with unlike denomi-nators, mixed numbers, and so forth), and by whether or not regrouping is involved. If the student has difficulty with basic addition of single-digit numbers, the teacher needs to determine if the student understands the concept of combining sets of objects. The special education teacher obtains help in performing subskill task analysis of content areas by referring to scope and sequence charts that accompany curriculum materials. Information on how the student performs different subskills comes from standardized assessment tools, classroom work samples, and teacher developed informal probes. (Additional information about assessing subskills appears in Part Three.)

Once specific subskills are identified, the special education teacher needs to know what stage of learning the student is at with respect to the subskill. Smith (1981) discussed five *stages of learning:*

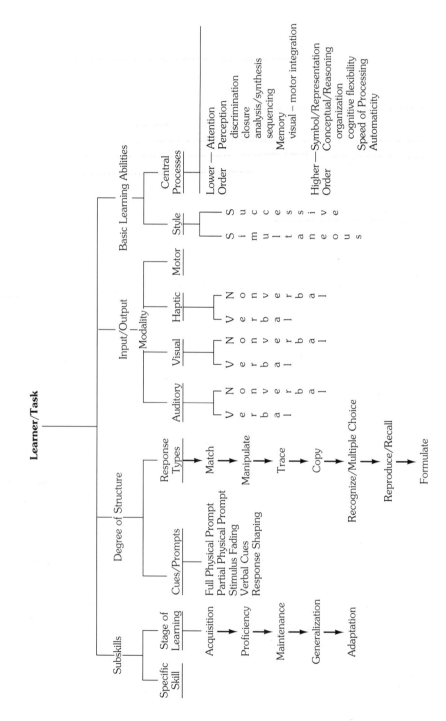

FIGURE 6-1 Components of analytical thinking about learner and task characteristics

- acquisition,
- proficiency,
- maintenance,
- generalization, and
- adaptation.

5 STAGES OF LEARNING

In the *acquisition* stage the aim of instruction and practice activities is to develop accuracy. During the *proficiency* stage, the aim of frequent practice activities is to develop speed or fluency with the material while maintaining a high rate of accuracy. In the *maintenance* stage, practice is periodic rather than frequent. The goal is to help students maintain what they have learned. In the *generalization* stage, students transfer their knowledge to new settings or responses. The *adaption* stage occurs when the student extends and modifies the skill, creating a higher level of knowledge than existed previously. Special education teachers can determine the student's stage of learning relative to a specific subskill through informal probes.

Degree of Structure

The degree of structure or level of assistance the student needs to successfully perform an emerging skill is another component of analytic thinking used by special education teachers. The importance of this component is illustrated by a frequent exchange between special and regular classroom teachers. The special education teacher will excitedly describe the success a student is having in demonstrating a newly learned skill. The regular classroom teacher expresses disbelief, claiming the skill is not demonstrated in the mainstreamed class. Often this discrepancy can be traced to the difference in structure or assistance provided in the two classrooms. The special education teacher has to be consciously aware of how much structure is being provided and gradually withdraw it, so the level of assistance matches that available in the regular classroom.

The degree of structure component can be divided into two aspects, cues/prompts and response types. Cues/prompts are usually used during the acquisition stage of learning. The teacher may physically assist a student through an activity like buttoning or using scissors. This assistance is considered a full or partial *physical prompt* depending on how much physical assistance is given. The teacher may provide a stimulus in which the key feature stands out and gradually provide stimuli that are more similar, for example, "Are these words the same: window–pin?" vs. "Are these words the same: pin–pen?" as questions presented during a sound discrimination activity. Moving from dissimilar stimuli to similar stimuli is called *stimulus fading*. The teacher may supply some type of verbal cue such as the first sound of the target word. *Response shaping* is accomplished when the teacher asks a student a successive set of questions until the obtained response is of the quality desired. The teacher reinforces those aspects of the student's responses that are in the direction of the target response. When the teacher is using errorless learning procedures, a question will be posed and, if the student does not respond immediately, the teacher will supply the correct answer. As the student has more practice opportunities with the material, the teacher may lengthen the time delay between posing the question and supplying the answer. The list of cues/prompts that appears in Figure 6-1 is not comprehensive nor are the items listed in a particular order. The list does, however, provide a sample of the wide range of cues/prompts a teacher might use during dynamic assessment or during the acquisition stage of teaching a new concept or skill.

Response types is the other aspect of the degree of structure component teachers must consider. The arrows in Figure 6-1 denote that the types listed are hierarchical. Matching is the lowest level response type and deals primarily with perceptual material. Students may be asked to identify two pictures that are the same. The student may make the identification by underlining, marking, or answering a yes–no question. Manipulating requires that the student move objects, gesture, or pantomime to respond. When a student traces as a way of responding, he or she follows lines of a sample with either a finger or pencil. Copying requires that a student make an exact duplicate of print or of a drawing. Recognizing is the same as answering when a multiple choice is provided; it requires higher level thinking than perceptual matching. High school students are frequently given tests in which they must match a word to the correct definition. Even though the directions for the activity say "match," it is a recognition response type. Similarly, if the student is directed to pick one of four pictures that best illustrates the meaning of a word, the response type is recognition because the goal is to assess word knowledge rather than the ability to note perceptual similarities and differences. Reproduce/recall responses require that the student retrieve information previously learned. Examples of reproduce/recall responses include fill-in-the-blank questions (when a word bank is not present), short answer questions, and paraphrasing material that has been read previously. A formulation response requires that the student generate unique information, as in writing a narrative essay or applying learned information to novel situations, such as comparing characters in a novel or predicting an ending to a story.

It is very important for special education teachers to think about response types. Initially, teachers should use low-level response types to ensure that the student understands concepts. Instruction in the special classroom, however, should gradually require response types that are similar to those required in the regular classroom so the student can make a successful transition. Thinking about response types can also help explain discrepancies between standardized test scores and classroom performance. Many standardized tests require responses at the recognition level or below. In contrast, students are often required to produce recall or formulation responses in the regular classroom. Considering this factor can help in determining eligibility, planning instruction, and planning modifications for the regular classroom.

Input/Output

Another component of analytical thinking the special education teacher must consider is the input and output task demands and strengths of the learner. Like subskills and degree of structure, the teacher must consider two aspects of the input and output task demands and learner abilities. Unlike subskills and degree of structure, the two aspects, modality and nature of the content, are not separable. They must be considered simultaneously.

Modality refers to the sensory channels through which information is received.

Table 6-1 Examples of intramodality and intermodality tasks used in language intervention

Modalities		
Stimulus	Response	Task
Intramodalities		
Auditory	Auditory	Listen to these words. Repeat the word with the sound *d. Man, egg, dog.*
Visual	Visual	Look at this figure. Now draw one just like it.
Tactile	Tactile	Touch what is under this cloth. Make sure you know what it feels like. Now touch each of the things under this cloth. Find the one that is just like the one you touched first.
Intermodalities		
Auditory	Visual	Listen to the word I say. Now look at these pictures/words and find the one that goes with the word I said.
Visual	Auditory	Read this word. Now say as many words as you can think of that sound like it (rhyme).
Auditory	Tactile	Listen to what I tell you about how one of the things under the cloth feels. Now touch each thing under the cloth. Find the one that feels the way I told you.
Tactile	Auditory	Touch one of the things under this cloth. Tell me what it feels like. After you tell me, I will guess which one you touched.
Tactile	Visual	I will draw a shape/letter on your hand. Now look at these shapes/letters. Find the one I drew.
Motor	Auditory	I will walk the way one of the animals walks. Look and tell me the name of the animal.
Auditory	Motor	I will tell you to draw some lines/connect some points. Draw what I tell you. You will end up with a picture of something you know.

Source: Reprinted with the permission of Merrill, an imprint of Macmillan Publishing Company from LANGUAGE ASSESSMENT AND INTERVENTION FOR THE LEARNING DISABLED, Second Edition by Elizabeth Hemmersam Wiig and Eleanor Semel p. 61. Copyright © 1984 by Bell & Howell company.

Auditory information is heard or spoken. *Visual* information is seen or written. *Haptic* information involves touch and movement, such as tracing something with a finger or feeling objects. Motor information deals with movements only, such as when a coach moves a student's arms through the pattern of the breast stroke in swimming. Academic tasks typically entail information that is auditory or visual, and occasionally haptic. Teachers need to consider the modality of the input and the modality of the output. Some tasks have input and output demands requiring the same type of modality. These tasks are intramodality tasks. Other tasks have one type of modality for the input but a different output modality. These tasks are intermodality tasks. Table 6-1 provides examples of intramodality and intermodality tasks.

Information is delivered through primary modalities, but some learners have difficulty associated with one modality or another. Achievement areas that can be affected by auditory processing problems include spelling, phonetic analysis in reading decoding, reading rate, reading comprehension, foreign language acquisition, lecture comprehension, and notetaking during lectures. Achievement areas that can be affected by visual processing problems include spelling, handwriting, proofing and fluency in written language, developing a sight vocabulary in reading, reading rate, reading comprehension, notetaking during lectures, and mathematics—especially computation numeration, geometry, and measurement. Notice that there is overlap among the achievement areas affected by auditory and visual processes. Another problem when considering modality difficulties is that some students have both auditory and visual processing problems. A third problem is that some students

Table 6-2 Modality and nature of content inputs and outputs

	Technical Language	Real-World Examples
INPUT	Auditory verbal	Listening/understanding oral languages, i.e., oral directions, listening to stories, lecture comprehension.
	Auditory nonverbal	Listening/understanding environmental sounds, i.e., fire alarm and other warning signals, intonations in speech, music.
	Visual verbal	Reading/understanding print.
	Visual nonverbal	Understanding graphic signs.
OUTPUT	Auditory verbal	Speaking.
	Auditory nonverbal	Humming, imitating animal sounds.
	Visual verbal	Writing.
	Visual nonverbal	Drawing, underlining, marking.

(handwritten margin notes: "Differs from info I taught"; "motor")

are able to perform intramodality tasks but have difficulty with intermodality tasks or vise versa. The special education teacher should not try to train or strengthen a modality that is difficult for the student. Instead, the teacher should match learner needs and task demands in the way most beneficial to that student's learning abilities.

In addition to modality, the teacher needs to consider the nature of the content when thinking about input and output. Content can be either verbal or nonverbal. Verbal content involves language, either spoken or written. Nonverbal content does not involve language but includes gestures, facial expressions, signs, intonation, and environmental sounds. Some students will have difficulty primarily with verbal or with nonverbal content. When the teacher is thinking about task demands and learner needs, the modality and nature of the content should be considered together. Table 6-2 provides examples of input and output that consider both.

The assessment team must look across different data sources to determine strengths and weaknesses specific to modality and the nature of the content. Reports from the classroom teacher provide the initial data the team uses. The team looks across work samples, classroom observations, and the demands of standardized tests to explore hypotheses relative to modality and the nature of the content. The team looks for a consistent pattern suggesting a strength or a weakness rather than a single test score.

Basic Learning Abilities

Basic learning abilities are the processes people use to think about information. Two aspects of basic learning abilities are style of processing information and how information is manipulated (that is, central or integrative processes). Two styles of processing are frequently discussed in the literature: the successive style and the simultaneous style. The *successive style of processing* deals with information in a stepwise fashion. Successive processing has also been called sequential or serial processing. Real-world activities that require successive processing include assembling a puzzle, imitating gestures, sounding out an unknown word, and following the steps of written directions. The *simultaneous style of processing* deals with information in a holistic or gestalt fashion. It has also been called parallel processing. Real-world activities that require simultaneous processing include language comprehension, reading comprehension, picture interpretation, and social perception.

The second aspect of basic learning abilities, how information is manipulated, refers to what is believed to happen to information in the mind. *Lower order processes* involve attending selectively to stimuli, perceiving or encoding it, and storing it. *Higher order processes* involve attaching meaning and relating information to existing information, and the speed and flexibility with which information can be manipulated. Difficulties in lower order processing can interfere with higher order processing. The development of higher order processes can influence functioning of lower order processes. A real-world example will help illustrate this point. Suppose a person learns the meaning of a word. That word existed in print and in conversation before this individual learned the meaning, but because the meaning was unknown the word was probably ignored when it was encountered. After the person learns the meaning of the word, that particular word seems to show up frequently in conversations and in things the person reads. Because the word is now meaningful, it stands out for awhile. The person attends to it more. Later, as the person gets used to knowing the meaning of the word, it no longer seems to stand out as much. Attention is not so specifically focused on it because the meaning is integrated and it is no longer novel.

Lower Order Basic Learning Abilities

Lower order basic learning abilities include selectively attending to stimuli, encoding the perceptual features of the stimuli, and storing perceptual information. The stronger the meaning of the stimuli, which involves higher order processes, the less cognitive energy is needed to perform the lower order abilities. Primary *lower order processes* include selective attention, perception, and memory. Since visual–motor integration is important in producing responses and was of interest early in the field of learning disabilities, it will also be discussed as a lower order process.

Attention

Parents, teachers, school psychologists, and researchers in the fields of education and psychology use the term *attention*. But despite such wide use, attention is difficult to define as a process. Goldstein and Goldstein (1990) attribute this difficulty to the fact that there are different aspects to the attentional process. This notion is supported by Taylor's (1980) observation that the reason statistically weak correlations exist between tests of attention is that different tests may be assessing different aspects of attention. Therefore, it is important to make a distinction between attention problems that may underlie a learning disability and generalized attention problems.

Attention problems, which are part of the profile of a learning disability, are a specialized dysfunction affecting specific features of language or print, or affecting one of the channels conveying visual or auditory information (Conners, 1987). Therefore, the individual may have difficulty selectively focusing on auditory or

Table 6-3 Tests of attentional processes

Figure–Ground
    Selective Attention Subtest, Goldman–Fristoe–Woodcock
    Auditory Skills Battery
    Visual Figure–Ground Subtest, Test of Visual Perceptual Skills

Selective Attending
    Rapidly Recurring Target Figures Test
    Cross Out Subtest[1]
    Visual Matching Subtest[1]

Divided Attention
    Halsted Trail-Making Test
    Arithmetic Subtest[2]
    Digit Span Subtest[2]
    Numbers Reversed Subtest[1]

Notes: 1. Woodcock–Johnson Psychoeducational Battery–Revised, Tests of Cognitive Ability (Woodcock and Johnson, 1989).
       2. Wechsler Adult Intelligence Scale–Revised (Wechsler, 1981b) and Wechsler Intelligence Scale for Children–III (Wechsler, 1991).

visual information, but not have difficulty in both areas. For example, a student may have trouble listening to a teacher lecture when there is noise in the hall. The student has problems selecting and focusing on the lecture (the "figure") when there is competing auditory stimuli like the noise in the hall (the "ground"). This type of auditory figure–ground problem may exist without a similar figure–ground problem for visual information. Students with attention problems may have difficulty identifying identical geometric designs because of a failure to attend to all the features of the designs. Attention problems may also be manifest as difficulty simultaneously focusing on two sources of information, referred to as divided attention by Goldstein and Goldstein (1990). Students with this type of problem will probably have difficulty taking notes while listening to a lecture.

There are no tests of pure selective attention. Tests that examine attentional processes also frequently tap perceptual discrimination or memory. To assess attentional processes, the examiner must make systematic comparisons between the student's performance on auditory versus visual discrimination and memory tasks. This information can then be compared to the observed classroom behaviors reported as concerns. A list of tests that may help document attention problems appears in Table 6-3.

Students may also experience attention problems that are not indicative of learning disabilities. These attention problems are generalized rather than specific. Generalized attention problems affect all levels of information selection. Common teacher concerns suggesting generalized attention problems include:

- staying on task,
- listening,
- concentrating,
- frequent, careless errors,
- low tolerance for frustration,

- daydreaming,
- inappropriate or nondirected activity, and
- excessive talking.

When these concerns are the reason for referral, the assessment team must determine the cause of the generalized attention problems. The most common cause of generalized attention problems is anxiety, the second most common cause is depression, and the least common cause is attention deficit disorder (ADD) or attention deficit hyperactivity disorder (ADHD) (Silver and Conners, 1989; Weinberg and McLean, 1986). Of the students with learning disabilities, only 20 to 25 percent also have ADHD, while 60 to 85 percent of the students with ADHD also have learning disabilities (Silver and Conners, 1989).

The assessment team must first determine if the cause of the attention problems is anxiety or depression. (Help in learning how to rule out these factors can be obtained in chapter 7.) When making the diagnosis of ADHD, the assessment team looks for the presence of four factors. One component is either hyperactivity or overarousal. Students with ADHD tend to be overactive, excessively restless, or easily aroused (Goldstein and Goldstein, 1990). Arousal has to do with the speed and intensity with which these students go to emotional extremes. The second component is the presence of distractibility or inattention. Students with distractibility problems have difficulty sustaining attention on the task at hand. Irrelevant stimuli appear too appealing to be ignored. Impulsivity is the third component considered in the diagnosis of ADHD. Impulsivity is the inability to delay responding. Parents and teachers complain that students who are impulsive act before they think and answer before the question is finished. The fourth component is the presence of a chronic or pervasive history of attention problems (Silver and Conners, 1989). Silver and Conners (1989) contend that students who have a history of attention problems prior to age 7 most likely have neurologically based ADD and are good candidates for medication. Attention problems that emerge later are frequently symptomatic of anxiety or depression related to school failure or environmental stress. Sometimes medications relieve these attention problems because they treat the affective problem.

The assessment team should gather data from standardized tests as part of the diagnosis of ADHD. The team will need three other types of data. A detailed case history is needed to determine when the attention problems were first observed. Observations in the regular classroom and during testing are needed to verify the distractibility, the impulsive style of responding, and the hyperactivity or overarousal. Finally, the team needs behavior inventories and rating forms from the student's parents and all the teachers who work with the student to document that the problem occurs across settings and people. A problem in only one setting or with one person may be solved with environmental modifications or changes in expectations.

Perception

Perception is the process of extracting information from objects, people, and events in the environment (Gibson and Levine, 1975). It involves sorting out the distinctive features of stimuli in an attempt to differentiate them. This differentiation is dependent on the ability to selectively focus or attend to some stimulus. It is also a necessary step toward assigning meaning to environmental stimuli.

Perceptual processes are frequently discussed in terms of more specific skills such as discrimination, closure, analysis, synthesis, and sequencing. These specific skills are further analyzed according to the modality through which the stimuli are received. Literature in the fields of education and psychology can be found that addresses auditory discrimination, visual discrimination, auditory closure, visual closure, auditory analysis, visual analysis, auditory sequencing, and visual sequencing. When making decisions in the assessment process, it is important that the special education teacher have an understanding of what these abilities are, how they would show up in the regular classroom, and what tests are available for use in the data-gathering process.

Discrimination is the ability to perceive similarities and differences among features of stimuli. Visual discrimination involves detection of similarities and differences among nonverbal forms like geometric shapes and pictures, and among verbal forms like letters and words. Auditorially, it involves differentiation of speech and environmental sounds, tone, rhythm, volume, and direction of sound (that is, localization). A visual discrimination problem may be suspected when the classroom teacher reports that a student has trouble with letter and number reversals, problems attending to details of words (that is, reading "foot" as "feet"), and confusing operator signs in mathematical calculation (for example, $\times$ confused as $+$). Auditory discrimination problems might be hypothesized if the classroom teacher reports the student has articulation problems, misunderstands oral directions, has difficulty with rhyming words, has problems learning and using phonics, has spelling problems, or has difficulty assigning voices to people. These classroom difficulties may exist for many different reasons, and the assessment team should systematically consider each reason. Evaluating discrimination abilities should be part of that systematic consideration. Haptic and motor discrimination problems may also exist but may not affect academic situations as much as auditory or visual discrimination problems. Haptic and motor discrimination problems may be more noticeable in daily living, vocational, and recreation/leisure skill development. Discrimination may require either a simultaneous or successive style of processing.

Closure is the ability to identify the complete stimuli from partial information. It is an ability that emerges with development and experience. For example, young infants (younger than 4 months) recognize a nursing bottle only if they see most of the bottle and it is oriented in the way they typically view it. As infants develop, they gain the ability to recognize the bottle even if most of it is obscured and only the bottom shows. Piaget's investigations led him to believe that this ability emerges between the ages of 4 and 10 months (Ginsburg and Opper, 1969).

In classroom situations, auditory closure is needed for listening if the classroom is noisy. Visual closure is needed to read poorly produced work sheets. Closure tends to require a simultaneous processing style.

Analysis and synthesis are often considered together. Analysis involves breaking an item into its component parts, while synthesis requires integrating parts into a whole. Analysis and synthesis require simultaneous processing of whole–part and part–whole relationships. Real-world activities such as sounding out a word and then saying the complete word, dividing words into syllables, and assembling puzzles and models require analysis and synthesis. Visual analysis and synthesis underlie a person's skill with manipulating spatial relationships. Such relationships are required in geometry and in occupational activities like sewing, carpentry, mechanics, factory assembly, and wrapping merchandise.

Sequencing is the ability to perceive order. It tends to require a successive processing style. Sequencing ability is often influenced by attention and memory. Classroom activities involving sequencing include pronouncing multisyllabic words, spelling, writing multidigit numbers, reciting the days of the week or months of the year. Perceptual sequencing is a lower order basic learning ability that contributes to the higher order ability of organization.

To assess sequencing ability, the evaluation team should contrast the student's performance on memory tasks where sequencing of the recalled items does and does not affect scoring. The team needs to perform an error analysis on all memory tasks to determine whether the student lost credit on items because he or she failed to recall items or recalled items out of order. Classroom work samples should be analyzed to determine the frequency of letter and number transpositions in words and multidigit numbers.

Selecting tests of perceptual processes.   The assessment team must listen carefully to the concerns of the regular classroom teacher to form hypotheses about whether or not perceptual processing is problematic for a student. If perceptual basic learning abilities are suspected of contributing to the student's academic difficulties, the team needs to systematically examine the various aspects of perceptual processing for the different types of modalities. The tests listed in Table 6-4 can be used to systematically gather data that supports or rules out the hypothesis that a type of perceptual disability exists. When selecting the perceptual test to be used, the team needs to look at the technical adequacy of the instrument. The Woodcock–Johnson Psychoeducational Battery–Revised, Tests of Cognitive Ability (Woodcock and Johnson, 1989) have good technical adequacy and contain subtests that assess perceptual processes. Two tests, Developmental Test of Visual Perception (Frostig, Lefever, and Whittlesey, 1966) and Illinois Test of Psycholinguistic Abilities (Kirk, McCarthy, and Kirk, 1968) were very popular early perceptual tests in the field of learning disabilities. These tests are rarely used now because of their weak technical adequacy. When interpreting the results of the tests, the team needs to compare the student's test performance to observed classroom behavior and to teacher concerns. The team should only identify a perceptual disability when there is some agreement across test performance, classroom behaviors, and teacher concerns that this explains the academic, vocational, or social difficulties.

Memory

Memory is the ability to retain and retrieve information. It is influenced by attention and the perceptual processes of discrimination and sequencing. A memory problem might be suspected if the teacher expresses concerns that a student forgets material

Measures to utilize to rule out or support perceptual processing problems)!!

Table 6-4 Selected tests of perceptual processes

Test (Author)	Ages	Discrimination	Closure	Analysis/ Synthesis
Auditory Discrimination Test (2d ed.) (Reynolds, 1987; Wepman, 1975)	4 to 8–11	A		
Detroit Tests of Learning Aptitude–3 (Hammill, 1991)	6 to 17			
design sequences		V		
picture fragments			V	
Goldman–Fristoe–Woodcock Auditory Skills Battery (Goldman, Fristoe, and Woodcock, 1976)	3 to adult	A		
auditory discrimination				
recognition				A
analysis				A
sound blending				A
Kaufman Assessment Battery for Children (Kaufman and Kaufman, 1983a)	2–6 to 12–16			
magic window			V	
Gestalt closure			V	
triangles				V
Motor Free Visual Perception Test (Colarusso and Hammill, 1972)	4 to 8–11	V	V	V
Stanford–Binet–4 (Thorndike, Hagen, and Sattler, 1986)	2 to adult			
pattern analysis				V
Test of Language Development–2 Primary (Newcomer and Hammill, 1988)	4 to adult			
word discrimination		V		
Test of Visual Perceptual Skills (Gardner, 1988)	4–0 to 12–11			
visual discrimination		V		
visual–spatial relationships		V		
visual closure			V	
Wechsler Intelligence Scale for Children–R (Wechsler, 1974a)	6 to 5–11			
block design				V
object assembly				V
Woodcock–Johnson Revised Tests of Cognitive Ability (Woodcock and Johnson, 1989)	2 to 90			
visual matching		V		
cross out		V		
incomplete words			A	
sound blending				A
sound patterns		A		
visual closure			V	
spatial relations				V

V = Visual Stimuli   A = Auditory Stimuli

learned the previous day, has difficulty following all the steps in multistep directions, has problems recalling details of material read, and makes frequent excuses for things not remembered (for example, homework). Memory deficits often have an impact on recalling content knowledge, literal reading comprehension, notetaking, and written language.

Memory is a multidimensional ability. The assessment team should consider the various dimensions of memory when selecting assessment instruments. Some tasks assess short-term memory and others assess long-term memory. Short-term memory is needed to recall assignments and directions, to hold in mind ideas being developed in a written essay, to take notes during a lecture, and to answer literal comprehension questions over material just read. Long-term memory is needed to recall content that has been learned. The student's conceptual understanding of the material determines how it is organized and may facilitate or inhibit long-term recall.

A second dimension of memory tasks is whether the material to be retrieved is meaningful or nonmeaningful. Examples of nonmeaningful content include strings of random words, letters, or digits; objects or pictures of objects; and position in space. Meaningful content involves sentences or paragraphs, oral directions for a task, and people's faces. Meaning often helps a person retrieve information. Other dimensions of memory tasks were addressed in the discussion of the components of analytic thinking.

The team must decide whether memory problems are influenced by the modality of the material to be recalled (auditory, visual, haptic). The team must also consider what kind of response type is demanded by the task. Most memory tasks require a reproduce/recall response. The examiner says something or shows the student something, removes the stimulus, and then asks the student to tell or write what was presented. Some memory tasks use a recognition/multiple choice response. Finally, the team must decide if it is interested in the style of processing demanded by the memory task. Most memory tasks require a successive style of processing. The team needs to know if the material must be remembered in the order it was presented or remembered in any order for credit to be earned. Table 6-5 lists selected memory tests in a way that helps clarify some of these dimensions. Note that few tests assess long-term memory. Most tests that tap long-term memory also assess exposure to knowledge, making it difficult to determine why a score might be low. Examples of such subtests include basic information from the Detroit Tests of Learning Aptitude–3 (Hammill, 1991), faces and places from the Kaufman Assessment Battery for Children (Kaufman and Kaufman, 1983a), and information from the Wechsler scales (Wechsler, 1991; 1989; 1981b).

Visual–Motor Integration

Visual–motor integration is the ability to synchronize visual perceptual input with the movements of the hand and fingers. It is required for handwriting, typing, drawing, cutting, coloring, threading a needle, and such self-grooming tasks as zipping, buttoning, and applying makeup. It can be hypothesized that a student has a visual–motor integration problem when the teacher expresses concerns about difficulty copying from a blackboard or book, hand trembling during fine motor

Table 6-5 Selected measures of memory

Most are for STM not LTM

Test (Author)	Auditory (A) Visual (V)	Meaningful (M) Nonmeaningful (NM)	Recognition Recall	Short-Term (ST) Long-Term (LT)
Clinical Evaluations of Language Fundamentals–Revised (Semel, Wiig, and Secord, 1987)				
oral directions	A	M–directions	recall	ST
recalling sentences	A	M–sentences	recall	ST
Detroit Test of Learning Aptitude–3 (Hammill, 1991)				
design sequences	V	NM–geometric designs	recall	ST
sentence imitation	A	M–sentences	recall	ST
reversed letters	A	NM–letters	recall	ST
design reproduction	V	NM–designs	recall	ST
word sequences	A	NM–words	recall	ST
Goldman–Fristoe–Woodcock Auditory Skills Battery (Goldman, Fristoe, and Woodcock 1976)				
auditory memory–recognition	A	NM–words	recognition	ST
auditory memory–content	A	NM–words	recognition	ST
auditory memory–sequence	A	NM–words	recognition	ST
Kaufman Assessment Battery for Children (Kaufman and Kaufman, 1983a)				
word order	A	NM–words	recognition	ST
number recall	A	NM–numbers	recall	ST
hand movements	V	NM–movements	recall	ST
face recognition	V	M–face	recognition	ST
spatial memory	V	NM–position	recall	ST
Stanford–Binet–4 (Thorndike, Hagen, and Sattler, 1986)				
memory for sentences	A	M–sentences	recall	ST
memory for digits	A	NM–numbers	recall	ST
memory for objects	V	NM–pictures	recognition	ST
bead memory	V	NM–pattern	recall	ST
Test of Adolescent Language–2 (Hammill, Brown, Larsen, and Widerholt, 1987)				
speaking/grammar	A	M–sentences	recall	ST
Test of Language Development 2–Primary (Newcomer and Hammill, 1988)				
sentence imitation	A	M–sentences	recall	ST
Test of Visual–Perceptual Skills (Gardner, 1988)				
visual memory	V	NM–shapes	recognition	ST
visual sequential memory	V	NM–shapes	recognition	ST
Wechsler Intelligence Scale for Children–R (Wechsler, 1974a)				
digit span	A	NM–numbers	recall	ST
Woodcock–Johnson–Revised Tests of Cognitive Ability (Woodcock and Johnson, 1989)				
memory for sentences	A	M–sentences	recall	ST
memory for words	A	NM–words	recall	ST
memory for names	A & V	NM–characters	recognition	ST & LT
numbers reversed	A	NM–numbers	recall	ST
visual/auditory learning	A & V	M–sentences	recall	ST & LT

tasks, difficulty aligning numbers in math problems, or deterioration of the appearance of the student's work from the beginning to the end. The task of the team is to determine whether these concerns reflect a lack of effort or care on the part of the student or a visual–motor difficulty. Observation and analysis of classroom work samples are very important. Two tests that can provide some standardized data are the Bender Visual–Motor Gestalt Test (Bender, 1938) and the Developmental Test of Visual–Motor Integration (Beery, 1989b). On both tests the student must copy geometric designs.

Higher Order Basic Learning Abilities

The *higher order processes* involve meaning and reasoning. Higher order basic learning abilities may be affected by problems with lower order processes or may be deficient themselves. While various terms are used to denote higher order processes, and there is considerable overlap between the different processes, it is helpful to think about four broad processes:

- symbolization/representation,
- conceptualization/reasoning,
- speed of processing, and
- automaticity.

Symbolization/Representation

Different terms are used to refer to the process of attaching meaning to experiences. Two of the most frequently used terms are symbolization (Johnson, 1982, 1987; Johnson and Myklebust, 1967; Myklebust, 1954, 1960) and representation (Bruner, 1973; Piaget, 1962). *Symbolization/representation* is the ability to associate experiential meaning with culturally agreed upon arbitrary signs. It allows two people to share meaning in the absence of concrete experience. Meaning can be shared even if the people are separated by a great distance. Like many of the lower order basic learning abilities, symbolization/representation can be verbal or nonverbal. Verbal symbolization/representation involves attaching meaning to oral or written language, spoken and printed words. Nonverbal symbolization/representation involves attaching meaning to signs that can be shared by people who speak different languages. Examples include notes and signs in music, mathematical symbols and numbers, national flags, and international aid symbols (for example, restroom, no parking, first aid).

Students who have deficits in the process of symbolization/representation may have difficulty learning vocabulary words and language structures, may have problems developing a meaningful sight vocabulary, may word call in reading but not develop comprehension skills, or may have trouble translating from a verbal system like language to a nonverbal symbol system like mathematical signs. Some students may learn to play a musical instrument "by ear" but have extreme difficulty learning to read music despite direct instruction and effortful practice.

Remember!

use obs. & informal probes

There are no standardized tests of pure symbolization/representation. The assessment team must look at teacher concerns, classroom observations, and language tests. Language tests often involve labeling concepts and, therefore, tend to examine both symbolization/representation and conceptualization/reasoning. The assessment team can develop informal probes that require the student to translate between symbol systems (for example, written language to oral language, mathematical symbols to oral language, mathematical language to written language) as a way to demonstrate an understanding of meaning.

Conceptualization/Reasoning

Conceptualization/reasoning is the ability to construct relationships among experiences that are not observable (Johnson and Myklebust, 1967), make inferences, generalize, and anticipate outcomes. It is classifying and categorizing. If one thinks of symbolization/representation as assigning a culturally agreed upon sign one step removed from the actual experience, then conceptualization/reasoning can be thought of as two steps removed from the observable experience. Johnson and Myklebust (1967) provided an example when they wrote:

> . . . in early life the child's experience "chair" refers only to a specific chair, perhaps his own which is present and observable. Later he generalizes "chair" to include other chairs, whether or not they are observable. Still later he learns to classify and categorize his experience "chair" relative to the concept "furniture"; he conceptualizes it in terms of a group or groups of experiences. Another distinction to be noted is that experiences that are abstracted (such as the experience "chair") can be observed, whereas the class of category that forms a concept is not in itself observable. (p. 43)

Teachers' descriptions of their concerns for a particular student provide a good first step in hypothesizing that the student has difficulty with conceptualization/reasoning. In the area of oral language, the teacher may observe that the student has a limited, concrete vocabulary that is inconsistent with his or her environmental background. The student may appear to have only a literal or concrete understanding of language or may have problems following directions. In reading comprehension, the student may have extreme difficulty grasping the main idea of text and may have problems with inferential comprehension. Other comments may include a concern that the student does not see things as a whole, has difficulty applying knowledge to new situations, does not recognize cause–effect relationships, has a poor sense of time, has difficulty developing a plan for solving problems such as finding lost belongings or resolving peer problems, or has social perception difficulties.

symptoms

These teacher concerns are the first step in identifying a conceptualization/reasoning deficit. Formal standardized tests can provide further data. Most oral language tests assess a combination of symbolization/representation and conceptualization/reasoning, so performance on these tests should be an important consideration. The assessment team should conduct an error analysis that considers how well the student is able to understand and use abstract language like idioms, metaphors, and figurative language, and how well the student manipulates multiple meanings of words and ambiguous language. (See chapter 9 for a discussion of language tests.)

Table 6-6 Selected conceptualization/reasoning tests

Test (Author)	Age	Verbal Content	Nonverbal Content
Columbia Mental Maturity Scale (Burgemeister, Blum, and Lorge, 1972)	3–6 to 10		X
Raven's Progressive Matrices (Raven, Court, and Raven, 1977)	5 to adult		X
Leiter International Performance Scale (Leiter, 1948; Arthur, 1952)	2 to 18		X
Test of Nonverbal Intelligence–2 (Brown, Sherbenou, and Johnsen, 1990b)	5–0 to 85–11		X

Detroit Tests of Learning Aptitude–3 (Hammill, 1991)
   word opposites
   symbolic relations
   story sequences
	6 to 17	X	
			
			X
			X

Test of Problem Solving (Zachman, Jorgensen, Huisingh, and Barrett, 1984)	6 to 12	X	X
Wisconsin Card Sorting Test (Heaton, 1981; Grant and Berg, 1948)			X

Stanford–Binet–4 (Thorndike, Hagen, and Sattler, 1986)
   comprehension
   matrices
   number series
   paper folding and cutting
   verbal relations
	2 to adult	X
		
		X
			
			X
			X
			X

Woodcock–Johnson Revised Tests of Cognitive Ability (Woodcock and Johnson, 1989)
   analysis–synthesis
   concept formation
   verbal analogies
	2 to 90+	
		
		X
			
			X
			X

Wechsler Intelligence Scale for Children–R (Wechsler, 1974a)
   similarities
   comprehension
   picture arrangement
	6 to 5–11	
		X
		X
			
			X

Kaufman Assessment Battery for Children (Kaufman and Kaufman, 1983a)
   matrix analogies
   photo series
	2–6 to 12–6		
			X
			X

The assessment team should also look at the student's performance on reasoning subtests of batteries assessing intelligence and cognitive ability. Table 6-6 provides a list of selected tests with reasoning subtests.

Two important components of conceptualization/reasoning are organization and cognitive flexibility. *Organization* is the ability to impose structure and systematically arrange elements into a plan. Perceptual sequencing can influence it, but organization is more comprehensive and involves the use of relationships. Organization deficits may manifest themselves as difficulty with the use of time, with position and awareness of space, task preparation, task completion, returning homework, keeping belongings, and arranging the immediate physical environment. Deficits in organization are particularly noticeable in reading comprehension, written language, and math problem solving.

In assessing organization problems, it's important for the assessment team to observe the appearance of classroom products and the spatial organization of the designs on the Bender Visual–Motor Gestalt Test. The succinctness of the student's oral and written language is another clue. Is the student able to come to the point quickly? Or does either the oral or written language ramble, and is it hard to follow? The assessment team should note discrepancies on structured versus unstructured tasks. The team should also note the student's problem solving approach. Is it random or strategic? When organization problems are present, the team should determine whether they are chronic, situation specific, or if they emerged at a particular point in time. Chronic or pervasive organization problems suggest that they are due to processing deficits. Typically, parents can provide examples of organization problems that existed prior to school. Situation specific problems suggest that the student is unfamiliar with the content or material and has not had enough support in relating the unfamiliar with what is already known. If organization problems emerge later in school or life, they may be due to affective problems like anxiety or depression or be a result of having too much to do at one time. In these situations, dealing with the affective issues and setting limits and priorities helps alleviate the problems.

Cognitive flexibility, another component of conceptualization/reasoning, is the ability to rapidly switch a mind-set. It requires simultaneous processing. It can be hypothesized that a student may have a problem with cognitive flexibility when the teacher reports some of the following concerns:

- problems organizing self during transitions,
- problems understanding directions on novel tasks,
- difficulty on math work sheets of mixed problems,
- poor brainstorming ability,
- talks about the same topics over and over,
- asks questions or makes comments about subjects previously discussed after the topic has changed, or
- becomes stuck on problem solving tasks if the first solution does not work and has difficulty generating alternatives.

The assessment team can gather documentation of a problem with cognitive flexibility when analyzing work samples and making observations in the one-to-one testing situation. The examiner may note that the student has trouble understanding directions on novel tasks. The student may miss several early test items before seeming to "catch on" to the nature of the task. Another frequent observation is a perseverative response style. The student appears to give the same response or select the same item number on multiple choice questions for several successive questions. On tasks requiring changes in problem solving strategies (for example, analysis/synthesis subtest and concept formation subtest of the Woodcock–Johnson Psychoeducational Battery–Revised Tests of Cognitive Ability, Wisconsin Card Sorting Test), the student may appear surprised and easily frustrated when changes are necessary. On tests assessing knowledge of multiple meanings of words and language (for example, listening vocabulary subtest of the Test of Adolescent Language–2, multiple meanings subtest of the Language Processing Test, ambiguous sentences subtest of the Test of Language Competence–Expanded), the student can typically think of one meaning of the word or language but has trouble generating the second meaning, even though posttest probing reveals that the second meaning is known.

Speed of Processing

Speed of processing is the rate at which a person is able to understand the meaning of stimuli as they are being presented. Deficits in speed of processing result in a generalized slow rate of dealing with information. Often times the problems are modality specific (that is, slow auditory processing, or slow visual processing). Chi and Gallagher (1982) subdivide speed of processing into four sequential stages: encoding or recognition, manipulation and decision, response selection, and response execution. Their review of the literature and research lead them to tentatively conclude that the major breakdown in speed of processing occurs at the response selection stage. Speed of processing has been grouped with the higher mental processes because in many instances the stages of mental manipulation and decision making, and response selection require symbolization and conceptualization.

It can be hypothesized that a student has a speed of processing problem when the teacher observes that the student is slow completing assignments even when consistently on task, is slow answering questions even when the student raised his or her hand to respond, rarely or never finishes timed tests, or has a slow rate of reading despite adequate sight vocabulary and word analysis skills. During formal assessment, the examiner can gather further observational data to document a speed of processing problem. The examiner may note that the student cannot be rushed even when told a task is timed and speed is important, or that the student is able to solve timed test items, but typically after the time limit expires. Compared to other students who are evaluated, the student with speed of processing problems completes only part of the planned assessment during a standard testing session. The examiner should conduct a task analysis when the student receives a low score on a speed of processing task (for example, visual matching subtest and cross out subtest from the Woodcock–Johnson Psychoeducational Battery–Revised Tests of Cognitive Ability) to determine if the low score was a function of missed items (a possible visual discrimination problem) or a function of completing only a few items (a possible speed of processing problem or compensating for a discrimination problem). This task analysis should be compared with other task analyses to document the problem.

Automaticity

As we learn and become familiar with certain tasks, we are able to perform those tasks almost without thinking about them—they become "automatic." Some learning disabled individuals have difficulty gaining this *automaticity of tasks and task components*. Sternberg and Wagner (1982) found that the learning disabled individual continues to have to perform in a controlled way (i.e., with conscious attention) tasks that a normally functioning individual will long ago have automatized. The disabled person again and again must devote attention to tasks and task components that others have long ago mastered. Processing resources that in others have been freed and used to master new tasks are in the disabled person devoted to tasks that others have already mastered. (p. 2)

NOTE: It is inappropriate to identify an automaticity problem when material is being introduced and the student is still in the acquisition stage of learning. All students need to expend considerable conscious energy during this early stage of learning new material. The process of learning new material often involves all of the lower order and higher order processes.

Automaticity problems appear to affect the proficiency stage of learning. An example of this type of problem is helpful in understanding it. One frequently reported automaticity problem is mastering the multiplication facts. Parents and teachers report that the student understands the concept of multiplication and can demonstrate it with concrete materials and semiconcrete tally marks. The student knows the meaning of the numerals and operator signs signaling multiplication. Given time, the student can figure out the correct answer to multiplication facts. However, despite repeated effortful drill, the student does not seem able to become automatic in recalling the facts. Parent and teacher reports are the primary means of documenting this problem.

Learning Strategies

Studies have found that some students with learning disabilities have deficits in basic learning behaviors that have a severe impact on academic achievement (Shankweiler, Liberman, Mark, Fowler, and Fisher, 1979; Swanson, 1986; Torgesen and Houck, 1980). But the population with learning disabilities is very heterogeneous and a single explanation for learning problems does not seem satisfactory. Therefore, it is not surprising that others have found that academic problems are related to a failure to be actively involved with the material to be learned and to apply procedures to help learning (Bauer, 1979a,b; Lewis, 1983; Tarver, Hallahan, Kauffman, and Ball, 1976; Schumaker, Deshler, Alley, and Warner, 1983; Torgesen, 1977, 1979, 1980; Torgesen and Greenstein, 1982). This active involvement typically means using learning strategies to aid learning. Alley and Deshler (1979) define learning strategies as "techniques, principles, or rules that will facilitate the acquisition, manipulation, integration, storage, and retrieval of information across situations and settings" (p. 13). McLoughlin and Lewis (1990) point out that it is important to distinguish study skills from learning strategies. They note that study skills require basic reading and writing fluency and are often related to specific academic tasks. In contrast, learning strategies are not dependent on reading and writing but are behaviors the student uses to learn. These behaviors include deploying attention, rehearsing material to be learned, and generating and evaluating solutions to problems.

Assessing Learning Strategies

While the literature cited above describes some students with disabilities as ineffi- cient learners, there are no standardized assessment tools for evaluating learning strategies. Deshler, Schumaker and their colleagues (1983, 1984a, 1984b) have developed the Learning Strategies Curriculum, which is designed to teach specific strategies. That curriculum has an assessment component useful for targeting strate- gies for instruction, but it does not provide any normative data. Informal evaluation techniques tailored to specific assessment questions remain the most popular proce- dure for assessing learning strategies.

The first step in developing an informal assessment of learning strategies is to review the referral problem and the behaviors of concern to the classroom teacher. Next, the evaluation team should interview the classroom teacher to determine what strategies the student may be using. Questions that might help start the interview include:

How does the student compare to classmates in the ability to start a task? . . . to remain on task?

What does the student do when assistance is needed?

Can the student ask specific questions if directions are not understood, or does he or she complain, "I don't get it"? Give examples of questions the student does ask.

Does the student spontaneously review completed work for errors?

What does the student do when a first attempt at solving a problem is unsuccess- ful?

What is the student's response to positive feedback? Constructive suggestions? Unsolicited peer help?

What types of assignments are most difficult for the student to do independently?

After interviewing the teacher, a member of the evaluation team should observe the student in the classroom to obtain further documentation of the behaviors described by the teacher. Next, it is extremely important to interview the student. Interviews can be conducted while the student is working on an assignment or shortly after the student has finished one. McLoughlin and Lewis (1990) suggest using the following questions:

Think about the things you just did in studying _____. What did you do first?

Did you begin by looking over the information to be learned?

Did you try to organize the information in any way? If so, how did you organize it?

Was there anything in the material that you didn't understand? If there was, how did you try to figure it out?

In your studying, did you do anything to help you remember the information? What did you do? Did you look at it? Say it to yourself? Picture it in your mind? Take notes? Outline the information?

Can you recall the information now? Do you think you'll be able to remember it tomorrow?

Will you study this information again? If so, will you use the same study methods? (p. 245)

The answers to these questions provide information on how the student approaches a task, if the student uses organization and rehearsal strategies in studying, and whether the student is aware of the need for help and how to get it.

Information from a student interview can be used to construct a dynamic assessment. The examiner forms a hypothesis about a learning strategy the student may or may not use. The examiner then presents a learning task and gradually cues the student to use components of the strategy to determine whether the strategy would be helpful.

Steps in the Assessment Process

Develop Purpose for the Assessment

The first step in assessing basic learning abilities and learning strategies is to determine if problems in these areas exist. The evaluation team should review the referral information, talk with the classroom teacher, and examine work samples to determine if any basic learning behaviors or strategies are problematic. From this review and discussion, the team will form hypotheses about the existence of any deficits. Assessment procedures can then be used to reject or affirm the hypotheses.

Develop Data Sheets to Record Assessment Results

The data on a student's basic learning abilities and learning strategies should be organized in a way that will ensure that no data are lost and that all data are considered systematically. Developing data sheets that can be used throughout the evaluation will help the assessment team structure the assessment and systematically consider the information from numerous sources. Table 6-7 provides a sample data organization sheet.

Conduct an Integrated Assessment

A variety of assessment procedures should be used to document the student's basic learning abilities and use of learning strategies. Observation, work sample analysis, and interviews with the student, parents, and teachers are very important steps in forming the hypotheses that will guide the selection of standardized tools. In many cases, observation, work sample analysis, and interviews are the only documentation for some of the higher order processes and learning strategies. Where standardized tools exist, it is important to select tests carefully to be sure the team has the data needed to explore specific hypotheses. This requires, for example, that the team has test data that will permit a comparison of the student's performance on a specific process relative to different modalities and to verbal or nonverbal content.

Analyze the Errors

Error analysis is required to make some determinations about processing abilities. Suppose a student obtained low scores on the visual matching and cross out

Table 6-7 Sample data organization sheet

Student's Name _____ Age _____ Grade _____

Basic Learning Behavior	Behaviors Cited in Referral and Teacher Interview	Standardized Test Data				Classroom Observation and Work Samples
		Auditory Verbal Content	*Auditory Nonverbal Content*	*Visual Verbal Content*	*Visual Nonverbal Content*	
Attention						
Perception						
discrimination						
closure						
analysis/synthesis						
sequencing						
Memory						
long-term						
short-term						
Visual–motor integration						
Symbolization/ representation						
Conceptualization/ reasoning						
organization						
cognitive flex						

	Behaviors Cited by Teachers	*Observation During Testing*	*Classroom Observation*
Speed of processing			
Automaticity			

Student Interview			
Learning strategies			
Approaching tasks			
Sustaining on-task behavior			
Seeking assistance			
Asking questions			
Accepting assistance			
Generating solutions			
Selecting solutions			

subtests from the Woodcock–Johnson Psychoeducational Battery–Revised Tests of Cognitive Abilities. These low scores could suggest a problem with visual discrimination for nonverbal material or with speed of processing. To make a decision about the probable cause of the poor score, the team should first look at the test protocol to determine if the low score was the result of marking wrong items, suggesting a discrimination problem, or the result of completing only a few items, suggesting a speed of processing problem. Next, the team should compare these scores with scores obtained on untimed visual discrimination tests. Finally, the team should compare their analyses with teacher concerns and observational data. When a consistent pattern emerges across these comparisons, the team has the type of documentation needed to identify a deficit in one of the basic learning abilities.

Develop Annual Goals, Instructional Objectives, and Modifications

Data from the evaluation of learning strategies can be used to develop specific annual goals and instructional objectives that will help the student become a more efficient learner. Data on basic learning abilities is used differently. The team does not develop goals and objectives for basic learning abilities. Special education teachers should not try to train deficit basic learning abilities. Instead, the special education teacher should use that information to select instructional materials dealing with academic content that will capitalize on the strengths of the student. Special education and classroom teachers also use these data to collaboratively develop modifications that facilitate student success in the mainstream setting. These modifications are intended to provide the student with disabilities with an equal educational opportunity. They do not give the student an unfair advantage or a watered-down curriculum. For example, a student with a speed of processing problem may be given untimed tests or fewer items to complete on an assignment. A student with visual–motor integration problems may be excused from copying from the board or text and given a copy of the material. This student may be required to use a typewriter or word processor so that final products are legible. A student who has extreme difficulty becoming automatic with basic math facts may be permitted to use a calculator or facts table when working on applied problems.

Summary

What Are Basic Learning Abilities?

1. Basic learning abilities are the specific cognitive behaviors individuals use to collect, sort, store, and retrieve information.
2. Basic learning behaviors have receptive and expressive functions.
3. Current, common terms for basic learning abilities include cognitive processes, central processes, basic learning behaviors, and specific learning abilities.

Why Should Teachers Know about Basic Learning Abilities?

1. Teachers need to know about basic learning abilities to read and critically evaluate the literature in the field of learning disabilities.
2. Special education teachers need to plan direct instruction in academic content areas that optimize the student's basic learning abilities.
3. Special education teachers need to know about basic learning abilities to assume their equal role in the assessment process.
4. Special education teachers need to know about basic learning abilities to be effective consultants to regular classroom teachers and parents.

A Framework for Thinking about Learners and Tasks

1. Special education teachers engage in analytic thinking about the learner and task characteristics of subskills, degree of structure, input and output demands, and basic learning abilities.
2. When considering subskills, teachers think about specific skills that need to be taught and the student's stage of learning for each skill.
3. The degree of structure can be changed by using different cues/prompts and by requiring different types of responses, depending on the student's stage of learning and processing abilities.
4. Teachers can manipulate how the content is presented and how the student demonstrates knowledge depending on the student's processing abilities.
5. Two aspects of basic learning abilities that teachers should consider are the style of processing and how the information is manipulated.

Lower Order Basic Learning Abilities

1. Lower order basic learning abilities entail selectively attending to stimuli, encoding the perceptual features of the stimuli, and storing the perceptual information.
2. Selective attention problems are a specialized dysfunction affecting specific features of language or print, or affecting one of the channels conveying visual or auditory information (Conners, 1987).
3. Generalized attention problems affect all levels of information selection.
4. Perception is the process of extracting information from objects, people, and events in the environment.
5. Perception is often subdivided into discrimination, closure, analysis and synthesis, and sequencing.
6. A perceptual processing deficit should only be identified when a consistent pattern of data is identified across teacher concerns, observations, and technically adequate standardized tests.
7. Memory is the multidimensional ability to retain and retrieve information.
8. Visual–motor integration is the ability to synchronize visual perceptual input with the movements of the hand and fingers.

Higher Order Basic Learning Abilities

1. The higher order processes involve meaning, the relationships among meaning, and reasoning.
2. Symbolization/representation is the ability to associate experiential meaning with culturally agreed upon arbitrary signs.
3. Conceptualization/reasoning is the ability to construct relationships among experiences that are not observable (Johnson and Myklebust, 1967).
4. Important components of conceptualization/reasoning are organization and cognitive flexibility.
5. Speed of processing is the rate at which a person is able to understand the meaning of stimuli as it is being presented.
6. Automaticity is the ability to perform a task without having to think about it consciously.

Learning Strategies

1. Learning strategies are behaviors a student uses to facilitate learning across tasks and settings.
2. Learning strategies are different from study skills in that they are not dependent on basic reading and writing skills and are not related to specific academic tasks.
3. Because of the absence of standardized tools, learning strategies are best assessed through observation, dynamic assessment, and interview procedures.

Steps in the Assessment Process

1. Develop the purpose of the assessment by forming hypotheses about possible deficits in basic learning abilities and learning strategies from the referral information.
2. Develop data sheets to record assessment results and facilitate systematic consideration of information from numerous sources.
3. Conduct an integrated assessment, drawing information from observation, work sample analysis, interviews, and technically adequate standardized tools.
4. Analyze errors across tests and compare the results with teacher concerns and observational data.
5. Data on learning strategies can be used to develop annual goals and instructional objectives.
6. Data on basic learning abilities can be used to develop modifications and to guide the preparation of instructional activities in content areas.

Assessing Social, Behavioral, and Affective Functioning

Key Terms

Affective functioning
Attitudes
Behavior
Behavioral approaches
Checklists
Completion techniques
Direct assessment
Drawing techniques
Ecological approaches
Environment-focused
    assessment

Indirect assessment
Interests/values
Life space interview
Likert-type format
Locus of control
Performance deficit
Picture-based techniques
Projective techniques
Rating scales
Self-control deficit

Self-control performance
    deficit
Self-esteem/self-concept
Semistructured interview
Skill deficit
Social skills
Structured interview
Student-focused assessment
Traditional approach

Johnny used to stand alone on the school playground, sucking on one finger and twisting a lock of hair. Most of the sixth graders were too engrossed in the game to even notice that Johnny wasn't playing with them, but he wouldn't have been missed anyway. And most of the time Johnny wasn't even watching. He was standing too far away—where no one could see the occasional tear in his eye.

Osman, 1979, p. 67

Few people would argue that reading, mathematics, and written language are academic subjects that fall within the domain of public school instruction. But the responsibility for developing social, behavioral, and affective functioning is not as clear. Some members of the general public argue that parents and clergy have the primary responsibility for social, behavioral, and affective aspects of a student's development. Others push for the school to share in the responsibility to develop some common standard for the future work force. Others express concern about the changing nature of the American family and the diversity of American society. This latter group frequently states that the school should take a leadership role in development of the student's social, behavioral, and affective functioning.

In the context of these various viewpoints, some research suggests that teachers tend to see themselves as more responsible for a student's academic development than for his or her social development (Kauffman, Lloyd, Landrum, and Wong, 1988). The debate about how the responsibility should be shared will undoubtedly continue for some time to come. But teachers cannot wait for such philosophical discussions to resolve themselves. They need guidance on when and how they should respond to a student whose social, behavioral, and affective functioning is problematic. When should the home be held responsible? When should the school act? And are there times when other agencies should be contacted?

Literature in the field of special education contains numerous strong arguments supporting teacher involvement in addressing social, behavioral, and affective development. Witt, Elliott, Gresham, and Kramer (1988) provide the following scenario:

> Phil is a behavior problem in Ms. Adams' fourth-grade classroom. His behavior disrupts the class and makes it difficult for Ms. Adams to teach and for the other children to learn. Phil is frequently out of his seat, he bothers other children during reading and math periods, he often gets into fights on the playground, and he is currently failing all of his academic subjects. Ms. Adams wants Phil out of her class because his behavior makes teaching a difficult if not impossible task.
>
> Children like Phil are not uncommon. One child like Phil in a class of thirty children can interfere with the learning and academic performance of almost everyone in the class, not to mention the mental health and stress level of their teachers. (p. 305)

Black (1974) conducted a study that found that self-concept was directly related to achievement. In that study, it was also found that students with learning disabilities had lower self-concepts than their peers. Similarly, Wallace and Kauffman (1986) reported that students with learning disabilities frequently have negative or poor self-concepts. Others have found that students with learning disabilities often demonstrate a variety of social and behavioral problems (Bryan, Pearl; Donahue, Bryan, and Pflaum, 1983; Deshler and Schumaker, 1983).

Students with behavior disorders and learning disabilities are not the only ones who may experience social, behavioral, and affective problems. Several researchers have found that students at risk for failure do not learn critical social and affective skills on their own and, as a result, suffer from poor peer relationships, loneliness, and poor self-esteem (Coie and Dodge, 1983; Dodge, 1983; Luftig, 1987a, 1987b, 1989). Hodgkinson (1991) points out "that at least one-third of the nation's children are at-risk of school failure even before they enter kindergarten" (p. 10). McLoughlin and Lewis (1990) believe that the dimensions of classroom behavior, self-concept, self-esteem, peer acceptance, and the student's interests and attitudes toward school are important variables that should be considered for all students referred for special education assessment.

Definition of the Area

Evaluation teams need to examine three specific components: social skills, behavior, and affective state. While there is overlap between these components, there are also some distinctions. If these distinctions are ignored, it will be difficult to obtain a balanced perspective of the problem, making effective programming very difficult.

Social Skills

Social skills are the behaviors, language, and attitudes a person conveys during interaction with one or more other people. The appropriateness and effectiveness of social skills tend to be judged by unwritten societal standards that vary depending on the age and cognitive development of the participants, their roles in relation to each other at a specific time, and the current environment. Competencies necessary for maintaining adequate social relations were identified by Strayhorn and Strain (1986) and include:

- the ability to be kind, cooperative, and appropriately compliant, as opposed to having a prevailing habit of being hostile and defiant;
- the ability to show interest in people and things, to be appropriately outgoing, to socialize actively, as opposed to being withdrawn, fearful, and shy; and
- the ability to use language well, to have a command of a wide range of vocabulary and syntax such that ideas may be both comprehended and expressed with facility (p. 288).

Cairns (1986) conducted an extensive review of the literature on social skills and found that five assumptions about social skill development and functioning seem to be prevalent. The first assumption is that social relationships are always developing and changing. Close friends in grade school drift apart in high school and form new circles of friends. Compatible college roommates find they have little in common a few years after graduation. Couples need to constantly renegotiate interactional styles as each partner matures and develops new interests.

A second assumption identified by Cairns is that observable social behavior is simultaneously influenced by internal, affective variables and external, environmental variables. For this reason, individuals may respond very differently to praise. A student with low self-esteem may view accomplishments as a function of luck and someone else's effort. In this case, a teacher's praise may be viewed as insincere and be received with suspicion and anger. A student with better self-esteem and an internal locus of control can accept the teacher's praise with a pleasant sense of satisfaction.

Cairn's third assumption is that people tend to form social relationships across all stages of development. This is the premise that underlies Vygotsky's theory of cognitive development. Humans seek and respond to interactions with others. This tendency can be documented from very early in life and becomes the foundation for cognitive development (Vygotsky, 1962).

The fourth assumption Cairns abstracted from the literature is that social patterns and interactional styles are resistant to change once they become established. This assumption has direct implications for early intervention in the classroom. When a student and teacher develop an interactional style characterized by frustration and anger, it is hard to change that style. Both the student and the teacher become accustomed to interacting with each other based on that frustration and anger. Changing that style, even if the style is counterproductive, may initially feel unfamiliar and, therefore, uncomfortable.

Finally, Cairns found that the literature supports the notion that social interactions are a multifaceted and dynamic process. Interactions are shaped by the activity at hand, the age and development of the participants, the roles of the individuals for a specific situation, and the environmental context. For these reasons, the assessment of social skills must take place across settings and interactional partners. No single evaluation tool is adequate for social skill assessment.

Phillips (1978) points out that very few people are completely competent or wholly lacking in interactional skills in every social situation. Therefore, the goal of assessment should be to identify strengths on which to build, as well as weaknesses that should receive direct instruction. Evans, Evans, and Schmid (1989) affirm that social skills are responsive to direct instruction.

To plan for direct instruction in social skills, it is helpful to know whether a student has a skill deficit or a performance deficit. These terms emerged from Gresham's (1981a, 1981b, 1981c) expansion of Bandura's work (1969, 1977). A *skill deficit* exists when the student does not have a particular skill needed in a specific social situation. For example, the student may not have had adult models who demonstrated how to introduce someone. Because of this lack of exposure, the student does not know how to make introductions and has never demonstrated appropriate introducing behaviors. The instructional plan for addressing this skill deficit involves directly teaching the student how to introduce people to each other in different social situations and providing naturalistic opportunities to practice making introductions. In contrast, a student with a *performance deficit* has demonstrated that the skill is within his or her repertoire of social behavior but is used inconsistently, inappropriately, or at unsatisfactory levels. For example, a student may be able to initiate a conversation with known peers. However, the student may attempt to start a conversation when it is obvious to other people that the peer is engaged in a very private conversation with someone else.

Strayhorn and Strain (1986) identified the effective use of oral language as one competency needed in social relationships. The previous example of a student trying to initiate a conversation with friends who are conferring privately illustrates the need for nonverbal communication competencies as well. Researchers have estimated that between 60 and 65 percent of the meaning in a given social situation is communicated nonverbally (Archer and Akert, 1977; Burgoon, 1985; Gitter, Black, and Fishman, 1975; Seay and Altekruse, 1979; Zahn, 1973). Nonverbal social signals include gestures, body movements, posture, facial expressions, eye contact, proximity and spatial position, bodily contact, and tone of voice. Students with disabilities may have difficulty understanding the meaning of and producing nonverbal social signals, yet these signals are important communication supports that provide illustrations, feedback, and synchronizing signals. (These issues are discussed further under pragmatics in chapter 9.)

Various authors have developed programs or curricula to teach social skills to students. Reviewing the scope and sequence of these programs can help the evaluation team identify areas that may need to be examined. Some of the available programs include *Social Skills in the Classroom* (Stephens, 1978), the *Skillstreaming* series (Goldstein, Sprafkin, Gershaw, and Klein, 1980; McGinnis and Goldstein, 1984), *ACCEPTS Program* (Walker, McConnell, Holmes, Todis, Walker, and Golden, 1983), *Let's Talk Inventories* (Wiig 1982a, 1982b), *Getting Along with Others* (Jackson, Jackson, and Monroe 1983), and *Socially Appropriate and Inappropriate Development (SAID): Social Skills Assessment and Instruction Program* (Armstrong, Mulkerne, and McPherson, 1988). Tables 7-1, 7-2, and 7-3 illustrate the range of behavior encompassed by social skills. These tables also identify the overlap between social skills, behavior, and affective functioning. The classroom skills listed could be considered as behavioral functioning because not all the items listed address interaction between people. Skills listed under the headings of dealing with feelings and with coping skills address issues of affective functioning.

Behavior

The focus of social skills assessment is examination of a student's ability to interact appropriately with different people across settings. Assessing *behavior* entails evaluation of a student's ability to comply with rules established by authority figures for different environments. In the classroom setting, the assessment team is concerned with the student's behaviors related to staying on task; following directions; completing work; following classroom routines for obtaining assistance from the teacher, aid, or peers; and following routines for using free time appropriately, obtaining work materials, and taking care of personal needs for water and the

Table 7-1 Skills taught in the Skillstreaming series

I. Classroom Survival Skills	*IV. Skill Alternatives to Aggression*
1. Listening	36. Using self-control
2. Asking for help	37. Asking permission
3. Saying thank you	38. Responding to teaching
4. Bringing materials to class	39. Avoiding trouble
5. Following instructions	40. Staying out of fights
6. Completing assignments	41. Problem solving
7. Contributing to discussions	42. Accepting consequences
8. Offering help to an adult	43. Dealing with an accusation
9. Asking a question	44. Negotiating
10. Ignoring distractions	
11. Making corrections	*V. Skills for Dealing with Stress*
12. Deciding on something to do	45. Dealing with boredom
13. Setting a goal	46. Deciding what caused a problem
	47. Making a complaint
II. Friendship-Making Skills	48. Answering a complaint
14. Introducing yourself	49. Dealing with losing
15. Beginning a conversation	50. Showing sportsmanship
16. Ending a conversation	51. Dealing with being left out
17. Joining in	52. Dealing with embarrassment
18. Playing a game	53. Reacting to failure
19. Asking a favor	54. Accepting no
20. Offering help to a classmate	55. Saying no
21. Giving a compliment	56. Relaxing
22. Accepting a compliment	57. Dealing with group pressure
23. Suggesting an activity	58. Dealing with wanting something that
24. Sharing	isn't mine
25. Apologizing	59. Making a decision
	60. Being honest
III. Skills for Dealing with Feelings	
26. Knowing your feelings	
27. Expressing your feelings	
28. Recognizing another's feelings	
29. Showing understanding of another's feelings	
30. Expressing concern for another	
31. Dealing with your anger	
32. Dealing with another's anger	
33. Expressing affection	
34. Dealing with fear	
35. Rewarding yourself	

Source: From *Skillstreaming the Elementary School Child: A Guide for Teaching Prosocial Skills* (pp. 43–44) by E. McGinnis and A. P. Goldstein, 1984, Champaign, IL: Research Press. Copyright 1984 by the authors. Reprinted by permission.

restroom. In addition to looking at behavior relevant to learning and personal needs, the evaluation team will consider the student's behaviors that are disruptive or harmful to others or to property. The team will examine the occurrence of unnecessary and distracting noises (for example, singing, pencil tapping, clapping, and whistling), damage or destruction of property, aggression toward others, and interfering with others' attempts to work. Sometimes these overt, observable, and recordable behaviors are related to the student's affective state. However, the focus

Table 7-2 ACCEPTS social skills

AREA I. Classroom Skills
  1. Listening to the teacher when the
    teacher asks you to do something
  2. Doing your best work
  3. Following the classroom rules
	AREA IV. Making Friends Skills
	  1. Good grooming
	  2. Smiling
	  3. Complimenting
	  4. Friendship-making

AREA II. Basic Interaction Skills
  1. Eye contact
  2. Using the right voice
  3. Starting
  4. Listening
  5. Answering
  6. Making sense
  7. Taking turns talking
  8. A question
  9. Continuing
	AREA V. Coping Skills
	  1. When someone says "No"
	  2. When you express anger
	  3. When someone teases you
	  4. When someone tries to hurt you
	  5. When someone asks you to do
	    something you can't do
	  6. When things don't go right

AREA III. Getting Along Skills
  1. Using polite words
  2. Sharing
  3. Following rules
  4. Assisting others
  5. Touching the right way	

Source: From *The Walker Social Skills Curriculum: The ACCEPTS Program* by H. M. Walker, S. McConnell, P. Holmes, B. Todis, B. J. Walker, and N. Golden p. 25. Copyright © 1983 by PRO-ED, Inc. Reprinted by permission.

of the evaluation is not to infer those states but to identify positive, learning-relevant behaviors so they can be increased, and to identify negative, counterproductive behaviors that need to be decreased. These assessment data are used to establish clear, consistent consequences designed to foster the desired behavioral change. It is often easier and faster to design and implement consequences that promote behavioral change than it is to teach social skills or change affective states. For this reason, intervention programs often start with strategies for addressing behavior. However, successful adjustment in the mainstream requires that social skills and affective states also be addressed, even though they may require longer interventions and are not as easily observable.

Affective States or Functioning

Teachers may feel a certain level of comfort assessing social skills and behavior because these components can be defined in objective terms and observed directly in ordinary environments. When it comes to assessing affective states or functioning, teachers are often uneasy because the internal nature of this component requires more inferences and less direct observation. Teachers can, however, develop an understanding of this component and skill in gathering information on affective functioning that will help in developing effective intervention programs.

A person's affective state consists of that individual's pervasive and longstanding emotions (for example, complex feelings of fear, anger, joy, or grief) (Brown,

Table 7-3 Sample skills covered in the *Let's Talk* inventories

Ritualizing
   Greets others appropriately
   Asks for persons appropriately when telephoning

Informing
   Asks others appropriately for the location of events
   Responds appropriately to requests for preference or wants

Controlling
   Suggests places for meetings appropriately
   Asks appropriately for reasons

Feelings
   Expresses agreement appropriately
   Expresses negative feelings and attitudes appropriately

1987a). A person's affective state influences how the individual interprets environmental events and how the individual responds based on that interpretation (that is, *affective functioning*). Four variables contribute to a person's affective state: attitudes, interests/values, self-concept/self-esteem, and locus of control. *Attitudes* are an individual's learned feelings associated with specific activities, people, environments, objects, or ideas (Aiken, 1985; Brown, 1987a). Everyone strives to feel comfortable and personally satisfied. When someone has repeated experiences with a specific environment, for example, that makes him or her feel angry, sad, or fearful, that person learns to expect and dread those feelings each time that environment is encountered. This is how a student develops a negative attitude toward school, a certain teacher, or a particular subject.

Interests/values are learned preferences. Individuals seek things that are pleasurable. Over time, the individual learns which activities, people, events, or objects produce comfort, joy, or satisfaction. These experiences then influence the choices that person makes. Teachers need to know about a particular student's interests to select appealing instructional materials and to develop options for reinforcing positive changes in the student's behavior.

Self-concept/self-esteem refers to how one views oneself. Like attitudes and interest/values, self-concept/self-esteem is learned gradually over time from comments and actions by other people and influences a student's willingness to take risks in academic and social situations. For example, if a student's primary caregiver has a parenting style characterized by constant or harsh criticism, that student internalizes the frequently heard criticism and develops a poor self-concept. The student will then try to avoid situations involving risk and that might trigger the internalized negative criticism. Avoidance can take the form of an unwillingness to try, withdrawal, development of real or imaginary physical symptoms, or acting out behavior.

Locus of control has to do with how the student accepts and assigns responsibility for his or her behavior (Brown, 1987a). It entails the student's understanding of cause–effect relationships relative to consequences the student encounters. Locus of control may be either internal or external. A student who has a strong internal locus of control believes that his or her actions and efforts have a direct relationship to the consequences the student experiences. A student with a strong external locus of control often perceives that consequences experienced have little relationship to his or her behavior. Let's consider the situation in which a student obtains a poor grade on an assignment. The student with a strong internal locus of control will consider why the poor grade was obtained. That student may examine how much effort was used in studying and whether or not he or she asked the teacher for help on unclear aspects of the assignment. The student with a strong external locus of control will try to generate reasons outside of himself or herself that explain the poor grade (for example, incorrect directions, unfair grading procedures, poor parental tutoring, bad luck). Locus of control, like attitudes, interests, and self-concept, develops over time, but it also depends on the student's cognitive ability to understand cause–effect relationships.

Understanding that affective state variables are learned over time or depend on the student's understanding of cause–effect relationships helps teachers begin to see how and why a student's affective functioning can be addressed in an academic setting. Situations can be arranged for students that allow them to learn different attitudes, develop a different self-concept, and develop a balanced sense of locus of control. These situations need to be planned based on an assessment of affect functioning strengths and reinforced with a menu of options reflecting the student's interests. Teachers are in a good position to arrange appropriate learning situations.

The evaluation team needs to take several steps in assessing a student's affective functioning. Interest inventories and observation of the student's preferences help the team identify what can be used to reinforce progress toward target behaviors. Next, the team uses observations, interviews, inventories, and self-rating measures to determine whether social skills or behavior problems are a function of self-control deficits or self-control performance deficits. As with skill deficits and performance deficits, these terms come from Gresham's (1981a, 1981b, 1981c) expansion of Bandura's work (1969, 1977). *Self-control deficits* are an inability or difficulty learning appropriate social skills or behavior because an affective state blocks learning. Evans, Evans, and Schmid (1989) provide an excellent example of a self-control deficit.

> Tyrone, for example, seethes with anger much of the time. Nearly every interaction with adults ends in a shouting match followed by Tyrone's sullen withdrawal. With other children, Tyrone curses, shouts, and often explodes with a flurry of shoves and blows. He is so antagonistic to others that they avoid him whenever possible. As a consequence, Tyrone probably will not learn appropriate social interaction until interventions are introduced to reduce his anger to a manageable level and appropriate skills are systematically taught to him. (p. 135)

Self-concept performance deficits are like performance deficits in that the desired social skills or behavior is known but performed inconsistently or inappropriately. The difference between the two is that affective states interfere with consistent performance in the case of self-control performance deficits. Suppose a student knows that to obtain assistance in reading class he or she must raise a hand and wait to be recognized. The student has demonstrated the ability to remember that rule on many occasions. Yet just before tests, the student blurts out questions and starts working on items before instructed to do so. In this situation, anxiety about the test may underlie breaking the rule and responding impulsively. The student may have learned that he or she performs well on daily assignments but poorly on tests. Repeated experiences of this type could lead to anxiety about testing situations that results in the inappropriate behavior. In cases like this, intervention focuses on awareness of the anxiety and strategies for managing it, while simultaneously developing study skills and effective test taking strategies. Over time, the improved study skills and test taking strategies should lead to more successful test performance, which will in turn reduce the anxiety.

Traditional, Behavioral, and Ecological Approaches

School-based assessment of social skills, behavior, and affective functioning has taken a variety of approaches since the passage of PL 94–142. These approaches are still being used to varying degrees by different school systems and by different agencies that serve individuals under the age of 21. The approach that dominates in a particular agency or school often depends on the training background of the people who conduct the assessments. If students stayed in one school system for their entire school career, special education teachers could learn the approach used in that system and function fairly well. However, we live in a mobile society. It is not uncommon for students to change schools several times during their academic careers. It is also more common for young people to have help from several agencies outside the school system. Therefore, special education teachers need to know the underlying assumptions, the data sources used, and the strengths and weaknesses of various approaches to assessing social skills, behavior, and affective functioning. While teachers focus on those problematic social skills, behaviors, and affective states that interfere with academic performance, it is important to know how assessment results from nonacademic agencies can be used to consider the total individual and aid program planning.

Traditional Approaches

Traditional approaches to assessing social, behavioral, and affective functioning are based on a medical model (Witt, Elliott, Gresham, and Kramer, 1988) and are called psychoanalytic. From this perspective, behaviors are considered a sign of an underlying trait much like physical symptoms are viewed as a sign of disease. Traditional assessment approaches tend to rely on the reports of others as well as projective and objective personality tests. Intervention then focuses on personality issues, similar to the treatment of a medical disease. Psychiatrists, some psychologists, and some mental health facilities use this type of approach.

The advantage to this approach is that it can help identify affective problems that result in self-control deficits and self-control performance deficits. Since affective functioning is learned over time and influenced by others' responses to the student, once affective problems are identified an intervention program can be established to provide the student with supportive feedback and an opportunity to learn to respond differently. However, there are several disadvantages to this approach. From this perspective, the problems or difficulties are owned by the student. They are considered internal student variables. Social, behavioral, and affective difficulties are frequently perpetuated by environmental responses to the student, a fact that is not fully considered in traditional approaches. A second problem with this approach is the reliance on *indirect assessment* procedures. These procedures require the examiner to infer the basis of the student's difficulties based on responses to unstructured stimuli and reports by others. Interviewing the student directly helps solve some of these problems but requires that the student have the cognitive skills to be insightful and to report those insights accurately. A third problem with traditional approaches to assessing social, behavioral, and affective functioning is that they emphasize classification rather than intervention. Traditional approaches may result in a diagnosis of depression; however, such a label communicates little information about how to intervene.

Behavioral Approaches

Behavioral approaches to assessing social, behavioral, and affective functioning focus on observable behaviors rather than internal student traits. While traditional approaches tend to focus on classification, behavioral approaches focus on intervention, making them very popular with teachers. Behavioral approaches use *direct assessment* methods to obtain data: the examiner counts or measures behavior in the actual environments in which the student functions. Since the examiner is not required to make inferences about what motivates the behavior, there is less chance for bias or error.

While counting behaviors in an actual setting sounds relatively straightforward, using consistent procedures to obtain reliable data across observers requires training and time. The meaning of the data is sometimes difficult to communicate unless there are similar data on the student's peers. Well-trained observers can overcome these problems; however, school systems often face a shortage of such observers. Inexperienced observers can introduce systematic bias to data collection, reducing its usefulness. Newcomer (1980) identifies a second weakness of behavioral approaches when she writes, "behavior cannot be understood from the examination of simple observable events" (p. 44). Newcomer points out that observed behaviors are based on the student's perceptions of specific situations, and these perceptions are intrinsically related to self-concept. Therefore, effective interventions must consider the affective states that motivate observed behavior.

Ecological Approaches

Ecological approaches blend traditional and behavioral approaches. Brown (1987b) writes, "ecological assessment recognizes that behaviors do not occur in a vacuum but are highly related to situational or ecological variables" (p. 599). Ecological approaches not only consider the situational variables but also the student's perceptions of specific situations. These approaches blend the best of the traditional and behavioral approaches and consider the dynamic, interactive dimensions of social, behavioral, and affective functioning. During the assessment process, the evaluation team examines social, behavioral, and affective strengths as carefully as it evaluates weaknesses. These strengths become an important foundation for the intervention program designed to improve self-concept and shape appropriate social and behavioral responses in different settings. Ecological approaches are being used more widely in public schools and will probably continue to grow in popularity. They require an assessment of both the student and the environment.

Assessing the Student

The complex and dynamic nature of social, behavioral, and affective functioning demands that assessment information be gathered from a variety of sources and examined across different settings. There is no single test or procedure that reliably assesses a student's social, behavioral, and affective functioning across all settings. Therefore, the evaluation team needs to use a variety of procedures to develop an ecologically sound picture of the student's abilities in this domain. Procedures that can provide useful *student-focused assessment* information include ratings by others, self-report inventories, observation, interviews, and projective assessments. The exact instruments used depend on the nature of the problem and the cognitive level of the student. The strengths and weaknesses of various procedures as well as the availability of technically adequate instruments will guide the evaluation team in planning and carrying out the evaluation.

Ratings by Others

A student often comes to the attention of an evaluation team because people who have contact with the student view his or her social, behavioral, or affective functioning as problematic. A first step in the assessment process involves gathering data to determine who perceives a problem and how severe the perceived problem is. Checklists and rating scales are used to gather this data. *Checklists* typically pose a series of yes/no questions and help establish whether a problem exists. They are useful screening devices. *Rating scales* generally require the rater to make a qualitative judgment about the severity or frequency of an observed behavior by using a *Likert-type format* (that is, 1 = never, 2 = rarely, 3 = occasionally, 4 = frequently, 5 = always). The rater's judgments are then compared to a normative sample to determine whether the problem is outside the average range for the student's age. Teachers need to be aware that the terms "checklist" and "rating scale" are not used consistently: some checklists provide normative data.

Checklists and rating scales offer several advantages in the assessment of a student's social, behavioral, and affective functioning. Typically, they are easy to use and score. Because of this advantage, they can be given to everyone who has regular contact with the student. Having data from multiple informants helps the evaluation team determine how severe the problem is and if it occurs across settings. This fast screening information is invaluable in planning observations that will be made later in the assessment process. Many rating scales and some checklists provide normative data, making the information obtained from them superior to interview data (Mattison and Hooper, 1992), especially if interviews are conducted by inexperienced or poorly trained personnel. This normative data aids in making judgments about how typical or atypical the behavior is for an age or developmental level. The normative data also facilitate communication between professionals about the nature and severity of the problem. Finally, all of these advantages contribute to the cost effectiveness of using checklists and rating scales during evaluation. Selected, commonly used checklists and rating scales are listed in Table 7-4. Some instruments are general, surveying two or three components. Others are very specific, surveying narrow dimensions like depression or hyperactivity within one component.

While checklists and rating scales offer many advantages, teachers need to be aware of some potential problems when using them. One major problem is the technical adequacy of individual checklists and rating scales. Some instruments are well standardized and have a sound theoretical basis. Others do not. This problem raises the question, What does the obtained score really mean? Teachers need to attend to the adequacy of the instruments they choose to use. See chapter 3 for further information on technical adequacy.

A second disadvantage is the fact that checklists and rating scales are indirect methods of obtaining data. Because a teacher or parent endorses an item on an instrument does not mean that the behavior actually occurs or occurs with the frequency indicated by the rater. For this reason, the obtained data needs to be verified with more direct methods, like observations.

A third disadvantage is that despite the apparent objectivity of checklists and rating scales the obtained results may appear to be erratic. If several people complete checklists or rating scales, it is possible that the results will vary greatly. Several factors contribute to this problem. Depending on the reading level of the caregiver, some instruments may not be suitable for use. In these cases, interviews may be the only way to gather data from the family. Some raters may have a limited knowledge of the student. Others may hesitate to endorse items describing problematic behavior because they feel they should be able to manage the student better or may not want to present the student in a bad light. Finally, teachers need to be aware that parents and teachers who complete rating scales may be biased, may be part of the problem, or may contribute to its severity (Beck, 1986; Humphreys and Ciminero, 1979). Studies have revealed that abusive parents (Reid, Kavanagh, and Baldwin, 1987) and mothers who are depressed (Friedlander, Weiss, and Taylor, 1986) have trouble accurately reporting the behaviors of their sons and daughters.

Self-Report Instruments

Self-report instruments are similar in format to checklists or rating scales, but they are completed by the student who is being evaluated. Self-report rating scales and inventories are norm-referenced. By comparing the student's pattern of responses to a norm group, the examiner is able to determine if the student is like nondisabled peers or has characteristics of special groups needing intervention. Like checklists

Table 7-4 Social skill, behavioral, and affective checklists and rating scales completed by others

Scale (Author)	Age or Grade	Checklist (C) or Rating Scale (R)	Informant			Component		
			Parent	Teachers	Peers	Social	Behavioral	Affective
Behavior Evaluation Scale—2 (McCarney & Leigh, 1990)	Grs. K–12	R	X			X	X	X
Behavior Rating Profile—2 (Brown & Hammill, 1990)	6–6 to 18–6	R	X	X	X	X	X	
Burks Behavior Rating Scales (Burks, 1977)	Grs. 1–9	R	X	X		X	X	X
Child Behavior Checklist (Achenbach, 1986, 1981)	2 to 16	R	X	X		X	X	X
Comprehensive Behavior Rating Scale for Children (Neeper, Lahey, & Frick, 1990)	6–0 to 14	R		X		X	X	X
Conners Rating Scales (Conners, 1989)	3–3 to 17	R	X	X		X	X	X
Devereux Adolescent Behavior Rating Scale	Ages 13–18	R	X			X	X	X
Devereux Child Behavior Rating Scale	8 to 12	R	X			X	X	X
Devereux Elementary School Behavior Rating Scale–II (Swift, 1982)	Grs. 1–6	R		X		X	X	X
Revised Behavior Problem Checklist (Quay & Peterson, 1987)	Grs. K–8	R		X		X	X	X
Social–Emotional Dimension Scale (Hutton & Roberts, 1986)	5–6 to 18–6	R		X		X	X	X
Social Skills Rating System (Gresham & Elliott, 1990)	3–0 to 18	R	X	X		X	X	X
Test of Early Socio-emotional Development (Hresko & Brown, 1984)	3–0 to 7–11	R, C	X	X	X	X	X	
Walker–McConnell Scale of Social Competence and School Adjustment (Walker & McConnell, 1988)	Grs. K–6	R		X		X		
Walker Problem Behavior Identification Checklist (Walker, 1983)	Grs. K–6	C		X		X	X	X

and rating scales completed by others, self-report instruments are most appropriately used as an initial screening device to determine possible problems that must be explored in more detail with other procedures. However, self-report instruments

Table 7-5 Self-report instruments

Scale (Author)	Age (A)/Grade (G)
Affective Issues	
Beck Depression Inventory (Beck, 1987)	(A) 13–18
Children's Depression Inventory (Kovacs & Beck, 1977)	(A) 6–17
Children's Depression Scale (Tisher & Lang, 1983)	(A) 9–16
Children's Depression Scale–Revised (Reynolds, Anderson, & Bartell, 1985)	(A) 8–13
Depression Self-Rating Scale (Birleson, 1981)	(A)7–13
Revised Children's Manifest Anxiety Scale (Reynolds & Richmond, 1985)	(A)6–19
Reynolds Adolescent Depression Scale (Reynolds, 1987)	(A) 13–18
State-Trait Anxiety Inventory for Children (Spielberger, Edwards, Lushene, Montuori, & Platzek, 1973)	(G) 4, 5, & 6
Attitudes/Interests	
Estes Attitudes Scale (Estes, Estes, Richards, & Roettger, 1981)	(G) 2–12
School Interest Inventory (Cottle, 1966)	(G) 7–12
Survey of School Attitudes (Hogan, 1975)	(G) 1–8
Woodcock–Johnson Psychoeducational Battery, Tests of Interest (Woodcock–Johnson, 1977)	(A) 3–80+
Personality	
Analysis of Coping Style (Johnson & Boyd, 1981)	(G) K–12
Children's Personality Questionnaire (Porter & Cattell, 1982)	(A) 8-0—12
High School Personality Questionnaire (Cattell, Cattell, & Johns, 1984)	(G) high school
Index of Personality Characteristics (Brown & Coleman, 1988)	(A) 8-0—17–11
Personality Inventory for Children (Wirt, Lachar, Klinedinst, & Seat, 1984)	(A) 3–16
Self-Concept	
Coopersmith Self-Esteem Inventories (Coopersmith, 1981)	(A) 8–adult
Culture-Free Self-Esteem Inventories (Battle, 1992)	(A) 5-0—adult
Dimensions of Self-Concept (Michael, Smith, & Michael, 1984)	(G) 4–12 & college
Multidimensional Self-Concept Scale (Bracken, 1992)	(A) 9-0—19
Piers–Harris Children's Self-Concept Scale (Peirs & Harris, 1984)	(G) 4–12
Self-Descriptive Questionnaire I, II, & III (Marsh, 1988)	(A) 8–adult
Self-Esteem Index (Brown & Alexander, 1991)	(A) 7-0—18–11
Tennessee Self-Concept Scale (Fitts & Roid, 1988)	(A) 12—adult

tend to have a narrower focus than do tools completed by others. Self-report instruments dealing with social skills are rare and tend to be experimental (Luftig, 1989). Similarly, there are few self-report instruments dealing primarily with behavior. The majority of self-report instruments deal with affective issues, specifically feelings, attitudes, and interests, personality and self-concept. For this reason, teachers are not usually the ones selecting and administering self-report instruments. They are used primarily by psychologists in the schools and by a variety of mental health professionals in private practice and in agencies outside the school. However, teachers need to assist psychologists in selecting self-report measures. Teachers can supply valuable information about the student's language skills and reading level. Some self-report instruments are not appropriate for some students because of the complexity of the language used. For students with poor reading or language skills, interviews may be a more accurate method for gathering data because the student's intent can be explored if his or her language is not clear. Selected self-report instruments appear in Table 7-5.

Most of the advantages and disadvantages of checklists and rating scales completed by others also apply to self-report instruments. However, there are a few other factors regarding self-report instruments that should be kept in mind. One advantage is that the self-report instrument may help identify a problematic area for which the student does not have a label. Students may not have the language to talk about a poor self-concept or being depressed. Self-report instruments typically have many items that contribute to a score suggesting, for example, poor self-concept or depression, so these problem areas can be highlighted for additional assessment and intervention even though the student cannot talk about it.

Just as the problem of bias is a disadvantage of scales completed by others, the issue of accuracy is important in using self-report instruments. Research findings indicate that students misinterpret, misunderstand, or lie on items on self-report instruments (Cartledge and Milburn, 1986; Gresham and Elliott, 1984). Sometimes this occurs because the student does not have the reading skills needed to use the instrument or does not have the language skills to understand all the words. Barnett and Zucker (1990) list several other factors that can influence accuracy on self-report measures, including embarrassment about private thoughts or experiences, a desire to convey a particular impression, indifference, or hostility about the evaluation process that prompts random or thoughtless responding, and the degree of self-knowledge that a student possesses. These factors, along with the technical adequacy of the tool, need to be considered carefully when deciding whether to use self-report instruments and in selecting the measure to use.

Observation

Data obtained from ratings completed by others or self-report instruments are useful first steps in documenting social skill, behavioral, and affective problems, but they are not sufficient for a diagnosis or for planning interventions (Barnett and Zucker, 1990; Garner, Shafer, and Rosen, 1992). These data need to be verified within the setting in which the student must function. Observational procedures are used to obtain that verification. This direct method of data gathering can avoid some of the problems of inference and bias if conducted carefully. Using checklist, rating scale, and self-report information, the observer identifies specific social skill or behavior problems. With a clear, objective description of the problem behaviors in mind, the observer spends time in different settings in which the student functions. The observer should confirm the presence of the problem behaviors in each setting. This is accomplished by recording occurrence of the behaviors with techniques such as time sampling or event sampling. Careful recording using established techniques will help communicate observational data to other professionals. However, these techniques cannot completely resolve the problems of low reliability and validity that are the primary disadvantages of observation.

The observer is also interested in how the environment contributes to or maintains the problem behavior. The observer should note the circumstances leading to occurrence of certain behaviors and how undesirable behaviors may be unconsciously reinforced by other people in the setting. Finally, the observer will form an impression of how the student compares to peers within a particular setting. If peers

A special education teacher verifies problems identified on checklists and rating scales by observing a student in the regular classroom setting.   *Source:* © Elizabeth Crews

behave similarly, the reported problem may be an issue of the teacher's tolerance for a particular student rather than of deviant behavior. More detailed information on preparing for and conducting observations is presented in chapter 2.

Interviews

Information from ratings by others, self-report instruments, and observation can be further refined through interviews. Interviews are the oldest, most widely used, and most valued assessment technique for evaluating social and affective functioning (Aiken, 1985; Haynes and Jensen, 1979; Korchin and Schuldberg, 1981; Swan and MacDonald, 1978). They serve as important aids in interpreting the formal data from other-completed ratings and self-report inventories (Brooks, 1979; Fischer, 1985). With respect to social, behavioral, and affective functioning, Barnett and Zucker (1990) identified four specialized functions of interviews:

- a formal diagnostic technique,
- a method to study private experiences,
- a data-gathering technique critical to the assessment–intervention process, and
- an educational technique.

Who conducts the interview and when depends on the function the interview serves.
    Interviews have been used extensively as a formal diagnostic technique in diagnosing social, behavioral, and affective problems. The purpose of such an interview is to determine whether an individual has symptoms that warrant the diagnosis of

various mental health problems such as depression. Interviews used for this function are conducted with both the individual and those closest to the person, such as a parent or spouse. The interviewer is typically a mental health professional who has had considerable training and experience in interview techniques. Some mental health professionals use a *structured interview* format. This involves using a list of specific questions that correspond to formal diagnostic criteria. Other mental health professionals prefer a *semistructured interview* that lists questions but provides opportunities to explore issues uncovered during the interview. There are published structured and semistructured interviews for use with students. Often these published interview formats have a companion interview to be used with the student's parents. When the student is very young or functioning below the average range cognitively, the mental health professional may use toys and play situations to obtain the diagnostic interview data. Teachers typically do not have the training to conduct formal diagnostic interviews. However, the school psychologist may. Teachers and school psychologists may see interpretations of these types of interviews in reports on students from psychiatrists or clinical psychologists in private practice and in mental health agencies.

Interviews as a method for studying private experiences sometimes occur during an initial evaluation. However, they are more commonly used in the course of counseling. Trained and experienced mental health professionals conduct these interviews.

Interviews as a data-gathering technique employed during the assessment–intervention process are used extensively in public school settings. These interviews seek data on the perceptions of all involved on the nature of the problem, the reasons for the problem, attempted interventions and barriers to other interventions, the beliefs of key individuals about changes that could solve the problem, and the motivation of key individuals to participate in the changes needed to solve the problem. These interviews tend to be problem focused, but the interviewer does not ascribe the cause of the problem to a single source. The interviewer is concerned with all components of the system of interactions where the social, behavioral, or affective problem occurs. The purpose of the interview is to determine how the student, parents, and teachers view the problem behaviors, ascribe responsibility or blame, and believe that change is possible. Special education teachers, school psychologists, and school social workers conduct these interviews. Since the student, parents, and teachers all need to be interviewed, the evaluation team members share the interview responsibilities. The broad questions asked during the interview should be planned before starting the interview and should be based on the nature of the problem and who is being interviewed. The guided interview recommended by Peterson (1968) provides a format for these interviews. This format appears in Table 7-6.

Finally, the interview is used as an educational technique on a regular basis to help a student develop skill in considering antecedents, consequences, and responsibility for various problem situations. The teacher or school counselor generally conducts these interviews when social and behavioral problems occur. These interviews are a part of the intervention process and are discussed more fully in texts on intervention methodology, often under the name of *life space interviews* (Coleman, 1992; Gardner, 1990; Long, 1990; Redl, 1959; Rizzo and Zabel, 1988; Wood, 1975).

Table 7-6 Guided interview from Peterson

A. Definition of Problem Behavior
  1. Nature of problem as defined by client
     a. *As I understand it, you came here because* . . . (discuss reasons for contact as stated by referral agency or other source of information).
     b. *I would like you to tell me more about this. What is the problem as you see it?* (Probe as needed to determine client's view of his own problem behavior, i.e., what is he doing, or failing to do, which he or somebody else defines as a problem?)
  2. Severity of the problem
     a. *How serious is this as far as you are concerned?* (Probe to determine perceived severity of problem.)
     b. *How often do you* . . . (exhibit problem behavior if a disorder of commission, or have occasion to exhibit desired behavior if a problem of omission. The goal is to obtain information regarding frequency of response.)
  3. Generality of the problem
     a. Duration
        How long has this been going on?
     b. Extent
        Where does this problem usually come up? (Probe to determine situations in which problem behavior occurs; e.g., Do you feel that way at work? How about at home?)
B. Determinants of Problem Behavior
  1. Conditions that intensify problem behavior
     Now I want you to think about the time when . . . (the problem) *is worst. What sort of things are going on then?*
  2. Conditions that alleviate problem behavior
     What about the times when . . . (the problem) *gets better? What sorts of things are going on then?*
  3. Perceived origins
     What do you think is causing . . . (the problem)?
  4. Specific antecedents
     Think back to the last time . . . (the problem occurred). *What was going on at that time?*
     As needed:
     a. Social influences
        Were any other people around? Who? What were they doing?
     b. Personal influences
        What were you thinking about at the time? How did you feel?
  5. Specific consequences
     What happened after . . . (the problem behavior occurred)?
     As needed:
     a. Social consequences
        What did . . . (significant others identified above) *do?*
     b. Personal consequences
        How did that make you feel?
  6. Suggested changes
     You have thought a lot about . . . (the problem). *What do you think might be done to* . . . (improve the situation)?
  7. Suggested leads for further inquiry
     What else do you think I should find out about to help you with this problem?

Source: From Donald R. Peterson, THE CLINICAL STUDY OF SOCIAL BEHAVIOR, copyright © 1968, pp. 121–122. Reprinted by permission of Prentice Hall, Englewood Cliffs, New Jersey.

Interviews can provide very rich data not available from rating scales and self-report inventories. They enable the evaluation team to probe responses and to explore discrepancies in responses on norm-referenced measures. They also provide a vehicle for gathering data when the parents or student do not have the reading skills to allow them to complete rating scales and self-report inventories. If an interview is conducted following an observation, the interviewer can learn how key individuals perceived the events that occurred. The interviewer can learn if the observed session was representative of the usual interactional style and behavior. Observed problems can be referred to and explored in terms of perceived cause and feelings during the situation.

While interviews have many advantages, teachers need to be aware of some of the disadvantages. Compared to norm-referenced data, interviews have relatively low reliability and validity. These problems result from inherent interviewer bias due to the interviewer's own values and training orientation and the tremendous variability in interviewing skills. Another disadvantage is the time-consuming nature of gathering interview data. The interview must be planned and requires some extended uninterrupted time to conduct. This time requirement can make interviewing an expensive data-gathering technique. A final disadvantage is the fact that it can be difficult to succinctly communicate interview data to other professionals. More time is required to present results of interviews than to review norm-referenced data.

The focus of this section has been on interviews used to explore social, behavioral, and affective problems. Interviews can also be used to gather developmental and academic histories, to define problem areas, and to examine academic difficulties. These other types of interviews are discussed in chapter 2 along with recommendations for setting up and conducting interviews.

Projectives

Ratings completed by others, self-report inventories, observation, and interviews are all techniques widely used in public schools to assess social, behavioral, and affective problems. *Projective techniques,* which involve unstructured or ambiguous stimuli, are occasionally used by school psychologists but are more commonly used by psychiatrists and clinical psychologists in private practice and at mental health agencies. Special education teachers do not have the intensive training required to use and interpret projective measures. However, teachers will see reports from the school psychologist or mental health professionals that discuss results of projective measures. Therefore, it is helpful for teachers to have some understanding of the variety of techniques and the advantages and disadvantaged of projectives.

Projective techniques involve giving the student some type of unstructured stimuli and requiring a response to that stimuli. The thinking behind projective techniques is that the person's responses will help the examiner form hypotheses about the individual's dominant view of life, beliefs about self and others, and style of thinking. These hypotheses can then be explored in more depth during intervention interviews.

Projective techniques are grouped into three broad categories: completion techniques, drawing techniques, and picture-based techniques. In *completion techniques* the individual is given the beginning of sentences or stories and is asked to finish them. Typically, the sentences are written for the student, requiring that the student read the sentence stem and write the rest of the sentence (Hart, 1972; Lanyon and Lanyon, 1980; Rotter and Rafferty, 1950). When reading or written language skills are not well developed, the task is sometimes modified by the exam-

A student draws a picture of his family.   *Source:* © Mimi Forsyth/Monkmeyer Press Photos

iner reading the stems and acting as the student's "secretary," recording verbatim responses. Stories are sometimes presented as unfinished cartoons. The pictures depict a variety of interactional scenes, and the student fills in the dialogue "balloon" above the person's head (Rosenzweig, 1978).

Drawing techniques are used primarily with young children and grew out of the use of drawings to study cognitive development (Barnett and Zucker, 1990). In using drawing projectively, the student is asked to draw something specific (for example, a person, house, tree, or family), then the examiner analyzes the drawing, forming a global impression and noting special details. The examiner is guided in the analysis by an extensive literature on interpreting drawings. The degree to which the examiner is aware of and uses this literature can influence the interpretation.

Picture-based techniques require that the individual look at inkblots or pictures and either identify what is seen or tell a story to accompany the picture. The examiner then scores the responses or stories based on common themes, relation-

Table 7-7 Picture-based projective techniques

Instrument (Author)	Age/Grade	Description
Children's Apperceptive Story-Telling Test (Schneider, 1989)	Age 6–13	31 colored pictures, racially sensitive, equivalent boy/girl stimulus pictures; objective scoring system and nationally representative standardization samples
Children's Apperception Test (Bellak & Bellak, 1974)	Age 3–10	10 black line drawings of animals
Michigan Picture Test–Revised (Hutt, 1980)	Grades 1–12	15 cards, 7 given to both boys and girls and 8 gender specific cards; normative data for some grades
Roberts Apperception Test (McArthur & Roberts, 1982)	Age 6–15	27 black line drawings 16 of which are administered at any one time; scoring system and psychometric data provided
Thematic Apperception Test (Murray & Bellak, 1973)	Age 7–adult	31 black and white pictures, 10–12 are chosen for use based on age and sex; several scoring systems exist but none are used widely

ship of the stories to the pictures, whether the response focuses on details or the gestalt, and unusualness of responses. With the exception of the Exner Comprehensive Scoring System (Exner, 1986) used with the Rorschach inkblot test (1921), published scoring systems for different sets of picture stimuli are not widely adopted because of the time needed to use them (Barnett and Zucker, 1990). Examiners often prefer to form a general impression of the themes that cross several stories developed by the individual. These techniques are used with both children and adults. A list and brief description of picture-based techniques that can be used with students appears in Table 7.7.

Proponents of projective techniques believe that the unstructured and ambiguous nature of the stimuli help guard against response sets, faking, and lying that may invalidate the results of more objective affective measures (Aiken, 1985). Projectives can also be helpful in exploring very sensitive domains of an individual's personal experience (Barnett and Zucker, 1990). Finally, projectives provide a framework for examining such thought processes as organization of thoughts, appropriateness of thoughts, conventionality of thoughts, bizarre or distorted thoughts, interest in social contact, and outlook on life. Projective techniques provide important qualitative data and, when used with other information, can enhance the overall understanding of an individual (AERA, APA, and NCME, 1985).

The primary disadvantage of projective techniques is their technical adequacy. Scoring or interpretation of responses tends to be very subjective. When scoring systems exist, they have limited reliability and validity data and are not widely used. Therefore, it is vital that examiners who use projective techniques have extensive training and experience and remain current on new interpretations of responses. Finally, projective techniques tend to be time-consuming data-gathering procedures relative to the quality of information obtained. Often the techniques require that the examiner probe selected responses with follow-up questions, and scoring/interpretation may result in only general impressions that might be effectively documented with more direct methods of data-gathering. Because of these weaknesses, projective techniques should be used cautiously and only by specially trained examiners.

Assessing the Environment

Student-focused assessment of social, behavioral, and affective functioning examines the degree of deviance of the student's behavior and feelings and the impact of social, behavioral, and affective variables on the student's ability to function. *Environment-focused assessment* examines environmental expectations of and tolerance for the student and how environmental interventions can resolve the problem, preventing "labeling" a student as deviant. Observations, interviews of key individuals, and informal checklists are the primary means of gathering information on the environmental contribution to problem behaviors. These procedures were covered in the previous section on assessing the student and in chapter 2. This section describes the five areas that should be assessed: the physical environment, behavioral expectations, instructional demands, interactions, and tolerance and cultural diversity.

Physical Environment

The nature of the physical environment influences learning. Light, temperature, space, and noise level can make the learning environment conducive to learning. People have preferences about these variables and have varying degrees of tolerance for deviations from their preferences. A student who is struggling academically may have less tolerance for deviations or for an unattractive environment. Therefore, the physical environment should be evaluated for the comfort level of temperature and light. The noise level can also promote or inhibit learning. Noise levels should be considered for different types of activities. Quiet and noisy activities are best alternated. The classroom should be evaluated for features that control noise level during quiet activities, such as carpet on the floor and filled bookcases or bulletin boards against walls. Space is another key feature. People who feel crowded together will get on each others' nerves faster than people who have individual space. The furniture in the classroom should be the right size for the students; there needs to be enough for the number of students. It should be organized to provide different areas for different activities (that is, small group instruction, large group instruction, quiet independent work stations, activity centers) and to facilitate movement around the classroom. Table 7-8 provides a checklist for the physical environment that can be used during an observation.

Behavioral Expectations

Another environmental variable that influences a student's social, behavioral, and affective functioning is the level of expectations held by authority figures. If a student does not know the expectations or is unable to meet high expectations, behavior and affective problems can develop. The primary caregiver and the student's teachers should be interviewed to determine what expectations they have for a particular student. These expectations need to be compared to the student's cognitive and language levels to determine if they are reasonable for that student. During the interview, the examiner will also want to explore how the expectations are communicated to the student. Many times, behavioral expectations are communicated in

Table 7-8 Checklist of physical environment

	Yes	No
Temperature		
Comfortable		
Too hot (frequent request for open windows or fans, students fanning themselves)		
Too cold (students wearing coats, shivering)		
Inconsistent		
Light		
Adequate		
Glare (obscures blackboard or charts)		
Shadows		
Flicking or burned out lights		
Noise		
Quiet/noisy activities alternated		
Noise control features		
carpeting		
drapes		
bulletin boards		
filled bookcases		
Distracting noises present (hum from lights, hallway noise)		
Regular shouting is heard (teachers or students)		
Students complaints about noise		
Space		
Organized for different activities		
small group		
large group		
quiet, independent work		
leisure, free time		
Uncrowded, personal space preserved		
Adequate and convenient storage of supplies, materials, equipment		
Direct traffic patterns control distractions		
Furniture appropriate size for students		
Enough furniture for number of students		
Flexible, can be rearranged periodically		

the form of rules. Classroom and home rules should be few in number, simply stated, and stated in terms of what is expected rather than prohibited (that is, "Raise your hand" versus "Don't call out") to promote understanding and compliance (Affleck, Lowenbraun, and Archer, 1980). Rules should have a clear rationale based on cooperation and respect for the individual, other people, and property. Rules should have appropriate consequences and should be consistently enforced. Students should have opportunities for input in the development of rules and the chance to negotiate rules when circumstances or development changes. Table 7-9 lists questions that can be considered when evaluating classroom management systems.

In addition to rules, expectations are communicated by responses to the student and to his or her work. The evaluator can obtain this information by observing

Table 7-9 Questions for evaluating classroom management systems

1. Do students have a clear understanding of the expectations for classroom conduct? Are they aware of which behaviors are considered acceptable and which are considered unacceptable?
2. Are students aware of the consequences of appropriate and inappropriate behavior?
3. What happens in the classroom when students behave appropriately? Is appropriate behavior rewarded in some way?
4. What types of rewards or reinforcers are provided? Are students rewarded with social reinforcers like teacher praise? Can they earn activity reinforcers such as free time in the media center or the opportunity to do a special art project? Are tangible rewards like stars, notes home to parents, or school supplies used for reinforcement? Are edible rewards provided?
5. Is there a formal system for rewarding appropriate behavior? For example, do students earn points for good behavior and later trade their points for reinforcers? If a formal system is in place, does it include provisions for inappropriate behavior?
6. What happens in the classroom when students behave inappropriately? Is inappropriate behavior ignored or are there consequences?
7. What are the consequences of inappropriate behavior? Does the teacher verbally rebuke the student? Does the student lose privileges or previously earned rewards? Is the student sent to the principal or kept in at recess or after school?
8. Are consequences delivered consistently to all students at all times?
9. How does the classroom behavior management system relate to the rules of the school and the school's behavior management system?

Source: Reprinted with the permission of Merrill, an imprint of Macmillan Publishing Company from ASSESSING SPECIAL STUDENTS, Third Edition by James A. McLoughlin and Rena B. Lewis pp. 280–281. Copyright © 1990 by Macmillan Publishing Company. Originally published by Merrill Publishing Company.

interactions between the student and teacher or between the student and the primary caregiver. Information can also be obtained during the interview by asking what happens when the student brings home a failing paper, a C or an A on the report card, and by asking what the interviewee thinks will be going on for the student three to five years from now.

Instructional Demands

Students placed in academic situations in which they have little chance for success become unhappy, may develop a poor self-esteem that impacts on their willingness to try new things, and may demonstrate their frustration by acting out. No one likes to feel inadequate. When those feelings emerge, the person tries various strategies to escape them. For these reasons, it is important that the evaluation team consider that the problematic behaviors have emerged because the student is being asked to function independently beyond his or her capabilities. The team needs to have information on the student's cognitive, language, and academic skills so they can compare those skills with the academic skills required in the regular classroom to see if there is a match.

Consider the following scenario. Sam, a fifth-grade student, has problems with reading comprehension. He is aware that other students do not struggle as he does. Sam's social studies teacher conducts class by calling on students to read portions of the text aloud, then asks the students oral questions on the material. During social studies class, Sam frequently fools around, cracks jokes, and does anything to get a laugh from the other students. This behavior often results in Sam being sent to the principal's office. From the teacher's perspective, Sam is unruly and disrupts the class. However, from Sam's perspective, he has discovered a strategy to entertain his peers and prevent them from discovering he has reading problems. Sam has been placed in a situation in which the academic requirements exceed his skill level. Being sent to the office reinforces the disruptive behavior because Sam escapes the aversive situation and has earned a certain admiration from some peers because of his clowning. Sam's behavior is not going to change under these circumstances.

Sam's situation illustrates why instructional demands must be considered as a motivator of problematic behavior. The evaluation team should consider the materials and the type of instruction that takes place in classrooms where problematic behaviors occur. Are the reasons for learning the material presented? Is there direct instruction on new skills; is there sufficient group practice and feedback before the student must perform independently? When is feedback given, and what is the nature of that feedback? And what are the characteristics of the instructional group (that is, size, homogeneity of skill level)? McLoughlin and Lewis (1990) suggest exploring the following questions:

Do the learning activities match the instructional goals and objectives for the student?

Has the student mastered the prerequisite skills necessary for the learning activity?

Are the directions for the activity clear and comprehensible?

Does the activity present information in a way appropriate for the student? For example, if the task requires the student to read, is the level of the reading material appropriate for the student?

Are the types of responses required by the activity appropriate for the student?

Does the activity provide adequate opportunity for practice of newly learned skills and information?

Is there adequate feedback to students about the accuracy of their responses?

Is the activity motivating? Is some type of reinforcement provided for successfully completing the activity?

Is the classroom environment conducive to participation in and completion of the learning activity? (p. 281)

If it is determined that the instructional demands are the driving factor behind the problem behavior, the evaluation team should try to modify the instruction. Table 7-10 provides suggestions for making adaptations. Note that the last resort is giving the student a different task. Every attempt should be made to support the student in completing the task required of other students.

Interactions

Interactions with others help shape how people feel about themselves in various situations. When people are uncomfortable about a situation they do something to manage those feelings or escape. Students engage in problematic behaviors to manage feelings or escape uncomfortable situations. Therefore, the evaluation team needs to examine interactions. A student's interactions with both parents and teachers are important. However, school-based personnel will have little or no opportu-

Table 7-10 Ways of adapting instructional activities

IF students experience difficulty in task performance, TRY these adaptations of . . .

Materials and Activities:

1. clarify task directions
2. add prompts
3. teach to specific student errors

Teaching Procedures:

4. give additional presentation of skills and information
5. provide additional guided practice
6. make consequences for successful performance more attractive
7. slow the pace of instruction

Task Requirements:

8. change the criteria for successful performance
9. change task characteristics
10. break tasks into smaller subtasks

BEFORE selecting an alternate task.

IF NECESSARY, substitute a similar but easier task or a prerequisite task.

Source: Reprinted with the permission of Merrill, an imprint of Macmillan Publishing Company from TEACHING SPECIAL STUDENTS IN THE MAINSTREAM, Second Edition by Rena B. Lewis and Donald H. Doorlag p. 80. Copyright © 1987 by Merrill Publishing Company.

nity to observe or change parent–child interactions. That is best handled in family counseling. Teacher–student and student–student interactions can be observed and suggestions for changes made. During classroom observations, the evaluation team member should record the number of interactions the student has and with whom they occur. An interactional observational checklist like the one in Table 7-11 facilitates recording important data.

In the first column the observer records a consecutive number each time the student interacts with anyone. Checks are placed in each of the other columns to indicate who started the interaction, who interacted with the student, and the type and the nature of the interaction. There are four different types of interactions. Interactions about procedures deal with obtaining supplies and equipment, when and where to turn in completed work, requests to leave the room, and discussions about how to use time. Content interactions focus on specific academic material and skills for a particular subject. They may involve requests for help on work, clarifying information presented during instruction, or a dialogue about a skill. Interactions regarding behavior is the third type. These are specific comments about the student's behavior and compliance with classroom rules. When interactions concern matters not related to school or functioning in the classroom, they are classified as social interactions. Making plans with friends, telling the teacher or peers about an upcoming event, and discussing family or friends with the teacher or classmates are examples of social interactions. The nature of the interaction has to do with the tone or impact of the interaction on the student.

Look at Table 7-11 to get an idea of the interactions Sam had in Mr. Wilson's social studies class. During the 15-minute observation period, Sam had four interactions. Sam initiated the first interaction, so an X is placed in the student column as the initiator. The interaction partner was the teacher, so an X is placed in that

Table 7-11 Interaction observation checklist

Name ___Sam___ Teacher/Class ___Mr. Wilson—Social Studies___ Date ___12/15/91___ Observation Time ___15 mins.___

Interaction Count	Initiator			Interaction Partner			Type				Nature		
	Student	Peer	Teacher	Other	Peer	Teacher	Other	Procedure	Content	Behavior	Social	Positive	Negative	Neutral
1	X					X		X						X
2	X								X					X
3	X				X					X		X		
4	X									X	X			X

column in the section on interaction pattern. Sam asked the teacher about the time available for working on an assignment. This question deals with a procedure, so an X is placed in that column indicating type of interaction. Mr. Wilson responded to Sam's question by stating there would be a 15-minute work period. Such a response would be considered neutral in tone. The next interaction started when a classmate asked Sam a question about an answer for part of the assignment. The peer column is checked as initiator, because a classmate started the interaction. Nothing is checked in the interaction partner column, because Sam did not start the interaction, he only responded. Since the classmate's question to Sam had to do with the material being studied, an X is placed in the content column indicating type of interaction. Finally, this content related question from a classmate resulted in Sam simply responding. The exchange was, therefore, considered neutral.

Observations of interactions are direct means of gathering data. However, it is equally important to consider the student's perceptions of interactions. The evaluation team should discover whether the student's perceptions match the observations. Student-completed interaction checklists supply that information. Samples of these checklists appear in Figure 7-1.

Tolerance and Cultural Diversity

The evaluation team must also consider the issue of tolerance when assessing the environment. Teachers have varying abilities in tolerating differences. Some teachers have difficulty adjusting rules and instructional demands to meet individual needs. Other teachers individualize most of the work in their classrooms. The evaluation team may encounter a situation in which the student's disabilities are mild but the student is in a classroom where the teacher tends to use one instructional style and has difficulty adjusting to others. In this situation, the student may develop inappropriate behaviors to cope with the instructional rigidity. The same student may show few behavior problems in a classroom where the teacher has more flexibility in adjusting instructional style and demands. Teachers also differ in how much noise and movement is acceptable in the classroom. In one situation, a teacher may complain that a student is hyperactive and disruptive. In a different classroom, the student's activity level may not be considered an interfering factor. Sometimes, just moving a student from one classroom to another resolves problems.

The issue of tolerance is especially important considering the cultural diversity in many schools. Sometimes there are differences between the student's cultural background and the teacher's in behavioral expectations, communication patterns, and the value of formal academics. Unless these differences are understood and the diversity appreciated, classroom problems may occur.

Diagnosis and Classification

All students who have been referred to an evaluation team should have their social, behavioral, and affective functioning assessed. Students with primary problems of mental retardation, language disorders, or learning disabilities may have social, behavioral, or affective difficulties as well that need to be addressed to maximize

Interaction Checklist (Elementary)

	Always 3 ☺	Seldom 2 😐	Never 1 ☹
1. I can get extra help from the teacher when I need it.	☐	☐	☐
2. The teacher praises me when I do well.	☐	☐	☐
3. The teacher smiles when I do something well.	☐	☐	☐
4. The teacher listens attentively.	☐	☐	☐
5. The teacher accepts me as an individual.	☐	☐	☐
6. The teacher encourages me to try something new.	☐	☐	☐
7. The teacher respects the feelings of others.	☐	☐	☐
8. My work is usually good enough.	☐	☐	☐
9. I am called on when I raise my hand.	☐	☐	☐
10. The same students always get praised by the teacher.	☐	☐	☐
11. The teacher grades fairly.	☐	☐	☐
12. The teacher smiles and enjoys teaching.	☐	☐	☐
13. I have learned to do things from this teacher.	☐	☐	☐
14. When something is too hard, my teacher makes it easier for me.	☐	☐	☐
15. My teacher is polite and courteous.	☐	☐	☐
16. I like my teacher.	☐	☐	☐

Interaction Checklist (Secondary)

The teacher	Always 5	Sometimes 4	Often 3	Seldom 2	Never 1
1. is genuinely interested in me.	☐	☐	☐	☐	☐
2. respects the feelings of others.	☐	☐	☐	☐	☐
3. grades fairly.	☐	☐	☐	☐	☐
4. identifies what he or she considers important.	☐	☐	☐	☐	☐
5. is enthusiastic about teaching.	☐	☐	☐	☐	☐
6. smiles often and enjoys teaching.	☐	☐	☐	☐	☐
7. helps me develop skills in understanding myself.	☐	☐	☐	☐	☐
8. is honest and fair.	☐	☐	☐	☐	☐
9. helps me develop skills in communicating.	☐	☐	☐	☐	☐
10. encourages and provides time for individual help.	☐	☐	☐	☐	☐
11. is pleasant and has a sense of humor.	☐	☐	☐	☐	☐
12. has "pets" and spends most time with them.	☐	☐	☐	☐	☐
13. encourages and provides time for questions and discussion.	☐	☐	☐	☐	☐
14. respects my ideas and concerns.	☐	☐	☐	☐	☐
15. helps me develop skills in making decisions.	☐	☐	☐	☐	☐
16. helps me develop skills in using time wisely.	☐	☐	☐	☐	☐

FIGURE 7-1 Student rating scales for evaluating the teacher's performance   *Source:* Reprinted with the permission of Merrill, an imprint of Macmillan Publishing Company from THE EXCEPTIONAL STUDENT IN THE REGULAR CLASSROOM, Fourth Edition by Bill R. Gearheart, Mel W. Weishahn and Carol J. Gearheart p. 107. Copyright © 1988 by Merrill Publishing Company.

success in the regular classroom. These difficulties are often disturbing to teachers and peers in the mainstream but are not necessarily disorders. Teachers and peers also have differences in tolerance levels for these behaviors.

When a student's social, behavioral, or affective problems are frequent, intense, occur over time, and have an impact on learning, the student is identified as having a disorder that warrants special services under PL 94–142. The federally recognized term for these students is "seriously emotionally disturbed" (*Federal Register*, 1977). Educators across the country have varying degrees of acceptance for this term. Some feel uncomfortable with the term *emotional* and prefer to focus on observable behaviors. For this reason, students with social, behavioral, and affective disorders may be called seriously emotionally disturbed, emotionally disturbed, emotionally conflicted, emotional/behavior disordered, behavior disordered, or behaviorally handicapped. The controversy behind these labels and the characteristics of students so labeled is more appropriately discussed in texts on behavior disorders.

It is important for educators to recognize that a student with social, behavioral, or affective disorders may be seen by mental health professionals in agencies outside the school. Mental health practitioners tend not to use the labels from PL 94–142. Mental health professionals use diagnostic labels from the *Diagnostic and Statistical Manual of Mental Disorders—Third Edition Revised* (DSM–III–R) (American Psychiatric Association, 1987). This manual and its predecessors define various mental disorders and provide a standardized terminology for developmental, academic, social, behavioral, and affective disorders. Labels from the DSM–III–R that may be applied to students include separation anxiety disorder, attention deficit hyperactivity disorder, conduct disorder, anorexia nervosa, and major depression. To determine if the student is eligible for special education services, the evaluation team should review both the documentation provided by the mental health agency and the student's classroom performance. If the student's classroom performance is affected by the social, behavioral, or affective disorder, then the student is eligible for special education. However, sometimes a student has a diagnosed mental health problem but is not eligible for special education. For example, this may be the case with anorexia nervosa. In this situation, the student clearly needs therapeutic support, but if the student's academic performance is within the normal range, then the help must come from a mental health professional outside the school. Hopefully, school personnel (teachers, counselors, school psychologists) and mental health professionals from outside agencies will cooperate to meet the student's needs, but those from the outside agency have the leadership responsibility for this kind of intervention.

Steps in the Assessment Process

Objectively Describe the Concern

The first step in assessing social skills, behavior, and affective functioning is to describe the concern as clearly as possible. Getting a clear description of the concern allows formation of a hypothesis about which area (social skills, behavior, affective functioning) needs to be evaluated first. A clear description of the concern also permits trial modifications before a comprehensive evaluation is conducted.

Pre-Evaluation Intervention

Labeling a student as having a social skill, behavioral, or affective disorder is very stigmatizing. The label and provision of services to the student may not resolve the problem if environmental variables contribute to the problem. Therefore, attempts should be made to modify the environment or the student–teacher interactions before conducting a comprehensive evaluation. These attempted modifications convey the message that the problem may be a shared difficulty rather than an inherent student deficit. Such modifications may make the problem less severe but not resolve it completely. That outcome will help refine hypotheses about the problem and can provide invaluable information for planning the comprehensive evaluation.

Develop Data Sheets to Record Assessment Results

Part of planning a comprehensive evaluation is developing data sheets to ensure that both the student and the environment are assessed using multiple procedures. When assessing the student, it is important to examine social skills, behavior, and affective functioning from the perspective of the student, the parents, and the teacher. When assessing the environment, it is important to examine the physical environment, expectations, instructional demands, and interactions. Table 7-12 provides one format for organizing summaries of this information.

Conduct a Systematic Assessment

A variety of procedures should be used to document a student's strengths and weaknesses and the environmental contributions to social skill, behavioral, and affective functioning. Checklists and ratings completed by the student and significant others provide screening information that can be explored in more detail with observations and interviews. Conducting a systematic assessment is a lengthy process during which a pattern of behaving emerges. Attempting shortcuts in the process may result in a score that qualifies the student for special services but does not reveal the pattern of behaving and the environmental contributors, information needed to plan effective interventions.

Planning Interventions

Interventions should be based on a pattern of behavior that emerges across settings rather than a single score on a rating form. Interventions should have a two-pronged approach, one focused on the student and one focused on the environment. When prioritizing the objectives for intervention, the first objective should be directed at the social skill, behavior, or affective state considered the most disturbing by the people directly involved. Progress on this objective will provide relief from stress and engender hope that a long-term solution is possible. Simultaneous to considering the most disturbing problem, the team should consider the commitment of the student and significant others to working on a particular problem. If commitment to finding a solution is high, the probability of success is increased. When the most disturbing problem and commitment to a problem-specific solution are different, the

Table 7-12 Data organization

| | Student Assessment | | | | | | |
| | Rating | | | Interview | | | |
	Student	Parents	Teacher	Observation	Student	Parents	Teacher	Projectives	Summary
Social Skills									
Behavior									
Affective									
Environmental Assessment									
Physical Environment									
Expectations									
Instructional Demands									
Interactions									

planning team will probably use level of commitment as the main criteria for ordering intervention objectives. Making these decisions requires the professional judgment of the planning team.

Summary

Introduction

1. A case can be made for involvement of teachers in dealing with social skill, behavior, and affective problems of students.
2. The social skill, behavior, and affective functioning of all students referred for comprehensive evaluation should be explored, not just those students who are referred with identified difficulties in these areas.

Definition of the Area

1. Social skills are a person's behavior, language, and attitudes conveyed during interaction with one or more people.
2. Social skills are judged by unwritten societal standards that vary depending on the participants and the environment.
3. Behavior refers to the ability to comply with rules established by authority figures for different environments.
4. A person's affective state consists of an individual's pervasive and longstanding emotions.
5. Four variables that contribute to a person's affective state are attitude, interests/values, self-concept, and locus of control.
6. Attitudes are learned feelings regarding something specific.
7. Interests/values are learned preferences.
8. Self-concept refers to how one views oneself.
9. Locus of control has to do with how the student accepts and assigns responsibility for his or her behaviors.

Traditional, Behavioral, and Ecological Approaches

1. Traditional approaches to social skill, behavior, and affective functioning are based on a medical model that views problems as person-centered.
2. Behavioral approaches focus on observable behaviors rather than internal student traits.
3. Ecological approaches consider the interaction of the student and the environmental variables.

Assessing the Student

1. No single test or procedure reliably assesses a student's social skill, behavior, and affective functioning across settings.
2. Ratings by others provide screening information in a cost-effective manner.

3. Self-report measures are norm-referenced measures that typically deal with affective issues and are used to provide screening information.
4. Observation is a direct method of gathering followup data on concerns that emerge from the screening tools.
5. Interviews help interpret formal screening data and can serve four functions.
6. Teachers use interviews primarily to gather data on perceptions of problems, perceived causes of problems, and factors that have an impact on problem-solution.
7. Projective techniques are used by specially trained mental health professionals to gather information on a student's dominant view of life, beliefs about self and others, and style of thinking.

Assessing the Environment

1. Environment-focused assessment examines environmental expectations of and tolerance for the student and how environmental factors contribute to problem behaviors.
2. The physical environment is examined for light, temperature, space, and noise levels.
3. Data is gathered on the nature and appropriateness of expectations and how they are communicated to the student.
4. The nature and appropriateness of instructional demands must be examined.
5. The quality of student–teacher and student–student interactions must be assessed.
6. Tolerance for differences in learning style and behavior must be explored.

Diagnosis and Classification

1. Some students have problematic behaviors that need attention but do not warrant the label "seriously emotionally disturbed."
2. Some students have disordered behavior and are given the label "seriously emotionally disturbed."
3. Agencies outside the school often use diagnostic labels that do not indicate the student's eligibility for special education services.
4. Some social skill, behavior, and affective problems require intervention but should be addressed outside the school.

Steps in the Assessment Process

1. Describe the concern in objective, observable terms.
2. Attempt to solve the problem by making environmental modifications.
3. Develop data sheets to facilitate data organization and remind the evaluation team of the numerous variables to be examined.
4. Conduct a systematic assessment that examines both student and environment variables and uses several different data-gathering techniques.
5. Order intervention objectives based on the most disturbing problems and the commitment of key participants to finding a solution.

PART THREE

Assessing Skills

Assessing Adaptive Behavior

Key Terms

Adaptive behavior

Developmental milestone model

Developmental theory-based model

Ecological inventories

Functional model

Informant

Maladaptive behavior

Mobility

Positive adaptation

Priority matrix

Self-care

Self-direction

Independent functioning as an adult typically means that a person can live on his or her own by performing some task for pay and using that money to provide basic needs such as food, clothing, and shelter. The independent adult can do these tasks without regular supervision or help from someone else. The independent adult can also interact with other people in a way that maintains social contact and considers differences in the roles between people such as employee/employer, casual acquaintances, or close friends. Independent functioning means that the adult can organize and use his or her time for a variety of purposes. Independent functioning is the goal for all adults. However, people with disabilities are often at risk for not reaching this goal. Professionals in special education try to facilitate attainment of this goal. Knowing how a person is progressing toward the goal of independence, however, is often very difficult. The intermediate steps toward the goal of independence can be described as *adaptive behavior*. Therefore, it is very important to know how to assess adaptive behavior so that activities can be planned to help develop independence.

Definition of the Area

There are many definitions of adaptive behavior. Its multidimensional nature is reflected in Nihira's definition, "a composite of many aspects and a function of a wide range of specific abilities and disabilities" (1976, p. 83). Leland (1978) defined it as the "ability to adapt to environmental demands" specifically in the areas of independent functioning, personal responsibility, and social responsibility. Adaptive behavior is described in *Classification in Mental Retardation* (Grossman, 1983) as "the effectiveness or degree with which an individual meets the standards of personal independence and social responsibility expected for age and cultural group" (p. 157).

These selected definitions present a general view of adaptive behavior, but to assess a person's adaptive level of functioning you need to consider some of the components inherent in the term. Sloan and Birch (1955) conducted a study now considered a classic in the area of adaptive behavior. They identified three components of adaptive behavior that should be measured: maturation, learning capacity, and social adjustment. Others have analyzed the Adaptive Behavior Scale by the American Association on Mental Deficiency to identify important components. Lambert and Nicoll (1976) based their analysis on a public school population and identified the components of functional autonomy, social responsibility, interpersonal adjustment, and intrapersonal adjustment. In contrast, Nihira's (1969) analysis used an institutional population and found three factors: personal independence, social maladaptation, and personal maladaptation. After reviewing a number of definitions of adaptive behavior, Witt and Martens (1984) concluded that most definitions include components of independent functioning and social responsibility.

In addition to the variety of definitions for adaptive behavior and the components inherent in the definitions, assessment is further complicated by the variety of terms that exist for this concept. The term *adaptive behavior* is used by the American Association on Mental Deficiency (Grossman, 1983) and is the most widely used term. However, the same basic concept has been called social competence (Cain, Levine, and Elzey, 1963), social maturity (Doll, 1953), adaptive capacity (Fullan and Loubser, 1972), and adaptive fitting (Cassel, 1976).

Complexity of Adaptive Behavior

The variety of terms, the components inherent in the concept, and the numerous definitions of adaptive behavior suggest the complexity of this area. However, the complexity becomes even more apparent when an assessment of adaptive behavior is being planned. Some of the issues that have to be considered are the purposes for the assessment, the model on which the assessment will be based, the setting for the assessment, the subskill areas to be assessed, the age of the individual, and the type and severity of the disability. Each of these issues must be considered carefully to obtain the most useful information from the assessment process.

Reason for Assessing Adaptive Behavior

Assessment of adaptive behavior, like all educational assessments, serves two primary functions: identification and placement, and planning educational programs and intervention (Coulter and Morrow, 1978). These functions must be considered when selecting instruments to use in assessing adaptive behavior. A norm-referenced measure is often required as part of the documentation of a disability. Norm-referenced measures use age equivalents or standard scores so a student's functioning level can be judged as average or below expectations compared to that of a sample of individuals of the same age. But norm-referenced measures are often not specific enough for planning educational programs and intervention. For planning interventions the teacher needs information from criterion-referenced measures or ecological inventories.

Models Underlying Assessment Tools

Developers of adaptive behavior assessment tools typically ascribe to a model of functioning that helps them structure the items to be used. Three models are used frequently: the developmental milestone model, the developmental theory-based model, and the functional model (Bailey and Wolery, 1984, 1989; Gast and Wolery, 1985). The *developmental milestone model* is most often reflected in trade books for parents about child development. This model is based on the perspective that as children grow certain skills and abilities emerge in an orderly, stepwise fashion. Parents come to expect that their child will roll over, sit, stand, walk, talk, and be toilet trained at certain ages. Several researchers have described this perspective and the milestones normally expected at certain ages (Bayley, 1969; Cattell, 1940; Gesell, 1928, 1938, 1940; Gesell and Amatruda, 1947; Havinghurst, 1972). Norm-referenced tests constructed on this model are intended to identify children who exhibit developmental delays. However, there are numerous critics of the developmental milestone model, because many of the assessment items have little relevance to direct instruction (Bailey and Wolery, 1984, 1989; Brooks–Gunn and Lewis, 1981; Browder, 1991; Gaussen, 1984; Keogh and Sheehan, 1981). This specific concern was clearly articulated by Gaussen (1984) when he wrote:

> The milestones of development which are so much a part of the common currency of clinical practice, and indeed of parenthood, are at risk of becoming conceptual millstones hung round the necks of parents, professionals, and infants alike. As such they serve to restrict the process of assessment and remediation by focusing on aspects of developmental change which are more fixed and less open to intervention. (p. 103)

Planning an instructional program on the basis of developmental stage fails to consider the age-appropriateness of the activities and the environmental expectations. This is particularly true when disabilities are more severe (Browder, 1991).

The *developmental theory-based model* has also been used to construct assessment measures. This model is based on the assumption that researchers have accurately described the sequence of skills that culminates in a specific ability (Gast and Wolery, 1985). These descriptions are often presented as stages of development. Piaget's work on the development of logic (Piaget and Inhelder, 1958) and of moral judgment (Piaget, 1965) are examples of such models. In his work, Piaget provides careful descriptions of behaviors that occur at four broad stages: sensorimotor stage, pre-operational stage, concrete operational stage, and formal operational stage. These careful descriptions have been used to develop assessment tools such as the Ordinal Scales of Psychological Development (Dunst, 1980; Uzgiris and Hunt, 1975). However, the quality and usefulness of such tools rests on the assumption that the underlying theory is correct and is free of cultural bias. Another disadvantage to the use of theory-based models for assessment purposes is the relatively few tools available for use in evaluations (Gast and Wolery, 1985).

An assessment model that produces data that can be used directly in planning intervention programs is the *functional model*. This model does not focus on typical sequential development but rather on age-appropriate expectations for functioning as independently as possible in specific environments. A functional model of assessment requires that both the individual's skill and the environment be evaluated. Because people function in several environments, each one must be evaluated. Therefore, multiple assessments tailored to the specific student and the student's various environments are conducted when the functional model is used. Instead of using norm-referenced, commercially produced tools, evaluators use ecological inventories that have been carefully developed for each child. While these procedures are beneficial for all children with disabilities, they are most commonly used with individuals who have severe disabilities.

Environment

Leland's (1978) definition of adaptive behavior contained the key provision of being able to adapt to environmental demands. This suggests that it is critical to consider environmental demands when assessing adaptive behavior. The importance of this issue is highlighted when attempts are made to evaluate students from minority groups or individuals from different socioeconomic backgrounds. Many times these children learn to function very well at home and in their neighborhoods. However, when these students are in the school environment and are compared to middle-class students from the dominant culture, they may appear to be disabled. The term "six-hour retarded child" has been used to describe such situations (President's Committee on Mental Retardation, 1970). Similarly, a student who has been in a very structured, self-contained classroom may have developed adaptive skills for that setting but have extreme trouble meeting expectations in a less structured setting. Special education teachers frequently praise a student's ability to do something in the special education classroom only to have the mainstream teacher complain that the skill is not demonstrated in the regular classroom. For these reasons, it is critical to consider the environmental demands and supports across all environments in which the individual must function when assessing adaptive behavior.

Multiple Abilities and Skills

Adaptive behavior is not a single entity but a composite of a wide range of abilities (Nihira, 1976). Looking across definitions and studies, two broad components of adaptive behavior emerge: positive adaptation and maladaptive behavior. *Positive adaptation* is reflected in descriptions of adaptive behavior that include terms such as personal independence (Nihira, 1969), functional autonomy, social responsibility, interpersonal adjustment, intrapersonal adjustment (Lambert and Nicoll, 1976), and social adjustment (Sloan and Birch, 1955). However, meeting social expectations for one's age, environment, and cultural group also means not engaging in *maladaptive* or inappropriate behaviors. When planning an assessment of adaptive behavior, both positive adaptation as well as maladaptive behaviors should be examined. Many adaptive behavior assessment tools help examine both components. These two broad divisions are routinely broken down into skill areas. Since no assessment tool evaluates all areas, it is important to have an idea of what skills could be included. Table 8-1 describes skill areas that might be included in adaptive behavior measures.

Age of the Individual

Grossman's (1983) widely used definition of adaptive behavior states that standards of personal independence and social responsibility must be considered with respect to a

Table 8-1 Skill areas of adaptive behavior

Positive Adaptation

Self-Care	Includes dressing, feeding/eating, and personal hygiene such as washing and toileting. This area is also called self-help, self-maintenance, or independent functioning.
Domestic	Includes household chores related to cooking and storage of food, cleaning, care of clothes, and minor home maintenance.
Communication	Includes gestures, sign language, use of alternative communication systems, oral language (both listening and speaking), and written language (use of letters, newspapers, and catalogues).
Motor Skills	Includes both gross and fine motor development related to mobility, recreational activities, and tool use.
Physical Fitness	Includes stamina, endurance, and appropriate use of recreational and leisure time.
Mobility	Ranges from physical mobility in a controlled environment to the ability to plan and take trips.
Consumer Skills	Includes shopping, handling money, banking, and budgeting. This area is also called economic functioning.
Self-Direction	Includes initiating tasks without direction or assistance from others, persevering until tasks are completed, and offering assistance to others. This area is also called initiative or responsibility.
Socialization	Includes interpersonal interactions, telephone skills, and dealing with feelings in appropriate ways.
Vocational	Includes punctuality, work habits, job performance, and supervising other work.
Academic	Includes understanding number and time concepts, performing calculations, and recognizing letters of the alphabet through reading comprehension.

Maladaptive Behavior

Activity Level	Includes hyperactivity, inactivity, and withdrawal.
Impulsivity	Difficulty waiting, problems inhibiting responses.
Self-Stimulating Behaviors	Includes rocking, masturbating, hand flapping.
Aggressive/Destructive Behavior	Includes hitting, temper tantrums, destruction of property.
Self-Injurious Behavior	Includes head banging, eye gouging.
Untrustworthy Behavior	Includes stealing and lying.
Antisocial Behavior	Includes swearing, bossiness, disruption/negative attitudes toward authority, noncompliance with rules and requests. This is also called rebellious behavior.
Eccentric Habits or Mannerisms	Includes smelling everything, nail biting, inappropriate undressing, and hording specific items.

person's age. Adaptive behavior is not the same at all age levels but is defined differently depending on the life stage of the individual. During the preschool years, the emphasis in adaptive behavior tends to be in the areas of motor skills, communication, self-care, and emerging socialization skills. Maturation figures prominently in the development of these skill areas and, therefore, has a stronger influence on adaptive behavior than during any other life stage. Parents watch eagerly for their infant to roll over,

The role of special education teacher includes teaching self-care skills such as face washing. *Source:* © Robert Finken/Jeroboam, Inc.

sit up unsupported, pull to a standing position, and begin walking. Delays in motor development are often the first signal that a disability may be present.

The next skill area to emerge is communication. Although maturation and mental ability are important to the development of language, environmental stimulation is also critical to language development. Some parents stimulate language development by talking to and playing language games with their young child. These parents may direct the child to wave bye-bye, point to various facial features, and offer toy or food choices that encourage gesturing or labeling. Such activities help parents observe emerging receptive language. Parents also label things for children and urge the child to imitate the words. They repeat a child's two-word utterance, expanding it and modeling more complete sentences. Other parents do not spontaneously engage in these language stimulating activities. Sometimes parents are busy with work, other family demands, personal problems, or have limited language skills themselves, and they do not engage the child in interactions. In the development of communication skills, maturation, intelligence, oral motor coordination, and environmental stimulation play equal roles.

Self-help skills develop during the preschool years for nondisabled children.

Between ages 2½ and 3, most nondisabled children gain bladder and bowel control and learn to use language or gestures to indicate the need to go to the toilet. Around this time, nondisabled children also show an interest in feeding themselves. Awkward attempts to finger feed are gradually refined, and skills at using a spoon or fork emerge. Nondisabled children also begin to develop skills at undressing and dressing themselves. Dressing behaviors requiring fine motor skills—such as operating snaps, buttons, zippers, and tying shoes—are still developing when the child enters school. Intelligence, motor development, and environmental stimulation and modeling are all critical for the emergence of self-help skills. For children with physical and mental disabilities, these basic self-help skills require considerable training throughout elementary school. Individuals with severe disabilities may require assistance with some of these skills even as adults.

Socialization skills also begin to develop very early in life. Eye contact, cuddling, smiling, and the ability to be soothed are factors that influence bonding between the infant and the primary caregiver, and these are the foundation for the development of socialization skills. During the toddler stage, there is a great deal of overlap between socialization and communication skills as children are taught to use gestures and language rather than tears to make their needs understood. Children are encouraged to use language rather than hitting, biting, pushing, and crying to express anger and frustration. Children are introduced to other children and, through these contacts, begin to learn how to wait for turns, share, and engage in both parallel and interactive, imaginative play. These basic skills are expected to have developed by the time the child enters kindergarten. But for these skills to develop, the child must have a certain level of cognitive ability, communication skills, environmental opportunity, and environmental models.

Motor skills, communication, self-care, and socialization skills continue to be refined and developed throughout life. Expectations for these skill areas gradually increase depending on the age of the individual. During the elementary school years, emergence of new skill areas is very important. Adaptive behavior shifts from an emphasis on maturation and environmental stimulation to learning capacity during the school years. Academic competence is evaluated from the time the student enters school. Within the school environment there is tremendous overlap between academic competence and communication skills. Academic tasks introduce students to the concepts needed for later independence.

Because students are now in contact with people outside the family, socialization skills are extremely important. The socialization skill of waiting your turn is gradually expanded to *self-direction* skills of offering help to others and working independently. *Self-care* skills are expanded from eating, dressing, and personal hygiene to include keeping track of personal belongings and organizing oneself. Through physical education programs at school, students learn a variety of skills that provide the foundation for the physical fitness area. However, physical fitness skills are reinforced by family preferences for recreation and leisure activities.

Family routines are also important during the elementary school years in the introduction to and development of domestic skills, through assignment of chores, and consumer skills, through awarding allowances. While most nondisabled elementary school children gradually develop skills in many areas of adaptive behavior by watching others and requesting greater independence, children with disabilities,

A special education teacher helps a student with autism communicate through facilitated communication. Without giving direction, the teacher gently supports the student's arm while the student types out her message.   *Source:* © Carey/The Image Works

especially those with moderate and severe disabilities, need direct instruction to develop these skills. The instructional program should focus on age-appropriate skills needed to meet expectations that help the child be as independent as possible at home, at school, and in the community settings most often frequented by the family. The instructional program should also anticipate future environmental settings the student may encounter and begin developing entry-level skills.

During the high school years, nondisabled students begin dating, driving, and working at part-time jobs. Earning money expands opportunities for students to develop consumer skills. While academic competence, communication, and socialization skills remain priorities, the emerging consumer, vocational, and *mobility* skills reflect the independence that will be expected of students as adults. Students with mild disabilities frequently do not have part-time jobs because extra time is needed to maintain academic performance or learning, and behavior problems interfere with performing entry-level jobs. These students may need an instructional program that directly teaches a variety of vocationally related academic skills and consumer skills. For students with moderate and severe disabilities, academic skills are de-emphasized and instructional programs focus on domestic, vocational, mobility, consumer, and self-direction skills.

Type and Severity of Disability

The assessment of adaptive behavior is important whenever a student is suspected of having a disability. However, it is a critical component in the identification of mental retardation. Two essential components of the definition on mental retardation proposed by the American Association on Mental Deficiency (Grossman, 1973, 1977, 1983) are subaverage intelligence and impairment in adaptive behavior. Therefore, data on a student's adaptive behavior are necessary if a diagnosis of mental retardation is being considered. But even within the category of mental retardation there is a great deal of heterogeneity. Some children are not identified as being retarded until they fail to meet the demands of the academic environment. For these children, adaptive behavior scales with school editions may be appropriate tools for diagnosis. Other children are identified during infancy and often exhibit severe disabilities. In these cases, adaptive behavior assessment tools should be selected that assess very low functioning. Some tools have special editions for use in institutional settings. Commercially produced, norm-referenced tools are not particularly helpful in program planning for children with severe disabilities. For these children, teacher/ caregiver-developed ecological inventories provide the most useful information.

Almost all other disabling conditions can have some impact on one or more areas of adaptive behavior. Eligibility regulations typically do not require assessment of adaptive behavior when disabilities other than mental retardation are being considered. However, such information can prove invaluable in program planning. The 1990 amendments to PL 94–142, referred to as the Individuals with Disabilities Education Act (IDEA, PL 101–476), require that transition goals be included on all IEPs for all students served by special education. This requirement will probably foster an increase in the use of adaptive behavior scales for students with diagnoses other than mental retardation.

Types of Assessment Tools

There are two reasons to assess adaptive behavior: to diagnosis the presence of a disabling condition, and to plan intervention programs. To determine the presence of a disability, it is critical that some type of standardized tool be used to help the evaluation team determine whether the condition has an impact on adaptive behavior. Standardized tools assist team members by helping them make comparisons between a particular individual and other individuals of the same age. Scores from standardized tools measuring adaptive behavior are often required during the eligibility process, particularly if problems are believed to be due to mental retardation.

As important as standardized tools are during the process of diagnosis and eligibility, often they do not contain specific enough information for instructional planning. Standardized tools help identify broad areas of adaptive behavior that might require direct instruction, but they do not indicate what subskills the student possesses—that is, the information needed as an instructional base. Teacher developed ecological inventories are better suited for instructional planning.

Procedures Used on Standardized Tools

During the process of assessing intelligence, cognitive processes, or academic areas, an examiner will typically ask the student questions and the student will respond.

The standardized assessment process for adaptive behavior is different. Rather than giving specific tasks directly to the student, the examiner will typically work with someone who knows the individual well or will observe the student. These approaches to gathering data for a student have strengths and weaknesses that should be considered when interpreting the data.

One of the most common ways of collecting information on adaptive behavior is interviewing a parent, caregiver, or teacher who knows the student well. The advantage of this data collection procedure is that it can be a very efficient use of time. Another advantage is that the information comes from the perspective of someone who has expectations of the student. Obtaining information from an *informant* (person being interview) can also pose some problems. Someone who has not accepted the student's disability may try to present the student in a very positive light and, in so doing, overestimate what the student does independently. Someone who may be more rejecting of a student with disabilities may supply information that severely underestimates the student's capabilities. Underestimates of the student's capabilities may also be obtained if the informant does not know the student well or if the person only knows the individual's behavior or skills from one setting.

The quality of the information obtained during an interview also depends on the skill of the person conducting the interview. Interviewing requires careful preparation. The interviewer should take the time to carefully review the student's records. During this preparation time, the interviewer can begin to hypothesize about what kind of expectations the child may be facing so that those hypotheses can be explored in the interview. The interviewer should also be familiar with characteristics of nondisabled people the same age as the student. Such information helps the interviewer maintain a perspective of age-appropriate expectations. If the interviewer is not familiar with normal development at a particular age, someone else should conduct the interview or the interviewer will need to review normal development as part of the preparation process.

The interviewer prepares the format for the interview. Adaptive behavior can be assessed informally with an interview. In these situations, the interviewer should plan open-ended questions that encourage the informant to talk freely about the student's capabilities. The interviewer should avoid questions that require only a yes–no response or one-word answers. The interviewer might also prepare an outline of areas of functioning and skills that need to be explored. Such an outline keeps the interview from digressing too much and ensures that critical areas are not omitted from discussion. An open-ended format may not satisfy the need for norm-referenced information on a student's adaptive behavior. When scores are needed for eligibility, the interviewer may choose to use one of the standardized tools that has an interview format, such as the Adaptive Behavior Inventory for Children (Mercer and Lewis, 1977), the Scales of Independent Behavior (Bruininks, Woodcock, Weatherman, and Hill, 1984), the Vineland Adaptive Behavior Scales, interview edition (Sparrow, Balla, and Cicchetti, 1984), or the Cain–Levine Social Competency Scale (Cain, Levine, and Elzey, 1977). Advanced preparation is especially needed when using these standardized interviews. The interviewer should be familiar with the types and organization of the questions and know when and how probing for more information is acceptable within the standardized format.

Beside skills in preparing for interviews, the interviewer should also have the skill to set up an appropriate environment for the interview and to establish rapport with the informant. It is important that the setting contain adult-sized furniture arranged in a manner that conveys the message of equality among participants (that is, the interviewer is not behind a desk). Simpson (1990) stresses that it is important for the interviewer to be relaxed and maintain a natural demeanor throughout the session and to be sensitive to the emotions of the informant.

Few interviewers have the skill and memory capabilities to recall everything said during the interview. For this reason, the interviewer should explain that notes will be made or the session will be tape recorded to preserve the accuracy of the shared information. This explanation can reduce anxiety that may be caused by note taking or tape recording. It also allows the informant the opportunity to request note taking rather than tape recording.

A second method of gathering data on adaptive behavior is through the use of questionnaires or checklists. One advantage of using these procedures is the efficiency with which information can be obtained. Very little time is required from the assessment team member who merely explains to the informant the purpose of the instrument and how to fill it out. Preparation time is still required, however, as the team member needs to select a questionnaire that is appropriate for the age of the student and that covers a sufficient number of skill areas. One disadvantage of questionnaires and checklists is that they require that the informant have reading skills beyond the functional level. This can be a problem for parents who lack basic literacy skills. This problem may be circumvented if the questionnaire or checklist is completed during an interview. Another issue to consider is how well the informant being asked to complete a checklist or questionnaire knows the student. Manuals that accompany these tools specify how long the informant should have known the student for the results to be valid. If questionnaires or checklists are the primary data base on a student's adaptive behavior, then they should be obtained from several informants so information can be compared across people and environments. Adaptive behavior measures that use a checklist or questionnaire format include the Normative Adaptive Behavior Checklist (Adams, 1984b), the AAMR Adaptive Behavior Scales–School, second edition (Nihira, Lambert, and Leland, 1993), the Adaptive Behavior Inventory (Brown and Leigh, 1986), the Vineland Adaptive Behavior Scales, classroom edition (Sparrow, Balla, and Cicchetti, 1984), and the Weller–Strawser Scales of Adaptive Behavior for the Learning Disabled (Weller and Strawser, 1981).

Some adaptive behavior instruments use a combination of observation and direct measure to assess adaptive behavior. Examiners who use such instruments present tasks to the student to perform much as they would if administering an intelligence test. The examiner may also set up the natural environment so the student is required to perform some task and then observe how successful the child is. This type of format is often used with young children on criterion-referenced measures of self-help skills such as the Early Learning Accomplishment Profile (Glover, Preminger and Sanford, 1978), the Adaptive Performance Instrument (CAPE, 1980), and the Battelle Development Inventory (Newborg, Stock, Wnek, Guidubaldi, and Svinicki, 1984). Observation/direct measure instruments appropriate for children beyond 5 years of age include the Children's Adaptive Behavior Scale (Richmond and Kicklighter, 1980), and the Comprehensive Test of Adaptive Behavior (Adams, 1984a).

Selecting a Standardized Measure

The examiner selecting a standardized measure of adaptive behavior must consider several variables. One variable is the age of the individual being assessed. Many developmental inventories exist that are appropriate for assessing the self-help skills of young children with suspected disabilities. However, these inventories are not appropriate for assessing self-help skills of older, severely involved students.

Another important variable in selecting adaptive behavior assessment tools is the setting in which the individual is seen most frequently. Some instruments, such as the Balthazar Scales of Adaptive Behavior (Balthazar, 1976), are designed for individuals with severe disabilities in residential settings. Other instruments, such as the AAMR Adaptive Behavior Scales—School, second edition (Nihira, Lambert, and Leland, 1993) and the Vineland Adaptive Behavior Scales, classroom edition (Sparrow, Balla, and Cicchetti, 1984), are specifically designed for use in school settings. Many instruments with an interview format are not setting-specific.

The technical adequacy of the instrument should also be reviewed carefully before selecting an adaptive behavior instrument. Examiners should consider the characteristics of the standardization population and the validity and reliability of any instrument they select. Some adaptive behavior instruments have limited technical adequacy and should only be used for screening purposes. Examples of such measures include the Cain–Levine Social Competency Scale (Cain, Levine, and Elzey, 1977), the Camelot Behavioral Checklist (Foster, 1974), the Normative Adaptive Behavior Checklist (Adams, 1984b), and the TARC Assessment System (Sailor and Mix, 1975).

The assessment questions needing to be answered and the available resources for obtaining information are also important instrument selection issues. When adaptive behavior is assessed, it is important that the tool selected covers the subskill areas of particular interest for a specific individual. There is tremendous variability in the areas covered on different instruments. When resources are limited, the evaluation study team may decide to use a questionnaire format rather than a more time-consuming interview format. The type of format used may be determined by the availability of the student's primary caregiver. Some instruments may not be used if school personnel have extreme difficulty contacting a particular student's parents/caregivers.

Examiners charged with the task of selecting appropriate tools for assessing adaptive behavior should review the manual and technical documentation accompanying the instrument. If critical information is not contained in the instrument's manual, this should be considered a weakness of the instrument. Table 8-2 lists adaptive behavior instruments.

Ecological Inventories

Examination of the student's records and the use of standardized adaptive behavior assessment instruments are two important sources of information invaluable in

Table 8-2 Measures of adaptive behavior

Name (Author)	Ages	Type of Measure	Publisher
AAMR Adaptive Behavior Scale, Residential and Community, second edition, (Nihira, Leland, and Lambert, 1993)	3 to 69	I, Q	PRO-ED
AAMR Adaptive Behavior Scales, School, second edition (Nihira, Lambert, and Leland, 1993)	3–3 to 17.2	I, Q	PRO-ED
Adaptive Behavior Inventory (Brown and Leigh, 1986)	5 to 18–11	Q	PRO-ED
Adaptive Behavior Inventory For Children (Mercer and Lewis, 1977)	5 to 11	I	Psychological Corporation
Adaptive Performance Instrument (CAPE, 1980)		O, DM, I	University of Idaho
Balthazar Scales of Adaptive Behavior (Balthazar, 1976)	5 to 57	O	Consulting Psychologist Press
Cain–Levine Social Competency Scale (Cain, Levine, and Elzey, 1977)	5 to 13	I	Consulting Psychologist Press
Callier–Azusa Scale (Stillman, 1978)	Birth–5	O	University of Texas
Camelot Behavioral Checklist (Foster, 1974)	2–Adult	C	Edmark
Children's Adaptive Behavior Scale (Richmond and Kicklighter, 1980)	5 to 10	DM	Humanics
Comprehensive Test of Adaptive Behavior (Adams, 1984a)	Birth–60	DM, Q	Merrill
Normative Adaptive Behavior Checklist (Adams, 1984b)	Birth–21	C	Merrill
The Pyramid Scales (Cone, 1984)	Birth–78	I, O	PRO-ED
Scales of Independent Behavior (Bruininks, Woodcock, Weatherman, and Hill, 1984)	Infants–40+	I	DLM Teaching Resource
TARC Assessment System (Sailor and Mix, 1975)	3 to 16	C, O	H & H Enterprises
Vineland Adaptive Behavior Scales, Interview Edition (Sparrow, Balla, and Cicchetti, 1984)	Birth to 18–11	I	American Guidance Service
Vineland Adaptive Behavior Scales, Classroom Edition (Sparrow, Balla, and Cicchetti, 1984)	3 to 12–11	Q	American Guidance Service
Weller–Strawser Scales of Adaptive Behavior for the Learning Disabled (Weller and Strawser, 1981)	6 to 8	Q	Academic Therapy Publications

I = Interview
O = Observation
Q = Questionnaire
DM = Direct Measure or Testing
C = Checklist

determining a student's eligibility for special education services. However, these approaches to gathering data do not provide the information needed to plan a functional curriculum for a specific student. Ecological inventories are very helpful sources of information for curriculum planning.

Ecological inventories use interview, survey, and observation procedures to iden-

A special education teacher tries to determine what skill these students have in using public transportation.   *Source:* © Diana Mara Henry, Carmel, CA.

tify environments and skills important for a particular student. The child study team tries to identify particular environments a specific student is currently in and future environments the student is moving toward. Primary environments for many students are the home, school, and the community. Subenvironments within each of these primary ones are identified for a specific individual. For example, home subenvironments might include the bedroom, the kitchen, and the living room. A community environment might be a vocational setting with subenvironments of the work station, the restroom, the cafeteria, and the break area.

Within each of the environments and subenvironments, the evaluation team must determine the skills and subskills the student has and needs to develop to become more self-sufficient. In making these decisions, standardized developmental assessments may provide a starting point, but they are not specific enough and do not help in identifying age-appropriate functional skills. For example, in assessing a 12-year-old student with severe multiple disabilities, a standardized developmental assessment may indicate that the student functions in the infancy range. It would not be appropriate to try to train skills in the normal developmental progression. Rather, the teacher needs to focus on how to use the skills the student has to function as independently and as age-appropriately as possible. Skill areas that should be considered include motor skills, communication skills, social skills, and domestic/community skills. The teacher should also determine whether the student exhibits behaviors that interfere with developing target skills.

Selecting the skills for instruction depends on the expectations of significant people in the various environments in which the student functions. Ecological inventories are used to obtain information on what those expectations are and what next steps toward self-sufficiency are most desired by caregivers or supervisors. By using ecological inventories, the teacher can select skills for instruction that match expectations by significant others in critical environments (Browder, 1991). The teacher can then structure skill development so the student has real opportunities in natural environments for using the skill. Figure 8-1 provides an example of an ecological inventory that uses a survey format to obtain information from a student's parents. In addition to surveying or interviewing significant people, the teacher may observe the student in critical environments, may observe nondisabled peers in target environments, or may interview or use a written survey with nondisabled peers to learn about age-appropriate, popular activities, interests, or clothes.

Steps in the Assessment Process

Determine the Purpose of the Assessment

The first step in the assessment process is to have a clear understanding of why a particular student is being evaluated. Oftentimes one major question is whether or not the student has a disabling condition. If there is a disabling condition, an equally important question is whether the condition has so severe an impact on academic performance that special education is required. Some students with disabilities have learned compensatory strategies that enable them to maintain a level of academic performance such that special education services are not considered necessary. Federal money allocated for special education services must be used for students with the most severe levels of each disabling condition. Only 12 percent of the school population can be served under PL 94–142. Therefore, state eligibility regulations are periodically revised so the 12 percent cap is maintained and so that the most severely involved students in each disability area are served. For this reason, a student found eligible for special education services after an initial evaluation may be found ineligible following a reevaluation three years later. When the focus of the evaluation is on eligibility for services, the evaluation team must gather standardized, norm-referenced data to document that the student has not developed intellectually, socially, behaviorally, or academically like nondisabled peers. The team begins the evaluation process by examining referral information and the student's records. This information helps the team form hypotheses about the reasons for the academic problems and helps in selection of appropriate norm-referenced tools.

Student's name: Dennis   Date: 9/3/85
Teacher: Ms. K   Parents or Caregiver: Ms. T

This survey was developed to assist the teacher in developing a comprehensive educational assessment. The information you provide can help make this assessment relevant to this student.

1. What are Dennis's favorite activities and leisure materials?

2. What other preferences has Dennis expressed (for example, preferred and nonpreferred food, clothing, temperature)?

3. Where does your family typically go, or where would your family like to go to, for each of these activities?
   Shopping:
   Clubs, Church:
   Medical appointments:
   Visit friends and relatives:
   Family recreation:
   Other:

   For each of the above, circle the places that your family frequently goes, stating the places that Dennis has frequently gone.

4. What skills were previously taught to Dennis that you would like to see maintained in his future instruction?

5. What changes need to be made in Dennis's educational program?

6. Who in the home provides most of Dennis's care? Who would be willing and have time to implement some instruction for Dennis at home that would be designed by the teacher? How much time would be realistic for his home instruction (for example, 30 minutes daily)?

7. Attached please find a survey of adaptive behavior. Please follow the instructions to indicate the skills that Dennis currently has.

8. Please feel free to make any general comments about Dennis's educational needs.

THANK YOU FOR YOUR TIME IN COMPLETING THIS SURVEY

FIGURE 8-1 Example of a form that can be sent to parents to solicit their input in developing the comprehensive educational plan. (In this example, an adaptive behavior scale has not yet been used, so the parent survey of the Comprehensive Test of Adaptive Behavior will be included with this form.) *Source*: From *Assessment of Individuals with Severe Handicaps*, by D. M. Browder, p. 32. Copyright © 1987 by Paul H. Brookes Publishing Company. Reprinted by permission.

Even when the main focus of the evaluation is on eligibility, the evaluation team should incorporate assessment tools that can help in program planning. Therefore, criterion-referenced tools and ecological inventories are extremely important components of the assessment battery. The team should strive for a balance of types of data across all hypothesized areas affected by the disability.

Develop Data Sheets to Record Assessment Results

This chapter has provided a description of the many components to consider in assessment of adaptive behavior. It is vital that information on adaptive behavior be gathered

Teacher: **Ms. P**   Student: **Ann**

Skill Areas	Previous records	Caregiver inventory	Other ecological inventory	Teacher-made checklists or adaptive behavior scales	Current testing and observations
Home Personal Maintenance	Eating skills Toilet-training	Drinking from glass Dressing Toilet-training		Using restroom alone Eating with spoon	Panting up/ down Eating finger foods
Housekeeping		Wiping table	Work center: discarding trash		Opening containers
Recreation/Socialization		Music	Adult peer: playing piano		Using radio, tape player
Other (e.g., travel, shop)	No awareness of danger	Eating in restaurant	7–11, Restaurant bus station: selecting choice grasping/ releasing	Pedestrian skills	Communicating basic needs Using wallet
Related Skills Communication		Need for help Conversing	Making choices Using I.D. card	Imitating social comments	Yes/no
Motor	Grasp/release Thumb–finger opposition	Walking faster	Walking to restroom Carrying bag	Opening doors	
Academics					
Social			Imitating social		
Interfering behavior	Decreasing swearing	Choking when eating		Inappropriate comments	

FIGURE 8-2 Illustration of skill selection process to plan a comprehensive assessment and curriculum chart   *Source:* From *Assessment of Individuals with Severe Handicaps*, by D. M. Browder pp. 31-32. Copyright © 1987 by Paul H. Brookes Publishing Company. Reprinted by permission.

from several people across a variety of environmental settings. Therefore, it is important to have a way to organize the data that will highlight the most critical areas for intervention. Figure 8-2 illustrates one data organization system that can be helpful.

Conduct an Integrated Assessment

Adaptive behavior requires communication, motor, and social skills. It requires the intellectual ability to develop these skills and to adjust the use of these skills to different environmental settings that have unique demands and expectations. Therefore, assess-

Critical Functions	School Classroom	School Lunchroom	Domestic Area	Communicative Center
Eating	Chew snack foods, finger feed appropriate foods	Chew meals	Chew meals, finger feed appropriate foods	
Toileting	Answer "yes" or "no" to "Do you need to go to the bathroom?"	Answer "yes" or "no" to "Do you need to go to the bathroom?"	Answer "yes" or "no" to "Do you need to go to the bathroom?"	Answer "yes" or "no" to "Do you need to go to the bathroom?"
Expressive Communication	Request snack Greet teacher and fellow students	Request mild	Request toy Greet visitors	Greet people in appropriate situations
Receptive Communication	Follow one-step commands Point to specified toy			
Hygiene/Appearance		Open mouth when teeth are brushed and hold toothbrush	Extend arms and legs during dressing	
Recreation/Leisure	Toy play 5 minutes		Play 5 minutes social interaction with parents	Float in swimming pool
Social Interactions	Initiate social interaction with teacher		Initiate social interaction with parents	
Gross Motor	Extend arms to front, left, and right during protective extension exercises			

FIGURE 8-3 Priority matrix environmental domains   *Source:* From *An Introduction to Special Education,* 2/e by William H. Berdine and A. Edward Blackhurst. Copyright © 1985 by William H. Berdine and A. Edward Blackhurst. Reprinted by permission of HarperCollins Publishers.

ment of adaptive behavior requires that the evaluation team gather standardized data and ecological data across significant people and settings. The team must organize the data to highlight the patterns of skills that have been developed as well as the skills that are most critically needed for success in current environments. The team must understand how the different domains of adaptive behavior overlap and be able to conduct an assessment that explores the interrelationships of the domains.

Develop Annual Goals and Instructional Objectives

Once the data have been gathered and organized, decisions must be made about what skills to teach first. Typically, those skills required across several environments should receive the primary focus of training. A *priority matrix* can help identify those skills from the available assessment data (Sailor and Guess, 1983). Various functional behaviors are listed on one dimension of the matrix, with the student's environments listed on the other dimension. Figure 8-3 is a sample priority matrix

DOMAIN: Domestic	ENVIRONMENTS:	Current: Medical residence Grandmother's home Future: Group home
Subenvironments Bedroom	*Priority Activities* Participating in dressing	*Priority Skills for IEP* 1. Communicate choice 2. Move arms to help put shirt on
	Ringing buzzer for help	1. Activate switch 2. Respond to yes/no questions
Bathroom	Participating in bathing	1. Move arms on command 2. Maintain head control 3. Participate in face washing
	Participating in personal hygiene	1. Communicate need to be changed
Dining room	Eating	1. Communicate choice 2. Indicate when full 3. Drink from a straw
	Socializing	1. Eat in presence of people and noise 2. Communicate greetings 3. Wait turn to be fed without crying

DOMAIN: Recreation	ENVIRONMENTS:	Current: Medical residence Grandmother's home Future: YM/YWCA Events at theater or college
Subenvironments Living room	*Priority Activities* Listening to tapes	*Priority Skills for IEP* 1. Select tape 2. Activate switch to turn tape player on/off 3. Ring buzzer to help to change tape
Library/living room	Listening to stories read from books	1. Select book 2. Respond to yes/no questions about book
Outdoors	Swinging in wheelchair swing	1. Indicate desire to swing and to stop 2. Maintain head control on swing
	Taking walks in wheelchair	1. Maintain head control 2. Tolerate chair for longer periods of time 3. Respond to yes/no questions about outdoors
Pool	Swimming	1. Indicate desire to get in/out of pool 2. Tolerate water 3. Move arms independently
Theater/bleachers	Observing events	1. Maintain head control 2. Indicate needs (e.g., thirst, hunger, personal hygiene) 3. Respond to yes/no questions about the event

(continued)

FIGURE 8-4 Format for prioritizing goals and objectives for an IEP *Source:* From ''A New Curriculum for Tommy'' by D. M. Browder and D. K. Martin, *Teaching Exceptional Children,* Summer 1986, Volume 18, Pages 264 to 265. Copyright © 1986 by The Council for Exceptional Children. Reprinted with permission.

DOMAIN: Community	ENVIRONMENTS:	Current: Travel
		     Senior Citizens Home
		Future: Shopping Mall
		     Restaurant
		     Community
		     Physician's Office

Subenvironments Car or van	*Priority Activities* Traveling without one-to-one assistance	*Priority Skills for IEP* 1. Maintain head control 2. Tolerate chair 3. Maintain body alignment
Senior citizens lounge	Socializing	1. Give gifts 2. Use yes/no communication with strangers 3. Play cassette tapes for others
Stores	Buying clothes	1. Communicate choice 2. Maintain head control 3. Tolerate chair
Physician's office	Cooperating with examination	1. Use yes/no with doctor 2. Tolerate examination
Dining area of restaurant	Eating	1. Drink with straw 2. Eat in strange setting 3. Communicate choices
DOMAIN: Vocation	ENVIRONMENTS:	Current: Medical residence Future: Senior Citizens center or other residences as audiovisual assistant

Subenvironments
Lounge/living room
	Priority Activities
	Running audiovisual equipment that
	    has been setup
		Priority Skills for IEP
		1. Activate switch for on/off
		2. Ring buzzer when equipment malfunctions or movie
		    or tape is completed

FIGURE 8-4 (continued)

for a student with severe disabilities during middle childhood. Another format for listing priority activities and skills is shown in Figure 8-4. This format provides more detail regarding subenvironments and very specific skills that should be included in the IEP. This sample was developed for a 12-year-old boy with severe motor, communication, and health problems. Using organizational systems like those depicted in Figures 8-2, 8-3, and 8-4 helps the assessment team focus on the interrelationships within the domains of adaptive behavior, conduct an integrated assessment, and plan goals and objectives for the student's IEP that are functional and age-appropriate for various critical environments.

Summary

Definition of the Area

1. Adaptive behavior encompasses the many skills required for independent functioning within specific environments as socially prescribed for a given life stage.
2. Most definitions of adaptive behavior include components of independent functioning and social responsibility.

3. Other terms related to the concept of adaptive behavior include social competence, social maturity, adaptive capacity, and adaptive fitting.

Complexity of Adaptive Behavior

1. Assessing adaptive behavior serves two functions: identification and placement, and planning educational programs.
2. Three models are used in developing adaptive behavior tools: the developmental milestones model, the developmental theory-based model, and the functional model.
3. The developmental milestones model is based on the perspective that as children grow certain skills and abilities emerge in an orderly, stepwise fashion.
4. Developmental theory-based models are predicated on the assumption that researchers have accurately described the sequence of stages that culminates in a higher order ability or skill.
5. Functional models focus on age-appropriate expectations for functioning as independently as possible in specific environments.
6. It is important to consider the nature of environmental demands when assessing adaptive behavior.
7. When planning an assessment of adaptive behavior, positive adaptation skills as well as maladaptive behaviors should be examined.
8. During the preschool years, the emphasis in adaptive behavior tends to be in the areas of motor skills, communication, self-care, and emerging socialization.
9. During the elementary school years, adaptive behavior demands tend to be in areas of communication, academic competence, and socialization.
10. During the high school years, consumer, vocational, and mobility skills become the main focus.
11. Assessment of adaptive behavior is required for a diagnosis of mental retardation, but the impact of other disabilities on adaptive behavior should also be assessed.

Types of Assessment Tools

1. Standardized assessments of adaptive behavior are available in interview, questionnaire/checklist, and observation/direct measure formats.
2. Evaluators must consider the characteristics of the standardization population, the validity, the reliability, and the subskill areas included on any adaptive behavior instrument selected for use with a particular student.
3. Teacher developed ecological inventories use interview, survey, and observation procedures to identify specific environments and skills important for a particular student.

Steps in the Assessment Process

1. Determine the purpose of the assessment.
2. Develop data sheets to record assessment results.
3. Conduct an integrated assessment.
4. Develop annual goals and instructional objectives.

Assessing Oral Language

Key Terms

Articulation
Auditory discrimination
Bilingualism
Dialect
Discourse
Discrimination

Expressive language
Functionalist approach to language
Morphology
Nonverbal language

Oral language sample
Phonology
Pragmatics
Receptive language
Sociolinguistics

"I wish someone had realized and helped me understand that the basis of my learning difficulties lay in the fact that I use a different language system than most people. I wish someone had taken the time to help me understand my system and how it differed from the one most people use. I wish someone would have worked with me to find my language strengths rather than trying to change my system to theirs."

C. Lee and R. Jackson, 1992

Oral communication is the activity of dialogue that involves the interaction of perceptions, ideas, and feelings. Encompassed under the rubric of oral communication are the processes governing speech and language. The verbal means of expressing ideas and feelings is termed speech. Language, however, refers to the rules governing the representation of ideas through symbols. These symbols can be words or pictures or gestures. Parents, classroom teachers, special educators, psychologists, and speech pathologists are all involved on a daily basis with analyzing and coding oral communication competency. Oral language performance is influenced by a student's physical environment as well as by the people in that environment. Some children express themselves more fluently at home, where they feel more comfortable and protected. If home life is dysfunctional, however, children may feel more at ease and become more fluent in the school setting. The special educator assessing a student's oral communication should collect observations of the student's language proficiency across settings and between significant others (that is, parent, teacher, peer).

Speech and language development are the result of an individual interacting with his or her milieu. The ability to communicate is a process that begins at birth. The importance of the role of context on the developing communicator cannot be overestimated. In recent years, language specialists have focused on the interactions of adult/child and child/child across contexts. Such a focus on interactions in specific contexts is called a *sociolinguistic* approach, suggesting that oral communication requires both linguistic (speech and language) and social abilities. The assessment of oral communication requires observations of language users in a variety of contexts implementing a myriad of sociolinguistic abilities. A major premise of this chapter is that language assessment is not the domain of any one profession. Specialists from different fields (that is, linguistics, psychology, education) are all needed to code oral communication behaviors. In addition, observations from parents, peers, and the individual language user are important in making assessment and programming decisions. Therefore, the special educator who interacts often with various individuals who play significant roles in a student's life (that is, parents, classroom teachers, peers) plays a vital role in collecting observations about a student's oral communication competence.

The assessment of oral communication depends on the special educator's willingness to arrange and change contexts (that is, classroom, playground, cafeteria) for the observation of oral speech and language behavior. In addition, evaluation of language competence requires integration of data collected from norm-referenced measures, oral language samples, and dynamic assessment measures. No single measure of oral language is appropriate for deciding a student's current oral language competence or predicting future performance.

Methods of Assessment

Primary Mode

Communication requires both verbal (words) and nonverbal (body language, gestures) symbols. A student's preference for words or gestures is influenced by that individual's developmental age, functional level, and disabilities. Young children use eye gaze, spatial proximity, gestures, physical manipulation, and vocalization to regulate interactions with significant others (Argyle and Ingham, 1972; Linder, 1989). The special educator should note the mode of communication a student is most comfortable using to express needs or ideas. A child with autism may use verbalization but little eye contact with people, while an individual who is physically impaired may depend on eye contact and verbalization to communicate. Students with language disorders rely heavily upon gestures to supplement attempts to use speech and language. During an assessment, the examiner should determine whether a student is using the most effective mode or all the modes of communication available to him or her. This determination is best met by using dynamic assessment measures, discussed later in this chapter. With advances in technology, many children who in the past were felt not to have an efficient means of expressing themselves can now express their needs and ideas through alternative modes of communication. Information about a student's most effective mode of communication should be determined during an assessment of language.

Nonverbal Communication

Communication requires the use of both verbal and nonverbal symbols. As Lyon (1975) noted, however, there is not always a clear dichotomy between verbal and nonverbal indices. To understand what someone says to us requires that we read the verbal and nonverbal cues, each elaborating the intent of the speaker. Therefore, no assessment of oral communication is complete without observing the individual's understanding and use of *nonverbal language*.

Nonverbal communication has been investigated by many researchers (Argyle, 1969; Argyle and Cook, 1976; Birdwhistle, 1952, 1970; Harper, Wren, and Matarzzo, 1978; Scheflin, 1967). These studies reveal that language users access a sophisticated network of communication skills that include kinetics (body language), facial expression, paralanguage (tone of voice, sighs, cries), proxemics (use of space), and chronemics (use of time). Each of these areas can operate independently or together with verbal communication. Table 9-1 lists areas of nonverbal communication along with possible messages these nonverbal behaviors relay to the listener. During an assessment of oral communication, the special educator must consider whether the

Table 9-1 Nonverbal communication

Name	Area	Message
Kinetics	Body Movement body hands legs head	Superior/Inferior Attitude Interest/Disinterest Tension/Ease Defensive Negative/Positive Acceptance Understanding
Facial Expressions	Face Eye Contact Mouth Tilt of Head Nodding	Positive/Negative Active/Passive Like/Dislike Listening/Speaking Turn-Taking
Paralanguage	Tone of Voice Sigh Cries Laughs	Feelings/Attitudes
Proxemics	Use of Space	Intimate Zone Personal Zone Social Zone Public Zone
Chronemics	Use of Time	Discount Person Value Person's Home

speaker's oral language matches his or her nonverbal language as well as whether the student appears to understand the meaning of nonverbal messages received from others during conversation. For instance, a student with difficulties coding nonverbal messages will not pick up the meaning during a conversation when the listener looks at his or her watch to indicate the discussion should stop soon. These students often do not understand the meaning behind disapproving looks unless the looks are accompanied by verbalization. Difficulty interpreting nonverbal messages can be caused by emotional or neurologically based cognitive deficits (Gregg, Jackson, Hoy, and Hynd, 1989; Myklebust, 1975; Rourke, 1985). These individuals usually demonstrate severe adaptive and vocational limitations, emotional instabilities, social inadequacies, and tendencies to panic during problem-solving tasks. They also tend to rely heavily on others for support (Gregg and Jackson, 1989). The special educator must compare observations of nonverbal behaviors to results gathered during assessment of cognitive functioning as well as to social–emotional and adaptive behavior functioning. Nonverbal behavior is directly influenced by a student's culture and background experiences. Therefore, the special educator must be sensitive to a student's age, socioeconomic, and cultural background.

Input/Output

The verbal language components (i.e., pragmatics, discourse, phonology, syntax, semantics) we will discuss next are vital for successful communication competency and must be evaluated in terms of input and output requirements on the part of the

Table 9-2 Input and output skills needed for oral communication

Category	Meaning	Difficulties Noted When Deficit
Expressive Skills	Production of oral language	Blending sounds together into syllables Producing specific sounds Producing words in correct order within sentences Producing complex sentences
Receptive Skills	Understanding oral language	Understanding meaning of age-appropriate words Understanding abstract words Understanding spoken messages Understanding story plots Understanding humor Understanding indirect requests
Organizational and Integrative Skills	Understanding and using oral communications in an integrative plan	Following directions Completing assignments Explaining events Learning new games Coordinating two activities simultaneously Integrating information across sense modalities (visual–auditory)
Combinatorial Skills	Combinations of breakdowns with receptive, expressive, and organizational skills	Mixtures of previous behaviors

language user (speaker) and the listener. For each component of verbal language, the special educator must investigate the expressive, receptive, organizational, and combinatorial skills required of the task and the speaker's mastery of those skills. Table 9-2 summarizes these input/output skill requirements relative to oral communication, describing possible behaviors that could be indicative of a breakdown in any one of these areas.

Expressive skills. Expressive skills allow language users to accurately produce the sounds, words, and meanings that represent the intent of their message and that are appropriate for the situation. A breakdown in the expression of content results in inappropriate or inadequate use of words and word relationships. Expressive deficiencies often include problems with oral language structures (phonology, morphology, or syntax). Behaviors noted frequently by classroom teachers that could be indicative of expressive language problems include the inability to blend sounds into syllables, difficulty producing some phonemes (misarticulated sounds), grammatical errors in speaking, or using sentences that have restricted length, complexity, or structure. The special educator should observe whether the test or task given to a student puts additional receptive or expressive demands on his or her oral language system. For instance, when an examiner asks "What is this?" or "Give me the name for this," expressive language skills are being evaluated. However, if the examiner says "Show me an apple" or "Point to the picture of the boy under the table," receptive rather than expressive language skills are being evaluated. Many students in special education classes demonstrate discrepancies between their proficiency with expressive and receptive language tasks. A child with word finding problems cannot recall the label for a word (such as "pen") but could tell the examiner that pen "Is the thing you use for story writing." The child understands the language concept but cannot recall the label. Conversely, some students can imitate words and language structures but do not understand their meanings or the multiple meanings across contexts; this problem is more receptive than expressive.

Receptive skills.   *Receptive language* skills refer to the oral comprehension of words, language structures, and discourse. At one time, language professionals felt that receptive language skills were a prerequisite for the use of (expressive) language skills. Recent research has showed that children can and do use words and structures that are beyond their comprehension by remembering and repeating words and phrases in an appropriate context. Leonard (1976) advocates that to receive credit for a language structure, a child should demonstrate the ability to use the structure across different situations.

Receptive language ability significantly correlates with an individual's cognitive development. Therefore, a child's ability to understand temporal words (before, after), relational words (more/less, same/different), locational words (behind, in front of), or prepositions related to self or others is dependent upon the child's conceptual understanding of these words. Behaviors a classroom teacher might observe that could be the result of receptive language disorders include the child not knowing the meaning of spoken words on grade or age level, not understanding abstract words, not understanding spoken messages, not understanding story plots, and confusing word types (number, color, quantity). In addition, these students often demonstrate problems comparing and contrasting ideas and events as well as using inferencing, indirect requests (for example, "*Someone* needs to clean his or her desk"), and understanding humor. When reading, these children often substitute words that do not make sense in the context of the story (for example, "The boy rode the garage").

Organizational skills.   Oral communication also requires the ability to plan and execute tasks directed toward a predetermined goal. Such a skill requires the use of both expressive and receptive language skills in an integrated plan. Some students with special needs demonstrate adequate expressive and receptive language skills when asked to use them in isolation; however, if required to use these skills in an integrated or organized manner, they demonstrate significant problems. Such children have extreme difficulty monitoring their own actions, focusing their attention, planning ahead, and completing directions. Difficulty arises with both initiating and maintaining the task requirements over time. Behaviors often noted by classroom teachers observing individuals with organizational or integration problems include difficulty following directions, completing assignments, explaining events, learning new games, executing/coordinating two simultaneous activities (reaching for a piece of paper while erasing), and integrating information from one sensory pathway to another (copying the directions off the blackboard while listening to the teacher). Many language tests require a student to integrate both receptive and expressive skills to complete tasks. The special educator must be careful to observe where the breakdown in language use actually occurs (that is, in receptive, expressive, or integrative tasks).

Combinatorial skills.   Some language users demonstrate breakdowns across receptive, expressive, and integrative processes. Wood (1982) labels this combinatorial skill use. The language system is a highly sophisticated and integrative network of skills, increasing the possibility that one or several types of cognitive processes are deficit among language users. Combinations of processing breakdowns are common, and the range of severity (mild to severe) of the deficit must be noted by the special educator.

Components of Oral Language

For many years, language was studied as if sound (phonology), meaning (semantics), and form (syntax and morphology) existed in isolation from the context (environment) of the language user. Recent research has shown the dramatic impact of context on the language user's application of meaning and structure, thereby illustrating that language cannot be assessed in isolation from the interaction of speaker and listener. The study of the effects of context on oral language is called pragmatics. It has been investigated and described by numerous researchers (Duchan, 1984; Lund and Duchan, 1988; Simon, 1985) in an attempt to develop alternative approaches and methods for analyzing oral language competence. According to a functionalist approach to oral language (Lund and Duchan, 1988), pragmatics is the catalyst for a student's choice of word meanings and structures; therefore, pragmatics maintains a vital role in understanding a student's expressive and receptive language proficiency (Bates and MacWhinney, 1979). Since we support a *functionalist approach* to understanding oral language competence, the first component of oral language we will discuss is pragmatics.

Pragmatics

Pragmatics is the study of the impact of different contexts on speaker/listener communication. Currently, two perspectives govern research in the area of pragmatics. The formalist perspective views pragmatics as one of five equal parts of the language system: semantics, syntax, morphology, phonology, and pragmatics. The functionalist perspective considers that pragmatics is the overall organizing principle of language (Owens, 1984). As such, pragmatics governs the word choice and the structures used to communicate effectively. Oral communication governed by pragmatics suggests that intent (purpose) and context (environment) be viewed as an interactive process. Pragmatic skills first involve the intent a speaker wants an event to accomplish, then the specific event in which the intent is embedded, and finally, how communication is altered to accommodate the status of the listener.

To understand language from a pragmatics perspective, it is imperative to understand the sequence of events defining the significant interest in pragmatics. During the 1970s, pragmatics was viewed from the speech act approach, which looked at children's language from the aspect of communicative intents (purposes). The 1980s brought more of a concern for the way children and adults cooperated in conversation, the interactional approach. Also during the 1980s, the event focus approach surfaced, which viewed language from its event context (Lund and Duchan, 1988). The special educator investigating the oral language of students should consider all these perspectives—that is, the intent (purpose), interaction, and context (environment) of the language setting being observed. Therefore, to better understand the oral language competence of a student, the special educator should consider all three aspects of pragmatics: the student's understanding of the language activity, the student's intent of the language activity, and the adjustment strategies demonstrated during the activity.

Understanding language activity.   The special educator needs to first determine how the student is making sense (Lund and Duchan, 1988) of the ongoing language activity. In other words, the student's perceptions of the event are investigated to determine what is going on for the student that makes the observed behaviors understandable. Asking a child, "What is going on here?" can help the adult observer understand whether the child felt it was a game, an examination, or a lesson. An adult (teacher) may view a language activity as a "lesson" whereas the child might view it as a "game." How the individual makes sense of the language activity can influence the vocabulary or language structures used to convey ideas in that context.

A student makes sense of a language activity based on his or her understanding of person(s) and event(s). Schank and Abelson (1977) were the first to propose that individuals possess mental images of events that organize experience; they called these images "scripts." Examples of scripts children use include meal time, getting ready for school, or going to bed. Researchers (Nelson, 1985; Schank and Abelson, 1977) agree that even infants recognize and become upset if a script routine is not followed. Many students in special education follow scripts in a very rigid, inflexible manner. These individuals have difficulty handling even the slightest change to their perceptions of the sequence in which events should occur. Understanding a student's knowledge of a script for a particular event usually requires asking that student to report on the event as well as gathering information from others who observe the student on a daily basis and know the student's experience with certain activities.

A student's success during a language activity is also based on his/her perceptions of the persons the student is talking to during the language activity. This requires the student to understand how much knowledge about a topic the listener has, what language structures are appropriate, the social status of the listener, and whether the listener shares the same environment as the student. All these features require that a student be able to see things from another's viewpoint (perspective). During conversation, a speaker must take the perspective of the listener to adjust vocabulary or syntax choice as well as to evaluate the amount of information needed. To draw conclusions about pragmatics competency, the special educator should compare evaluation results from the cognitive and the social–emotional functioning of the student.

Intent of the activity. Oral communication is carried out by adults and children for a purpose or with a specific intent in mind. The intent of conversation is one of the three components of a communicative act (Searle, 1969). The choice of words and syntax helps determine the intent of a conversation. Many times a speaker's intent is misinterpreted by a listener. For instance, a student with specific types of language disorders who does not understand sarcasm can easily misunderstand the classroom teacher's intent during a discussion in which sarcasm is used.

Adjustment of language during an activity. The third aspect of pragmatics that the special educator should observe relates to the speaker's and listener's abilities to adjust their language for each other. For the speaker, this includes the person's understanding and use of conversational rules (for example, turn-taking, topic introduction and maintenance, and conversational repair).

The special educator must also observe the type of language (words and structures) used with the individual being observed. Research studies have shown that the language spoken to young children is different from that being spoken to older students and adults (Broen, 1972; Drach, 1969; Ferguson, 1978; Newport, 1977; Snow, 1972). Language spoken to young children has been called motherese. Motherese does not mean, however, that only mothers adjust their language structures. Fathers (Rondal, 1980), other adults (Snow, 1972), and older children (Sachs and Devin, 1976) appear to adjust their language for younger children as well. Table 9-3 lists some of the characteristics of motherese. However, cross-cultural research (Brice–Heath, 1983) has indicated that many of the features of motherese are culturally specific. Cultural differences will be discussed later in this chapter.

The important thing for the special educator to observe is whether the speaker and the listener are adjusting their language patterns for each other during a conversation. An assessment of the phonology, prosody (versification), syntax, vocabulary, and discourse strategies should be recorded across different settings. A classroom teacher might be using syntactic structures that are too complex for a student with special needs. If the classroom teacher modified her own language structures, the student might better understand the content being discussed in the classroom setting. In addition, the special educator should observe the student's adjustment of language for the listener. A student in special education might not be adjusting his or her vocabulary, syntax, and intonation when speaking to authority figures (the principal). If a student uses the same vocabulary and syntax with the principal that he or she uses with peers, the lack of adjusting verbal and nonverbal language could be interpreted as an "attitude" or "behavior" problem.

Discourse

Discourse refers to aspects of language that are a function of talking. Discourse requires using all the components of language (phonology, syntax, semantics, prag-

Table 9-3 Features of motherese with young children of middle-class families

Component of Language	Features
Discourse	Self-repetition Repetition of child's language
Phonology	Very clear enunciation Reduplication (go bye-bye)
Prosody	High pitch Exaggerated conversation Slow rate of speech Long pauses between sentences
Syntax	Short, choppy sentences Telegraphic speech Frequent questions
Semantics	Restricted vocabulary Concrete nouns Vocabulary present in child's language

Source: Gleason, 1975; Rondal, 1980; Sachs & Devin, 1976; Snow, 1972.

matics) together to communicate ideas. Students are involved in several types of discourse structures (Lund and Duchan, 1988) during the course of a school day. These include stories, conversations, and school discourse or lessons. With each discourse structure, it is the speaker's responsibility to engage in referencing, attending, and perspective-taking activities that will lead to an effective exchange of information. As Lund and Duchan (1988) point out, communication is an interactive process and, to complete the exchange efficiently, the listener's inferencing skills must also be accessed and employed efficiently.

Stories. Stories differ from conversational discourse structures in several ways. Stories require elaborated or extended units of text, introductory and closing statements, and an orderly presentation of events leading to a logical conclusion. As the one responsible for the continuity and completeness of information, the speaker is expected to maintain an oral monologue that is organized, coherent, and interesting. In their research on narration (story telling), Roth and Spekman (1986) found that children demonstrating a specific learning disability usually have an intact knowledge of story structure, but they generally mismanage the episodic structures. Since the episode is considered to be the basic building block of the story, analysis at this level provides more meaningful information. They also suggest that the problem these children have with narratives often centers around perspective-taking and reflects problems with the use of clear referents and cohesive ties.

By the age of 5, children should be able to tell entertaining stories that contain the components necessary for story grammars (Applebee, 1978; Botvin and Sutton–Smith, 1977; Westby, 1984). Such story grammars include (1) an introduction, including a setting; (2) development of a problem to be solved; (3) a description of a goal and a solution; and (4) construction of an ending. By around 6 years of age, the student should be able to identify with the characters in the story. This can be observed by noting statements made by the student about the characters' thoughts and feelings (Botvin and Sutton–Smith, 1977). However, it is not until age 11 that students' narratives contain multiple episodes or embedded episodes.

Conversation.   Conversations differ from stories in that they do not follow a story grammar or structure and are not employed simply for entertainment. (Many of the features of conversation—topic introduction, turn-taking, topic mainte-nance—were discussed in the previous section under pragmatics.) Wiig (1990) views many students' difficulties with conversation as the result of strategic language competencies. She suggests that many of these students have adequate conversa-tional skills but have difficulty using or accessing the sophisticated strategies neces-sary for effective communication. These students use less sophisticated techniques to maintain conversations with peers.

Lesson or school discourse.   School discourse refers to the rules of discourse that govern how teachers and children communicate in a variety of school contexts. Discourse strategies apply to school discourse just as to any discourse form. Each school discourse context has its own set of discourse requirements. While some of the rules are similar from setting to setting, others differ significantly. For example, children's informal interaction with peers and teachers on the playground is vastly different from the more formal interaction of the classroom (Ripich and Spenelli, 1985). Discourse rules vary within settings depending on whether the interaction is small- or large-group based. Teacher directed or student directed activities present other sets of discourse rules. The special educator should evaluate a special educa-tion student across different types of school contexts (playground, lessons, teacher directed activities) to observe the student's pragmatic skills (understanding, intent, adjustment) with different types of school discourse. During such observations, the student's nonverbal behaviors, choice of vocabulary, syntactic structures, and orga-nizational skills should be noted. Table 9-4 is a checklist for observing a student's use of oral language across contexts (environments).

Phonology

The study of the sound system of language is called *phonology*. In recent years, there has been a recognition that phonological development is dependent upon many of the same cognitive processes (for example, rule generalization) as syntax, semantics, or pragmatics. Traditionally, assessment of phonological disorders was left completely to the speech pathologist, who often tested and provided therapy in isolation from other academic or social contexts. However, special educators have now realized the significant impact phonological errors have on reading and written language development. Therefore, the special educator should observe and code phonological behaviors of students.

This section describes the characteristics of phonological receptive problems (auditory discrimination deficits) and types of phonological expressive problems (articulation). Articulation problems are often among the first signs detected by parents and professionals. In Box 9-1, Lee and Jackson (1992) describe the percep-tions many students with such problems feel.

Table 9-4 Informal oral language checklist

Name of Student: _____

Age: _____

Grade: _____

	Context									
		Informal							Formal	
Oral Language Behaviors Observed Across Context	With peers	With teachers	With family	With other adults in school	Role-playing activities	In large class activities	In small group activities	One-to-one activities with teachers	Oral reports with other adults
Does the student speak too low?									
Does the student speak too softly?									
Does the student willingly participate orally?									
Does the student demonstrate more expressive language problems?									
Does the student demonstrate more receptive language problems?									
Does the student demonstrate more organizational problems?									
Does the student attend to others?									
Does the student's nonverbal behavior match his/her oral communication?									
Does the student appear to understand nonverbal cues?									
Does the student respond relevantly to the topic?									
Does the student appear responsive to others?									
Does the student use nonstructural forms?									
Does the student adjust word choice and grammar intervention for appropriateness to the audience?									
Does the student demonstrate the components of story grammar when telling stories?									
begin with a setting?									
build a problem to be solved?									
describe a goal and solution?									
construct an ending?									
Does the student appear to demonstrate deficits in any specific component of language use?									
pragmatics									
phonology (sounds)									
semantics (meaning)									
syntax (word order)									

Box 9-1   *Remembering Speech Problems*

''Basically my speech disability was the first sign that something deeper was wrong; however, it was many years before another diagnosis was made. I had not made much progress in language development by the time I reached school, but the school had the answer. They suggested I had a simple articulation problem that could easily be fixed by a speech teacher. I was placed in speech classes almost immediately, the first of many times that I would be separated from my friends to attend a ''special'' class. When I think back on it, it would have been nice if all I had had was a simple speech problem that could have been cured with a few hours of speech lessons each week.''

Source: From C. Lee and R. Jackson, *Faking It: A Look into the Mind of a Creative Learner* (Portsmouth, NH: Boynton/Cook, 1992), pp. 59–60.

Auditory discrimination.   Auditory perception or, more accurately, speech sound discrimination requires the ability to discriminate individual sounds. Such a skill is certainly needed in oral language to hear the differences between words as children attach meaning to words. In addition, it is a necessary skill for development of phonetic skills needed for reading and later for success in spelling. Speech sound *discrimination* is a receptive language process.

The special educator assessing a student's perception of speech sounds must observe the individual's ability to discriminate words across a variety of contexts by varying both the nature of the input and the responses. Harris–Schmidt and Noell (1983) discuss eight factors that the clinician should consider when assessing auditory discrimination. We will discuss several of these factors in relation to the role of the special educator. All eight of the factors are listed in Table 9-5.

First, Harris–Schmidt and Noell (1983) encourage examiners to evaluate the student's ability to discriminate both their own and someone else's speech. Most evaluation tools, however, only test the individual's ability to discriminate someone else's speech and not his or her own misarticulated sounds. In addition, Harris–Schmidt and Noell (1983) stress the need for the clinician to consider the student's familiarity with the words given, the length of the words (single syllable or multisyllable), and whether the words are given in or out of context (sentences). Many older

Table 9-5 Systematic analysis of speech sound discrimination

Phonemic vs. Phonetic Discriminations
Others' Speech vs. Self-Speech
Pictures vs. No Pictures
Familiar Words vs. Unfamiliar Words
Meaningful Words vs. Nonsense Words
Single Syllable Words vs. Multisyllable Words
Single Words vs. Words in Context
Linguistic vs. Metalinguistic

Source: Harris–Schmidt and Noell, 1983, p. 59. From *Language Learning Disabilities,* by C. Wren (ed.). Copyright © 1983 by PRO-ED, Inc. Reprinted by permission.

special education students can discriminate single syllable words but cannot discriminate multisyllabic words (for example, conversation/conservation). In addition, some students can discriminate words out of context but when given in context (sentences or discourse) cannot discriminate sound differences. When students hear words inaccurately, they have difficulty attaching meaning to the words and in understanding directions or discourse used with them. Another very important factor that Harris–Schmidt and Noell (1983) point out is to note whether the stimulus given to the student to discriminate between words is given only orally (Are "big" and "pig" the same in sound?) or whether a visual stimulus (picture) accompanies the oral command. Some children who have a history of otitis media (inflammation of the ear) do better when a visual cue (picture) is used together with an oral command.

Phonemic production (articulation).   *Articulation* disorders are often first noted by a trained observer of language such as the special educator. The special educator who identifies a student with possible articulation disorders should refer the student to the speech pathologist for further testing. Currently, two systematic schemas exist for assessment of phonemic articulation disorders. One system, developed by Chomsky and Halle (1968), proposes a system of distinctive features. The more traditional analysis of speech articulation focuses on isolated sounds and types of errors: omission, substitution, distortion, and addition. The most common phonological errors demonstrated by children have been described in depth by Ingram (1976). These errors include (1) deletion errors, (2) assimilation errors, and (3) substitution errors. Again, the special educator observing a student's articulation errors must be sure to do so across contexts. Culture and dialectical variability must also be factored into the special educator's observations.

In addition to observing a student's development of phonological rule knowledge, the special educator should also observe the student's use of phonological strategies. Lund and Duchan (1988) discuss several general phonological strategies normally achieving children use during their development of language skills. These strategies include ignoring words with unattainable phonological structures (Ferguson and Farwell, 1975), using sounds or words with favorite sounds (Ferguson, 1978), modifying an adult form to fit a limited phonology, selecting single sounds as the target around which to organize phonology, and concentrating on learning forms or sound combinations (Peters, 1983). In Box 9-2, Lee and Jackson (1992) clearly describe a strategy (visual imagery) some students with language disorders use to help them recall sounds or words.

Syntax and Morphology

Syntax.   Syntax refers to the linguistic rules for combining words to make sentences, in other words, the order words must be in to make correct sentences. The special educator assessing the oral language of students will soon recognize the large number of special education students demonstrating significant syntactic disorders (for example, hearing impaired, learning disabled). Wiig and Semel (1975) estimate that "between 75 percent and 85 percent of youngsters with learning

---

Box 9-2   *Seeing Sounds*

"The way I hear (see) sounds is similar to the difference between reading and writing printed and cursive letters. When sounds are spoken clearly and crisply in a straightforward manner, I picture them in my mind as being printed letter combinations. When people speak rapidly or in different tones of voice, the sounds come into my mind written in cursive, making them difficult to distinguish."

Source: From C. Lee and R. Jackson, *Faking It: A Look into the Mind of a Creative Learner* (Portsmouth, NH: Boynton/Cook, 1992), p. 61.

---

disabilities may experience significant delays in the acquisition of language" (p. 578). The impact of oral syntax problems on a student's academic and social development cannot be overestimated. Oral syntax problems affect a student's listening comprehension, reading, written language, and social skill success.

It is not certain how children learn such a complex body of rules governing word order. Research suggests that meaning has a significant impact on syntactical development (Bloom, 1970; Bloom and Lahey, 1978; Bowerman, 1976). From language modeled by significant others in their environment, children abstract categories of meaning from words with similar functions in the sentence structure. Oral syntax, however, does not develop receptively and expressively at the same time. Students must comprehend a syntactic structure before they can use it consistently. For example, a child will be able to answer the question "Is that a dog?" before he or she can formulate the question structure.

Syntax, combining words into larger units, involves combining ideas with distinctive syntactic structures. Noun phrases and clauses are the primary units that result from word combinations. A sentence is made up of one or more clauses, each of which includes a subject and a predicate. The subjects and predicates are composed of noun and verb phrases. Syntax development begins at the one-word stage, with the word acting like a complete sentence. *Holophrase* is the term given to the idea of single words that express what adults say in a sentence. Around the age of 18 to 20 months, children begin to combine words and between the ages of 2 and 3 multiple clause utterances appear. By the age of 4, most children are using complex sentence structures and are able to deal with structured ambiguities.

Five basic sentence patterns (see Table 9-6) are the foundation from which all the different sentence types in the English language are developed. These sentence types are created through a process of applying various transformations (see Table 9-7) according to a set of transformational grammar rules (Chomsky, 1957).

The transformations create negative, passive, interrogative, and imperative sentences. The special educator should evaluate a student's ability to understand (receptive) as well as to produce (expressive) these different sentence structures. Some students can understand different syntactic structures but cannot accurately produce them. Other students can accurately produce sentence structures but do not understand the meaning of them.

Table 9-6 Five basic sentence patterns for English

NP	+	VP	+	Advp
Boys		run		home

NP	+	V	+	Adj.
The boy		is		tall

NP	+	VP	+	NPz
Boys		play		games

NP	+	Vpe	+	NP2
The boy		is		my brother

NP	+	Vp	+	Adj./NP
The boy		became		ill

Common errors often indicative of syntax disorders that the special educator might observe in a student's oral language include omission, substitutions, and reversal of word order. Table 9-8 gives some examples of oral syntax errors. The clinician, however, must keep in mind the student's age, background, and dialect, as well as experience working with such a task format. In addition, the student should be observed across several contexts (classroom, playground, art class).

During an evaluation, the special educator must control the amount of structure different receptive and expressive syntax tasks require of the student. Some students can understand and produce syntax patterns if given a significant amount of structure but could not use these same patterns in spontaneous conversation. Table 9-9 illustrates language tasks with varying degrees of structure. Any assessment of syntax competence should include at least one task across these varying degrees of structure (sentence imitation, sentence production, and spontaneous language). Additional assessment formats typically used in the measurement of sentence formation include grammatical contrast tests, parallel sentence production tests, and comparison of meaning tests (see Table 9-10). Grammatical contrast tests contain sentence pairs presented in association with two or more picture choices. The student identifies the picture or pictures that best represent the meaning of the sentence. Parallel sentence production tests require the examiner to present a spoken sen-

Table 9-7 Sentence transformations

Active	*Passive*
The swing hit Susie.	Susie was hit by the swing.
Affirmative	*Negative*
The swing hit Susie.	The swing did not hit Susie.
Declarative	*Interrogative*
The swing hit Susie.	What hit Susie?
Simple	*Complex*
The swing hit Susie.	Susie was walking to the sandbox when she was hit by the swing.

Table 9-8 Selective types of syntactic errors

Behavior	Stimulus Sentence	Student's Error
Omission of Words and Phrases	John likes cars with shiny, bright hubcaps.	John likes cars. John likes cars with hubcaps.
Reversal of Word Order	Mary likes salt on her french fries.	Mary likes french fries on her salt.
Substitution of Related Words	Tom likes steak and potatoes with butter.	Tom likes steak and rice with butter.

tence that includes a target structure. The spoken sentence is accompanied by a picture. After the model sentence is presented, a second picture designed to elicit the same sentence structures is shown. Comparison of meaning tests require the student to recognize and match sentences with close proximity in meaning despite different surface/structural differences. The special educator should always include syntax tasks that measure both receptive and expressive syntax skills. If the special educator feels that the student demonstrates syntactic problems, further evaluation by the speech pathologist is recommended.

Morphology. Words are made up of one or more basic units of meaning called morphemes, and the rules for developing words from morphemes is called *morphology*. Morphological rules alter the meaning of words by changing number and case (boy/boys), verb tense (drop/dropped), and possession (mother/mother's). In addition, morphological rules change word classes such as verbs (teach-er), adjectives (dirt-y), adverbs (slow-ly), and diminutives (book-let). Morphological rules also extend the meaning of root words by adding prefixes (re-turn). Common errors indicative of morphological disorders that the special educator might observe in a student's oral language include omission of noun plurals; possessives; third person present tense endings; verb, adjective, and adverb endings; substitution of incorrect verb, adjective, and adverb endings; and the use of inappropriate or no prefixes.

Assessment of a student's morphological development requires the use of rule extension. A stimulus word is presented to observe whether the student can use the rules for its inflection correctly. Nonsense words are the purest way to evaluate inflectional and derivational rules. Unfortunately, the standardized communication tests available to evaluate morphological development usually measure the exten-

Table 9-9 Syntax tasks

Task	Requirement	Structure
Sentence Imitation	Student must repeat sentence that the examiner has said.	Most structured
Sentence Production	Student is given words to put together into a sentence.	
Spontaneous Language	Student's oral language is recorded during a conversation with another person.	Least structured

Table 9-10 Sentence formation assessment formats

Spontaneous Language Sample

Grammatical Contrasts

    A sentence or a sentence pair is presented in association with two or more picture choices. The student identifies the picture or pictures that best represent the meaning of the sentence.

Parallel Sentence Production

    The examiner presents a spoken sentence that includes a target structure. The spoken sentence is accompanied by a picture. After the model sentence is presented, a second picture is shown designed to elicit the same sentence structures.

Sentence Imitation

    The examiner reads selected sentence structures, and the student is asked to repeat the sentence.

Producing Formulated Sentences

    The student is given isolated words, and the student must put them together to make a sentence.

Comparison of Meaning

    The student must recognize and match sentences with close proximity in meaning despite different surface/structural differences.

sion of rules with real words. Sentence completion (cloze formats) are the most effective means by which to evaluate morphology. One item uses nonsense words and the other real word items. A student's word formation knowledge must always be evaluated against his or her dialectical background to evaluate whether the deviation is due to a language disorder or a language difference.

Semantics

Semantics is the study of the meaning of words and word relationships. In recent years, research studying word meaning has moved from a unidimensional perspective based on quantitative measures of evaluation (vocabulary counts) to a more qualitative means of investigating the broader aspects of word meaning. Cognitive prerequisites of vocabulary development and the semantic intentions (purposes) of children have become the major focus of researchers in the last few years. Psycholinguists agree that development of word meaning is linked to the development of concepts by mapping words onto the knowledge individuals already possess about their world.

    Brown (1958) was the first to discover that children are guided in the types of words they learn by the naming practices of adults. Later, Clark (1973) found that what a word means to a child is not necessarily what it means to an adult. She described the evolution of children's word meaning by the types of errors they demonstrated. Children first learn word meaning by attending to the functional features of the word (what the object does) (Nelson, 1973). Later, the perceptual features such as shape and size appear to have an impact on a child's development of word meanings. The choice of whether to attend to functional or to perceptual features is not consistent across all normally achieving children; individual personality styles influence preference. Some children begin learning more expressive types of words—that is, words concerned with self and other people. Other children begin

Table 9-11 Normal semantic development levels

10–15 Months Sloban, 1967; Smith, 1926	30–10 word vocabulary.

18–24 Months
Bowerman, 1979; Lenneberg, 1967; McCarthy,
  1954; Nelson, 1973; Sloban, 1967; Smith, 1941
	Over 50 words (usually 200–400 word
	  vocabulary). Combine words into
	  multi-utterances.

3–5 Years Lenneberg, 1967; McCarthy, 1954; Sloban, 1967; Smith, 1941	800–1,000 word vocabulary.
High School Graduate Carroll, 1964	60,000–80,000 word vocabulary.

by learning more referential words, requiring more of a concern with naming objects and people (Nelson, 1973). By around 4 or 5 years of age, children begin to develop word meanings by the use of relational concepts, wherein the meaning of a word can only be understood in relation to another concept. Examples of relational concepts include such linguistic functions as prepositions (in, on, above), grammatical categories (noun, verb), and pronouns. As children increase their experience with words, meanings change. Therefore, the semantic system is ever changing. Table 9-11 describes normal semantic developmental levels as a guide for the special educator planning assessment priorities.

Two important strategies children use to extend word meaning are called overextension and underextension. Overextension refers to the child's application of a word to a referent that according to adult language would be outside that semantic category. For instance, all men are called "Daddy." Underextension is when a child restricts a semantic category to only a subset of referents. For example, only the child's dog can be called "dog." Overextension and underextension strategies continue to be seen in older handicapped students. Such students have significant difficulty with adjectives such as "sweet" that can mean "something sweet to eat" or a "person is very sweet."

One recent concern under study is how this knowledge is stored in the memory structure. Rummelhart, Lindsay, and Norman (1972) describe semantic knowledge as a network of information. This organizational network controls how an individual retains, relates, and retrieves meaningful information. For some individuals, the breakdown is a receptive problem, not understanding the meaning of the word. Other individuals understand the meaning of the word but cannot retrieve the word label from the network, an expressive problem. These students know what a pen is but cannot recall the label "pen." Rather, they say, "You know, that thing you write with." Lee and Jackson (1992) provide an excellent description of the impact of word finding problems on an individual's daily life (see Box 9-3).

The special educator evaluating a student's semantic skills should measure both receptive and expressive semantic skills. Investigation of receptive semantic skills includes basic vocabulary, category structure, abstract language, word retrieval, and word relationships. Expressive semantic skills to assess include spontaneous lan-

Box 9-3   *Impact of Word Finding Problems*

"All people have trouble from time to time calling up the words they need. I often hear people joking about the 'tip of the tongue syndrome.' This is no joke to me. The disorganized filing cabinet in my brain causes me to lose entire thoughts and subjects while I am searching for one heading. It affects me not only when I am speaking, but also when I am listening. I often seem to get behind when listening to others because I misunderstand or don't know the meanings of key words. My vocabulary words are not stored in a manner that I can grasp immediately, so I am always having to search for meaning. Over the last few years I have learned that words are usually put together in a certain way so that there is a root that helps locate the heading it should be filed under. I never knew this before so I had no clue as to how to file a word away in my memory so that I could recall it later. I would learn a new word and hear it the next day and not know that I had *ever* heard it before. It is like having one shoe in a closet—eventually you throw it out because it's useless. I have learned now to tear new words apart to see where the word comes from, making them easier to store. The meanings are not always clear at first, but at least I am building a system where there was once only chaos.

"Sometimes I have trouble pulling up words because I am not sure of the way the sentence should be structured. This is called a syntax problem."

Source: From C. Lee and R. Jackson, *Faking It: A Look into the Mind of a Creative Learner* (Portsmouth, NH: Boynton/Cook, 1992), p. 71.

guage, definitions, and sequencing/organization skill measures. In addition, the clinician should explore how specific semantic problems could be interfering with other academic and social areas. When students demonstrate difficulty understanding the meaning of words they read, reading comprehension scores are low. Combinations of word meaning skills are necessary to express oneself in written language. In addition, many mathematical concepts are based on verbal concepts of size, shape, and quantity. The ability to understand these concepts may be impaired significantly by semantic deficits.

Developmental Progression

Foundation for Learning

The acquisition of language requires the development of linguistic competence, which includes unconscious knowledge of phonological, syntactic, and semantic rules, and communicative competence, which encompasses the knowledge that language is used differently across contexts (Genishi and Dyson, 1984). Sociolinguistics is the study of how linguistic forms are used in different communicative situations. Sociolinguists view language development as part of general social or interactional abilities. Age, cognitive development, experiential knowledge, and culture are all factors that affect an individual's linguistic and communicative competence. Research is beginning to stress the importance of language experience as playing an even greater role in language acquisition than does cognitive ability (Ortony, Turner, and Larson–Shapiro, 1985). Language, therefore, must always be evaluated in light of social context (school, play).

The contrast between early and later language competence is significant to the observer (see Table 9-12). The development of syntax, phonology, and semantic skills during the preschool years is fairly obvious to parents and teachers. However, the growth that occurs in older children and adolescents is more subtle and requires one to look beyond conversational context to discourse and pragmatic skills. For, as Nippold (1988) said, "it is the cumulative effect of many subtle changes that makes the 19-year-old talk and write differently than the 9-year-old" (p. 88). For instance, syntax complexity grows by one word per year from second to third grade, not a change that would be obvious to parents or teachers. The oral language of the elementary, middle, and high school student has not been investigated as thoroughly as preschool children's oral language since for some time a bias existed that the bulk of language is acquired by the age of four.

Investigation of the oral language of older children has broadened the exploration of language areas such as pragmatics and discourse. Recent research (Nippold, 1988) has shown that significant oral language growth occurs in the areas of discourse, pragmatics, figurative language, and linguistic ambiguity throughout the preadolescent and adolescent years. In addition, investigation of the language demonstrated by older children and adolescents has generated a more sophisticated understanding of the linguistic basis of classroom activities such as reading, writing, and mathematics, as well as social skill attainment (Wallach and Liebergott, 1984; Wolf and Dickinson, 1985). The older child's oral language development is aided by reading and written language activities. Certainly, language development does not end at the conclusion of preschool; rather, it is important to consider the impact of "language through the life-span" (Obler, 1985).

Preschool.   The major language goal of the preschool years is acquisition of oral communication skills. Spoken language is the major source of stimulation for the development of speech and language skills. Preschoolers learn their language primarily from hearing and using it in nondirected settings. Rather than teaching oral language to preschoolers, adults often simplify their language input (use motherese) and reinforce the child's attempts (Owens, 1988).

The preschool child develops phonological rules that govern sound discrimination and sequencing. Learning the sounds that can be put together, which sounds can be put in different parts of words, and which sounds should be stressed constitutes a large part of the preschool child's language learning (Ingram, 1976; Oller, 1974). The growth rate of the preschool child's syntactic skills is remarkable. Between 18 months and 3 years of age, children acquire basic sentence structure (subject clause and verb clause) and basic sentence forms (declaratives, imperatives, negatives, and questions). The use of compound sentences joined by a conjunction (I drank my milk and I ate my cookie) is noted between 2 and 2½ years of age. By 2 and 3 years of age, many preschoolers are using complex sentence structures (I ate

Table 9-12 Oral language developmental sequence

	Pragmatics	Discourse	Syntax	Semantics
Preschool	Self-oriented, nonadaptive listener	One- or two-word utterances	Brown's 14 morphemes acquired Acquired 5 basic sentence patterns Production > (pr. of sentence patterns)	Meaning tied to functional and concrete actions Speech is holophrasic Words declare, question, exclaim Attends to one attribute at a time
Elementary School	Beginning perception and awareness of listener needs Undifferentiated adaption to listener needs Adjusts language Awareness of listener's role Sustains topic	True narrative structure used	Syntax added by reading t-unit length—7.6 spoken (Loban, 1967) Spoken sentences contain subordinate clauses about 22%—one in every five (Nippold, 1988) Clauses of time (when) reason (because) and purpose (to) account for most of adverbial subordination and condition if existent (Scott, 1984) 2.6 rel. clauses per 100 t-units (O'Donnell, 1976)	Vocabulary level added by reading Word definitions tied to sentence context Difficulty conversing about events not visible Develop reversible thinking and is able to perceive more complex word relationships
Middle School	Differentiated adjustment to listener needs Provide greater contextual and background information	Multiple episodes Embedded episodes	Reversible and nonreversible passives Increased use of *would* and *could* (Scott, 1984) Use of adverbials decreases (Rubin, 1982) Syntax added by writing 3.3–3.9 rel. clauses per 100 t-units (O'Donnell, 1976) Verb phrase complexity increases	Definitions at an adult level Uses abstract language Uses verbal inferences and causal reasoning Development of CPR of facuitive noun verbs (Scoville & Gordon, 1980) Vocabulary development added by reading and writing
High School	Continued differentiated adjustment to listener needs Provide greater contextual and background information	Development of sophisticated judgment or evaluation of narrative (Nippold, 1988)	t-unit length = 11.7 (Loban, 1967) Use subordinate clauses 67% time (Nippold, 1988) Syntax added by reading	Vocabulary development added by experience, reading, and writing

the cookie that was in the jar). In addition to syntax development, dramatic gains are also seen in the use of grammatical morphemes.

A child's increasing development of word meaning is closely connected to the development of cognitive abilities. The preschool child's understanding of word meanings is usually tied to the referent's functional and perceptual attributes, and the child's discourse consists more of labeling or describing activities. Sentences are usually simple, declarative, and in the present or present progressive tense. Stories told are often chains of associated events as one thought leads to another. Words begin to replace gestures that were used to express language functions. By the age of 3 or 4, the preschool child demonstrates turn-taking and is becoming more aware of the social aspects of dialogue.

Elementary age.   Elementary school presents a variety of settings for children to interact. Both formal, teacher directed activities and informal activities are available to enhance oral language skills. While spoken communication is the major language goal of the preschooler, the acquisition of written communication skills (Wolf and Dickinson, 1985) becomes the focus of elementary school. However, the ability to learn to read and write requires a strong background in oral communication (Rees, 1988; Wallach and Liebergott, 1984). During about the fourth-grade level, children begin to use their reading skills to learn advanced vocabulary (Miller and Gildea, 1987), complex syntax, text discourse, and figurative language (Nippold, 1988). The ability to read allows the child to develop linguistic skills more independently. Children will often read a lot of books around a special topic. For instance, a child may develop a special "horse vocabulary" from having read so many books related to horses. These specialized vocabularies make it difficult for researchers to accurately map language development.

The elementary child's definitions are closely tied to the sentence context. There is still difficulty conversing about events not visible; therefore, descriptions continue to be concrete. The humor of the elementary age child tends to be very concrete. For example, they often tell and laugh at jokes or riddles stemming from phonological, lexical, or syntactic ambiguity (McGhee, 1979). The sentence complexity of both oral and written language structures is increasingly more sophisticated. The elementary child's spoken sentences contain subordinate clauses about 22 percent of the time (Nippold, 1988), with time (when), reason (because), and purpose (to) accounting for most of the adverbial clauses (Scott, 1984). The average t–unit length for the elementary child, a measure of syntactic complexity, is 7.6 words (Loban, 1976).

The elementary age child's oral and written discourse demonstrates true narrative structure. Such narratives include an introduction, development of a problem, description of a goal and solution, and an ending (Bovin and Sutton–Smith, 1977). The elementary school child also demonstrates more advanced pragmatic skills as sensitivity to the listener's needs develops. The elementary school child can adjust his or her language, turn-take, and is able to initiate and maintain topics.

Middle/secondary school.   The older student demonstrates more capability to deal with the abstract. This is certainly noted in the types of new vocabulary words individuals acquire, words that represent abstract notions (Dale and Eichholz,

1960). In addition, reasoning abilities show evidence of a transition from concrete to abstract (Scheibe and Copndry, 1987). This can be noted in the humor of students in this age group. By sixth or seventh grade, students begin to appreciate linguistic ambiguity (Nippold, Cuyler, and Braunbeck–Price, 1988).

The discourse of the older student contains all the elements of a story grammar that were obtained by the elementary school child. In addition, the older student's story contains multiple and embedded episodes as well as demonstrating empathy for the characters. By the secondary school years, the student develops a sophisticated ability to judge or evaluate narratives (Nippold, 1988). Middle and secondary school students demonstrate ability to differentiate the listener's needs. They also provide greater context and background information when needed during conversation.

Concerns Expressed by Classroom Teachers

Oral language deficits cause serious problems with both social and academic goals. The inability to understand (*receptive*) or utilize (*expressive*) language can lead to underachievement in various areas of oral language (for example, syntax, discrimination, semantics, discourse). Receptive and expressive language disorders often lead to problems with reading, writing, mathematics, and social skills. The oral language deficits of many students with special needs are subtle and often are not obvious to the classroom teacher. Classroom teachers are not expected to diagnose or remediate oral language disorders; however, they are expected to be cognizant of behaviors students display that may suggest the presence of a language problem. Students who have language disabilities may experience one or more of the following problems.

1. Difficulty labeling. Appears to know the concept but cannot recall the specific word to express it.
2. Difficulty following multistep directions.
3. Difficulty relating information in sequence.
4. Difficulty restating what someone just said.
5. Difficulty responding appropriately to questions.
6. Difficulty maintaining the topic of a conversation.
7. Difficulty shifting the topic during a conversation.
8. Difficulty making ideas understood.
9. Frequent stops, starts, and hesitations when they talk.
10. Limited vocabulary.
11. Difficulty with multiple meaning words.
12. Difficulty understanding humor.

Types of Assessment Tasks

Facilitating Language Assessment

Preassessment.   The special educator evaluating the speech and language skills of any student should gather information about the individual before the first formal testing session. In the past, case histories were the means by which teachers gathered information regarding a student's past. Case histories consisted of questions answered by parents regarding the developmental history of their children. Etiology and normative milestones were usually the focus of the questions on these case histories. Recently, researchers (Gallagher, 1983; Lund and Duchan, 1988; MacDonald, 1978) advocate that teachers collect preassessment interviews that question parents and classroom teachers specifically about their observations of the child's language performance across different contexts. Since the special educator does not have time to observe the student across all these contexts (home, playground, small classroom activities, study hall), these observations are invaluable.

Observe student in the natural environment. The special educator should observe the student being evaluated in several activities to document the influence of context on language proficiency. Norm-referenced, dynamic, criterion-based, and curriculum-based assessment all present contrived testing formats. They do not allow the special educator to observe the student using language in a setting that is natural to the individual. It is suggested that the special educator observe the student in the classroom, during a nonstructured school activity (for example, playground, lunch, pep rally), with friends, and with an unfamiliar person. During the observation, a sample of language should be collected by recording either on audiotape or videotape. This will allow the special educator to go back and listen for types of language errors. The special educator might also want to collect a language sample by initiating a conversation with the student. Speech patterns should always be evaluated according to their function in the student's repertoire. For example, Peter, age 4 and diagnosed as mildly autistic, would often use language (verbal and nonverbal) in which the form was inappropriate but the pragmatics context was correct. While trying to get Peter to feel comfortable in the testing situation, the examiner began singing a nursery song to Peter between tests. Unknown to the examiner, Peter hated music. To get the examiner to stop singing, Peter bent over to her and made a nonverbal gesture like he was turning off a radio and said, "turn off." Most striking in this case is the appropriateness of the pragmatics intent.

Norm-Referenced Tests of Oral Language

Norm-referenced tests for the assessment of oral language have received a significant amount of negative criticism (Darley, 1979). Many oral language tests have very poor reliability and validity. Therefore, it is very important that the special educator be aware of a test's shortcomings when interpreting an individual's performance. In addition, the special educator should work in cooperation with the speech pathologist in the assessment of oral language. While the speech pathologist's major role is assessment of oral language, the special educator's testing is needed for supplementary documentation and for application to academic and social performance. Some students may not qualify for a speech/language assessment. In this case, the special educator is the professional responsible for completing the language assessment.

The special educator administering tests of oral language should recognize that standardized tests measure language skills in a contrived, unnatural manner. Language is taken out of an interaction context, and a student is required to focus on aspects (semantics, syntax) of language devoid of social context. Therefore, as Van Kleech (1983) noted, such tests tell us more about how an individual "deals with decontextualized uses of language than how he or she is able to deal with language effectively as a social-interactive tool" (p. 187). Therefore, any assessment of oral language must include samples of spontaneous language (language used in discourse) as well as contrived language samples (norm-referenced tests) so an accurate and complete observation is made of a student's language competence. Both measures help the special educator investigating a student's oral language skills and the impact of the student's performance on social and academic tasks. Table 9-13 contains a list of some of the most commonly used oral language norm-referenced assessment tools along with the age level and a brief description to aid the special educator in choosing assessment tools.

Dynamic Assessment of Oral Language

The main goal of dynamic assessment is to help the special educator explore the variables that contribute to a student's errors. These variables can include motivation, social interaction, complexity of task, length of task, linguistic context, and social context. Through systematic control and observation of the student's performance, task, and teacher performance, the special educator can identify points at which a student breaks down and might with specific prompting obtain a stated linguistic goal. Our discussion of dynamic assessment has some similarities to what Wiig and Semel (1984) call *extension testing*. Both dynamic assessment and extension testing are used in an "effort to establish a baseline at which the youngster can respond correctly" (Wiig and Semel, 1984, p. 52). However, dynamic assessment puts specific emphasis on the teacher/learner interaction, whereas extension testing focuses more on modification of the linguistic task or strategies deficits across the student's performance.

The mediated learning experience (MLE) is the essence of dynamic assessment. Research suggests that a student's competence is highly correlated with the variety and quality of interaction the student has with adults as resources (Lidz, 1987a; White, Kabon, and Attanucci, 1979). Such parent/child or teacher/child interaction is central to development of linguistic concepts. Dynamic assessment is equally concerned about the behavior of the examiner (teacher), such as requesting, reporting, reinforcing, controlling, as well as the behavior of the student, and the nature of the task. To record task performance only (standard score, competency checklist) and not observe the teacher/child dialogue contributes to the possibility of missing the focal reason for success or failure at the task.

The first step in conducting a dynamic assessment is to administer a pretest. In the following example, Linguistic Concepts, a subtest of the CELF–R (Semel,. Wiig, and Secord, 1987) was used to record baseline data. The Linguistic Concepts subtest was administered to a 10-year-old male demonstrating learning and behavior problems in school. The subtest was scored, and the majority of errors indicated a

Table 9-13 Norm-referenced oral language assessment tools

Test	Age Range	Description	Phonology	Semantics	Syntax	Pragmatics	Word Finding
Analysis of Language Learning (Blodgett & Cooper, 1987)	5–10	Assesses the child's awareness of the structural aspects of language: language concepts, sentences as sequences of words, words as sequences of sounds, initial and final phonemes of words, and repairing incorrect utterances.	×	×	×		
Assessing Children's Language Comprehension (Foster, Gidden, & Stark, 1972)	3 to 6–5	Evaluates how many critical elements a child can understand when these elements are presented in increasing difficulty from one to four critical elements in a picture identification format.		×			
Bankson Language Test–Two (Bankson, 1990)	3–7	Evaluates young children's psycholinguistic skills in three general areas: semantic, morphological syntactical rules, pragmatics.		×	×	×	
Bracken Basic Concept Scale (Bracken, 1984)	2–5 to 8	Measures concept attainment in the following categories: color/letter identification, numbers/counting, comparisons, shapes, direction/ position, social/emotional, size, texture/material, quantity, and time/sequence.		×			
Carrow Elicited Language Inventory (Carrow–Woolfolk, 1974)	3–8	Measures a child's productive control of grammar with a sentence imitation format that includes basic sentence constructions and specific grammatical morphemes.			×		
Clinical Evaluation of Language Fundamentals–Revised (Semel, Wiig, & Secord, 1987)	5–17	Identifies children who lack the basic foundations of form and content that characterize mature language and word meanings, word and sentence structure, and recall and retrieval.	×	×	×		
Expressive One-Word Picture Vocabulary Test–Revised (Gardner, 1985a)	2–11	Assesses a child's ability to label a series of pictures.		×			
Expressive One-Word Picture Vocabulary Test–Upper Extension (Brownell, 1985)	12 to 15–11	Assesses older student's ability to label a series of pictures.		×			
Fullerton Language Test for Adolescents (Thorum, 1986)	11–18	Evaluates auditory synthesis, morphological competence, oral commands convergent production, divergent production, syllabication, grammatic competency and idioms.	×	×	×		
Language Processing Test (Richard & Hammer, 1985)	5–12	Assess a child's ability to label, state functions, make associations, categorize, explain similarities, differences, multiple meanings, and attribution.		×			

(continued)

Table 9-13 Norm-referenced oral language assessment tools *(continued)*

Test	Age Range	Description	Phonology	Semantics	Syntax	Pragmatics	Word Finding
Miller–Yoder Test of Grammatical Comprehension (Miller & Yoder, 1984)	3–6	Measures grammatic comprehension through a picture selection format.			×		
Northwestern Syntax Screening Test (Lee, 1971)	3–8	Screens receptive and expressive use of syntactic form.			×		
Peabody Picture Vocabulary Test–Revised (Dunn & Dunn, 1981)	2–6 to 41	This is an individually administered, norm-referenced, wide-range power test of hearing vocabulary. The subject is to select the picture considered to best illustrate the meaning of a stimulus word presented orally by the examiner.		×			
Porch Index of Communicative Ability in Children (Porch, 1971)	3–12	Assesses and quantifies certain verbal, gestural, and graphic abilities. The clinician obtains general and specific levels of expressive ability and makes inferences about receptive and integrative ability.		×	×		
Preschool Language Assessment Instrument (Blank, Rose, & Berlin, 1978)	3–6	Assesses the preschool child's discourse skills in four subgroups: matching perception, selective analysis of perception, reordering perception, and reasoning about perception.	×	×			
Quick Screen of Phonology (Bankson & Bernthal, 1990)	3–7	Screens for phonological production.	×				
Receptive One Word Vocabulary Test (Gardner, 1985b)	2–11	Assesses a child's understanding of single words.		×			
Receptive One-Word Vocabulary Test–Upper Extension (Gardner, 1985c)	12 to 15–11	Assesses a student's understanding of single words.		×			
Sequenced Inventory of Communication Development (Hedrick, Prather, & Tobin, 1976)	4 mos–4 yrs	Screens communicative behaviors including speech awareness, discrimination, and understanding as well as imitating, initiating, and responding.	×				
Structured Photographic Expressive Language Test–II (Werner & Kresheck, 1974)	4 to 9–5 yrs	Measures a child's production of specific morphological and syntactical structures.			×		
Test of Adolescent Language–2 (Hammill, Brown, Larsen, & Weiderholt, 1987)	12–18	Assists in identifying students who have problems in vocabulary and grammar as they relate to listening, speaking, reading, and writing.		×	×		
Test for the Auditory Comprehension of Language–Revised (Carrow–Woolfolk, 1985)	3–10	Tests auditory comprehension of word classes, grammatical morphemes, and elaborated sentences.		×	×		

(continued)

Table 9-13 Norm-referenced oral language assessment tools *(continued)*

Test	Age Range	Description	Phonology	Semantics	Syntax	Pragmatics	Word Finding
Test of Early Language Development (Hresko, Reid, & Hammill, 1981)	3–8	Measures syntactic, semantic, and phonologic systems as they relate to listening and speaking.	×	×	×		
Test of Language Competence–Expanded (Wiig & Secord, 1989)	5–18	Assists in identifying students who have not acquired the expected levels of metalinguistic competence in semantics.		×	×		
Test of Language Development–Intermediate (Hammill & Newcomer, 1988)	8–6 to 12–11	Measures syntactic, semantic, and phonologic systems as they relate to listening and speaking.	×	×	×		
Test of Language Development–Primary (Newcomer & Hammill, 1988)	4–0 to 8–11	Measures syntactic, semantic, and phonological systems as they relate to listening and speaking.	×	×	×		
Test of Problem Solving (Zachman, Jorgensen, Huisingh, & Barrett, 1984)	4–8	Assesses children's thinking and reasoning abilities critical to events of everyday living: explaining inferences, determining causes, negative why questions, determining solutions, and avoiding problems.		×			
Test of Word Finding (German, 1986)	6–12	Assesses older child's ability to produce target words in a variety of tasks: picture naming, sentence completion, and description naming.					×
Test of Word Finding: Adolescents and Adults (German, 1991)	12–0 to 80–0	Assesses an adolescent/adult's ability to produce target words in a variety of tasks: picture naming, sentence completion, and description naming.					×
Token Test for Children– (Disimoni, 1978)	4–0 to 12	Evaluates the retention and recall of oral directions that increase in length and size of units.			×		
Token Test for Adults (McNeil & Prescott, 1978)	13 to 89	Evaluates the retention and recall of oral directions that increase in length and size of units.			×		
Utah Test of Language Development (Mecham, 1989)	3–11	Evaluates expressive and receptive language skills.	×	×	×		

difficulty with conditional word relationships (if, until, when). It is at this point that the mediated learning experience is initiated by the diagnostician. Prior to beginning the MLE, the examiner should analyze the task to determine what cognitive processes are involved in completing the task. According to Wiig and Semel (1983), the subtest evaluates comprehension of fifty linguistic concepts representing comparative, passive, temporal–sequential, spatial, and familial relationships. In addition to comprehending linguistic relationships, the task involves

Table 9-14 Dynamic assessment using extension testing and strategic teaching

Step 1: The conditional linguistic concepts *when* and *if* are practically used and labeled.

    Teacher: What happens *when* I turn this radio on?
    Student: It plays music.
    Teacher: Right, *when* I turn the radio on, you hear music. (Several more examples given.)
    Teacher: What will happen *if* I take the batteries out of the radio?
    Student: It won't work.
    Teacher: Right, *if* I take the battery out it will not work. (Several more examples given.)

Step 2: Generalization of the conditional linguistic concepts are presented to the student by showing a picture of a motorcycle and asking if/when questions.
    (Dialogue between teacher and student accompanied examples.)

Step 3: Application of conditional linguistic concepts are presented to the student by sharing a picture of an event and asking the student to tell what happened using *if* and *when* statements.
    (Dialogue between teacher and student accompanied examples.)

Step 4: Present the conditional linguistic concepts (*if, when*) in a similar task to the CELF–R Linguistic Concepts subtest by presenting the student with attribute blocks and asking if/when questions.
    (Dialogue between teacher and student accompanied examples.)

Step 5: Extend the application of the linguistic concepts (*if, when*) by talking to the student about experiences in his or her own social environment (music, play, home life).
    (Dialogue between teacher and student accompanied examples.)

- the ability to classify,
- the ability to sequence,
- the ability to learn temporal seriation, and
- the ability to learn conditional relations.

The results of the pretest indicated that the student performed poorly in understanding conditional references. In addition to scoring the student's performance, the examiner videotaped herself administering the test. The special education teacher's supervisor evaluated her performance using an adaptation of Feuerstein's (1980) published criteria for evaluating the interactive behaviors of the teacher and learner during a testing situation. It became apparent that during the evaluation little regulation of the student's impulsivity and attention to the task was provided by the teacher. Therefore, the next step in the MLE was to consistently direct the student's attention to the task. Next, to address the possible problem with conditional linguistic concepts, the teacher followed steps adapted from Wiig and Semel's (1984) extension testing and Wiig's (1989) strategic teaching (described in Table 9-14).

The final step in the MLE was to readminister the CELF–R Linguistic Concepts subtest. When the teacher changed her behavior, helping the student focus and attend to the task and teaching the student strategies (Wiig, 1989) in approaching such a task, the student did not demonstrate a linguistic disorder. The initial low performance on the pretest resulted from a lack of strategies to use with conditional linguistic relationships as well as poor self-directive behavior. Such quick improvement on a task clearly illustrates a breakdown between understanding the "sense" of the task and how to interact (attend). The special education teacher should evaluate this student's long-term maintenance of this skill by presenting similar tasks to the student over time. Students with significant disorders with language or generalized attentional disorders would not have made significant progress so quickly and would have been easily identified as handicapped learners.

Multicultural Assessment of Oral Language

The assessment of oral language for language minority students presents challenges to special educators, particularly in light of the lack of extensive research investigating bilingual special needs individuals. In addition, tests of language proficiency have been found to have significant technical and construct-related problems (Merino and Spencer, 1983; Ulibari, Spencer, and Rivas, 1980). However, language minority students are often referred for special education evaluations due to regular educators' interpretations of linguistic, cultural, economic, or other background characteristics as deviant (Ortiz and Yates, 1983, 1984). In addition, the majority of what is known about first language acquisition in English is based on studies of white middle-class individuals and is not always appropriate in drawing conclusions about language competence across cultures.

Different cultural or socioeconomic groups place varying degrees of emphasis on verbal dialogue in early childhood. A special educator must not only evaluate a student's linguistic competence and knowledge of phonological, syntactic, and semantic rules but also must evaluate the student's communicative competence, the ability to use language across contexts (Hymes, 1972).

All individuals are socialized to show verbal adroitness as valued by their culture. Heath (1982) investigated the impact of cultural variation on the acquisition of oral language. She studied several working-class communities in the Piedmont Carolinas, which included a mainstream middle-class community (Maintown), a white working-class community (Roadville), and a black working-class community (Trackton). The results of this ethnographic research study illustrated the impact of culture on the acquisition and function of language structures. Other research with native Americans (Scribner and Cole, 1973) and non-Western cultures (Harkness, 1977) found similar results to those of Heath.

Lobov (1970) rejected the myth that poor children are nonverbal and culturally deprived. He studied the impact of types of dialect on language acquisition. According to Lobov (1970), the social situation was the most powerful determinant of verbal behavior. He illustrated this by the example of Leon (Lobov, 1970, p. 163). Leon was a young black student with whom Lobov set up three situations to evaluate his use of oral language. In the first situation, Leon was interviewed by a white male about a toy plane. This resulted in very little dialogue between the participants. Second, Leon was interviewed by a black male about a popular TV show. An increase in verbal behavior was noted. Finally, a black male brought Leon's close friend with him as well as providing potato chips for the group. They all sat on the floor and talked. During this social interaction, Leon's oral language skills were certainly appropriate to the context. Therefore, by manipulating the participants, topic, and purpose of the encounter, different samples of oral language were obtained. Shultz, Florio, and Erickson (1982) have stressed that teachers need to recognize the importance of mediating learning to enhance communication and that many classroom situations may be contrived and senseless to some students. They stress that students may have different notions of "interactional etiquette" (p. 120).

Dialect

Dialect has an impact on all areas of oral language (phonology, syntax, morphology, and pragmatics). Distinctions are made between dialects based on social stratification and geographical area (Williams and Wolfram, 1977). Geographical dialects can be noted by observing the speech patterns of New Englanders or Southerners. Social dialects are often highly correlated with race, ethnic group, and economic status levels. Some examples of nonstandard dialects are Black English Vernacular, Appalachian English, Puerto Rican English, or West Indian Creole English. Social dialects reveal "consistent and predictable patterns of variation irrelevant to regional boundaries" (Reed, 1981, p. 140). Therefore, not all blacks speak Black English Vernacular. Yet low-income blacks, whether they live in Philadelphia or Atlanta, are likely to use nonstandard Black English Vernacular. It must be emphasized, however, that everyone speaks a dialect, and the number of features that dialects share is greater than the number they do not share. The special educator should keep in mind that Standard English is called standard precisely because it is socially and economically preeminent over other dialects of English and not because it is inherently superior in grammar or phonology (Whiteman, 1976, p. 155). Baratz (1969) described some dialect or code differences that differentiate Black English Vernacular from Standard English:

1. Numerical quantifier. When one has a numerical quantifier such as two or seven-fifty, you don't need to add the morphemes for plural, for example, fifty cent or two foot.
2. Possessive marker. The nonstandard speaker would say, "John cousin." The possessive is marked by the contiguous relationship of John and his cousin.
3. The conditional. This is expressed by word change rather than by "if." Standard English: "I asked if he wanted to go." Nonstandard English: "I asked did he want to go."
4. Third person. The third person singular has no obligatory morphological ending in nonstandard English. "She works here" becomes "She work here."
5. Verb agreement differs with usage. A Black adolescent might say, "She have a bike" or "They was going."
6. The use of the copula is not obligatory. "I going." "He a bad boy."
7. Rules of negation. The double negative is used a great deal. "I don't have none."
8. Use of "ain't." "Ain't" is used mainly in the past tense. "I didn't go yet" becomes "I ain't go yet."
9. Use of "be." "Be" is used to express habitual action. "He workin' right now" becomes "He be workin' every day." *Source:* From *Teaching Black Children to Read,* edited by J. C. Baratz and R. Wishuy, p. 127. Copyright © 1969 by Center for Applied Linguistics. Reprinted by permission.

Dialect differences also occur in students for whom the primary language is not English. The special educator must recognize when regional variations of a language, social class distinction, and informal popular speech of the first language influence language performance. Regional variations are noted in word differences used by Mexicans in the Southwest and by Puerto Ricans or Cubans. For instance, the English word "kite" is "papalote" in Mexico, Texas, and California but also "huita" in Texas, "cameta" in Spain and Colombia, and "chiringa" in Puerto Rico (Valadez, 1981, p. 168). At the phonological and syntactical level, differences due to regional variation can be noted. Dialects of Spanish can be nonstandard in the same way dialects of English are considered nonstandard (that is, Vernacular Black English or Appalachian English). Characteristics concerning other dialect variations of English can be found by referring to Wiig and Semel (1984) for descriptions of Appalachian English and Southern White dialects, Adler and Birdsong (1983) for the phonological characteristics of Mountain English, and Cheng (1987) for Asian dialect. During an assessment, the special educator should determine what dialects of English a student understands and uses as well as what dialects of the student's primary language is understood and used across contexts.

Bilingualism

Bilingualism is often misunderstood by professionals. Woolfolk and Lynch (1983) define the term to "reflect two language capabilities in a range of degree" (p. 422). Diglossia, as defined by Penalosa (1975), pertains to when two different languages or varieties of the same language are used in the same society. Minority language students often utilize three different strategies in recalling a second language: code-switching, borrowing, and mixing. Code-switching occurs when a speaker uses two or more languages or dialects, each associated with specific activities, social situations, or speakers (Gumperz and Hernandez–Chavez, 1975). For instance, in many Mexican-American neighborhoods, a change from English to Spanish signals a change in the relationship between the parties involved. Another typical strategy used by second language learners is borrowing: words for new concepts not in one language are borrowed from another. Mixing is a strategy used when words from one language are interspersed into the other, but not consistently. A Spanish/English bilingual child may say, "Yo quiero play" (I want to play) or "Yo estaba playendo" (I was playing). This is an example of mixing English vocabulary and English grammar with a Spanish linguistic context (Garcia, 1990).

Research has shown that the processes involved in learning a second language are similar to the processes involved in learning the first language (Celee–Murica, 1978; Krashan, 1982). Learning two languages together should not present problems. Bilingual students, both at early and late periods of development, do not differ significantly from monolinguals in vocabulary development, phonological development, syntactic development, and pragmatics (Garcia, 1990; Hakuta, 1986). However, if the models (significant others) at home or school are not available or if a language disorder is apparent, a student will not reach optimum competence in either language. It is important to keep in mind that it is not possible for a bilingual individual to have a language disorder in only one of the two languages (Juarez, 1983; Ortiz, 1984). Typical errors demonstrated by normal learners acquiring a second language include: (1) use of forms, structures, or vocabulary from the first language to substitute for forms in the second language not yet learned (Wool-folk–Carrow and Lynch, 1983); and (2) overgeneralization of semantic features identified with a word, particularly prepositions. Research suggests that errors of the second language learner often look like errors of a child with learning disabilities (Damico, Oller, and Storey, 1983; Mattes and Omark, 1984; Ortiz and Maldo-nando–Colon, 1986). The special educator must carefully investigate whether the errors are a language difference or a language disorder.

Oral language assessment of multicultural students must control for five specific factors:

1. the competency of the student in both languages;
2. semantic, syntactic, and pragmatic differences between the first and second languages;
3. the linguistic and social milieu;
4. cognitive factors; and
5. affective factors.

In addition, a student's strategic competence can be identified. Strategic competence includes the student's mastery of verbal and nonverbal communicative strategies that circumvent deficiencies in grammatical and sociolinguistic competence. Interestingly, Mexican-American students have been found to increase their level of task engagement when activities draw upon the expression of personal interest, experience, and language background (Willig, Swedo, and Ortiz, 1987). Gonzalez (1986) found that Mexican students excel in literary activities that are meaning based, intended for real audiences, and allow for peer collaboration.

PL 94–142 mandates that all children are to be evaluated in a nondiscriminatory manner. "Nonbiased testing simply means reducing the chance that a child is incor-rectly placed in special classes and increasing the use of intervention programs which facilitate his or her physical, social, emotional and academic program" (Tucker, 1980, pp. 93–104). Special educators need to evaluate whether specific standardized assessment tools are nonbiased measures of language competence and when dynamic assessment or language samples are better measures of ability.

The two types of tests used to assess oral language for minority language students are integrative and discrete point assessment tools. Integrative tests are tasks that "obtain evidence of students' overall control of the language by having them pro-duce connected discourse in some meaningful context" (Dietrich and Freeman, 1979). Examples of integrative task formats include picture descriptions, open-ended questions, cloze, or dictation. Discrete point tests evaluate a number of specific structures or rules, the discrete points in the language system (Dietrich and Freeman, 1979). This format could include imitating sentences, completing senten-ces, choosing pictures to match orally presented sentences, or paraphrasing stories. McLoughlin (1985) cautions that many of the standardized measures used in evalu-ating the listening and speaking skills of language minority students possess poor reliability and validity. Research by Damico, Oller, and Storey (1983) found that inclusion of integrative (pragmatics) and discrete point behaviors together resulted in the most effective index of language/learning difficulties as measured by academic and social progress over one academic year (Ortiz and Polyzoi, 1989).

Assessing Special Education Language Minority Students

Research supports the concept that the assessment of language minority students should focus on communicative competence rather than only on language proficiency (Duran, 1989; Figuero, 1989; Jax, 1989). The emphasis should be on student/teacher, student/significant other, student/peer interaction rather than on the results taken from contrived assessment tools. Dynamic assessment tasks appear to be one of the most effective means of assessing oral language for language minority students.

The first step in evaluating the oral language of language minority students is to collect a language background questionnaire. The purpose of the language background questionnaire is twofold: (1) to gather information pertaining to the dominant language used at home; and (2) to collect preassessment data pertaining to the student's use of language across context. However, as Payan (1989) concludes, "The type of questions commonly presented in language background questionnaires will not directly identify the language the child commands readily but describes the child's linguistic environment, the amount of language input received, and impressions of the child's communicative abilities" (p. 132). The special educator needs to design effective preassessment questionnaires and interviews so a better evaluation of the student's language competence can be collected. In addition, during this preassessment period, the special educator should observe the student's instructional milieu (classroom), the teaching styles of the referring teacher, and the experience the referring teacher has with the child's dominant culture. Additional information required to plan an effective assessment includes the reasons for referral (that is, family perceptions, teacher perceptions, student perceptions), background information (family history, health history, developmental milestones), school history, length of residence in the United States, and cognitive and social-emotional functioning.

The second step in the assessment of the language minority student is to determine language proficiency. Table 9-15 lists several tests used for this purpose. As can be seen, the majority of these tests are specifically designed for assessment of Spanish competence. While Spanish-speaking students represent the largest group of language minority students, there are approximately fourteen other minority language groups in the United States whose children in 1980 comprised almost 2,400 students between the ages of 5 and 14 (Yates, 1987). Lynch and Lewis (1987) state that educators will be at a particular disadvantage when assessing the ever-growing population of Pan-Asian students entering schools. Cheng (1987) provides a description of the best practices (formal and informal) for assessing Pan-Asian students.

The technical adequacy and educational usefulness of many language assessment tools used with language minority students has been questioned. Payan (1989) and DeAvila and Havassy (1974) have argued against direct translations of English language tests. DeAvila and Havassy (1974) state the following problems with direct translations of English language tests:

1. Regional differences within a language make it difficult to use a single translation in a standardized testing situation where examiner and examinee are permitted virtually no interaction.

2. Monolingual translations are inappropriate because the language familiar to non-English speaking children is often a combination of two languages.

Table 9-15 Norm-referenced oral language tests for non-English speaking populations

Test	Age/Grade Range	Language(s)	Phonology	Semantics	Syntax	Pragmatics	Word finding
Basic Inventory of Natural Language (Herbert, 1977, 1979, 1983)	K–12 grades	32 languages		•			
Ber–Sil Elementary and Secondary Spanish Tests (Beringer, 1987, 1984)	5–12 years 13–17 years	Spanish, Tagalog, Ilokawo, Cantonese, Mandarin, Korean, & Persian		•			
Bilingual Syntax I and II (Burt, Dulay & Chavez, 1978)	PreK–12 grades	Spanish, English			•		
Dos Amigos Verbal Language Scales (Critchlow, 1973)	5–13 years	Spanish, English		•			
Language Assessment Scales–Oral (DeAvila & Duncan, 1975–85)	K–12 grades	Spanish, English	•	•			
Prueba de Desarrollo Inicial del Lenguaje (Hresko, Reid, & Hammill, 1982)	3–7 years	Spanish		•	•		
Woodcock Language Proficiency Battery, English and Spanish Form (Woodcock, 1980, 1981)	3–80 years	Spanish, English		•			

3. Many non-English speaking children have never learned to read in their spoken language. For example, many Chicano children speak Spanish but have had no instruction in reading Spanish. (pp. 77–78)

In addition to translation problems, the special educator will soon learn that standardization of many minority language tests is inadequate. It is inappropriate to use English language norms for non-English speaking students. Therefore, local norms must be constructed, or the test can only be used as an informal measure. If the special educator does locate minority language norms for a specific instrument, careful inspection must be made of these norms. As Lynch and Lewis (1987) caution, "Spanish-language tests prepared for use in Mexico may not be appropriate for Cuban refugees in urban areas of Florida or for Mexican-American students in the rural southwest" (p. 404).

The use of interpreters to assist in administering tests to language minority students may be the only option available to school systems, particularly if the student's primary language is not common. However, the special educator must keep in mind that when English language tests are administered by an interpreter, test norms are no longer applicable. Plata (1982) describes several problems in the use of interpreters for test administration. These problems include:

1. On-the-spot translation is very difficult, especially when the interpreter does not know the technical language found in test items.

2. Many words lose their meanings in the translation process.

3. The interpreter may not know all the possible terms or dialects applied to a word or concept, especially if the child being tested is from a different geographic region than that of the interpreter.

4. There may be hostile feelings toward the examiner on the part of an interpreter who feels that he or she is "being used" to "cover up" inadequacies of the examiner or if the interpreter perceives the remuneration to be minimal for doing the work of a highly paid professional. (p. 4)

In addition, the interpreter may not have had experience working with some of the behaviors demonstrated by special needs students. Specific acting out or withdrawal behaviors might be seen negatively by the interpreter and affect the evaluation of the student's language competence. The special educator should talk with the interpreter prior to the test administration concerning some strategies in managing behaviors that could interfere with the test administration.

The assessment of language minority students is currently inadequate, particularly when norm-referenced measures are the only tools used to make decisions of eligibility (Galagan, 1986; Huntze, 1985; Walker and Fabre, 1987). There has been a shift among language professionals to move away from traditional language assessment approaches and to emphasize evaluation of pragmatic skills. Damico (1985) developed a procedure, Clinical Discourse Analysis, that "incorporates clinical observation and analysis of data obtained from conversation samples to identify behavior patterns that interfere with interpersonal communication" (Ortiz and Ployzoi, 1989, p. 35). Evaluation criteria using this type of analysis included linguistic nonfluencies, nonspecific vocabulary, poor topic maintenance, and inappropriate responses (see Table 9-16).

Researchers have concluded that neither a pragmatic nor a norm-referenced approach to assessment alone is accurate in identifying language disorders among language minority students (Damico, Oller, and Storey, 1983; Ortiz and Polyzoi, 1989). The special educator should use both approaches together with a dynamic assessment model to determine an effective index of language learning abilities.

Steps in the Assessment Process

Students with special needs often demonstrate some kind of mild to moderate language impairment that is associated with poor academic and social success. With some special needs students, difficulties are noted both in their understanding of the language of others and in their own expression of language. Oral language assessment is also a concern for special educators working with students speaking nonstandard English or languages other than English.

Table 9-16 Pragmatic criteria used in analysis of the HMRI language samples

1. **Revisions:** Is the child's speech constantly disrupted by numerous false starts or self-interruptions?

   Example:
   E: "How big is your little brother?"
   C: "He's about half...he comes... he's here on me." (points to shoulder)

2. **Linguistic nonfluencies:** Is the child's speech characterized by a disproportionately high number of repetitions, pauses, or hesitations?

   Example:
   C: "Sh...She...She comes...She comes at dinner time."

3. **Delays before responding:** Is the child's speech characterized by pauses of inordinate length?

   Example:
   E: "And what did you do then?"
   C: "...(pauses approximately 3 seconds) We played tag."

4. **Nonspecific vocabulary:** Does the child make frequent use of expressions such as "it," "thing," "stuff," "this/that," etc., when the listener has no way of knowing what is being referred to?

   Example:
   E: "So, did you help them move?"
   C: "Yeah..but they were mad cuz I dropped it."
   E: "Oh? What did you drop?"
   C: "That thing of Rosa's."

5. **Inappropriate responses:** Does the child have trouble attending to the examiner's prompts or probes and continue to respond inappropriately?

   Example:
   E: "How do you like school?"
   C: "I don't know him yet."

6. **Poor topic maintenance:** Does the child tend to keep changing the topic without providing transitional clues to the examiner?

   Example:
   C: "I went to bed at 6:30."
   E: "That early? You must have had a hard day."
   C: "Yeah."
   E: "What made it such a hard day?"
   C: "The raking. Our teacher said, whoever wins in checkers – I won – goes to McDonalds."

7. **Need for repetition:** Does the child constantly ask the examiner to repeat questions or information due to lack of comprehension?

   Example:
   E: "What did the boy do then?"
   C: "..."
   E: "What did the little boy do?"
   C: "Wh..What?"
   E: "What did the little boy do after he saw the bunny rabbit?"

E = Examiner
C = Child

Source: From "The Diagnosis of Language Disorders in Bilingual Children," by T. S. Damico, T. W. Oller, and M. E. Storey, *Journal of Speech and Hearing Disorders, 48.* Copyright © 1983 Journal of Speech and Hearing Disorders. Reprinted by permission.

In the last decade, it has become clear that communication is an intentional and interactive process intricately bound to the context in which it occurs. One of the most serious flaws in the research investigating oral language in handicapped students has been the general, artificial, and contrived nature of the tasks used to assess communication (Habiger, 1990). The time for analyzing oral language with only norm-referenced measures is long past. The intricate processes of communication cannot be studied using quantitative methods alone. It is not the end product of language that eludes quantification, it is the nature of the interactive process that is difficult to mold into standard scores. The time has come to focus on the process: intent embedded in specific events and the discourse rules that apply to those events. Norm-referenced and dynamic assessment together provide the tools to accurately describe the variables that enhance or sabotage communication attempts. New oral language models view individuals as active and responsible participants in constructing their own communication event. The special educator must become competent in the use of both norm-referenced and dynamic assessment techniques.

We have stressed the influence of different contexts on a student's oral language competence. Some students with special needs demonstrate better oral language abilities depending on their level of comfort with the environment. The special educator must be sure to collect information about a student's oral language skills as noted in the classroom, at home, and in social contexts. In addition, the impact of oral language performance on academic and social performance must be evaluated. For many students, underachievement in reading, written language, or mathematical performance is the direct result of underlying oral language deficits. In addition, oral language ability has a significant impact on an individual's feelings of self-worth and his or her ability to socialize. Oral language performance must not be examined in isolation from the individual's overall cognitive, emotional, and academic strengths and weaknesses.

Determine the Purpose of the Assessment Process

The selection of the language tests or testing procedures to be used during an assessment should be guided by the purpose and questions the special educator is asking. Different questions require the use of different methods of testing. Unfortunately, some teachers guide their choice of a test battery by what tests are available in their schools or what tests they were taught to give during their training programs. These teachers are likely to find that the tests chosen provide little useful information to help develop effective instructional goals.

Identification. One purpose for an assessment is to determine whether the student has an oral language problem. The focus of this testing should be on identification, to be used as eligibility for services. To answer such a question, the special educator must compare the student's performance to the performance of a group average. Utilizing direct observation of the student as well as normative tools, the special educator then determines "how much" variation determines deviance. Some language tests have cutoffs defining the amount of deviation from the average that indicates a language disorder. Other types of language measures leave it to the examiner to determine what is considered a disorder. Most norm-referenced tests do not provide the teacher with a "yes or no" answer but describe results in some of the following ways: below the 6th percentile, 70 standard score, 14 months' delay, age-equivalent of 4½, or below average.

Cause.   The search for the etiology (cause) of the language disorder is another purpose for much of the assessment done with special needs students. Such a pathological approach focuses on the physical and psychological reasons for the student's poor performance. A significant amount of weight is placed on case history information such as birth history, developmental milestones, health history, and family history. However, there has been a trend to avoid making inferences about the cause of language disorders. Special educators must be careful to avoid implying a causal relationship between the language problem and some behavioral or social description of the student. The cause of a language disorder is often not known, and even when it is, this information is not always helpful in program planning.

Areas.   One purpose for evaluation is to evaluate behavior across the different areas of oral language to observe inter- (between language areas) and intra- (within one areas of language) oral language competence. A student's language skills acquire significance in direct proportion to the model used to view language and communication interaction. The two most common models used to view language abilities are the formalist and the functionalist model. From a formalist perspective, there are five equal parts of the language system: phonology, semantics, syntax, morphology, and pragmatics. Considered from a functionalist perspective, as we have done here, pragmatics is the overall organizing principle of language (Owens, 1988). Pragmatics is the force behind the choice of structures used to communicate effectively. It is an interactive process in which intent and context form the basis from which communicative competence is viewed. Therefore, the special needs student's pragmatic competence should be the first area observed by the examiner. The other areas of language (phonology, morphology, syntax, and semantics) should be evaluated in the context of the information gathered about the student's pragmatic competence.

The special educator assessing the oral language skills of a student should, however, describe explicitly what the student can or cannot do. Lund and Duchan (1983) advocate a method they term *structural analysis* in which the evaluator describes "what is correct and what is missing or incorrect" (p. 11). Performance is described in behavioral terms rather than as abstract categories. For instance, rather than saying that the student has a grammatic closure problem, the examiner would record that the student has no plural or past tense endings.

Program planning.   One of the major reasons special educators carry out oral language assessment is to develop more effective instructional programs for students. Assessment is an ongoing process that should not be used only to determine eligibility. Traditionally, diagnostic procedures have been static, leading only to diagnostic labels and placement decisions. Recently, the concept of process or dynamic assessment has lead clinicians to reevaluate diagnostic models. Dynamic assessment is based on the following principles (Meyers, 1987):

- there must be link between assessment and intervention,
- assessment must be tied to the environment,
- assessment must focus on the process as well as the product of behavior, and
- assessment must involve a means of generating and testing hypotheses.

Every interaction with a student becomes part of the assessment that will help develop a realistic and effective instructional program.

Develop Record Sheets to Record Assessment Data

Oral language sample. The special educator should begin the assessment by observing the student and recording a sample of the student's language across several contexts to determine strengths and weaknesses. The student should be observed interacting with a familiar partner and with an unfamiliar partner. In addition, the student should be engaged in an activity with the partner while the observation is completed. There is no way to force an individual to talk. It is the role of the special educator to create a situation in which the student feels there is a reason to talk in an atmosphere that is safe. Roberts and Crais (1989) offer suggestions for encouraging students to communicate verbally.

1. Limit your own talking, especially asking questions. Pause often to encourage the child to initiate communication and take a turn.
2. Watch for and encourage any mode of communication demonstrated by the child (eye gaze, point, shrug, or word).
3. Parallel play with the child, mimicking his or her actions. Play animatedly with an object or a toy, and occasionally comment on an object or action.
4. Place a few items within eye gaze but out of reach; partially hide a few objects as well. If necessary, point to or comment on objects to encourage a comment or request by the child.
5. Let the child choose objects or activities, particularly in the beginning (and throughout the interaction if possible). Be prepared to watch and interact/comment when the child shows interest.
6. Include a parent or another child to help break the ice. Stay in the background and slowly get into the interaction.
7. Begin the interaction with activities that require little or no talking, and gradually move into more verbal tasks.
8. Be genuine in your questions, and stay away from asking what is obvious to both you and the child.
9. Follow the child's lead in the interaction by maintaining the child's focus on particular topics and meanings.
10. Show warmth and positive regard for the child, and value his comments.
    Source: Reprinted with the permission of Merrill, an imprint of Macmillan Publishing Company from *Assessing Infants and Preschoolers with Handicaps* by Donald B. Bailey, Jr. and Mark Wolery, p. 351. Copyright © 1989 by Merrill Publishing Company.

After the special educator has elicited an *oral language sample,* the next step is to transcribe the sample. Lund and Duchan (1988) describe three types of oral transcripts: a running transcript, a listing transcript, and a multilevel transcript.

Norm-referenced and dynamic testing.   After the special educator has collected oral language samples, determination of specific oral language areas (phonology, semantics, morphology, syntax) needing further investigation can be made by the special educator. Throughout both norm-referenced and dynamic testing, the student's error patterns must be accurately recorded on a data sheet.

Conduct an Integrated Assessment Utilizing Norm-Referenced Tests, Oral Language Samples, and Dynamic Diagnostic Measures

The need for an integrated assessment of oral language performance utilizing norm-referenced tests, oral language transcripts, and dynamic assessment measures has been discussed throughout this chapter. A special educator must remember that standard scores or percentage correct scores that a student receives are not as important as how the student arrives at his or her responses. Regardless of whether norm-referenced tests, oral language transcripts, or dynamic assessment measures are used, the student's verbal and nonverbal behaviors should be recorded for analysis. The special educator must note task demands (structured, nonstructured) as well as strategies the student either successfully or unsuccessfully employs while attempting to communicate.

The assessment of oral language performance should include observation of all the areas (pragmatics, phonology, semantics, morphology, and syntax) within a naturalistic context (classroom, playground). From the data collected in natural settings, specific areas needing further probing through norm-referenced and dynamic assessment can be determined by the special educator. The main goal of the assessment process must always focus on future intervention. The special educator should view all language assessment (norm-referenced tests, oral language transcripts, or dynamic assessment) as a means of generating and testing hypotheses. Assessment is an ongoing process, not just an exercise for eligibility statements.

Analyze the Error Patterns

Steps one through three have focused on selecting, recording, and transcribing information pertaining to a student's oral language competence. The next step is for the special educator to discover error patterns, both strengths and weaknesses, across the different areas of language (phonology, semantics, morphology, syntax, and pragmatics). Behaviors recorded using different types of measurements (norm-referenced tests, language samples, and dynamic assessment) can be useful here.

Error patterns are behaviors that can be grouped together or classified by type (for example, omission of "ing" endings). As Lund and Duchan (1983) state, "They can be regarded as aspects of knowledge, located in the mind of the child—knowledge which the child can use to understand or produce language" (p. 33). It is equally important for the special educator to note structures that are omitted, substituted, or added as well as incorrect structures. In addition, the examiner must always note the student's "sense" or understanding of the purpose of the activity. If a student perceives an activity or an event to be a game, a very different vocabulary or syntax may be utilized to convey ideas.

The special educator must note whether errors recorded cause a breakdown in the pragmatics so that interaction between the student and the language partner is impaired. Errors that confuse or mislead the intent of the conversation are more serious than if students simply "sound" different in the way they pronounce words. Next, the evaluator must note errors within different language areas, across language areas, and across tasks. The different areas of language should be seen in relationship to each other rather than as isolated units. The impact of a disorder in one area should be noted along with its effect on other areas of language. For instance, students with difficulty hearing sound differences (phonology) often attach inaccurate meanings (semantics) to words since they hear the wrong word. This is very different from students whose semantic problems are the result of conceptual deficits. Finally, the special educator should evaluate the impact of specific oral language errors on the cognitive, social, and academic performance of students.

Develop Instructional Objectives Based on Careful Analysis

The final step in the assessment process is development of instructional objectives for the purpose of intervention. Information gathered from careful analysis of error patterns is used to determine the objectives. According to Lund and Duchan (1988) a structure is a good candidate for change through language intervention if it:

- is consistent—lacks in sturdiness;
- changes when the child is presented with the adult model—is stimulatable;
- is not generalized to new contexts—lacks generativity;
- changes when it fails to communicate—improves under repair; and
- carries more communicative impact for the child—is functionally significant. (p. 39)

The objectives for instruction are influenced by the special educator's approach to intervention. Wiig and Semel (1984) discuss five common instructional approaches: process-oriented, task-analysis, behaviorally oriented, interactive–interpersonal, and total environmental system. The process-oriented approach to language intervention attempts to remediate cognitive processes (perception, memory, selective attention) that have an impact on verbal communication. The psycholinguistic approach (Bush and Giles, 1966) and the neurosensory approach (Johnson and Myklebust, 1967) are examples of this kind of intervention. Task-analysis approaches focus on "increasing the complexity of meaning (semantics), structure (morphology and syntax), or function (pragmatics) of the language input–output that child can handle" (Wiig and Semel, 1984, p. 63). Examples would be the Peabody Language Development Kit (Dunn and Smith, 1965, 1966, 1967; Dunn, Smith, and Horton, 1968), Developmental Syntax Program (Coughran and Lieles, 1974), Fokes Sentence Builders (Fokes, 1976), and the Clinical Language Intervention Program (Semel and Wiig, 1982). Behavior and performance-oriented approaches are based on applying operant conditioning principles to teaching oral language structures. This approach has not proved useful for remediation of mild to moderate language disabilities, particularly with older students (Wiig and Semel,

1984). The main goal of the interactive–interpersonal approach to language instruction is to strengthen pragmatic abilities. An example of this approach is the Let's Talk intervention program (Wiig, 1982b, 1982c; Wiig and Bray, 1983). Finally, the total environmental systems approach to language instruction focuses on the use of the natural environment to enhance oral communication. "These approaches may consider within-child, within task, within context, and within-listener-speakers characteristics and the dynamic interactions among these factors" (Wiig and Semel, 1984, p. 67). A total environmental program makes use of all the other approaches discussed as well as considering the social–emotional needs of the student and the family. Meta-analysis of studies with preschool children found that modeling approaches within the natural environment were a more efficient instructional method than imitation or focused stimulation (Nye and Seaman, 1985). In the area of adolescent language assessment and intervention (Schwartz and McKinley, 1984; Simon, 1985; Wiig, 1985, 1989; Wiig and Secord, 1985), an awareness of the need to teach metalinguistic strategies has been noted. Wiig and Secord (1989) feel such a teaching strategy is also necessary for preschool and elementary students demonstrating language disorders.

Regardless of the instructional approach the special educator feels is most appropriate for a student clear behavioral objectives must be written. In addition, normal language development, as well as the goals of the school curriculum, must be consistent during the creation of a student's oral language instructional program. Systematic recording and monitoring of behavior must be an ongoing component of the special educator's role such that constant reevaluation of the appropriateness and effectiveness of instructional methods can be determined.

Communicative competencies (Mathinas, 1988) are elaborate and complex puzzles that affect all aspects of an individual's life. Students become who they are, not in isolation, but by communicating and interacting with others. Communication involves everything about students as individuals—emotion as well as knowledge, thought as well as action, and mind as well as body. The assumption that only the speech/language pathologist can adequately address these complex issues is naive. Special educators play a significant role in collecting, recording, and analyzing oral language competencies for special needs students. Professional barriers that restrict exchanges between and among the very people who can put the pieces of the puzzle together must be removed—for the good of the students we are all trying to help.

Summary

Introduction

1. Language refers to the rules governing the representation of ideas through symbols.
2. Speech and language development are the result of an individual interacting with his or her environment.
3. Assessment of oral communication requires observation of language users in a variety of contexts, implementing a myriad of sociolinguistic abilities.

Methods of Assessment

Primary Mode

1. Communication requires both verbal (words) and nonverbal (body language, gestures) symbols.
2. Individuals use eye gaze, spatial proximity, gestures, physical manipulation, and vocalization to regulate interactions with others.
3. During assessment, a determination should be made as to whether students are using the most effective or all the modes of communication available to them.

Nonverbal

1. To understand what someone says to us requires that we read the verbal and nonverbal cues, each elaborating the intent of the speaker.
2. Language users implement a sophisticated network of communication skills that include kinetics, facial communication skills, paralanguage, proxemics, and chronemics.
3. It is important to match the verbal language interaction with the nonverbal behaviors from both the perspective of the person initiating the conversation and from the perspective of the person responding.

Input/Output

1. Expressive skills allow language users to accurately produce the sounds, words, and meanings that represent the intent of their message.
2. Receptive language skills refer to the oral comprehension of words, language structures, and discourse.
3. Oral communication requires the ability to plan and execute tasks directed toward a predetermined goal.
4. The language system is a highly sophisticated and integrative network of skills. The chance for one or more cognitive processes to be deficit is more common than not among language users.

Components of Oral Language

Pragmatics

1. Pragmatics is the study of the impact of different contexts on speaker/listener communication.
2. The special educator needs to determine how the student is making sense of the language activity that is ongoing.
3. Oral communication is carried out by adults and children for a purpose or with a specific intent in mind.
4. The special educator should observe whether the speaker and the listener are adjusting their language patterns for each other during a conversation.

Discourse

1. There are several types of discourse structures that students are involved in during the course of a school day. These include stories, conversation, and school lessons.
2. Stories require elaborated or extended units of text, introductory and closing statements, and an orderly presentation of events leading to a logical conclusion.
3. Conversations differ from stories in that they do not follow a story grammar or structure and are not employed simply for entertainment.
4. School discourse refers to the rules of language that govern how teacher and students communicatively interact in a variety of school contexts.

Phonology

1. The study of the sound system of language is called phonology.
2. Auditory perception or, more accurately, speed sound discrimination, requires the ability to discriminate individual sounds.
3. Articulation refers to the ability of a student to produce individual sounds.

Syntax and Morphology

1. Syntax refers to the linguistic rules for combining words to make sentences.
2. Oral syntax does not develop receptively and expressively at the same time.
3. Common errors the special educator might observe in a student's oral language that often indicate syntax disorders include omission, substitutions, and reversal of word order.
4. During an evaluation, the special educator must control the amount of structure different receptive and expressive syntax tasks require of students.
5. Words are made up of one or more basic units of meaning called morphemes; the rules for developing words from morphemes is called morphology.

Semantics

1. Semantics is the study of the meaning of words and word relationships.
2. Overextension refers to a student's application of a word to a referent that according to adult language would be outside that semantic category.
3. Underextension is when a student restricts a semantic category to only a subset of referents.
4. Investigation of receptive semantic skills should include basic vocabulary, category structure, abstract language, word retrieval, and word relationships.
5. Expressive semantic skills to assess include spontaneous language, definitions, and sequencing/organization skill measures.

Developmental Progression

Preschool

1. The major goal of the preschool years is acquisition of oral communication skills.
2. Preschoolers learn their language primarily from hearing and using it in nondirected settings.

Elementary Age

1. The acquisition of written rather than oral language becomes the focus of elementary school.
2. The ability to learn to read and write requires a strong oral language foundation.

Middle/Secondary Age

1. The older student demonstrates more capability to deal with abstract language.
2. By the secondary school years, the student will develop more sophisticated abilities to evaluate language and language use.

Types of Assessment

1. The special educator evaluating the speech and language of any student should gather information about the person before the first formal testing session.
2. A student being evaluated should be observed across several activities to document the influence of context on language proficiency.
3. Many norm-referenced tests for assessing oral language have very poor reliability and validity.
4. The special educator administering tests of oral language should recognize that standardized tests measure language skills in a contrived, unnatural manner.
5. Dynamic assessment has some similarities to what Wiig and Semel (1984) call extension testing.
6. Dynamic assessment puts specific emphasis on the teacher/learner interaction, whereas extension testing focuses more on the modification of the linguistic task or strategies deficits across the student's performance.

Multicultural Assessment of Oral Language

1. Different cultural or socioeconomic groups place varying degrees of emphasis on verbal dialogue in early childhood.
2. Dialect has an impact on all areas of oral language.
3. Distinctions are made between dialects based on social stratification as well as those associated with geographical areas.
4. The special educator must recognize when regional variations of a language, social class distinction, and currently popular speech of the first language influence language performance.

5. It is not possible for a bilingual individual to have a language disorder in only one of the two languages used.
6. Assessment of language minority students should focus on communicative competence rather than only language proficiency.

Steps in the Assessment Process

1. Develop the purpose of the assessment process.
2. Develop record sheets to record assessment data.
3. Conduct an integrated assessment utilizing norm-referenced tests, oral language samples, and dynamic diagnostic measures.
4. Analyze the error patterns.
5. Develop instructional objectives based on careful analysis.

T E N

Assessing Reading

Key Terms

Automaticity of letter
Basal reading series
Basic sight words
Cloze procedure
Comprehension
Decoding
Emergent literacy skills

Maze procedure
Miscue analysis
Phonetic analysis
Reading fluency
Semantic system
Sight words
Story grammars

Structural analysis
Syntactic system
Text structure
Topological analysis
Word analysis
Word calling
Word identification

I feel like a prisoner of the printed word. If I lived in a society in which the printed word were not important I would have no learning disability. . . . Students like me find themselves behind bars of words. It is imperative that teachers and parents find a way to remove the bars and set our minds free to explore our potential.

Lee and Jackson, 1992, p. 40

Reading is a complex, language-based process that is learned over a number of years. During the elementary grades, more time is spent on reading instruction than on any other subject area. In the primary grades, students spend tremendous time learning the subskills necessary to read and understand what they are reading. In later grades, students are expected to have developed sufficient reading skills so that new material can be learned by reading. Reading failure, therefore, can have an impact on what and how much the student learns in content areas throughout the student's academic career. Not only will reading problems create difficulties academically for the student, but they can also have a significant impact on independent functioning as an adult. Obtaining a job or credit requires that the applicant have sufficient reading skills to understand and complete the application. Job performance standards and safety precautions are frequently in written manuals. Manuals accompany appliances purchased for the home. Even spending an evening with friends often requires that one read a menu or newspaper listings of movies or concerts. An inability to read or long-term reading problems will often have a psychological impact. Poor readers are quickly labeled by peers as being "dumb" and are at risk for developing low self-esteem. Low self-esteem can affect peer relationships, motivation, and an individual's willingness to try new things. Because of the tremendous, long-range impact of reading difficulty, it is one of the most frequent reasons for special education referral.

Definition of the Area

Decoding versus Meaning

A special educator who looks at the numerous tests on the market that assess reading can discover a variety of definitions of reading. Some tests require the student to read long lists of words, identify the sounds heard at the beginning or end of words, or divide words into syllables. From these kinds of tasks, the special educator might define reading as *word calling* or *word analysis*. But these *decoding* skills are only one part of the reading process. If other tests were examined, the special educator would find tasks requiring the student to answer *comprehension* questions or to supply a single word missing from one of several sentences. These tasks suggest that reading is understanding the meaning of what is read. The special educator must keep in mind that reading is a complex process that requires both decoding skills and skill in attaching meaning to what is being read. The relative importance of these skills depends on the model of reading used as a framework for assessing and teaching reading. There are three broad types of models of the reading process to consider: bottom-up models, top-down models, and interactive models.

Bottom-Up Models of Reading

Bottom-up models of reading are text driven. Reading begins with the letters on the page. The reader perceives the lines, curves, and angles that denote a specific letter. Once the features of letters are recognized, the spelling pattern is noted and the word is recognized or decoded as a word from oral language. Comprehension occurs as an automatic outcome of word recognition. Bottom-up models, like LaBerge and Samuel's (1974, 1976) model, are hierarchical; that is, the sequence of noting letters, spelling patterns, and finally recognizing the word follow one after the other. These models suggest that comprehension does not occur when steps in the sequence are missed. Mature readers have developed so much automaticity with the early steps in the sequence that it appears that those steps do not occur. Many programs for teaching reading, especially those for poor readers, are based on bottom-up models of reading. Decoding skills are taught first, usually beginning with instruction on individual letters and the sounds represented by them. Instructional programs in reading fashioned after bottom-up models include linguistic approaches, phonics-based approaches, and programmed instruction.

Top-Down Models of Reading

Comprehension is the emphasis in top-down models of reading. In these models, the reader abstracts meaning from print by using oral language competency, prior knowledge, previous experiences, questioning, and hypothesis testing. The reader attends to just enough of the graphic information to either support or reject a hypothesis about the meaning of the text. A model proposed by Goodman (1965, 1976) exemplifies a top-down model of reading. In Goodman's model, three decoding systems are used simultaneously. The *semantic (meaning) system* consists of the reader's prior experiences brought to the print along with the reader's concepts and vocabulary. The *syntactic system* is made up of sentence patterns, pattern markers, and grammatical rules. Within this system, sentence patterns are the sequences that typically occur in English (for example, Article + Noun + Verb). The pattern markers are function words (the, to, an), inflections, or common affixes, like "ed" and "ing," and punctuation marks that represent the pitch, stress, and juncture of speech. The third system, the graphophonic system, includes graphic information (letters, spelling patterns), phonological information (sounds, sound patterns), and phonic information. Phonic information is the complex set of relationships between specific sounds and letters that represent language. Using these three systems simultaneously, the reader scans a line of print, picking up clues to meaning based on graphic features of the print, language knowledge, reading strategies, and previous context. Based on these graphic clues and expectations, the reader forms perceptual images of the words. Memory is then checked by the reader for related phonological, syntactic, and semantic cues. From this check, a tentative word choice is made. If this choice fits, decoding is confirmed, and meaning is assimilated. If the choice is semantically, syntactically, or phonologically unacceptable, the reader goes back and picks up additional graphic cues until an acceptable choice is found. When meaning is attached, the cycle is repeated (Goodman, 1976).

Instructional approaches in reading that emphasize meaning are based on top-down models. The language experience approach and individualized reading instruction are two such approaches.

Interactive Models of Reading

Interactive models of reading are based on the belief that both bottom-up and top-down processing styles are necessary. In interactive models, comprehension is believed to be dependent on both graphic information and the knowledge and experiential information the reader brings to the reading task. Bottom-up and top-down processing occur simultaneously in an interactive model. Reading is viewed as "an interactive process where the reader strategically shifts between the text and what he already knows to construct his response" (Walker, 1988, p. 6). Most basal reading series teach phonics and comprehension skills simultaneously.

Developmental Progression

Foundations for Reading

Cognitive Ability

Reading is a complex process requiring many cognitive skills. Therefore, it might be expected that estimates of intelligence reflected in IQ scores would be good indicators of how well a student will do in reading. However, the research results are mixed. Kirk (1940) felt that intelligence could have a limiting factor on a child's ability to read, indicating a strong relationship. The relationship between reading and intelligence was investigated by Hammill and McNutt (1981). They reviewed one hundred research studies that suggest a high correlation between reading and intelligence. However, Harris (1972) pointed out that the degree of the relationship between intelligence and reading depends on the stage of reading that is being examined. Harris noted that "the relation between intelligence and reading is low to moderate at the beginning level, but increases as children get older. . . . As the nature of the reading task becomes more one of comprehension and interpretation, intelligence becomes a stronger determining factor" (p. 42).

Spache and Spache (1977) expressed a similar viewpoint: "Research studies of school beginners show that intelligence test results are not highly predictive of early reading success" (p. 156). In 1981, Spache did note that the intelligence/reading relationship increases as the age of the pupil increases and reading tasks require reasoning. Ekwall (1976) found that "many children with low IQs become good readers and many children with medium and high IQs become disabled readers" (p. 12). Despite the apparent inconsistency of the research results, most researchers agree that a child with a very low IQ is at a disadvantage in learning to read (Ekwall and Shanker, 1983).

Oral Language

Oral language difficulties are often strong predictors of reading problems. But, just as with intelligence, oral language skill development does not automatically suggest reading skill development. Many agree that reading is a language-based process (Carroll, 1977; Johnson and Myklebust, 1967; Myklebust, 1978; Noell, 1983; Risko, 1981; Stauffer, 1976; Strauss and Lehtinen, 1947). Researchers have described how important oral language skills are to the development of reading (Dechant, 1964; Harris, 1970; Heilman, 1972; Loban, 1963; Strickland, 1969; Zintz, 1970). Deaf children who must struggle to learn language rarely learn to read well (Gibson and Levine, 1975). Children with language delays often have difficulty learning to read later on (Vogel, 1974, 1975; Wiig and Semel, 1976). Therefore, it is important that oral language skills be assessed to determine whether oral language problems are contributing to the student's reading difficulties. In these situations, special educational services should address both the oral language and the reading problems. While oral language difficulties may suggest later reading problems, well-developed oral language skills do not guarantee that the student will be a functional reader (Hammill and McNutt, 1981).

Emotional Factors

It is very difficult to determine the exact relationships between reading and emotional problems. Regarding the development of reading skills, Fernald (1943) noted, "Some children fail to learn because they are emotionally unstable; others become emotionally unstable because they fail to learn" (p. 7). All children who have reading problems do not also have emotional problems. Similarly, there are many children with emotional problems who have no difficulty with reading. However, reading problems do place a child at risk for developing self-esteem and peer relationship problems. Rabinovitch (1968) wrote, "no discussion of reading problems in children should avoid mention of the inordinate suffering experienced by otherwise normal youngsters, cut off from communication channels that are increasingly vital for survival today" (p. 10). Researchers have found a significant positive relationship between reading achievement and self-concept (Cohn and Kornelly, 1970; Padelford, 1969). Success in learning to read contributes to a positive self-concept, while reading failure tends to have a negative impact on the self-concept. The psychodynamic symptoms of anxiety, depression and low self-esteem, hostile-aggressive behavior, learning block, and passive-withdrawn behavior were cited by Richek, List, and Lerner (1983) as problems associated with poor readers. Emotional problems contributing to reading difficulties listed by Harris and Sipay (1980) include: conscious refusal to learn, overt hostility, negative conditioning to reading, displacement hostility, resistance to pressure, clinging or depen-

Table 10-1 Stages of reading

Bush and Huebner (1970)	Chall (1983)	Doehring and Aulls (1979)	Evans, Evans, and Mercer (1986)
Prereading Stage, Birth–6 yrs.	Prereading Stage, Birth–6 yrs.	Prereading	Readiness for Reading Stage
Beginning Reading Stage, K–Gr 2	Initial Reading or Decoding Stage, Grs 1–2; Ages 6–7	Stage 1: Beginning Reading	Beginning Reading Stage
Beginning Independent Reading Stage	Confirmation, Fluency, Ungluing from Print Stage, Grs 2–3; Ages 7–8	Stage 2: Transitional Reading	Rapid Development Stage
Transition Stage, Grs 2–4			
Intermediate or Low Maturity Stage, Grs 4–6	Reading for Learning the New Stage, Middle School; Ages 9–13		
Advanced Reading Stage, Grs 7–12	Multiple View Points Stage, High School; Ages 14–18 Construction and Reconstruction Stage, College; Ages 18 and Above	Stage 3: Proficient Reading	Wide Reading Skills

dency, quick discouragement, a belief that success is dangerous, extreme distractibility or restlessness, and absorption in a private world. Because it is possible that emotional problems may result from reading failure as well as be the cause of reading problems, it is important that a comprehensive assessment of a student examine emotional development whenever reading is a presenting problem.

Reading Skill Development

The development of reading skills is best considered in stages. At any one grade level, the teacher is likely to find students whose skills reflect different stages of development. Therefore, students are typically assigned to different groups for reading instruction. Teachers strive to make these groups as homogenous as possible. Many researchers and educators have identified stages believed to reflect the development of reading skills, but there is no consensus about what to call the stages or when various stages begin and end. Table 10-1 shows four different ways researchers have partitioned reading skill development into stages. In some cases, ages or grades are assigned to each stage; in others, they are not. The stages discussed here reflect a blending of the works included in Table 10-1.

Prereading Stage

This stage generally covers the years from birth through age 6 or the preschool to kindergarten years. It is the stage in which children develop the skills prerequisite to learning to read. Language activities are very important during this stage. Young children learn to communicate by observing and imitating the communication attempts of others. Children construct implicit grammar rules that shape oral language use. During this period, the amount and type of language a child hears contributes to later reading achievement.

Parents help young children develop beginning literacy skills when they read to them. *Source:* © Carol Palmer/The Picture Cube.

Children also develop the ability to play imaginatively during this stage. Through imitative or imaginative play, children construct rules governing "beginning," "middle," and "end" sequences of play. These rules form the basis for rudimentary *story grammars,* which will later aid reading comprehension. Story grammars and other *emergent literacy skills* are further developed when adults read to young children. Through these very important adult–child reading experiences, the child develops an interest in books and reading (Strickland and Morrow, 1990). The child requests favorite books to be read aloud and demonstrates an interest in listening to stories. The child talks about or tells others favorite stories. These comments about familiar stories demonstrate an ability to recall the sequence of events, to recall details, to understand the main idea of a book (this book is about _____), and to understand basic cause and effect. The child holds the book right side up, turns pages front to back, and appears to "read" a story out loud.

These emergent literacy skills tend to develop when there are reading materials in the home and adults are observed reading. However, even children not exposed to books and adults reading develop important literacy skills from TV and the environment. Children develop an awareness of print in the environment from street signs, restaurant signs, advertisements for toys and foods, and packages of food. By the end of this stage, children should have the ability to identify objects and letters that match (visual discrimination skills) and to identify words and sounds that are the same or different (auditory discrimination skills). At the end of this stage, a child will have acquired the readiness skills listed in Table 10-2, a

Table 10-2 Reading skills network

Word Recognition and Analysis Skills

Readiness for Reading Stage

- recognizes common colors
- identifies common body parts
- sees likenesses and differences in shapes, directionality, letters, and words
- hears differences in words (same or different? hat–hit)
- recites alphabet
- names upper- and lowercase letters
- matches letters (uppercase to lowercase letters)
- recognizes own name in print
- counts from 1 to 10
- identifies numerals 1 through 10

Beginning Reading Stage

- identifies words with both upper- and lowercase letters at the beginning
- identifies words usually found in preprimers
- identifies single consonant sounds in initial, final, and medial position
- identifies sounds of two-letter consonant blends in initial position (*bl, br, fl, fr, gr, st, tr, cl, dr, pr, sl, sp, pl, gl, sk, sm, sn, sw, wr, tw, sc, dw*)
- identifies sounds of two-letter consonant digraphs in initial position (*sh, wh, th, ch*)
- knows common word families (*all, at, it, et, en, in, an, ill, ell, ay, ake*)
- recognizes word endings (*d, ed, t, s, ing*)

Rapid Development Stage

- recognizes complete list of 220 Dolch Basic Sight Words
- uses word-form clues (configuration and visual similarity)
- knows contractions
- recognizes and uses synonyms, antonyms, and homonyms
- can use elementary school dictionary to find word meanings
- alphabetizes words to the second letter
- knows additional word families (*ou, er, ow, ur, ir, oi, oy, oo, eck, ick, aw, ew, ight, ind, ack, uck, ing,* and *ike*)
- knows short-vowel sounds (*a, e, i, o,* and *u*)
- knows long-vowel sounds (*a, e, i, o,* and *u*)
- understands function of *y* as a consonant at the beginning of a word and as a vowel anywhere in a word
- knows soft and hard sounds of *c* and *g*
- knows two-letter consonant blends in final and medial position
- knows two-letter consonant digraphs in final and medial position
- knows three-letter initial blends (*str, sch, thr, spr, spl, chr*)
- understands silent consonants in *kn, wr, gn*
- recognizes root words
- recognizes word endings (*en, er, est, ful, y, ly*)
- recognizes compound words
- recognizes and uses possessives
- knows basic phonics rules:
  - a single vowel in a word or syllable is usually short
  - a single *e* at the end of a word makes the preceding vowel long
  - a single vowel at the end of a word is usually long
  - where there are two vowels together, the first is long and the second silent
  - in attaching a vowel sound, try first the short sound, then the long sound
- knows basic rules for changing words (adding *s, es, d, ed, ing, er, est;* dropping final *c* and adding *ing,* doubling the consonant before adding *ing,* changing *y* to *i* before adding *es*)
- knows basic rules for forming plurals (adding *s, es, ies;* by changing *f* to *ve* before adding *es*)   *(continued)*

Table 10-2 Reading skills network *(continued)*

Word Recognition and Analysis Skills

- knows basic syllabication rules:
  - there are usually as many syllables in a word as there are vowels
  - where there is a single consonant between two vowels, the vowel goes with the first syllable (*pa-per*)
  - when there is a double consonant, the syllable break is between the two consonants and is silent

Wide Reading Stage

- knows new vocabulary in content areas (math, science, social studies)
- knows multiple meanings of words
- uses context clues
- knows accent clues:
  - first syllable is usually accented, unless it is a prefix
  - endings that form syllables are usually unaccented (skipp*ing*)
  - *ck* following a single vowel is accented (*rack-et*)
- knows and uses prefixes and suffixes
- recognizes similarities of known words such as compound words, root words, suffixes, prefixes, plurals, and hyphenated words
- knows additional rules for syllables:
  - each syllable must contain a vowel; a single vowel can be a syllable
  - suffixes and prefixes are syllables
  - root words and blends are not divided
  - if the first vowel is followed by two consonants, the first syllable usually ends with the consonant
  - if the first vowel is followed by a single consonant, the consonant usually begins the second syllable
  - if a word ends in *ie* preceded by a consonant, that consonant begins the last syllable
  - the letter *x* always goes with the preceding vowel to form a syllable
  - the letters *ck* go with the preceding vowel and the end the syllable
  - when there is an *r* after a vowel, the *r* goes with the vowel
- understands homophones and homographs
- understands and recognizes figurative expressions including metaphors and similes

Comprehension Skills

Readiness for Reading Stage

- wants to learn to read
- likes to be read to
- can work independently for short periods
- can follow three-part directions
- can sequence events logically
- can recall main ideas and names of characters from story read aloud

Beginning Reading Stage

- can follow printed directions
- can draw conclusions from given facts
- can recall major details and sequence of story read aloud
- can recall main ideas, names of characters, major details, and sequence of story after silent reading
- can distinguish between real and imaginary events
- can suggest or select an appropriate title for a story
- can relate story content to own experiences

Rapid Development Stage

- can draw logical conclusions
- can predict outcomes
- can see relationships in story

(continued)

Table 10-2 Reading skills network *(continued)*

Comprehension Skills

- can classify items
- can read for a definite purpose (for pleasure, to answer a question, to obtain general idea of content)
- can use table of contents, index, glossary, encyclopedia (to locate a topic), telephone directory
- knows technique of skimming
- knows technique of scanning
- can determine what source to use to obtain information (dictionary, encyclopedia, index, glossary, etc.)
- uses maps, graphs, charts, diagrams, and tables

Wide Reading Stage

- can take notes from lectures and reading
- can outline using main idea headings (I, II, III) and subordinate idea headings (A, B, C)
- can talk from an outline
- can locate information (periodicals, reference materials, other library skills)
- reads creatively to (a) interpret story ideas, (b) see relationships, (c) identify the mood in a story, (d) identify the author's purpose, and (e) identify character traits
- reads for pleasure from a variety of sources

Oral and Silent Reading Skills

Readiness for Reading Stage

Oral Reading Skills
- gives name and age
- speaks in complete sentences
- is able to remember a five-word sentence

Beginning Reading Stage

Oral Reading Skills
- uses correct pronunciation
- uses correct phrasing
- uses proper voice intonation to give meaning
Silent Reading Skills
- reads without vocalization, lip movements, or whispering
- reads without head movements
- reads without pointing

Rapid Development Stage

Oral Reading Skills
- reads clearly and distinctly
- reads with adequate volume
Silent Reading Skills
- reads more rapidly silently than orally

Wide Reading Stage

Oral Reading Skills
- reads with understanding and expression
- varies rate depending on reading material
- reads without constantly looking at reading material
Silent Reading Skills
- reads with good comprehension
- adjusts rate depending on reading material

Source: From Susan S. Evans, William H. Evans, and Cecil D. Mercer, ASSESSMENT FOR INSTRUCTION, pp. 169–172. Copyright © 1986 by Allyn and Bacon. Reprinted by permission.

reading skills network. Children who do not have these skills are not ready for formal reading instruction.

Beginning Reading Stage

This stage tends to cover children ages 6 to 8 or kindergarten through third grade. It is the stage when formal reading instruction begins. Where that instruction begins will depend on the philosophy of the primary grade teacher. Some will begin by having the class develop stories from classroom experiences and have children identify whole words or sentences, reflecting a top-down model of reading. Others will begin by teaching sound/symbol relationships, reflecting a bottom-up model of reading. No matter how this instruction begins, before the stage ends the child has developed several word analysis skills, has a growing *sight word* vocabulary, and has had his or her attention focused on the meaning of words, sentences, passages, and short stories. By the end of this stage, children are expected to have sufficient reading skills to be able to read and follow directions independently on classroom assignments. Children are introduced to the library and are encouraged to select and read books independently. Some of the skills developed during this period are listed in Table 10-2.

Rapid Development or Transition Stage

This stage roughly covers ages 9 to 13 or grades four through eight. Direct instruction in reading continues, tending to focus on mastering word analysis skills, developing a wide variety of comprehension skills, and learning about different styles or types of literature. Although direct reading instruction continues, it is during this stage that there is a shift in how much reading is expected of a student. In the beginning reading stage, much of the reading done was for the purpose of learning skills. During this transition stage, students are expected to read content textbooks (that is, science, social studies) to learn new material. Students also read for recreation. Reading instruction includes teaching *text structure,* library skills, and study skills. The instructional emphasis is clearly on the meaning of what is read. Table 10-2, under the headings of rapid development and wide reading, lists some of the skills developed during this stage.

Advanced or Proficient Reading Stage

Ages 14 and beyond, or the high school and college years, are covered by this stage. Students no longer receive direct instruction in reading. That instructional time is now used for vocabulary development and the study of various types and periods of literature. Students have mastered word identification techniques and developed evaluative and critical reading skills. Students are refining the reference and study skills that allow independence with complex and technical reading material.

Concerns Expressed by the Classroom Teacher

Students referred by regular classroom teachers because of difficulty with reading are usually not progressing well through the adopted reading curriculum. Since regular classroom teachers have other students for comparison, the concerns they

This student is in the proficient reading stage and can study periods of literature since she no longer needs direct instruction in word attack skills and comprehension strategies. *Source:* © Cleo Freelance Photo/New England Stock Photo

express about individual students indicate problems beyond what can be reasonably expected for students who have had similar instructional experiences. Common concerns expressed by classroom teachers can be divided into three categories: reading behaviors, word analysis difficulties, and comprehension difficulties. Box 10-1 lists some of the difficulties experienced under each of these broad categories.

Types of Assessment Tasks

What Are You Measuring and Why?

Tremendous emphasis is placed on learning to read and using reading skills to learn content material. Because of this emphasis, the progress students make in reading is closely monitored. Reading curriculum materials frequently include student workbooks, skill development work sheets, and periodic tests to assess skill mastery. These study aids are routinely used in the regular classroom. In the early elementary grades, regular classroom teachers spend time listening to students read orally. In addition, most school districts follow a specific schedule for administering group

Box 10-1   *Characteristics that Signal Possible Reading Difficulties*

Reading Behaviors

- Reads in a slow word-for-word manner
- Reads rapidly, ignoring punctuation
- Points to each word with a finger
- Repeats words, phrases and sentences, or lines
- Looses place when reading
- Reads the pictures instead of the words
- Uses poor phrasing when reading orally
- Lacks expression when reading orally
- Uses a monotonous tone of voice when reading orally
- Uses a voice that is too high or low during oral reading
- Uses a voice that is too loud, too soft, or sounds strained during oral reading
- Enunciates poorly during oral reading
- Head moves during reading tasks
- Approaches all reading tasks the same
- Appears anxious or nervous in a reading situation
- Is easily distracted from reading
- Tries to avoid reading anything
- Is unable to sit still when reading
- Gives up easily on reading tasks
- Misbehaves or asks for frequent breaks during reading class

Word Analysis Difficulties

- Reverses words (for example, *saw* for *was*)
- Reverses or inverts letters in words (for example, *b* for *d*, *g* for *q*, *u* for *n*, *p* for *b*) beyond age 8
- Has difficulty pronouncing many words in reading and oral language
- Substitutes words that are either visually alike or are similar in meaning
- Makes guesses about unknown words instead of demonstrating any decoding strategies
- Has difficulty identifying rhyming words
- Cannot produce rhyming words automatically
- Does not correctly associate letters with their sounds
- Cannot identify words beginning with a particular sound
- Cannot distinguish between long and short vowel sounds
- Has difficulty hearing the number of vowel sounds in words (for example, cannot clap out the syllables)
- Cannot remember sight words
- Requires extra time to complete a reading assignment

(continued)

Comprehension Difficulties

- Adds words or leaves words out in oral reading
- Stops at the end of each line whether punctuation dictates it or not
- Ignores discrepancies when reading makes no sense
- Cannot recall basic story details
- Cannot sequence the events from a story
- Cannot predict possible endings to sentences or stories
- Has difficulty retelling a story just read
- Answers comprehension questions based on personal experience rather than on information presented in the story
- Does not make inferences
- Has difficulty making conclusions about information read
- Has difficulty identifying the main idea of a passage just read
- Has difficulty locating specific information within a text
- Cannot answer questions relating to vocabulary from a reading selection
- Has difficulty giving either the synonyms or antonyms of given words
- Has difficulty following written directions

achievement tests containing subtests on reading comprehension, word analysis skills and, in the intermediate and upper grades, study skills. In some parts of the country, state- or district-wide competency tests in reading are criteria for promotion to selected grades or for graduation.

When a student fails to meet the expectations of the regular education reading curriculum, reading becomes a focus for individualized assessment. Depending on the stage of the assessment process, many questions can be raised concerning a student's reading abilities. Early in the assessment process, questions typically deal with eligibility for special education and determining if reading is a general strength or weakness. Later in the process, questions focus on specific skills in word analysis and reading comprehension for which special instructional objectives are needed. Assessment of reading continues to be an important issue throughout the student's special education program as progress is monitored, special instruction adjusted, and plans made for reintegrating the student into the regular classroom or for transition to a postsecondary training program, school, or job site. A combination of norm-referenced, criterion-referenced, curriculum-based, and dynamic assessment tools are used, depending on the particular questions that need to be answered.

Norm-Referenced Tools and Inventories

The first question asked about reading performance is whether the student is under-achieving compared to age or grade peers and compared to the student's mental ability. Some norm-referenced data will already be available from subtests on group and individually administered achievement tests. These tests were discussed in chapter 2. Additional, in-depth norm-referenced data may be required for special education eligibility, depending on the state regulations and procedures for various types of disabilities, and examiners will then use diagnostic reading tests. Performance on these tests is usually reported as a percentile rank, some type of standard score, or an age-equivalent or grade-equivalent score. Since diagnostic reading tests often have several subtests assessing different aspects of reading, several scores may be available. It is important that the evaluator understand the numerous variables that may affect the student's performance as reflected in the scores. Sometimes a student may obtain surprisingly different scores on subtests whose names suggest they assess the same thing. Similarly, the classroom teacher may report that a student is failing reading, yet individually administered test results may indicate that the student's reading ability is in the normal range. These discrepancies are often attributed to the structure and format of the subtests.

Oral Reading Tests and Subtests

Diagnostic reading tests are typically divided into subtests measuring oral reading, decoding skills, and comprehension skills. Tasks measuring oral reading ability can be found on several norm-referenced tests. Typically, the student is given a series of passages of increasing difficulty. Without any opportunity to scan the passage, the student is told to read it out loud. The examiner marks the errors the student makes while reading. Sometimes examiners tape-record the student's oral reading and double check the accuracy with which errors were marked at a later time. The examiner frequently times the student's reading. The number of errors and reading rate are usually considered together in deriving a score. On most oral reading tests the examiner will ask the student comprehension questions about the story.

Word Analysis Tests and Subtests

Assessments of decoding skills measure the student's ability to recognize letters and words in print. The examiner is usually interested in identifying how automatic letter and word identification is and the student's proficiency in using various word analysis skills. *Automaticity of letter* and *word identification* is assessed by using a "flash" or tachistoscopic presentation of a list of letters and lists of words arranged according to difficulty. When letters are presented, there is usually a mix of uppercase letters, lowercase letters, and letters of different types (for example, italic, script, gothic print). When lists of words are presented tachistoscopically, the examiner is interested in learning about the student's sight word vocabulary.

Sometimes word identification tasks are not timed. These tasks are used to determine the approximate level of the student's independent reading vocabulary. The absence of timing allows the student to employ various word analysis skills. These untimed tasks have different formats. One format presents lists of isolated words of increasing difficulty. The student simply reads the list while the examiner marks the words as correct or incorrect. Some examiners tape-record the student reading the words so they can examine the types of errors the student made at a

Table 10-3 Word analysis skills

Phonetic Analysis
   Single consonant sounds
   Initial consonant blends (for example, *bl, fr, st, thr, sch*)
   Final consonant blends (for example, *sh, th, wh, ck, ph*)
   Long and short vowel sounds
   Sounds of vowel combinations
   Rules governing vowel sounds
Structural Analysis
   Prefix recognition and meaning
   Suffix recognition and meaning
   Rules for adding prefixes and suffixes
   Compound words
   Multisyllabic words formed with prefixes and suffixes (for example, professional, detective,
      tremendous)
   Syllabication rules
Context Clues
Dictionary Skills
   Alphabetical order
   Alphabetizing words to the third letter
   Using guide words
   Selecting appropriate definition for context
   Using diacritical marks to aid pronunciation
   Identifying parts of speech

---

later time. When examiners do this, they typically have more information for later instructional planning than is normally available from these norm-referenced tasks. Another word identification or recognition format provides the student with a picture and a list of possible word choices. The student selects the word or words that go along with the picture. Still other formats require the student to select one of four words the examiner reads orally.

Word analysis refers to the skills used to decode unknown words. Table 10-3 identifies four broad categories of decoding skills and gives examples of the types of skills required within each category. Many norm-referenced tasks assess these skills. *Phonetic analysis* refers to the ability to associate sounds with particular letters. In the area of phonetic analysis, students are sometimes shown single letters, blends, diagraphs, or vowel combinations and asked to say the sound represented. On other tasks, students are given several choices of letters and asked to identify the letters that represent the beginning and ending sounds of words the examiner says. Sometimes the same basic task requires students to circle one of several letters that represent the sound heard at either the beginning or the end of a word illustrated by a picture. Young children may be required to circle two of several pictures whose names begin or end with the same sound. Older students may be given several printed words and asked to circle the two with the same vowel sound. Another common task requires that students orally read nonsense words. The student is expected to use correct phonics rules to properly pronounce the nonsense word.

Readers relying on structural analysis to decode unknown words use their knowledge of prefixes, suffixes, root words, and syllabication rules. One test format presents the student with words and asks the student to identify a particular attribute of the word (for example, underline a prefix, suffix, or root word; tell the number of syllables in a word). Other subtests require students to divide words into syllables. Still others provide several syllable choices for each item. The student must then circle the two or three syllables that go together to form a real word. To assess knowledge of compound words, the student is given a stimulus word and several word choices. The student must identify one of the choices that can be put with the stimulus to make a compound word. Knowledge of contractions is assessed by providing a contraction and having the student identify the two words the contraction stands for, or present the two words and have the student form the contraction. Finally, on some tests requiring the student to read nonsense words, the words are best decoded by using *structural analysis*. The examiner should do an item analysis of the nonsense word reading task to determine whether structural analysis could be used.

The use of context clues is best assessed on oral reading tasks or reading comprehension tests that use a *cloze procedure*. While the student is reading orally, the examiner may notice the student struggling with a difficult word and then spontaneously correcting an initial mispronunciation. This type of self-correction suggests that the student has used a combination of decoding skills including the use of context clues. However, only an analysis of the types of errors and self-corrections made by the student will provide any clues to the student's ability to use context clues.

Cloze tasks are usually used to assess reading comprehension. The student is given a sentence or short passage to read that has one or more missing words. The student is required to read the passage and supply the missing word or words. Again, error analysis is critical to understanding the student's ability to use context clues. Sometimes the selected word may fit grammatically within the sentence even if the choice had to be counted wrong because it reflects a lack of understanding of specific details given earlier in the passage. Other times the selected word will not fit syntactically or with the previous details. In fact, the word may be grossly out of context. Determining the frequency of each type of error provides information on context clues.

Dictionary skills are rarely assessed on norm-referenced diagnostic reading tests. Sometimes these skills are measured on group administered, multisubject achievement tests. (Chapter 2 contains a list of such tests.) At other times, dictionary skills are included on tests of study skills. Chapter 14 provides additional information on those tests.

Comprehension Tests and Subtests

Assessments of comprehension skills measure the student's ability to gain meaning from print. These tests and subtests examine the various skills listed in Table 10-4. In the early grades, vocabulary tests and some word analysis tests may be identical. On these subtests, the student is given a picture and several word choices. The student is required to mark the words that go with each picture. In later grades, the student may be given a sentence with a single missing word and asked to supply the word that best fits into the sentence. On other vocabulary tests for higher grades, the student may be given a set of several words as the stimulus. The student must think how those words are alike and select two of four possible choices that go along with the stimulus set of words. Other vocabulary comprehension subtests provide definitions, and the student must select one of several choices that fit the specific definition, or the student is given

Table 10-4 Comprehension skills

Vocabulary Development
Literal Comprehension: Recognition and Recall of
  Details
  Main ideas
  Sequence
  Comparisons
  Cause–effect relationships
  Character traits
Inferential Comprehension
  Predicting outcomes
  Interpreting figurative language
  Forming hypothesis about story making identifying cause–effect relationships
  Identifying or comparing character traits
Evaluative or Critical Comprehension
  Reality versus fantasy
  Fact versus opinion
  Adequacy of information
  Worth, desirability, and acceptability of ideas
Appreciation

---

the word and must select one of several definitions that best matches the word. At times, students are required to select the synonyms or antonyms of specific words.

Some comprehension subtests examine the understanding of single sentences or short phrases. Children are given a sentence and asked to select one of several pictures that best illustrates the sentence, or are given a picture and asked to pick one of several single sentences that best matches the picture. Sometimes the student is given a phrase or short sentence and asked to pantomime or follow the directions. On other tests, students are given several single sentences and asked to mark the two that have the same basic meaning.

As children move through school they are required to read longer passages, and comprehension subtests reflect that shift. Many such subtests provide the student with a passage consisting of several paragraphs. The student is required to read the passage and answer multiple choice questions about the content of the passage. Most of these types of tasks are timed, so rate of reading is also reflected in the score. On individually administered subtests, the student answers the questions orally and is not provided with choices of responses. The questions typically require a mix of literal, inferential, and evaluative comprehension skills. An error analysis is necessary to learn whether the student has different abilities depending on the type of comprehension needed. Table 10-5 provides a list of norm-referenced diagnostic reading tests that assess word analysis and comprehension skills.

Criterion-Referenced Tools and Inventories

Criterion-referenced tools and inventories are commercially produced and assist in identifying instructional objectives the student has mastered and those that require further work. An analysis of errors a student makes on norm-referenced tests helps to broadly identify areas in which further instruction might be needed. Criterion-

Table 10-5 Norm-referenced measures of reading performance

Name (Authors)	Ages or Grades	Group/Individual	Publisher
Diagnostic Reading Scales (Spache, 1981a)	Grs. 1–8	I	CTB/McGraw-Hill
Doren Diagnostic Reading Test of Word Recognition Skills (Doren, 1973)	Grs. 1–6	G	American Guidance
Durrell Analysis of Reading Difficulty (Durrell and Catterson, 1980)	Grs. 1–6	I	Psychological Corporation
Formal Reading Inventory (Wiederholt, 1986)	Ages 7–18	I	PRO-ED
Gates–MacGinitie Reading Tests (MacGinitie, 1978)	Grs. K–12	G	Riverside Publishing
Gates–McKillop–Horowitz Reading Diagnostic Tests (Gates, McKillop, and Horowitz, 1981)	Grs. 1–6	I	Teachers College Press
Gilmore Oral Reading Test (Gilmore and Gilmore, 1968)	Grs. 1–8	I	Psychological Corporation
Gray Oral Reading Tests Diagnostic (Bryant and Wiederholt, 1990)	Grs. K–6	I	PRO-ED
Gray Oral Reading Tests Revised (Wiederholt and Bryant, 1986)	Grs. 1–12	I	PRO-ED

referenced reading tests and inventories help pinpoint specific areas where instruction should occur. Performance results on these measures are sometimes reported as grade- or age-equivalents. Other times, no score is available. In either situation, the examiner will be able to identify specific instructional objectives in reading that can be used to develop the student's IEP. Criterion-referenced tools and inventories in reading can be found that assess a variety of word analysis and comprehension skills. However, the examiner needs to consider the numerous variables mentioned previously when selecting a criterion-referenced measure or inventory. Another important factor in selecting a criterion-referenced measure in reading is the fact that some measures are keyed to particular reading textbook series.

Once an objective needing further work is identified, the examiner can locate the pages in the *basal reading series* where that objective is taught. When objectives are not keyed to basal series, sometimes instructional activities for specific objectives are suggested. Table 10-6 lists criterion-referenced measures and inventories available in reading. Unlike norm-referenced tests that may be group or individually administered, criterion-referenced tests and inventories are typically individually administered. The grade levels that appear in Table 10-6 do not refer to actual grade placement as much as to functional grade level. Students placed in tenth grade can be given a criterion-referenced test or an inventory at an eighth-grade level if their reading skills are significantly below grade placement.

Curriculum-Based Reading Assessments

Curriculum-based assessments of reading typically include measures of word attack skills, word recognition or sight vocabulary, oral reading fluency, and reading com-

Table 10-6 Criterion-referenced measures and inventories of reading performance

Name (Authors)	Grades	Criterion-Referenced or Inventory
Advanced Reading Inventory	Primer–Gr. 9	I
Analytical Reading Inventory, 4th ed. (Woods and Moe, 1989)	Grs. 1–6	I
Bader Language and Reading Inventory (Bader, 1983)	Grs. 1–6	I
Boder Test of Reading–Spelling Patterns (Boder and Jarrico, 1982)	Preprimer–adult	I
Botel Reading Inventory (Botel, 1978)	Grs. 1–8	I
BRIGANCE Diagnostic Comprehensive Inventory of Basic Skills (Brigance, 1983)	Grs. K–9	CR
BRIGANCE Diagnostic Inventory of Essential Skills (Brigance, 1981)	Grs. K–6	CR
BRIGANCE Diagnostic Inventory of Basic Skills (Brigance, 1977)	Grs. 4–12	CR
Classroom Reading Inventory, 5th ed. (Silvaroli, 1986)	Preprimer–Gr. 8	I
Criterion-Referenced Curriculum–Reading (Stephens, 1982b)	Grs. K–6	CR
Diagnosis: An Instructional Reading Aid (Shub, Carlin, Friedman, Kaplan, and Katien, 1973)	Grs. K–6	I
Ekwall Reading Inventory, 2nd ed. (Ekwall, 1986)	Preprimer–Gr. 9	I
Fountain Valley Teacher Support System in Reading (Zweig, 1971)		CR
Hudson Educational Skills–Reading (Hudson, Colson, and Welch, 1989b)	Grs. K–12	CR
Multilevel Academic Skills Program Inventory: Reading (Howell, Zucker, and Morehead, 1982)	Grs. 1–8	CR
New Sucher–Allred Reading Placement Inventory (Sucher and Allred, 1981)	Primer–Gr. 9	I
Prescriptive Reading Inventory (CTB/McGraw–Hill, 1972)	Grs. 1–8	CR
Reading Comprehension Inventory (Giordano, 1988)	Grs. K–6	I
Reading Miscue Inventory (Goodman, Watson, and Burke, 1987)	Grs. 1–8+	I
Standardized Reading Inventory (Newcomer, 1986)	Preprimer–Gr. 8	CR
System FORE (Bagai and Bagai, 1979)	Grs. K–12	CR
Wisconsin Tests of Reading Skill Development (1972, 1977)	Grs. K–6	I

prehension. The point at which the teacher begins the assessment will depend on whether the adopted reading curriculum uses a bottom-up or a top-down model as its theoretical basis. If the curriculum uses a bottom-up model, the teacher will probably begin by assessing word attack skills such as knowledge of beginning consonant sounds, knowledge of long vowel sounds, and knowledge of short vowel sounds in the order in which the skills are introduced in the curriculum. The teacher would then move to sight vocabulary, oral reading fluency, and reading comprehension. If the adopted curriculum uses a top-down model, the teacher may begin by assessing sight vocabulary, reading comprehension, and then word attack skills.

These informal, teacher developed probes must be based on the curriculum the student is expected to use to provide guidance in developing appropriate instruction.

Curriculum expectations depend on the age and ability level of the student. Peers of younger students are themselves still learning how to read. Therefore, younger students served in special education are still expected to attempt a standard developmental curriculum, typically a basal reading series used across several grade levels. Older students who have mild degrees of various handicapping conditions might also be expected to continue working in a standard developmental curriculum. In these situations, the teacher should draw sight vocabulary and material to assess reading comprehension from the basal series. Older students with moderate to severe degrees of handicaps and young students with severe or profound degrees of handicaps are often expected to follow a functional curriculum. This curriculum is typically used only in special education and focuses on reading tasks required for adult independence. The teacher concentrates on developing sight vocabulary from safety (danger, warning, poison, hot), vocational (name, employer, employee, date of birth), transportation (bus stop, taxi stand) and environmental (restroom, women, men, enter, exit) vocabularies. Reading comprehension focuses on phrases needed to read job applications, want ads, and menus. In these situations, the informal assessment tools the teacher develops focus on this specialized vocabulary.

Word attack skills.   Teachers need to consider the time (that is, when skills are introduced in the curriculum), the order, and the sequence of different word attack skills when developing assessments. These factors dictate the specific content of teacher developed assessment tools for word attack skills. Typically, the teacher will develop assessment tasks that examine some of the subskills that appeared under phonetic and structural analysis in Table 10-3. The teacher can vary the tasks developed by requiring both recognition and recall responses. For example, if the teacher is interested in the student's knowledge of single consonants, the teacher could present a list of consonants and ask the child to point to the letter that makes the /t/ sound. This task requires a recognition response from the student. On the other hand, the teacher could say the /t/ sound to the student and require that the student say or write the letter that makes the sound. This requires recall of the letter name or letter formation and is a more difficult task. To determine whether the student is able to apply the rules governing letter sounds or syllabication rules, the teacher may want to use phonetically regular real words from the basal series that are well beyond the child's sight word reading level or use nonsense words that require the application of specific rules. Initial assessments and instructional objectives should focus on the student's accuracy with letter sounds and application rules. As the student develops accuracy, assessment and instruction can shift to development of speed/automaticity.

Word recognition.   When a teacher decides to examine a student's word recognition skills, the teacher is really concerned with the extensiveness of the child's sight vocabulary. The teacher first needs to determine whether the child is in a developmental or functional curriculum. If the child is in a developmental curriculum, the teacher should select words from the basal series as target words for assessment and instruction. In the teacher's edition, many basal series contain lists of words that are introduced at each level. If the purpose of the curriculum-based assessment is to identify the approximate level of the child's sight vocabulary, the teacher presents lists of about twenty words from each level. Such a sampling helps the teacher place the student in an appropriate level. Once the level is identified, the teacher may choose to present a more extensive list of words from that particular level to target words for direct instruction.

Some authors make the distinction between *sight words* and *basic sight words* (Ekwall and Shanker, 1983). The procedures discussed in the preceding paragraph will help the teacher identify a particular student's sight word vocabulary in relation to a specific curriculum. Basic sight words are high-utility words that often appear on lists not associated with a particular curriculum. The Dolch List (Dolch, 1948, 1950) is one example of such a list. Basic sight word lists are typically found in college level reading methods textbooks. These lists contain words that the student is likely to encounter in a wide variety of basal series and trade books.

Whether the teacher is assessing the student's sight vocabulary or basic sight vocabulary, the speed with which the student names the words is a factor. Sometimes the teacher constructs an oaktag tachistoscope, which allows presentation of one word at a time from a word list through the use of a small slot or window. The teacher may also print the words on small cards and expose each card for a very brief period of time (for example, one second). The words the child reads during such a brief presentation are considered to be the student's sight vocabulary. Longer exposures allow the student to apply word attack skills to decode the words.

Reading fluency. A third area that may be included in teacher developed curriculum-based assessments is *reading fluency,* which is the rate and accuracy with which a student is able to read connected text. To construct a reading fluency assessment, the teacher selects a beginning passage from each basal reading text that is representative of the language and vocabulary of that level within the adopted series. Evans, Evans, and Mercer (1986) recommend that a fifty-word selection be used at the preprimer level, a one hundred-word passage be used at the primer and first grade levels, and that 200-word passages be selected at second grade and above. Once the passages are selected and typed so there is one passage per page, the student is given the passages, one at a time, and asked to read them out loud. The teacher tape-records the reading for careful analysis later. The teacher follows along on another copy of the passage as the student reads and begins noting types of errors. Once the student has read several passages, the teacher calculates the percentage of words read correctly. Table 10-7 illustrates the calculation of the percentage of words read correctly and how those percentages translate into reading levels. The assessment goal is to identify the instructional level for the student.

Error analysis is an important component of the assessment process, providing information that can be invaluable in planning instruction. Everyone makes occasional random or careless errors, and these errors can be overlooked. However, poor readers or students just learning to read make errors that reflect strategies they are trying to use to decode words. These errors provide information on what strate-

Table 10-7 Calculating reading accuracy and accuracy levels

	Accuracy Level
Independent Reading Level	95% or better
Instructional Reading Level	85%–95%
Frustration Reading Level	Below 85%

$$\frac{\text{Total Correct Words}}{\text{Total Number of Words}} = \text{Percentage Accuracy}$$

gies the student has developed and may be using inappropriately. The primary way the teacher learns about these strategies is by analyzing errors the student makes as the student orally reads connected text.

Salvia and Hughes (1990) discuss two broad types of error analysis: topological analysis and miscue analysis. *Topological analysis* examines how accurately the student reproduces the text while reading orally. For this type of analysis, the teacher provides a text for the student to read orally. As the student reads, the teacher tape-records the oral reading and follows along on a copy of the text. The teacher marks the errors the student makes. After the student has finished all reading, the teacher uses the tape recording to double check the marking system and to pick up any errors that may have gone undetected while the student read orally. Several authors have studied students' oral reading errors and suggested notational systems for marking errors (D'Angelo and Wilson, 1979; Ekwall, 1976, 1981; Swaby, 1984). Table 10-8 lists various error types and provides examples of how to mark them.

Table 10-8 Oral reading errors

Error Type	Notation	Example
Insertions	Indicate with a caret and write in the insertion.	straight The girl had long ˄ black hair.
Omissions	Circle omitted word, word part, or punctuation.	The girl had (long) black hair.
Substitutions	Write substituted real word above the target word.	blond The girl had black hair.
Mispronunciations	Write phonetic pronunciation of the nonsense word above the target word.	gil The girl had black hair.
Aid	After waiting briefly, supply the unknown word and draw a line under it.	The truck <u>careened</u> around the mountain curve.
Repetition	Draw a wavy line under the word or phrase repeated	The truck careened <u>around</u> the mountain curve.
Hesitations	Note with a slash mark.	The truck / careened around the mountain curve.
Reversals	Draw a line indicating the transposition of words	The boy ran slowly.
Self-Corrected Errors	Mark the original errors and then place a C above the error.	C gil The girl had black hair.

Topological analysis aids the teacher in identifying error types; it does not help the teacher understand substitution errors that distort or change the meaning of the text. *Miscue analysis* will help the teacher develop that understanding by considering the semantic (meaning) and syntactical (grammar) relationship between the target word and the word the student substituted for it. Again, several authors have examined miscue analysis (Goodman, 1969; Goodman and Burke, 1972; Hammill and Bartel, 1986). Table 10-9 provides one type of miscue analysis that considers why substitution errors may have occurred.

The rate of reading is obtained by timing the student as the passage is read out loud. It is less distracting to the student if the timing is done when the teacher listens to the tape recording of the student reading. The time needed to read the passage is simply recorded on the bottom of the teacher's copy of the passage. Scoring the rate is done by counting the number of words the student read correctly and the number of words read incorrectly. Each of these numbers is then divided by the number of minutes the student needed to read the passage, resulting in a words per minute score. Mercer and Mercer (1985) suggest that when reading words in connected text, the teacher should look for the level at which the student is able to read 100-words per minute with two or fewer errors. Sometimes a student's accuracy reading level is higher than the student's rate of reading level. For example, a student may be reading at the sixth grade level with respect to accuracy yet only be reading at a fifth grade level with respect to rate. The better placement is probably the fifth grade level because, as several investigators have found, the number of words read correctly during timed oral reading is closely related to how much is understood (Deno, 1985; Deno, Mirkin, and Chiang, 1982; Fuchs, Fuchs, and Maxwell, 1988).

Reading comprehension. The final goal in reading is understanding and using the material read. Therefore, evaluating reading comprehension is an important part of curriculum-based assessment. Several evaluation procedures can be used in teacher developed, curriculum-based assessments. One very direct procedure is to ask the student questions based on a passage the student has just read. First, the teacher selects passages representative of the different levels of difficulty in the basal series. Oftentimes the teacher uses the same series of passages selected to assess oral reading fluency. Next, the teacher decides whether the questions will be asked orally or whether the student must answer written questions. Oral questions require a recall type of response. Written multiple choice questions require a recognition type of response. Open-ended written questions require writing skills that might also be difficult for the student with reading problems. When written questions are used, the teacher must be sure that the questions are written at the same difficulty level as that of the text. Once the decision is made about whether oral or written questions will be used, the teacher must develop the questions. Five to ten questions should be developed for each passage. The number of questions prepared depends on the length of the passage and the level of difficulty of the material. Questions that can be answered either "yes" or "no" should not be used. The types of questions the teacher develops will depend on the aspect of comprehension to be assessed. To decide this, the teacher compares the various kinds of literal, inferential, and evaluative skills depicted in Table 10-4 with the scope and sequence of

Table 10-9 A sample miscue analysis chart

Types of Summaries Analysis	Examples	Hypothesis of "What the Teacher Does Next."
I. Graphic Analysis a. No discernible similarity (no shared letters)	King/Lady	Probe whether the student is just guessing. Student may have virtually no word attack skills (test further with commercial or teacher-made word analysis test).
b. Words similar in overall configuration	Leg/Boy	Student may be utilizing configural clues. This is a strength that needs to be built on and supplemented with other word analysis skills.
c. Reversal of single letter	Bad/Dad	Recheck student's ability to discriminate between b and d, also between other pairs, such as p and q. Provide left–right activities, also specific exercises for discrimination training. See also section on grammatical appropriateness.
d. Reversal of two or more letters	Was/Saw	Provide activities as indicated in I.c.
e. Beginning letters similar	Play/Plant	Student is correctly utilizing initial consonant blend cue. He or she needs to be encouraged to utilize middle and ending graphic cues, also to attend to context. Check other initial letters.
f. Middle letters similar	Good/Food	Same as I.e. except with middle letters.
g. Ending letters similar	That/What	Same as I.e. except with ending letters; also extra exercises with "wh" and "th" letters.
h. Single letter omission, deletion, or substitution	Very/Every	Student needs to be encouraged to look at entire word, also needs help using syntactic and semantic cues.
i. Similar root word; suffix/prefix miscue	Toys/Toy	Check for presence of dialect; then use activities dealing with singular and plural, also encourage attention to word endings.
II. Syntactic Analysis a. Beginning position in sentence	The boy . . . Who . . .	Check whether student can discriminate between these words when they occur later in the sentence; if so, he or she is relying heavily on syntactic cues (which is good) but needs more help on word analysis skills.
b. Middle or ending position in sentence	Mary ran far/ Mary ran fast	Student is using syntactic and semantic features of the sentence (good); needs help as in I.e.
c. Grammatical appropriateness (Substituted word has same rate of occurrence as stimulus word? Sentence grammatical up to and including miscue?)	John found his pet/John found his play	Student relying on initial letter cue (good) but is not showing grammatical awareness. Does student have mastery of oral language? If so, further testing and activities with cloze technique and "guess the end of the sentence game" might be used.
III. Semantic Analysis a. Stimulus word and child's response unrelated or only partially related	Peter could Peter cold	Student is using fairly sophisticated word analysis skills (teacher can build on this) but needs sequential sentence, speaking, and reading opportunities. Other activities as in II.c.
b. Meaning of student's response acceptable in sentence, but not related to stimulus sentence or paragraph	Jerry went home/Jerry went away	Student is thinking about the internal meaning of the word (good) but is not relating it to the meaning of the story. Student lacks word analysis skills.

Note: Category types are not mutually exclusive. In each example, the printed text or expected response precedes the diagonal line; the child's miscue or the observed response follows.

Source: From Donald D. Hammill and Nettie R. Bartel, TEACHING STUDENTS WITH LEARNING AND BEHAVIOR PROBLEMS, Fifth Edition, pp. 45–46. Copyright © 1990. Reprinted by permission of Allyn and Bacon.

comprehension skills from the basal series. The teacher develops one or more questions for each kind of comprehension skill expected at each grade level. Next the teacher asks the student to read the text and answer the questions. The text should be available to the student so that memory is not a confounding variable. The teacher then determines what percentage of questions the student answered correctly at each level. Salvia and Hughes (1990) report that a score of 90 percent correct answers on the comprehension questions indicates the material is at the student's independent reading level, 75 percent to 89 percent indicates an instructional reading level, and below 75 percent is the student's frustration level.

Another procedure for evaluating reading comprehension uses a cloze technique. It requires that the student use context clues to supply missing words in graded passages. To construct cloze materials, the teacher selects passages of approximately 250 words from the different levels of the basal series. Slightly shorter passages may be selected from books for the first and second grades, and slightly longer passages can be selected from upper grade texts. The teacher then types each passage on a separate page. When typing, the first and last sentences of the passage are left intact. Every fifth word is deleted from all other sentences. The student is then directed to read the passage and supply the missing words. If several students are being tested, they are directed to write the words. Completion of the exercise is not timed. The teacher scores the passages by counting the number of missing words the student supplied that match the original text. To ensure that different teachers scoring the same passage are consistent, synonyms of words are not counted as correct. However, when the students are required to write their answers, misspellings are not counted as errors. The teacher calculates the percentage of correctly supplied words. Ekwall (1976) recommends that 58 to 100 percent correct responses indicates that the passage is at the student's independent reading level, 44 through 57 percent correct indicates the instructional reading level, and 43 percent or below indicates the frustration reading level.

Teachers may chose to vary the way they construct the cloze passages. For example, every third, eighth, or tenth word can be omitted. Ekwall's recommended percent correct scores should not be used under these circumstances. When constructing the cloze passage, the teacher may decide to delete all of a specific type of word (for example, pronouns or conjunctions) rather than every *n*th word. For younger students, the teacher may supply the first letter of every missing word. For students for whom the traditional cloze technique is too difficult, the teacher may supply three word choices for each blank. This modification is called the *maze procedure* (Guthrie, Seifert, Burnham, and Caplon, 1974) and is a recognition task rather than a recall task. Gillet and Temple (1982) suggest that the three word choices include the correct word, an incorrect word from the same grammatical class, and an incorrect word from a different grammatical class.

Teachers can also assess how much a student understands of what has been read by having the student retell or paraphrase the passage. To employ this method, the teacher selects representative passages from each of several levels of the basal reading series. For each passage, the teacher identifies the main ideas and critical details. The student is directed to read the passage silently and then paraphrase the passage. The teacher should not be concerned about the student's ability to use the exact words in retelling the story since such skill may be rote memory and not true understanding. The teacher counts the number of main ideas and critical details the student includes in the paraphrase. There are no hard rules or recommended percentages of material retold for suggested placement. The teacher is looking for the level at which the student can paraphrase at least half of the key points. The teacher uses these results in conjunction with other curriculum-based assessments to determine the precise level.

Students with oral language expression problems may have extra difficulty with the paraphrase method of assessing reading comprehension. For these students the teacher should select direct questioning or the cloze method. A modification of the paraphrase procedure requires that the student write the retelling of the passage. The written language demands of this response type make such a modification more difficult; however, increased difficulty may be appropriate at the high school level or if this type of task is routinely required in the regular classroom.

Dynamic Assessment

Dynamic assessment methods are used to learn more about how a student deals with information while engaged in a specific task. Unlike traditional assessment methods that focus on the end product of learning, dynamic assessment methods help clarify the interaction of the student, the task, and the environment. These methods have also been called process assessment (Kratochwill and Severson, 1977; Meyers, 1987; Meyers and Lytle, 1986; Meyers, Pfeffer, and Erlbaum, 1985) and learning potential assessment (Feuerstein, 1979a; Lidz, 1987a; Meyers and Lytle, 1986) because of the attempt to examine how a student thinks about tasks while doing them and to estimate the student's readiness to use different strategies.

One dynamic assessment technique that assesses the strategies students use in reading comprehension is Think-Aloud Protocol Analysis (Afflerbach and Johnson, 1984; Bereiter and Bird, 1985; Lytle, 1982; Meyers, 1987; Meyers and Lytle, 1986; Olshavsky, 1976/77). To use this technique, the examiner first identifies the student's instructional reading level using curriculum-based assessment. Next, the examiner selects a couple of passages of fifteen to twenty sentences each from the latter part of the text being used. The examiner retypes the passages so each sentence is on a separate line. The passage is covered by a blank piece of paper and given to the student with instructions to read each sentence and think out loud or verbalize all thoughts after reading each sentence. The examiner records verbatim the think-aloud responses that the student makes. After the student has read the entire passage, the student is asked to summarize what was read. The examiner then analyzes the think-aloud responses the student made to determine the kinds of thinking the student has used. Lytle (1982) identified six major categories of thinking strategies:

1. Signaling Understanding (paraphrasing)
2. Monitoring Doubt (indicating partial or lack of understanding)
3. Analyzing Text Features (analyzing aspects of style)
4. Elaborating the Text (imagery)
5. Judging the Text (judging the ideas presented)
6. Reasoning (hypothesizing)

Student: Age: Grade Placement: Date:
Textbook and Level Used:
Teacher Concerns About:
   Reading Behaviors
   Word Attack Skills
   Comprehension Skills
Current Group Achievement Test Results in Reading   Test Name:
                                                      Date Given:

Decoding   PR¹=   SS²=   Comprehension   PR¹=   SS²=

	Norm-Referenced Data	Criterion-Referenced Objectives Passed	Criterion-Referenced Objectives Failed	Sample Errors	Error Hypothesis
Word Attack Phonetic Analysis					
Structural Analysis					
Letter/Word					
Reading Comprehension Vocabulary					
Literal					
Inferential					
Evaluative					

¹Percentile rank
²Standard score

FIGURE 10-1 Sample reading data sheet

Following the analysis, the examiner can point out and reinforce the strategies the student has used. Then the examiner can provide brief instruction using the second typed passage to show how to use one of the strategies not used spontaneously. This approach reinforces the idea that reading is an interactive process requiring reflective thinking (Baron, 1981). It has been used with students as early as the fourth grade (Meyers and Lytle, 1986).

Steps in the Assessment Process

Determine the Purpose for Assessment

The reasons for evaluating a student must be clearly identified before administering any assessment instruments. The evaluator must consider the history of reading instruction the student has had prior to the evaluation, the age of the student, and the types of concerns the regular classroom teacher has expressed about the student's reading skills. While one purpose of assessment may be to determine the student's level of reading, specific strengths and weaknesses need to be identified before an appropriate IEP can be developed. Therefore, in the area of reading, the assessment must be planned so that word attack skills and reading comprehension skills are examined systematically.

Develop Data Sheets to Record Assessment Results

The data on a student's reading strengths and weaknesses must be organized in a way that ensures that no data are lost and that all data are considered systematically. Developing data sheets to be used throughout the evaluation helps the assessment team structure the assessment and systematically consider the information from numerous sources. Figure 10-1 illustrates a data sheet for reading.

Conduct an Integrated Assessment

A variety of assessment tools are used to conduct an integrated assessment. Classroom observation helps the evaluation team look at environmental variables that may be contributing to a student's learning problems. Norm-referenced tests can help determine the general reading performance level. This is needed to indicate whether special educational services are needed in reading. Criterion-referenced tools, curriculum-based measures, and dynamic assessment techniques are necessary for refining the IEP goals and objectives. During the process of assessing reading performance, the evaluation team should keep the following questions in mind:

- Is reading performance consistent with cognitive abilities?
- Are there deficits in selected learning behaviors that could have an impact on reading performance?
- Are oral language skills affecting reading?
- Have behavior problems or emotional concerns affected the motivation to read or the cognitive availability to learn reading?
- What environmental situations are contributing to reading difficulties?
- Has there been direct, systematic instruction to teach the deficit reading skills?

It is also important for each evaluation team member to record observational notes while working in the one-to-one testing situation. These observations can provide important informal information about the student's behavior that may be contributing to learning problems or the strategies the student uses when working on reading tasks.

Analyze the Errors

Recording the exact responses a student makes during oral reading tasks, whether reading a list of words or an extended text, provides the examiner with miscues that can be analyzed to determine the skills and strategies the student tries to employ. Errors from norm-referenced tools, criterion-referenced tools, and classroom work samples provide hypotheses that can be tested through the use of teacher developed, curriculum-based and dynamic assessment tasks. Data from these tasks often indicate where instruction should begin.

Develop Annual Goals and Instructional Objectives

Annual goals and short-term objectives are based on data from the entire assessment process. Once the assessment team determines that the student is eligible for special education, the IEP committee members use the same data to determine whether the student's level of performance in reading requires special instruction. The committee should systematically consider the student's level of performance on assessments of word attack skills and reading comprehension appropriate for the grade level in which the student is placed. Annual goals may be written for either or both of these skill areas. Next, the committee develops several short-term objectives for each of the annual goals in reading. In developing these objectives, the committee uses the norm-referenced and criterion-referenced assessment data and the results of initial error analysis of the reading subtests. When the IEP committee has completed the goals and objectives, a placement decision is made based on which setting is least restrictive for providing the special instruction needed to reach the specific goals and objectives.

Once reading goals and objectives are written into the IEP and the student is placed in special education, the special educator continues the assessment/instruction process. The special educator is already familiar with the existing data on the student's skills in word attack and reading comprehension. Using that existing data, the teacher can develop short curriculum-based tasks and dynamic probes that specify where special instruction should begin. The data from these curriculum-based and dynamic tasks become the baseline measure for the student's performance for a specific reading objective.

Summary

Definition of the Area

Decoding versus Meaning

1. Decoding tasks assess the student's word calling ability.
2. Meaning tasks assess the student's reading comprehension skills.
3. The relative importance of these skills depends on the model of reading used.

Bottom-Up Models

1. These models are text driven.
2. Reading begins with attention to the features of print.
3. Comprehension is an automatic outcome of word recognition.

Top-Down Models

1. These models conceptualize reading as based on oral language competency and prior experience.
2. Three systems are used simultaneously: the semantic system, the syntactic system, and the graphic system.

Interactive Models

1. These models are based on the belief that both bottom-up and top-down processing styles are important to reading. .
2. Basal reading series are often based on interactive models of reading.

Developmental Progression

Foundations for Reading

  I. Cognitive Ability
   1. Low intelligence is correlated to reading problems.
   2. Good intelligence does not guarantee good reading skills.
 II. Oral Language
   1. Problems with oral language often foreshadow reading problems.
   2. Good oral language skills do not guarantee good reading skills.
III. Emotional Factors
   1. The relationship between reading and emotional factors is difficult to identify.
   2. Some emotional problems may contribute to difficulty learning to read.
   3. Reading failure may contribute to the emotional problems.

Reading Skill Development

1. Preschool language development and early experiences with print in the environment lay the foundation for a readiness to read.
2. Early reading instruction focuses on developing word analysis skills, a basic sight vocabulary, and an understanding that the purpose of reading is to gain meaning.
3. During the transition stage of reading, students are expected to read for recreation and learn new material while refining decoding and comprehension skills.
4. A student in the advanced stage of reading development has mastered decoding skills, has developed evaluative and critical reading skills, and is refining reference and study skills.

Concerns Expressed by the Classroom Teacher

1. The concerns expressed by regular classroom teachers can be broadly divided into the areas of reading behaviors, word analysis difficulties, and comprehension difficulties.

2. These concerns can help shape hypotheses about a student's reading ability that will underlie critical assessment questions.

Types of Assessment Tasks

1. Group administered, standardized reading achievement tests are designed to provide only a broad estimate of reading skill development.
2. Norm-referenced diagnostic tests measure an array of reading subskills such as oral reading fluency, differential word analysis techniques, and various types of comprehension skills.
3. Commercially produced criterion-referenced tests and inventories of reading are keyed to specific objectives that can facilitate instructional planning.
4. Curriculum-based assessments help identify specific reading skills needed for success in a particular curriculum.
5. Dynamic assessment in reading allows the examiner to point out and reinforce the student for effective use of various reading skills and trial teaching of a skill not used.

Steps in the Assessment Process

1. Determine the purpose for the assessment process.
2. Develop data sheets to record assessment results.
3. Conduct an integrated assessment.
4. Analyze the errors.
5. Develop annual goals and instructional objectives.

Assessing Written Language

Key Terms

Communicative competence
   tasks
Controlled stimulus passage
Discrete-point tests
Expressive writing
Handwriting
Ideation/abstractness

Identification tasks
Mechanical errors
Prewriting
Quasi-integrative tests
Sense of audience
Sentence combining

Spelling
Spontaneous writing
Symbolic play
Text organization
Word usage
Written syntax

Writing is beautiful.
It can express the depths of a person's soul.
It is a way of talking without opening the mouth.

(Lee and Jackson, 1992)

Written language is the expression of ideas and feelings in written form. It is one of the most difficult of the communication arts to master as it calls for the integration of several discrete and individually complex skills. Writing requires the writer to code experience/ideas into symbols (words) that a reader can understand. Therefore, writing is much more than words or sentences on paper; it requires important transformations (Moffett and Wagner, 1983). These transformations include changing experiences into ideas, changing ideas into oral language, and finally changing oral language into written language. Writers must first organize their experiences and ideas in their minds before initiating any paper or pencil activities. Such a process requires communicating with self. Next, writers code these thoughts into oral language symbols. Oral language, however, is not always external since a writer is often guided by internal speech (Vygotsky, 1962). Finally, writers code their thoughts and oral symbols into a form of written language. Printed symbols represent the oral symbols, and ideas are transformed through handwriting, spelling, and punctuation skills. Figure 11-1 illustrates the changes involved in the writing process: experiences are translated into ideas, ideas are transformed into oral symbols, and oral symbols are coded as written symbols. Students demonstrating underachievement in written language often have problems stemming from thinking and oral language deficits such that the breakdown occurs early in the transformation of writing skills (that is, experience to thoughts or thoughts to language). However, teachers often focus on the basic skills of literacy (spelling, handwriting, punctuation) and ignore the real core of the problem.

Written language requires that the writer simultaneously deal with thoughts, text, and a reader; breakdowns in the system may occur for several different reasons. Underlying conceptual or thinking disorders can have an impact on how a student attempts to organize ideas or the degree of abstractness of those ideas. Problems in oral language and reading are often precursors to difficulties with the writing process (Johnson and Myklebust, 1967). Difficulty with the integration of subject, text, and reader, however, is not always due to an underlying thinking or oral language problem. It may be the result of poor instruction, lack of adequate experience in manipulating language structures, or the result of overall intellectual or emotional functioning. Careful investigation of the transformations required to produce written

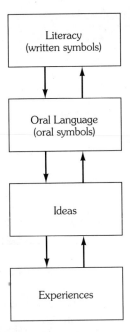

FIGURE 11-1 Development of written language

text allows the special educator to document the primary cause of written language underachievement. Understanding the etiology (instructional, cognitive, and emotional) has direct implications for effective program planning.

Areas of Written Language

A written language disorder can affect one or several areas of written language depending on the number, type, and severity of the deficit. Assessing written language requires understanding each of these areas and the skills most necessary to complete task demands in each area. No single standardized assessment tool is currently available that provides an evaluator with the information necessary to investigate all these areas. A diagnostician must have a broad understanding of all aspects of written language to utilize the tools on the market in combination with qualitative measures to make an accurate assessment of written language achievement. The areas of written language most commonly affected by a writing disorder include spelling, syntax, text organization, sense of audience, ideation, and handwriting (Gregg, 1990; Myklebust, 1965). Each of these areas will be discussed generally prior to a more specific discussion of evaluation tools and methods.

Spelling

An individual's *spelling* strategies change as a function of knowledge and experience. In addition, the complex process of spelling requires an individual to spell both

Table 11-1 Analysis of spelling errors of individuals with developmental writing disorders

Type of Error	Description
Phonological	In some respects these spelling errors resemble the sound of the target word when pronounced (for example, yrx/works, fihin/fishing).
Visual	These errors preserve the general shape or look of the word, but pronunciation does not lead to a similar sound (for example, went/wind, in/on, famly/family).
Morphological	These errors are problems with the morphological form of the word (for example, answrd, seard, ofcors).
Spelling Rule	Errors in this category include suffix-adding rules, doubling rules for final letters, the end rule, and other spelling rule errors (for example, runing/running, comeing/coming).
Segmentation	These errors describe incorrect segmentation, usually one word written as two (for example, away/a way).
Context	Words in this category were spelled correctly when observed in isolation, but in the context of the text they were incorrect. These errors include homonyms and other word substitutions. (Cromer's analysis did not include this category.)

Source: From R. F. Cromer, Spontaneous spelling by language-disordered children. In U. Firth, ed., *Cognitive Processes in Spelling* (London: Academic Press, 1980), pp. 402–422.

phonetically predictable and unpredictable words. Phonetically predictable words are spelled like they sound (for example, cat, dip). To spell words that are phonetically predictable, a student must be able to analyze and discriminate sounds heard in words. The student must then attach the correct symbols to these sounds. On the other hand, to spell words that are phonetically irregular or unpredictable, a student must be able to remember letters and letter sequences. Irregular or unpredictable words are not spelled exactly the way they sound (for example, the, were, enough). The student must rely on visual imagery to spell irregular or unpredictable words.

Two of the most commonly used spelling tasks are those that investigate the recall and recognition of single words. A student's ability to recognize correctly spelled words is largely a measure of reading ability (Smith, 1980). But it is a very important skill in correcting or proofing written text as well. On recall tasks, a student must remember the spelling words from memory and either spell it out loud or produce it in written form. Gregg, Hoy, and Sabol (1988) found that a recall spelling task was a better discriminator of spelling deficits when compared with performance on a standardized recognition spelling test.

The ability to copy text either from a paper or a chart also provides significant information about transcription abilities. Students often make spelling errors when asked to copy correctly spelled words from one paper to another or to copy from the board. Unfortunately, teachers examine spelling achievement primarily by giving the student a standardized spelling measure that usually requires the teacher to orally prompt the individual. Cromer (1980) stresses the necessity for examination of spontaneous writing samples to observe spelling strategies that might not be utilized on single-word recall or recognition spelling tasks. Gregg, Hoy, and Sabol (1988) adapted the Cromer analysis when investigating spontaneous writing. Table 11-1 describes categories of errors the special educator can use to help identify patterns or strategies indicative of a student's writing abilities.

The special educator must remember that no single standardized or informal

Box 11-1 *Description of Spelling Problems*

"My eye is trained not to worry about spelling. I do not misspell a word the same way each time. My spelling is not at all consistent. Every time I write a word it could be different. I am really strong with words that start with "b" and "d." I don't always put them in the right place, but I know they have a place somewhere in the word. **A, i, e, k, ph, f, j, o, u,** and **y** are letters that seem to give me the most trouble in spelling and reading. Notice here that all the vowels are included in this list and there are no words that do not contain vowels. Basically words that I spell right consistently are words that I have been exposed to over and over again, and they are usually short. The longer the word, the more confusing it is for me. Words that I can usually spell correctly include 'the, if, was, has, were, funny, time, nice, please, people, girl, friends, Georgia, and Florida.' Not many people my age can list the sum total of words they can spell with confidence within a couple of lines of print."

Source: From C. Lee and R. Jackson, *Faking It.* (Portsmouth, NH: Boynton/Cook Publishers, 1992) p. 27.

spelling assessment can adequately identify all the different types of spelling errors students can make in writing. A recognition, recall, copying, and spontaneous writing sample provides the teacher with a valid examination of the spelling processes required with different types of academic tasks. Lee and Jackson provide a good description of the difficulties experienced by writers demonstrating spelling problems (see Box 11-1). The emotional component of spelling disorders cannot be overestimated by the special educator.

Written Syntax

A student must understand and use the rules of written language that govern punctuation and capitalization usage, word form and order, and sentence structure. Many reasons exist for a student's inability to acquire or produce the rules applicable to formulating ideas within sentences (*written syntax*) and assigning appropriate punctuation. Breakdowns may be the result of cognitive processing deficits, oral language deficits, or a lack of instruction. Behaviors often indicative of written syntax disorders include word omissions, word substitutions, inappropriate verb or pronoun use, omission and substitution of word endings, lack of punctuation, and a discrepancy between oral and written syntax (Gregg, 1990). Box 11-2 illustrates common written syntax problems in examples of student writing.

The assessment of written syntax should include tasks measuring both receptive (identification) and expressive (production) syntax. Standardized measures of written language can supplement informal measures in obtaining this information. An evaluator should begin by comparing the student's oral syntax to the student's written syntax to identify receptive and expressive oral language disorders in written language. (See chapter 9 for a discussion of oral language assessment.)

Box 11-2   ***Examples of Student Writing Demonstrating Significant Syntactic Deficits***
What is love? I want to friend with somebody to make people feel better to have love. Love is kind of feeling to be friend.
(15-year-old male)

What is Love? means to love ride bike and tricks, ride with friends.
   I love ride and read freestyle books for many tricks with friends of mine. My goal love is ride freestyle bike to win for team's company. In California I would like to be new champion of freestyle trick and on ramp and I want to set world record for highest feet to about 70 feets.
(15-year-old male)

Sentence combining.   In the last several years, research efforts have been devoted to discovering the impact on sentence combining as an evaluation measure of syntactic maturity. *Sentence combining* is an approach designed to allow students to manipulate language to improve the maturity of the syntactic structures. A student is given sets of kernel sentences that must be combined and written out as single complex sentences. Exercises may contain grammatical cues (Mellon, 1969), nongrammatical cues (O'Hare, 1973), or no guiding cues (Strong, 1973).

Controlled stimulus passage.   A *controlled stimulus passage* (O'Donnell and Hunt, 1975) attempts to measure the syntactic complexity of a student's writing by controlling such writing variables as topic, verbosity, and lack of information. Such a task requires a student to rewrite material that contains short, choppy sentences. It is similar to sentence combining except that the student is provided with a complete paragraph and must make decisions about which sentences to combine or eliminate. Syntax, mechanical organization, and spelling errors should be noted by the evaluator and compared to the types of errors made on a spontaneous writing sample.

Spontaneous writing.   Evaluation of a student's syntactic maturity should always include a sample of *spontaneous writing*. In determining whether an individual's spontaneous writing displays syntactic errors, the special educator should also evaluate sentence mechanics (punctuation, word usage, patterns, and transformations). See Tables 11-2 and 11-3 for a list of word usage errors and mechanical errors to investigate.

Identification tasks.   Multiple choice word usage, punctuation, and style subtests on many of the achievement tests provide a way to determine whether a student understands the syntactic rules by *identification tasks* as well as on production tasks. The information from these contrived writing tasks should be compared to the individual's spontaneous writing samples.
   The special educator investigating the written syntax of a student should begin by administering tasks that tap different components of the cognitive processing sys-

Table 11-2 Word usage to observe in written language samples

	Omission	*Insertion*	*Substitution*	*Tense*	*Not Used*
Noun					
Verb					
Adjective					
Adverb					
Functors					
Prepositions					
Pronouns					
Conjunctions					

tem. Such formats might include sentence combining, controlled stimulus passage, identification, and spontaneous writing. Specific syntactic structure should be examined to determine if any were used appropriately, omitted, substituted, added, or rarely used in written text. By presenting the student with different task formats, an examination of syntactic development and punctuation can be made in both a contrived and a spontaneous manner.

Text Organization

The ability to organize ideas in written language and arrange them to create an organizational plan involves many linguistic and cognitive skills (Scardamalia, Bereiter, and Goelman, 1982). A writer's cognitive development has been found to have a significant impact on the ability to create different organizational patterns with written text (Applebee, 1978). According to Applebee, a child at the preoperational stage (ages 2 to 6) tells stories in whole or in part with very little sense of the overall structure of the plot. By the time the child reaches the concrete operational stage (ages 7 to 11), the writer's ability to summarize and categorize in story-telling becomes apparent to the reader. However, it is not until a writer reaches the formal operational stage (12 to adult) that analyses of story structure and characters as well as generalization of theme or point of view are noted.

Text organization focuses on the structure of meaning within a student's writing that supersedes the sentence. Narrative is one type of organizational scheme students use in school, particularly in the elementary and middle school years. Other types of text forms (genre) commonly used in schools include descriptive, persuasive, and expository forms. Each genre has specific rules governing its overall organization. In describing events, people, or ideas through different genre, a student establishes causal, temporal, and motivational relationships between people, things, and events. A student's spontaneous writing sample becomes a better predictor of written language performance for a teacher than isolated and contrived written language tasks (for example, spelling and punctuation) since it is a measure of language competency more than language proficiency.

Table 11-3 Mechanical behaviors to observe in written language samples

Punctuation	Omission	Substitution	Insertion	Not Used/Not Necessary
Periods				
end of sentence				
abbreviations				
initials				
numbers in lists				
Capitals				
beginning sentences				
proper nouns				
I				
titles				
beginning quotations				
Question Marks				
Underlining				
Quotation Marks				
quotations				
titles				
Commas				
dates				
city/state				
listing				
explanatory words				
appositives				
direct address				
transitional words				
Apostrophes				
possession				
contractions				
Indentations				
beginning paragraphs				
quotations				
Colons				
writing time				
listing				

Stein and Glenn (1979) identified seven types of story structures (sequences and episodes) most commonly found in the narratives of young writers. These included (1) descriptive sequences, (2) action sequences, (3) narrative sequences, (4) abbreviated episodes, (5) complete episodes, (6) complex episodes, and (7) interactive episodes. Table 11-4 lists these types of story structures with the cognitive skills related to them, highlighting the cognitive and linguistic demands required to write stories.

The special educator investigating an individual's ability to produce written text must first consider the genre (narrative, expository, persuasive, descriptive), age of the student, logical reasoning ability of the student, and the experience the student

Table 11-4 Story structures

Story Structure	Purpose of Sequence of Event	Cognitive Skills Required
Descriptive sequences	Describes character(s) and setting.	Comprehend setting information in text.
Action sequences	Provides a chronological list of actions.	Comprehend setting information in text.
Reactive sequences	Indicate circumstance(s) that cause change but no planning.	Process information that causes change.
Episode sequences	Presents goal of the protagonist but planning is not included.	Account for goals, plan applications and temporal or causal relationships.
Complete	Provides evidence of planning and includes consequences. Includes at least two narrative components (initiating event, internal response, attempt).	
Complex	Elaboration of complete episodes by embedding episodes.	
Interactive	Goals and attempts of two characters. Characters influence each other, and complete episodes from perspective of each character are provided.	

Source: Adapted from Hedberg and Stoel-Gammon (1986) and Stein and Glenn (1979)

has had with the topic. Then a teacher should compare the writer's sentences and inter- and intra-paragraph organization across different writing samples.

Sense of Audience

A *sense of audience* requires the writer to make the necessary adjustments and choices in writing that take into account the intended reader(s). A student demonstrating difficulty with this aspect of written language often does not elaborate or provide the reader with enough information to understand the meaning of the written text. This student's writing often appears disorganized and without purpose. Such writers do not define the audience and effectively imagine the response of that audience. Therefore, an egocentric perspective on the part of the writer results in an inadequate concern for the reader's needs.

In the past, audience awareness has been treated as a "monolithic" rather than a "multidimensional" construct (Rubin, 1984, p. 239), that is, as one skill rather than a combination of several skills. Gregg and McCarty (1989) adapted the subskills from Rubin's research to be useful for the special educator. They identified six social cognitive subskills as good predictors of sense of audience ability (see Table 11-5). It must be noted, however, that while these subskills have been identified in theory as separate activities, some are so interrelated that one written statement can illustrate more than one subskill. They clearly illustrate that a sense of audience is not as simple as "keep your audience in mind."

Britton, Burgess, Martin, McLeod, and Rosen (1975) advocate that students need experience communicating directly to specified audiences for different purposes. Examples of a few types of audiences are writer to teacher, writer to friend, writer to unknown audience, or writer to examiner. It is important for the evaluator to assess an individual's writing across different audiences. Some writers produce more elaborate and better organized texts when they feel comfortable with the audience.

Table 11-5 Audience awareness subskills important for assessment

Writer Ability for Successful Use of Sense of Audience	*Influencing Use of Writer Ability*
Content	
Knowledge/value base.	Language deficits
"I know something about what I'm going to write about."	Reading deficits
	Long-term memory deficits
	Pragmatics deficits
	Conceptual deficits
	Nonverbal deficits
	Limited experience
Execution	
Actual linguistic resources.	Word finding deficits
"I have the skills to express my ideas to meet the demands of	Oral receptive syntax deficits
this audience."	Oral expressive syntax deficits
	Semantic deficits
	Written syntax deficits
	Phonological deficits
	Spelling disorders
	Text structure deficits
Construct Differentiation	
Transferring the mental image of the audience into	Distractibility
communication strategies that aid message delivery.	Pragmatics deficits
"In order to communicate my ideas, I need to do it this way	Oral language deficits
using these strategies."	Conceptual deficits
	Organizational deficits
	Low self-esteem
	Nonverbal deficits
	Limited experience
Perspective	
Realizing that the reader has a perspective different from the	Egocentricity
writer's.	Pragmatic deficits
"She may look at this problem in a different way than I do."	Conceptual deficits
	Nonverbal deficits
	Limited experience
Maintenance of Perspective	
Interaction between text and reader.	Egocentricity
"How well I say what I know depends on the words I can have	Rigidity of thought
to choose and who continues to read my product."	Pragmatics deficits
	Oral deficits
	word finding
	syntax
	semantics
	Organizational deficits
	Nonverbal deficits
	Limited experience
Role-Taking	
Engaging in social inference.	Pragmatics
"I have something to say, but my reader is thinking a certain	Conceptual deficits
way. I have to consider this."	Rigidity
	Egocentricity
	Nonverbal deficits
	Limited experience

Source: Adapted from D. Rubin, Social Cognition and Written Communication. *Written Communications, 1,* (2), 1984, pp. 211–243.

Table 11-6 Aspects of ideation/abstractness

Assessment Area	Components
Type of discourse	Drama/recording Description Exposition Argument/persuasive
Temporal aspect	What is happening? What happened (or will happen)? What happens? What might/shall happen?
Degree of decentering	Egocentric Well-known audience Unknown audience Emotions projected Emotions focused
Basis of abstraction	Sensations Perceptual Memory Generalization Inferences
Communication mode (ideas)	Implicit Explicit
Communication mode (vocabulary)	Implicit Explicit

Source: From N. Gregg and N. Henry (1988). *Ideational Abstractness—Assessment Areas,* Unpublished manuscript, University of Georgia, Department of Special Education, Athens, GA.

Ideation/Abstractness

Integral with sense of audience and text organization is the concept of *ideation/ abstraction.* Moffett and Wagner (1983) define abstractness as the umbrella structure of written language, the set of relations between the speaker–listener–subject involved in referential and rhetorical communication. Referential relations are defined as how someone abstracts from raw phenomena, and rhetorical relations are how someone abstracts from an audience. Moffett and Wagner suggest that abstraction reduces the stress of an individual by selecting and ranking the elements of experiences (that is, sensations, memory, generalizations, and inferences). According to Moffett and Wagner, increased consciousness of abstracting has as much to do with developmental growth as does progress up the abstraction ladder.

Ideation/abstractness is a very difficult area to assess and should not be evaluated in isolation from other areas of written language. Myklebust's (1965, 1973b) Abstraction Quotient is one of the few standardized measurements of ideation/abstraction in written language. He developed an abstract–concrete scale to be used with the Picture Story Language Test (Myklebust, 1968). However, there are problems with this scale, including the type of task specified, lack of sensitivity to audience, and validity and reliability issues (Gregg, 1990). Therefore, the special educator trying to evaluate this very important area of written language is not left with many standardized tools. Table 11-6 provides some aspects of ideation an evaluator should consider while probing a student's written language abstraction skills.

The special educator must investigate the type of discourse (that is, narrative, descriptive, et cetera), tense, degree of decentering, and the communication mode (implicit or explicit). In addition to this information, the evaluator must determine the means by which the student organizes ideas (that is, sensation, perception, memory, generalization, inferences). Students demonstrating low ideation tend to organize their ideas through sensory or perceptual constructs, while students with high ideation organize ideas using generalizing and inferencing techniques. However, the type of discourse (narrative or descriptive), the topic, and the tense can significantly affect the level of abstraction that is appropriate to a specific task.

The special educator should be sensitive to the fact that sometimes students' problems in spelling or syntax can have an impact on their fluency or ideation level. Chris Lee describes this problem with writing in the text he wrote with Rosemary Jackson called *Faking It: A Look Into the Mind of a Creative Learner.*

> Sometimes I turn words or phrases around; sometimes they come out completely backwards. Sometimes the sentences are just wordy because I am trying to get back on track with my thoughts. I cannot really explain why I write like this except that I am concentrating so much on the spelling and meaning of individual words that fluency is impossible. (1992, p. 33)

Handwriting

The ability to produce legible *handwriting* is fundamental to other writing skills. Without the ability to transform experiences, ideas, and oral words into written text, the student has little access to his thoughts through written language. The inability to produce legible text can make an individual appear "slow" or "backward" to the classroom teacher, yet this same student can present abstract and interesting ideas when speaking. For many special education students, the basic cognitive processes (motor skills, visual discrimination, and visual memory) required in handwriting never become automatic; thus, illegible handwriting remains a problem for them throughout their schooling.

Special education students have at times been identified by poor handwriting performance (Sovik, 1984; Sovik, Arntzen, and Thygesen, 1986). However, many factors can influence a student's ability to produce legible text. These factors include motivation, instruction, motor coordination, memory, oral language skill, and reading ability. Distinguishing the cause for an individual's poor handwriting performance is, to say the least, quite difficult. Research exploring the association between memory for letters, motor coordination, and oral language ability is lacking (Sovik, Arntzen, and Thygesen, 1986). The ability to produce legible handwriting, however, utilizes to the greatest extent those cognitive processes that allow for discrimination and identification of shapes by sight and touch as well as the cognitive processes involved with muscular movement. Since visual and motor abilities must be coordinated in handwriting, this skill is often called *sensorimotor.*

Because the special educator involved in assessing handwriting skills has very few reliable standardized indices available, he or she must depend on informal measures (see Table 11-7). Handwriting should be measured using recall, copy, and spontaneous writing tasks since each of these tasks calls upon different cognitive processes.

Table 11-7 Handwriting assessment

Tool	Task Demand	Critique
Ayers Handwriting Scale (Ayers, 1917)	Measure of quality and speed of handwriting. Timed. Copy Gettysburg Address at near point from a paper directly in front of student. Number of letters written correctly in one minute is converted to a grade level equivalent.	Significant degree of subjectivity. Poor reliability and validity. Content not always relevant or motivating. Advanced reading level required.
Handwriting Scale of the Test of Written Language (Larsen and Hammill, 1988)	Assesses cursive writing only. Score derived from examining student's writing and comparing to samples in the manual.	No stated criteria for levels from which standard scores ranging from 1–10 are derived. Poor reliability, often no match sample.
Test of Legible Handwriting– TOLH (Larsen and Hammill, 1989)	Any writing sample may be used. Student's handwriting is matched with one of three scoring guides.	Grades 2–12. Nationally standardized manuscript and cursive standard scores and composite scores. Reliability–Strong; Validity–Weak.
Children's Handwriting Evaluation Scale–CHES (Phelps, Stempel, and Speck, 1982)	Near point copy task. Scoring obtaining by counting the number of letters written correctly in two minutes.	Standardized on 1,372 Dallas County students in grades 1–8. Subjective quality. No validity and reliability reported. Measures general appearance, slant, rhythm, letter formation, and spacing.
Slingerland Screening Tests for Identifying Children with Specific Language Disabilities (Slingerland, 1970)	Far point copy tasks. Near point copy tasks. Visual memory for letters and nonverbal symbols. Auditory memory for letters and nonverbal symbols. Auditory discrimination. Auditory–visual translators.	Informal measure, no validity or reliability data. Attempts to look at writing across tasks. Attempts to identify underlying processing disorders.

Error patterns should be noted in letter formation, letter size, proportion and alignment, spacing, line quality, slant, and rate (Mercer, 1983). However, the special educator must first identify the handwriting program from which the student has received the majority of his or her instruction. More important than complete accuracy of letter formation is identification of handwriting competencies that are difficult for the student. Table 11-8 lists several of the competencies the evaluator should assess to determine a student's handwriting performance. It is important to identify whether the student can identify letters by name, draw figures (circles and squares), trace letters, copy letters, write letter symbols from oral dictation, translate

Table 11-8 Handwriting competencies necessary for written composition

Ability to draw circular, rectangular, and curving shapes.
Ability to trace letters.
Ability to copy letters.
Ability to identify individual letters by name.
Ability to write letters from an oral response.
Ability to translate small printed letters to capital printed letters.
Ability to translate small cursive letters to capital cursive letters.
Ability to translate from printing to cursive.

manuscript to cursive and vice versa, and translate capital to small letters. In addition, the special educator should observe the student's rate of writing across these tasks.

Developmental Progression

Foundations for Learning

The ability to produce written language is built upon a foundation consisting of experiences, oral language skills, conceptual skills, and emotional maturity. A special educator assessing a student's written language skills must consider each of these building blocks in relation to the individual's developmental age and level of written language instruction. As Moffett and Wagner (1983) state: "Comprehending and composing concern nothing so much as trying to match private minds by means of a public vehicle called language" (p. 4). In the previous section, discussion of the areas of written language (spelling, syntax, text organization, et cetera) illustrated the impact on oral language and conceptualization on written language performance. In addition to these building blocks, the special educator must also consider a student's motivation, emotional maturity, and general experiences with the skills demanded by specific written language tasks. A readiness for written language requires that a student has been read to, talked to, and taken different places. The special educator cannot assume that all students share a common experiential base. The importance of considering sociocultural influences is discussed in greater detail later in this chapter.

Preschool Focus

The development of writing skills begins prior to picking up a pencil to record symbols on paper. Vygotsky (1978a) discusses the development of representation that leads to symbolization in writing and the importance of the development of gesture, play, and drawing to the ability to write. The cognitive and emotional deficits that will later have an impact of written text show up early in these other modes of representation. Therefore, the special educator is able to identify high-risk children for written language disorders before such children are required to use pen and paper.

Many children experiment with writing before anyone provides them with formal instruction; however, little is known about the precise age at which those who write early do begin or exactly what motivates them to write. The special educator interested in evaluating predictors for later written language problems should begin by focusing on investigating preschoolers play and drawing skills.

Symbolic play.   Vygotsky (1978a) felt that children learn to write as a result of more general representational competence beginning with the ability to master *symbolic play*. Play requires integrating oral language, thinking, and social skills. When children use these skills in play, they often are attempting to sound and act like adults. As a result, they often expand the forms and functions of their oral language, thinking, and social skills. In addition, play provides a more naturalistic or real context to evaluate a child's emerging abilities. Black (1979) found that children's language during play showed a greater variety of word meanings and language structures as well as utilizing more functions of language. In addition, Black found that children demonstrated a greater knowledge of appropriate social and language rules during play than was noted on standardized testing.

The special educator should observe a child's ability to integrate language, thinking, and social skills during dramatic or social play. Garvey (1974) suggested that for children to take part in social play they must be able to understand the difference between reality and play; understand and develop abstract rules for structuring play; and understand, use, and share a theme common to all the players. Play provides the setting for the special educator to evaluate a child's competence in an environment that is sometimes less anxiety-producing and one in which the child has control. However, some special education children find play too unstructured and overwhelming, leading to a demonstration of negative, acting-out behaviors.

A child also learns to play with words; this is usually demonstrated by repetitious and rhythmic play with the sounds of language. Garvey (1977) gives an excellent illustration of this type of play.

Boy: Teddy bear's mine.
Girl: The fishy fishy is mine.
Boy: No, the snakey snakey is yours. 'Cause it's fishy too. 'Cause it has fishes.
Girl: And it's snakey too 'cause it has snakes and it's beary too because it has bears.
Boy: And it's and it's hatty 'cause it has hats. (pp. 69–70)

Language play influences language development, thinking, and social skill interaction. Such play helps the child develop an awareness that language is an entity separate from its reference. This understanding is referred to as metalinguistics. Children learn that language can be analyzed in terms of sounds, syllables, pitch, intonation, and words. In addition, they learn the ambiguity of word meanings and word structures. Vygotsky (1978a) and, more recently, Pellegrini and Galda (1990) indicate that children's early symbolic play necessitates the use of metalinguistics. Metalinguistic skills are very important to later reading and written language performance.

Drawing.   Drawing has long been used as a means to investigate a child's developing cognitive, social, and language competence (Luquet, 1913). According to Dileo (1977), children demonstrate the ability to draw lines and arcs between 15 months and 3 years of age; this is followed with the emergence of the circle at 3

A young student's drawing and painting activities are precursors to writing.   *Source:* © Karen Gilborn/Omni Photo Communications, Inc.

years of age. Children quickly learn that their circle can represent something (for example, a face) in their reality. Just as symbolic play represents their world, a child between 3 and 4 years of age uses drawing to represent people and objects. While the 4-year-old's drawing is recognizable as a person, the legs often stem from the head. By 5 years of age, the child adds a trunk, arms, fingers, and hair. Luquet (1913) noted that children of this age draw by means of "intellectual realism," drawing what is understood rather than what might have been seen. For example, a person is never drawn in profile but always from the front perspective. Drawings at this age also begin to tell a story and reflect a child's emotional state.

The special educator can also observe the child's ability to manipulate a pencil during drawing exercises. Children between the ages of 2 and 3 should be able to copy circles, vertical lines, horizontal lines, and crosses. Cohen and Gross (1979) note that by age 5 a child can copy squares, triangles, diamonds, and most letters and numbers. However, development of drawing ability depends on more than just fine motor ability. Specific cognitive and affective competencies also affect a child's prewriting performance.

Young children learning to write use pictures to tell their stories. Graves (1975) discusses the activity of drawing as "rehearsal" for later writing skills. Initially, children draw and use graphic forms or letters as secondary to the pictures. Gradually, the letter forms take a primary role in the picture. Ferreiro (1984) describes the close relationship between logical thinking and drawing/writing skills of young children. According to her research, a child's ability to utilize the concepts of one-to-one correspondence,

Table 11-9 Sequence of prewriting skills

1. Imitate features of writing.
2. Draw graphic forms of characters more similar to conventional forms.
3. Write with one letter standing for syllable—syllabic writing.
4. Write with one letter standing for a single sound—alphabetic writing.

Source: From E. Ferreiro, The Underlying Logic of Literacy Development. In H. Goelman, A. Oberg, and F. Smith, eds., *Awakening to Literacy* (London: Heindemann Educational Books, 1984), p. 154–173.

totality and its constituent parts, serial order, conservation, classification, and permutation and commutation directly affect the child's ability to develop written language skills. Therefore, the special educator should first investigate the oral language and thinking abilities of a child prior to judging written language performance.

Children appear to make the transformation from drawing to writing in a very predictable sequence (see Table 11-9). First, they identify features of writing characters by imitating the motor and graphic forms of adults. Therefore, beginning writing often takes two forms, continuous wavy lines ⌒ ⌒ ⌒, imitating cursive writing, or a series of small circles or vertical lines 𝑜𝑏𝑞𝑜𝑜, imitating manuscripts. Gradually a child's graphic forms of letter characters move to the more conventional letter forms. Ferreiro (1984) discusses how these graphic forms are first inserted into the child's drawing, then gradually move to outlining the drawing. Next, graphic shapes, while still outside the drawing, take on meaning based on spatial proximity. Soon the graphic forms match the number concept in the picture, and finally the form stands for a word. Gardner (1980) gives an excellent example of a child's transition from drawing to writing when he describes a child seen by Gertrude Hildreth at Columbia Teacher's College in the 1930s. The child was apparently obsessed with trains and over a ten-year period drew thousands of them. In the child's preschool years, letters were used as decoration around the train, but by school age the picture was decorative to the writing.

Once children have learned to associate a graphic form with a letter, they begin to assign a sound value to each of the letters that comprise their writing. However, at this point the letter stands for one complete syllable. Following this stage, children make the transition from syllabic writing to alphabetic writing by assigning individual phonemes to letter forms.

A child's oral language, conceptual, and social skills bear directly on his or her ability to develop *prewriting* skills. Peter, a child with autism described in Box 11-3, illustrates the splinter abilities many special education students demonstrate in the area of prewriting. Looking only at Peter's fine motor skills, the evaluator could be misled in predicting future writing abilities. The assessment of written language requires that the special educator have a strong theoretical foundation in the area of writing processes and written language development. The majority of special education students are high risk for written language disorders. In addition, the systematic instruction currently practiced in school systems assumes that students enter school with a sophisticated conceptualization of the writing process that many special education students lack. Symbolic play and the drawing abilities of students can provide the special educator with information needed to identify appropriate

---

Box 11-3   *Autistic Prewriter*

Peter, a 4-year-old child with autism, loved to draw circles and squares all over his papers at school. However, he could not be encouraged to draw a person or even graphic form(s) symbolic of a piece of a person (that is, eye, hand). Peter's ability to manipulate his paper and pencil to draw circles and squares appeared to be superior to his symbolic play. Therefore, while he could perform the visual–motor skills required of prewriting, his lack of knowledge of self and others, as well as weak interpersonal skills, affected his ability to tell stories.

---

prewriting instructional objectives for many special education students who are chronologically, but not conceptually, past the preschool years.

Elementary Focus

Students in the elementary grades are becoming increasingly sophisticated writers. The development of writing abilities is rather dramatic in the early elementary years. As Gundlach (1982) noted, the young child "extends the functions of several sym-

The development of writing abilities is rather dramatic in the early elementary years.
Source: © Jeffrey High/Image Productions

FIGURE 11-2 Normally achieving kindergarten writer

bol systems—of speaking, drawing, and play—into the new activity of writing, and uses written language for purposes already important to him'' (p. 136). However, the special educator must keep in mind the diversity of performance in written language among normally achieving children. For instance, some children entering first grade write sentence-length or longer stories, often inventing spellings. Other children are totally dependent on assistance from teachers, peers, reading books, or posters in the classroom. In addition, the special educator must investigate the written language curriculum a child has been exposed to as well as the experiences a child has with the written word (that is, read to, reading). Figure 11-2 illustrates the writing of a high achieving kindergarten student who had been introduced to the Rebus reading program; this is reflected in her choice of symbols. The writing of many special education students matches the linguistic structures and choice of vocabulary they were introduced to in their reading text.

Expressive writing.   In the elementary years, the focus is on moving away from dependence on drawing as the only means of symbolizing communication. In many instances, a young student's initial independent writing will be single words or clusters of well-known words or repetitive sentence structures, often written in a list fashion (Clay, 1975; McGaig, 1981). The writing of a normally achieving first

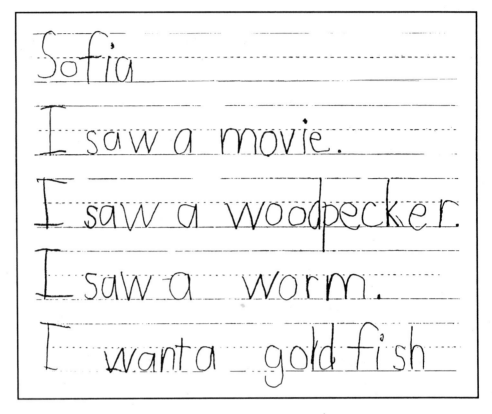

FIGURE 11-3 Normally achieving first-grade writer

grader illustrates such a structured writing technique (see Figure 11-3). Adolescent students demonstrating specific writing disabilities are often observed writing single words, word clusters, or lists (see Figure 11-4). While this is an appropriate step in the writing process for the young elementary child, in the older child it indicates a developmental delay or disorder.

As a child's oral language develops and his or her experience reading books increases, the child's written sentences become more complex grammatically. However, as the child's sentences and ideas become more sophisticated, the chance of making errors increases. Therefore, early in the school year a child might make fewer *mechanical errors* than when the child takes new risks expressing ideas with more complex vocabulary and syntax. In addition, as a child becomes a better writer, the child incorporates more talk-like style into his or her writing, demonstrating a recognition between the child's own talk and writing. The discovery of this written voice appears to be a means for the child to code experiences. Such writing is often egocentric and unintelligible to any reader who has not shared the child's experiences. In addition, the child's use of vocabulary words is closely connected to his or her conceptual development. Words naming things (nouns) develop first, followed by names for time–space relationships (prepositions), and finally words naming logical relations (if, because, prepositions). Many elementary age children have

FIGURE 11-4 Adolescent writer demonstrating specific learning disabilities

acquired the meanings for a large number of prepositions and conjunctions, but often these children do not explicitly use them in their writing since they egocentrically assume that the reader shares their knowledge base.

Elementary age writers learn to use a variety of word forms and sentence constructions in their written language. However, the majority of children know how to comprehend and compose word forms in oral language before they come to school. While there is a significant ability range among elementary age children with respect to success at using written syntax, the majority learn how to write with independent clauses and coordinating clauses during their early elementary years. By late elementary grades, children are experimenting with subordinating clauses and embedding. However, the special educator evaluating the written syntax of children must recognize that many errors attributed to a breakdown in syntax use are really differences in dialect, poor punctuation, pronoun reference, vocabulary, and coherence rather than grammar usage.

Elementary age children's writing is usually self-expressive (Genishi and Dyson, 1984). Their stories are often accompanied by a picture, and the picture conveys more detail than the text. Gradually, as children develop more confidence with written language, their text will move from a general description to include more specific details. Interestingly, researchers (Genishi and Dyson, 1984; Martin, 1971) have discovered that when children are asked to write fantasy or make-believe stories they produce more sophisticated writing structures. However, the elementary writer tends to write in the progressive present (what is happening). Generally, the early elementary age child's writing style is simple, general, egocentric, and concrete. By later elementary years, children develop stories using conventional story structures consisting of a setting, an initiating event, an internal response, an attempt, a consequence, and a reaction. Stein (1979) illustrates such a child's story schema in the following example:

Setting: Once there was a big gray fish named Albert. He lived in a big icy pond near the edge of a forest.

Initiating Event: One day, Albert was swimming around the pond. Then he spotted a big juicy worm on top of the water.

Internal Response: Albert knew how delicious worms tasted. He wanted to eat that one for his dinner.

Attempt: So he swam very close to the worm. Then he bit into him.

Consequence: Suddenly, Albert was pulled through the water into a boat. He had been caught by a fisherman.

Reaction: Albert felt sad. He wished he had been more careful.

    Spelling.   Spelling often presents a barrier to the elementary age child since he or she is just recognizing the sound–symbol relationships required by written spelling. Unfortunately, many classroom teachers place such a great deal of stress on "getting it spelled right" that they inhibit the child's motivation to write. Attempting to get their ideas down on paper, many children invent their own spellings (Read, 1971). Often, a child's first invented spellings omit vowels (ct = cat). Next the child invents spelling words that match his or her perceptions of sound–symbol associations (enuf = enough), which often result in an overgeneralization of patterns (groe = grow). This is a normal developmental pattern among young elementary children that should not be diagnosed as a deficit unless it continues into late elementary, middle, and secondary grades.

    Mechanics.   While the primary focus in schools is on the purpose or function of the writing task, development of punctuation and capitalization rules is also important. By the end of the elementary school years, a writer should be able to recognize and use the following conventions of written language spontaneously: begin sentences with a capital letter, end sentences with a period, end questions with a question mark, use commas in a list, and use apostrophes in contractions.

Middle School Writers

The writing curriculum at the middle school level stresses style, organization, and ideation with less concern for teaching mechanics. It is assumed that the writer in middle school has learned the majority of basic rules of mechanics and spelling

The middle school student begins to conceptualize the function of writing as a means of communicating.   *Source:* © Shelley Rotner/Omni Photo Communications

necessary to become a competent writer. Again, the special educator needs to investigate the oral language, thinking, and social skills of the young adolescence writer prior to making any statements regarding written language performance.

Expressive writing: The middle school writer is better equipped to incorporate multiple meanings and ambiguity into written text, particularly with a noted decline in egocentric thinking. Such writers become more sensitive to what has not been made explicit for the reader. In addition, the middle school writer has learned that a concept is often named by more than one word; therefore, diction, in the sense of word choice, increases. Greater versatility and originality of vocabulary is noted in the writing of the middle school student. As vocabulary increases so does the writer's ability to combine words in more original phrases, resulting in a more individualistic style. The middle school writer incorporates an ever-expanding repertoire of clause-connecting sentence structures in his or her writing.

The middle school writer is able to write more in the past tense (what happened) in comparison to the elementary writer who tends to use the present tense (what is happening). Therefore, the writing curriculum for the middle school writer stresses the literary modes of autobiography, memoir, biography, reportage, chronicles, and history (Moffett and Wagner, 1983).

Role-taking skills are observable in the oral language of middle school children but have not stabilized in their written text (Crowhurst and Piche, 1979). Therefore, middle school children have significant difficulty writing in the modes of expositions and persuasion. Exposition and persuasion also require more of the writer in terms of logic, analysis, and reasoning than the middle school student has developed in both cognitive and affective skills. The middle school child is still more comfortable with the demands required by narrative and descriptive writing. In fact, Crowhurst and Piche (1979) feel that the narration "places the fewest demands on writers to make use of their syntactic resources" (p. 107).

The middle school child begins to conceptualize the function of writing as a means of communicating both with self (personal) and others (public) rather than just a means of telling stories. Teachers note an increase among middle school writers in using writing to express feelings that are beginning to be explored in the middle school child's family and peer relationships.

Secondary School Writers

The secondary school writing curriculum varies according to the vocational goals of the individual student. Students interested in vocational/technical careers will be introduced to technical writing skills (for example, business education) required for their future profession. Those students interested in a college career receive a literature/composition writing curriculum. In addition, more and more high schools are developing basic writing classes that teach the mechanical skills of writing to students who either for lack of instruction or due to disabilities have never automatized writing skills. Regardless of the focus of the writing class in which these different groups of students are placed, they must all write in their other content classes (history, social science, science). Therefore, many high schools stress a curriculum that focuses on writing across the content classrooms rather than seeing writing as something that is only done in English classrooms. Such a focus on writing puts an additional pressure on the student demonstrating written language disorders.

Expressive writing.   Cognitively, the secondary school student should be ready to produce written discourse at a higher abstraction level than the middle or elementary child. Writing assignments are often in the future tense (what might or could happen) as compared to the dependence in lower grades on the perfect and past tense modes. The ability to cognitively deal with the future tense corresponds with the genre demands of the secondary school student. Articles of factual generalization, essays of idea generalization, and essays of argumentative theory are often required assignments (Moffett and Wagner, 1983). Literature, particularly contemporary realism and poetry, become the means by which students begin to model types of writing styles. In addition, the secondary school student is better able to analyze the structure of literary works and the motives of the story characters. In turn, by late secondary years, the student can generalize about literature, science, theological, and philosophical works and can consider themes or points of view different from his or her own. The second-

Table 11-10 Written language skill development

Level	Focus of Writing Program
Prewriting	Symbolic play Drawing
Elementary School	Spelling Mechanics Syntax Narrative story scheme Introducing sense of audience (egocentric stage) Tense (present) Function (story telling)
Middle School	Style individualized and more flexible Narrative and descriptive story schema Increased sense of audience skills with writing Versatility with vocabulary Tense (past) Function (communication of feelings)
Secondary School	Style continues to be individualized Expository and persuasive writing schema Greater versatility with vocabulary and syntax Social role-taking skills affect sense of audience Tense (future) Function (communication of ideas and feelings)

ary student is expected not only to generalize but to categorize and summarize ideas in writing by retelling ideas in whole or part, depending on the function or purpose of the writing task. Therefore, there is an increase in the student's ability to write more in the expository and persuasive genre. Crowhurst and Piche (1979) found that sentence structure is more elaborated when writers use exposition and persuasion rather than with narration and description. Crowhurst and Piche (1979) found that exposition and persuasion also are more demanding since the writer needs to use conditionals (if/ then), resultants (therefore), and other language structures requiring significant interaction between the writer and the content.

The secondary school student's social role-taking skills increase from ninth to twelfth grade. Ritter (1979) found that twelfth graders devised more complex strategies and appeals than did ninth grade students. In addition, Ritter found that by secondary school, adolescents can elect or choose to role-take when motivated and are more likely to develop their role-taking abilities with close friends. Throughout the secondary school years, motivation continues to assume a major role in writing performance. Table 11-10 summarizes the focus of typical writing curricula from preschool through secondary grades.

Concerns Expressed by Classroom Teachers

Disorders in the area of written language are normally not identified until a child reaches the age of 9 or 10. More often than not teachers ignore the impact of symbolic play and drawing competence as red flags for later writing problems.

Spelling difficulties and letter reversals resulting from visual–motor or sound–symbol problems often draw the classroom teacher's attention to a student's writing performance. However, it isn't until the student is expected to write stories or reports that production problems become a concern for the teacher. Quite often the classroom teacher focuses on handwriting, spelling, and punctuation errors and ignores the possible strengths with organization, ideation, or sense of audience. The evaluation that occurs in the regular classroom can provide the basis for an in-depth and objective analysis of written language skills. The special education teacher should be familiar with and utilize both formal and informal techniques to achieve a precise and useful assessment, looking at obvious performance deficiencies and other variables of written language such as ideation, sense of audience, and organization. The special education teacher should collect written language samples from the student's classroom assignments as well as a student's own spontaneous writing, the most accurate tool for evaluating writing.

Types of Assessment

What Are You Measuring?

Area.   Written language disorder(s) can have an impact on one or several areas of written language depending on the number, type, and severity of the oral language, cognitive, or emotional deficits. The assessment of written language requires investigation of the abilities necessary to complete task demands required in spelling, syntax, text structure, sense of audience, ideation, and handwriting. No single standardized assessment tool will provide an evaluator with the necessary information to investigate all of these areas. However, understanding the areas allows the special educator to utilize the tools available in combination with qualitative measures to make a more accurate assessment.

Format.   To evaluate the different areas of written language, Luria (1980) suggests dividing tasks into three formats: copying, dictation, and spontaneous writing. Such formats allow the special educator to examine the different cognitive and affective abilities of the student confronted with very different task demands. These formats will be discussed fully later in this chapter. To determine a student's level of functioning in written expression, Zigmond, Vallecorsa, and Silverman (1983) discuss a hierarchy of task formats that the evaluator should investigate when assessing a student's writing abilities. The highest level, writing continuous text, includes writing a series of thematically related sentences (that is, paragraphs). Level two, writing single sentences, requires the student to write sentences that are not organized into paragraphs or connected thematically. To meet the requirements of levels 3 and 2, the student must think of something to say, write it down, spell the words correctly, and use appropriate conventions of print. Level 1 demonstrates component skills of written expression and presumes that the student is not yet able to combine the discrete skills necessary to express ideas in written form, although the student may be able to perform these skills in isolation.

Structure.   The special educator must also control for the amount of structure specific task demands make on a student. Zigmond, Vallecorsa, and Silverman (1983) discuss a writing continuum that begins with tasks requiring the greatest amount of structure and moves to tasks requiring the least amount of structure. These tasks include assignments with no teacher direction, topics assigned, story starters, picture starters, and finally writing from a sequence of pictures. Writing from a sequence of pictures puts the least demand on the student. To determine which category to start with, the student's age and oral language skills should be considered.

Interest/motivation.   In addition to the area of written language and amount of task structure, the special educator should consider the interests of the student being tested. If students are allowed to write about something that is intriguing or motivating to them, a longer writing sample is more likely to be generated. The special educator using pictures as a story stimulus should identify topics of interest to the student, considering age and ability level. The pictures should include at least one central character engaged in some obvious activity. At some point during the evaluation, the special educator may want to conduct an informal interview with the student to determine the individual's attitude toward writing as well as areas of interest.

Topic.   Students should always be given a choice of writing topics during an evaluation of their performance. For example, when using story starters or picture stimuli, there should be several to choose from that include age-appropriate themes and culture-appropriate experiences (Zigmond, Vallecorsa, and Silverman, 1983). In addition the special educator might be prepared to tape-record the student reading his or her own written text. This assists the evaluator later in accurately interpreting the student's intent so a thorough error analysis can be completed.

Audience.   Britton, Burgess, Martin, McLeod, and Rosen (1975) advocated that students need experience communicating in writing directly to specified audiences for different purposes. They claimed that the student "must have a lively representation of this audience in mind—or, if he does not, he will fail in his intent" (p. 59). Therefore, it is important for the special educator to assess an individual's writing across different audiences. These different audiences could include student to teacher, student to student, student to trusted friend, student to examiner, or student to an unknown audience. Some writers produce much more elaborate and better organized text when they feel comfortable with the audience.

Norm-Referenced Assessment in Written Language

The majority of standardized test batteries used in schools contains at least one subtest that measures reading (the receptive component to written language) and some measure of grammar and vocabulary; however, considerably fewer have subtests measuring written expression abilities. Standardized achievement tests in written language are typically designed to provide a broad estimate of written

Table 11-11 Achievement tests with written language sections

Test	Area Assessed	Receptive (R) Expressive (E)	Grade Level
California Achievement Tests (Tiegs and Clark, 1978)	Capitalization Punctuation Word usage Sentence structure	R	3–12
Stanford Achievement Tests (Madden and Gardner, 1990)	Mechanics Grammatical structure	R	3–12
Iowa Test of Basic Skills (Hieronymus, Hoover, and Lindquist, 1986)	Capitalization Punctuation Word usage Spelling–proofreading	R/E	— 1–9
Iowa Test of Basic Skills Language and Writing Supplement—Form G & H Level 12–14 (ITBS)	Description Explanation Narration Report Persuasion	R/E	12–14
Metropolitan Achievement Tests (Prescott, Balon, Hogan, and Farr, 1987)	Spelling Dictated–word Proofreading	R/E	2–4 4–9
Otis–Lennon School Ability Test (Otis and Lennon, 1979)	Syntax Cohesion Text structure Spelling	R/E	K–12
SRA Achievement Series (Naslund, Thorpe, and Lefever, 1985)	Capitalization Punctuation Spelling–proofreading Sentence structure	R/E	1–12
Wide Range Achievement Test–Revised (Jastak and Jastak, 1986)	Spelling–dictated	E	3–12
Cognitive Abilities Test (Thorndike and Hagen, 1986)	Syntax Cohesion Text structure Spelling	R/E	K–12
Kaufman Test of Educational Achievement (Kaufman and Kaufman, 1985)	Spelling	E	6–18-11
Test of Achievement and Proficiency (Hieronymus, Hoover, and Lindquist, 1982)	Spelling	E	5-2–18-3

language achievement level, usually receptive knowledge of written skills. Scores are given as percentiles, standard scores, or grade equivalents with the intent of comparing a student's functioning to that of the student's peer group. These tests may be useful in documenting an individual's progress through the school grades, but they offer little diagnostic information to the special educator. Table 11-11 lists achievement tests with written language sections that are used by schools today. The majority of these standardized achievement tests consist of a contrived writing format. Skills such as capitalization, punctuation, and word usage are presented in isolation from the general written product, and no attempt is made to evaluate the adequacy of the student's own written composition.

Compared to written language achievement tests, diagnostic tests measure a wider range of skills associated with written language as well as investigating these skills across different formats (receptive and expressive). The oldest diagnostic measure in the field of special education used to assess written language is Myklebust's (1965) Picture Story Language Test (PSLT). The measure is no longer considered a reliable or valid measure of written expression, and the cognitive processes he identified as disordered and resulting in dysgraphia have been questioned by current research. But the contributions of Myklebust's work in the area of developmental writing disorders cannot be overestimated today. While terminology and etiology continue to be debated, the impact of cognitive processes on written language among students with handicapping conditions (for example, hearing impaired, emotionally disturbed, learning disabled, mentally retarded) was thoroughly addressed by Myklebust in light of available research. In addition, Myklebust was one of the pioneers in addressing areas of written language other than handwriting and spelling. While it is easy today to discount the PSLT as an unsound psychometric instrument, its importance to the development of current assessment instruments cannot be ignored.

The more commonly employed diagnostic tests as well as the purpose of each, the format of the tests, areas of written language investigated, and the appropriate age range for each are presented in Table 11-12. There is some overlap in the measures presented in this table as it is difficult to separate the components of written language actually being measured. Although formal standardized tests provide a starting point for evaluation, they must be followed with dynamic assessment, curriculum-based assessment, and observation to accurately pinpoint written language deficiencies affecting a student's performance.

Criterion-Referenced Measures of Written Language

Criterion-referenced measures (CRM) of written language can be integrated into the special educator's assessment battery to contribute to better program planning. However, as with standardized tests, the teacher must evaluate the area of written language addressed, the amount of structure of the tasks, the task format, the topic, the motivational level of the writer, and the audience the writer must consider. In addition, few criterion-referenced measures in the area of written language are currently available to teachers. Those published CRMs assess the mechanical components of written language (that is, spelling, sentence structure, capitalization, and punctuation). No CRM to date addresses issues such as text organization, sense of audience, or ideation. Table 11-13 lists CRMs used most frequently by special educators today.

Criterion-referenced measures often lack a sound theoretical foundation. Quite often these measures ignore the concern for function and interaction so important in assessing written language. The special educator should be very careful in utilizing criterion-referenced measures in the decision-making process pertaining to written language disorders.

Table 11-12 Standardized diagnostic measures of written language

Measure	Formats		Areas of Written Language Assessment	Age Range
	Spontaneous	*Contrived*		
Picture Story Language Test (Myklebust, 1965, 1973b)	X		Productivity (Total words, total sentences, words per sentence)	7–17 yrs.
	X		Syntax (Word usage, grammatical endings, punctuation)	
	X		Abstract–Concrete (Rating of ideational level)	
Test of Written Language–2 (Larsen and Hammill, 1988)	X	X	Vocabulary (Semantics)	7–11 yrs.
	X		Thematic Maturity	
	X		Thought Units	
	X		Handwriting	
	X		Style (Capitalization, punctuation, spelling)	
		X	Spelling	
		X	Logical Sentences (Syntax, Semantics)	
		X	Sentence Combining (Syntax)	
Test of Adolescent Language–2 (Hammill, Brown, Larsen, and Wiederholt, 1987)		X	Vocabulary: Write sentences using specific words (Semantics)	11–18 yrs.
		X	Grammar (Syntax)	
		X	Sentence combining (With two or more stimulus statements)	
Test of Early Written Language (Hresko, 1988)		X	Ideas	3–0 to 7–11 yrs.
		X	Language	
		X	Spelling	
		X	Style	
		X	Handwriting	
Test of Legible Handwriting (Larsen and Hammill, 1989)	X		Handwriting	7–6 to 7–11 yrs.
Test of Written Spelling–2 (Larsen and Hammill, 1986)		X	Spelling	7–0 to 17–11 yrs.
Woodcock–Johnson Psychoeducational Battery–Revised, Achievement Battery (Woodcock and Johnson, 1989)		X	Spelling	3–81 yrs.
		X	(Dictation)	
		X	Proofing	
		X	Word Usage	
		X	Productivity	
		X	Formulation	
Peabody Individual Achievement Tests–Revised (Markwardt, 1989)	X	X	Spelling	5–18 yrs.
	X		Handwriting	
	X		Organization	
	X		Syntax	
	X	X	Mechanics	

Table 11-13 Criterion-referenced measures for written language

Test	Areas	Grade Level
BRIGANCE Diagnostic Inventory of Basic Skills (Brigance, 1977)	Write complete and correct sentences that incorporate several stimulus words	Elementary
BRIGANCE Diagnostic Comprehensive Inventory of Basic Skills (Brigance, 1983)	Comprehensive basic skills	K–9
BRIGANCE Diagnostic Inventory of Essential Skills (Brigance, 1981)	Handwriting Syntax Mechanics Text structure (letter writing only) Spelling	Secondary
Hudson Educational Skills: Reading (Hudson, Colson, and Welsh, 1989)	Capitalization Punctuation Grammar Vocabulary Paragraphs	Elementary

Curriculum-Based Measures of Written Language

Curriculum-based assessment (CBA) in written language should be developed by the special educator and integrated into the evaluation process. Since instruction in written language is dependent upon a combination of a student's ability and achievement level, a teacher's theoretical concept of written language, and the school's curriculum, CBA can aid in a systematic investigation of written language needed for program planning. The development of curriculum-based measures has been hampered in the area of written language due to a lack of agreement regarding the essential knowledge and skills required of all writers. Systematic assessment using a CBA model should include all the areas of written language (that is, spelling, syntax, handwriting, text organization, sense of audience, and ideation). The special educator should also consider the need to evaluate all these areas to develop a spiral curriculum for students in the area of written language. Such an approach allows each rule or principle to be repeated and practiced over time as a review for more advanced instruction. In addition, as with the administration of standardized and criterion-referenced measures, the teacher developing CBA must consider the area of written language to be assessed, the amount of structure a task requires, tasks formats, topics, motivational level of the student, and the audience the student will address.

Curriculum-based assessment in written language helps the special educator formulate future program objectives. It requires that the evaluator specify a specific area to assess, analyze the school's curriculum, formulate behavioral objectives, assess, chart data, and interpret errors for program decisions. However, this rather behavioral approach to the assessment of written language ignores some of the underlying reasons for student errors such as cultural diversity or emotional, language, and cognitive functioning. CBA focuses on the skill performance needed for curriculum success rather than on the underlying causes for poor achievement. Another weakness of CBA is the difficulty collecting information across student writers, teachers, and programs for evaluation decisions. CBA is most effective

---

Box 11-4   ***Writing of a College Student Demonstrating a Specific Learning Disability***
Private Pain
by Beth Bailey

As I sit here, a rush of pain comes over me.
Then the sadness and depression set in.
You don't understand why I am sad.

I cry today for all the things I should have done.
I cry for all those things I must still do.
These things may seem simple or even trivial to the average person;
But, to me they are life and death.
I am possessed with drive to succeed when I could say "I can't."
I *must* strive to overcome this thing.

You may never know why I weep, or even that I do.
Please, just be there for me when I feel I must do more than cry.

Source: "Private Pain," a previously unpublished poem by Beth Bailey of Athens, Georgia. Reprinted by permission.

---

when all the students are learning the same skill(s), a luxury few teachers in special education experience in their program planning. As Deno (1985) noted, "Unless CBA can achieve a level of generality that enables aggregation across curricula, they are not likely to supplement the more general, commercially produced achievement tests for making all programming and evaluation decisions" (p. 231). The strength of CBA is its concern for systematic data collection and realistic program planning.

Dynamic Assessment

Dynamic assessment allows the teacher to become equally involved in the writing process—a partnership in dialogue. Part of the role of dynamic assessment in written expression should be consideration of public versus private writing. Public writing is geared toward the expected product, whereas the value of private writing lies in the actual process of expression. A teacher who is sensitive to the intensity, feelings, fears, and frustration of students will encourage their written expression without always stressing conventional standards of assessment. The poem in Box 11-4, written by a college student with a specific learning disability, reveals powerful feelings that are real and meaningful. It lends insight into the psyche of the student writer that no contrived measure of written language could generate.

A most important component of dynamic assessment of written language is learning how the student feels about each stage in the writing process. How does the student see himself or herself as a writer? By interacting (dialogue) with the student and using interactive assessment techniques, the special educator may be able to determine how attitudes toward the writing experience affect the individual's performance.

As in the assessment of other areas of academic ability, the interaction between examiner/teacher and student writer is of critical importance. Analysis of the task, the student's approach to that task, the examiner's approach, and the specific testing situation are key factors in the dynamic assessment concept. Respect for sharing inner feelings and personal ideas must be conveyed in a form as enduring as written language. A positive one-to-one interaction between teacher and student may create an atmosphere in which written expression that had seemingly become stagnant can begin to flourish. Such an atmosphere allows the special educator to capture the student writer's peak performance in written language.

Luria (1980) describes a series of tasks that the special educator could utilize in assessing written language through a dynamic approach. To evaluate the different areas of written language, Luria suggested dividing tasks into three formats: copying, dictation, and spontaneous writing. These different formats allow the special educator to examine the cognitive processing abilities of the individual confronted with very different task demands. Each area of written language should be examined using each of these formats.

Copying.   Luria (1980) points out several ways to vary the coping task to observe different cognitive processing abilities of the writer. The first suggestion is to have the individual, if developmentally appropriate, copy individual letters, single words, isolated sentences, and paragraphs. Spelling, syntax, and organizational deficits can be noted as the task demands increase the need for integration of specific cognitive processing abilities. Luria also recommends varying the type of script (size, density, and type) to assess specific motor and visual processing abilities accurately. Copying nonsense figures (Roeltgen, 1985) is also valuable because it is more difficult to transcribe figures with no apparent symbolic meaning. Luria (1980) also encourages varying the distance between the presentation of the stimuli and when the individual is allowed to reproduce the information as a means to evaluate specific motor, memory, and spatial abilities. Monitoring the strategies an individual uses (auditorization, tracing, et cetera) as well as the amount of time necessary to complete the task is significant information in drawing conclusions regarding a disorder versus a cognitive style difference.

Dictation.   The ability to complete a dictation task requires the individual to integrate linguistic, visual–spatial, and motor skills in an automatic manner. Therefore, dictation tasks should begin by requesting the person to write individual letters, syllables, and sentences. To distinguish between linguistic and motor disorders, the examiner should vary the client's response by the use of anagrams (blocks with single letters written on them).

Spontaneous writing.   A spontaneous writing sample requires that the individual write either a sentence, a paragraph, or a story on a familiar topic. Many researchers have indicated that the complexity of such a task requires extensive integration of several cognitive processing abilities (Cromer, 1980; Luria, 1980; Roeltgen, 1985). It is suggested that the topic or picture be standard from client to client so performance can be compared. However, the type of task (sentence starter, picture, or topic) significantly influences individual performance. Ideally, the evaluator should collect samples of the individual's writing across different audiences (for example, peer, teacher) and types of genre (for example, letter, narrative, descriptive).

Cultural Issues in Written Language Assessment

Minority children are frequently referred by classroom teachers to special education on the basis of oral and written language behaviors that do not correspond to the expectations of the dominant culture (Ortiz and Yates, 1983, 1984). The referral is often made as the result of teacher perceptions that linguistic, cultural, economic, and other background characteristics are deviant. In addition, research (Damico, Oller, and Storey, 1983; Mattes and Omark, 1984; Ortiz and Maldonando–Colon, 1986) has suggested that many of the oral and written language behaviors demonstrated by children normally acquiring a second language are similar to the characteristics demonstrated by children with developmental language disorders. Therefore, the special educator must learn to discriminate between poor comprehension, limited vocabulary, or grammatical and syntactical errors signifying a handicapping condition and those same errors signifying a lack of English proficiency.

The input hypothesis (Krashen, 1982) currently advocated by researchers studying second language acquisition purports that individuals acquiring a second language go for meaning first, acquiring language structures as a byproduct. Assessment and instruction for second language learners should focus on evaluating the development of comprehension and text structure more than on surface features (that is, spelling and syntax) of written language. In addition, current research findings (Cummins, 1982, 1984) stress that speech and language disorders affect common language processes that underlie the surface structure of the language spoken or written by the child. The special educator must keep in mind that it is not possible for a bilingual child to have a language disorder in one language and not in the other (Juarez, 1983; Ortiz, 1984). This highlights the need for the special educator to always obtain test results from the individual's primary language as well as the secondary language prior to making decisions regarding written language competence.

The majority of research investigating the development of written language in English is based on studies of white middle-class children. Anglo-American or British families tend to place a high value on their children's oral and written language competencies. However, because American society is so heterogeneous, all groups within it do not share the same values regarding oral and written language competency. The special educator must be sensitive to cultural variation and consider the contrasting values that underlie normal processes of written language acquisition among different groups of students.

Hildreth (1936) conducted the first systematic developmental study of preschool writers, charting development of nonwriters between the ages of 3 and 6. Through parent interviews, Hildreth concluded that these white middle-class children acquired writing skills by "begging to know how to write when seeing others write" (p. 79). Also highlighting the high correlation between an active learner, a responsive environment and writing success was studied by Hall, Mortez, and Statom (1976). Parents in this study reported that help with writing was given at the child's request. Most frequently, help was requested with letter formation, spelling, and words, or recording a child's diction. Recently, however, researchers (Anderson and Stokes, 1984; Harste, Burke, and Woodward, 1982) have drawn attention to how children develop literacy skills (reading and writing) from interaction with the print in their environment outside of their homes or parental guidance. They noted the significant impact of advertisements, TV, and church on the development of children's written language competency. The special educator must remain sensitive to the impact of cultural variation on the ways in which children use and talk about print.

Assessment of written language performance of culturally diverse populations presents a challenge to the special educator because little has been written about this subject. Conventional written language proficiency tests typically measure the minority child's mechanical skills (spelling and syntax) in written language. Recent research (Duran, 1989; Figuero, 1989; Jax, 1989) advocates that special educators begin looking at "*communicative competence*" rather than "language proficiency" during assessment of written language performance. The emphasis would be more on the student/teacher or student/peer interaction than on discrete performance on contrived written language tasks. Duran (1989) suggested that the "successful functioning of Hispanic and other ethnic minority students can be affected dramatically by interactional competencies" (p. 154). Communicative competence models are based on a dynamic assessment model that assumes that the interactions and strategies used during student/teacher or student/peer dialogue are more accurate assessments of student competency. Carrasco, Vera, and Cazden (1981) discussed a Hispanic first-grade student who was capable of teaching a language arts spelling task to a peer but was not able to reply to the teacher's questions about the task. Tharp and Gillmore (1988), based on their experiences teaching reading to high-risk Hawaiian children, discuss how communicative competence models can be incorporated into school assessment and instruction.

Assessment in written language for the language or cultural minority child falls into three categories (Erickson and Omark, 1981). The first category, which they label *discrete-point tests,* is a standardized assessment of written language. Such measures reflect a structuralist point of view in that samples of finite units of written language (that is, word usage, sentence structure, and spelling) serve as a measure for overall written language ability. The second category includes *quasi-integrative tests* (for example, Developmental Sentence Scoring) where spontaneous writing samples are used to obtain scores such as t–unit, word counts, and sentence types. The third category highlights the functional use of language through a pragmatics framework. Cloze procedures, which omit every *n*th word in a discourse sample, or story constructions are typical measures used in this kind of written language assessment.

Utilizing story construction as a reliable measure of written language competence for language minority students has been supported by Jax (1989). Story writing or narration allows the student to discuss experiences from a world of people, events, and time periods familiar to the student. Peterson and McCabe (1983) discuss seven types of narrative story structures that emerged in the collaborative research of Stein

Table 11-14 Assessment data needed for the diagnosis of written language performance among culturally diverse populations

Area	Components
Reason for Referral	Family perception Teacher perception Student perception

Background Information	Family history
	Health history
	Developmental milestones
	School history
	   attendance record
	   types of classes
	Length of residence in United States
	Referring teacher's experience with culture

Cognitive Functioning	
Oral Language Functioning	Primary language Second language

Social-Emotional Functioning	Peer comparisons
	Motivational level
	   school related
	   home/work related
	Self-confidence
	Anxiety
	Depression

Written Language Functioning	Competence in primary language
	Competence in second language
	   Discrete-point tests
	   Quasi-integrative tests
	   Integrative tests
	   Communicative competence tasks
	      story telling, narrative
	      teach task to another

and Glenn (1979): descriptive sentences, action sequences, narrative sequences, abbreviated episodes, and interactive episodes. These categories can be especially helpful to the special educator when evaluating the story structures of language minority children and adolescents. The story patterns are listed logically from least to most complex. Narrative discourse structures are important when considering written language competencies. As Applebee (1978) noted, these patterns reflect the cognitive stages of individual growth.

The special educator must not only analyze the type of written language format (that is, discrete point, quasi-integrative, or integrative) used in assessment of a language minority student but also must analyze the relevance of the process of obtaining that information. As Erickson (1985) noted, ''being tested is a middle-class activity that may be unfamiliar to minorities who are overrepresented in lower socioeconomic groups'' (p. 13). In addition, the special educator must evaluate his or her own biases, attitudes, skills, training, and knowledge of the culture of the student being evaluated. Table 11-14 lists additional information needed for a thorough and nonbiased assessment of culturally different children and adolescents. Benavides (1989) suggests that placement in special education is often related to socioeconomic, linguistic, and cultural bias rather than sound psychoeducational factors. The special educator's role, therefore, demands reconsideration of diagnostic strategies for evaluating the written language of minority students.

Steps in the Assessment Process

The lack of empirical research defining the written language characteristics of individual demonstrating different handicapping conditions as well as a lack of valid and reliable measurement tools to assess spelling, written syntax, handwriting, text organization, sense of audience, and ideation makes the job of the special educator investigating a student's written language performance very difficult. Qualitative indices (dynamic assessment, curriculum-based assessment, and criterion-referenced measures) and clinical judgment should always be incorporated into the assessment process as diagnostic supplements to standardized measurements to develop realistic school-based instructional objectives.

The special educator preparing to assess a student's performance in the area of written language should follow the five steps discussed on the following pages. A consistent and systematic approach should be followed at all times. Efficient and effective assessments require that the examiner be prepared, organized, and flexible in his or her approach. In addition, the special educator must control and analyze every test or task given for the following variables:

- Area of written language addressed (prewriting, spelling, syntax, text organization, sense of audience, ideation).
- Structure of interaction between the student and teacher.
- Structure of task format (copy, dictation, spontaneous writing).
- Task format (receptive or expressive).
- Topic of writing task.
- Motivational level of student writer.
- Audience the writer is addressing.

Develop the Purpose of the Assessment Process

The special educator must begin the assessment process by determining the purpose of the evaluation. Isaacson (1988) discussed four main purposes for assessing a student's writing competence: interindividual comparison (distinguishing between successful and unsuccessful writers), instructional planning, monitoring student progress, and providing student feedback. The purpose of the assessment should dictate the extent of the evaluation process. For instance, interindividual requires an extensive exploration of the student's cognitive, language, and social–emotional functioning compared with the student's academic achievement across various types of written language formats. In making these comparisons, student feedback regarding specific areas of written language performance might be obtained by behavioral checklists.

Once the special educator has determined the purpose of the evaluation, specific goals should be developed prior to the evaluation process. When setting the goals, the special educator should identify appropriate developmental milestones for the student writer and coordinate them with the content of the school's written language curriculum. While goals should be set that investigate specific referral issues (for instance, spelling), assessment goals should also evaluate all other areas of written language (syntax, text structure, et cetera). The main purpose of assessment is to provide the teacher with specific guidelines in establishing a student's curriculum needs, in this case in the areas of written language. Therefore, the teacher should address a student's strengths as well as areas of below average performance.

Develop Record Sheets to Record Assessment Data

The special educator must record the data of the assessment in an organized and systematic manner to quickly identify error patterns; the importance of good record keeping cannot be overemphasized. From the information recorded on the teacher's assessment data sheets, areas of written language needing further probing or standardized testing can be identified. As well, this information is used to develop instructional goals. The forms should summarize all the areas of written language, the student's performance level, and other quantitative (ability level, age, grade) and qualitative information (motivational level) pertinent to the evaluation process. Some teachers prefer to record data in a chart fashion while other teachers prefer to record data on detailed error sheets. The more detailed the information recorded the easier it will be to develop performance-based objectives for instructional planning.

Conduct an Integrated Assessment Utilizing Standardized, Curriculum-Based, and Dynamic Diagnostic Measures

The need for an integrated assessment of written language performance utilizing standardized, curriculum-based, and dynamic diagnostic measures has been discussed throughout this chapter. We have stressed that the score or the percentage correct a student receives is not as important as how the student arrives at the response. Special educators must be recording the student's behaviors throughout the evaluation process, noting interaction and format differences across tasks. During a writing task, the student should be encouraged not to erase but to cross out answers he or she feels are incorrect. This allows the diagnostician to explore some of the possible strategies a student uses to obtain answers. Error analysis can provide an interesting exploration of the student's thinking processes.

The assessment of written language performance is not complete until all the areas of written language (spelling, syntax, text structure, sense of audience, and ideation) are evaluated with both contrived and spontaneous writing tasks. Since very few standardized diagnostic tests are available in the area of written composition, the special educator must become knowledgeable about written language processes and disorders so informal measures can be developed that will tap into different areas and levels of written language performance.

Analyze the Error Patterns

The special educator investigating written language competence must consider the importance of evaluating such students across several tasks designed to investigate different aspects of the writing process. Error patterns can vary according to task demands. The special educator must be cognizant that the type of task can influence a student's written performance and that the writing abilities of an individual using copying, dictation, and spontaneous writing tasks (see dynamic assessment section) should be investigated. Each task investigates a different cognitive demand required for the writing process.

Currently there is a dearth of information regarding the types of written language errors indicative of different handicapping conditions as well as appropriate instruments useful in documenting types of errors (Gregg, Hoy, McAlexander, and Hayes, 1981). Understanding the source of the errors exhibited by writers demonstrating different handicapping conditions would help in developing more appropriate identification procedures and instructional strategies. As Shaugnessy (1977) points out, error-laden work must be viewed in light of its intentional structures as errors evidence systematic, rule-governed behavior.

The special educator must investigate possible cognitive and affective deficits that could affect a student's writing performance. It is advantageous for the diagnostician to learn more about the cognitive processing mechanisms that support or share the input and output processes involved in writing (Gregg, 1990). Kosslyn (1981) outlined an account that included sharing resources and cognitive skills between perpetual and productive processes. While specific cognitive resources might be shared in the writing process, investigation of functionally distinct processes also needs to continue for a better understanding of the components of the system. Current research (Caramazza, 1988; Hill and Caramazza, 1989; Rapp and Caramazza, 1989) supports the significant contributions of both linguistic and visual–spatial processes in the act of writing. Problems with oral language and reading are often precursors to difficulties with the writing process (Johnson and Myklebust, 1967).

Difficulty with the integration of subject, text, and reader, however, is not always due to an underlying processing problem. It may be the result of poor instruction, lack of adequate experience manipulating language structures, or the result of overall intellectual or emotional functioning. Writing involves not only knowledge of the topic, rhetorical knowledge, and metacommunication skills (Burleson, 1984) but awareness of an audience (reader) and sensitivity to the reader's needs. Therefore, specific personality and affective disorders can seriously impair a student's success with written communication.

The special educator must determine the source (cognitive, affective, or instructional) of a student's written language errors. Patterns across writing areas (for example, spelling, syntax, and text organization) and types of task formats (for example, copy, dictation, or spontaneous) need to be carefully investigated by the special educator. Instructional objectives are dependent on a careful analysis of error source, frequency, and severity. For instance, spelling errors due to an instructional deficit require very different instructional techniques than spelling errors that are due to underlying cognitive processing deficits (for example, phonetic analysis or visual–spatial processes). Careful investigation of error patterns will lead to realistic instructional goal setting.

Develop Instructional Objectives Based on Careful Analysis of Diagnostic Findings

The special educator must translate the diagnostic information collected during standardized and dynamic assessment into behavioral instructional objectives. This requires specifying instructional goals in the writing curriculum, under what conditions those goals should be performed, and exactly what a student must do to demonstrate attainment of that instructional goal. According to Mager (1975), behavioral objectives must have three components: the behavior to be demonstrated, the conditions under which performance will be demonstrated, and the criterion for successful competence.

The special educator must be sure to include behavioral objectives in all the areas (spelling, syntax, text discourse, sense of audience, and ideation) of written language. In addition, normal developmental skill acquisition and the goals of the school curriculum in written language must be considered when creating a student's written language instructional program. Systematic monitoring of the student's behavioral objectives in written language will often lead to discovery of additional errors types as well as to a better understanding of the source of some errors. At that point, the special educator should reevaluate the appropriateness of instructional objectives and methods for that student.

Summary

Areas of Written Language

1. A written language disorder can affect one or several areas of written language depending on the number, type, and severity of the deficit.
2. Currently, no single standardized assessment tool provides the special educator with the necessary information to investigate all areas of written language.
3. The areas of written language most commonly affected by a writing disorder include spelling, syntax, text organization, sense of audience, ideation/abstractness and handwriting.

Spelling

1. Phonetically predictable words are spelled like they sound (for example, cat, dip).

2. Phonetically irregular or unpredictable words are not spelled exactly like they sound (for example, the, were, enough).
3. Two of the most commonly used spelling tasks are those that investigate the recall and recognition of single words.
4. A recognition, recall, copying, and spontaneous writing sample provides the special educator with a valid examination of the spelling processes required with different types of academic tasks.

Written Syntax

1. Behaviors often indicative of written syntax disorders include word omissions, word substitutions, inappropriate verb or pronoun use, omission and substitution of word endings, lack of punctuation, and a discrepancy between oral and written syntax.
2. The assessment of written syntax should include tasks measuring both receptive (identification) and expressive (production) syntax.
3. The special educator investigating the written syntax of a student should begin by administering various types of tasks that tap different components of the cognitive processing system. The formats for such tasks might include sentence combining, controlled stimulus passage, identification, and spontaneous writing.

Text Organization

1. Text organization focuses on the structure of meaning within a student's writing that supersedes the sentence.
2. The special educator investigating an individual's ability to produce written text must first consider the genre (narrative, expository, persuasive, descriptive), age of the student, logical reasoning ability of the student, and the experience the student has had with the topic.

Sense of Audience

1. A sense of audience requires the writer to make the necessary writing adjustments and choices that take into account the intended reader(s).
2. Students learn to adapt their writing to different audiences (such as teachers, friends, unknown audiences, or examiners).
3. It is important to evaluate a student's writing across different audiences.

Ideation/Abstractness

1. Students demonstrating low ideation tend to organize their ideas through sensory or perceptual constructs, while students with high ideation organize ideas using generalizing and inferencing techniques.
2. The type of discourse (narrative or descriptive), the topic, and the tense can significantly affect the level of abstraction that is appropriate to a specific writing task.

Handwriting

1. Many factors, such as motivation, instruction, motor coordination, memory, oral language skill, and reading ability can affect a student's handwriting performance.
2. Handwriting error patterns should be noted in letter formation, letter size, proportion and alignment, spacing, line quality, slant, and rate of writing.
3. It is important to identify whether the student can identify letters by name, draw figures, trace letters, copy letters, write letters or words from dictation, translate manuscript to cursive, and translate capital to small letters.

Developmental Progression

1. The ability to produce written language is built upon a foundation consisting of experiences, oral language skills, conceptual skills, and emotional maturity.
2. A child's ability to gesture, play, and draw are all representational systems that are prerequisites for written expression.
3. The symbolic play and drawing abilities of students can provide the special educator with information needed to identify appropriate prewriting instructional objectives for many special education students who are chronologically, but not conceptually, past the preschool years.
4. By the end of the elementary years, the writer should be able to recognize and use the following conventions of written language spontaneously: begin sentences with a capital letter, end sentences with a period, end questions with a question mark, use commas in a list, and use apostrophes in contractions.
5. The writing curriculum at the middle school level emphasizes the development of style, organization, and ideation with less concern on teaching mechanics.
6. The secondary school writing curriculum varies according to the vocational goals of the individual student.

Types of Assessment

1. The special educator must evaluate a writing task according to the area of written language it measures, the type of format it uses (copying, dictation, or spontaneous writing), the amount of structure the task requires, the student's interest in the task, the writing topic, and the audience.
2. Standardized achievement tests in written language are designed to provide a broad estimate of written language achievement, usually receptive knowledge of written skills.
3. Diagnostic tests measure a wider range of skills assigned with written language as well as investigating these skills across receptive and expressive tasks.

4. Criterion-referenced measures of written language usually deal only with the mechanical components of written language.
5. Curriculum-based assessment focuses on the skill performance needed for curriculum success rather than on the underlying causes for poor achievement.
6. Dynamic assessment allows the teacher to become equally involved in the writing process—a partnership in dialogue.

Cultural Issues in Written Language Assessment

1. Language minority children are frequently referred by classroom teachers to special education on the basis of oral and written language behaviors that do not correspond to the expectations of the dominant culture.
2. It is not possible for a bilingual individual to have a language disorder in one language and not in the other.
3. Research advocates that special educators begin looking at "communicative competence" rather than "language proficiency" during assessment of language minority students.
4. Utilizing story construction as a reliable measure of written language competence for language minority students has been supported by research.

Steps in the Assessment Process

1. Develop the purpose of the assessment.
2. Develop record sheets to record assessment data.
3. Conduct an integrated assessment utilizing standardized, curriculum-based, and dynamic diagnostic measures.
4. Analyze the error patterns.
5. Develop instructional objectives based on careful analysis of diagnostic findings.

Assessing Mathematics

Key Terms

Abstract level
Algorithms
Application
Arithmetic
Calculation
Comparative relationships
Concepts

Concrete level
Conservation of number
Consumer math
Counting
Enumerating
Mathematics
One-to-one correspondence

Positional relationships
Semiconcrete level
Spatial relationships
Temporal relationships
Temporal–sequential relation-
ships

The fact that mastery of the number concept and of numerical operations is the result of instruction does not mean we can examine it as a simple skill. It is obvious that instruction in any science is never merely the simple mastery of elementary skills but always turns out to be a complex process resulting in the reorganization of the given material and related to a profound change in the methods of intellectual activity. We thus have no grounds for thinking that scientific concepts, once they have arisen during instruction, will break down as simple memories or skills do. On the contrary, in the deterioration of scientific concepts we should expect to discover a process corresponding in complexity to the process of their formation and revealing the complexity of their structure.

(Luria, 1969, p. 40)

Difficulties with mathematics can significantly interfere with a person's ability to function independently as an adult. Managing personal income, paying rent, purchasing food, clothing, and entertainment, cooking, even measuring detergent before washing clothes require basic mathematical skills. Yet in our society, problems with mathematics are often viewed as failures and not manifestations of disabilities (Cawley, 1981). Since one of the goals of special education is to help students become functional adults capable of making a contribution to society, it is important that special education teachers realize the need to develop the mathematical skills of all students with disabling conditions. Special education teachers should have information on the mathematical ability of all students receiving special services. The assessment process is the way to obtain that important information.

Definition of the Area
Mathematics versus Arithmetic

The terms *mathematics* and *arithmetic* are frequently used interchangeably. However, there is an important distinction between them. Reid and Hresko (1981) define mathematics as "the study or development of relationships, regularities, structures, or organizational schemata dealing with space, time, weight, mass, volume, geometry, and number" (p. 292). They define arithmetic as "the computational methods used when working with numbers" (p. 292). Mathematical knowledge is the foundation on which arithmetical skills are developed. Even before children receive formal instruction, they are constructing mathematical knowledge through their experiences with objects of different sizes, shapes, and weight. Young children quickly learn that they want "more" cookies and not "fewer," and students of all ages must solve problems that involve relationships between objects. It is important for special educators who are part of the assessment process to understand that some tests measure narrowly defined arithmetic skills while others tap mathematical knowledge.

Curriculum Strands

The field of mathematics is typically broken down into three broad strands that help organize the curriculum. Those strands are concepts, calculation, and application. *Concepts* are the way that objects, events, actions, and situations are related to each other (Kameenui and Simmons, 1990). Students construct concepts by comparing and contrasting the similarities and differences between objects, events, actions, and situations. Learning concepts requires that students have opportunities to manipulate examples and nonexamples of concepts and relate new information about objects, events, actions, and situations to knowledge they have already constructed. Conceptual learning requires a great deal of time as students continually refine their understanding of a concept and gain proficiency in generalizing that concept to novel situations. For example, the concept of number may be as basic as the label used to denote how many objects are in a set, or as complex as the ability to define and identify examples of the four types of numbers: real, rational, integer, and counting.

The second area, calculation, also consists of arithmetic processes or procedures. *Calculation* may be as fundamental as knowing the basic facts in addition, subtraction, multiplication, and division, or as complex as demonstrating proficiency with various algorithms. *Algorithms* are the steps used to carry out computational operations such as multiplying two fractions or dividing a four-digit number by a two-digit number. Much of the mathematics curriculum at all grade levels is devoted to developing calculation skills. Skill deficits in this area are easier to circumvent with the use of a calculator than problems with conceptual understanding and application.

The third broad strand in the mathematics curriculum is *application*. This strand includes estimating; measuring time, distance, weight, volume, and temperature; using and budgeting money; reading, interpreting, and constructing tables, charts, and graphs; using probability and statistics to predict; and solving a variety of problems ranging from simple, one-step story problems to complex, multistep, real-world problems. Independent functioning as an adult requires application skills.

Developmental Progression

Foundations for Learning Mathematics

Oral Language

The study or development of relationships is one aspect of mathematics (Reid and Hresko, 1981). Oral language is used to describe those relationships. Examples of words denoting various relationships include:

Spatial Relationships: long, tall, short, near, far, thin, wide, narrow
Temporal Relationships: first, last, early, late, before
Positional Relationships: under, on, in, over
Comparative Relationships: shorter, longer, bigger, heavier
Temporal–Sequential Relationships: between, after

Students who have language disabilities may have difficulty understanding the oral language used to describe mathematical relationships or may have problems using words to discuss mathematics. These students may have problems attaching multiple meanings to the same word. For example, the word "circle" may function as a noun, "Point to the circle," or as a verb, "Circle the set with 3 in it." They may also have problems understanding that the same operation can be described with several synonyms: subtract, take away, minus, and less than (Wiig and Semel, 1984). Language disabilities may also interfere with the student's ability to understand story problems, especially as the problems use longer sentences and more complex vocabulary. Finally, it is important to remember that mathematics is expressed as a symbolic language and that children who have had trouble learning to use other symbolic languages, like reading, may have problems learning the symbolic language of mathematics (Reisman and Kauffman, 1980).

Hendrickson (1983) writes, "In the development of comprehension of mathematical language and symbolism, it is important to maintain a constant interrelationship between oral description, written description, pictorial representation, symbol representation, and real situation" (p. 105). Students with oral language problems often have trouble understanding the oral and written descriptions, resulting in difficulty attaching meaning to the mathematical symbolic representation. Language problems that may have an impact on mathematics are often found in students who have severe hearing impairments, mental retardation, specific learning disabilities, autism, or language disabilities (see chapter 9 for a more detailed discussion of oral language assessment.)

Cognitive Factors

Reisman and Kauffman (1980) discuss cognitive factors as "core influences on learning" (p. 3). They believe that knowing about a student's core or generic factors is much more important to planning appropriate mathematics instruction than knowing the student's diagnostic label. Some of these cognitive factors have already been alluded to in the previous section on oral language. The remaining cognitive factors that Reisman and Kauffman (1980) describe as having an impact on learning mathematics are:

- the rate and amount of learning compared to age peers;
- the speed of learning related to specific content;
- an ability to retain information;
- a need for repetition;
- the ability to form relationships, concepts, and generalizations;
- the ability to attend to salient aspects of a situation;
- the use of problem-solving strategies;
- an ability to make decisions and judgments;
- an ability to draw inferences and conclusions and to hypothesize; and
- an ability, in general, to abstract and to cope with complexity.

Students with disabilities often have problems with one or more of these cognitive factors. Information on these cognitive factors can be obtained through an interview with the student, the student's classroom teacher, classroom observation, and observation of the student during the assessment process, particularly during assessment of intelligence (see chapter 5) and assessment of basic learning abilities (see chapter 6).

Emotional Factors

Writing on the role of emotions in learning mathematics, Krutetskii (1976) stated:

> The emotions a person feels are an important factor in the development of abilities in any activity, including mathematics. A joy in creation, a feeling of satisfaction from intense mental work, and an emotional enjoyment of this process heighten a person's mental tone, mobilize his powers, and force him to overcome difficulties. An indifferent person cannot be a creator. (p. 437)

Similarly, Reisman (1978) wrote:

> Failure in arithmetic can be caused by emotional problems but it also can cause emotional problems. Some children already have developed a fear of arithmetic before they come to school. They may have heard a parent talk about his difficulty or failure in arithmetic and subconsciously may identify with this parent. . . . Sometimes, a parent's occupation is mathematically oriented. Such children may have difficulty in arithmetic either because they would rather fail than compete with their parents, or because they try so hard to succeed that they block their learning. (pp. 22–23)

A variety of affective problems can lead to failure in mathematics. Anxiety or depression often produce disorientation, confusion, a feeling of being overwhelmed, memory loss, and an inability to concentrate that can interfere with the student's ability to attend to instruction. The student's beliefs about mathematics as a subject, or about himself or herself as a learner will influence the student's approach to and efforts in mathematics (Underhill, 1988). Such beliefs can produce anxiety or blocks to learning the content. Stress from life events such as moving, illness or death of a family member or pet, divorce, and social isolation can also interfere with the student's ability to learn (Burton, 1987). Long-term stress may lead to depression or anxiety.

Mathematical Skill Development

Preschool

Prior to going to school at age 5 or 6, young children learn a lot about the size, shape, weight, and number of objects. They engage in four processes that help develop a meaningful understanding of number: describing, classifying, comparing, and ordering (Reid, 1988). Young children describe toys they want according to a variety of attributes. They sort or classify toys or candy by color or size. They can compare two cookies so as to obtain the larger one or pick the heaviest package from among birthday presents to open first. They often repeat the order of events in favorite stories or line up toys by size. Through these experiences, young children learn the meaning of quantitative concepts like "more," "the same," "biggest," and "first."

One-to-one correspondence and conservation of number also become established during the preschool years (Piaget, 1952). *One-to-one correspondence* allows the child to compare one set of objects with another set by matching one object from set one to one object from the other set. If eight M&Ms are laid out in a set and the child

This preschool youngster learns a lot about amount, size, shape, and weight through play activities.   *Source:* © Elizabeth Crews

is told to use more M&Ms to make a set the same size, the child uses one-to-one correspondence to construct the second set. The child usually places one M&M next to each M&M in the first set. *Conservation of number* is the ability to understand that the amount in a set remains the same even when the physical arrangement is changed. Consider the activity with the M&Ms just described. After the child has constructed a second set of M&Ms of equal size, a teacher spreads out the second set the child constructed so that it covers more of the table. When asked if the sets are the same size, the child who cannot conserve number will claim that the set that is spread out has more in it. This child is distracted by the spatial arrangement of the M&Ms. A child who can conserve will state that the two sets are the same size even though one covers more space than the other. Generally, children 4 years old and younger cannot conserve. By 5 or 6 years of age many nondisabled children are able to conserve number.

Table 12-1 Mathematical knowledge typical of nondisabled children by first grade entrance

- One-to-one correspondence established.
- Conservation of number established.
- Can demonstrate understanding of quantitative concepts of more, same, first, big, and little.
- Can match objects by size, shape, and color.
- Can sort objects by size, shape, and color.
- Can compare sets of objects by amount (more, most) and size (biggest, smaller).
- Can make sets containing up to ten objects.
- Can count to ten in correct sequence.
- Can solve simple, real-life addition and subtraction problems using counting procedures.
- Can recognize numerals to ten.

During the preschool years, children also learn to count and enumerate. *Counting* means that the child can say a series of numbers in correct sequence. Initially, this is a rote activity Fuson and Hall (1983) refer to as using sequence words. *Enumerating* means that the child has learned how to use numbers to count things (Ginsburg, 1987), an activity that Fuson and Hall (1983) refer to as counting. Counting forms the basis for preschoolers' ability to solve basic, real-life addition and subtraction problems (Gelman and Gallistel, 1978). Table 12-1 lists the mathematical knowledge nondisabled children have developed prior to entering first grade.

Elementary Grades (Kindergarten through Grade 4)

Preschool children develop informal mathematical knowledge (Ginsburg, 1987) through activities with objects, by playing with other children, watching adults, or watching TV. Formal mathematics instruction begins when children enter kindergarten. It is at this point in time that teachers have some guidance as to what skills should be taught and in what sequence the skills should be taught. This guidance comes in the form of scope and sequence charts accompanying math textbook series or sometimes developed by state departments of education for statewide use. Guidance can also be obtained from professional organizations concerned about teaching mathematics. One such organization is the National Council of Teachers of Mathematics.

During the elementary grades, children construct concepts, learn basic arithmetic facts, and learn how to perform simple algorithms. Instruction is sequenced in a way that assumes that the knowledge listed in Table 12-1 is already established. Students are introduced to the written notational system in the elementary grades. One of the key tasks in these grades is to resolve three conflicts surrounding written numbers (Kamii, 1981). One conflict is the clash between the spoken and written systems of representing number. Children learn to sound out words in reading at the same time that they are learning to write numbers. When sounding out a word, the child learns to match sounds to symbols (letters) and pronounce the word based on the order in which the symbols appear. Unfortunately, a similar rule cannot be applied to written numbers. Consider, for example, the number 16. When saying this number, the first sounds one hears is "six," yet that symbol is written last. The same is true for all the numbers in the "teens." When writing larger numbers, children have to learn that digits are not written for every word that is spoken when the number is said orally. Some children mistakenly write "100203" for the number 123.

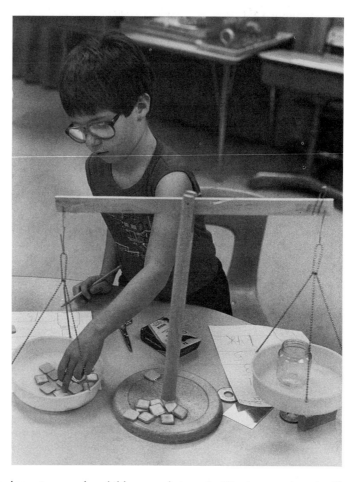

During the elementary grades children need opportunities to experiment with size, shape, weight, and amount as a way of constructing important mathematical concepts.   *Source:* © Michael Siluk

A second set of conflicts that must be resolved during the elementary grades is the conflict between the principles underlying number and those underlying the notational system for recording numbers (Kamii, 1981). Children who have constructed the conservation of number know that the spatial arrangement of objects in a set does not change the quantity in the set. If there are twelve items in a set, it does not matter if the items are arranged in a row, in a circle, or scattered in random order. The "twelveness" or amount remains the same. However, when writing numbers, the order and spacing between digits makes a great deal of difference. The written numbers 1, 2, 12, and 21 represent very different quantities.

A third conflict that must be resolved during the elementary grades is the conflict between arithmetic operations and written computations (Kamii, 1981). Children often come to understand that multiplication is just repeated addition. They know that if one has 3 plates with 4 cupcakes on each plate the situation can be repre-

Table 12-2 Selected mathematical skills developed in kindergarten through grade four

---

Concepts

    Matching, sorting, and ordering objects.

    Combining and separating sets.

    Comparing whole numbers to millions.

    Comparing fractions with like denominators.

    Identifying two-dimensional geometric shapes.

    Rounding numbers to the nearest 100.

Calculation

    Recalling basic math facts.

    Adding and subtracting whole numbers without and with regrouping.

    Multiplying by three-digit numbers.

    Dividing by three-digit numbers.

    Translating fractions to decimals.

Application

    Solving one-step story problems involving operations on whole numbers and fractions.

    Computing averages.

    Estimating sums, differences, and products.

    Interpreting simple graphs.

    Comparing inches, feet, yards, miles, ounces, pints, and gallons.

    Locating points on maps or grids.

---

sented as $4 + 4 + 4 = 12$ or as $3 \times 4 = 12$. Yet the repeated addition notion of multiplication does not "fit" if one is concerned with finding the area of a rectangle 3 inches by 4 inches, even though the number sentence would be $3 \times 4 = 12$.

Nondisabled children may need several elementary grade years to resolve these conflicts. They also need time to "master" the basic facts for addition, subtraction, multiplication, and division. The concept of place value, which underlies regrouping (that is, borrowing and carrying), is constructed slowly, as are all the concepts developed during these years. Table 12-2 lists some of the skills children must learn in the elementary grades.

Middle Grades (Grades 5 through 8)

Just as teachers of elementary grades struggle with a wide range of developmental abilities, so to do middle school teachers. Some middle school students continue to struggle with basic arithmetic facts, while others are eager to explore probability, geometry, and prealgebra. The mathematics curriculum at the middle school level tries to balance the diversity of instructional demands, with varying degrees of success. The report from the Commission on Standards for School Mathematics (1989) notes that "many students view the current mathematics curriculum in grades 5–8 as irrelevant, dull, and routine" (p. 65). The commission argues that although development of certain computational skills is important, development of basic mathematical skills extends far beyond computational proficiency. The commission urges that the middle school curriculum contain the following features:

> Problem situations that establish the need for new ideas and motivate students should serve as the context for mathematics in grades 5–8. Although a specific idea might be forgotten, the context in which it is learned can be remembered and the idea re-created.

Table 12-3 Selected mathematical skills developed in grades five through eight

Concepts

Rounding to nearest millions and billions.
Comparing whole numbers beyond millions.
Comparing fractions with unlike denominators.
Comparing and ordering decimals.
Identifying three-dimensional geometric shapes.
Using set notation.
Identifying relations and properties of numbers: prime and composite numbers, ratio, and proportion.

Calculation

Adding, subtracting, multiplying, and dividing whole numbers of three or more digits.
Adding, subtracting, multiplying, and dividing fractions, mixed numbers, and decimals.
Adding, subtracting, multiplying, and dividing integers.

Application

Solving multistep story problems involving whole numbers, fractions, mixed numbers, and decimals.
Estimating time, volume, and weight.
Graphing ordered pairs.
Finding equivalent standard measures.
Finding unit price, sales tax, and installment payments.

In developing the problem situation, teachers should emphasize the application of mathematics to real-world problems as well as to other settings relevant to middle school students.

Communication with and about mathematics and mathematical reasoning should permeate the 5–8 curriculum.

A broad range of topics should be taught, including number concepts, computation, estimation, functions, algebra, statistics, probability, geometry, and measurement. Although each of these areas is valid mathematics in its own right, they should be taught as an integrated whole, not as isolated topics; the connections among them should be a prominent feature of the curriculum.

Technology, including calculators, computers, and videos, should be used when appropriate. These devices and formats free students from tedious computations and allow them to concentrate on problem solving and other important content. They also give them new means to explore content. As paper-and-pencil computation become less important, the skill and understanding required to make proficient use of calculators and computers become more important.[*]

Table 12-3 lists some of the skills developed under the headings of concepts, calculation, and application during the middle school grades.

High School (Grades 9 through 12)

During the high school years, students have the option of selecting the amount of mathematics they take. Some students elect to take mathematics, considered necessary for independent functioning as an adult. This course, often called *consumer math,* focuses on the skills needed for day-to-day consumer problems. The content

[*]From "Curriculum and Evaluation Standards for School Mathematics," report by the Commission on Standards, 1989, pp. 66–67, National Council of Teachers of Mathematics. Reprinted by permission.

Some high school students with mild disabilities study algebra, goemetry, and trigonometry.
Source: © Lew Lause/Uniphoto

focus tends to be on ratios, percents, and proportion, because those are the major areas underlying such consumer activities as calculating the best buy, comparing interest rates, and buying something through installment payments.

Other high school students elect a college preparatory course of study. This group may include students served in special education under the label of learning disabled or behavior disordered. These students encounter algebra, geometry, and possibly trigonometry during the high school years. Table 12-4 lists selected skills these students will be developing.

Concerns Expressed by Classroom Teachers

Children with severe disabling conditions are often identified during the preschool years and begin receiving special services before or during kindergarten. Other students start school in regular classrooms and must be identified by the regular classroom teacher as having difficulties beyond what might typically be expected. Therefore, regular classroom teachers are often the first to notice problems in mathematics that may indicate the need for special education. Since regular classroom teachers have other students for comparison, the concerns they express about individual students indicate problems beyond what can be reasonably expected for students who have had similar instructional experiences. Common concerns expressed by classroom teachers include:

- difficulty copying problems from the board or textbook, either taking too long or copying inaccurately;

Table 12-4 Selected mathematical skills developed in grades nine through twelve

---

Concepts
    Identifying formal properties of the real number system.
    Identifying types of angles.
    Identifying properties of trigonometric functions.
    Simplifying a variable expression using properties of addition and multiplication.
    Identifying the meaning of mathematical symbols.

Calculation
    Adding, subtracting, multiplying, and dividing integers.
    Adding, subtracting, multiplying, and dividing polynomials.
    Factoring polynomials.
    Simplifying variable expressions using properties of addition and multiplication.

Application
    Finding area of triangles, quadrilaterals, and regular polygons.
    Finding volume spheres and cube of cubes, tetrahedron, right prisms, cylinders, cones, and spheres.
    Graphing points on a rectangular coordinate system.
    Solving uniform motion problems.
    Solving percent mixture problems.

- problems aligning numbers in computation problems;
- skipping problems on a work sheet;
- reversing numerals;
- failure to attend to the operator sign on work sheets with mixed problem types;
- counting on fingers long after peers have stopped;
- difficulty remembering basic facts;
- losing place in column addition;
- starting computational problems in the wrong column;
- forgetting the sequence of steps in computational problems involving multidigit numbers;
- persistent difficulty using regrouping procedures;
- difficulty telling time, recalling the months of the year or the days of the week;
- problems reading multidigit numbers;
- problems writing multidigit numbers from dictation;
- difficulty selecting the correct operation for solving story problems; and
- difficulty ignoring irrelevant information in story problems.

Types of Assessment Tasks

What Are You Measuring and Why?

A student's progress in learning mathematics is routinely monitored in regular education. Typically, chapter or unit tests accompany commercially produced mathematics textbook series and are used at the completion of the chapter or unit to assess mastery of the material covered. In addition, most school districts follow a specific schedule for administration of group achievement tests containing subtests on mathematics. In some areas, state- or district-wide competency tests in mathematics are part of the criteria for promotion to the next grade or for graduation.

When a student fails to meet the expectations of the regular education mathematics curriculum, mathematics becomes a focus for individualized assessment. Many questions can be raised concerning a student's mathematical knowledge and skill. Early in the assessment process, questions may deal with eligibility for special education and determining whether mathematics is a general strength or weakness. Later in the process, questions focus on specific skills in conceptual understanding, calculation, or application for which special instructional objectives are needed. Assessment of mathematics continues to be an important issue throughout the student's special education program as progress is monitored, special instruction adjusted, and plans made for reintegrating the student into the regular mathematics classroom or for transition to a postsecondary training program, school, or job site. A combination of norm-referenced, criterion-referenced, curriculum-based, and dynamic assessment tools are used, depending on the particular questions that need to be answered.

Norm-Referenced Tools

The first question about mathematics performance that needs to be answered is whether the student is underachieving compared to age or grade peers and compared to the individual's mental ability. Some norm-referenced information is obtained from subtests of group and individually administered achievement tests. Depending on the state's regulations and procedures for special education eligibility, additional in-depth, norm-referenced data may be required such as mathematics diagnostic tests. Performance on these tests is usually reported as a percentile rank, a standard score, or an age or grade equivalent score. These tests often have multiple subtests assessing different aspects of mathematics. Each subtest may result in a separate score. It is important that the evaluator understand the numerous variables that may affect the student's performance and be reflected in these scores. A student may obtain surprisingly different scores on subtests whose names suggest that they assess the same thing. Similarly, the classroom teacher may report that a student is failing mathematics, yet individually administered test results may indicate mathematical ability in the normal range. These discrepancies can often be attributed to the structure and format of the subtests.

Depending on the particular test, conceptual knowledge may be assessed on one subtest, as on the Stanford Diagnostic Mathematics Tests (Beatty, Madden, Gardner, and Karlsen, 1984), or across several subtests, as on the KeyMath–Revised (Connolly, 1988) or the Sequential Assessment of Mathematics Inventories–Standardized Inventory (Reisman, 1985). Sometimes conceptual knowledge test items are scattered throughout the test, as on the Test of Early Mathematics Ability–2 (Ginsburg and Baroody, 1990), rather than having a separate subtest. On some subtests dealing with mathematical vocabulary, as on the Test of Mathematical Abilities (Brown and McEntire, 1984), the manner in which the vocabulary is assessed really requires a conceptual understanding. Sometimes subtests assessing mathematical vocabulary are found on instruments whose title would not even suggest the evaluation of mathematics, as on the Test of Reading Comprehension (Brown, Hammill, and Wiederholt, 1986) or the Bracken Basic Concept Scale (Bracken, 1984).

Subtests examining calculation skills also vary considerably. Tests of computation may be timed or untimed. To a certain extent, timed tests measure how automatic the calculation ability is. Students who have trouble memorizing basic facts or working quickly may appear to have poorly developed calculation skills if assessed on a timed subtest but may seem to have better skill development if assessed on an untimed subtest. Computation subtests also vary in the way problems are organized. Sometimes problems requiring a single operation are grouped together. Other calculation subtests mix problems requiring addition, subtraction, multiplication, and division, demanding that the student attend closely to operator signs. The format of the calculation test is a third way these subtests vary. Some subtests have many problems on each page, which can intimidate students and increase anxiety. Some subtests provide multiple choice responses, while others require the student to generate an answer. Some subtests place each problem in a separate box, but other subtests have no barriers between problems. The vehicle for student response is the final variable to consider. Most calculation subtests require the student to write or mark the answer. A few subtests do not use a paper-and-pencil format but require an oral answer to problems presented on an easel. Students with motor problems may perform better on easel subtests.

Subtests assessing application skills also differ widely. Some test authors define application skills as solving word problems, and the subtest reflects that definition. In these cases, it is important to note whether the examiner or the student reads the problems. When students are required to read problems on their own before solving them, reading difficulties can interfere. Hence, the score may not accurately reflect mathematical application skills. Although some tests require students to read the problems themselves, directions encourage them to ask for help on unknown words. Despite this encouragement, some students will not ask for help and their score may be depressed because of their reading problems. Some test authors define application skills much more broadly. These tests generally contain several subtests assessing different aspects of mathematical application. Table 12-5 lists a variety of norm-referenced tests for assessing mathematical skills.

Criterion-Referenced Tools and Inventories

Criterion-referenced tools and inventories assist in identifying which instructional objectives the student has mastered and which need further work. An analysis of the errors a student makes on norm-referenced tests can help identify areas where further instruction is needed. Criterion-referenced mathematics tests and inventories help pinpoint specific areas where instruction should occur. Performance results on these measures are sometimes reported as grade or age equivalents, and on other measures no score is available. In either situation, the examiner will be able to identify specific instructional objectives in mathematics that can be used to develop the student's individualized educational program.

Criterion-referenced tools and inventories in mathematics can be found that assess a variety of concepts, calculation skills, and application skills. However, the examiner needs to consider the numerous variables mentioned previously when selecting a criterion-referenced measure or inventory. Another important factor in

Table 12-5 Norm-referenced measures of mathematics performance

Name (Authors)	Ages or Grades	Group/Individual	Publisher
Cooperative Mathematics Tests (CTB/McGraw–Hill, 1965)	Grs. 7–14	G/I	CTB/McGraw–Hill
Diagnostic Screening Test: Mathematics (Gnagey, 1980)	Grs. 1–12	G/I	Slosson Educational Publications
KeyMath-Revised (Connolly, 1988)	Grs. K–9 Ages 5–0 to 16–0	I	American Guidance Service
Sequential Assessment of Mathematics Inventories—Standardized Inventory (Reisman, 1985)	Grs. K–8	I	Psychological Corporation
MAT6 Mathematics Diagnostic Tests (Hogan, Farr, Prescott, and Balow, 1986)	Grs. 1–0 to 9–9	G/I	Psychological Corporation
Orleans–Hanna Algebra Prognosis Test—Revised (Hanna and Orleans, 1982)	Grs. 7 to adult	G/I	Psychological Corporation
Peabody Mathematics Readiness Test (Bassler, Beers, Richardson, and Thurman, 1979)	Grs. K–1 Mental age 4 to 6	G/I	Scholastic Testing Service
Standard Diagnostic Mathematics Test, 3rd ed. (Beatty, Madden, Gardner, and Karlsen, 1984)	Grs. 1–12	G/I	Psychological Corporation
Test of Early Mathematics Ability–2 (Ginsburg and Baroody, 1990)	Ages 3–0 to 8–11	I	PRO–ED
Test of Mathematical Abilities (Brown and McEntire, 1984)	Grs. 3–12 Ages 8–6 to 18–11	G/I	PRO–ED

selecting a criterion-referenced measure in mathematics is the fact that some measures are keyed to particular mathematics textbook series. Once an objective needing further work is identified, the examiner can locate the pages in the basal math book where that objective is taught. When objectives are not keyed to basal series, instructional activities for the objectives are often suggested. Table 12-6 lists criterion-referenced measures and inventories available for mathematics.

Curriculum-Based Tools

Commercially produced criterion-referenced measures and inventories can provide invaluable information during development of an individualized educational program with specific instructional objectives. However, the special education teacher must be aware that these measures may not match the mathematics curriculum used in a particular school. Therefore, it is the responsibility of the special education teacher to examine the mathematics curriculum to ensure that the student has had an opportunity to learn the objectives identified as weaknesses by criterion-referenced measures. The special education teacher uses both the mathematics curriculum scope and sequence chart and the student's textbook for this examination. The scope and sequence chart is typically found in the teacher's manual that accompanies the specific mathematics curriculum. This chart identifies the array or scope of topics covered and the order or sequence in which the topics are presented. Different mathematics

Table 12-6 Criterion-referenced measures and inventories of mathematics performance

Name (Authors)	Ages or Grades	Group/Individual	Publisher
Adston Mathematics Skills Series: Common Fractions (Adams, 1979)	Any gr. after instruction in fractions	G/I	Adston Educational Enterprises
Adston Mathematics Skills Series: Readiness for Operation (Adams and Sauls, 1979)	Preschool—Gr. 2	G/I	Adston Educational Enterprises
Adston Mathematics Skills Series: Working with Whole Numbers (Adams and Ellis, 1979)	Any gr. after instruction in a basic operation	G/I	Adston Educational Enterprises
BRIGANCE Diagnostic Comprehensive Inventory of Basic Skills (Brigance, 1983)	Grs. K–9	I	Curriculum Associates
BRIGANCE Diagnostic Inventory of Basic Skills (Brigance, 1977)	Grs. K–1	I	Curriculum Associates
BRIGANCE Diagnostic Inventory of Essential Skills (Brigance, 1981)	Grs. 4–12	I	Curriculum Associates
Classroom Learning Screening Manual (Koenig and Kunzelmann, 1980)	Grs. K–6	G/I	Psychological Corporation
Criterion-Referenced Curriculum—Mathematics (Stephens, 1982)	Grs. K–6	G/I	Psychological Corporation
Criterion Test of Basic Skills (Lundell, Brown, and Evans, 1976)	Grs. 1–6	G/I	Academic Therapy Publications
Diagnosis: An Instructional Aid: Mathematics (Guzaitis, Carlin, and Juda, 1972)	Grs. 1–6	I	Science Research Associates
Diagnostic Mathematics Inventory (Gessell, 1977)	Grs. 1–5 to 8–5	G/I	McGraw–Hill
Diagnostic Test of Arithmetic Strategies (Ginsburg and Mathews, 1984)	Grs. 1–6	I	PRO–ED
Enright™ Diagnostic Inventory of Basic Arithmetic Skills (Enright, 1983)	Less than gr. 7 functioning	G/I	Curriculum Associates
Fountain Valley Teacher Support System in Mathematics (1976)	Grs. 1–8	I	Zweig Associates
Hudson Educational Skills Inventory— Mathematics (Hudson, Colson, and Welch, 1989a)	Grs. 1–12	I	PRO–ED
Multilevel Academic Skills Inventory: Math Program (Howell, Zucher, and Morehead, 1982)	Grs. 1–8	I	Psychological Corporation
Steenburger Diagnostic Prescriptive Math Program (Steenburger, 1978)	Grs. 1–6	I	Academic Therapy Publications
System FORE (Bagai and Bagai, 1979)	Grs. K–12	I	Fireworks Publication

curricula have vastly different scopes and sequences. It is also important for the teacher to inspect the student textbooks for the curriculum being used. Sometimes there are subtle discrepancies between the scope and sequence chart and the actual presentation of material in the student text. Even when no discrepancies exist, it is important to determine how new material is introduced and how much practice is provided. Some students receiving special education services need a different introduction to concepts, more work on concept development, or more practice of a particular skill than that offered by the mathematics series being used.

The special educator may need to develop additional diagnostic assessments that more closely match the content covered in the mathematics curriculum than do commercially produced criterion-referenced measures and inventories. These educator developed tools based on a particular series are curriculum-based assessments. Not only will such assessments be used in planning instruction, but they will be developed and used throughout the instructional process. For example, before beginning a unit of instruction, the teacher should administer a pretest to ensure that the unit does not cover material the student already knows. Periodic practice tests and an end-of-the-unit test provide additional data on the progress a particular student is making.

Curriculum-based assessments in mathematics allow the special educator to examine factors important to learning mathematics that are typically not found on norm-referenced and criterion-referenced tools. One of these poorly assessed factors is the level of learning. Much of mathematics instruction and assessment requires the student to manipulate numerals and symbols to solve problems. Underhill, Uprichard, and Heddens (1980) call these kinds of learning activities "abstract," the highest level of learning. Students who are having difficulty learning activities at the *abstract level* probably lack a meaningful understanding of the mathematical concepts involved. These students need many more experiences at the concrete and semiconcrete levels. At the *concrete level,* the student manipulates real objectives to illustrate relationships and solve problems. If given the problem, "Sam has 12 marbles but loses 3. How many marbles does Sam have now?," the student may need to use counters of some type, laying out 12 counters and then removing 3 and counting the remaining counters. Children who need more experiences at the concrete level will count on their fingers. Connors (1983) found that students with learning problems use concrete experiences like counting on their fingers more often than do their normally achieving peers. Concrete experiences are critical to the development of all mathematical concepts regardless of the grade level at which the concepts are first introduced.

At the *semiconcrete level* of learning, students are able to solve problems using aids that are slightly more abstract than three-dimensional manipulatives. The student is now able to solve problems by drawing a diagram, drawing a picture, or making tallies to represent the numbers. Math workbooks and work sheets that match number sentences to pictures of groups of objects are at the semiconcrete level. Students who experience particular difficulty in mathematics may need more practice with this type of activity than is offered in the regular curriculum.

The special education teacher can develop short assessment tools to examine how proficient the student is in performing tasks at the concrete, semiconcrete, and abstract levels for specific concepts taught at the student's grade level in the regular curriculum. With the use of such curriculum-based tools, the teacher will quickly be able to identify where the student's understanding breaks down and plan instructional activities at the appropriate level.

Clinical Interviews and Dynamic Assessment

Norm-referenced, criterion-referenced, and curriculum-based measures tend to be product-oriented in mathematics. That is, a question is posed and a specific answer is given. That answer is identified as either correct or incorrect. However, the evaluator does not know the process by which the student arrived at the answer. Sometimes a student invents a strategy for solving a particular type of problem that is based on a conceptual misunderstanding. The invented strategy may result in a correct answer some of the time, so it is reinforced. The teacher may also believe that the student understands the problem because a correct answer was obtained. For example, suppose a student thought that, like reading, one was supposed to start at the left side of a problem. When the student solves problems where regrouping is not required, the student produces the correct answer. The teacher may not be aware that the student has an incorrect idea about the solution of problems because the student's answers are correct many times. Unless the student discusses with the teacher the process used to obtain the answer, the mistaken procedure will not be discovered. Considerable time may elapse before the student is required to solve a problem requiring regrouping that allows the teacher to notice the mistaken procedure. Through the process of clinical interviewing, special education teachers can discover how the student is thinking mathematically.

Clinical interviewing provides the special education teacher with the opportunity to discover the thought processes and metacognitive strategies a student uses in solving computational problems or the level of conceptual understanding the student has developed about specific concepts. Clinical interviewing can be used at any grade and with any area of mathematics. The special education teacher prepares for a clinical interview by looking at the types of errors the student has made on the more product-based, norm-referenced tests, criterion-referenced tests, and classroom work samples. From this information the teacher can form some hypotheses about the level of conceptual understanding or about a particular computational skill. Next, the teacher develops broad, open-ended questions about carefully selected problems or a set of manipulative materials. These questions and problems are diagnostic probes. Then the teacher works with the student in a one-to-one situation using the carefully prepared materials. For example, the teacher may present three problems similar to problems the student missed in another situation and ask the student to solve the problems, explaining what is being done at each step of the solution. In another situation, the teacher may ask the student what a fraction is, have the student read several fractions and explain what each one means, and then illustrate various fractions using drawings (for example, a circular region, a rectangular region) and different types of manipulative materials (counters or Cuisenaire rods). The teacher may pose the same basic questions in different ways to determine the student's flexibility with the concepts being probed. The teacher should gently push the student for an explanation of thinking processes but should not criticize the student.

Clinical interviews should focus on one topic at a time. They may be conducted while the student is engaged in an activity or after the activity is completed. Ashlock (1986) recommends using a combination of both approaches. Table 12-7 provides several suggestions for interviewing.

Dynamic assessment is closely related to clinical interviews. As with a clinical interview, the teacher prepares by looking at the errors the student has made. The teacher also develops some hypotheses about the student's thinking process and conceptual understanding. Before working with the student, the teacher develops a

Table 12-7 Suggestions for clinical interviewing

To Establish Rapport
- The setting should be quiet and free from distractions.
- You should be the only adult present.
- Spend time with the student before the interview.
- Before beginning the interview, put the student at ease with small talk or, if the student is young, by letting him or her engage in activities like drawing.
- If the student will not talk to you, bring in another student and have the pair work as a team.
- Explain the purpose of the interview in an honest way that the student can understand. "I want to know how you do your math. If I find out why you're having trouble, I can help you learn better."
- Be warm and supportive. Encourage effort. Do not criticize wrong answers.

To Discover Thinking Processes
- Begin by observing the student's behavior in the classroom.
- Find out what material is being covered in the classroom.
- Ask the student to devise and solve some problems reflecting material being taught in class at the present time. "What kinds of addition are you working on now?" "What did your teacher show you today in math?"
- Ask the student to indicate the areas in which he or she is having difficulty. "What are you having trouble with now?" "Why do you think you are having trouble with that?"
- Make the tasks as open-ended as possible. "What do you do with this problem?"
- Request information concerning how the student solves the problems. "How did you do this one?" "How did you get that answer?" "Can you tell me more about it?"
- Nod, smile, pause, or say "uhmm" when you want the student to talk more.
- Repeat the student's last statement in the hope that he or she will elaborate on it.
- Follow up on the student's last response until you are sure of his or her strategy.
- Don't put words in the student's mouth.

To Describe How Thinking Operates
- When you have an idea about how the student is solving problems, prepare some tasks that will test your hypothesis.
- Try to use tasks that the student will solve in one way if using one strategy and in another way if using a different strategy.
- The tasks should proceed from general ("What do you do with these numbers?") to specific ("Can you add these up with carrying?")
- The tasks should proceed from easy to hard.

To Assess Competence
- Encourage effort and display interest in the student's work.
- Don't criticize or push too hard if the student is having a hard time. If the student seems tired, take a break or change tasks.
- Use language suitable to the student's level of understanding.
- If the student does not seem to understand the question, vary the wording. "Can you do subtraction? Can you do take-away?"
- If the student seems to be parroting the teacher or test, ask him or her to rephrase the answer. "Can you put that in your own words?"
- To determine the strength of belief, challenge the student's answer. "How could that be true?" "Johnny doesn't do it that way."

General Advice
- Start your flexible interviewing slowly and on a small scale.
- Get your initial questions by expanding on existing tests.
- Later, devise some of your own problems.
- Do short interviews concentrating on a limited amount of material.

Source: From H. Ginsburg, Assessment Techniques, Tests, Interviews, and Analytic Teaching in *Assessing the Abilities and Instructional Needs of Students,* edited by D. D. Hammill, p. 460. Copyright © 1987 by PRO-ED, Inc. Reprinted by permission.

series of cues or prompts that gradually provide more direction and support. The initial part of dynamic assessment is similar to clinical interviewing. The teacher and the student work in a one-to-one situation, using problems and materials designed to probe the student's thinking. When the student encounters difficulty, the teacher introduces the first cue or prompt. If the student continues to have difficulty, the other cues are gradually introduced. The goal in dynamic assessment is to determine how much prompting the student needs to perform accurately. The structured cues or prompts help the teacher determine what support the student needs to perform correctly. This information is invaluable in determining how to proceed with instruction. These dynamic procedures also provide a nonbiased approach to assessing the mathematical knowledge and skills of students from culturally diverse backgrounds.

Steps in the Assessment Process

Determine the Purpose for the Assessment

Before administering any assessment measures, the reasons for testing a student must be clearly identified. Each measure used should be selected based on the age of the student, the presenting problem, and the history of instruction the student has had up to the referral. In mathematics, the most common objectives are:

- identify the level of general math performance;
- identify conceptual knowledge strengths;
- identify conceptual knowledge weaknesses;
- identify calculation strengths;
- identify calculation weaknesses;
- identify application strengths; and
- identify application weaknesses.

Develop Data Sheets to Record Assessment Results

So much information is collected during the assessment process that important data may not be considered fully unless there is a system for organizing it. Having data sheets for each area assessed ensures that no valuable information is lost. Developing the data sheets prior to beginning work with an individual student ensures that all the assessment objectives are met. Figure 12-1 illustrates a sample data sheet for mathematics.

Conduct an Integrated Assessment

An integrated assessment means that a variety of assessment tools are used. Norm-referenced tests provide the general performance level for math needed to determine eligibility for special education and to determine if mathematics will need to be addressed on the IEP. For some students referred for indivdualized assessment, mathematics performance may be at grade level and no further assessment will be needed. If performance in mathematics is below grade level, analysis of errors made on math subtests provide guidance as to what other math measures should be selected and the area of math (concepts, calculation, or application) needing further

Student: Age: Grade Placement: Date:

Textbook and Level Used:
Current Group Achievement Test Results in Math—Test Name:

          Concepts   PR= SS= GE=
          Calculation PR= SS= GE=
          Application PR= SS= GE=

Teacher Concerns about Math:

Errors Noted on Classroom Work Samples:

	Norm-Referenced Data	Criterion-Referenced Objectives Passed	Criterion-Referenced Objectives Failed	Sample Errors	Error Hypotheses
Concepts					
Calculation					
Application					

FIGURE 12-1 Sample math data sheet

exploration. Criterion-referenced measures, curriculum-based tools, and dynamic assessment techniques are necessary to refine IEP goals and objectives. During the assessment process, the evaluation team should consider the following questions:

Are cognitive abilities consistent with math performance?
Are there deficits in selected learning behaviors that could have an impact on math?
Are oral language skills having an impact on math?
Have behavior problems or emotional concerns affected the motivation to do math or the cognitive availability to learn math?
Are math difficulties a reflection of reading problems?
What environmental situations are contributing to math difficulties?
Has there been direct, systematic instruction to teach deficit math skills?

Sometimes the student's behavior during testing or the manner in which the student undertakes completion of math subtests provides important informal data that helps answer these questions. Therefore, it is important for the evaluator to record observational notes while working with the student.

Analyze the Errors

The grade on math homework or the score on a norm-referenced test provides a global level of performance but does not suggest what should be taught next. From criterion-referenced and curriculum-based measures, the special educator can generate a list of objectives that can direct the planning of instruction, but these results do not explain the nature of a particular student's misunderstandings. Error analysis provides that insight. All students make careless errors. Typically, when these are pointed out, the student quickly recognizes the error and may feel foolish for making it. Other errors, however, are made because of conceptual or procedural misunderstandings. When these are pointed out, the student may feel frustrated or confused about why a problem was not correct. Examining the errors a student makes provides direction for developing clinical interviews and dynamic assessments and pinpoints where instruction should begin.

The analysis of mathematical errors has been an interest of investigators across many years (Ashlock, 1986; Brueckner, 1930; Buswell and John, 1925; Cox, 1975; Engelhardt, 1977; Enright, 1983; Osborn, 1925; Roberts, 1968). Examining the many systems for classifying errors reveals several broad types.

1. Mechanical errors. Incorrect responses resulting from perceptual–motor difficulties or motor problems. Students may misread poorly formed numbers or make errors because the columns of numbers are misaligned.

2. Conceptual or missing skill errors. Incorrect responses that reflect an absent or misunderstood concept. (See Figure 12-2.)

3. Incorrect number fact error. Incorrect responses reveal that a number fact has been learned incorrectly or recalled incorrectly.

4. Defective algorithm or procedural error. Incorrect responses resulting from skipping a step, applying steps in the wrong sequence, or using an inaccurate method. (See Figure 12-2.)

5. Incorrect operation error. Incorrect responses resulting from selecting the wrong operation (that is, adding instead of subtracting). The student may not attend to the operator sign for computation problems or may select the wrong operation for story problems.

6. Random or careless errors. Incorrect responses due to a lack of attention to the problem.

Looking across the student's incorrect responses on norm-referenced, criterion-referenced, and teacher produced curriculum-based measures, the teacher should look for patterns of errors. Once the teacher has identified patterns of errors, hypotheses can be formed about why those errors were made. These hypotheses provide the basis for an interview with the student. Data gathered during the interview help the teacher identify poorly developed concepts and missing broad ideas that tie mathematical knowledge into a structured, organized whole.

Develop Annual Goals and Instructional Objectives

When the IEP committee gathers to develop annual goals and short-term objectives, data from the assessment process will be used. The assessment team will have already met to determine that the student is eligible for special education, and the IEP committee members use the same data to determine whether the student's level of performance in mathematics requires special instruction. The committee should systematically consider the student's level of performance in

Conceptual Errors

$\begin{array}{r} 20 \\ -13 \\ \hline 10 \end{array}$	inappropriate concept of zero

$\begin{array}{r} 13 \\ +\ 4 \\ \hline 8 \end{array}$	no concept of a multidigit number

$$\begin{array}{r} \dfrac{1}{2} \\ + \\ \dfrac{1}{5} \\ \hline 9 \end{array}$$ no concept of fractions; adds all numbers

Procedural Errors

$\begin{array}{r} 3^{1}2 \\ +83 \\ \hline 16 \end{array}$	adds from left to right

$\begin{array}{r} 41 \\ -28 \\ \hline 27 \end{array}$	subtracts smaller number from larger number

$\begin{array}{r} 5^{1}8 \\ -35 \\ \hline 23 \end{array}$	unnecessary regrouping

$\begin{array}{r} 2 \\ 35 \\ \times\ 5 \\ \hline 255 \end{array}$	adds regrouped number before multiplying

$\begin{array}{r} 14 \\ 3\,\overline{)123} \\ 12 \\ \hline 3 \end{array}$	records answer from left to right

$$\begin{array}{r} \dfrac{1}{4} \\ + \\ \dfrac{3}{5} \\ \hline \dfrac{4}{9} \end{array}$$ adds numerators and denominators

FIGURE 12-2 Examples of selected error types

each of the three broad areas of mathematics: concepts, calculation, and application. Annual goals can be written for each of the broad areas in which special instruction is needed. Developing only one annual goal, intended to cover all of mathematics at a particular level, is inappropriate because the goal would be entirely too broad. Next, the committee develops several short-term objectives for each of the annual goals in mathematics. In developing these objectives, the committee uses the norm-referenced and criterion-referenced assessment data and the results of preliminary error analysis of the math subtests. When the IEP committee has completed the goals and objectives, a placement decision is made based on which setting is least restrictive for providing the special instruction needed to reach the specific goals and objectives.

Once math goals and objectives are written into the IEP and the student is placed in special education, the special educator continues the assessment/instructional process. The special educator is already familiar with the existing data on the student's math knowledge and skills. Using that information, the teacher develops short, curriculum-based tasks and dynamic probes to determine where special instruction should begin. The data from these curriculum-based tasks and dynamic probes become the baseline measure of the student's performance for a specific math objective.

Summary

Definition of the Area

1. Mathematics is a broad term covering the study of relationships involving space, time, weight, mass, volume, geometry, and numbers.
2. Arithmetic is narrower, is subsumed under mathematics, and means computational methods.
3. Mathematical curricula contain three broad strands: concepts, calculation, and application.
4. Concepts are the relationships between things and are constructed by students.
5. Calculation involves operational procedures with numbers.
6. Application requires the use of concepts and calculations to solve real-world problems.

Developmental Progression

1. Students who have oral language problems may have difficulty understanding the language used to describe mathematical relationships or may have problems using words to discuss mathematics.
2. Students with disabilities may have problems with one or more cognitive factors that have an impact on mathematics.
3. A variety of emotional problems can lead to failure in mathematics.
4. The student's beliefs about mathematics as a subject or about himself or herself as a learner influence the student's approach to and efforts in mathematics.
5. Preschool aged children describe, classify, compare, and order environmental objects. This helps them develop a basic understanding of numbers.
6. During the elementary grades, children need to construct concepts, learn basic arithmetic facts, and learn how to perform simple algorithms.
7. Some middle school students continue to struggle with basic arithmetic facts, while others are eager to explore probability, geometry, and prealgebra.
8. During the high school years, some students select consumer mathematics, while others elect the college preparatory curriculum of algebra, geometry, and trigonometry.

Types of Assessment Tasks

1. Group administered mathematics achievement tests provide a broad estimate of a student's mathematical skill development.
2. Norm-referenced diagnostic tests of mathematics typically contain subtests dealing specifically with concepts, calculation, and application skills.
3. Commercially produced criterion-referenced tests and inventories of mathematics can help identify specific objectives that can facilitate instructional planning.
4. The special educator may need to develop additional assessment tasks that more closely match the math curriculum than the commercially produced criterion-referenced measures.

5. Curriculum-based mathematics tools help determine whether the student understands concepts at the concrete, semiconcrete, or abstract level.
6. Dynamic assessment in mathematics focuses on the processes students use to solve problems.

Steps in the Assessment Process

1. Determine the purpose for the assessment.
2. Develop data sheets to record assessment results.
3. Conduct an integrated assessment.
4. Analyze the errors.
5. Develop annual goals and instructional objectives.

Transitional Assessment: Postsecondary Education and Employment

Key Terms

Aptitude
Behavioral analysis
Career awareness
Career simulation
Individualized College Plan
  (ICP)

Individualized Transition Plan
  (ITP)
Interest inventory
Learning style
Personal transition profiles

Person variable
Strategy variable
Task variable
Transitional services

In my freshman year in college, I had a choice: either leave because I could not do the work alone or accept the fact that I needed help. I could no longer hide. My learning disabilities had finally caught up to me.

(Lee and Jackson, 1992, p. 7)

The number of students receiving special education services has grown steadily since the passage of the Education of the Handicapped Act (PL 94–142) in 1975, increasing from 3.7 million in the school year 1976–77 to 4.4 million in 1986–87 (Hayward and Wirt, 1989). Data collected by the Office of Special Education Programs (OSEP) for the school year 1986–87 indicated that at the high school level 7.1 percent of the nation's 16-year-olds, 6 percent of 17-year-olds, and 3.4 percent of 18-year-olds received special education services either in resource or self-contained settings. The increase of students with special needs in secondary settings has resulted in investigation of effective transitional competencies for students from secondary settings to postsecondary job or training programs that lead to competitive employment. Yet there continues to be a serious problem with the transition from school to work for all disability categories. Special educators have not been successful in identifying and teaching the competencies necessary for future success and satisfaction in the world of work. Teachers working with students demonstrating special needs on employment skills often focus on program or curricula activities and ignore the role of vocational evaluation in developing career goals (Hursh, 1989). Quite often students with special needs receive no career or vocational assessment. If they have evaluation information, it is frequently not used by teachers to plan curriculum objectives or guide students in decision making. A lack of familiarity with career assessment is often the reason teachers do not make use of or request vocational evaluations.

Hayward and Wirt (1989) found that on average students with disabilities spent a greater share of their time in vocational education and earned more credit in these programs than did the nondisabled. Yet they were not better prepared for the transition from school to work. Special educators need to have a better understanding of career assessment for special needs students. In addition, counseling must be improved to eliminate ethnic or gender bias in the development of college and career placement goals. As Hayward and Wirt (1989) state:

Moreover, our data suggest that these continuing problems may affect female handicapped students disproportionately. That is, while male handicapped students enroll in trade and industry in about the same proportions as male students, female handicapped

Many students with special needs are unaware that support systems are available for them should they wish to go to college.   *Source:* ©Dede Hatch/The Picture Cube

students are more likely to take consumer and homemaking education and more training for service occupations than any other group, and black students are less likely to earn credits in specific labor market preparation. Greater efforts are required to ensure that all students have access to programs that will help to maximize their postschool employment and educational opportunities. (p. 49)

Limited expectations by teachers, parents, and the students themselves result in a lack of consideration of many postsecondary choices available to students with special needs as well as a focus on careers that do not necessarily utilize the student's strengths. Evaluation of cognitive ability, affective functioning, style of learning, academic performance, vocational abilities, and interests can help the special educator develop effective transitional plans for students with special needs. In addition, careful consideration must be given to the selection of evaluation tools that are free of bias toward the growing number of minority students represented by the special education population.

Transitional planning includes helping students with special needs become familiar with their rights as adults with disabilities. Federal and state laws regulate support services for adults with disabilities in areas such as accommodations, affirmative action, counseling, fringe benefits, high technology, housing, medical assistance, training, and transportation. Many students with special needs are unaware that support systems are available for individuals with disabilities should they wish to continue their education. A large percentage of students with special needs are used to environments in which their disabilities are understood and problems are solved for them. Many have no idea how to find out what services are available to them or how to ask for appropriate help. Students with disabilities have spent considerable time working toward short-term goals but often have not considered how to formulate the long-term goals that come with adult responsibility (Nay, 1979). Quite often one of the greatest problems facing students with special needs nearing the transitional level in their educational programs is their lack of awareness and acceptance of their disability. One of the primary objectives of evaluation should be to help students understand their disabilities so they can clearly describe them to others. Self-understanding is as important to a student with learning disabilities who is going on to college as it is to a student with mild physical handicaps who is preparing for a factory job. Understanding their strengths and weaknesses will help students prepare themselves and devise strategies or accommodations to help them deal with "real-world" problems.

Unfortunately, many students with special needs assume that their problems will disappear upon graduation. In addition, the transitional process is often more difficult for parents than for the student with the disabling condition. Many parents are still confused about the capabilities of their children, often setting expectations unrealistically high or low. Effective career assessment can help the entire family better understand the student's vocational goals and aspirations. Career assessment results help identify potential postsecondary opportunities that could include university/college training, technical school training, immediate entry into the work world, on-the-job training with a job coach, or a sheltered workshop training program.

Legislation Promoting Transitional Assessment for Postsecondary Education and Employment

Career assessment for students with special needs has been addressed by several federal legislative mandates. Such legislation has been the result of litigation concerning testing and the application of diagnostic labels to individuals (*Hobson v. Hanson,* 1967; *Arreola v. Santa Ana Board of Education,* 1968; *Spangler v. Pasadena Board of Education,* 1970; *Diana v. California State Board of Education,* 1970; *Stewart et al. v. Phillips et al.,* 1970; *Covarrubias v. San Diego Unified School District,* 1971; *Larry P. v. Riles,* 1971). The three main issues surrounding this early litigation centered on bias and discriminatory assessment tools, incompetent test administrators, and lack of parental input during placement decisions. The majority of this litigation was concerned with equal educational opportunity and violations of the Fourteenth Amendment of the Constitution. Therefore, the assessment and placement of students with special needs received extensive congressional attention. For example, the Education Amendments Act (PL 93–380) approved by Congress in 1974 directly addressed assurance of nondiscriminatory assessment.

Education of All Handicapped Children Act (PL 94–142)

One year after enactment of PL 93–380, PL 94–142 was signed into law. PL 94–142 required accurate, reliable, and effective evaluation of an individual to determine the presence of a disability. The law required state and local educational agencies to use assessment practices that were neutral with regard to cultural or ethnic bias as well as communication mode. It also prohibited the use of tests or testing practices for which validity had not been established. Finally, the law specified that tests be administered by trained personnel in conformance with the instructions provided by the test author. Without a doubt, PL 94–142 has had a profound effect and will continue to influence practices used in the educational and psychological diagnosis of students with special needs.

Secondary Education and Transitional Services for Handicapped Youth Act (PL 98–199)

Section 626 of PL 98–199 is often called the Transition Amendment. The intent of the law was to "stimulate and improve the development of secondary special education programs to increase the potential for competitive employment . . ." (Senate Report on the EHA Amendment of 1983, p. 20). The discretionary sections (C through H) of the Education of the Handicapped Act (PL 99–427), which include section 626, are currently being reauthorized through 1994. There has been an attempt by the Senate to broaden the definition of transition to include "the various transitions that a child with a disability may face throughout such child's years in school. . . . " Such a broadened definition dilutes the original intent of 626, which was to focus on employment preparation and transition from school to adult life. Accordingly, transition could be viewed as a phase of career development that involves individual preparation for success in employment and other adult roles.

Transition section 626 advocates implementation of statewide systems to help students with special needs make the transition into employment, postsecondary education, or other appropriate settings. Section 626 focuses on starting the transition process early and establishing interagency links for cooperative services. Appropriate planning for students reaching the age of 14, as mandated by section 626, will require effective assessment and special educators trained to understand and translate assessment information gathered from several agencies (that is, vocational rehabilitation, psychology, and mental health). Proposed changes to section 626 reflect the need for effective assessments and the definition of transitional services:

> The coordinated set of activities shall be based upon the individual student's needs, taking into account each student's preferences and interests, and shall include, but not be limited to, instruction, community experiences, the development of employment and other post-school adult living objectives, and when appropriate acquisition of daily living skills and functional vocational evaluation.

Vocational Education Act: PL 482 (1976)

PL 482 built on the provisions of the Vocational Education Act of 1963 and the Vocational Education Amendments of 1968 (PL 90–576) by requiring that students with special needs be involved in vocational education and that regular educators be involved in the student's curriculum. In addition, IEPs in the area of vocational and career development are required by PL 482 for each student with special needs. PL 482 also requires states to spend at least 10 percent of the federal/state grant-in-aid funds on students with special needs. In addition, it allows that the 10 percent set-aside monies be matched with 50 percent from state and local funds.

Rehabilitation Act Amendments of 1973 (PL 93–112)

Disability was defined much more broadly under PL 93–112 than it was in PL 94–142. According to PL 93–112, a person with a disability meant "any person who (1) has a physical or mental impairment which substantially limits one or more major life activities, (2) has a record of such impairment, or (3) is regarded as having such impairment." Thus, PL 93–112 included populations with disabilities defined under PL 94–142 and in addition qualifies drug and alcohol addiction, ADD/ADHD, head injured, other health needs, communicable diseases, and "otherwise qualified" individuals as eligible for special education services.

Section 504 of PL 93–112 directly dealt with issues of assessment as well as accessibility to programs, rights to a public education, and elimination of discriminatory admissions procedures. Evaluation was cited as necessary before any subsequent change in placement (34 CFR 104.35).

Carl D. Perkins Vocational and Applied Technology Education Act

The Carl D. Perkins Vocational and Applied Technology Education Act (1990) updates the Carl D. Perkins Vocational Technical Education Act of 1984 (PL 98–524), which was designed to "assure that individuals who are inadequately served under vocational education programs are assured access to quality vocational education programs." A major change in the update legislation is elimination of set-aside monies from vocational education funds that were only allotted to students with disabilities. The law now allows local educational agencies (LEAs) to simply try to use set-aside monies with "assurances" to "enhance participation" of persons with disabilities. This was a significant loss to students with special needs, since it allows LEAs to decide how to distribute money among special populations. In addition, the new law applies the Chapter One formula from the Elementary and Secondary Education Act, based on poverty level, for distribution of basic grant funds to meet greatest needs.

A primary mandate of both the old and new acts is that all students receiving vocational education must participate in an evaluation to assist in developing appropriate career objectives. Such evaluations should measure career interests, aptitudes, abilities, and learning styles. Both secondary and postsecondary programs are responsible for assuring ready accessibility to their programs. Postsecondary programs will be required to offer transition services and will be held responsible for assisting individuals with special needs with applications to their programs.

Individuals with Disabilities Education Act of 1990 (PL 101–476)

PL 94–142 was recently amended by Congress in several important ways. The term *handicapped* has been eliminated from the law and replaced with the term *disabilities*. The definition of "children with disabilities" now includes autism and traumatic brain injury. Related services have been expanded to include therapeutic recreation, social work services, and rehabilitation counseling. For the first time, transition services will be required to be written into the annual individualized educational program for every child age 16 and over (age 14 when appropriate). The term *transitional services* has significant meaning to special educators involved with the career assessment of individuals with special needs. According to PL 101–476[*] transitional services are defined as:

> a coordinated set of activities for a student, designed within an outcome-oriented process, which promotes movement from school to post-school activities, including post-secondary education, vocational training, integrated employment (including supported employment), continuing and adult education, adult services, independent living or community participation. The coordinated set of activities shall be based upon the individual student's needs, taking into account the student's preferences and interests, and shall include instruction, community experiences, the development of employment and other post-school adult living objectives, and when appropriate, acquisition of daily living skills and functional vocational education.

Emerging Legislative Directions

Recent legislation such as the Americans with Disabilities Act (PL 101–336), the Civil Rights Act of 1990 (H.R. 4000), and the Targeted Jobs Tax Credit (H.R. 452, S.766) all reflect a paradigm shift in transforming disability in America, as well as redefining disability in the social/cultural context of the 1990s (Kochhor, 1990). The new paradigm advocates individual rights rather than focusing on individual deficits. As Kochhor (1990) states, "the way to promote productivity and independence of people with disabilities is to remove the barriers that our society has created and restore the rights of citizens with disabilities to partake of the opportunities available to Americans" (p. 3). This change directs attention to overcoming disabilities through education, rehabilitation, and technology. Special educators need to provide accurate, nonbiased assessment to help persons with disabilities plan future career goals. Systematic and attitudinal barriers can be better faced when individuals have accurate perceptions of their strengths and weaknesses.

In the past, the majority of professional concern for career assessment has centered on vocational training for students with special needs. But today more and more students with special needs are continuing their education past high school at colleges and universities around the country. Currently, 7.7 percent of all first year students on American campuses are disabled. Many of these students have not received adequate transitional services to prepare them for the college curriculum. Appropriate career assessment in secondary schools would help students recognize their strengths and weaknesses as well as the types of modifications appropriate for them. Special educators need to work cooperatively with other professionals to develop career assessment at the secondary level to help students with disabilities to be better prepared for postsecondary training.

[*]Amendments to PL 94–142 are referred to by this new number.

Transitional and Postsecondary Assessment Areas

A career assessment for students with special needs considering either immediate employment or postsecondary schooling should be an ongoing and systematic process that utilizes standardized, dynamic, and curriculum-based tools as well as work and simulated work activity. It may focus on evaluating the competencies needed for success at a university or college or those competencies needed for success at any entry-level job. In either case, the assessment should provide an understanding of the student's developing career potential and help in formulating decisions for career direction. Above all else, a career assessment should provide the special educator with curriculum and program planning information needed to enhance the student's future career performance. According to Hursh (1989), a career assessment should yield the following outcomes:

- evaluation of career maturity;
- identification of preferred learning styles;
- identification of cognitive and academic ability;
- identification of social and interpersonal skills;
- identification of accommodations, compensation strategies, and job or training modifications;
- identification of career interests;
- organization of occupational information; and
- recommendation for career planning.

The Assessment Process

The special educator plays a significant role as a case manager during a career assessment for a student with special needs by helping to collect and interpret information that will be used for career decisions. Quite often, the special educator has worked with a student over a period of time and is the best observer of the student's abilities across tasks and settings. The special educator brings background knowledge concerning the possible impact of a student's disability on different types of job training requirements. In addition, the special educator is often aware of a student's strengths, which might not be apparent on standardized assessments.

A college or vocational career assessment requires collecting and integrating a variety of data. To better understand how this information can be used to determine appropriate career goals, we have broken the assessment process down into three main stages: the foundation, interests and style, and career simulation. The data collected at each of these stages is compiled by many different professionals (that is, psychologist, speech and language specialist, and school counselor). Often, students with special needs receive feedback from these different specialists in a very fragmented and isolated manner. This leads to confusion and misunderstanding of the suggestions presented for career decision making. It is imperative that the special educator take the lead in helping the student integrate all these data prior to formulation of an Individualized Transition Plan (ITP). (The ITP is discussed in detail at

```
┌─────────────────────────────┐
│       Stage Three           │
│     Career Simulation       │
│                             │
│       Job/Work Samples      │
│     Academic Work Samples   │
│                             │
└─────────────────────────────┘

┌─────────────────────────────┐
│        Stage Two            │
│     Interest and Style      │
│                             │
│      Career Awareness       │
│      Career Interests       │
│       Work Aptitude         │
│      Learning Style         │
│                             │
└─────────────────────────────┘

┌─────────────────────────────┐
│        Stage One            │
│        Foundation           │
│                             │
│      Cognitive Data         │
│    Social/Emotional Data    │
│     Communication Data      │
│       Academic Data         │
│        Medical Data         │
│       Interview Data        │
│                             │
└─────────────────────────────┘
```

FIGURE 13-1 Stages of assessing college and vocational career skills

the end of this chapter.) In addition, the special educator must see that a student receives an appropriate career assessment, one that includes the information listed in Figure 13–1 and discussed throughout the rest of this chapter.

The Foundation

The first stage includes gathering information pertaining to cognitive level, social/emotional functioning, appropriate communication modes, academic levels, and medical history. In addition, interviews and data from cumulative files are collected at this time. A majority of the data collected during this stage should be available from a student's psychological file. However, the special educator might determine that it is time for a student to be reevaluated or that diagnostic information is not available from past evaluations. In this case, the special educator should help facilitate the process to obtain missing data.

Cognitive assessment. A career assessment should include measure(s) that investigate a student's verbal and nonverbal problem solving abilities. This broad estimate of cognitive potential helps to determine a student's strengths and weaknesses. Examination of a student's problem solving across novel/learned, time/untimed, integrative, and metacognitive tasks can then be compared to academic, personality, and work samples to determine similarities and discrepancies across performance. (See chapters 6 and 7 for specific information pertaining to broad cognitive assessment.)

Social/emotional assessment.   Students with special needs are high risk for depression and anxiety disorders that can significantly affect work performance. In addition, some students demonstrate disorders (for example, schizophrenia, pervasive developmental disorder, or nonverbal learning disabilities) that have a significant impact on social/emotional functioning. The special educator needs to be sensitive to such personality and neurological disorders as postsecondary options are planned. The special educator also needs to consider the impact addictive disorders have on the overall social/emotional functioning of students with special needs. If not already identified, addictive disorders (for example, drug, alcohol, or eating disorders) can often be documented during an assessment. Helping a student deal with such addictions is necessary prior to developing career goals. (See chapter 8 for specific information pertaining to social/emotional assessment and chapter 9 on adaptive behavior assessment.)

Communication skills.   The ability to utilize oral language to understand as well as to express ideas is a vital requirement for career success whether working at McDonald's or selling computer software. Many students with special needs demonstrate significant problems on the job due to disabilities that interfere with their ability to communicate. While the impact of some language disorders associated with disabilities (deafness or cerebral palsy) appear clearer with regard to career adjustment, many students with mild mental handicaps also have subtle language disorders that cause a breakdown in communication. Working with speech and language specialists, the special educator should evaluate the different areas of oral language (phonology, semantics, syntax, and pragmatics) to determine the impact of specific language disorders on career training and job placement. In some situations, the employer may need to make modifications for the individual with a disability. For other students, the burden rests on learning strategies and improvement of their communication skills. (Review chapter 10 for a thorough discussion of the assessment of oral language.)

Academic skills.   The special educator will more than likely have the most information available pertaining to the academic performance of a student with special needs. Achievement and diagnostic test data documenting a student's reading, written language, and mathematics performance are very important in making training and job placements. The special educator must determine the appropriate modifications and substitutions a student would require if placed in a setting where academic learning is a demand (for example, technical school, college, or university). In addition. the special educator needs to help the student understand his or her strengths and weaknesses to determine strategies that could be used if academic requirements become a problem on a job or during further postsecondary training. (Review chapters 11, 12, and 13 for a discussion of the assessment of reading, written language, and mathematics.)

Medical.   The special educator should gather information pertaining to a student's medical history during a career assessment. Neurological, physical, or psychological problems in a student's past that could affect his or her well-being on a job or during a training program is vital information for the decision-making process. Careful consideration must be given regarding any prescription drugs a student takes that have side effects that could affect performance or endanger the student or others on a job. It is recommended that a special educator encourage a student to receive a current physical, particularly if there is a history of any neurological, physical, or psychological problems.

Interviews.   The special educator often has information pertaining to a student that has been collected during interviews with parents, teachers, and sometimes employers. While this information must be considered from the perspective of the person interviewed, it can often provide insight into a student's motivation, work or learning habits, and adaptability skills that is vital in determining future career goals. Student interviews play an important role in career assessment.

Interest and Style

Career awareness.   The second stage in a career assessment for students with special needs involves collecting data pertaining to career awareness, interests, aptitude, learning style, work habits, and learning strategies. Some of this information can best be obtained from structured interviews and dynamic assessment rather than from a standardized assessment tool. The special educator's professional expertise is invaluable in the administration, collection, and interpretation of such information.

The second stage in any career assessment of students with special needs begins with the collection of data documenting *career awareness.* Many students with special needs are not encouraged to pursue careers that require postsecondary training or jobs other than entry-level, low-paying positions. This low expectation of the population with disabilities leads to a large percentage of underemployed individuals with disabilities. Success at entry-level jobs is more difficult for some students than mid-management roles. Jim, described in Box 13-1, is an excellent example of such a case. Due to Jim's specific cognitive processing deficits (perceptual and auditory memory), taking orders at McDonald's was a disaster. However, his creative and conceptual skills made him invaluable to a computer software business. If Jim's resource teacher had not encouraged him to pursue college, he more than likely would currently be among the unemployed in our society. Therefore, a part of every special needs student's curriculum should be career awareness units, not only describing blue-collar jobs but also white-collar opportunities for employment. The special educator should assess a student's career awareness as part of the evaluation process. This can be handled during a structured interview with the student, probing his or her knowledge of career opportunities both at the local and the national level. Many students limit career selection to opportunities available to them within their own communities. Some students with special needs who have been given appropriate transitional guidance can handle training or job opportunities that require traveling to a new and different location.

Box 13-1   *Jim's Story*

Jim was diagnosed in third grade as having a specific learning disability that had an impact on reading and written language. Specific cognitive processing deficits were identified in spelling, punctuation, and syntax difficult for Jim. However, he demonstrated strengths with verbal and nonverbal reasoning tasks. His listening comprehension and problem solving strategies were above average across content areas. In addition, on verbal and figural creativity tasks, Jim was in the superior range.

Jim's learning disabilities resource teacher provided many opportunities for him to enhance his writing by using the Macintosh computer. Since reading was difficult due to decoding, Jim's teacher made sure he obtained additional content through Books-on-Tape. The use of the computer and listening to tapes helped nourish his excellent reasoning and problem solving skills. Convinced of his above average intelligence, Jim was encouraged to participate in college preparation courses during high school.

During the summer of Jim's junior year in high school, he decided to work at McDonald's. Unfortunately, due to his significant auditory memory and speed of processing deficits, this experience was a disaster. Jim could not take the orders quickly and certainly could not spell them well enough to write them down so anyone else could read and decipher the meaning. Jim's resource teacher contacted the owner of one of the local computer stores. Explaining Jim's superior creativity and problem solving as well as his knowledge of the Macintosh, she encouraged the owner to try Jim out as a salesperson for a week on a trial basis. Jim was an instant success. He was able to work well with the public and illustrated some creative uses of the computer for both business and educational purposes. Within three months, Jim was asked to be one of the store managers.

Career awareness includes not only becoming knowledgeable about types of careers but also about the skills required to be successful at those jobs. Students with special needs require help breaking down the job skills specific careers require and matching this to their knowledge of their personal strengths and weaknesses. Information obtained in the first stage of the career assessment process is necessary to make these comparisons. Developing realistic expectations is part of any transitional program. However, the special educator must be careful not to set goals based solely on standardized test scores. Information gathered from dynamic criterion-referenced, and curriculum-based assessment will help develop an appropriate prediction of career success. In particular, social/emotional development must be considered very carefully. As Rappleyea and Choppa (1989) point out, the primary reasons people are unable to hold jobs are (1) inappropriate social behaviors and (2) the inability to adapt to changes in the work place while maintaining quality work performance. Therefore, postschool success is dependent upon the ability to learn new skills and adapt to changing situations. Information from social/emotional assessment as well as adaptive behavior testing can aid the special educator in

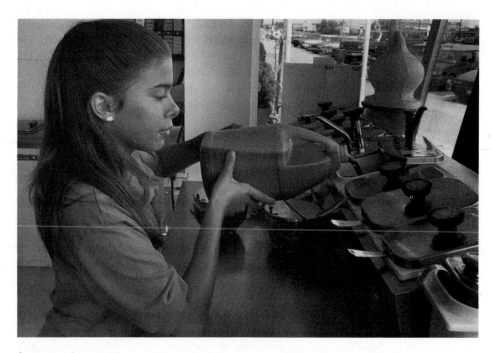

Some students with special needs limit career selection to opportunities within their community, when, with appropriate transitional guidance, they can handle more demanding jobs that may require traveling to a new location.   *Source:* © Joel Gordon, 1988

helping the student recognize his or her abilities to ease job adjustment. Motivation is another factor that cannot be overestimated in predicting postsecondary success. A student's cognitive and academic standardized scores often do not reflect that student's motivation and desire to learn new information or the student's skill in learning how to work around deficit areas.

Postsecondary training.   Teachers, parents, and the students themselves often hold limited expectations that result in a lack of consideration of college or technical schooling as a postsecondary choice for students with special needs. This leads to a lack of preparation for college and a lack of career planning. Individualized transitional plans for students with special needs should consider interest in postsecondary training.

Students with special needs should begin inquiring about a technical or college education during their junior year of high school. It is important to identify the support services available for students in these settings. For instance, does the institution provide separate courses for students with disabilities? Are notetakers, books on tape, signers, tutors, special testing arrangements, support groups, or high school to college transition programs available? Above all else, prior to applying, determine how barrier free an institution is for a student with a specific disability. In addition, the admission criteria should be evaluated to determine whether the student has the prerequisites for regular admission and whether "special" admissions exist for students with disabilities. If scholastic testing such as the Scholastic Achievement Test (SAT) is required, special administration of the test, depending on the student's disabilities can be obtained and should be encouraged. Special accommodations include braille formats, extended times, readers, or separate rooms during administration of the test. The special educator will be involved in helping the student obtain all this background information.

Interest inventories.   The first step in helping a student identify preferences for specific vocations is awareness of career options. In addition to the suggestions presented in the previous section, the special educator might consider administering an *interest inventory* to help match career options with a student's preference for future vocational goals. Interest inventories are usually paper-and-pencil tasks, which immediately sets limitations for many students with special needs. The special educator should carefully examine the strengths and weaknesses of an interest inventory, particularly in relation to the student's special needs. The vast majority of interest inventories available to the special educator were not designed specifically for the disabled population; therefore, specific modifications will need to be provided and generalization should be made with caution in predicting a student's specific interests. Table 13-1 provides a list of the most commonly used interest inventories.

The special educator should consider several aspects of interest inventories that pertain to their construction and application for special needs populations. Simply choosing an interest inventory from a list presented in an assessment text can lead to confusing results and inappropriate suggestions for career planning. The special educator must use knowledge about the student's specific abilities and disabilities and then match information available about the interest inventory. Mary's story (see Box 13-2) illustrates the problem that can arise when careful consideration has not been given to selection of a measurement in relation to the student's known disability. While able to read at the level indicated appropriate by the test constructors, Mary had significant difficulties with receptive syntax (understanding the meaning of specific syntactical structures); therefore, her responses on the inventory were the result of not understanding the questions presented to her. To avoid this problem, the special educator should critique the following aspects prior to selecting any inventory to be used with an individual with special needs.

1. *Format.* Some interest inventories are presented in picture format rather than in words. An example is the GEIST Picture Interest Inventory (Geist, 1988). However, the special educator must be aware that pictures can be confusing for some students with disabilities. Careful consideration should be given to picture clarity and whether the student has visual acuity or visual perceptual problems that would make interpretation difficult. In addition, some low-functioning individuals have difficulty abstracting the concepts presented in the pictures and need help from the special educator to interpret the meaning behind the illustrations.

2. *Prerequisites.* The special educator should carefully examine the reading, oral language, and response mode requirements for successful completion of any interest

Table 13-1 Interest inventories

Inventory (Author)	Requirements and Focus	Time Required to Administer	Minority Adaptations
Gordon Occupational Checklist (Gordon, 1981)	Noncollege-bound clients Requires sixth-grade reading level No special adaptations for individuals with disabilities	25 minutes	None
Strong–Campbell Interest Inventory (Strong, Campbell, and Hansen, 1985)	Requires sixth-grade reading level Twenty-three occupational scales included in SCII Oriented toward professional, semi-professional, or managerial occupations that attract college graduates Computer scored	25 minutes	None
Kuder General Interest Survey, Form DD (Kuder, 1960)	Requires sixth-grade reading level Ten occupational areas assessed Applicable for college bound and shorter training interests No special adaptations for individuals with disabilities	30 minutes	None
The Self-Directed Search, SDS (Holland, 1985)	Self-administered, self-scored, and self-interpreted Form E published in 1970 is designed for students as young as fourth grade or adults with limited reading skills Regular form requires a sixth-grade reading level No special adaptations for individuals with disabilities	40 minutes	None
Career Assessment Inventory (CAI), Enhanced Version (Johansson, 986)	Requires a sixth-grade reading level Developed to explore occupations requiring less than a four-year college degree Enhanced version was written for an eighth-grade reading level and focuses on college occupations Computer scored No special adaptations for individuals with disabilities	20–40 minutes	None
Interest Checklist (U.S. Department of Labor, 1981)	Requires a sixth-grade reading level Purpose is to serve as interviewing aid No special adaptations for individuals with disabilities	20–30 minutes	None
GEIST Picture Interest Inventory–Revised (Geist, 1988)	Self-administered Pictorial Inventory Noncollege-bound clients No special adaptations for persons with disabilities other than those with reading disabilities	15 minutes	Norms did include Puerto Rican and Hawaiian schools

inventory. Reading levels are usually indicated in the manual. But the special educator must be very careful in accepting the accuracy of printed reading competency levels. It is often difficult to determine what type of reading formula was used to determine grade levels, and consideration of independent rather than guided reading ability is usually not presented.

Box 13-2   *Mary's Story*

Mary was diagnosed as having a language learning disability in the first grade. Through help from a speech pathologist and a learning disability teacher, she made significant academic gains over the years. During the first through third grade, Mary was in a self-contained learning disability class; however, by fourth grade she was served by a resource teacher. Mary received resource help through high school. Specific cognitive processing deficits had an impact on her understanding of words (semantics) and word order (syntax). These oral language problems in turn made reading comprehension very difficult for her.

By the time Mary was a sophomore in high school, her reading comprehension score was at the sixth-grade level for literal content. However, text that required the interpretation of figurative or abstract language was very difficult for her. In addition, Mary had a significant problem with double negatives, subordinate clause structures, adverbial clauses, and complex sentence structures. She was very concrete in the interpretation of sarcasm, ambiguity, indirect enquiries, and double meaning words.

Mary's guidance counselor wanted to explore career options with her as they began investigating postsecondary job opportunities. Without consulting Mary's learning disability teacher, he administered an interest inventory to her. The results came back indicating a high lie factor, leading to an invalid score. Mary was extremely upset when the counselor confronted her with the lie factor score because she felt her answers to the questions were honest estimations of her feelings and interests. Mary went to her learning disabilities resource teacher with the test results. As the teacher examined the questions on the interest inventory, she realized that many of the questions involved language structures that Mary had difficulty understanding (for example, double negatives, adverbial clauses, figurative language). The learning disabilities teacher administered an interest inventory developed for students with limited reading skills that contained simpler language structures and vocabulary. The results of this inventory provided a significant amount of information that was used in the development of Mary's Individualized Transition Plan (ITP).

The complexity of the language structures of the questions presented to the student throughout an inventory should be assessed by the special educator. Very often questions are asked using double negatives or with vocabulary students do not commonly use in their social environment. The response mode required by most inventories is to check a statement with a pencil mark. However, new inventories are often computer scored and require the student to use "bubble forms"; these can be confusing to students with organizational or perceptual deficits. Modification of the answer sheet might be appropriate for such a student.

3. *Group/individual administration.* Most inventories, whether in picture or word format, can be administered either to a group or to an individual. It might

be appropriate for several students with special needs to take a particular inventory at one time. Some students with special needs will require individual administration as a result of the types of modifications necessary for fair implementation of the tools. For example, a student might require someone to read the inventory aloud, need extended time to take the inventory, or request administration in a separate room so distractibility does not interfere with the test results.

4. *Age/grade level.* The special educator should identify the appropriate age or grade level for which the test was developed. Typically, interest inventories are designed for eighth grade through adulthood. However, some inventories, such as the Kuder General Interest Inventory—Form E (Kuder, 1988) and the Wide Range Interest Opinion Test (Jastak and Jastak, 1979) include sixth and seventh grade levels.

5. *Occupations targeted.* Interest inventories are not always targeted for the same occupations. The special educator should determine whether the interest inventory is surveying a student's interest for manual labor, technical training, or jobs requiring two to four years of college. For instance, the Kuder Occupational Interest Survey—Form DD (Kuder, 1985) and the Strong–Campbell Interest Inventory (Strong, Campbell, and Hansen, 1985) both critique the student's interest for vocations that require a minimum of a four-year college degree. These inventories are appropriate for use with students with learning disabilities or behavior disorders who have been preparing for college throughout their high school curriculum, but they would be inappropriate for a student with a mild mental handicap.

6. *Time to administer.* It must be kept in mind that time estimates found in the test manual are obtained by determining the work time a nondisabled student needs. Therefore, administration of an interest inventory to a special needs student will often take much longer, particularly if modifications for test administration are needed. The majority of interest inventories require 20 to 60 minutes to administrate. In addition, the special educator should consider the time needed to score the inventory prior to purchasing any instrument. Some inventories are computer scored, either by the test company or by software purchased by the school system, while other inventories require elaborate hand scoring that might not be cost effective to the special educator.

7. *Norms.* Careful consideration should be given to the norms available in the technical manual for the interest inventory. Norms are often outdated or do not incorporate populations with disabilities. Not only should norms on different disabilities be available, but data across gender, geographical regions, and socioeconomic levels should be published in the technical manual. The validity of test results depends on the attention to detail used in collecting and presenting the psychometric data to the test user. Gender and cultural bias can easily influence the results of poorly constructed inventories.

8. *Reliability and validity.* Many interest inventories have poor reliability and validity data available to the test user. The special educator must be very careful in reviewing test manuals to determine the criteria used to report reliability and validity. If data are not available, generalizations from inventory results should be made with care. (See chapter 4 for a further discussion of reliability and validity.)

9. *Cost.* The cost of any instrument is a concern of professionals working under very tight budgets. Special educators should determine if any inventory could be hand scored rather than sent back to the company for computer scoring. If large numbers of students will be administered certain inventories, it might save a school system money to purchase the software for computer scoring rather than use company scored sheets. The special educator must also consider what information is provided for the cost of an inventory. Some inventories cost slightly more but provide a significant amount of feedback concerning career interests that is important during transitional planning. The cost must be evaluated relative to the total amount of feedback provided on each student's interest profile.

Aptitude.   The assessment of career aptitude is a vital component of any evaluation for students with special needs. Information regarding career aptitude can be interpreted from information gathered during the initial stage of an assessment. *Aptitude* pertains to the investigation of a student's innate capacity to learn and solve problems, and the student's speed or proficiency learning new and novel information. The cognitive and affective components of an evaluation (see chapters 6, 7, and 8) provide the special educator with much of this information. It is important that dynamic assessment be incorporated into any cognitive testing, since the focus of dynamic assessment is to look past standard scores to evaluate a person's ability to learn new information.

The purpose of aptitude testing is different from achievement testing. Achievement tests evaluate previously learned material, reflecting more on an individual's ability to recall information from school-learned material. Aptitude testing attempts to match a person's learning potential or problem solving to specific occupations and vocations. For instance, does a student have the numerical aptitude or ability to perform the arithmetic operations required to be a carpenter? A student may not have the educational skills but, if taught, could learn the arithmetic operations required of a job. Another student, no matter how much instruction on specific numerical skills he or she received, would have difficulty applying this knowledge on a job. This student would not appear to demonstrate an aptitude for mathematics.

Success in a career involves much more than just aptitude. For instance, motivation, life experiences, social/emotional functioning, and medical history all affect future success. Aptitude is only one component of the entire process of evaluation. Unfortunately, many students with special needs are given a single aptitude test that is then used as the sole predictor of career success. While these single batteries provide information for the decision-making process, the information gathered during each stage of a career assessment should also be considered when defining transitional choices. Table 13-2 lists some of the single aptitude batteries commonly used in career assessment. Much of the data collected from these tools can also be obtained from data collected during the initial stage of an assessment. Single aptitude batteries are a gross estimation of a student's possible job potential. The special educator will gain little new information from single

Table 13-2 General aptitude test batteries

Battery	Special Adaptations	Components Measured	Time Required for Administration	Targeted Populations	Minority Use
General Aptitude Test Battery (GATB) (U.S. Department of Labor, 1970)	No special adaptations for individuals with disabilities other than reading All subjects are highly speeded (Anatasi, 1982)	General Learning Ability Verbal Aptitude Numerical Aptitude Spatial Aptitude Form Perception Clerical Perception Motor Coordination Finger Dexterity Manual Dexterity	2 1/4 hours	Adults who have not chosen a field	Spanish version
Differential Aptitude Test, Fifth Edition, (Bennett, Seashore, and Wesman, 1982)	Minimal reading Software scoring available No special adaptations for individuals with disabilities	Verbal Reasoning Numerical Ability Abstract Reasoning Clerical Speed and Accuracy Mechanical Reasoning Space Relations Spelling and Language Usage	3 hours	Level 1: Grades 7–9 Level 2: Grades 10–12 Predictor of engineering, science, and math ability	None
Flanagan Aptitude Classification Test (Flanagan, 1953)	Each test is published in a separate booklet Multiple choice responses are recorded in booklets Requires eighth-grade reading level No special adaptation for individuals with disabilities	Inspection Coding Memory Precision Assembly Scales Coordination Judgment and Comprehension Arithmetic Patterns Components Tables Mechanics Expression Reasoning Ingenuity	10 hours for total administration	Education population Useful for individuals considering college	None
Minnesota Clerical Test (Andres, Paterson, and Longstaff, 1961)	No special adaptation for individuals with disabilities	Number Checking (200 items) Name Scoring (200 items)	Less than 30 minutes	Grades 8–12	None
Crawford Small Parts Dexterity Test (Crawford and Crawford, 1975)	No special adaptations for individuals with disabilities	Designed to measure fine motor coordination.	Less than 15 minutes	Adult norms only	None
Purdue Pegboard (Tiffin, 1948)	No special adaptations for individuals with disabilities	Measures finger and hand dexterity.	10–15 minutes	Adult norms	
Scholastic Aptitude Test (SAT)	Untimed version	Verbal and quanitative reasoning	3 hours	High school seniors Individuals interested in college	None
Graduate Records Examination	Untimed version	Verbal and quanitative reasoning	4 hours	College students Graduate school	None

aptitude batteries, and the majority of these batteries are focused on technical or manual labor jobs.

Habits.   Observation of a student's work and study habits should be an integral part of any career assessment. Such information is collected from teacher/employer observations, student interviews and observations, and behaviors demonstrated during the assessment process. Systematic record keeping will help identify the transitional competencies needed for success after secondary school. The special education teacher should be especially alert to the following student behaviors:

1. *Appropriateness:* determining the appropriateness of a response, an interaction, or dress.
2. *Perseveration:* continuing an action or a conversation longer than necessary.
3. *Disinhibition:* difficulty inhibiting an action or response that may not be appropriate for the situation.
4. *Attention:* difficulty attending to directions for work-related tasks.
5. *Anticipation:* difficulty anticipating problems that might arise on the job.

Under the best of circumstances the job world is a very stressful place. The stress can be somewhat reduced for individuals with special needs if they know what to expect and understand some of the unwritten rules that govern job performance. Observation of a student's work and study habits help the special educator determine where disabilities might have an impact on job success. Once the problems are identified, the special educator can work with the student to develop strategies to work around ineffective work or study habits. The following factors are significant problems often demonstrated by students with special needs that should be observed during an assessment to determine their impact on a specific student's level of performance.

1. *Time Concept:* For students with disabilities affecting time orientation, being on time for a job or managing time for studying can be a problem. The first step during an evaluation is to determine whether the student is aware of this difficulty and the impact it has on his or her performance. Next the special educator should investigate strategies the student has developed to help with the problem. Finally, the special educator should match the student's strengths and weaknesses to time management strategies to develop a comprehensive system of skills that can help the student manage time more effectively as well as recognize the importance being on time plays in job success.

2. *Dressing:* Some students need guidance on the appropriateness of dress for job success. The student's appropriateness of attire should be observed across school, work, and social situations. The unwritten rules of dress should be explored with a student during an interview to determine the knowledge the student has picked up from daily living.

3. *Language:* Students with oral language disabilities (see chapter 10) have difficulty understanding and expressing themselves on a job. Role playing situa-

tions can be used by the special educator to evaluate specific language problems critical to the communication process. In addition, the special educator might have a student listen to audiotapes or view videotaped interviews of "good" or "bad" interview applicants. Such exercises help determine whether the student is even aware of potential bad habits.

4. *Rejection:* Being turned down for a job or receiving negative feedback on a job is difficult for everyone. Students with special needs who have experienced academic difficulties may find a rejection from the work world to be devastating. This can significantly interfere with future attempts at job success. How a student will react to criticism or rejection can be predicted from information collected from teachers, employers, observations, and psychological testing. If dealing with constructive criticism or rejection is a problem for a student with special needs, the special educator should help the student develop coping strategies based on that individual's profile of strengths and weaknesses.

Knowledge of what to communicate.   Skill strengths and weaknesses are personal and private information. The special educator must decide how much of this information to communicate to an employer or a college professor. Obviously, it is important not to place the student on a job or at a task that the disability prevents the student from accomplishing. It is also important that the student not place himself or herself on a task that focuses attention on the disability. An effective way to observe a student's ability to provide or withhold personal information is to provide role playing activities in the student's vocational interest area. For example:

1. The student demonstrates good mechanical skills. His disability is in the area of reading, although given enough time he can decipher much of what he is expected to read. New car dealers get modification orders and specialized repair instructions on newly designed mechanical units. During a role playing activity, the special educator could pose the question: "What would be your response if you are asked, 'Can you handle modification orders?' "

2. The student has been cleaning off tables in a large cafeteria and seems happy in her job. Her disability makes it difficult for her to process verbal information quickly. She becomes flustered when work instructions are given too rapidly. Because she is doing well in her job, the manager is likely to ask if she would like the higher paying job of serving food behind the counter. This job requires quick response to customer orders, frequently two or three items long. The special education teacher could pose the question during a role playing activity: "What would be your response if you are asked, 'Do you want the counter job on vegetables?' "

Communication skills, both verbal and nonverbal, are frequently very difficult for students with special needs (see chapter 10). This problem is compounded when the information to be communicated is negative, ego destructive, or potentially damaging to an immediate goal. It is imperative that the special educator thoroughly evaluate the impact of oral language skills on job performance during a career assessment.

Study skills.   Despite the importance of study skills for success at postsecondary institutions, very limited research exists pertaining to specific study skills assessment or training procedures that prepare students with disabilities for college. Lecture presentations are a pervasive form of instruction in secondary and college classrooms (Carrier, Williams, and Dalgaard, 1988; Westendorf, Cape, and Skrtic, 1982), therefore, the ability to acquire content from lectures is imperative for postsecondary students. Gathering content information, organizing and remembering it, and providing corrective feedback are all cognitive areas that affect a student's success in college.

A term associated with the realm of study skills is "metacognition," an awareness about how we learn. For instance, if you have weak memory skills you might find that making notes to yourself will help you remember important tasks. Metacognitive abilities are vitally important in developing effective study skills. Flavell and Wellman (1977) identify three variables important in developing a person's metacognitive ability:

1. *Person variable:* knowledge about one's strengths and weaknesses.
2. *Task variable:* knowledge of tasks that are harder or easier to learn.
3. *Strategy variable:* knowledge of which strategies facilitate learning.

The role of the special educator working with a student on transitional goals is to help that student identify person, task, and strategy variables that have an impact on different types of study skill requirements. Table 13-3 lists broad and specific skills that should be investigated during an assessment of a student's study skills.

Few standardized tools sensitive to populations with special needs exist to help the special educator in the area of study skills assessment. Special educators may need to develop their own curriculum-based assessment tools to measure study skills. Table 13-4 is an example of a teacher made assessment developed to investigate organization and graph reading skills important for success at the postsecondary level. Figure 13-2 is an example of a teacher made visual cue strategy designed to help determine whether mapping (visual cues) would help a student studying Virgil's *Aeneid.* Some students are significantly aided by having a visual cue to use in conjunction with verbal cues in remembering information.

Assessment is an ongoing process. Special educators are constantly required to develop curriculum-based assessment measures of content and evaluate the effectiveness of learning strategies with students they work with on a daily basis. Standardized tests offer only limited help with many of the facets of evaluation that are necessary in helping students with special needs meet the demands of academic and vocational environments.

Learning style.   Students with special needs have individual styles of learning that are distinct from their disabilities. All people, with or without disabilities, exhibit differences in the way they learn and act. Such differences are not good or bad, rather they are styles of learning. The manner in which people differ in temperament or *learning style* is just as unique as their body build. Unfortunately, quite often differences in behaviors or learning styles are interpreted as flaws or disabilities. A student's reflective style of approaching problems could easily be interpreted as a disability in the area of processing information quickly (automaticity). The special educator must

Table 13-3 Study skill areas requiring assessment

Broad Areas	Specific Area	Research
Gathering Information	Brainstorming Skills	Feldhusen and Treffinger, 1978
	Generalizing Skills	Fraenkel, 1973
		Alley and Deshler, 1979
	Hypothesizing Skills	Fraenkel, 1973
		Alley and Deshler, 1979
	Offering Alternatives	Fraenkel, 1973
	Predicting and Explaining Skills	Fraenkel, 1973
	Questioning Strategies	Fraenkel, 1973
		Torrance and Myers, 1970
Remembering Information	Mnemonic Devices	Devine, 1981
	Associative Devices	Reid, 1981
		Reid, 1988
	Orienting Tasks	Torgesen, 1979
	Metamemory Devices	Reid, 1988
Organizing Information	Manipulating Information	De Bono, 1967
	Perceiving Organization	De Bono, 1967
		Berthoff, 1982
	Listing, Grouping, and Labeling	Fraenkel, 1973
		Berthoff, 1982
		Alley and Deshler, 1979
	Categorizing	Berthoff, 1982
		Fraenkel, 1973
	Differentiating and Defining	Berthoff, 1982
		Fraenkel, 1973
		Alley and Deshler, 1979
	Planning and Organizing Multiple Tasks	Uris, 1970
	Metacognitive Study Strategies	Reid, 1988
Corrective Feedback and Evaluation	Self-Administrating Reinforcement	Hoy, 1987
		Alley, Deschler, Clark, Schumaker and Warner, 1983
	Setting Goals	Hoy, 1987
		Reid, 1988
	Developing Plans that Identify Problems	Hoy, 1987
		Alley, Deschler, Clark, Schumaker, and Warner, 1983
Specific Notetaking Skills	Taking Notes	Cowen, 1988
	Deciding What Information to Record	Suritsky and Hughes, 1990
	Recording Notes Quickly	Bireley, Landers, Vernooy, and Schlaerth, 1986
	Identifying Lecture Cues	Hartley and Fuller, 1971
		Locke, 1977

become sensitive to styles of learning and problem solving that might affect a student's task performance or interactive skills. In addition, during observations in the classroom, the special educator should determine the match between a teacher's learning style and the student's. It is possible that a teacher and a student have learning styles that make successful communication difficult. A teacher's own learning style can influence his or her perceptions about a student, which in turn can have an impact on the accuracy of the information provided to the special educator about a student's behavior during class. Table 13-5 on page 440 provides a description of various

Table 13-4 Organization assessment

Directions: Imagine that in addition to eating, sleeping, and attending class your current state of affairs includes the following:

- Clean laundry is running low.
- A movie you've been wanting to see opens Tuesday at the mall.
- Georgia plays Auburn at home on Saturday.
- You have a science class Monday, Tuesday, and Friday, 5th period with a 3-hour lab on Wednesday from 6th to 8th periods.
- You have your eye on a new CD at Turtles, and your roommate owes you money.
- You're running low on bread, peanut butter, and shampoo.
- You have a quiz in your 2nd period history class on Thursday.
- You have a three-page paper due in your 4th period Literature class on Friday.
- *The Color Purple* will be discussed in your Lit class on Tuesday.
- Your roommate wants you to go to a party Saturday night.
- There is an extra-credit seminar Monday night from 8–10 p.m.
- Midterms begin next week.
- Counseling and Testing is having a self-hypnosis seminar you've been wanting to attend on Monday from 3:30 to 5:00 p.m.
- You'd like to ask out the cute person who sits next to you in History.

How would you organize your week?

You have three choices of how to do this task:

1. Orally (into a tape recorder)
2. Written
3. Diagram

Make your choice. The examiner will provide you with the necessary materials and answer any questions you may have.

Hours	Sunday	Monday	Tuesday	Wednesday	Thursday	Friday	Saturday

Source: From: Wahlers, D. and Jackson, R. (1993). *Organization Assessment.* University of Georgia Learning Disabilities Center.

learning styles and the type of classroom management teachers employing these styles are most comfortable with, as well as the type of student they are most successful in helping. Careful observation of a student's learning style helps determine when behavior is the result of style rather than disability.

The *Myers–Briggs Type Indicator* (Keirsey and Bates, 1984) is one of the most commonly used learning style inventories. It identifies sixteen different patterns of learning styles based on Jung's (1923) theory of psychological types. The typology distinguishes between four types of temperament or learning styles. It is important for the special educator to keep in mind that a student is not always one or the other of these four types—degree and situation are closely correlated to temperament type. The four personality types used in the Myers–Briggs include:

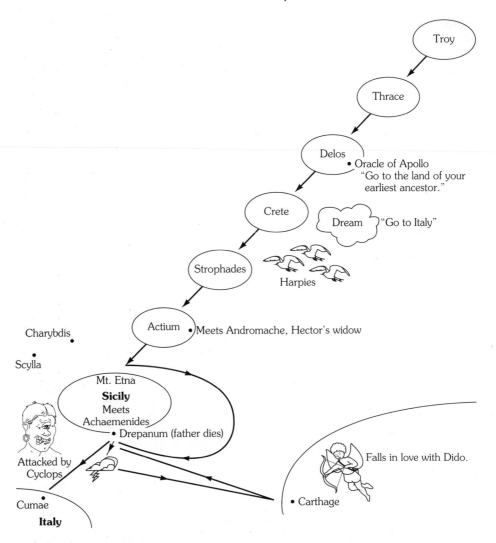

FIGURE 13-2 Visual cue strategy for Virgil's *Aeneid* (Jackson, 1992)

- Extraversion versus Introversion
- Sensation versus Intuition
- Thinking versus Feeling
- Judging versus Perceiving

Through the use of pairs of words and phrases, Table 13-6 defines these four personality types. If the special educator understands a student's type, a better estimate can be made of the student's anticipated behavior in a given situation, and it is not as likely that differences in behavior will be diagnosed as a disability. Vocationally it is important for students to be aware of their own learning styles when considering job preferences and aptitude. In addition, a competency that a student needs to acquire during the transitional stage of schooling centers on the

Table 13-5 Teaching style summary

	Prime Value in Education	Percentage of Teachers and Length of Service	Favored Teaching Areas		Favored Instructional Techniques	
SPs	Growth of spontaneity and freedom	4% Short stay in teaching	Arts Crafts Sports	Drama Music Recreation	Projects Contents Games	Demonstrations Shows
STs	Growth of responsibility and utility	56% Long stay in teaching	Agriculture Clerical Business Sports Social Sciences	Political Science Homemaking History Geography	Recitation Drill Composition	Tests/Quizzes Demonstrations
NTs	Growth of knowledge and skills	8% Medium stay in teaching	Philosophy Science Technology	Communications Mathematics Linguistics	Lectures Tests Compositions	Projects Reports
NFs	Growth of identity and integrity	32% Long stay in teaching	Humanities Social Sciences Theater Music	Foreign Languages Speech Theology	Group Products Interaction Discussion	Shows Simulations Games

Source: From *Please Understand Me: Character and Temperament Types,* by D. Keirsey and M. Bates, p. 79. Copyright © 1978 by Prometheus Nemesis Book Company. Reprinted by permission.

ability of the student to understand and respect the differences of temperament of others. Student awareness of why a person might react to a situation based on their temperament will help in developing solutions to problems presented during a normal working day.

Career Simulation

The purpose of *career simulation* is to observe a student's behavior and occupational assets and liabilities during a real-world situation (Sitlington, 1979). Rehabilitation counselors use this approach both at job sites and in sheltered workshops. The simulation of career roles allows for the observation of work and school aptitude. In addition, specific cognitive, language, and affective competencies can be evaluated in a real-world setting. For instance, a student could have mastered the ability to complete all clerical skills required of an office manager but specific social/emotional problems prohibit success when actually faced with time constraints and dealing with other people on a job. Special educators should play a significant role in collecting observations from career simulation tasks. Working cooperatively with rehabilitation counselors, special educators can contribute their knowledge of the impact of specific disabilities on job performance and help develop strategies for the student to work around obstacles that are causing unsatisfactory job performance. The diagnostic and instructional skills background of the special educator will add to the counseling and employment knowledge of the rehabilitation counselor.

Table 13-6 Myers–Briggs personality types

Extraversion (75% of population)	versus	Introversion (25% of population)
Sociability		Territoriality
Interruption		Concentration
External		Internal
Breadth		Depth
Extensive		Intensive
Multiplicity of relationships		Limited relationships
Expenditure of energies		Conservation of energies
Interest in external events		Interest in internal reaction

Sensation (75% of population)	versus	Intuition (25% of population)
Experience		Hunches
Past		Future
Realistic		Speculative
Perspiration		Inspiration
Actual		Possible
Down-to-earth		Head-in-clouds
Utility		Fantasy
Fact		Fiction
Practicality		Ingenuity
Sensible		Imaginative

Thinking (50% of population)	versus	Feeling (50% of population)
Objective		Subjective
Principles		Values
Policy		Social values
Laws		Extenuating circumstances
Criterion		Intimacy
Firmness		Persuasion
Impersonal		Personal
Justice		Humane
Categories		Harmony
Standards		Good or bad
Critique		Appreciate
Analysis		Sympathy
Allocation		Devotion

Judging (50% of population)	versus	Perceiving (50% of population)
Settled		Pending
Decided		Gather more data
Fixed		Flexible
Plan ahead		Adapt as you go
Run one's life		Let life happen
Closure		Open options
Decision making		Treasure hunting
Planned		Open ended
Completed		Emergent
Decisive		Tentative
Wrap it up		Something will turn up
Urgency		There's plenty of time
Deadline		What deadline?
Get show on the road		Let's wait and see

Source: From *Please Understand Me: Character and Temperament Types,* by D. Keirsey and M. Bates, p. 25. Copyright © 1978 by Prometheus Nemesis Book Company. Reprinted by permission.

Career simulation has focused primarily on job readiness and ignored postsecondary schooling readiness. Many students with special needs are not prepared to deal with the demands of postsecondary training. While they may be working independently in a secondary school resource room, when placed on a college campus they become overwhelmed and often are not able to function productively in their classrooms. Special educators working with students with special needs in secondary settings should include career simulation tasks as part of these students' ITP. In addition, many students not planning on attending college or university are required as part of their job to attend technical training sessions or schools. Prior observation of their ability to learn in such settings and development of strategies to deal with "training classes" can lead to increased career success.

Most work that has been done with the career simulation approach has ignored the training or schooling aspect of career success and focused primarily on the simulation of entry-level job skills. Therefore, the special educator will be required to develop many of the suggested activities in this chapter without the luxury of commercial programs. The special educator should help students develop better transitional competencies based on systematic observations of behaviors and diagnostic assessment of the competencies required for specific careers. Limiting career simulation to only job and not classroom observations encourages many students with special needs to accept underemployment and cease striving to reach their true potential.

Behavioral analysis.   A key to assessing job or classroom simulation activities is systematic observation and record keeping of behaviors. The purpose of career simulation is twofold: (1) simulation of actual work settings or postsecondary classroom environments, and (2) manipulation of as many variables as possible to elicit as many work behaviors as possible from the student. According to Sitlington (1979), the instruments used for recording the data should focus precisely on the behaviors and attitudes of concern. These instruments should report the data as objectively as possible. Some guidelines that facilitate the process of observation include:

1. Use only observable terms to describe behaviors.
2. Describe the situation in which the behavior was observed.
3. Describe only what occurred, not your hypothesis as to the etiology of the behavior.
4. Use behavioral terms in reporting information rather than professional jargon. "The student demonstrated difficulty remembering three-word directions when presented orally," rather than, "The student had poor auditory memory skills."
5. Record frequency, rate, and duration data whenever possible.
6. Record baseline data on the student's performance.
7. Continue observation over a period of time to establish maintenance, generalization, and improvement data.
8. Provide observations on the manipulation of work variables.

   a. environmental conditions (that is, noise, number of people the student must interact with, gender of supervisor)

b. instructional methods employed (that is, verbal, nonverbal, computer)

c. reinforcement and reinforcement schedule

The Material Development Center at the University of Wisconsin–Stout developed a measurement device (MDC Behavior Identification Format, 1974) that can be very helpful to the special educator in deciding which behaviors to observe during a job or classroom simulation. While this instrument is somewhat outdated in relation to its norms, it does provide an excellent outline of behaviors to assist in identifying, observing, and recording behavior during simulation activities. In addition, the device provides sample descriptions and examples of behavioral observations. The twenty-two behaviors this instrument identifies as important to measure during a career assessment are:

- hygiene
- grooming and dress
- irritating habits
- odd or inappropriate behaviors
- communication skills
- attendance
- punctuality
- work-coping skills
- personal complaints
- vitality
- stamina
- work consistency
- distractibility
- conformity
- reactions to change in work assignments
- reactions to monotonous or unpleasant tasks
- social skills (relating to coworkers or other students)
- required supervision
- recognition/acceptance of authority
- reactions to close supervision, criticism, and pressure from supervisors or professors
- need for assistance
- organizational skills

Job simulation.   The most common approach used to observe a student on a job is called situational assessment, conducted on job sites or in sheltered workshops. According to Neff (1968), the difference "between situational assessment . . . and ordinary employment . . . is that it is possible to alter all of the customary conditions of employment without the overriding concern for efficient production" (p. 207). The special educator works with the rehabilitation counselor to collect data on a student's ability to perform a job with minimal supervision while at the same time yielding quality production.

Job site assessment is another evaluation technique used to observe a student's competencies in the world of work. This technique differs from situational assessment as it is always carried out at actual job settings. It is a more realistic and ecologically sound estimate of an individual's ability to deal with all the variables that influence job performance. Poor (1975) list some advantages of this technique:

• Business and industry are directly involved with problem solving to integrate a person with disabilities into the world of work.
• Additional equipment or finances are not needed.
• Students have the opportunity to really assess the job.
• Students develop better self-awareness leading to more independent living competencies.

The special educator and the rehabilitation counselor must work together to integrate additional information about the student prior to job placement. Background information collected during the career assessment process is vital to create a positive work experience. Such background information can help anticipate problem areas, strengths, and special concern areas. Rehabilitation counselors have the skills necessary to help the special educator with employer-oriented communications to obtain the best utilization and goodwill of community resources. Due to the diverse nature of job sites, few assessment instruments provide accurate recording of this observational data. The special educator and the rehabilitation counselor must work together to develop a systematic way to observe the student on a job site that will include information from the perspective of the student, the employer, the special educator, and the rehabilitation counselor.

Work sample technique.   Work samples can be either self-developed or commercially prepared tools that help evaluate one or several aspects of a particular work skill. They simulate an actual job skill(s) before placing a student in the work situation with all the other social variables that influence job performance. This provides the special educator or rehabilitation counselor the opportunity to observe a student's ability to actually perform a job task. Work sample techniques have been defined as "a well defined work activity involving tasks, materials, and tools which are identical or similar to those in an actual job or cluster of jobs" (Vocational Evaluation and Work Adjustment Association, 1975, p. 52). While commercially developed work samples provide standardization and statistical data supporting the predictive validity of samples to community jobs (Bitter, 1979), they often become obsolete because of rapidly changing technology. Self-developed work samples are more economically feasible and can be adapted easily to individual students and job descriptions. However, self-developed work samples often do not have any norming or predictive data to back up the performance score. If a special educator is interested in developing work samples, Sitlington (1979) proposes six basic steps for preparing a work sample:

1. determine the samples to develop;
2. conduct job analysis to include task description, work requirements, and environmental demands (content validity);
3. design and construct work samples;

4. develop work samples manual;
5. establish norms; and
6. establish estimates of reliability and validity.

Work samples can be used to observe many diverse skill activities. They can be utilized to sample an actual work activity, observe a job that has been modified in structure, assess specific skills common to a larger group of jobs, or observe clusters of traits inherent in a job or variety of jobs. The special educator will need to use all the information collected in the early stages of a college and vocational career assessment when interpreting the performance of a student on any work sample. Work samples do not provide all the necessary information for evaluation and must be supplemented by other information and techniques.

Commercially based job simulation systems are increasing in demand due to the standardization and limited personnel time for administration they provide. In addition to recognizing that such systems provide only part of the data needed to help students with special needs choose careers, the special education teacher should evaluate a system's control for:

• cognitive limitations;
• language limitations;
• academic limitations; and
• behavior/emotional limitations.

College/training simulation. The middle and secondary school special educator concerned about a student's ability to meet the demands required of a postsecondary training program should develop some situations that simulate activities required of college or university students. Evaluation of an individual's performance on these simulation activities can help in development of appropriate transitional goals as well as in decisions regarding choice of a specific college or university. Identifying problem areas can help the special educator work with a student to develop compensation strategies and determine needed modifications for survival at a postsecondary institution. For instance, notetaking is often difficult for students with disabilities. The special educator can help the student learn strategies around the problem depending on the student's specific disabilities (for example, notetakers, tape recorder). In addition, the special educator might need to include objectives in a student's ITP that pertain to learning how to develop a timeline to carry out multiple projects and prioritize study tasks.

Computers in Career and Vocational Assessment

Computers have taken on an increasingly important role in college and vocational career assessment. One of the most significant contributions computers have added to assessment is their ability to assist persons with a disability in taking standardized tests through such modifications as voice-operated response units (Growick, 1983). For students with milder disabilities, such as learning disabilities, the ability to express their thoughts using the computer rather than a paper/pencil task often provides a more accurate assessment of their overall potential. If such a student is

Table 13-7 Select computer programs for vocational assessment

Program	Requirements and Focus	Time Required to Administer	Minority
MESA Program (Valpar International, 1982)	Criterion- and norm-referenced Short form available Vocational screening	30–50 minutes	None
APTICOM Program (Vocational Research Institute, 1989)	Only 2 of 11 tests require reading Measures vocational aptitudes	70–90 minutes	None
Talent Assessment Program (Instant Report, 1988)	No reading required Norms nondiscriminatory Initial screening device		None
System of Interactive Guidance and Information Program (Educational Testing Service, 1988)	Interactive assistance in career decision making Designed primarily for students considering two- or four-year colleges	60 minutes	None
Discover Program (American College Testing, 1989)	Designed for counseling students in grades 7–12	60 minutes	None

allowed to use spell-check or a grammar check, the final product may represent a better estimate of the student's level of cognitive thinking. Maze (1984) suggests that computer systems also contribute to vocational assessment in the following ways:

1. *Self-Assessment.* Computers provide a means for administering and scoring evaluative instruments that provides quick feedback of information to the client. In addition, Power (1991) discusses the ability of computers to provide subjective exercises with prompts and extra assistance for individuals having difficulty understanding instructions.
2. *Occupational Selection.* One of the most common uses of the computer in a career assessment is to aid in sorting occupational titles leading to the selection of appropriate vocational categories for a student.
3. *Informational Component.* Computers provide the special educator with an excellent information retrieval device. Information such as facts about educational programs, industries, occupations, financial aid, and job openings can easily be accessed on the computer.

Table 13-7 lists selected computer-assisted assessment systems that might be useful to the special education teacher working with a rehabilitation counselor to provide the most appropriate instructional program for a student with special needs. The cost of many of these systems is relatively high. A school system must weigh the initial cost of the system against the large number of students with and without disabilities who could benefit from such programs as well as the savings in time necessary to track down even a small portion of the information quickly accessed by the computer. Special educators must become knowledgeable about the different adaptive devices that provide students with special needs with a nonbiased assessment. They must also become aware of the use of the computer for testing, scoring, and information retrieval.

Transition from High School to the Real World

Statistics from follow-up studies indicate that many students with special needs are not as successful as they should be once they leave high school. More than 70 percent of students with disabilities graduate from high school without employment or postsecondary prospects. Those who seek employment have more difficulty finding and keeping jobs than do their peers. They are more likely to be employed in unskilled, semiskilled, or service-oriented jobs with a lower mean income than that of their peers. Statistics also show that they are less satisfied with their jobs and change jobs more frequently than do their coworkers. Only about half of the students with special needs who pursue postsecondary training programs ever graduate. It is apparent from such statistics that many students with special needs are leaving high school without the necessary skills, self-image, and self-awareness to make the transition to a successful adult life.

The special educator must help students with special needs identify the competencies they need for successful employment and career development. This requires review of all the information collected throughout the career assessment (see Figure 13-3). After data on performance levels, interests, and motivation are used in the decision-making process, the special educator must work with the student and his or her parents to develop an Individualized Transition Plan (ITP) and a Transition Profile. Development of an ITP is the end product of careful career assessment. Formal, dynamic, and criterion-referenced data should be used to develop the ITP. The following steps can be used to develop an ITP for a special needs student:

Step One: The needs and concerns of a student should be the first information used in developing the ITP. A transition plan should be designed with the specific intention of making the transition from high school to post–high school as successful and anxiety-free as possible. To do this, the student must be actively involved in the planning process. The special educator should probe the following areas:

1. *The student's awareness and acceptance of his or her disability.* Since many students with disabilities do not clearly understand their strengths and weaknesses, they are not prepared to devise coping strategies or accommodations to help them through "real-world" problems.
2. *The student's awareness and acceptance of postsecondary knowledge.* Many special needs students are unaware that support systems are available for students with disabilities should they wish to continue their education.
3. *The student's self-advocacy skills.* Many students with special needs are used to the environments in which their disabilities are solved for them. Many of these students have little understanding of what services are available to them or how to ask for appropriate help.
4. *The student's long-term goal planning.* Many students with special needs have never considered how to formulate the long-term goals that come with adult responsibility.

```
┌─────────────────────────────┐
│      Stage Three            │
│    Career Simulation        │
│                             │
│     Relationship with       │
│  supervisors and coworkers  │
│       Social skills         │
│   Job-seeking and keeping   │
│        behaviors            │
│      Job performance        │
│    Response to pressure     │
│      Transfer of skills     │
└─────────────────────────────┘

┌─────────────────────────────┐
│       Stage Two             │
│    Interest and Style       │
│                             │
│   Independent functioning   │
│   Adjustment and maturity   │
│      Job-seeking skills     │
│      Readiness to work      │
│        Motivation           │
└─────────────────────────────┘

┌─────────────────────────────┐
│       Stage One             │
│       Foundation            │
│                             │
│   Realistic expectations    │
│       Self-concept          │
│   Problem-solving ability   │
│     Interpersonal skills    │
│      Language skills        │
│       Adaptability          │
│    Response to pressure     │
│       Energy level          │
│     Physical limitations    │
│    Academic functioning     │
└─────────────────────────────┘
```

FIGURE 13-3 Relationship of assessment stages to career comptencies

Step Two: The second step in developing an ITP is to involve parents or care-takers. Parents of special needs students often view their children as less capable of functioning independently than are students with no disability and do not encourage postsecondary options appropriate to their child. On the other hand, some parents have unreasonably high expectations that might be inappropriate for a specific student. Many parents are too willing to leave their child's special education concerns completely up to the school system. As the student with special needs progresses through school, the teacher's role is to shift the sense of transitional empowerment gradually toward the parent and student and finally, if mature enough, to the student alone.

Step Three: The third step in developing an ITP is consideration of all postsecondary possibilities available to a student and building into the ITP opportunities to be ready to handle any specific postsecondary options (school or job).

Forming ITP Goals: Vocational Orientation

An ITP for vocationally oriented students should address the following areas for a special needs student:

- postsecondary residential accommodations;
- recreation and leisure activities;
- job/career plans;
- legal needs;
- transportation needs; and
- medical needs.

Diagnostic and background information collected during the career assessment process should be used to develop individualized competencies for:

- communication skills;
- coping/compensation skills;
- social skills;
- problem solving skills;
- job related skills specific to a student's career interest; and
- knowledge of rights and responsibilities.

The ITP for many students with mild disabilities includes integration of career and academic curricula. Diagnostic psychological, cognitive, and academic information collected to support eligibility can be used in conjunction with further vocational testing. The special educator will often be the case manager in pulling together the diagnostic information from different professionals (that is, psychologist, speech and language specialist, medical doctor) involved in the foundation stage of a college and vocational career assessment. The interest and learning style portion of a career assessment might find the special educator or rehabilitation counselor administering an interest inventory, conducting an interview with the student, or observing a student's work habits. Finally, the special educator could provide a work sample or job-site evaluation of a student's ability to perform a specific job. The data collected from each of the stages of assessment can be used to develop transitional competencies necessary to a specific student and that can be written into the student's ITP.

Forming ITP Goals: Academic Orientation

A larger percentage of special needs students are now attempting education and training after high school. Postsecondary education includes any education beyond high school, trade or business schools, vocational or technical schools, colleges, universities, and continuing education programs. Success for special needs students at postsecondary schooling depends on careful transition plans. Once a student with learning disabilities has determined that postsecondary schooling is a viable option, the student, parents, and special education teacher should sit down together and develop an *Individualized College Plan* (ICP). An ICP should assist students with special needs to:

1. identify appropriate modifications needed for academic success;
2. identify available resources;
3. identify coping skills necessary for postsecondary training programs;
4. minimize obstacles for learning (personal, social, and environmental);
5. offer a plan of study and preparation that opens the widest horizons;
6. explore different career goals;
7. assess strengths and weaknesses in relation to postsecondary schooling; and
8. develop a Personal Transition Profile.

Development of an ITP for a student with an academic orientation will obviously be directed more toward the academic competencies, modifications, and substitutions necessary for an individual considering postsecondary academic training. A special educator will, however, follow the same stages in the career assessment that would be followed for a student with a more vocational orientation. The difference rests in the types of tasks administered to the student. Besides the information gathered during the first stage of assessment, the special educator also needs to evaluate the student with an academic orientation in the areas of:

1. study skills (independent and guided);
2. computer literacy;
3. academic modifications needed across different subject matter (for example, extended time, books on tape, notetakers, reduced course load);
4. time management and organization skills;
5. independent living skills; and
6. knowledge of effective learning strategies.

Personal Transition Profiles

Students with special needs will be asked to provide background information about themselves, their disabilities, and the types of assistance they have received in the past as they enter postsecondary jobs and schooling. The special educator should work with the student to develop all this information into an organized plan for the student to take on interviews for jobs or school programs. A *Personal Transition Profile* containing all the important information about the student and can reduce frustration and save time and repetitive testing. The profile should contain the following information:

- latest academic testing results, including the test names;
- grade point average, or final high school transcript;
- SAT results, if taken;
- vocational or aptitude tests, if available;
- description of a student's learning style;
- description of a student's strengths and weaknesses without the use of professional jargon;
- assistance provided in secondary programs;
- modifications and accommodations provided during secondary schooling;

- career goals;
- description of work and study skill habits;
- verification of disability; and
- recommendations from teachers or other professionals who have worked closely with the student.

It is important for the student with special needs to recognize that the school or job placement cannot make modifications or accommodations without a psychological evaluation. The student and parents should be made aware of the importance of the report and should be cautioned to keep a copy on hand, but this information should be considered confidential and should not be released by the school without a written release. In addition, the student should be very careful about releasing confidential psychological information at a school or job. Only professionals with proper credentials should review this information. The special educator is an integral team member in the development of ITPs for students with special needs. Unfortunately, many professionals working on employment competencies with individuals demonstrating disabilities focus on program and curricula activities and ignore the role of evaluation in developing career goals (Hursh, 1989). Evaluation of cognitive ability, affective functioning, style of learning, academic performance, vocational abilities, and interests must be considered in developing effective college and vocational career transition programs. The special educator must learn to recognize appropriate evaluation tools that will provide the most efficient and effective information for planning career goals.

Summary

Introduction

1. Teachers working with students demonstrating special needs often focus on program or curricula activities and ignore the role of vocational evaluation in developing career goals.
2. Limited expectations for students with special needs on the part of teachers, parents, and the students themselves results in lack of consideration of many postsecondary choices available and focuses on careers that do not utilize students' strengths.
3. One of the primary objectives of evaluation should be to help students understand their disabilities so they can clearly describe them to others.
4. Career assessment results help evaluate all potential postsecondary opportunities, which include university or college training, technical school training, immediate entry into the work world, on-the-job-training with a job coach, or a sheltered workshop training program.

Legislation Promoting Postsecondary Education and Employment

1. PL 94–142 requires accurate, reliable, and effective evaluation to determine the presence of a disability.

2. PL 98–199 is often called the Transition Amendment because the intent of the law was to stimulate and improve development of secondary special education programs to increase the potential for competitive employment.

3. Section 504 of PL 93–112 deals directly with issues of assessment, accessibility to programs, rights to a public education, and elimination of discriminatory admissions procedures. Evaluation is cited as necessary before any subsequent change in placement.

4. The Carl D. Perkins Vocational and Applied Technology Education Act (1990) requires that all students receiving a vocational education participate in an evaluation to assist in developing appropriate career objectives.

5. The Individuals with Disabilities Education Act of 1990 (PL 101–476) requires for the first time that transition services be written into the annual IEP for *every* child 16 years of age and over (age 14 when appropriate).

6. A new paradigm in America is emerging that advocates an individual's rights rather than focusing on an individual's deficits.

The Assessment Process

1. Stage one of a career assessment includes gathering information pertaining to cognitive level, social/emotional functioning, appropriate communication modes, academic levels, and medical history.

2. The second stage in a career assessment involves collecting data pertaining to career awareness, interests, aptitude, learning style, work habits, and learning strategies.

3. The third stage in a career assessment is to observe an individual's behavior– occupational assets and liabilities during a real-world situation.

4. One of the most significant contributions computers have added to assessment is their ability to assist persons with disabilities in taking standardized tests through such modifications as voice-operated response units.

Transition from High School to the Real World

1. Statistics from follow-up studies indicate that many students with special needs are not as successful as they should be once they leave secondary settings.

2. The special educator works with a student and his or her parents in developing an Individualized Transition Plan (ITP).

3. The data collected from each of the stages of a career assessment is used to develop transitional competencies that are individualized to a specific student and written into that student's ITP.

4. An ITP that is written with an academic orientation is called an Individualized College Plan (ICP).

5. A Personal Transition Profile is a portfolio containing all the important information about a student, which he/she can take on interviews for jobs or school programs.

6. The special educator must be knowledgeable, recognizing appropriate evaluation tools that provide the most efficient and effective information for planning career goals.

Using Results

Critique and Integration of Assessment Data

Key Terms

Academic achievement
Background information
Behavioral observations
Cognitive functioning
General recommendations

Identifying information
Oral language functioning
Percentile rank
Person-oriented statements
Precision ranges

Professional judgment
Reason for referral
Social/emotional functioning
Specific recommendations
Test-oriented statements

Critique of Assessment Data

The special educator involved in the assessment of individuals with special needs should carefully evaluate assessment data from all past or current evaluations. Interpretation of assessment findings is generated by a variety of professionals and can easily lead to inappropriate recommendations if safeguards are not in place. Evaluation of the appropriateness of test tools and scores or interpretation of scores requires a sophisticated knowledge of psychometric assessment. It is the special educator's professional and ethical obligation to understand psychometric principles and assessment instruments and to update that knowledge. At times, the special educator may need to question the appropriateness of instruments used by other professionals. For instance, if a student demonstrates significant language or hearing problems, certain intelligence measures can be discriminatory if used as a measure of cognitive ability. In addition, a psychologist with little understanding of language disabilities may misinterpret an individual's performance. The special educator must advocate for administration of nonbiased assessment instruments for students with special needs.

The special educator is the most qualified member of the assessment team to translate psychological data into instructional recommendations. Application of assessment findings to teaching strategies requires a thorough understanding of the meaning of scores and knowledge of what the tests purport to measure. A critique of the appropriateness of psychometric data should include an evaluation of the following:

- reliability and validity of tests;
- test scores;
- clinical decisions;
- damaging findings; and
- recommendations based on the assessment findings.

Reliability and Validity

Members of the assessment team should ask whether the performance of the individual tested was a reliable indicator of that person's ability. Psychological reports provided to the assessment team from an outside evaluator (that is, a person not part of the school's assessment team) should contain a statement explaining the impact of the student's behavior during the testing on test accuracy. Members of the assessment team must consider the reliability and validity of all assessment tools used during an evaluation. This requires careful reading of test manuals and the literature from professional journals pertaining to the effectiveness of specific test instruments with certain populations of learners. (See chapter 3 for a thorough discussion of the principles governing reliability and validity.) It is important to consider the reliability and validity of all test instruments used during an assessment, not just those tests the special educator administers.

Evaluation of Test Scores

Precision Ranges

Whether a test measures broad cognitive ability or achievement, the special educator should always consider a student's score in relation to the test's precision range. The *precision range* is a combination of the standard error of measurement and the test's confidence level. Tests with lower reliability (higher confidence levels) have wider precision ranges. The special educator can identify precision ranges at different percent levels of precision by looking for charts in the test manual. For instance, if Mary, a 13-year-old student, received a Full Scale IQ of 100 on the WISC–III and a 90 percent level of precision was considered appropriate, the confidence interval would be 5. The precision range would be reported by stating that Mary obtained an IQ of 100 ± 5. Therefore, the chances that her range of scores from 95–105 includes her true IQ are about 90 out of 100. It is inappropriate to interpret a single score without looking at a student's precision range due to the reliability problems inherent in assessment tools. The special educator should identify or ask for a student's precision range on any test data being interpreted during an assessment staffing.

Subtest Scores

An individual's performance should be evaluated using both a normative comparison (age comparison) and an intraindividual comparison (individual profile). For instance, the average *percentile rank* for scores spans from the high average of the 84th percentile rank to the low average of the 16th percentile rank. Scores between the 25th percentile rank and the 75th percentile rank reflect average ability. Scores above the 84th percentile or below the 75th percentile are strengths or weaknesses relative to an individual's age peers. Quite often, however, the special educator will note strengths or weaknesses in an individual's own profile of scores. The majority of a student's scores on a reading measure might be at or below the 16th percentile, with the exception of one subtest score at the 40th percentile; this one subtest indicates a strength relative to the student's overall ability. While an individual's strengths or weaknesses must be evaluated in light of some standard (that is, comparison to the individual's age peers or to the individual's own performance), it is important that the comparison standard be clearly identified.

Interpretation of Test Data

The special educator often has the role of interpreting past or current psychological data to parents or students. This information can be presented by test-oriented statements or person-oriented statements (Sattler, 1988). The statement, "Peter obtained a standard score of 100 + (50th percentile) on a reading subtest" is an example of a *test-oriented statement*. As an alternative, the *person-oriented statement* would be, "Peter obtained an average score on a reading subtest." The choice of test-oriented or person-oriented statements depends on the purpose of the test interpretation. If the special educator is writing information for other professionals who will be working with a student, a test-oriented statement provides more specific information useful for decision-making or instructional purposes. On the other hand, if a special educator is talking with a parent or the student, a person-oriented statement provides adequate information in an understandable fashion to describe an individual profile of strengths and weaknesses.

Test information provided by either test- or person-oriented statements should be followed by discussion of the cognitive, social/emotional, or achievement skills required to complete a specific task. The score gives only one piece of information: functional level. Additional information is needed to understand a person's performance.

It is important that the special educator make clear that while a test might be labeled one thing (for example, reading comprehension) the problem a student has on that task might actually be caused by something unrelated to the name of the task (for example, receptive language skills). In addition, an individual might obtain discrepant scores on two tasks that purport to measure the same ability. It is the responsibility of the special educator to interpret the cause(s) of this discrepancy in performance.

Clinical Decisions

Unfortunately, professionals often put more faith in the "statistical" reliability and validity of test instruments than in their own professional judgments. As Smith (1988) stated, "where there is no need for professional judgment, there is no need for professionals" (p. 62). The entire evaluation process, from data collection to interpretation of results, falls within the providence of *professional judgment*. While much of the diagnostic evaluation is data-based, professional interpretation of results is a vital part of this process. Special education and school psychology programs provide graduate training to guide professionals in the best practices, policies, and professional ethics surrounding professional judgments. Given the imprecision, the theoretical vagueness, and the poor ecological validity of many norm-referenced measures available to professionals, the informed judgment of professionals will often be the most reliable means of measurement of a student's ability.

Damaging Information

The assessment team decides what information about a student's performance to present, either in a written or an oral report. No rules exist that specify what information should be included or excluded; rather, the use of good judgment and discretion is required of all professionals involved in the assessment process. According to Sattler (1988), "No matter how interesting or true it is, any information that does not contribute to an understanding of the referral question and to the clinical and psychoeducational evaluation is irrelevant and consequently should be left out of the report" (p. 733). For instance, is it important to report that the mother has had extramarital affairs or that the father was hospitalized ten years ago for manic depression? These questions must be considered carefully and, if presented, there should be a direct correlation to the diagnostic questions being addressed in the assessment process.

Student:_____   Grade Placement:_____
Date of Birth:_____   Special Education: _____yes   _____no
                                                     Area:_____

Assessment Section	Data Source	Content	Date of Assessment	Results
Background				

Activity
  Visual
  Auditory				

Behavioral Observations				
Social/Emotional				
Cognitive	Standardized			
	Dynamic			
Oral Language	Standardized			
	Dynamic			
	Criterion-based			
Achievement	Standardized	Reading Written Language		
	Curriculum-based	Math		
	Criterion-based			
	Dynamic			

FIGURE 14-1 Assessment profile

Integrating Assessment Data

Assessment data provides information for teachers, the individual evaluated, and parents or guardians. This information can be presented as an oral report or more formally in a written report. Reporting data to the individual tested or to parents requires a more elaborate translation of information than if the special educator is using this material only for classroom use. While shorthand or idiosyncratic notations about behavior or response style are fine for the short term, these data can be misinterpreted in the long term and when filtered through others. Thus, the special educator is encouraged to always write complete behavioral observations on all test data. All test protocols should be double-scored prior to reporting data; scoring errors are not atypical and can make a significant difference in a student's total score. A profile sheet that lists a student's assessment results can make data more accessible for integration for oral or written presentations, particularly when the past evaluations and records that are part of a student's file are extensive. Figure 14-1 shows how this information can be recorded in a manner useful to the special educator. It is imperative to remember that these data are confidential and should be stored in a locked file system. The more organized and complete the information is, the easier it will be to illustrate a student's patterns of strengths and weaknesses.

Oral Reports

Oral reporting varies in formality, length, and interaction depending upon the school system and the diagnostic team. A clear, concise, organized presentation of the information is the goal of any oral report. The profile sheet in Figure 14-1 will help ensure that the special educator remains focused on the data in an organized manner. A professional presentation of information lends credibility to the special educator's role on the diagnostic team and helps the individual tested and the parents feel confident of the professional's abilities. Credibility during a staffing is enhanced by a professional presentation and by the completeness of the data presented (Guerin and Maier, 1983). The special educator should discuss performance in behavioral terms, describing the actions of the student under observable conditions. Other information about the student relevant during a reporting session include skill levels, norm comparisons (local and national), work samples, strengths as well as weaknesses, guidance and feedback on strategies that parents or other professionals have provided, and interventions attempted or suggested for the future. Telephone reporting is discouraged. Only brief information should be communicated over the phone, and negative or controversial data should not be presented in this manner. The special educator should remember that a lengthy and detailed presentation of assessment data can be confusing and frustrating to parents and to the individual tested. Critical elements of the report may be missed when information is poorly presented. It is not uncommon for parents of students with special needs to also have similar types of disabilities. Therefore, the special educator should structure the information and the language used so that detailed information can be understood by both the student and the student's parents.

Written Reports

The written report provides an archive of background history, interviews, behavioral observations, psychometric evaluations, and classroom data. At times, the written report is used in court as evidence of placement or service needs. A written report is more than a simple summary of test scores; it is the integration of behavioral and psychometric data collected over time and by numerous examiners. Written reports can be of two types. One type of report focuses on an area or domain (that is, oral language, reading, social/emotional); the other type of written report integrates all domains evaluated during the assessment process. Either type of report can organize performance around specific evaluation tools (for example, WISC–III, WJ–R) or areas (for example, semantics, syntax, text structure) assessed during the evaluation process. Each paragraph of the report should highlight the main finding of the test or domain, and a summary paragraph at the end of each section should integrate the findings. The special educator new to report writing will usually find test-by-test report writing easiest to organize.

A typical report organizes data and interpretation in the following categories:

1. Identifying Information
2. Reasons for Referral
3. Background Information
4. Behavioral Observations
5. Acuity
6. Assessment Results
   a. Social/Emotional Functioning
   b. Cognitive Functioning
   c. Oral Language Functioning
   d. Academic Achievement
      i. Reading
      ii. Writing
      iii. Mathematics
      iv. Other
7. Summary
8. General Recommendations
9. Specific Recommendations

Identifying information.   The purpose of this part of the report is to provide all the *identifying information* pertaining to the person assessed for quick reference and a record for the file. Information usually listed in this section includes: name of individual tested, date of examination (DOE), birthdate of the individual (DOB), chronological age of the individual (CA), sex of the individual, ethnicity, date of the report, grade or employment, examiners involved in the assessment and staffing process, and names of formal or informal tests administered during the evaluation.

Reason for referral.   The second section of the report contains the *reason for the referral*. This section should be brief and summarize the referral source's questions and other relevant data. Behaviors that led to the referral should be summarized in this section along with specific questions the referring agency or individual has about the student to be assessed. The reason for the referral guides an examiner in selecting the appropriate assessment battery and in assessing which professionals should be involved in the evaluation. This information helps others understand why specific expertise and assessment tools were chosen for the evaluation of the individual referred for assessment.

Background information.   Information included in the *background report* is gathered from interviews and past records (for example, school, psychological, and medical). A summary is then written of the individual's developmental and academic history, current family constellation, and relevant family history. Pertinent information about a parent's occupation, education, and history should be included in this section. The background section should note any changes in referral problems from prior evaluations. Box 14-1 shows the background information provided for Peter, a 7-year-old male with a history of attentional deficit disorder/hyperactivity.

Box 14-1   *Background Information Report for Peter*

Peter was born prematurely at approximately six months' gestation. He was hospitalized in a neonatal unit for three or four months after birth. His birth weight was three pounds. During that hospitalization, he had seizures and there was some concern about the serious nature of his illness at that time. In the first few years of his life, Peter was hospitalized numerous times for respiratory problems and seizures. He was also said to be hypothyroid, but his thyroid function is currently normal without medication. His mother states that Peter sat up at six to eight months of age but did not walk until age 2. In retrospect, she believes that he has been overactive since about age 2. Peter has had numerous episodes of destructive behavior, such as tearing up his bed and other items in his room. She is often fearful for his safety. For example, at home he has climbed up on the roof four or five times to play with the electrical wires. The behaviors noted by the mother are consistent with those noted by others, including his teachers and medical personnel. These behaviors are of longstanding duration and have to a large extent been resistant to educational, pharmacological, and behavioral interventions.

Behavioral Observations.   The purpose of the behavioral observation section is to summarize the individual's behaviors within the context of the setting in which the individual is evaluated. *Behavioral observations* help support the diagnostic team's decisions by providing objective examples of behaviors used to form impressions of strengths and weaknesses. It is important to summarize the observations of a student across examiners, times of day, and types of task. The special education teacher may need to explain to parents or other nonprofessionals that the behaviors noted in a highly structured situation like an assessment do not always generalize to the classroom or home, where structure is more difficult to control. However, the information summarized in the behavioral observations can have significant implications for intervention and classroom management. Box 14-2 is an example of behav-

Box 14-2   *Behavioral Observation Report for Mary*

Observation during testing indicated that Mary was increasingly impulsive, inattentive, and distractible as testing progressed. Eye contact decreased as fatigue increased. At times, Mary commented on the difficulty of a task, suggesting that she was anxious about her performance. During administration of the Wechsler Intelligence Scale for Children–III, Mary demonstrated a blunted affect with a narrow range of emotions. According to the examiner, Mary seemed somber, even slightly depressed. Although she seemed to want to please the examiner, at times Mary needed frequent redirection and structure to stay on task. Her off-task behavior was not deliberate but seemed to be beyond her control as she became fatigued.

Box 14-3   *Acuity Report for John*

John was administered the Keystone Vision Screening before the evaluation began. His results showed no acuity problems, although he had to struggle to focus on some items. Although the screening was performed without John's glasses, he wore his glasses throughout the evaluation as needed.

Audiological testing was completed at the Speech and Hearing Clinic. Test results indicated hearing sensitivity to be within normal limits bilaterally. Puretone averages and speech reception thresholds were in good agreement, suggesting hearing sensitivity to be within normal limits bilaterally. Speech discrimination scores were 100 percent in each ear, indicating excellent word recognition abilities in a quiet environment.

---

ioral observations made during the evaluation of Mary, an 8-year-old female referred due to underachievement in school.

Acuity.   A visual and auditory acuity assessment of the individual should follow the behavioral observation section. A description of the tasks administered, who did the administration, and the individual's performance throughout the evaluation in relation to visual and auditory acuity should be reported. Box 14-3 contains an example of an acuity section for a report on John, a high school male referred due to behavior problems.

Social/Emotional Functioning.   The *social/emotional functioning* section includes behavior rating scales, self-report inventories, projectives, incomplete sentences, personality inventories, and clinical interview data collected during the assessment. Description of significant items endorsed on particular measures can help support impressions of social/emotional strengths and weaknesses. Information collected on any adaptive behavior assessment should be included in this section. Box 14-4 shows an example of a section on a social/emotional functioning report on Susan, an 8-year-old female referred for behavioral and academic problems.

Box 14-4   *Social/Emotional Functioning Report for Susan*

Susan's social/emotional status was assessed through an analysis of behavior checklists completed by her parents and teachers, an in-depth parent interview, projective testing, and observation during testing. Historically, Susan has had a difficult time concentrating both at school and at home. She has had a history of daydreaming, fidgeting, and making frequent complaints about not feeling well. Her parents and teachers have been concerned about her anxiety and poor self-esteem. Indications are that Susan's social/emotional outlook may be complicating her learning progress.

The parental viewpoint of Susan's social/emotional status was derived from information on the Achenbach Child Behavior Checklist and from an in-depth

(continued)

parent interview. The checklist requires that parents individually rate their child in various settings (for example, academic, social, home) compared to other children. The respondent rates the child's behavior on a scale of 0–Not True, 1–Somewhat or Sometimes True, and 2–Very True. Overall, Susan's mother rated her as having more problems (36 out of 112 items were rated either "Sometimes True" or "Very True") than did Susan's father (14 out of 112 items were rated either "Sometimes True" or "Very True"). Whereas the father rated very few obsessive-compulsive and somatic complaint items, the mother rated Susan's behavior as indicative of significant obsessive-compulsive tendencies, such as poor sleep habits, nightmares, overtiredness, and perfectionism, as well as indicative of somatic complaints, such as dizziness, headaches, nausea, and fatigue. These behaviors suggest that Susan is internalizing her feelings in contrast to externalizing them.

Both parents characterized Susan as getting along well with her half-sister, her parents, and her friends. They also agreed that she was doing average work in the language arts subjects (reading, English, and spelling) but that she was doing below average work in math. Although both parents viewed Susan as demonstrating stubbornness, sullenness, or irritability at times, her father indicated that Susan sometimes had temper tantrums, bit her fingernails, lacked energy, and was poorly coordinated, whereas Susan's mother rated these items "Not True."

During the parent interview, the mother and father reported that they both work. The father's job requires him alternately to be away from home for three weeks and at home for one week. He expressed how difficult it was to re-adjust to the home routine. He indicated that he knows that Susan feels discouraged about the fact that she cannot seem to please her father. During the interview, it became evident that, according to the father, Susan's mother tended to be more easy going than he with disciplinary matters, although she, too, was becoming frustrated with Susan during homework time. The mother also noted that Susan confided her anxiousness to her about a cousin's recent death and about a pen pal's recent cancer diagnosis.

The teacher's viewpoint of Susan's social/emotional status was derived from information on the Achenbach Child Behavior Checklist. The math/social studies/science teacher rated Susan as significantly high in the area of inattentiveness. The reading/language arts/spelling teacher rated Susan as significantly high in inattentiveness and social withdrawal. During school-related activities, both teachers noted that Susan demonstrated a high frequency of fidgeting, confusion, difficulty following directions, incomplete work, restlessness, and difficulty learning. They also noted that she demonstrated a moderate frequency of disobedience and classroom disturbance. With regard to self-concept and peer relationships, both teachers indicated that Susan seemed to feel inferior, that she got into fights from time to time, and that she tended to choose friends who got into trouble. Although they characterize her conduct as having improved this year, both teachers view her quality of work as variable (that is, good one day and poor the next), with poor attention and an inability to concentrate listed as overriding problems.

(continued)

Projective tests used to interpret Susan's social/emotional status were the Bender Gestalt Test for Young Children, the Draw-a-Person, the Kinetic Family Drawing, and a Sentence Completion Test. On the Bender Gestalt Test for Young Children, Susan was given a blank sheet of paper and was asked to copy eight designs composed of lines, dots, and geometric figures. An analysis of Susan's drawings indicates the presence of three emotional indicators: (1) confused order, suggesting poor organization and lack of planning; (2) small size, suggesting anxiety or withdrawal; and (3) second attempts, suggesting impulsivity. On the Draw-a-Person Test, Susan was given several blank sheets of paper and was asked to draw a person. She completed two full-page drawings, one a male and one a female. The female had minimal detail except for the face, which contained eyelashes, hair, and a smiling mouth. Susan described the drawing as "a happy 10-year-old girl." The male figure also contained minimal detail but was drawn with clothing and shoes. Susan described this drawing as a "happy boy." Both figures were lopsided. Although the bodies were facing forward, the heads of both figures were turned in a profile perspective, possibly suggesting an avoidance in facing problems. They were drawn with thick, heavy lines, suggesting anxiety. The female drawing had several erasures, suggesting a desire to do a good job.

In the Kinetic Family Drawing, Susan drew a picture of all the members of her family standing in a row in the yard near the house and the car. She explained to her examiner that her father was working with a hoe, the children were playing in the dirt, and her mother was taking groceries out of the car. Although all members are physically present and doing something, there is no evidence of meaningful interaction among them, suggesting that Susan views her family members as acting independently from one another and not as a cooperative unit.

In summary, Susan's social/emotional status is characterized by internalized feelings of anxiety, inadequacy, and depression. Although her conduct has improved this year, Susan continues to be disruptive in class. Outside of class, she fights occasionally with peers. Susan's parents and teachers view her as being distractible, inattentive, and impulsive as well as having a poor self-concept. There is evidence that Susan's social/emotional outlook is adversely influencing her learning progress.

Cognitive functioning.   The *cognitive functioning* section of a written report should include information collected across several measures of cognitive ability. The general intelligence measure and other measures of cognitive processing abilities are discussed in this section. A description of the types of tasks performed should be included along with the scores. These test scores are difficult for the student and parents to understand unless a description of the task demands and what the task purports to measure are included. Box 14-5 is an example of the cognitive section of a report on Linda, a college female referred for concern as to whether a specific learning disability was affecting her college performance.

Box 14-5   *Cognitive Functioning Report for Linda*

Linda's cognitive abilities were assessed utilizing the Wechsler Adult Intelligence Scale–Revised (WAIS–R) and selected subtests of the Woodcock–Johnson Tests of Cognitive Abilities (WJ–R). On the WAIS–R, Linda attained a Verbal IQ score of 100 (75th percentile), a Performance (nonverbal) IQ score of 115 (84th percentile), and a Full Scale IQ score of 113 (81st percentile). There is a 95 percent probability that her true ability as reflected by this instrument falls within a range of the 70–88th percentiles in relation to her peers. This places Linda in the high average range of abilities. When last evaluated (1980), the Wechsler Intelligence Scale for Children–Revised (WISC–R) was utilized, and Linda scored in the superior range. Decreases of this nature are not unusual, and although there were some differences in the pattern of her scorings, her overall strengths and weaknesses were consistent.

The WAIS–R is comprised of eleven subtests. Six of these comprise the Verbal Component; five form the Performance Component. A scaled score of 10 is considered average on each of these subtests. Linda's average was 12. Linda scored significantly higher on two of the verbal and two of the performance subtests relative to her peers. On the Verbal Scale, these were Digit Span and Comprehension, both at the 84th percentiles. On the Performance Scales, Linda's strengths were in Object Assembly (84th percentile) and Block Design (95th percentile). Digit Span is a task in which the client is asked to vocally repeat series of numbers presented orally; half are repeated in the order presented, half are revised. Although scoring well, Linda's performance was inconsistent. She frequently recalled one set accurately and the next inaccurately. When asked after the test how she had remembered the series, Linda described an unusual approach. She stated that she attempted to remember the overall pattern of the number in terms of high versus low numbers rather than remembering the specific numerals. Digit Span is usually accomplished through some form of sequential processing. It appears that Linda attempted to utilize a simultaneous process with an unexpected level of success.

Comprehension is a measure of common sense and reasoning in social situations. Block Design and Object Assembly are nonverbal problem solving tasks. In Block Design the student is required to duplicate designs utilizing blocks. In Object Assembly, the student is asked to assemble puzzles from pieces without a model. Both require abstract reasoning abilities and good spatial visualization. Observing Linda's method of accomplishing these tasks revealed a strong tendency to utilize simultaneous processing skills. She appeared to synthesize the information needed to complete the task and to then produce the figure as a whole. This contrasts with the sequential method of breaking into parts and producing the figures in an ordered fashion. Simultaneous processing and reasoning skills appear to be personal strengths for Linda.

Linda's scores revealed no weaknesses in relation to her peers. However, she scored significantly low in relation to her overall score on two subtests, Arithmetic and Digit Symbol, both at the 37th percentile rank. Arithmetic

(continued)

requires that the individual mentally perform mathematical calculations often presented as oral word problems. It requires computational skills, concentration, sequential processing, and speed of numerical manipulation. Linda required several items to be repeated and appeared to feel pressured by her awareness that some items were timed. At one point she commented, "I can't believe it's taking me so long," when in actuality she took no more than half the allotted time. All errors occurred on timed items. As will be discussed later, computational skills with pencil and paper pose no problem for Linda. Digit Symbol is also a timed task that requires the individual to produce symbols matched with numerals. A key is provided as a guide. The task requires visual sequencing abilities, concentration, and psychomotor speed. Sequential processing, speed of processing, and concentration appear to be significant weaknesses for Linda.

Linda was administered twelve subtests of the WJ–R Cognitive Battery. Linda scored in the high average range on all but three subtests. Strengths included her scores on the Listening Comprehension and Sound Blending subtests (86th percentile), Visual–Auditory Learning subtest (85th percentile), and the Analysis/Synthesis and Concept Formation subtests (84th percentile). Listening Comprehension requires the individual to listen to a paragraph and orally fill in the last word. This requires skills in auditory memory and verbal comprehension. Sound Blending requires the client to synthesize isolated sounds into meaningful words. The Visual–Auditory Learning subtest requires the client to associate visual symbols with words and to then read sentences constructed from these symbols. The client is given instruction and feedback. Thus, it represents an example of learning to read. Linda's errors were all substitutions of words with similar meanings (such as "small" instead of "little"), suggesting that she utilized her strong verbal comprehension skills to assist her with this task.

Linda scored in the average range on two subtests requiring the perceptual ability to deduct the whole when given only a part or a distortion of the whole. One task was auditory (Incomplete Words, 50th percentile); the other was visual (Visual Closure, 53rd percentile). Linda scored in the low average range in Visual Matching (27th percentile), which represents a relative deficit for her compared to her overall abilities. This task requires the individual to identify and circle two identical numbers in a row of six numbers. It is a timed task that requires visual–perceptual fluency and accuracy. Linda's score was lowered primarily due to speed of processing, although she did make one sequencing error.

Due to Linda's very slow rate of processing any of the tasks requiring reading, a number of instruments, including the Beery Test of Visual Motor Integration were not given. Thus, only Digit Symbol and her handwriting were available as qualitative measures of visual–motor production. The quality of execution of the symbols on Digit Symbol and her handwriting were below the average quality seen in this clinic. On the last previous evaluation of her abilities (1980), Linda was administered the Bender Gestalt. She scored well below average for her age. The report suggested that her errors were related

(continued)

to visual perception and motor production. It is likely that Linda still experiences weaknesses, if not deficits, in visual–motor production.

In summary, Linda exhibited a pattern of strengths and weaknesses that is indicative of cognitive processing deficits. She has high average cognitive abilities and exhibits above average skills in reasoning, conceptualization, and simultaneous processing of information. Linda consistently exhibited difficulties with tasks requiring sequential processing, concentration, and psychomotor speed and fluency. She also exhibited weaknesses in both auditory and visual closure. These deficits are affecting Linda's ability to process information most efficiently processed in an ordered, step-by-step fashion. These deficits also affect her ability to quickly produce visual–motor operations and to scan symbolic information in a timely manner. Her weaknesses in closure may also affect her perception of what she sees and hears in situations in which the stimuli are incomplete or distorted. For example, even though Linda has excellent auditory discrimination skills in a quiet room, she may have difficulty understanding a lecture if background noise is present.

Oral language functioning.   The *oral language functioning* section of a diagnostic report varies in length depending on the referral problems. In this section, information on standardized oral language measures as well as analyses of informal language samples or dynamic assessment tasks are summarized. To support conclusions about an oral language profile, it is important to include a description of the task and the demands it places on the individual being tested. Box 14-6 is an example of the oral language section of a report on Kathy, a secondary school female underachieving in school.

Box 14-6   ***Oral Language Report for Kathy***

Kathy's ability to understand single-word vocabulary items places her in the high average range (Peabody Picture Vocabulary Test, 77th percentile; WAIS–R Vocabulary, 75th percentile). Kathy is also able to understand idioms and metaphors as indicated by her performance on the Figurative Language subtest of the Test of Language Competence–Expanded (TLC–E) (91st percentile). Skills of this kind suggest that Kathy is able to learn and understand the more abstract meanings of words and phrases when they are placed in atypical contexts. For example, she was able to quickly and accurately explain the meaning of, "He is as transparent as we thought." High school level texts contain countless idioms and metaphors. Kathy's reading comprehension should be significantly improved if she is not bound to the literal interpretation of these expressions. Kathy was further able to make inferences about the probable outcome of social situations as indicated by her performance on the Making Inferences subtest of the TLC–E (84th percentile). Skills of this kind suggest that Kathy is able to formulate answers to questions when the informa-

(continued)

tion is not explicitly stated in the text. For example, she was able to select two probable causes for the outcome of a social situation when provided with only the following information: "Jack went to a Mexican restaurant. He left without giving a tip." Academically, inferential difficulties should aid reading comprehension. High school level texts are filled with inferential material and the ability to go beyond stated information is a highly valued skill.

Kathy does experience significant problems with other sentence level tasks. She clearly has difficulty interpreting sentences that contain words or phrases with multiple meanings (TLC–E, Ambiguous Sentences, 17th percentile). On this subtest, Kathy was able to identify "drew a gun" in the contexts of "pulling a gun from a holster" and "drawing a picture of a gun with a pencil." However, she was unable to retrieve even one meaning for "I don't know about you, but visiting relatives can be a nuisance." Kathy was unable to retrieve the meaning related to "going to visit relatives." Neither was she able to explain the meaning in the context of "relatives who come to visit." Difficulties of this kind suggest that Kathy has problems shifting to a second meaning for a word once she has established an initial meaning. There may also be times when Kathy is unable to identify even one meaning for words or phrases that are ambiguous. Academically, these kinds of problems may impair reading comprehension if the initial meaning that Kathy assigns to a word or phrase is incorrect and she is unable to retrieve the correct meaning. The interpretation of test questions and following directions may also be problematic for the same reasons.

Kathy experiences difficulty formulating sentences when specific constraints are imposed on the task. Rather than simply providing a verbal description of the pictured stimulus, she had to formulate a sentence incorporating three specific words (TLC–E, Recreating Sentences, 2nd percentile). Kathy has problems formulating grammatically correct sentences. Kathy's errors occurred in the form of run-on sentences. For example, she generated the following sentence when required to incorporate the words "actually," "although," and "wrong": "Actually this isn't the jogging suit I saw, although I like this one too, but this is the wrong size." Kathy's sentence was really two sentences: "Actually this isn't the jogging suit I saw. Although I like this one too, it's the wrong size." When the sentences are more correctly formulated as two sentences, the conjunction "but" becomes an erroneous addition. Kathy could have received credit for a sentence such as, "Although it's the wrong size, I actually like this suit better."

Kathy's event description, her trip to New York City, was extremely long and convoluted. She related almost every aspect that led up to the event. In fact, seventeen minutes into the description she had spent only the last four minutes of that time talking about actually being in New York City. This is particularly significant in light of the fact that most *entire* event descriptions are completed well within a three- to five-minute period. As would be expected, without minimizing minor aspects, Kathy's description became long and somewhat convoluted, making it rather difficult to follow what she was saying. Difficulties of this kind indicate problems organizing and reorganizing information so that important aspects are highlighted and insignificant details omitted.

(continued*)*

Kathy's rendition of the narrative she chose to talk about, "Fried Green Tomatoes," was problematic in that the story contained many of the excessive, rambling details evident in her event description. There was evidence of episodic structure and even some parallel and interactive episodes, suggesting good reasoning skills. However, within these components, Kathy frequently included the excessive details noted previously. Kathy's use of episodic structure suggests that she has the ability to organize and reorganize information, but this frequently dissolves into the sequential rendition of unnecessary details. Academically, Kathy's problems in this area will, in all likelihood, make it difficult for her to understand reading passages and write well-organized papers. She may also have difficulty organizing information for short answer and essay questions. Kathy may also experience difficulties in formulating answers to questions in class even though she knows the answer.

Kathy's problems understanding directions and interpreting multiple choice questions are further indications of her problems organizing and reorganizing information. For example, on a history multiple choice test provided by Kathy, she had to respond to a question about a "republic." In attempting to select the correct answer, Kathy decided to compare the characteristics of a "republic" and a "democracy." In doing so, she listed a few things common to a republic, but then, inadvertently slipped into describing a democracy. Kathy was unaware that she was no longer describing a republic; she was listing characteristics of a democracy as though they were characteristics of a republic. Kathy's original attempt to answer the question by comparing a republic with a democracy was generally ineffective, since the multiple choice answers made it clear that all possible answers related to characteristics of a republic. A more effective organizational strategy would have been to organize the choices according to which one was most characteristic of a republic. Kathy was dealing with erroneous information because she had unknowingly slipped from describing a republic to describing a democracy. Kathy's difficulty understanding directions is also a manifestation of her organizational problems. Even though she understands the vocabulary and sentence structure the instructor uses, her lack of good organizational categories makes it difficult for Kathy to place all the information in the appropriate context.

Kathy was an interested and animated conversational partner who not only maintained conversational topics but spontaneously elaborated them with her own thoughts and ideas. Once again, there were instances of overly detailed information. Kathy engaged in conversational repairs and adapted to the conversational needs of her partner using turn-taking skills in a timely and appropriate manner. She also responded appropriately to a variety of conversational closes.

In summary, many of Kathy's oral language skills fell within the high average to above average range. However, she did have problems formulating sentences and retrieving multiple meanings for words. Her most significant difficulty lay in organizing and reorganizing information. These skills are important for understanding any kind of spoken or written text or generating a written language product.

Academic achievement.   The *academic achievement* section includes a summary of the individual's performance across areas of achievement if appropriate for the age level. A preschool child's report would not include reading, written language, or mathematics data but might include a section on symbolic play. Again, a description of the task and the demands on the individual being evaluated should be included. Work samples from the classroom can be utilized in the written report. Box 14-7 is an example of the written language section of a report on Wally, a graduate-level adult male concerned about the possibility that a learning disability might be contributing to his difficulty in the area of writing.

Box 14-7   ***Written Language Report for Wally***

Wally's skills in written language were assessed through a variety of measures, formal and informal, as well as across different types of tasks. Areas assessed included spelling, mechanics, syntax, text structure, ideation, and sense of audience. Wally's spelling was first investigated by administering two standardized spelling tests. On the first spelling test, the Wide Range Achievement Test–Revised (WRAT–R), Wally's score fell in the 4th to 32nd percentile range. There is a 95 percent probability that this range is his true ability in relation to his peers. This task measures the ability to recall a word presented orally and then to write down the correct spelling.

Consistent with the scores Wally obtained on the Slingerland College Level Screening Instrument, he demonstrated difficulty when required to code a visual–verbal symbol (spelling word) to information presented orally utilizing a visual–kinesthetic mode of response (handwriting). On a second standardized instrument of spelling, the Peabody Individual Achievement Test–Revised, Spelling (PIAT–R), Wally's score fell within the 4th to 18th percentile range. There is a 95 percent probability that this range is his true ability in relation to his peers. In comparison to his WRAT–R score (recall), the PIAT–R spelling subtest measures the ability to recognize the correct spelling of a word from four foils. Therefore, on isolated and contrived spelling tasks, Wally demonstrated difficulty with both recognition and recall spelling tasks. Wally's spelling abilities were also measured across writing samples, which included a short essay where he described his learning problems, a stimulus paragraph he was asked to copy, and a sample of expository writing that Wally wrote on the computer. Spelling errors were not noted on the sample of writing generated on the computer. However, on the other two writing samples, significant difficulties with spelling were noted. On Wally's description of his learning problems, he wrote 300 words, and of these, twenty-seven were misspellings. The majority of these errors were high-frequency words. In addition, Wally had a tendency to make more errors on open-class words (nouns, verbs, adjectives, adverbs), suggesting the problem is less likely the result of syntax or morphological errors. Further analysis of his spelling errors indicated that 70 percent of Wally's misspellings were phonographical in nature. Phonographical errors are those misspellings

(continued)

that are phonetically similar to the stimulus word (for example, effort/effert; description/discription). Of the 70 percent of his misspelled words that were phonographical, 33 percent were sound-related syllable errors (cinder/cylinder; long/along). Wally also demonstrated significant spelling problems on a simple transcription task where he was asked to copy a paragraph. His errors on this task appeared predominantly to be omission errors (I/it; the/they).

Wally appeared to overrely on the phonetic spelling of words, possibly because visual processing of letters appears to be a deficit area for him. This is supported by his scores on the DTLA–A Reversed Letters (37th percentile) and the DTLA Visual Attention Span for Letters subtest (AE = 10–4). Visual–motor processing (handwriting/copying) of stimuli is also a weakness for Wally. This problem was documented by Wally's performance on subtests V and VI of the Slingerland, where he was required to code either visual or auditory stimuli and then reproduce the verbal and nonverbal information in writing. Wally appears to have no difficulty with the phonological and lexical–semantic (meaning) processing required for spelling. Rather, his difficulties appear to center on the organization, storage, and retrieval of letters and words, as well as the motor patterns required for writing letters or words.

Written syntax was investigated across the writing samples collected (that is, description of the learning problem, lesson plan, and computer generated essay) as well as on sentence combining exercises. No significant written syntax errors were noted on any of the samples of writing. It was noted that on his description of the learning problem writing sample, Wally's most typical sentence type was simple sentences (56 percent), which is not indicative of his reasoning abilities. However, it was felt that this was the result of the type of task, in particular the emotional focus of the task. On the computer generated writing sample, Wally used a variety of sentence types, complex sentences being the most common. On sentence combining tasks, Wally was asked to utilize embedding, substitution, and addition transformations. No difficulties with written syntax were noted; Wally's errors on these tasks were predominately punctuation (for example, omission of periods) and spelling errors (women/wemen; quickly/quickley). Problems with punctuation were also noted throughout his spontaneous writing samples. It was felt that this was a function of visual and motor processing deficits rather than a result of syntax errors.

Text structure was measured on both receptive and expressive tasks. First, a receptive measure of text structure was administered (Logical Relationships) on which Wally's performance was within the 92nd to 94th percentile range. Sentence organization and interparagraph and intraparagraph organization were also investigated across Wally's samples of written language. No significant problems with cohesion or coherence were noted throughout his writing. In addition, Wally's writings were evaluated using behavioral ratings for ideation and sense of audience. No significant problems were noted in either of these areas.

In summary, Wally performs quite well in all areas of academics with the exception of written language. Wally appears to have no difficulty with the

(continued)

phonological and lexical–semantic (meaning) processing required for spelling. Rather, his difficulties appear to center on the organization, storage, and retrieval of letters and words and the motor patterns required for writing letters and words.

Summary. The summary section of a diagnostic report should be short, no longer than one or two paragraphs, integrating all the data presented from the entire evaluation. Diagnostic labels or eligibility statements are introduced in the summary section. The purpose of the summary is to review and integrate all the data, presenting the conclusions of the diagnostic team. No new information should be introduced in this section. The special educator might consider incorporating topic sentences or summaries from each of the sections of the report in writing the summary section. Some diagnosticians prefer to include the summary section at the beginning of the report after identifying information. The special educator should organize the diagnostic findings in the summary section by identifying common patterns through and across the procedures and assessment domains as well as by integrating the main findings. Nay (1979) discusses two sources of error during the integration stage. One error is to form hypotheses prematurely, and the second is to form hypotheses on too little information. Finally, the impressions and conclusions of a diagnostic evaluation should be based on a theoretical focus, and this focus should be easy to identify in the written report.

General and specific recommendations. Recommendations are the last section of a written report. The recommendations should be tailored to the individual needs of the student evaluated. *General recommendations* usually pertain to suggestions for referral for further evaluation (optometrist, vocational trainer) or related services that need to be consulted (social worker, behavior specialist) or placement decisions. *Specific recommendations* pertain to intervention suggestions, modifications, or substitutions required for academic or behavioral objectives. This is one of the most important sections of the report, and it should receive a great deal of discussion and care by the individual(s) writing the report. The recommendations provided to parents or to the student are important for long-range planning. Recommendations should never be canned statements that can generalize to all individuals. Rather, recommendations are based on the individual's own profile of strengths and weaknesses, functional level, and environmental demands. In addition, recommendations should always be realistic and presented in a manner that is understandable to both the parents and the student. Unfortunately, development of effective recommendations for students with special needs has often been neglected on oral or written reports. Traditionally, assessment procedures have been static, leading only to diagnostic labels and placement decisions with very little application to teaching techniques. Recently, the concept of dynamic assessment has led professionals to reevaluate diagnostic models. Dynamic and criterion-referenced models of assessment have encouraged a direct link between assessment and intervention. The special educator must also examine the student's strengths, age, and ability level when developing appropriate recommendations. Recommendations should also be made for those individuals involved in the student's milieu (that is, parents, teachers, tutors, and others). Recommendations might need to address behavior management or the social/emotional needs of the student even though the presenting problem is academic.

Summary

Critique of Assessment Data

Reliability and Validity

1. The special educator should always investigate whether the performance of an individual evaluated was a reliable indicator of that student's ability.
2. Members of the assessment team should always consider the validity and reliability of test instruments used during an evaluation.

Precision Ranges

1. A student's score should be considered in relation to the test instrument's precision range.
2. The precision range is a combination of the standard error of measurement and the test's confidence level.

Subtest Scores

1. An individual's performance should be investigated looking at both a normative comparison and an intraindividual comparison.
2. An individual's strengths or weaknesses must be evaluated in relation to some standard.

Interpretation of Test Data

1. Person-oriented and test-oriented statements are two different ways of interpreting test results. The purpose of the interpretation of information will determine the type of statement to use.
2. Interpretation of psychometric tasks should be grounded in information gleaned from recent professional literature and empirical research.

Clinical Decisions

1. Professionals often put more faith in the reliability and validity of test instruments than in their own professional judgment.
2. Clinical judgment will at times be a more reliable means to measure a student's ability given the imprecision, theoretical vagueness, and poor ecological validity of most of the norm-referenced measures available to professionals.

Damaging Information

1. There are no rules that specify what information to include or exclude from an oral or written report. The use of good judgment and discretion is required of all professionals involved in the assessment process.
2. There should be a direct correlation between information in the report and the diagnostic questions being addressed in the assessment process.

Integrating Assessment Data

Oral Reports

1. Oral reporting varies in formality, length, and interaction depending upon the school system and the diagnostic team.
2. A clear, concise, organized presentation of the information is the goal of any oral report.
3. A professional presentation of information lends credibility to the special educator's role on the diagnostic team and will help the individual tested and the parents feel confident in the professional's abilities.

Written Reports

1. The written report provides an archive of background history, interviews, behavioral observations, psychometric evaluations, and classroom data.
2. The identifying information section provides all the demographics pertaining to the individual being assessed.
3. The reason for referral section should summarize the referral source's questions and other relevant data.
4. The background information is a summary of the individual's developmental and academic history, family constellation, and other relevant family background.
5. The purpose of the behavioral observation section is to summarize the individual's behaviors in the context of the setting in which the individual is evaluated.
6. The acuity section is a summary of any relevant information pertaining to the individual's auditory or visual acuity performance; either formal or informal measures may be reported.
7. The social/emotional functioning section includes any behavior rating scales, self-report inventories, projectives, incomplete sentences, personality inventories, or clinical interview data collected during the assessment.
8. The cognitive functioning section includes a summary of any broad cognitive measures (IQ tests) as well as any specific cognitive processing assessment tools utilized during the evaluation.
9. The oral language section includes a summary of any standardized oral language tests administered as well as analyses of informal language samples or dynamic assessment tasks collected during the assessment.

10. The academic achievement section includes a summary of the individual's performance across areas of achievement.
11. The purpose of the summary is to provide a concise statement that integrates all the evaluation findings.
12. The recommendations should be tailored to the individual needs of the student evaluated.

Making Decisions

Key Terms

Annual goals
Individualized College Plan
(ICP)
Individualized Education Program (IEP)

Individualized Family Service
Plan (IFSP)
Individualized Transition Plan
(ITP)

Multidisciplinary team
Short-term objectives

The special education teacher is required by federal law to develop an individualized instructional plan for each student placed in special education based on specific assessment documentation. In addition to these formalized objectives, a means to monitor progress must also be incorporated into the plan. The *Individualized Educational Program* (IEP), a key component of Public Law 94–142, the Education for All Handicapped Children Act (EAHCA), provides the means by which this mandate can be operationalized. Recently, the Education of the Handicapped Amendments (PL 99–457) extended initiatives of PL 94–142 to infants, toddlers, preschoolers, and their families. PL 99–457 focuses on family-centered intervention rather than the student/school approach of the IEP. The *Individualized Family Service Plan* (IFSP) is the document of family goals and objectives used to monitor family support and training. In addition to concern for preschool children, the federal government recognized the need for providing better direction to secondary students making the transition from high school to either the work world or postsecondary schooling. Therefore, in the Education for the Handicapped Amendments of 1983, a section was included on Secondary Education and Transition Services (section 626). The Education for the Handicapped Amendments of 1986 further reinforced concern for transitional services. The *Individualized Transition Plan* (ITP) is the formalized document used to record goals and objectives for students in special education who require specific transitional services. Siperstein (1988) recommends that professionals develop *Individualized College Plans* (ICPs) for students with special needs who are entering colleges and universities. All of these individualized instructional plans were designed to comply with the law's intent of an appropriate education for students with special needs. Since the IFSP, ITP, and ICP are recent developments, this discussion will focus on the research pertaining to the IEP. Implications for the IFSP, ITP, and ICP will be discussed at the conclusion of the chapter.

Research investigating the effectiveness of the IEP over the last decade has led researchers to suggest that the intent of the EAHCA is not being met (Smith, 1990; Smith and Simpson, 1989). While Turnbell (1986) postulated that the IEP is reflective of special education's best thinking, there appears to be a discrepancy between theory and practice. Despite data to support a concern for the current IEP process, few position or research papers in the professional literature explore this problem. The few articles that have investigated problems with the IEP process appear to place the blame on mechanistic philosophies and bureaucracy (Heshusius, 1982; Mehaw, Hertweck, and Meihls, 1986). Whether these two variables will be supported by research as the source of the problem with the IEP process remains to be seen. The apathy, however, on the part of professionals to explore this problem to a greater extent is difficult to understand in light of the relationship between the IEP and classroom instruction. Direct design and delivery of instruction is, by mandate of federal law, to be piloted by the IEP. If the IEP is not a reliable mechanism for delivery of services, it raises questions about the effectiveness of "specially designed instruction" currently advocated in the field of special education. Certainly, the research for the validity of this instruction is suspect when the means to reach that goal are unreliable.

Chronicle of the IEP

An investigation of the history of the IEP can provide a better understanding of the current problems faced by professionals attempting to comply with the federal mandates. Smith (1990) reviewed the IEP literature from 1975 to 1989 and divided the research and position papers into three phases. The first phase, the normative phase, Smith defines as a period of time when professional literature focused on explaining the concepts and provisions of the EAHCA. At that time, authors such as Morrissey and Safer (1977) explicitly raised concerns about the lack of proper training of professionals for developing IEPs, paper compliance problems, and group variance. Smith (1990) labels the second phase of the history of the IEP as the analytic phase. During this phase, research focused on teacher perceptions of the IEP process and the effectiveness of the team approach required by the federal mandates. Researchers found little correlation between objectives developed for the IEP and psychoeducational assessment (Schenck, 1980). In addition, there was little connection made between assessment and instructional needs. This lack of synthesis between IEP objective and classroom activities lead Gerardi, Grohe, Benedict, and Coolidge (1984) to state that the IEP might be the "single most critical detriment to appropriate programming for these children" (p. 39), not because of philosophical or educational theory but due to the bureaucracy it tends to foster. The final phase that Smith (1990) discusses in the evolution of the IEP is the technology-reaction phase. During this phase the focus has been on development of computer-assisted systems to manage the data involved with the IEP process. The majority of studies conducted during this phase have focused on the time and cost-effectiveness of such data management systems (Davis, 1985; Ewell, 1983; Minick and School, 1982). The concern over "quality" has been replaced by "cost/time effectiveness" jargon. As Smith (1990) stated, "Use of technology to formulate IEPs represents a response to the failure of special education practice to conceptually embrace the concept of what we know about IEPs, versus what we do. Thus, efforts now are undertaken to ensure minimal compliance, the very nature of which the EAHCA was intended to preclude" (p. 11).

The IEP Multidisciplinary Team

A key concept in the IEP process is use of a *multidisciplinary team* for decision making and planning. Federal mandates call for a team of professionals and parents to make the important decisions for the IEP. The rationale is that different perspectives on the development of an individualized plan of instruction will ensure more effective and efficient objectives. Some critics of the multidisciplinary team have argued that the use of a team approach is based on logical assumptions rather than on empirical research (Crisler, 1979; Kehle and Guidubaldi, 1980). Certainly the low incidence of training programs in higher education that provide opportunities for school personnel to develop the competencies required to work effectively on multidisciplinary teams remains a problem. Thus, members often do not have clear expectations about what they and others are suppose to do at meetings. The level of perceived participation among members varies greatly. Often, the psychologist on the team is given total control of the meeting and encourages little input from other members of the team who have much more expertise in the areas of language, academics, instruction, and classroom management. Another problem that restricts the effectiveness of multidisciplinary teams is the high rate of absenteeism of key team members (Comptroller General of the United States, 1981; Smith, 1990; Smith and Simpson, 1989). Team members often give little attention to implementation of decisions made at IEP meetings, almost appearing to fear taking responsibility for decisions made regarding a student's IEP, even though "the IEP is not a performance contract which can be held against a teacher if the handicapped child does not meet the IEP objectives" (U.S. Department of Education *Policy Paper*, April 30, 1980, p. 27).

A central principle clearly articulated in the EAHCA is the positive impact on a student's instructional progress when parental participation is part of the planning process. Therefore, a key member of the IEP should be the parent(s) or guardian(s) of a student with special needs. Researchers investigating the role of parents during the IEP process have focused on professionals' perceptions of parent roles (Gilliam and Coleman, 1981), parents' real roles (Goldstein, Strickland, Turnbull, and Curry, 1980), and the perception of parents of their role (Lusthaus, Lusthaus, and Gibbs, 1981). The results of the research pertaining to parental roles supports the concept that parents are not encouraged to take an active role during the IEP process because they are perceived by school professionals as recipients of information (Smith, 1990). Witt, Miller, McIntyre, and Smith (1984) reported, however, that parents have generally been satisfied with the IEP process and its outcomes. More research is needed to explore the perceptions of parents across developmental ages, socioeconomic levels, geographic locations, severity of disabilities, and types of disabilities.

The regular education teacher has been neglected by researchers in their investigations of the usefulness of the multidisciplinary team. However, regular education teachers appear to be ranked as important members of the IEP team even though their contributions to decision making are considered minimal (Gilliam and Coleman, 1981). The few studies that have investigated regular education teacher participation in IEPs note their peripheral involvement in the process (Nevin, Semmel, and McCann, 1983; Pugach, 1982). Discussing the lack of regular education involvement during the IEP process, Pugach (1982) states, "It is unlikely that this

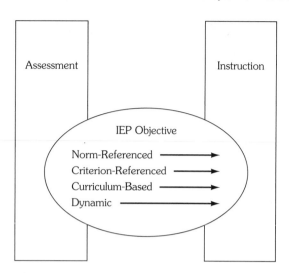

FIGURE 15-1 Connection between assessment, objectives, and instruction

approach promotes shared decision making or encourages consistent curricular modifications across instructional settings" (p. 374).

Research investigating the perception of special education teachers' concerns regarding the IEP generally conclude that many of these teachers feel that the IEP is a general guide to helping students with special needs. Yet these same teachers stress serious concern regarding the negative impact of the IEP on their workload, particularly the excessive amount of paperwork required by the process (Dudley–Marling, 1985; McGarry and Finan, 1982). Special education teachers often voice criticism toward their school administrations for not providing sufficient support, such as clerical assistance and time during the day, to accomplish the management of the IEP development and administration of services. Special education teachers state that they could teach and children could learn just as well without the IEP process as it is currently administered (Dudley–Marling, 1985; Joseph, Lindgren, Creamer, and Lane, 1983).

One problem special education teachers identify with the IEP process pertains to the lack of a relationship between the IEP goals and objectives and their own instructional plans. Unfortunately, it is rare when the IEP serves as the basis for developing a detailed instructional plan. This is not a problem with the IEP process itself as much as it is with the training of many special education teachers. Due to a lack of assessment knowledge, poor theoretically based teacher training programs, and weak observational skills, many special education teachers fail to see the interconnection between assessment, objectives, instruction, and the IEP (See Figure 15-1). With the growing popularity of dynamic assessment, it is possible that the perceptual gap between assessment and instruction will narrow.

Philosophical Perspectives and the Future of the IEP

The Regular Education Initiative (REI) and the full inclusion model are terms used to label current movements advocating "full access to a restructured mainstream" for students with special needs (Skrtic, 1987). Such models advocate for fewer pull-out (special) programs and stress working with students within the regular class-room. If special education moves toward inclusion of students with special needs the regular mainstream curriculum, the purpose and effectiveness of the IEP is certain to be questioned. Will the IEP be abandoned, or will it be used for all students with or without disabilities?

Considering the IEP process, Skrtic (1987) has encouraged the use of theory to guide future special education reform and decision making. The behavioral and constructivist theories are the two paradigms with a significant impact on assessment and instruction in the area of special education today. The behavioral model, as Reid and Hresko (1981) noted, was legalized in PL 94–142 through the mandate for quantitative measurement of goals and behavioral objectives (Heshusius, 1986; Poplin, 1985). According to Heshusius (1989), the behavioral model (a) assumes the problem is within the student; (b) segments learning into pieces; (c) is deficit driven; (d) regards teaching as unidirectional, that is, the teacher gives to the student; (e) assumes correct and incorrect strategies; and (f) regards school goals as life goals. The constructivist focuses on the individual as active, constructing learning on an ongoing basis. Purpose becomes the driving force for constructivist theory. According to Heshusius (1989), such a position holds that "It is not the case that the dynamics of the whole can be understood from the properties of the parts, but rather, that the properties of the parts can only be understood from the dynamics of the whole. The whole is both different from and more than the sum of its parts" (p. 412). Dynamic assessment is an example of constructivist theory. The question to special educators is how to best utilize theory, either in isolation or in combinations, to better develop the IEP process into effective and efficient individual instructional programs for the school of the future.

Individualized Education Program: Today's Model

The term *Individualized Education Program* was carefully chosen by the architects of PL 94–142. *Individualized* addresses the needs of a single individual. *Education* refers specifically to special education and related services. The word *program* means a statement of what will be provided to the individual receiving services. Following is the definition of the term IEP as written in PL 100–476, which was written from PL 94–142:

> The term individualized education program means a written statement for each individual with a disability developed in any meeting by representatives of the local educational agency or intermediate educational unit who shall be qualified to provide, or supervise the provision of, specially designed instruction to meet the unique needs of individuals with disabilities, the teacher, the parents or guardian of such individuals, and, whenever appropriate, such individuals, which statement shall include (a) a statement of the present levels of educational performance of such, (b) a statement of annual goals, including short-term instructional objectives, (c) a statement of specific educational services to be provided to such individuals, and the extent to which such individuals will be able to participate in regular educational programs, (d) the projected

date for initiation and anticipated duration of such services, an appropriate objective and criteria and evaluation procedures and schedules for determining, on at least an annual basis, whether instructional objectives are being achieved.

PL 100–476 clearly defines two components of the IEP process. First, there must be an IEP meeting in which school personnel and parents make decisions cooperatively pertaining to the educational program of the student with special needs. Second, as a result of this meeting, a written record of the decisions made by the IEP committee must be produced. The written service plan is the final product of the IEP commitee's job and should include the following data:

- student's current level of performance,
- annual goals to be met by the end of the academic year,
- short-term objectives that are steps in mastering the annual goal(s),
- documentation of specific special education and other related services to be provided for the student,
- identification of material and methods required to provide for the needs of the student,
- documentation of specific personnel who will implement the recommended instructional program,
- estimation of the time the student will spend in a regular education classroom,
- estimated time for the initiation and duration of services,
- evaluation procedures and schedules for the mastery of the student's short-term objectives, and
- identification of the IEP committee members' roles and their signature on the IEP.

The IEP is not restricted to academics. It is often appropriate for annual goals and short-term objectives to be written in the areas of social adjustment, vocational education, physical education, and adaptive behavior. A student's instructional program is designed around stated annual and short-term objectives.

Annual goals.   *Annual goals* refer to broad statements that define what the IEP committee expects the student to do or know by the end of the academic year. Annual goals should meet the following three criteria:

1. Be based on assessment data, including strengths/weaknesses and preferred learning style (White and Haring, 1980);
2. Be recognized by the IEP team, both parents and professionals, as high-priority items (White and Haring, 1980); and
3. Include cognitive, motor, and social/emotional skills as well as deal with vocational and self-help skills when applicable (Reid and Hresko, 1981).

Short-term objectives.   *Short-term objectives* pertain to how we specifically expect a student to get from point "a" to point "b." Short-term objectives are "measurable intermediate steps between the present levels of performance and the annual goals" (U.S. Department of Education, *Policy Paper,* April 30, 1980, p. 22). A short-term objective must include the following:

1. Provide a description of the desired performance,
2. Give conditions under which the desired performance should occur, and
3. List the criteria for adequate performance.

The special education teacher faces a problem when the goals and objectives developed for the IEP lead only to sanctified activities that are not sensitive to the dynamic changes going on in the classroom. Teaching is not doing preset activities but is a response to the needs of the individual students. Responsive teaching defies prescriptions for action. As Bussis, Chittenden, Amarel, and Klausneg (1985) state:

> The trick is sensing when to provide information, what to provide, how much to provide, and how long to keep on providing it. From what we have been able to observe, important clues for making these decisions come from the children. . . . Children are neither fragile nor prone to give up too easily. They will keep on signaling what information they need in one way or another." (p. 197)

An example of an IEP profile form is shown in Figure 15-2.

Extensions of the IEP

Individualized Family Service Plan (IFSP)

The major provisions of PL 94–142 were reaffirmed and expanded through PL 99–457, Education of the Handicapped Act Amendments of 1986. One of the most significant changes made through PL 99–457 was extension of services to children ages 3 to 5 by the 1990–91 school year, as well as providing incentives for initiation of networking among statewide interagency programming for infants and toddlers with disabilities and their families. PL 99–457 requires an Individualized Family Service Plan (IFSP), which describes the services to be provided to the child and to the family of the child. The law specifies that all the services be provided by qualified personnel, and the state must have a system for establishment and maintenance of standards, certification, and licensing policies (Ballard, Ramirez, and Zantal-Wiener, 1987). The IFSP is similar to the IEP with the exception that the plan must address the needs of both the child with a disability and his or her family. The federal mandate requires that the IFSP contain the following:

- performance levels across cognitive, oral language, psychosocial, motor, and adaptive behavior of the child;
- assessment of the family's current strengths and weaknesses in enhancing the child's development;
- short-term goals for child and family;
- long-term goals for child and family;
- criteria, procedures, and timelines for determining child and family progress;
- detailed description of early intervention services needed for both the child and the family;
- detailed description of the methods, frequency, and duration of services needed for both the child and the family;

Child's Name_____ Date of Birth_____

Parents' Names_____ Phone_____

Address_____

Grade_____ Teacher_____

School_____ District_____

I. **Present Level of Educational Performance** (academic, emotional maturity, self-help skills, vocational skills, prevocational skills).
   A. *Formal and Informal Assessment* (any evaluations done on this child. This includes psychological testing scores and interpretations, speech pathologist reports, occupational and physical therapy reports, physician reports, counselor reports).
   B. *Child's Learning Characteristics* (how the child learns).
   C. *Socioemotional Behaviors* (child's behavior with adults and peers).
   D. *Sensory and Motor Skills* (vision, hearing, fine and gross motor skills).
   E. *Physical and Medical Assessment.*
   F. *Current Teacher's Report.*

II. **Annual Goals** (overview of the student's program for the year).
   A. One goal should be written for each area of special instruction. The goals should be clearly stated.
   B. Consider: math, language, science, social studies, health, home economics, technology, art, music, physical education, library, lunch, recess periods, extracurricular activities, self-help skills, language, and motor development.

III. **Short-Term Objectives** (attached on separate sheets).
   Be sure that there is a hierarchical list of objectives for each of the annual goals listed.

IV. **Specific Special Education and Related Services to be Provided.**
   A. Remember to place the child in the least restrictive environment and with as many nonhandicapped children as possible.
   B. Consider whether the child needs occupational or physical therapy, speech therapy, notetakers, adaptive physical education, individual or family counseling.
   C. Consider transportation issues and accessibility of the building and the services.
   D. Determine whether any equipment will be required, such as hearing aids, touch talkers, wheelchairs, tape recorders, braille equipment, and so forth.

V. **Amount of Integration in Regular Education Classes.**
   Although the IEP does not have to specify goals for regular education classes, there should be at least a listing of the academic and nonacademic areas the child will be mainstreamed into for the year.

VI. **Projected Initiation Date and Anticipated Duration of Services.**
   The dates should be as specific as possible and include at least an annual review date.

VII. **Other Recommendations.**
   Consider anything not covered above.

Date:

Signature of Participants	Title
_____	_____
_____	_____
_____	_____
_____	_____
_____	_____

Everyone who was present at the meeting and had input into the IEP should sign the form to show their approval of the plan.

FIGURE 15-2 Example of an Individualized Education Program.   *Source:* Reprinted with permission from B. P. Tucker and B. A. Goldstein (1991), *Legal Rights of Persons with Disabilities: An Analysis of Federal Law* (pp. I-1 to I-3). Copyright © 1991 by LRP Publications (Horsham, PA). All rights reserved.

- projected dates for the beginning of services and expected duration of services needed for both the child and the family;
- name of the case manager; and
- procedures for transition from early intervention into the preschool program.

While the IFSP must contain all of the items listed above, it should also be designed to allow for flexibility in the implementation of services. The IFSP must be reviewed at least *every* six months and be fully evaluated at least annually (Ballard, Ramirez, and Zantal–Wiener, 1987).

Individualized Transition Plan (ITP)

The ITP grew out of a concern for providing transitional services to students with special needs as they move from the public school to community agencies or into the world of work. The process of moving from secondary programs to postsecondary opportunities is known as transition. In the Education of the Handicapped Amendments of 1983, a section was added called Secondary Education and Transition Services (section 626), which authorized funds for research, training, and demonstration programs in the area of transition. The Education of the Handicapped Amendments of 1986 further renewed the emphasis on transitional services. The ITP may be part of the IEP, but if so, it must be addressed differently. While the selection of personnel involved in development of a student's ITP will vary across individualized needs, there must be "joint involvement of school personnel who have the responsibility for training and job procurement as well as human service providers who could offer support and follow-up during the student's adulthood" (Wehman, Moon, Everson, Wood, and Barcus, 1988). The ITP must contain the following:

- short-term goals that include the skills necessary to function at home, in the community, and on the job;
- long-term goals that include the skills necessary to function at home, in the community, and on the job; and
- transitional services required such as appropriate agencies, job placement, or follow-up on the job.

The transition process should be one that evolves slowly over a period of time, beginning early, preferably in the ninth grade. The 1990 amendments of PL 94–142 require that transition goals be included in the IEP for any student age 16 or older. There should be no pressure for a family to make quick, final decisions. Parental involvement in the development of the ITP is mandated by federal law. Parents are encouraged to explore transitional programs and postgraduate options with their child. However, the student with special needs is the vital member of the ITP team. By allowing students more responsibility in planning vocational goals, the student learns to be more accountable, becoming independent and increasing his or her self-worth (Rappleyea and Choppa, 1989).

Some students with special needs develop the skills in their secondary programs that will allow them to be eligible to attend college and university. As mentioned earlier, Siperstein (1988) advocates development of Individualized College Plans (ICP) for such students. Since the needs of a student planning on college are somewhat different from those of students considering job/employment goals, the ICP is more specific to postsecondary goals. The ICP should include:

- substitutions and modifications needed for success in a college or university setting;
- coping skills necessary to learn effectively;
- resources available;
- plan of study;
- learning profile of a student's strengths and weaknesses; and
- learning strategies.

Future Needs

Research and professional perceptions support a need to question the efficacy of the IEP document and its relationship to the EAHCA. Recommendations from the literature advocate the need for more inservice (Nadler and Shore, 1980), better preservice training (Schenck, 1981), better coordinated compliance enforcement (Dodaro and Salvenmini, 1985; McGarry and Finan, 1982), a modification in parent involvement (Gerardi, Grohe, Benedict, and Coolidge, 1984), and a better system for allowing professionals to procedurally prescribe individualized education (Smith, 1990). Certainly, there is a need for a stronger interaction between instruction and assessment as it pertains to the IEP. IEPs of the future will also need to include more of a student's strengths, not just weaknesses, in an attempt to encourage the development of independence. The time has come to reevaluate the present format and theoretical concept of the IEP. As Smith (1990) states, "Alternative options to implementing special education, as the reform literature offers, may provide a recovery of the IEP to operate with its fullest intention. Perhaps the answers to the IEP problem can be found in the reform efforts divergent thought" (p. 12). The special educator has the opportunity to participate in this time of change. Knowledge of different assessment methods of evaluating students with special needs— norm-referenced, criterion-based, curriculum-based, and dynamic—will provide the vital link between the instructional needs of students and the assessment data such that the IEP of the future better meets the needs of students, parents, teachers, and others involved in striving to help a student meet his or her greatest potential.

Summary

Introduction

1. The special education teacher is required by federal law to develop an individualized education program for each student placed in special education based on specific assessment documentation.
2. The Individualized Education Program (IEP), a key component of Public Law

94–142, the Education for All Handicapped Children Act (EAHCA), provides the means by which this mandate can be operationalized.

3. Recently, the Education of the Handicapped Amendments (PL 99–147) extended initiatives of PL 94–142 to infants, toddlers, preschoolers, and their families.

4. Individualized programs for preschoolers focus on family-centered intervention rather than the student/school approach of the IEP. The Individualized Family Service Plan (IFSP) is the document of family goals and objectives used to monitor compliance with the federal law.

5. The Individualized Transition Plan (ITP) is the formalized document used to record goals and objectives for students in special education who require specific transitional services.

6. Individualized College Plans (ICP) are the formal plans developed for those students with special needs who are entering college or university.

7. Researchers investigating the effectiveness of the IEP over the last decade have indicated that the intent of the EAHCA is not being met.

Chronicle of the IEP

1. Smith (1990), reviewing the IEP literature from 1975 to 1989, divided the research and position papers into three phases. The first phase, the normative phase, Smith defines as a period of time when professional literature focused on explaining the concepts and provisions of the EAHCA.

2. Smith (1990) labels the second phase of the history of the IEP as the analytic phase. During this phase, research focused on teacher perceptions of the IEP process and the effectiveness of the team approach required by the federal mandates.

3. The final phase that Smith (1990) discusses in the evolution of the IEP is the technology-reaction phase. During this phase, the focus has been on development of computer-assisted systems to manage the data involved with the IEP process.

The IEP Multidisciplinary Team

1. A key concept in the IEP process is the use of a multidisciplinary team for decision making and planning.

2. The level of participation among members of the team varies greatly.

3. Parents are often not encouraged to take an active role during the IEP process because they are perceived by school professionals as recipients of information.

4. Regular education teachers are ranked as important members of the IEP team although their contribution to decision making is considered minimal.

5. Special education teachers stress concern regarding the negative impact of the IEP on their workload, particularly the excessive amount of paperwork required by the process.

6. One of the problems special education teachers identify with the IEP process pertains to the lack of relationship between the IEP goals and their instruction.

Philosophical Perspectives and the Future of the IEP

1. The behavioral and the constructionist theories represent the two paradigms that have a significant impact on assessment and instruction in the area of special education today.
2. The behavioral model (a) assumes the problem is within the student; (b) segments learning into pieces; (c) is deficit driven; (d) regards teaching as unidirectional, that is, the teacher gives to the student; (e) assumes correct and incorrect strategies; and (f) regards school goals as life goals.
3. The constructionist theory focuses on the individual as an active participant, constructing learning on an ongoing basis.
4. The question to special educators is how to best utilize theory, either in isolation or combinations, to better develop the IEP process into effective and efficient individualized education programs for the schools of the future.

Individualized Education Program: Today's Model

1. The term individualized education program was carefully chosen by the architects of PL 94–142. *Individualized* addresses the needs of a single individual. *Education* refers specifically to special education and related services. *Program* means a statement of what will be provided to the individual receiving services.
2. The IEP is not restricted to academics. Therefore, it is often appropriate for annual goals and short-term objectives to be written in the areas of social adjustment, vocational education, physical education, and adaptive behavior.
3. Annual goals refer to broad statements that define what the IEP committee expects the student to do or know by the end of the academic year.
4. Short-term objectives pertain to measurable steps between the present level of performance and the annual goal.

Extension of the IEP

1. One of the most significant changes made through PL 94–457 was extension of services to children ages 3 to 5 by the 1990–91 school year, as well as providing incentives for the initiation of networking among statewide agency programming for infants and toddlers with disabilities and their families.
2. PL 94–457 requires an Individualized Family Service Plan (IFSP) that describes the services to be provided to the child and the family of the child.
3. In the Education of the Handicapped Amendments of 1983, a section called Secondary Education and Transition Services was added (section 626), which authorized funds for research, training, and demonstration problems in the area of transition.
4. The Individualized Transition Plan (ITP) is developed during a student's secondary program and provides the student with the competencies to make the transition from school to the world of work.
5. An Individualized College Plan (ICP) should be developed for students planning to go on to a college or university setting. Such a plan is geared to preparing a student to handle the academic demands of postsecondary programs.

Future Needs

1. Research and professional perceptions support a need to question the efficacy of the IEP document and its relationship to EAHCA.
2. Recommendations from the literature advocate the need for more teacher inservice pertaining to the IEP, better coordinated compliance enforcement of the IEP, modification in parent involvement during the IEP process, and a better system for allowing professionals to procedurally prescribe individualized education.
3. Greater interaction between the IEP goals and instruction is needed.
4. The time has come to reevaluate the present format and theoretical concepts of the IEP.

APPENDIX A:
ADDRESSES OF TEST PUBLISHERS

ACADEMIC THERAPY PUBLICATIONS, 20 Commercial Blvd., Novato, CA 94949

AMERICAN ASSOCIATION ON MENTAL RETARDATION, 1719 Kalcrama Road, N.W., Washington, DC 20009

AMERICAN GUIDANCE SERVICE, Publishers' Building, P.O. Box 99, Circle Pines, MN 55014

ASPEN SYSTEMS CORPORATION, 1600 Research Blvd., Rockville, MD 20850

BEHAVIOR SCIENCE SYSTEMS, INC., P.O. Box 1108, Minneapolis, MN 55440

BER-SIL COMPANY, 3412 Seaglen Drive, Rancho Palos Verdes, CA 90274

BOBBS-MERRILL COMPANY, INC., 4300 West 62nd Street, Indianapolis, IN 46268

CHILDCRAFT EDUCATION CORPORATION, 20 Kilmer Road, Edison, NJ 08818

COMMUNICATION SKILL BUILDERS, P.O. Box 42050-D, Dept. 70, Tucson, AZ 85733

CONOVER COMPANY, P.O. Box 155, Omro, WI 54963

CONSULTING PSYCHOLOGISTS PRESS, INC., 577 College Ave., Palo Alto, CA 94306

NIGEL COX, 69 Fawn Dr., Cheshire, CT 06410

CTB/McGRAW-HILL (See Publishers Test Service)

CURRICULUM ASSOCIATES, INC., 5 Esquire Road, North Billerica, MA 01862–2389

DEVEREUX FOUNDATION, 19 South Waterloo Road, Box 400, Devon, PA 19333

DLM TEACHING RESOURCES, One DLM Park, Allen, TX 75002

EARLY RECOGNITION INTERVENTION SYSTEMS, P.O. Box 1635, Pawtucket, RI 02862

ECONOMY COMPANY, Box 25308, 1901 North Walnut, Oklahoma City, OK 73125

EDiTS, P.O. Box 7234, San Diego, CA 92107

EDMARK CORPORATION, P.O. Box 3903, Bellevue, WA 98009

EDUCATIONAL PUBLISHING SERVICE, INC., 75 Moulton Street, Cambridge, MA 02238–9101

EDUCATIONAL SERVICES, P.O. Box 1835, Columbia, MO 65205

EDUCATIONAL TECHNOLOGIES, INC., 1007 Whitehead Road-Exit, Trenton, NJ 08638

EDUCATIONAL TESTING SERVICE, Princeton, NJ 08541

FOREWORKS PUBLICATIONS, Box 9747, North Hollywood, CA 91609

HAHNEMANN UNIVERSITY, Department of Mental Health Services, Broad & Vine, Philadelphia, PA 19102

HARCOURT BRACE JOVANOVICH, INC. (See Psychological Corporation)

HAWTHORNE EDUCATIONAL SERVICES, INC., 800 Gray Oak Drive, Columbia, MO 65201

HOUGHTON MIFFLIN COMPANY, One Beacon Street, Boston, MA 02108

INSTITUTE FOR PERSONALITY AND ABILITY TESTING, P.O. Box 188, Champaign, IL 61820

JASTAK ASSOCIATES, INC., P.O. Box 4460, Wilmington, DE 19807

LADOCA PROJECT AND PUBLISHING FOUNDATION,

INC., East 51st Ave. & Lincoln St., Denver, CO 80216

LEARNING MULTI-SYSTEMS, INC., 340 Coyier Lane, Madison, WI 53713

LINGUI SYSTEMS, INC., P.O. Box 747, 3100 4th Ave., East Moline, IL 61244

MODERN CURRICULUM PRESS, 13900 Prospect Rd., Cleveland, OH 44136

NCE INTERPRETIVE SCORING SYSTEMS, 4401 West 7th St., Minneapolis, MN 55435

NCS PROFESSIONAL ASSESSMENT SERVICES, P.O. Box 1416, Minneapolis, MN 55440

NORTHWESTERN UNIVERSITY PRESS, 625 Colfax St., Evanston, IL 60201

PRO-ED, 8700 Shoal Creek Blvd., Austin, TX 78758

PSYCHOLOGICAL AND EDUCATIONAL PUBLICATIONS, INC., 1477 Rollins Road, Burlingame, CA 94010

PSYCHOLOGICAL ASSESSMENT RESOURCES, INC., P.O. Box 998, Odessa, FL 33556

PSYCHOLOGICAL CORPORATION, 555 Academic Court, San Antonio, TX 78204

PUBLISHERS TEST SERVICE, 2500 Garden Road, Monterey, CA 93940

RICHARD C. OWEN PUBLISHERS, INC., 135 Katonah Ave., Katonah, NY 10536

RIVERSIDE PUBLISHING COMPANY, 8420 Bryn Mawr Ave., Chicago, IL 60631

SCHOLASTIC TESTING SERVICES, INC., 480 Meyer Road, Bensenville, IL 60106

SCIENCE RESEARCH ASSOCIATES, INC., 155 North Wacker Dr., Chicago, IL 60606

SLOSSON EDUCATIONAL PUBLICATIONS, INC., P.O. Box 280, East Aurora, NY 14052

STANFORD UNIVERSITY PRESS, Palo Alto, CA 94305

STOELTING COMPANY, 1350 South Kostner Ave., Chicago, IL 60623

TALENT ASSESSMENT, INC., P.O. Box 5987, Jacksonville, FL 33247

TEACHERS COLLEGE PRESS, Teachers College, Columbia University, New York, NY 10027

UNITED EDUCATIONAL SERVICES, INC., P.O. Box 605, East Aurora, NY 14052

UNIVERSITY OF ILLINOIS PRESS, 54 East Gregory Drive, P.O. Box 5081, Station A, Champaign, IL 61820

UNIVERSITY OF IOWA, Publications Order Dept., Iowa City, IA 52242

UNIVERSITY OF MIAMI, c/o Dr. Herbert C. Quay, P.O. Box 248074, Coral Gables, FL 33124

UNIVERSITY OF MICHIGAN PRESS, P.O. Box 1104, Ann Arbor, MI 48106

VALPAR INTERNATIONAL CORPORATION, 2450 Ruthrauff Rd., No. 180, Tucson, AZ 85705

VOCATIONAL RESEARCH INSTITUTE, 2100 Arch St., Suite 6104, Philadelphia, PA 19103

VORT, P.O. Box 60132, Palo Alto, CA 94306

WESTERN PSYCHOLOGICAL SERVICES, 12031 Wilshire Boulevard, Los Angeles, CA 90025

WILLIAM C. BROWN PUBLISHERS, 2460 Kerper Blvd., Dubuque, IA 52001

ZANER-BLOSER, 2300 West 5th Ave., P.O. Box 16764, Columbus, OH 43216

APPENDIX B: TEST REVIEW FORM

Test Review Form
I. *Test Information*

A. Title of test _____

Acronym used to label test, if any _____

               Name   Position

B. Authors _____   _____

              _____   _____

              _____   _____

C. Publisher and Address _____

_____

D. Date of Publication _____   E. Number of Forms _____

F. Accompanying Materials (check)

    1. master manual _____   5. separate charts or profiles _____

    2. separate tables of norms _____   6. computer scoring _____

    3. separate directions for administration _____   7. other _____

    4. separate scoring keys _____

G. Age or Grade Levels _____

_____

H. Domain Sampled _____

I. Descriptive Titles of Parts (or subtests)

_____   _____

_____   _____

_____   _____

J. Purposes of the Test

    screening _____   diagnostic _____

    instructional planning _____   experimental _____

    other _____

K. Self-Administering _____Yes _____ No

L. Individual or Group Administration _____

M. Time

    1. Administration time _____ 2. Actual working time _____

N. Scoring Method

    1. Machine _____

    2. Computerized scoring program available _____ Yes _____ No

    3. Hand

             type of key _____

             special formula for scoring _____

    4. Other _____

O. Types of Scores Available

percentile rank _____ standard scores _____ (X = _____)

(SD = _____)

stanines _____ age equivalents _____ grade equivalents _____

P. Costs

1. Specimen set _____

2. Individual test booklets _____

3. Answer sheets _____

II. *Norms, Validity, and Reliability*

A. Norms

1. Types of Norms

By age level _____   Other _____

By age level _____   _____

2. Description and size of norm group(s) _____

_____

_____

_____

3. Describe diversity reflected in the norms _____

_____

_____

_____

_____

_____

B. Reliability _____

1. Description of groups used _____

_____

_____

2. Size of group used _____

_____

_____

3. How determined (check)

a. split half _____   c. alternate forms _____

b. test-retest _____   d. analysis of variance _____

4. Coefficients reported _____

_____

C. Validity (provide data for each type of validity found)

1. Type of validity _____ _____

_____ _____

How determined _____

_____

_____

_____

_____

Criterion used _____

Validity values reported _____

III. *Information Specific to Criterion-Referenced Tests*

Do the following for each objective.

Instructional Objective _____

_____

_____

_____

1. Do all of the test items sample the behavior specified in the instructional objective?   Yes_____   No_____
2. Does the test include the number of items called for in the criterion statement?   Yes_____   No_____
3. Do all of the items sample the content specified in the instructional objective?   Yes_____   No_____
4. Do the test items parallel the given conditions in the criterion statement?   Yes_____   No_____
5. Are the directions easy to understand?   Yes_____   No_____
6. Is the test format satisfactory?   Yes_____   No_____
7. Are the foils, if used, appropriate?   Yes_____   No_____
(Continue through all objectives)

IV. *Test Evaluation*

A. Principle References and Sources (primary and secondary sources)

B. Critical Comments (indicate name of critic and source of comments, including personal ones)

APPENDIX C:
BACKGROUND INFORMATION FORMS

Preschool–Kindergarten
Background Questionnaire

Child's Name _____ Today's Date _____

Birthdate _____ Age _____ Sex (Circle One)   Male   Female

Home Address _____ Phone _____

Home School _____

Referred By _____

Address _____

Person filling out form (Circle One)   Mother   Father   Stepmother   Stepfather   Other _____

Statement of the Problem

Describe the problem. _____

When was the problem first noticed? _____

What do you think caused the problem? _____

What has been done about it? _____

Family Data

Mother's Name _____ Age _____ Education _____

Occupation _____ Phone: Home _____ Business _____

Father's Name _____ Age _____ Education _____

Occupation _____ Phone: Home _____ Business _____

Stepparent's Name _____ Age _____ Education _____

Occupation _____ Phone: Home _____ Business _____

Marital status of parents. _____

If parents are separated or divorced, how old was child when the separation occurred? _____

List all people living in household.

Name	Relationship to Child	Age

If any brothers or sisters are living outside the home, list their names and ages.

_____

Primary language spoken in the home. _____

Other language spoken in the home. _____

Family income (if relevant). _____

Family Medical History

Place a check next to any illness or condition that any member of the immediate family has. When you check an item, please note the member's relationship to child.

Check	Condition	Relationship to Child	Check	Condition	Relationship to Child
_____	Alcoholism	_____	_____	Nervous or psychological problem	_____
_____	Cancer	_____	_____	Depression	_____
_____	Diabetes	_____	_____	Suicide attempt	_____
_____	Heart trouble	_____	_____	Mental handicap	_____
_____	Learning disability	_____			

Developmental History

During pregnancy, was mother on medication? Yes _____ No _____

If yes, please describe: _____

During pregnancy, did mother smoke? Yes _____ No _____

During pregnancy, did mother drink alcoholic beverages? Yes _____ No _____

During pregnancy, did mother use drugs? Yes _____ No _____

During pregnancy, did mother experience any problems with: _____ chronic disease, _____ poor nutrition, _____ vaginal bleeding, _____ toxemia, _____ viral infection, _____ trauma?

Were forceps used during delivery? Yes _____ No _____

Was a Caesarean section performed? Yes _____ No _____

Was the child premature? Yes _____ No _____

If so, by how many months? _____

What was the child's birth weight? _____

Were there any birth defects or complications? Yes _____ No _____

If yes, please describe: _____

Was there any special care? _____ incubator, _____ oxygen, _____ other

Were there any feeding problems? Yes _____ No _____

If yes, please describe: _____

Were there any sleeping problems? Yes _____ No _____

If yes, please describe: _____

As an infant, was the child quiet? Yes _____ No _____

As an infant, did the child like to be held? Yes _____ No _____

As an infant, was the child alert? Yes _____ No _____

Were there any special problems in the growth and development of the child during the first few years? Yes _____ No _____

If yes, please describe: _____

How did the family respond to the child? _____

The following is a list of infant and preschool behaviors. Please indicate the age at which your child first demonstrated each behavior. If you are not certain of the age but have some idea, write the age followed by a question mark.

Behavior	Age	Behavior	Age
Showed response to mother	___	Put several words together	___
Rolled over	___	Dressed self	___
Sat alone	___	Became toilet trained	___
Crawled	___	Stayed dry at night	___
Walked alone	___	Fed self	___
Spoke first word	___	Rode tricycle	___
Babbled	___		

How does the child let others know when she or he needs something (food, drink, toys, restroom)? Points _____ Other gesture or action (specify) _____ Single word _____ Sentence or several words together _____

Medical History

At what ages did any of the following illnesses or operations occur?

	Age	Severity		Age	Severity
Whooping Cough			CMV		
Mumps			Earaches		
Scarlet Fever			Measles		
Chicken Pox			Croup		
Chronic Colds			Pneumonia		
Head Injuries			Influenza		
Venereal Disease			Polio		
Diphtheria			Asthma		
Convulsions			Sinus		
Encephalitis			Rickets		
Meningitis			Headaches		
Rheumatic Fever			Typhoid		
Tonsillitis			Adenoidectomy		
Tonsillectomy			Mastoidectomy		

List physicians the child has seen. _____

Describe any other operations your child has had. _____

Describe any serious illnesses he or she has had. _____

What illnesses have been accompanied by an extremely high fever? _____

Temperature _____ Duration of fever _____

Describe any other serious injuries or deformities not already mentioned. _____

Has the child's vision been examined? _____ By whom? _____

Results _____

Has the child's hearing been examined? _____ By whom? _____

Results _____

Is he or she now under the care of a doctor? _____ For what reason? _____

Does the child have allergies? _____

Social and Behavior Checklist

Check

_____ Has difficulty with speech

_____ Has difficulty with language

_____ Has difficulty with coordination

_____ Prefers to be alone

_____ Does not get along well with brothers or sisters

_____ Is aggressive

_____ Is shy or timid

Check

_____ Has frequent tantrums

_____ Has frequent nightmares

_____ Has trouble sleeping (describe) _____

_____ Rocks back and forth

_____ Bangs head

_____ Holds breath

_____ Eats poorly

_____ Is stubborn

_____	Is more interested in things (objects) than in people	_____	Has poor bowel control (soils self)
_____	Engages in behavior that could be dangerous to self or others (describe) _____	_____	Is much too active
	_____	_____	Is clumsy
		_____	Has blank spells
_____	Has special fears, habits, mannerisms	_____	Is impulsive
	(describe) _____	_____	Shows daredevil behavior
	_____	_____	Is slow to learn
		_____	Gives up easily
_____	Wets bed	_____	Other (describe) _____
_____	Bites nails		_____
_____	Sucks thumb		_____

What are your child's favorite activities?

1. _____ 2. _____ 3. _____
4. _____ 5. _____ 6. _____

What activities would your child like to engage in more often than he or she does at present?

1. _____ 2. _____ 3. _____

What activities does your child like least?

1. _____ 2. _____ 3. _____

What disciplinary techniques do you usually use when your child behaves inappropriately? Place a check next to each technique that you usually use. There also is space for writing in any other disciplinary techniques that you use.

Check	Disciplinary Technique	Check	Disciplinary Technique
_____	Ignore problem behavior	_____	Tell child to sit on chair
_____	Scold child	_____	Send child to his or her room
_____	Threaten child	_____	Take away some activity/food
_____	Reason with child	_____	Other technique (describe) _____
_____	Redirect child's interest	_____	Don't use any technique

Which disciplinary techniques are usually effective? _____
_____

With what type of problem(s)? _____
_____

Which disciplinary techniques are usually ineffective? _____
_____

With what type of problem(s)? _____
_____

Does your child have behavior or discipline problems that are a frequent source of arguing between the parents? Yes _____
No _____

What are they? _____
How long have the problems been going on? _____
What have you found to be the most satisfactory ways of helping your child? _____
What are your child's assets or strengths? _____
_____

Is there any other information that you think may help us in working with your child? _____
_____

School-Age Background Questionnaire

Directions. This form is designed to be completed by the parents or guardian of children or adolescents prior to evaluation. Knowing as much as possible about the child's background and development helps team members select the most appropriate tests and interpret the results more accurately. Don't worry if you don't remember all the details asked for— even a guess is sometimes helpful. If you wish, you may let your child look at the form and help answer some of the questions.

I. *Identifying Information*

Child's name _____

                   (last)   (first)   (middle)   (name used)

Date of birth _____ Current Age _____ Sex _____ Adopted? _____

Father's name _____ Age _____

Address _____ Phone_____

Occupation _____ Education _____

Place of work _____ Work Phone _____

Mother's name _____ Age _____

Address _____ Phone _____

Occupation _____ Education _____

Place of work _____ Work Phone _____

Parents are   Married _____, Divorced _____, Separated _____, Single _____, Widowed _____

If divorced, child's age at time of divorce _____

Child lives with   Both Parents _____, Mother _____, Father _____, Other _____

Name of child's doctor _____ Phone _____

In case of emergency call (if parents cannot be reached).

Name _____ Phone _____

Brothers and sisters

Name	Sex	Age

Others living in the home

Name	Sex	Age	Relationship

Describe any learning problems noticed in other family members. _____

What language is spoken at home? _____

Does the child wear glasses? _____ When are they needed? _____

Does the child wear a hearing aid? _____ How long has it been worn? _____

Does the child wear any mouth appliances (braces, retainer, etc.)? _____

If yes, what type and for how long? _____

II. *Description of Problem*

Describe the child's problem, and the type of service you seek. _____

Describe any actions already taken to remedy the problem. _____

III. *Prenatal and Birth History*

During this pregnancy, did mother experience any unusual illness, condition, or accident, such as German measles, Rh incompatibility, false labor? _____

If yes, describe: _____

Were there any problems with the delivery, such as breech birth, Caesarian, etc.? _____
If yes, describe: _____

Infant's condition immediately following birth: _____ Did the infant have
difficulty starting to breathe? _____ Was the infant blue? _____ Jaundiced? _____ Did the infant
have sucking or swallowing difficulties? _____ Feeding problems? _____ Scars or bruises? _____
Other problems? _____

IV. *Developmental History*
At what age did your child do the following:
Sit without support: _____ Crawl: _____ Walk: _____. Describe anything noticeable about his or her
development of these abilities: _____

At what age was the child toilet trained:
Bowels (Day) _____ (Night) _____ Bladder (Day) _____ (Night) _____
Describe anything noticeable about toilet training. _____

As a baby did the child babble or enjoy vocal play? _____ How long did this last? _____ At what age did the child
say his/her first words? _____ What were they? _____ Describe anything noticeable about
your child's learning to talk (for example, especially noisy or quiet as a baby, or late in learning words or using
sentences). _____

Does the child seem to have any difficulty hearing? _____
If yes, explain: _____
Does the child seem to have trouble understanding speech? _____
If yes, describe: _____

Can the child remember things that happen? _____ Follow directions? _____
Can the child think of the words needed to explain something? _____

V. *Health History*

Illnesses	*Age*	*Severity*	*Temperature*
Measles			
Chicken Pox			
Mumps			
Scarlet Fever			
Croup			
Tonsillitis			
Bronchitis			
Ear Infection			
Allergies			
Poliomyelitis			
Encephalitis			
Meningitis			
Convulsions			
Other			
Hospitalization	*Age*	*Reason*	*Duration*

Were any of these illnesses followed by noticeable changes in the child's general behavior? _____ If yes, please describe:
_____

Describe any eating problems. _____

Does the child have difficulty chewing or swallowing? _____

Describe any sleeping problems. _____

Does the child fall or lose balance easily? _____
Is the child awkward in using his or her hands? _____
Is the child presently on any medication? _____ If so, what kind? _____
For what reason? _____
Prescribed by whom? _____
For how long? _____ Does the medication help? _____
Was the child previously on medication that has now been discontinued? _____
What medication? _____ For what reason? _____
Why was it discontinued? _____

Have you tried any special diets, food, vitamins, or other treatments? _____
If so, which, and what were the results? _____

Has the child had any of the following examinations:

	Date	*Place*
Educational	_____	_____
Speech	_____	_____
Psychological	_____	_____
Eyes	_____	_____
Hearing	_____	_____
Neurological	_____	_____
EEG	_____	_____
Other medical	_____	_____
Other medical	_____	_____

Describe the results. _____

VI. *School History*
School _____ Grade _____
Address _____ Principal _____
_____ Teacher(s) _____
Phone _____
Did the child attend nursery school? _____ Age _____
Kindergarten? _____ Age _____
At what age did the child start first grade? _____ Were any grades repeated? _____ Which ones?
_____ Why? _____

How many times has the child changed schools? _____ What necessitated the changes? _____
Are there any school subjects with which the child has particular difficulty? _____
Describe the difficulty. _____

What is the child's best school subject? _____
At this time is the child receiving any special help with school work? If so, describe. _____
How much time is spent doing homework? _____ At what time of day is homework done? _____
Does someone in the family work with the child on homework? _____ If so, who? _____ Does
someone in the family read to the child? _____ If so, who? _____

VII. *Social Development*
How does the child relate to parents? _____
To other adults? _____ To peers? _____

Are there specific things that make the child angry or afraid? _____

How does your child typically show anger? _____ How does your child react when
frustrated? _____

Do you feel the child is unusually dependent, nervous, fearful, irritable, depressed, etc.? _____ Describe ____

Are there any family problems that might be contributing to the child's problem? _____ If yes, explain: ____

Does the child enjoy jokes, cartoons, humorous situations? _____

Number of hours spent watching T.V. daily _____ What programs? _____
Number of hours spent in part-time employment _____
Describe employment _____
Does your youngster drive? Yes _____ No _____
Child's favorite outdoor play _____
Child's favorite indoor play _____
Names and ages of favorite playmates _____

Pets? _____
Does your youngster date? Yes _____ No _____ Age dating started _____
Is there any additional information that would contribute to a better understanding of your child? _____
_____
_____
_____

Signature of parent or guardian _____
Signature of person completing form, if not parent or guardian _____
Position or relationship to child _____

Date _____

APPENDIX D: CASE STUDY MATERIALS

To provide students with an opportunity to integrate data and apply assessment information to practical cases, two cases are presented for review.

I. Integrate the data to answer the following questions:
   A. Is student eligible for special education services? If so, what category?
   B. What modifications are needed for informal testing? Classroom instruction? This should include the most appropriate format.
   C. What modifications are needed to adapt teacher behaviors?
   D. Additional data requested that was not available.
II. Identify a skill objective(s) in the area the student appears to be deficient in and prepare the following:
   A. List of skill objectives.
   B. Task analysis (see chapter 6).
   C. Informal assessment that evaluates those skills chosen and also controls for all areas of a cognitive task analysis (see chapter 6).
   D. Programming suggestions.

Case Study: Tommy

You are a third-grade teacher in a regular classroom. You have become increasingly concerned about Tommy and his lack of progress in reading. Tommy is able to pronounce words phonetically, but his sight word recognition is limited. He performs approximately one year below his classmates on selection tasks for reading comprehension (multiple choice). More problematic, however, are his extremely weak production skills (fill in the blank and short answer), where he is two years below his classmates. Tommy does not readily participate in reading group discussions and becomes embarrassed if called upon to give an answer verbally. He often has trouble finding the right word and may speak in jumbled sentences.

Tommy is above grade level in arithmetic. He has well-developed fine motor skills and enjoys number games and manipulative puzzles. He follows classroom rules and presents no overt behavioral problems but appears shy and withdrawn around classmates.

Tommy is 8 years old and the youngest of four siblings. The family would be described as middle to upper middle class in socioeconomic status. The mother reports that reading is an activity that the family does together frequently.

Gray Oral Reading Sample

(Two) girls (went) to a farm for a visit. (There) (were) cows, pigs, (ducks,) (and) five hens. (The) girls gathered (the) eggs (every) morning. The farmer showed (the) girls (how) to milk a cow. (One) girl (said,) "The milk looks (good.) (But) it will be better after it's cold." (Then) (the) farmer showed (them) how to catch fish. (They) also helped the farmer pick (the) fat (ears) (of) corn. The farmer said, "Now you can see (where) we get (our) food."

Teacher's Notes: Circled words were not attempted, or were incorrect. Most other words were sounded out phonetically.

Time: 10 minutes

Psychometric Summary

Summary of Scores/Tommy

Visual Acuity—Within normal range.
Auditory Acuity—Within normal range.

Standardized Scores:

WECHSLER INTELLIGENCE SCALE FOR CHILDREN–III
Mean score = 100 (SS); 25%ile–75%ile, Standard Dev. = 15

Full Scale Score–93 (SS); 32%ile
Verbal Scale Score–75 (SS); 5%ile
Performance Scale Score–110 (SS); 75%ile

PEABODY PICTURE VOCABULARY TEST–REVISED
Mean score = 100 (SS); 25%ile–75%ile; Standard Dev. — 15

Standard Score–70; 2%ile

STANFORD DIAGNOSTIC READING TEST, RED LEVEL
Average performance = 100 (SS); 50%ile; Standard Dev. = 15; Subtests have Scaled Scores with average performance of 10

Decoding:	Auditory Discrimination–11
	Phonetic Analysis–10
Vocabulary:	Auditory Vocabulary–7
Comprehension:	Word Reading–6
	Reading Comprehension–6

GRAY ORAL READING TEST
Oral reading quotient–mean score = 100 (SS); 25%ile–75%ile; Standard Dev. — 15

Standard Score: 72; 3%ile

KEY MATH–REVISED
Mean score = 100; Standard Dev. = 15 for Total Test standard scores and Area standard scores

Total Test–106 (SS)
  Basic Concepts–110 (SS)
  Operations–115 (SS)
  Applications–95 (SS)

INFORMAL/CRITERION-REFERENCED

Oral Language Sample–Poor syntax (word order confused).
  Tommy speaks haltingly, taking time to find the word he needs. Often the word is not appropriate to the context. He speaks softly and appears embarrassed and uncomfortable.

BRIGANCE
(Competencies based upon grade level criterion)

Reading/Decoding–1.5 grade level
Comprehension–1st grade level

Organizational System for Data from School Records

Name __TOMMY__   Date __1|14|93__
Birth __June 7, 1983__   Current Grade Placement __third__

School Changes

How many school changes have occurred? __None__
Grade level when changes occurred? __Na__
Reasons for each school change: _____
Describe any fluctuations of grades following each change: _____

Attendance

Seasonal attendance problems during ____ fall, ____ winter, ____ spring.
Grade levels when attendance was problematic: __None__
Reasons for problematic attendance: _____
Attendance is becoming a problem but was not a problem before ____ yes ____ no
   Tardiness ____ is a problem now.
   ____ has been a problem in the past.
   __✓__ has never and is not a problem.
Reasons for tardiness: _____

Grades and Retention

Was this student ever retained? __✓__ yes ____ no
If so, what grade level(s)? __Kindergarten__
In what subjects are the poorest grades earned (list subject and grades)? __reading, written language__
When were poor grades first earned in these subjects? __Kindergarten__
Describe any annual pattern of grade fluctuations: _____

Group Administered Test Scores

Test Name	Date Given	Score (Standard Score or Percentile)
Otis-Lennon	April, 1992	PR = 28

Achievement Percentile Rank

Test Name & Date	Word Attack	Comprehension	Calculation	Problem Solving	Grammar/Spelling
Metropolitan Primary, Sept. 1991	PR = 4	PR = 2	PR = 63	PR = 54	PR = 4

School Records   Report Card for Fall

Reading = F	Language = D	Handwriting = S+	Social St. = C
Math = A	Spelling = D	Science = B	Conduct = S

Remedial Program

Tommy is currently enrolled in a remedial reading class. In addition, he has been assigned a peer tutor in his class to help him with his reading assignments.

Behavioral Observations

Name __TOMMY__   Date __January 14, 1993__

Chronological Age _____   Examiner __Ms. Morgan__

Assessment Time _____   Measures Given _____ __See__

__Psychometric Summary__

Handedness _____ right __✓__ left _____   variable, explain:

Reaction to New Examiner:
(yes - y or n or no - n)
__Y__ initially reserved
__Y__ eye contact within first 2 minutes
__N__ answers direct questions
__Y__ gradual warming
__N__ engages in spontaneous conversation
__Y__ nervous or fearful
__N__ overly friendly
_____ asks personal or inappropriate questions
__N__ resistant
__—__ other (describe on back)

Reaction to Novel Tasks:
(yes - y or n or no - n)
__N__ reasonably confident
__Y__ frustrated or discouraged
__Y__ requires repetition of directions
__N__ inclined to distrust own ability
__—__ other, explain

Need for Reassurance:
(yes - y or n or no - n)
__Y__ seeks feedback on responses
__Y__ needs encouragement to continue
__N__ indifferent to encouragement
__Y__ seems pleased by periodic encouragement
__—__ other, explain

Attention/Activity Level:
(yes - y or n or no - n)
__N__ lethargic
__Y__ attention/activity appropriate
__N__ activity level interferes with work
__N__ constantly moving, agitated
__Y__ frequent off-task comments
__Y__ variable depending on task
__Y__ needs frequent direction

Work Effort:
(yes - y or n or no - n)
__Y__ persists until task completed
__Y__ gives up after brief effort   *task specific*
__N__ complains, resists
__—__ other, explain

Work Style:
(yes - y or n or no - n)
__N__ impulsive, begins work before directions completed
__N__ reflects before answering
__N__ spontaneously self-monitors
__Y__ random approach to problem solving
—if reading involved
__N__ strategic approach to problem
__Y__ no self-monitoring
__—__ other, explain

Inappropriate or Resistant Behavior (Explain)   *NO*

Other Comments

Interview with Tommy

1. What does your teacher think is the most important subject? Reading
   How do you know? We read lots of times. A long time...

2. Which subject does your teacher think is the least important? (Shrugs?)
   How do you know? _____

3. Which school subject is the easiest for you? doing arithmetic on the computer (shrugs?)

4. Which school subject is the hardest for you? Reading group
   Why? It's too fast. I forget what the words say.

5. What does the teacher do that helps you learn the easiest? She lets me
   Describe? listen to headphones that tell stories.

6. What kind of answers are easiest for you? When I find a picture.

7. What else helps you learn? (Shrugs?) When my teacher says
   Why? the word.   I read it.

8. How do you feel about school? Okay. She's nice.
   Why? _____

9. When the teacher is busy, what is the hardest thing about doing your schoolwork? I
   Why? don't know how to start the worksheet.

10. How do you remember what your homework is? (shrugs?)
    How do you remember what to bring to school? My Mom!

11. Tell me about the last three times you got in trouble with your teacher? When I
    lost my spelling, I guess?

12. Name your three best friends: which one(s) are in your class? My friend at
    Boy Scouts, Jimmy. He's the one.

13. What do you most want to learn at school? Reading a story.
    Why? Myself, so I can do good.

Case Study: Shawna

Shawna is 12 years old and in the seventh grade at Fairview Middle School. This is her first public school experience after attending five different private schools in her seven-year school career. After being at Fairview for three months, Shawna is still having a difficult time adjusting, and teachers describe her as impulsive, with a low tolerance for frustration and a short attention span. She is not well accepted by her peers and often engages in attention-seeking behavior such as profanity and verbal aggression. Past school reports show sporadic improvements in behavior with behavioral modification plans, but these plans were not described in any detail.

Shawna's behavior is not the only concern, however. She is having extreme difficulty keeping up with her classmates, particularly in social studies and science, and she does very poorly on tests. In light of Shawna's educational background, ongoing behavior problems, and current academic problems, a complete assessment has been recommended for possible special education placement.

Psychometric Summary

Summary of Scores/Shawna

Visual Acuity—Waiting for records to be transferred.
Auditory Acuity—Waiting for records to be transferred.

Standardized Scores:

WECHSLER INTELLIGENCE SCALE FOR CHILDREN–III
Mean score = 100 (SS); Standard Dev. = 15

Full Scale Score–105 (SS); 63%ile
Verbal Scale Score–102 (SS); 55%ile
Performance Scale Score–106 (SS); 66%ile

PEABODY PICTURE VOCABULARY TEST–REVISED
Mean score = 100 (SS); Standard Dev. − 15

Standard Score–105; 63%ile

STANFORD DIAGNOSTIC READING TEST, RED LEVEL
Average performance = 100 (SS); 50%ile; Standard Dev. = 15; Subtests have Scaled Scores with average performance of 10

Decoding: Auditory Discrimination–8
                   Phonetic Analysis–9
Vocabulary: Auditory Vocabulary–9
Comprehension: Word Reading–8
                   Reading Comprehension–7

KEY MATH–REVISED
Mean score = 100; Standard Dev. = 15 for Total Test standard scores and Area standard scores

Total Test–95 (SS); 37%ile
   Basic Concepts–100 (SS); 50%ile
   Operations–93 (SS); 32%ile
   Applications–93 (SS); 32%ile

Organizational System for Data from School Records

Name **Shawna** _____ Date **2/93** _____
Birth _____ **March 1980** _____ Current Grade Placement ___ **7th** _____

School Changes

How many school changes have occurred? ___ **6** ____
Grade level when changes occurred? **See narrative**
Reasons for each school change: _____
Describe any fluctuations of grades following each change: _____

Attendance

Seasonal attendance problems during __✓__ fall, __✓__ winter, __✓__ spring.
Grade levels when attendance was problematic: **beginning with 5th grade**
Reasons for problematic attendance: _____
Attendance is becoming a problem but was not a problem before ____ yes ____ no
    Tardiness ____ is a problem now.
        __✓__ has been a problem in the past.
        ____ has never and is not a problem.
Reasons for tardiness: _____

Grades and Retention

Was this student ever retained? ____ yes __✓__ no
If so, what grade level(s)? _____
In what subjects are the poorest grades earned (list subject and grades)? **Social St., Study Skills,**
When were poor grades first earned in these subjects? _____ **Science**
Describe any annual pattern of grade fluctuations: _____
_____

Group Administered Test Scores

Test Name	Date Given	Score (Standard Score or Percentile)
Otis-Lennon	Sept. 1989	PR = 30

Achievement Percentile Rank

Test Name & Date	Word Attack	Comprehension	Calculation	Problem Solving	Grammar/Spelling
Metropolitan Intermediate April 1992	PR = 24	PR = 15	PR = 20	PR = 18	PR = 22

School Records   Report Card for Fall
    Reading = C-   Language = F   Handwriting = F   Social St. = D-
    Math   = C-   Spelling = B   Science = F   Conduct = U

Behavioral Observations

Name Shawna

Date February 1993

Chronological Age 12

Examiner Ms. Peoples

Assessment Time _____

Measures Given _____ See Psychometric Summary

Handedness ✓ right ____ left ____ variable, explain:

Reaction to New Examiner:
(yes - y or no - n)
- N initially reserved
- Y eye contact within first 2 minutes
- Y answers direct questions
- Y gradual warming
- Y engages in spontaneous conversation
- Y nervous or fearful anxious behavior noted
- N overly friendly
- N asks personal or inappropriate questions
- Y resistant - when problems got
- ___ other (describe on back) difficult or required to work independently.

Reaction to Novel Tasks:
(yes - y or no - n)
- Y reasonably confident
- Y frustrated or discouraged
- N requires repetition of directions
- Y inclined to distrust own ability
- ___ other, explain

Need for Reassurance:
(yes - y or no - n)
- Y seeks feedback on responses
- Y needs encouragement to continue
- N indifferent to encouragement
- Y seems pleased by periodic encouragement
- ___ other, explain

Attention/Activity Level:
(yes - y or no - n)
- N lethargic
- N attention/activity appropriate
- Y activity level interferes with work
- Y constantly moving, agitated
- Y frequent off-task comments
- Y variable depending on task
- Y needs frequent direction

Work Effort:
(yes - y or no - n)
- N persists until task completed
- Y gives up after brief effort
- Y complains, resists
- ___ other, explain

Work Style:
(yes - y or no - n)
- Y impulsive, begins work before directions completed
- N reflects before answering
- N spontaneously self-monitors
- Y random approach to problem solving —if reading involved
- N strategic approach to problem
- Y no self-monitoring
- ___ other, explain

Inappropriate or Resistant Behavior (Explain)

Other Comments
Very distractable; helped with structure.

Interview with Shawna

1. What does your teacher think is the most important subject? Ms. Small, Math - Mr. Peoples, Social St. - Ms. Jones, sitting on her ___ (she's a dork) - Mr. Evans, Basketball

2. Which subject does your teacher think is the least important? Anything fun, I guess - Sex Education

3. Which school subject is the easiest for you? Spelling. I can memorize spelling lists really fast. And computer math when they let me write poems, but not at school - and stories!

4. Which school subject is the hardest for you? I'm failing science (I Why? hate Ms. Jones) and Social St. (but Mr. Peoples is pretty cool)

5. What does the teacher do that helps you learn the fastest? Sends me to time Describe? out. So they can get rid of me

6. What kind of answers are easiest for you? It depends I'm pretty hyper - - -

7. What kind of work is the easiest for you? Math worksheets and computer games but I don't get computer time.

8. How do you learn best? I like talking to Terri - my tutor from the hi-school. She's cool + sometimes we even do Soc. St. But mostly we talk + stuff. Usually I work in carrels or go to time out.

9. Do you like school? I'd rather stay in bed or go to the mall. I hate to get up for the bus. Some parts of school are okay when I'm there.

10. When the teacher is busy, what is the hardest thing about doing your homework? I talk too much. Didn't they tell you? I'm hyper - - -

11. Do you ever get into trouble at school? Yea, it's usually for my language. You know... I "cuss like a boy or something" - that's what they say.

12. Do you have many friends? My best friend is a girl (Joan) in Florida - at my old school - one of my old schools - I've got 5 old schools. They all had a party OBSERVATION DURING INTERVIEW: when I moved.

During interview, Shawna was up and down from her seat, in and out the door, - she had to be stopped from going through the (teacher's) desk drawer in the room we used for the interview. She showed me pictures her dog who died (hit by car) last month or so.

Classroom Observation

Student's Name **Shawna**   Grade **7**   Date **Feb. 2, 1992**

School **Fairview Middle**   Teacher **Ms. Jones (Science)**   Observer **Ms. Sweet (Guidance counselor)**

Part A:

Target Behavior #1 **On task. Specifically – Student should remain in seat.**

Type of Observation

✓ Classroom Observation

Setting for Observation:

_____ Large group, total class   _____ Individual instruction

✓ Small group, direct instruction   _____ Individual seat work

Part B

Classroom Observation:

Interval-Time Recording: Frequency _____**1**_____ seconds (minutes)

Time of Observation **10 am**   Length of Observation **10 mins**

Target Student

+	−	−	−	+	−	−	−	−	−

Control Student

+	+	+	+	+	+	−	+	+	+

Summary of Observation:

Shawna was in seat 20% of time and out of seat 80% of time. She left the group completely after "why can't we have scissors to cut stuff out? Afraid I'll cut myself?" Control student in seat 90% of time, out 10% - She got up and began to walk toward Shawna - then returned to seat. Telling her to "shut up."

REFERENCES

ACHENBACH, T. M. (1981). *Child behavior checklist for ages 4–16*. San Antonio, TX: Psychological Corporation.

ACHENBACH, T. M. (1986). *Child behavior checklist for ages 2–3*. San Antonio, TX: Psychological Corporation.

ADAMS, G. L. (1984a). *Comprehensive test of adaptive behavior*. Columbus, OH: Merrill.

———— (1984b). *Normative adaptive behavior checklist*. Columbus, OH: Merrill.

ADAMS, S. (1979). *Adston mathematics skills series: Common fractions*. Baton Rouge, LA: Adston Educational Enterprises.

ADAMS, S., & ELLIS, L. (1979). *Adston mathematics skill series: Working with whole numbers*. Baton Rouge, LA: Adston Educational Enterprises.

ADAMS, S., & SAULS, C. (1979). *Adston mathematics skills series: Readiness for operations*. Baton Rouge, LA: Adston Educational Enterprises.

ADLER, S. (1979). *Poverty children and their language: Implications for teaching and treating*. New York: Grune & Stratton.

ADLER S., & BIRDSONG, S. (1983). Reliability and validity of standardized testing tools used with poor children. *Topics in Language Disorders, 3,* 76–81.

AERA, APA, & NCME (American Educational Research, American Psychological Association, & National Council on Measurement in Education) (1985). Standards of educational and psychological testing. Washington, D.C.: Author.

AFFLECK, J. T., LOWENBRAUN, S., & ARCHER, A. (1980). *Teaching the mildly handicapped in the regular classroom* (2nd ed.). Columbus, OH: Merrill.

AFFLERBACH, P., & JOHNSON, P. (1984). Research methodology on the use of verbal reports in reading research. *Journal of Reading Behavior, 16,* 307–322.

AIKEN, L. R. (1985). *Psychological testing and assessment* (5th ed.). Boston, MA: Allyn & Bacon.

ALBERTO, P. A., & TROUTMAN, A. C. (1986). *Applied behavior analysis for teachers* (2nd ed.). Columbus, OH: Merrill.

ALLEY, G., & DESHLER, D. (1979). *Teaching the learning disabled adolescent: Strategies and methods*. Denver, CO: Love Publishing.

ALLEY, G., DESHLER, D., CLARK, F., SCHUMAKER, J.

B., & WARNER, M. (1983). Learning disabilities in adolescent and adult populations: Research implications (Part III). *Focus on Exceptional Children, 15,* 1–12.

ALLEY, G., & FOSTER, C. (1978). Nondiscriminatory testing of minority and exceptional children. *Focus on Exceptional Children, 9,* 1–14.

AMERICAN ASSOCIATION OF SCHOOL ADMINISTRATORS (AASA) (1988). *Challenges for school leaders*. Arlington, VA: Author.

AMERICAN COLLEGE TESTING (1989). *Discover program*. Hunt Valley, MD: Discover Center.

AMERICAN PSYCHIATRIC ASSOCIATION (1987). *Diagnostic and statistical manual of mental disorders* (3rd ed., rev.). Washington, DC: Author.

AMERICAN PSYCHOLOGICAL ASSOCIATION (1981). Ethical principles of psychologists. *American Psychologist, 36,* 633–638.

———— (1985). *Standards for educational and psychological testing*. Washington, DC: Author.

ANASTASI, A. (1982). *Psychological testing* (5th ed.). New York: Macmillan.

———— (1992). Ethical prinicples of psychologists and code of conduct. *American Psychologist, 47,* 1597–1611.

ANDERSON, A. B., & STOKES, S. J. (1984). Social and institutional influences on the development and practice of literacy. In J. Goelman, A. Oberg, & F. Smith (eds.), *Awakening to literacy,* 24–37. London: Heinemann Educational Books.

ANDREWS, D. M., PATERSON, D. G., & LONGSTAFF, H. P. (1961). *Minnesota clerical test*. New York: Psychological Corporation.

APPLEBEE, A. N. (1978). *The child's concept of story: Ages two to seventeen*. Chicago: The University of Chicago.

ARCHER, D., & AKERT, R. M. (1977). Words and everything else: Verbal and nonverbal cues in social interpretation. *Journal of Personality and Social Psychology, 35,* 435–449.

ARGYLE, M. (ed.) (1969). *Social interaction*. Chicago: Aldine–Atherton.

ARGYLE, M., & COOK, M. (1976). *Gaze and mutual gaze*. Cambridge: Cambridge University Press.

ARGYLE, M., & INGHAM, R. (1972). Gaze, mutual gaze, and proximity. *Seminotica, 32–44.*

ARMSTRONG, S. W., MULKERNE, S., & MCPHERSON, A. (1988). *Socially appropriate and inappropriate development (SAID): Social skills assessment and instructional program.* Birmingham, AL: EBSCO Curriculum Materials.

ARRELOLA V. SANTA ANA BOARD OF EDUCATION (Orange County, CA) No. 160–577, 1968.

ARTER, J. A., & JENKINS, J. R. (1979). Differential diagnosis—prescriptive teaching. A critical appraisal. *Review of Educational Research, 49,* 517–553.

ARTHUR, G. (1952). *Arthur adaptation of the Leiter international performance scale.* Chicago: Stoelting.

ASHLOCK, R. B. (1986). *Error patterns in computation: A semi-programmed approach* (4th ed.). Columbus, OH: Merrill.

AYRES, J. (1975). *Southern California sensory integration tests.* Los Angeles: Western Psychological Services.

AYRES, L. P. (1917). *Ayres handwriting scale.* Princeton, NJ: Educational Testing Service.

BABAD, E. Y., & BASHI, J. (1978). On narrowing the performance gap in children. *Journal for Research in Mathematics Education, 9,* 221–227.

BADER, L. (1983). *Bader language and reading inventory.* New York: Macmillan.

BAGAI, E., & BAGAI, J. (1979). *System FORE handbook.* North Hollywood, CA: Foreworks Publications.

BAILEY, D. B., & WOLERY, M. (1984). *Teaching infants and preschoolers with handicaps.* Columbus, OH: Merrill.

_____ (1989). *Assessing infants and preschoolers with handicaps.* Columbus, OH: Merrill.

BALA, S. P., COHEN, B., MORRIS, A. G., ATKIN, A., GITTELMAN, T., & KATES, J. (1981). Saccades of hyperactive and normal boys during ocular pursuit. *Developmental Medicine and Child Neurology, 23,* 323–336.

BALLARD, J., RAMIREZ, B., & ZANTAL–WIENER, K. (1987). *P.L. 94–142, Section 504, and P.L. 99–457: Understanding what they are.* Reston, VA: Council for Exceptional Children.

BALTHAZAR, E. (1976). *Balthazar scales of adaptive behavior.* Palo Alto, CA: Consulting Psychologists Press.

BANDURA, A. (1969). *Principles of behavior modification.* New York: Holt, Rinehart & Winston.

_____ (1977). *Social learning theory.* Englewood Cliffs, NJ: Prentice–Hall.

BANKSON, N. W. (1990). *Bankson language test–two.* Chicago, IL: Riverside.

BANKSON, N. W., & BERNTHAL, J. E. (1990). *Quick screen of phonology.* Chicago, IL: Riverside.

BARATZ, J. (1969). Teaching reading in an urban negro school system. In J. C. Baratz, & R. Wishuy (eds.), *Teaching black children to read,* 27–42. Arlington, VA: Center for Applied Linguistics.

BARLOW, D. H., HAYES, S. C., & NELSON, R. O. (1984). *The scientist-practitioner: Research and accountability in clinical and educational settings.* New York: Pergamon.

BARNETT, D. W., & ZUCKER, K. B. (1990). *The personal and social assessment of children: An analysis of current status and professional practice issues.* Boston, MA: Allyn & Bacon.

BARON, J. (1981). Reflective thinking as a goal of education. *Intelligence, 5,* 291–309.

BARONA, A., & SANTOS DE BARONA, M. (1987). A model for the assessment of limited English proficient students referred for special education services. In S. H. Fraud & W. J. Tikunoff (eds.), *Bilingual education and bilingual special education: A guide for administrators,* 183–209. Austin, TX: PRO-ED.

BARSCH, R. H. (1967). *Achieving perceptual motor efficiency.* Seattle, WA: Special Child Publications.

BASSLER, O. C., BEERS, M. I., RICHARDSON, L. I., & THURMAN, R. L. (1979). *Peabody mathematics readiness test.* Bensonville, IL: Scholastic Testing Service.

BATES, E., & MACWHINNEY, B. (1979). A functionalist approach to the acquisition of grammar. In E. Ochs & B. Schieffeline (eds.), *Developmental pragmatics,* 46–62. New York: Academic Press.

BATTLE, J. (1992). *Culture-free self-esteem inventories* (2nd ed.). Austin, TX: PRO-ED.

BAUER, R. H. (1979a). Memory, acquisition, category clustering in learning disabled children. *Journal of Experimental Child Psychology, 27,* 365–383.

_____ (1979b). Recall after a short delay and acquisition in learning disabled and nondisabled children. *Journal of Learning Disabilities, 12,* 596–608.

BAYLEY, N. (1969). *Bayley scales of infant development.* New York: Psychological Corporation.

BEATTY, L. S., MADDEN, R., GARDNER, E. F., & KARLSEN, B. (1984). *Stanford diagnostic mathematics test* (3rd ed.). San Antonio, TX: Psychological Corporation.

BECK, A. T. (1987). *Beck depression inventory.* San Antonio, TX: Psychological Corporation.

BECK, S. (1986). Methods of assessment II: Questionnaires and checklists. In C. L. Frame & J. L. Matson (eds.), *Handbook of assessment in childhood pathology: Applied issues in differential diagnosis and treatment evaluation,* 79–106. New York: Plenum Press.

BEERY, K. E. (1989a). *Administration, scoring, and teaching manual for the developmental test of visual-motor integration* (3rd rev.). Cleveland: Modern Curriculum Press.

_____ (1989b). *Developmental test of visual-motor integration.* Cleveland, OH: Modern Curriculum Press.

BELL, W. (1990). *Children at risk due to exposure to alcohol, pediatric AIDS, and substance abuse.* Paper presented at the meeting of NASDSE Action Seminar: Infants exposed pre-natally to AIDS, Alcohol and Drugs, Decatur, GA.

BELLAK, L., & BELLAK, S. (1974). *Children's apperception test.* San Antonio, TX: Psychological Corporation.

BENAVIDES, A. (1989). High risk predictors and preferral screening for language minority students. In A. A. Ortiz & B. A. Ramirez (eds.), *Schools and the culturally diverse exceptional student: Promising practices and future directions,* 19–31. Reston, VA: Council for Exceptional Children.

BENDER, L. (1938). A visual motor gestalt test and its clinical use. *The Orthopsychiatric Association Research Monographs, 3.*

BENNETT, G. K., SEASHORE, H. G., & WESMAN, A. G.

(1982). *Differential aptitude test,* 5th ed. New York: Psychological Corporation.

BEREITER, C., & BIRD, M. (1985). Use of think aloud in identification and teaching of reading comprehension strategies. *Cognition and Instruction, 2,* 131–156.

BERINGER, M. (1984). *Ber-Sil Elementary Spanish test.* Rancho Palos Verdes, CA: Ber-Sil.

——— (1987). *Ber-Sil Secondary Spanish Test.* Rancho Palos Verdes, CA: Ber-Sil.

BERTHOFF, A. (1982). *Forming, thinking, writing: The composing imagination.* Montclair, NJ: Boyton Cook.

BERTHOZ, A., & JONES, G. M. (eds.) (1985). *Adaptive mechanisms in gaze control.* New York: Elsevier.

Better hearing is better living (1985). Union, NJ: Siemens.

BINET, A., & SIMON, T. (1976). *The development of intelligence in children* (E. S. Kit, trans.). Baltimore: Williams & Wilkins.

BIRDWHISTLE, R. L. (1952). *Introduction to kinesics.* Louisville: University of Louisville Press.

——— (1970). *Kinesics and context.* Philadelphia: University of Philadelphia Press.

BIRELEY, M. K., LANDERS, M. G., VERNOOY, J. A., & SCHLAERTH, P. (1986). The Wright State University program: Implications of the first decade. *Reading, Writing, and Learning Disabilities, 2,* 349–357.

BIRLESON, P. (1981). The validity of depressive disorder in childhood and the development of a self-rating scale: A research report. *Journal of Child Psychology and Psychiatry, 22,* 73–88.

BITTER, J. A. (1979). *Introduction to rehabilitation.* St. Louis, MO: C.V. Mosby.

BLACK, F. W. (1974). Self-concept as related to achievement and age in learning disabled children. *Child Development, 45,* 1137–1140.

BLACK, J. (1979). Formal and informal means of assessing the communicative competence of kindergarten children. *Research in the Teaching of English, 13,* 49–68.

BLANK, M., ROSE, S. A., & BERLIN, L. J. (1978). *Preschool language assessment instrument.* Orlando, FL: Grune & Stratton.

BLODGETT, E. G., & COOPER, E. B. (1987). *Analysis of language learning.* Illinois: Lingui Systems.

BLOOM, L. (1970). *Language development: Form and function in emerging grammars.* Cambridge, MA: The M.I.T. Press.

BLOOM, L., & LAHEY, M. (1978). *Language development and language disorders.* New York: John Wiley.

BODER, E., & JARRICO, S. (1982). *The Boder test of reading–spelling patterns.* San Antonio, TX: Psychological Corporation.

BORKOWSKI, J. G. (1985). Signs of intelligence: Strategy generalization and metacognition. In S. R. Yussen (ed.), *The growth of reflection in children,* 105–144. Orlando, FL: Academic Press.

BOTEL, M. (1978). *Botel reading inventory.* Chicago, IL: Follett.

BOTVIN, G., & SUTTON–SMITH, B. (1977). The development of structural complexity in children's fantasy narratives. *Developmental Psychology, 13,* 377–388.

BOWERMAN, M. (1974). Discussion summary—development of concepts underlying language. In R. Scheifelbusch & L. Lloyd (eds.), *Language perspectives—acquisition, retardation, and investigation.* Baltimore: University Park Press.

——— (1976). Semantic factors in the acquisition of rules for word use and sentence construction. In D. M. Moreland & A. E. Moreland (eds.), *Normal and deficient child language,* 52–97. Baltimore, MD: University Park Press.

——— (1979). The acquisition of complex sentences. In P. Fletcher and M. Garman (eds.), *Language acquisition,* 32–59. Cambridge, England: Cambridge University Press.

BRACKEN, B. (1984). *Bracken basic concept scale.* New York: Psychological Corporation.

——— (1992). *Multidimensional self-concept scale.* Austin, TX: PRO-ED.

BRADLEY–JOHNSON, S. (1986). *Psychoeducational assessment of visually impaired and blind students.* Austin, TX: PRO-ED.

BRICE–HEATH, S. (1983). *Ways with words: Language, life, and work in communities and classrooms.* New York: Cambridge University Press.

BRIGANCE, A. H. (1977). *BRIGANCE® diagnostic inventory of basic skills.* N. Billerica, MA: Curriculum Associates.

——— (1981). *BRIGANCE® diagnostic inventory of essential skills.* N. Billerica, MA: Curriculum Associates.

——— (1983). *BRIGANCE® diagnostic comprehensive inventory of basic skills.* N. Billerica, MA: Curriculum Associates.

BRINKLEY, R. C. (1989). Getting the most from client interviews. *Performance and Instruction, 28*(4), 5–8.

BRITTON, J., BURGESS, T., MARTIN, N., MCLEOD, A., & ROSEN, H. (1975). *The development of writing abilities.* London: MacMillan Education, Ltd.

BROEN, P. (1972). The verbal environment of the language learning child. *Monograph of the American Speech and Hearing Association.* No. 17.

BROOKS, R. (1979). Psycho-educational assessment: A broader perspective. *Professional Psychology, 10,* 708–722.

BROOKS–GUNN, J., & LEWIS, M. (1981). Assessing young handicapped children: Issues and solutions. *Journal of the Division for Early Childhood, 2,* 84–95.

BROWDER, D. M. (1987). *Assessment of individuals with severe handicaps: An applied behavior approach to life skills assessment.* Baltimore, MD: P. H. Brookes.

——— (1991). *Assessment of individuals with severe disabilities: An applied behavior approach to life skills assessment* (2nd ed.). Baltimore, MD: P.H. Brookes.

BROWDER, D. M., & MARTIN, D. K. (1986). A new curriculum for Tommy. *Teaching Exceptional Children, 18,* 261–265.

BROWN, A. L., & CAMPIONE, J. C. (1981). Inducing flexible thinking: A problem of access. In M. Friedman, J. P. Das, & N. O'Connor (eds.), *Intelligence and learning,* 515–529. New York: Plenum Press.

BROWN, A. L., & FRENCH, L. A. (1979). The zone of potential development: Implications for intelligence testing in the year 2000. *Intelligence, 3,* 255–273.

BROWN, L. (1987a). The nature of socioemotional development. In D. D. Hammill (ed.), *Assessing the abilities and instructional needs of students,* 507–523. Austin, TX: PRO-ED.

—— (1987b). An ecological perspective. In D. D. Hammill (ed.), *Assessing the abilities and instructional needs of students,* 599–609. Austin, TX: PRO-ED.

BROWN, L., & ALEXANDER, J. (1991). *Self-esteem index.* Austin, TX: PRO-ED.

BROWN, L., & COLEMAN, M. C. (1988). *Index of personality characteristics: A measure of affect in school-aged children.* Austin, TX: PRO-ED.

BROWN, L., & HAMMILL, D. D. (1990). *Behavior rating profile* (2nd ed.). Austin, TX: PRO-ED.

BROWN, L., & LEIGH, J. E. (1986). *Adaptive behavior inventory.* Austin, TX: PRO-ED.

BROWN, L., SHERBENOU, R. J., & JOHNSEN, S. K. (1990a). *Tests of nonverbal intelligence: A language-free measure of cognitive ability–revised.* Austin, TX: PRO-ED.

—— (1990b). *Test of nonverbal intelligence* (2nd ed.). Austin, TX: PRO-ED.

BROWN, R. (1958). How shall a thing be called? *Psychological Review, 65,* 14–21.

—— (1973). *A first language: The early stages.* Cambridge, MA: Harvard University Press.

BROWN, V. L., HAMMILL, D. D., & WIEDERHOLT, J. L. (1986). *Test of reading comprehension* (rev. ed.). Austin, TX: PRO-ED.

BROWN, V. L., & MCENTIRE, E. (1984). *Test of mathematical abilities.* Austin, TX: PRO-ED.

BROWN V. BOARD OF EDUCATION OF TOPEKA, KANSAS, 348 U.S. 886, 75 S. Ct. 210 (1954).

BROWNELL, L. (1985). *Expressive one-word picture vocabulary test–upper extension.* Chicago: Riverside.

BRUECKNER, L. J. (1930). *Diagnostic and remedial teaching in arithmetic.* Philadelphia: Winston.

BRUININKS, R. H., WOODCOCK, R. W., WEATHERMAN, R. F., & HILL, B. K. (1984). *Scales of independent behavior.* Allen, TX: DLM Teaching Resource.

BRUNER, J. S. (1973). *Beyond the information given: Studies in the psychology of knowing.* New York: W. W. Norton.

—— (1975). The ontogenesis of speech acts. *Journal of Child Language, 2,* 1–20.

BRYAN, T. H., PEARL, R., DONAHUE, M., BRYAN, J., & PFLAUM, S. (1983). The Chicago Institue for the Study of Learning Disabilities. *Exceptional Education Quarterly, 4*(1), 1–22.

BRYANT, B. R., & WIEDERHOLT, J. L. (1990). *Gray oral reading tests diagnostic.* Austin, TX: PRO-ED.

BUCKLEY, K., & OAKLAND, T. M. (1977). *Contrasting localized norms for Mexican American children on the ABIC.* Paper presented at the annual meeting of the American Psychological Association, San Francisco, CA.

BUDOFF, M. (1987). The validity of learning potential assessment. In C. S. Lidz (ed.), *Dynamic assessment: An interactional approach to evaluating learning potential,* 52–81. New York: Guilford Press.

BURGEMEISTER, B. B., BLUM, L. H., & LORGE, I. (1972). *Columbia mental maturity scale* (3rd ed.). San Antonio, TX: Psychological Corporation.

BURGOON, J. K. (1985). Nonverbal signals. In M. L. Knapp & G. R. Miller (eds.), *Handbook of interpersonal communication,* 344–390. Beverly Hills, CA: SAGE.

BURKS, H. F. (1977). *Burks' behavior rating scales.* Los Angeles, CA: Western Psychological Services.

BURLESON, B. R. (1984). The affective perspective taking process: A test of Furiel's role thinking model. In M. Burleson (ed.), *Communication yearbook II,* 473–488. Beverly Hills, CA: SAGE.

BUROS, O. K. (1938–1978). *Mental measurement yearbooks.* Lincoln, NE: University of Nebraska Press.

BURT, M. K., DULAY, H. C., & CHAVEZ, E. H. (1978). *Bilingual syntax measure 1 and 11.* San Antonio, TX: Psychological Corporation.

BURTON, G. M. (1987). Helping children control stress. *Focus on Learning Problems in Mathematics, 9* (4), 41–48.

BUSH, C. L., & HUEBNER, M. H. (1970). *Strategies for reading in the elementary school.* New York: Macmillan.

BUSH, W. J., & GILES, M. T. (1966). *Aids to psycholinguistic teaching.* Columbus, OH: Merrill.

BUSSIS, A. M., CHITTENDEN, E. A., AMAREL, M., & KLAUSNEG, E. (1985). *Inquiry into meaning: An investigation of learning to read.* Hillsdale, NJ: Erlbaum.

BUSWELL, G. T., & JOHN, L. (1925). *Fundamental processes in arithmetic.* Indianapolis: Bobbs–Merrill.

CAIN, L. F., LEVINE, S., & ELZEY, F. F. (1963). *Manual for the Cain-Levine social competency scale.* Palo Alto, CA: Consulting Psychologists Press.

—— (1977). *Cain-Levine social competency scale.* Palo Alto, CA: Consulting Psychologists Press.

CAIRNS, R. B. (1986). A contemporary perspective on social development. In P. S. Strain, M. J. Guralinick, & H. M. Walker (eds.), *Children's social behaviors: Development, assessment, and modification,* 3–48. Orlando, FL: Academic Press.

CAMPBELL, B., & BALDWIN, V. (1988). *Severely handicapped/hearing impaired students.* Baltimore: P. H. Brookes.

CAMPBELL, D. P., & HANSEN, J. (1985). *Manual for the SVIB—Strong–Campbell interest inventory.* Palo Alto, CA: Stanford University Press.

CAMPIONE, J. C., & BROWN, A. L. (1978). Toward a theory of intelligence: Contributions from research with retarded children. *Intelligence, 2,* 279–304.

—— (1984). Learning ability and transfer propensity as sources of individual differences in intelligence. In P. H. Brooks, R. D. Sperber, & C. McCauley (eds.), *Learning and cognition in the mentally retarded,* 265–294. Baltimore, MD: University Park Press.

—— (1987). Linking dynamic assessment with school achievement. In C. S. Lidz (ed.), *Dynamic assessment: An interactional approach to evaluating learning potential,* 82–115. New York: Guilford Press.

CAPE (CONSORTIUM ON ADAPTIVE PERFORMANCE EVALUATION) (1980). *Adaptive performance instrument.* Moscow, ID: Department of Special Education, University of Idaho.

CARAMAZZA, A. C. (1988). Some aspects of language processing revealed through the analysis of acquired aphasia. The lexical system. *Annual Review of Neurosciences, 11,* 395–421.

CARRASCO, R. L., VERA, A., & CAZDEN, C. B. (1981). Aspects of bilingual students' communicative competence in the classroom: A case study. In R. P.

Duran (ed.), *Latino language and communicative behavior*, 25–53. Norwood, NJ: Ablex.

CARRIER, C. A., WILLIAMS, M. D., & DALGAARD, A. R. (1988). College students' perceptions of notetaking and their relationship to selected learner characteristics and course achievement. *Research in Higher Education, 28*, 223–239.

CARROLL, J. B. (1964). *Language and thought.* Englewood Cliffs, NJ: Prentice–Hall.

——— (1977). Developmental parameters of reading comprehension. In J. T. Guthrie (ed.), *Cognition, curriculum and comprehension*, 1–19. Newark, DE: International Reading Association.

CARROW–WOOLFOLK, E. (1974). *Carrow elicited language inventory.* Allen, TX: DLM Teaching Resources.

——— (1985). *Test for the auditory comprehension of language–revised.* Allen, TX: DLM Teaching Resources.

CARTLEDGE, G., & MILBURN, J. F. (eds.) (1986). *Teaching social skills to children* (2nd ed.). New York: Pergamon.

CARTWRIGHT, G. P., CARTWRIGHT, C. A., & WARD, M. E. (1984). *Educating special learners.* Belmont, CA: Wadsworth.

CASSEL, T. Z. (1976). A social-ecological model of adaptive functioning: A contextual developmental perspective. In N. A. Carlson (ed.), *Final report: The context of life: A social-ecological model of adaptive behavior and functioning*, 26–53. East Lansing, MI: Institute for Family and Child Study, Michigan State University.

CATTELL, P. (1940). *The measurement of intelligence of infants and young children.* New York: Psychological Corporation.

CATTELL, R. B. (1963). Theory of fluid and crystalized intelligence: A critical experiment. *Journal of Educational Psychology, 54*, 1–22.

CATTELL, R. B., CATTELL, M. D., & JOHNS, E. (1984). *High school personality questionnaire.* San Antonio, TX: Psychological Corporation.

CAWLEY, J. F. (1981). Commentary. *Topics in Learning and Learning Disabilities, 1*(3), 89–94.

CELEE–MURICA, M. (1978). The simultaneous acquisition of English and French in a two-year-old child. In E. Hatch (ed.), *Second language acquisition: A book of readings*, 38–53. Rowley, MA: Newbury House.

CENTER FOR ASSESSMENT AND DIAGNOSTIC STUDIES (1988–1989).

CHALL, J. S. (1983). *Stages of reading development.* New York: McGraw–Hill.

CHEN, M. J., BRAITHWAITE, V., & HUANG, S. T. (1982). Attributes of intelligent behavior: Perceived relevance and difficulty by Australian and Chinese students. *Journal of Cross-Cultural Psychology, 13*, 139–156.

CHENG, L. L. (1987). *Assessing Asian language performance. Guidelines for evaluating limited-English proficient students.* Rockville, MD: Aspen.

CHI, M. T., & GALLAGHER, J. D. (1982). Speed of processing: A developmental source of limitation. *Topics of Learning & Learning Disabilities, 2*(2), 23–32.

CHOATE, J. S., ENRIGHT, B. E., MILLER, L. J., POTEET, J. A., & RAKES, T. A. (1992). *Curriculum-based assessment and programming* (2nd ed.). Boston, MA: Allyn & Bacon.

CHOMSKY, N., & HALLE, M. (1968). *The sound pattern of English.* New York: Harper & Row.

CHOMSKY, W. (1957). *Syntactic structures.* The Hague: Mouton.

CLARK, E. V. (1973). What's in a word? On a child's acquisition of semantics in his first language. In T. E. Moore (ed.), *Cognitive development and the acquisition of language*, 102–130. New York: Academic Press.

CLAY, M. (1975). *What did I write?* Auckland, New Zealand: Heinemann.

COAHLEY, D., & THOMAS, J. G. (1977). The ocular microtremor record and the prognosis of the unconscious patient. *Lancet, 1*, 512–515.

COHEN, M. A., & GROSS, P. J. (1979). *The developmental resource: Behavioral sequences for assessment and program planning.* New York: Basic Books.

COHN, M., & KORNELLY D. (1970). For better reading—a more positive self-image. *The Elementary School Journal, 70*, 199–201.

COIE, J. D., & DODGE, K. A. (1983). Continuities and changes in children's social status: A five-year longitudinal study. *Merrill-Palmer Quarterly, 29*, 261–282.

COLARUSSO, R. P., & HAMMILL, D. D. (1972). *Motor-free test of visual perception.* San Rafael, CA: Academic Therapy Publications.

COLEMAN, M. C. (1992). *Behavior disorders: Theory and practice* (2nd ed.). Boston, MA: Allyn & Bacon.

COLES, G. (1978). The learning disabilities test battery: Empirical and theoretical issues. *Harvard Educational Review, 48*, 313–340.

COMMISSION ON STANDARDS FOR SCHOOL MATHEMATICS. (1989). *Curriculum and evaluation standards for school mathematics.* Reston, VA: National Council of Teachers of Mathematics, Inc.

COMPTROLLER GENERAL OF THE UNITED STATES (1981). *Unanswered questions on educating handicapped children in local public schools.* Washington, DC: Author. (ERIC Document Reproduction Service No. ED 209 794).

CONE, J. D. (1984). *The pyramid scales.* Austin, TX: PRO-ED.

CONEN, S. W. (1988). Coping strategies of university students with learning disabilities. *Journal of Learning Disabilities, 21*, 261–264.

CONNERS, C. K. (1987, July). Dyslexia and the neurophysiology of attention. Paper presented at the meeting of the World Congress of Dyslexia, Crete, Greece.

——— (1989). *Conners' rating scales.* Austin, TX: PRO-ED.

CONNOLLY, A. J. (1988). *KeyMath revised: A diagnostic inventory of essential mathematics.* Circle Pines, MN: American Guidance Service.

CONNORS, F. P. (1983). Improving school instruction for learning disabled children: The Teachers College Institute. *Exceptional Children Quarterly, 4*(1), 23–44.

COOK, M. (1952). (trans.). *The origins of intelligence in children.* New York: International Universities.

COOPER, J. O. (1981). *Measuring behavior* (2nd ed.). Columbus, OH: Merrill.

COOPERSMITH, S. (1981). *Coopersmith self-esteem inventories.* Monterey, CA: Publishers Test Service.

COTTLE, W. C. (1966). *School interest inventory.* Chicago: Riverside.

COUGHRAN, L., & LIELES, B. V. (1974). *Developmental syntax.* Austin, TX: Learning Concepts.

COULTER, W. A., & MORROW, H. W. (eds.) (1978). *Adaptive behavior: Concepts and measurements.* New York: Grune & Stratton.

COVARRUBIAS V. SAN DIEGO UNIFIED SCHOOL DISTRICT (Southern California), No. 70–394–T, (S.D., Cal. February, 1971).

COWEN, S. E. (1988). Coping strategies of university students with learning disabilities. *Journal of Learning Disabilities, 21,* 161–164.

COX, L. S. (1975). Diagnosing and remediating systematic errors in addition and subtraction computations. *The Arithmetic Teacher, 22,* 151–157.

COYTE, W. R., & LISNON, F. (1985). The substance abuser in crisis: Evaluation and treatment. *The Counselor, 7*(2), 5–8.

CRATTY, B. J. (1969). *Perceptual-motor behavior and educational processes.* Springfield, IL: Charles C Thomas.

CRAWFORD, J. E., & CRAWFORD, D. M. (1975). *The Crawford small parts dexterity test.* New York: Psychological Corporation.

CRISLER, J. R. (1979). Utilization of a team approach in implementing Public Law 94–142. *Journal of Research and Development in Education, 12*(4), 101–108.

CRITCHLOW, D. C. (1973). *Dos amigos verbal language scales.* East Aurora, NY: United Educational Services.

CROMER, R. F. (1980). Spontaneous spelling by language-disordered children. In U. Frith (ed.), *Cognitive processes in spelling,* 402–422. London: Academic Press.

CROWHURST, M., & PICHE, G. L. (1979). Audience and mode of discourse effects on syntactic complexity at two grade levels. *Research in the Teaching of English, 13,* 101–109.

CTB/MCGRAW–HILL (1972). *Prescriptive reading inventory.* Monterey, CA: Author.

CUMMINS, J. (1982). The role of primary language development in promoting educational success for language minority students. In *California State Department of Education, schooling, and language minority students: A theorhetical framework,* 3–49. Los Angeles: Bilingual Education, Evaluation, Dissemination, and Assessment Center.

———— (1984). *Bilingual special education: Issues in assessment and pedagogy.* Clevedan, Avon, England: Multilingual Matters.

DALE, E., & EICHHOLZ, G. (1960). *Children's knowledge of words: An interim report.* Columbus, OH: Bureau of Educational Research and Service, Ohio State University.

DAMICO, T. S. (1985). Clinical discourse analysis. A functional approach to language assessment. In C. Simon (ed.), *Communication skills and classroom success: Assessment of language learning disabled students,* 165–204. San Diego: College Hill Press.

DAMICO, T. S., OLLER, T. W., & STOREY, M. E. (1983). The diagnosis of language disorders in bilingual children. *Journal of Speech and Hearing Disorders, 48,* 285–294.

D'ANGELO, K., & WILSON, R. M. (1979). How helpful is insertion and omission miscue analysis? *Reading Teacher, 32,* 519–520.

DARLEY, F. (1979). *Evaluation of appraisal techniques in speech and language pathology.* Reading, MA: Addison–Wesley.

DAS, J. P. (1973). Cultural deprivation and cognitive competence. In N. R. Ellis (ed.), *International review of research in mental retardation* (Vol. 6), 1–53. New York: Academic Press.

DAS, J. P., KIRBY, J., & JARMAN, R. F. (1975). Simultaneous and successive syntheses: An alternative model for cognitive abilities. *Psychological Bulletin, 82,* 87–103.

DAVIS, B. (1985). IEP management programs. *Reports to Decision Makers, 7* (ERIC Document Reproduction Service No. ED 266 610).

DEAVILA, E. A. (1977). *The cartoon conversation scales (CSS).* San Rafael, CA: Linguametrics.

DEAVILA, E. A., & DUNCAN, S. E. (1975–85). *Language assessment scales—oral.* Monterey, CA: CTB/McGraw–Hill.

DEAVILA, E. A., & HAVASSY, B. E. (1974). *Intelligence of Mexican-American children: A field study comparing neo-Piagetian and traditional capacity and achievement measures.* Austin, TX: Dissemination Center for Bilingual Bicultural Education.

———— (1975). Piagetian alternative to IQ: Mexican-American study. In N. Hobbs (ed.), *Issues in the classification of exceptional children,* 246–265. San Francisco: Jossey–Bass.

DEBONO, E. (1967). *New thinking.* New York: Basic Books.

DECHANT, E. V. (1964). *Improving the teaching of reading.* Englewood Cliffs, NJ: Prentice–Hall.

DENO, S. (1985). Curriculum-based measurement: The emerging alternative. *Exceptional Children, 52,* 219–232.

DENO, S., MIRKIN, P. K., & CHIANG, B. (1982). Identifying valid measures of reading. *Exceptional Children, 49*(1), 36–45.

DESHLER, D. D., & SCHUMAKER, J. B. (1983). Social skills of learning disabled adolescents: Characteristics and interventions. *Topics in Learning and Learning Disabilities, 3*(2), 15–23.

DESHLER, D. D., SCHUMAKER, J. B., & LENZ, B. K. (1984). Academic and cognitive interventions for LD adolescents: Part I. *Journal of Learning Disabilities, 17,* 108–117.

DESHLER, D. D., SCHUMAKER, J. B., LENZ, B. K., & ELLIS, E. S. (1984). Academic and cognitive interventions for LD adolescents: Part II. *Journal of Learning Disabilities, 17,* 170–187.

DEVINE, T. G. (1981). *Teaching study skills.* Boston, MA: Allyn & Bacon.

DIANA V. CALIFORNIA STATE BOARD OF EDUCATION, Civ. No. C–70 37 RFP (N. D. Cal. 1970, 1973).

DIETRICH, T. G., & FREEMAN, C. (1979). *Language in education: Theory and practice. A linguistic guide to English proficiency testing in schools.* Arlington, VA: Center for Applied Linguistics.

DILEO, J. H. (1977). *Child development: Analysis and synthesis.* New York: Brunner/Mazel.

DISIMONI, F. (1978). *Token test for children–revised.* Allen, TX: DLM Teaching Resource.

DODARO, G. L., & SALVENMINI, A. N. (1985). *Implementation of P.L. 94–142 as it relates to handicapped delinquents in the District of Columbia.* Washington, DC: U.S. General Accounting Office.

DODGE, K. A. (1983). Behavioral antecedents of peer social status. *Child Development, 54,* 1386–1399.

DOEHRING, B. G., & AULLS, M. W. (1979). The interactive nature of reading acquisition. *Journal of Reading Behavior, 11,* 27–40.

DOLCH, E. W. (1948). *Graded reading difficulty worksheet.* Champaign, IL: Garrard Press.

———— (1950). *Dolch word list.* Morristown, NJ: General Learning.

DOLL, E. A. (1953). *Measurement of social competence: A manual for the Vineland social maturity scale.* Circle Pines, MN: American Guidance Service.

DORE, J. (1974). A description of early language development. *Journal of Psycholinguistic Research, 4,* 423–430.

DOREN, M. (1973). *Doren diagnostic reading test of word recognition skills* (2nd ed.). Circle Pines, MN: American Guidance Service.

DRACH, K. (1969). *The language of the parent: A pilot study.* Working paper 14, Language–Behavior Research Laboratory, University of California, Berkeley, CA.

DUCHAN, J. (1984). Language assessment: The pragmatics revolution. In R. Navemore (ed.), *Language sciences.* San Diego: College Hill Press.

DUDLEY–MARLING, C. (1985). Perceptions of the usefulness of the IEP by teachers of learning disabled and emotionally disturbed children. *Psychology in the Schools, 22,* 65–67.

DUFFEY, J. G., SALVIA, J., TUCKER, J., & YSSELDYKE, J. (1981). Nonbiased assessment: A need for operationalism. *Exceptional Children, 47*(6), 427–434.

DUNN, LLOYD M., & DUNN, LEOTA M. (1981). *Peabody picture vocabulary test–revised.* Circle Pines, MN: American Guidance Service.

DUNN, L. M., & MARKWARDT, F. C., JR. (1989). *Peabody individual achievement test–2.* Circle Pines, MN: American Guidance Service.

DUNN, L. M., & SMITH, O. J. (1965). *Peabody language development kit–Level I.* Circle Pines, MN: American Guidance Service.

———— (1966). *Peabody language development kit–Level II.* Circle Pines, MN: American Guidance Service.

———— (1967). *Peabody language development kit–Level III.* Circle Pines, MN: American Guidance Service.

DUNN, L. M., SMITH, O. J., & HORTON, K. B. (1968). *Peabody language development kit–Level P.* Circle Pines, MN: American Guidance Service.

DUNST, C. J. (1980). *A clinical and educational manual for use with the Uzgiris and Hunt scales of infant psychological development.* Baltimore: University Park Press.

DURAN, R. P. (1989). Assessment and instruction of at-risk Hispanic students. *Exceptional Children, 56,* 154–159.

DURRELL, D. D., & CATTERSON, J. H. (1980). *Durrell analysis of reading difficulty* (3rd ed.). San Antonio, TX: Psychological Corporation.

DYSON, A., & PADEN, E. P. (1983). Some phonological acquisiton strategies used by two-year-olds. *Journal of Child Communication Disorders, 7,* 6–18.

EDUCATIONAL TESTING SERVICE (1988). *System of interactive guidance and information program.* Princeton, NJ: Author.

———— (1989). Scholastic Aptitude Test. Princeton, NJ: Author.

———— (1992–1993). Graduate Records Examination. Princeton, NJ: Author.

EHRENBERG, C. G. (1992). *Beliefs of regular and special education teachers regarding students at-risk: A qualitative case study of issues and professional roles.* Unpublished doctoral dissertation, University of Georgia, Athens, GA.

EKWALL, E. E. (1976). *Diagnosis and remediation of the disabled reader.* Boston, MA: Allyn & Bacon.

———— (1981). *Locating and correcting reading difficulties* (3rd. ed.). Columbus, OH: Merrill.

———— (1986). *Ekwall reading inventory* (2nd ed.). Boston, MA: Allyn & Bacon.

EKWALL, E. E., & SHANKER, J. L. (1983). *Diagnosis and remediation of the disabled reader* (2nd ed.), Boston, MA: Allyn & Bacon.

ENGLEHARDT, J. M. (1977). Analysis of children's computational errors: A qualitative approach. *British Journal of Educational Psychology, 47,* 149–154.

ENRIGHT, B. E. (1983). *Enright diagnostic inventory of basic arithmetic skills.* North Billerica, MA: Curriculum Associates.

ERICKSON, J. G. (1985). How many languages do you speak? An overview of bilingual education. *Topics in Language Disorders, 5,* 1–14.

ERICKSON, J. G., & OMARK, D. R. (eds.) (1981). *Communication assessment of the bilingual child: Issues and guidelines.* Baltimore: University Park Press.

ESTES, T. H., ESTES, J. J., RICHARDS, H. C., & ROETTGER, D. (1981). *Estes attitude scales.* Austin, TX: PRO-ED.

EVANS, S. S., EVANS, W. H., & MERCER, C. D. (1986). *Assessment for instruction.* Newton, MA: Allyn & Bacon.

EVANS, W. H., EVANS, S. S., & SCHMID, R. E. (1989). *Behavior and instructional management.* Boston, MA: Allyn & Bacon.

EWELL, N. C. (1983). *How to streamline your IEP: A special education handbook on computer-assisted individualized education programs.* Carmichael, CA: San Juan Unified School District. (ERIC Document Reproduction Service No. ED 236 859).

EXNER, J. E. (1986). *The Rorschach: A comprehensive system. Volume 1: Basic foundation* (2nd ed.). New York: John Wiley.

FALLOON, J., EDDY, T., ROPER, M., & PIZZO, P. (1988). AIDS in the pediatric population. In V. J. Devita, Jr., J. K. Sitellman, & S. A. Rosenberg (eds.). *AIDS: Diagnosis, treatment, and prevention,* 223–250. Philadelphia: JB Lippincott.

FARR, R. (ed.) (1973). *Iowa silent reading tests.* San Antonio, TX: Psychological Corporation.

FEDERAL REGISTER (1977, Aug. 23). Washington, DC: U.S. Government Printing Office.

FELDHUSEN, N., & TREFFINGER, S. (1978). *Teaching*

creative thinking and problem solving. New York: Kendall/Hunt.

FERGUSON, C. (1978). Learning to pronounce: The earliest stages of phonological development in the child. In F. Minifie & L. Lloyd (eds.), *Communicative and cognitive abilities—early behavioral assessment,* 273–297. Baltimore: University Park Press.

FERGUSON, C., & FARWELL, C. (1975). Words and sounds in early language acquisition. *Language, 51,* 419–439.

FERNALD, G. M. (1943). *Remedial technique in basic school subjects.* New York: McGraw–Hill.

FERREIRO, E. (1984). The underlying logic of literacy development. In H. Goelman, A. Oberg, & F. Smith (eds.), *Awakening to literacy,* 154–173. London: Heinemann.

FEUERSTEIN, R. (1979a). *The dynamic assessment of retarded performers: The learning potential assessment device, theory, instruments, and techniques.* Baltimore: University Park Press.

———— (1979b). *Instrumental enrichment: An intervention program for cognitive modificability.* Baltimore: University Park Press.

———— (1980). *Instrumental enrichment.* Baltimore: University Park Press.

FEUERSTEIN, R., RAND, Y., JENSEN, M. R., KANIEL, S. & TZURIEL, D. (1987). Prerequisites for assessment of learning potential: The LPAD model. In C. S. Lidz (ed.). *Dynamic assessment: An interactional approach to evaluating learning potential,* 35–51. New York: Guilford Press.

FIALKOWSKI V. SHAPP, 405 F. Supp. 946 (1975).

FIELDS, M. C., SPANGLER, K., & LEE, D. M. (1991). *Let's begin reading right: Developmentally appropriate beginning literacy* (2nd ed.). New York: Merrill/Macmillan.

FIGUERO, R. A. (1989). Psychological testing of linguistic-minority students: Knowledge gaps and regulations. *Exceptional Children, 56,* 145–153.

FISCHER, C. T. (1985). *Individualizing psychological assessment.* Pacific Grove, CA: Brooks/Cole.

FITTS, W. H., & ROID, G. H. (1988). *Tennessee self-concept scale.* Los Angeles, CA: Western Psychological Services.

FLANAGAN, J. C. (1953). *Flanagan aptitude classification test.* New York: Psychological Corporation.

FLAVELL, J., & WELLMAN, H. (1977). Metamemory. In R. V. Kail & J. W. Hagen (eds.), *Perspectives on the development of memory and cognition.* Hillsdale, NJ: Erlbaum.

FOKES, J. (1976). *Fokes sentence builder.* Hingham, MA: Teaching Resources.

FOSTER, C. R., GIDDEN, J. J., & STARK, J. (1972). *Assessing children's language comprehension.* Palo Alto, CA: Consulting Psychologists Press.

FOSTER, R. W. (1974). *Camelot behavioral checklist.* Bellevue, WA: Edmark Associates.

FOUNTAIN VALLEY TEACHER SUPPORT SYSTEM IN MATHEMATICS. (1976). Huntington Beach, CA: Zweig Associates.

FRAENKEL, J. R. (1973). *Helping students think and value: Strategies for teaching social studies.* Englewood Cliffs, NJ: Prentice–Hall.

FRENCH, J. L. (1964). *Manual: Pictorial test of intelligence.* Chicago: Riverside.

FRIEDLANDER, S., WEISS, D. S., & TAYLOR, J. (1986). Assessing the influence of maternal depression on the validity of the child behavior checklist. *Journal of Abnormal Child Psychology, 14,* 123–133.

FRIEND, M., & COOK, L. (1992). *Interactions: Collaboration skills for school professionals.* New York: Longman.

FRIENDLY, H. (1975). Some kind of hearing. *University of Pennsylvania Law Review, 123,* 1267–1317.

FROSTIG, M., & HORNE, D. (1964). *The Frostig program for the development of visual perception.* Chicago: Follett.

FROSTIG, M., LEFEVER, W., & WHITTLESEY, J. R. (1966). *Administration and scoring manual: Marianne Frostig developmental test of visual perception.* Palo Alto, CA: Consulting Psychologists Press.

FUCHS, L., FUCHS, D., & DENO, S. (1985). Importance of goal ambitiousness and goal mastery to student achievement. *Exceptional Children, 52,* 63–71.

FUCHS, L., FUCHS, D., & MAXWELL, L. (1988). The validity of informal reading comprehension measures. *Remedial and Special Education, 9*(2), 20–28.

FULLAN, M., & LOUBSER, J. J. (1972). Education and adaptive capacity. *Sociology of Education, 45,* 271–287.

FUSON, K. C., & HALL, J. W. (1983). The acquisition of early number word meanings: A conceptual analysis and review. In H. P. Ginsburg (ed.), *The development of mathematical thinking,* 50–109. New York: Academic Press.

GAGNÉ, R. M. (1965). *The conditions of learning.* New York: Reinhart & Winston.

GALAGAN, J. E. (1986). Psychoeducational testing: Turn out the lights, the party's over. *Exceptional Children, 52,* 288–299.

GALLAGHER, J. (1983). Pre-assessment: A procedure for accommodating language use variability. In T. Gallagher & C. Prutting (eds.), *Pragmatic assessment and intervention issues in language,* 10–28. San Diego: College Hill Press.

GALLAUDET UNIVERSITY CENTER FOR ASSESSMENT AND DEMOGRAPHICS STUDIES ANNUAL SURVEY (1988). Washington, DC: Gallaudet University.

GARCIA, E. E. (1990, Fall). Bilingualism, cognition, and academic performance: The educational debate. *Houghton Mifflin/Educator's Forum.*

GARDNER, H. (1980). *Artful scribbles: The significance of children's drawing.* New York: Basic Books.

———— (1983). *Frames of mind: The theory of multiple intelligences.* New York: Basic Books.

GARDNER, J. (1985a). *Expressive one-word picture vocabulary test–revised.* Chicago: Riverside.

———— (1985b) *Receptive one-word vocabulary test.* Chicago: Riverside.

———— (1985c) *Receptive one-word vocabulary test—upper extension.* Chicago: Riverside.

GARDNER, M. F. (1988). *Test of visual–perceptual skills.* San Francisco, CA: Health Publishing Company.

GARDNER, R., III (1990). Life space interviewing: It can be effective, but don't . . . *Behavioral Disorder, 15,* 111–119.

GARGIULO, R. M. (1985). *Working with parents of excep-*

tional children: A guide for professionals. Boston, MA: Houghton Mifflin.

GARNER, D. M., SHAFER, C. L., & ROSEN, L. W. (1992). Critical appraisal of the DSM–III–R diagnostic criteria for eating disorders. In S. R. Hooper, G. W. Hynd, & R. E. Mattison (eds.), *Child psychopathology: Diagnostic criteria and clinical assessment,* 261–304. Hillsdale, NJ: Erlbaum.

GARVEY, C. (1974). Some properties of social play. *Merrill–Palmer Quarterly, 20,* 163–180.

———— (1977). *Play.* Cambridge, MA: Harvard University Press.

GAST, D. L., & WOLERY, M. (1985). Severe developmental disabilities. In W. H. Berdine & A. E. Blackhurst (eds.), *An Introduction to Special Education* (2nd ed.), 469–520. Boston, MA: Little, Brown & Company.

GATES, A. I., MCKILLOP, A. S., & HOROWITZ, E. C. (1981). *Gates–McKillop–Horowitz reading diagnostic tests.* New York: Teachers College Press.

GAUSSEN, T. (1984). Developmental milestones or conceptual milestones? Some practical and theoretical limitations in infant assessment procedures. *Child: Care, Health and Development, 10,* 99–115.

GAYNÉ, R. M. (1965). *The conditions of learning.* New York: Holt, Rinehart & Winston.

GAZDA, G. M., ASBURY, F. R., BALZER, F. J., CHILDERS, W. C., WALTERS, R. P. (1991). *Human relations development: A manual for educators* (4th ed.). Boston, MA: Allyn & Bacon.

GEARHEART, B. R., WEISHAHN, M. W., & GEARHEART, C. J. (1988). *The exceptional student in the regular classroom* (4th ed.). Columbus, OH: Merrill.

GEIST, H. (1988). *GEIST picture interest inventory* (rev.). Los Angeles: Western Psychological Services.

GELMAN, R., & GALLISTEL, C. R. (1978). *The child's understanding of number.* Cambridge, MA: Harvard University Press.

GENISHI, C., & DYSON, A. (1984). *Language assessment in the early years.* Norwood, NJ: Ablex.

GEORGIA STATE CONFERENCE OF BRANCHES OF NAACP V. STATE OF GEORGIA ELEVENTH COURT OF APPEALS, 775 F. 2d. 1403 (1985).

GERARDI, R. J., GROHE, B., BENEDICT, G. C., & COOLIDGE, P. G. (1984). IEP-More paperwork and wasted time. *Contemporary Education, 56*(1), 39–42.

GERMAN, D. (1986). *Test of word finding.* Allen, TX: DLM Teaching Resource.

———— (1991). *Test of word finding: adolescents and adults.* Allen, TX: DLM Teaching Resource.

GESELL, A. (1928). *Infancy and human growth.* New York: Macmillan.

———— (1938). *The psychology of early growth.* New York: Macmillan.

———— (1940). *The first five years of life: A guide to the study of the preschool child.* New York: Harper & Row.

GESELL, A., & AMATRUDA, C. S. (1947). *Developmental diagnosis.* New York: Harper & Row.

GESSELL, J. (1977). *Diagnostic mathematics inventory.* Monterey, CA: CTB/McGraw-Hill.

GIBSON, E. J., & LEVINE, H. (1975). *The psychology of reading.* Cambridge, MA: The M.I.T. Press.

GILLET, J., & TEMPLE, C. (1982). *Understanding reading problems: Assessment and instruction.* Boston, MA: Little, Brown & Company.

GILLHAM, B. (ed.) (1986). *Handicapping conditions in children.* Dover, NH: Croom Helm.

GILLIAM, J. E., & COLEMAN, M. C. (1981). Who influences IEP committee decisions? *Exceptional Children, 47,* 642–644.

GILMORE, J. V., & GILMORE, E. C. (1968). *Gilmore oral reading test.* San Antonio, TX: Psychological Corporation.

GINSBURG, H. P. (1987). Assessment techniques: Tests, interviews and analytic teaching. In D. D. Hammill (ed.), *Assessing the abilities and instructional needs of students,* 412–503. Austin, TX: PRO-ED.

GINSBURG, H. P., & BAROODY, A. J. (1990). *Test of early mathematics ability* (2nd ed.). Austin, TX: PRO-ED.

GINSBURG, H. P., & MATHEWS, S. C. (1984), *Diagnostic test of arithmetic strategies.* Austin, TX: PRO-ED.

GINSBURG, H. P., & OPPER, S. (1969). *Piaget's theory of intellectual development: An introduction.* Englewood Cliffs, NJ: Prentice–Hall.

GIORDANO, G. (1988). *Reading comprehension inventory.* Bensemville, IL: Scholastic Testing Services.

GITTER, A. G., BLACK, J., & FISHMAN, J. E. (1975). Effect of race, sex, nonverbal communication and verbal communication on perception of leadership. *Sociology and Social Research, 2,* 376–389.

GITTLER, J. (1990). Infants born exposed to drugs: A problem growing at alarming rates. *Early Childhood Reporter, 1,* 1–5.

GLEASON, J. B. (1975). Fathers and other strangers: Mean's speech to young children. In D. Dato (ed.), *Developmental psycholinguistics,* 75–95. Washington, DC: Georgetown University Press.

GLOVER, M. E., PREMINGER, J. L., & SANFORD, A. R. (1978). *Early learning accomplishment profile.* Winston–Salem, NC: Kaplan School Supply.

GNAGEY, T. D. (1980). *Diagnostic screening test: Mathematics* (3rd ed.). East Aurora, NY: Slosson Educational Publications.

GOLDBERG, H. K., & SCHIFFMAN, G. B. (1983). *Dyslexia.* New York: Grune & Stratton.

GOLDBERG, S. S., & KURILOFF, P. J. (1987). Doing away with due process: Seeking alternative dispute resolution in special education. *Education Law Reporter, 43,* 491–496.

GOLDMAN, R. M., FRISTOE, M., & WOODCOCK, R. W. (1976). *Goldman–Fristoe–Woodcock auditory skills test battery.* Circle Pines, MN: American Guidance Service.

GOLDSTEIN, A. P., SPRAFKIN, R. P., GERSHAW, N. J., & KLWIN, P. (1980). *Skillstreaming the adolescent.* Champaign, IL: Research Press.

GOLDSTEIN, S., & GOLDSTEIN, M. (1990). *Managing attention disorders in children: A guide for practitioners.* New York: John Wiley.

GOLDSTEIN, S., STRICKLAND, B., TURNBULL, A. P., & CURRY, L. (1980). An observational analysis of the IEP conference. *Exceptional Children, 46,* 278–286.

GONZALEZ, L. A. (1986). *The effects of first language education on the second language and academic achievement of Mexican immigrant elementary school children in the United States.* Unpublished manuscript,

University of Illinois at Urbana Champaign, College of Education.

GOODMAN, K. S. (1965). Analysis of oral reading miscues: Applied psycholinguistics. *Reading Research Specialist, 6,* 126–135.

_____ (1969). Analysis of reading miscues: Applied psycholinguistics. *Reading Research Quarterly, 5,* 9–30.

_____ (1976). Behind the eye: What happens in reading? In H. Singer & R. B. Ruddell (eds.), *Theoretical models and processes of reading,* 283–325. Newark, DE: International Reading Association.

GOODMAN, Y. M., BURKE, C. L. (1972). *Reading miscue inventory.* New York: Macmillan.

GOODMAN, Y. M., WATSON, D. J., & BURKE, B. L. (1987). *Reading miscue inventory: Alternative procedures.* Katonah, NY: Richard C. Owen.

GORDON, L. V. (1981). *Gordon occupational checklist.* New York: Psychological Corporation.

GRANT, D. A., & BERG, E. A. (1948). A behavioral analysis of degree of reinforcement and loss of shifting to new responses in a Weigl-type card sorting problem. *Journal of Experimental Psychology, 38,* 404–411.

GRAVES, D. (1975). An examination of the writing processes of seven-year old children. *Research in the Teaching of English, 9,* 227–242.

GREEN, M. I. (1977). *A sigh of relief.* New York: Bantam Books.

GREEN, M. I., FORD, C., & FLAMET, T. (eds.) (1971). *Measurement and Piaget.* New York: McGraw–Hill.

GREGG, N. (1986). College learning disabled, normal, and basic writer's sentence combining abilities. *B. C. Journal of Special Education, 10,* 153–166.

_____ (1990). Written expression disorders. In L. Bailet, A. Bain, & L. C. Moats (eds.), *Written language disorders,* 65–98. Austin, TX: PRO-ED.

_____ (in press). Expressive writing disorders. In S. Hooper & G. Hynd (eds.), *Assessment and diagnosis of child and adolescent psychiatric disorders: Current issues and procedures.* New York: LEA.

GREGG, N., & HENRY, N. (1988). *Ideational abstractness—Assessment areas.* Unpublished manuscript, University of Georgia, Department of Special Education, Athens, GA.

GREGG, N., HOY, C., MCALEXANDER, P., & HAYES, C. (1991). Written sentence production patterns of college writers with learning disabilities. *Reading and Writing: An Interdisciplinary Journal, 3,* 169–185.

GREGG, N., HOY, C., & SABOL, R. (1988). Spelling error patterns of normal, learning disabled, and underprepared college writers. *Journal of Psychoeducational Assessment, 6,* 14–23.

GREGG, N., & JACKSON, R. (1989). Dialogue patterns of the nonverbal learning disabilities population—mirrors of self-regulation deficits. *Learning Disabilities: A Multidisciplinary Journal, 1,* 63–71.

GREGG, N., JACKSON, R., HOY, C., & HYND, G. (1989). *Nonverbal learning disabilities.* Neurological and psychiatric applications of topographic brain mapping of EEG and evoked potentials. Boston, MA.

GREGG, N., & MCCARTY, B. (1989). *Audience awareness: Subskills for assessment—an informal assessment.*

Unpublished manuscript, University of Georgia, Athens, GA.

GRESHAM, F. M. (1981a). Assessment of children's social skills. *Journal of School Psychology, 19,* 120–133.

_____ (1981b). Social skills training with handicapped children: A review. *Review of Educational Research, 51,* 139–176.

_____ (1981c). Validity of social skills measures for assessing the social competence in low-status children: A multivariate investigation. *Development Psychology, 17,* 390–398.

GRESHAM, F. M., & ELLIOTT, S. N. (1984). Assessment and classification of children's social skills: A review of methods and issues. *School Psychology Review, 13,* 292–301.

_____ (1990). *Social skills rating system.* Circle Pines, MN: American Guidance Service.

GROSSMAN, H. J. (ed.) (1973). *Manual on terminology and classification in mental retardation.* Washington, DC: American Association on Mental Deficiency.

_____ (ed.) (1977). *Manual on terminology and classification in retardation.* Washington, DC: American Association on Mental Deficiency.

_____ (1983). *Classification in Mental Retardation.* Washington, DC: American Association on Mental Deficiency.

GROWICK, B. (1983). *Computers in vocational rehabilitation: Current trends and future applications.* Washington, DC: NARIC.

GUADALUPE V. TEMPE ELEM. SCHOOL DISTRICT, 587 F. 2d. 1022 (1978).

GUERIN, G. R., & MAIER, A. S. (1983). *Informal assessment in education.* Palo Alto, CA: Mayfield.

GUILFORD, J. P. (1967). *The nature of human intelligence.* New York: McGraw–Hill.

GUMPERZ, J. J., & HERNANDEZ–CHAVEZ, E. (1975). Cognitive aspects of bilingual communication. In E. Hernandez–Chavez, A. D. Cohen, & A. G. Beltramo (eds.), *El-Lenguajge de los Chicanos,* 154–164. Arlington, VA: Center for Applied Linguistics.

GUNDLACH, R. A. (1982). Children as writers: The beginnings of learning to write. In M. Mustrand (ed.), *What writers know: The language process and structure of written discourse,* 129–145. New York: Academic Press.

GUSTAFSSON, J. E. (1984). A unifying model for the structure of the intellectual abilities. *Intelligence, 8,* 179–203.

GUTHRIE, J., SEIFERT, M., BURNHAM, N., & CAPLON, R. (1974). The maze technique to assess and monitor reading comprehension. *The Reading Teacher, 28,* 161–168.

GUYTON, A. C. (1977). *Basic human physiology: Normal function and mechanisms of disease.* Philadelphia, PA: W. B. Saunders.

GUZAITIS, J., CARLIN, J. A., & JUDA, S. (1972). *Diagnosis: An instructional aid (mathematics).* Chicago: Science Research Associates.

HABIGER, M. (1980). *Spelling analysis form.* Unpublished manuscript, University of Georgia, Department of Special Education, Athens, GA.

_____ (1990). *Pragmatics: A review of the literature.* Unpublished paper. Athens, GA: University of Georgia, Learning Disabilities Center.

HABIGER, M., & GREGG, N. (1991). *Pragmatic skills in*

children diagnosed as learning disabled: A critique of the literature. Unpublished manuscript, The University of Georgia, Department of Special Education, Athens, GA.

HAEUSSERMANN, E. (1952). Evaluating the developmental level of cerebral palsied preschool schildren. *The Journal of Genetic Psychology, 80*, 3–23.

HAKUTA, K. (1986). *Mirror of language: The debate on bilingualism.* New York: Basic Books.

HALL, M., MORTEZ, S., & STATOM, J. (1976). A study of early writing. *Language Arts, 53*, 582–585.

HALLIDAY, M. (1975). *Learning how to mean: Explorations in the development of language.* London: Edward Arnold.

HAMMILL, D. D. (1972). Training visual perceptual processes. *Journal of Learning Disabilities, 5*, 552–559.

———— (1991). *Detroit tests of learning aptitude* (3rd ed.). Austin, TX: PRO-ED.

HAMMILL, D. D., & BARTEL, N. R. (1986). *Teaching students with learning and behavior problems* (4th ed.). Boston, MA: Allyn & Bacon.

———— (1990). *Teaching students with learning and behavior problems* (5th ed.). Boston, MA: Allyn & Bacon.

HAMMILL, D. D., BROWN, L., & BRYANT, B. R. (1989). *A consumer's guide to tests in print.* Austin, TX: PRO-ED.

HAMMILL, D. D., BROWN, L., & LARSEN, S. C. (1980). *Test of adolescent language development.* Austin, TX: PRO-ED.

HAMMILL, D. D., BROWN, V. L., LARSEN, S. C., & WIEDERHOLT, J. L. (1987). *Test of adolescent language–2.* Austin, TX: PRO-ED.

HAMMILL, D. D., & LARSEN, S. C. (1974a). The effectiveness of psycholinguistic training. *Exceptional Children, 41*, 5–14.

———— (1974b). The relationship of selected auditory perceptual skills and reading ability. *Journal of Learning Disabilities, 7*, 429–435.

HAMMILL, D. D., & McNUTT, G. (1981). *Correlates of reading.* Austin, TX: PRO-ED.

HAMMILL, D. D., & NEWCOMER, P. (1988). *Test of language development intermediate.* Austin, TX: PRO-ED.

HANNA, G. S., & ORLEANS, J. B. (1982). *Orleans–Hanna algebra prognosis test–revised.* San Antonio, TX: Psychological Corporation.

HARKNESS, S. (1977). Aspects of social environment and first language in rural Africa. In C. E. Snow & C. A. Ferguson (eds.), *Talking to children: Language input and acquisition,* 27–52. Cambridge, MA: Cambridge University Press.

HARPER, R., WREN, A., & MATARZZO, J. (eds.) (1978). *Nonverbal communication: The state of the art.* New York: John Wiley.

HARRIS, A. J. (1970). *How to increase reading ability* (5th ed.). New York: David McKay.

———— (1972). Reading ability. In J. Harris & E. R. Sipay (eds.), *Readings on reading instruction* (2nd ed.), 1–23. New York: David McKay.

HARRIS, A. J., & SIPAY, E. R. (1980). *How to increase reading ability: A guide to developmental and remedial methods* (7th ed.). New York: Longman.

HARRIS–SCHMIDT, G. P., & NOELL, E. A. (1983). Pho-

nology. In C. Wren (ed.), *Language learning disabilities,* 39–84. Rockville, MD: Aspen.

HARSTE, J., BURKE, C., & WOODWARD, V. (1982). Children's language and world: Initial encounters with print. In J. Langer & M. Smith–Burke (eds.), *Reader meets author/bridging the gap,* 79–92. Newark, DE: International Reading Association.

HART, D. (1972). *The Hart sentence completion test for children.* Salt Lake City: Educational Support Systems.

HARTLEY, J., & DAVIES, I. (1976). Preinstructional strategies: The role of pretests, behavioral objectives, overviews and advance organizer. *Review of Educational Research, 46*, 239–265.

HARTLEY, J., & FULLER, J. (1971, Aug./Sept.). The value of slides in lectures: An exploration study. *Visual Education,* 39–41.

HAVINGHURST, R. J. (1972). *Developmental tasks and education* (3rd ed.). New York: Longman.

HAYNES, S., & JENSEN, B. (1979). The interview as a behavioral assessment instrument. *Behavioral Assessment, 1*, 97–106.

HAYWARD, B. J., & WIRT, J. G. (1989). Handicapped and disadvantaged students: Access to quality vocational education. *National Assessment of Vocational Education,* vol. V. Washington, DC: U.S. Department of Education.

HEATH, S. B. (1982). What no bedtime story means: Narrative skills at home and school. *Language in society, 11*, 46–76.

HEATON, R. K. (1981). *A manual for the Wisconsin card sorting test.* Odessa, FL: Psychological Assessment Resources.

HEDBERG, N. L., & STOEL–GAMMON, C. (1986). Narrative analysis: Clinical procedures. *Topics in Language Disorders, 7*, 58–69.

HEDRICK, D., PRATHER, E., & TOBIN, A. (1976). *Sequenced inventory of communication development.* Seattle, WA: University of Washington Press.

HEILMAN, A. W. (1972). *Principles and practices of teaching reading* (3rd ed.). Columbus, OH: Merrill.

HENDRICKSON, A. D. (1983). Prevention or cure? Another look at mathematics learning problems. In D. Carmine, D. Elkind, A. D. Hendrickson, D. Meichenbaum, R. L. Sieben, & F. Smith, *Interdisciplinary voices in learning disabilities and remedial education* (pp. 93–106). Austin, TX: PRO-ED.

HENRY, N. (1988a). *Text organization informal behaviors to observer.* Unpublished manuscript, University of Georgia, Department of Special Education, Athens, GA.

———— (1988b). *Ideational abstractness assessment areas.* Unpublished manuscript, University of Georgia, Department of Special Education, Athens, GA.

HENSING, E. D. (1972). *Children and drugs.* Washington, DC: Association for Childhood Education.

HERBERT, C. H. (1977; 1979; 1983). *Basic inventory of natural language.* Monterey, CA: Publishers Test Service.

HESHUSIUS, L. (1982). At the heart of the advocacy dilemma: A mechanistic world view. *Exceptional Children, 49*, 6–13.

———— (1986). Pedagogy, special education and the lives of young children: A critical futuristic perspective. *Journal of Education, 168*(3), 25–38.

———— (1989). The Newton law mechanistic paradigm, special education, and contours of alternatives: An overview. *Journal of Learning Disabilities, 22,* 403–415.

HIERONYMUS, A. N., HOOVER, H. D., & LINDQUIST, E. K. (1982). *Tests of achievement and proficiency.* Chicago: Riverside.

_____ (1986). *Iowa test of basic skills.* Chicago: Riverside.

HILDRETH, G. (1936). Developmental sequences in name writing. *Child Development, 7,* 291–302.

HILL, A. E., & CARAMAZZA, A. (1989). The graphic buffer and attentional mechanisms. *Brain and Language, 36,* 208–235.

HISKEY, M. S. (1966). *Manual for the Hiskey–Nebraska test of learning aptitude.* Lincoln, NE: Union College Press.

HOBSON V. HANSEN, 327 F. Suppl. 844 (1971).

HODGKINSON, H. (1991). Reform versus reality. *Kappan, 73*(1), 9–16.

HOGAN, T. P. (1975). *Survey of school attitudes.* San Antonio, TX: Psychological Corporation.

HOGAN, T. P., FARR, R. C., PRESCOTT, G. A., & BALOW, I. H. (1986). *MAT6 mathematics diagnostic tests.* San Antonio, TX: Psychological Corporation.

HOLLAND, J. (1985). *The self-directed search.* New York: Psychological Corporation.

HOLZMAN, P. S. LEVY, D. L., & PROCOTOR, L. R. (1976). Smooth pursuit eye movements, attention and schizophrenia. *Archives of General Psychiatry, 33,* 1715–1420.

HOLOWINSKY, I. Z. (1980). Qualitative assessment of cognitive skills. *The Journal of Special Education, 14*(2), 154–163.

HOLTZMAN, W. H., & WILKINSON, C. Y. (1991). Assessment of cognitive ability. In E. V. Hamayan & J. S. Damico (eds.), *Limiting bias in the assessment of bilingual students,* 248–280. Austin, TX: PRO-ED.

HOLVOET, J., & HELMSTETTER, E. (1989). *Medical problems of students with special needs: A guide for educators.* Boston: Little, Brown & Company.

HOWELL, K. W., ZUCHER, S. H., & MOREHEAD, M. K. (1982). *Multilevel academic skills inventory.* San Antonio, TX: Psychological Corporation.

HOY, C. (1986). Preventing learned helplessness. *Academic Therapy, 22*(1), 11–18. The article was reprinted with permission (1987) in *Mart Journal, 6*(4), 7–9.

HRESKO, W. (1988). *Test of early written language.* Austin, TX: PRO-ED.

HRESKO, W. P., & BROWN, L. (1984). *Test of early socioemotional development.* Austin, TX: PRO-ED.

HRESKO, W. P., REID, D. K. & HAMMILL, D. D. (1981). *Test of early language development.* Austin, TX: PRO-ED.

_____ (1982). *Prueba de desarrollo inicial del lenguaje.* Austin, TX: PRO-ED.

HUDSON, F. G., COLSON, S. E., & WELCH, D. L. H. (1989a). *Hudson educational skills: Mathematics.* Austin, TX: PRO-ED.

_____ (1989b). *Hudson educational skills: Reading.* Austin, TX: PRO-ED.

HUDSON, L. (1972). The context of the debate. In K. Richardson, D. Spears, & M. Richards (eds.), *Race and intelligence: The fallacies behind the race—IQ controversy.* Baltimore, MD: Penguin.

HUMPHERYS, L. E., & CIMINERO, A. R. (1979). Parent report measures of child behavior: A review. *Journal of Clinical Child Psychology, 8,* 56–63.

HUNTZE, S., & CCBD SUBCOMMITTEE ON TERMINOLOGY (1985). Statement to support replacing the term seriously emotionally disturbed with the term behaviorally disordered as a descriptor for children and youth who are handicapped by their behavior (Position Paper of CCBD). *Behavioral Disorders, 10,* 167–174.

HURSH, N. C. (1989). Vocational evaluation with learning disabled students: Utilization guidelines for teachers. *Academic Therapy, 25,* 201–215.

HUTT, M. L. (1980). *Michigan picture test–revised.* San Antonio, TX: Psychological Corporation.

HUTTON, J. B., & ROBERTS, T. G. (1986). *Social-emotional dimension scale: A measure of school behavior.* Austin, TX: PRO-ED.

HYMES, D. (1972). Introduction in C. Azden, V. John, & D. Hymes (eds.), *Functions of language in the classroom.* NY: Teachers College Press.

INGRAM, D. (1976). *Phonological disability in children.* London: Elsevier North–Holland.

INSTANT REPORT INSTANT SUMMARY SYSTEM (1988). *Talent Assessment.* Jacksonville, FL: Author.

IRWIN, J. W. (1991). *Teaching reading comprehension processes* (2nd ed.). Englewood Cliffs, NJ: Prentice–Hall.

ISAACSON, S. (1988). Assessing the writing product: Qualitative and quantitative measures. *Exceptional Children, 54,* 582–585.

JACKSON, N. F., JACKSON, D. A., & MONROE, C. (1983). *Getting along with others: Teaching social effectiveness to children.* Champaign, IL: Research Press.

JASTAK, J. F., & JASTAK, S. R. (1979). *Wide range interest opinion test.* Wilmington, DE: Jastak Associates.

_____ (1986). *Wide range achievement test–revised.* Wilmington, DE: Jastak Associates.

JAX, V. A. (1989). Understanding school language proficiency through the assessment of story construction. In A. A. Ortiz & B. A. Ramirez (eds.), *Schools and the culturally diverse exceptional student: Promising practices and future directions,* 45–49. Reston, VA: Council for Exceptional Children.

JENSEN, A. R. (1980). *Bias in mental testing.* New York: The Free Press.

JOHANSSON, C. B. (1986). *Career assessment inventory enhanced version.* Minneapolis, MN: National Computer Systems.

JOHNS, J. (1982). *Advanced reading inventory.* Dubuque, IA: Kendall–Hunt.

JOHNSON, D. J. (1982). Programming for dyslexia: The need for interaction analyses. *Annals of Dyslexia, 32,* 61–70.

_____ (1987). Principles of assessment and diagnosis. In D. J. Johnson & J. W. Blalock (eds.), *Adults with learning disabilities: Clinical studies,* 9–30. Orlando, FL: Grune & Stratton.

JOHNSON, D. J., & MYKLEBUST, H. R. (1967). *Learning disabilities: Educational principles and practices.* New York: Grune & Stratton.

JOHNSON, G. O., & BOYD, H. F. (1981). *Analysis of coping style.* San Antonio, TX: Psychological Corporation.

JOSEPH, J., LINDGREN, J., CREAMER, S., & LANE, K. (1983). *Evaluating special education: A study to pilot techniques using existing data in Skokie School District 68*. Skokie, IL: Skokie School District 68. (ERIC Document Reproduction Services No. ED 227 176).

JUAREZ, M. (1983). Assessment and treatment of minority-language handicapped children: The role of the monolingual speech–language pathologist. *Topics in Language Disorders, 3*, 57–66.

JUNG, C. (1923). *Psychological Types*. New York: Harcourt Brace.

KAMEENUI, E. J., & SIMMONS, D. C. (1990). *Designing instructional strategies: The prevention of academic learning problems*. Columbus, OH: Merrill.

KAMII, M. (1981). Children's ideas about written numbers. *Topics in Learning and Learning Disabilities, 1*(3), 47–59.

KARLSEN, B., MADDEN, R., & GARDNER, E. F. (1984). *Stanford diagnostic reading test* (3rd ed.) San Antonio, TX: Psychological Corporation.

KAUFMAN, A. S., & KAUFMAN, N. L. (1983a). *Kaufman assessment battery for children*. Circle Pines, MN: American Guidance Service.

———— (1983b). *Interpretive manual. Kaufman assessment battery for children*. Circle Pines, MN: American Guidance Service.

———— (1985). *Kaufman test of educational achievement*. Circle Pines, MN: American Guidance Service.

———— (1992). *Kaufman adolescent and adult intelligence test*. Circle Pines, MN: American Guidance Service.

KAUFFMAN, J. M., LLOYD, J. W., LANDRUM, T. J., & WONG, K. L. H. (1988). *Development of a scale for measuring teachers' beliefs about students' behavior: The teacher belief scale (TBS)*. Unpublished manuscript, University of Virginia.

KAVALE, K. (1981). The relationship between auditory perceptual skills and reading ability: A meta-analysis. *Journal of Learning Disabilities, 14*, 539–546.

———— (1982). Meta-analysis of the relationship between visual perceptual skills and reading achievement. *Journal of Learning Disabilities, 15*, 40–51.

KEHLE, T. J., & GUIDUBALDI, J. (1980). Do too many cooks spoil the broth? Evaluation of team placement and individual educational plans on enhancing the social competence of handicapped students. *Journal of Learning Disabilities, 13*, 552–556.

KEIRSEY, D., & BATES, M. (1984). *Please understand me: Character and temperament types*. Del Mar, CA: Prometheus Nemesis.

KEOGH, B. J., & SHEEHAN, R. (1981). The use of developmental test data for documenting handicapped children's progress: Problems and recommendations. *Journal of the Division for Early Childhood, 3*, 42–47.

KEPHART, N. C. (1960). *The slow learner in the classroom*. Columbus, OH: Merrill.

KIRK, S. A. (1940). *Teaching reading to slow learning children*. Boston, MA: Houghton Mifflin.

KIRK, S. A. & KIRK, W. (1971). *Psycholinguistic learning disabilities: Diagnosis remediation*. Urbana, IL: University of Illinois Press.

KIRK, S. A., MCCARTHY, J. J., & KIRK, W. D. (1968). *Illinois test of psycho-linguistic abilities* (rev. ed.). Urbana, IL: University of Illinois Press.

KNITZER, J. (1982). *Unclaimed children*. Washington, DC: Children's Defense Fund.

KOCHHOR, C. (1990). Message from the project director: Policy crossroads for the 1990's, *Policy Network Newsletter, 2*(1), 1, 4, 19.

KOENIG, C., & KUNZELMANN, H. (1980). *Classroom learning screening manual*. San Antonio, TX: Psychological Corporation.

KORCHIN, S. J., & SCHULDBERG, D. (1981). The future of clinical assessment. *American Psychologist, 36*, 1147–1158.

KOSSLYN, S. M. (1981). The medium and the message in mental imagery: A theory. *Psychological Review, 88*, 46–66.

KOVACS, M., & BECK, A. T. (1977). An empirical-clinical approach toward a definition of childhood depression. In J. G. Schulterbrandt & A. Raskin (eds.), *Depression in childhood: Diagnosis, treatment and conceptual models*, 1–25. New York: Raven Press.

KRASHEN, S. D. (1982). *Bilingual education and second language minority students: A theoretical framework*. Los Angeles: Bilingual Education Evaluation, Dissemination, and Assessment Center, School of Education, California State University.

KRATOCHWILL, T. R., & SEVERSON, R. A. (1977). Process assessment: An examination of reinforcer effectiveness and predictive validity. *Journal of School Psychology, 15*, 293–300.

KRUTETSKII, V. A. (1976). *The psychology of mathematical abilities in school children*. Chicago, IL: The University of Chicago Press.

KUDER, G. F. (1960). *Kuder general interest survey–form DD*. Chicago: Science Research Associates.

———— (1985). *Kuder occupational interest survey–form DD*. Chicago: Science Research Associates.

———— (1988). *Kuder general interest inventory–form E*. Chicago: Science Research Associates.

LABERGE, D., & SAMUELS, S. J. (1974). Toward a theory of automatic information processing in reading. *Cognitive Psychology, 6*, 292–323.

———— (1976). Toward a theory of automatic information processing in reading. In H. Singer & R. Ruddell (eds.), *Theoretical models and processes of reading*, 548–579. Newark, DE: International Reading Association.

LAMBERT, N. M., & NICOLL, R. C. (1976). Dimensions of adaptive behavior of retarded and nonretarded public school children. *American Journal of Mental Deficiency, 81*, 135–146.

LANYON, B. P., & LANYON, R. I. (1980). *Incomplete sentences task*. Chicago: Stoelting.

LARRY P. V. RILES, 343, Suppl. 1306 (1971).

LARRY P. V. RILES, 495, F. Supp. 926 (1979).

LARSEN, S. C., & HAMMILL, D. D. (1986). *Test of written spelling–2*. Austin, TX: PRO-ED.

———— (1988). *Handwriting scale of the test of written language–2*. Austin, TX: PRO-ED.

———— (1989). *Test of legible handwriting*. Austin, TX: PRO-ED.

LAU V. NICHOLS, 945. Ct. 786 (1974).

LAYZER, D. (1974). Heritability analyses of IQ scores: Science or numerology? *Science, 183,* 1259–1266.

LAZRUS, P., & STRICHART, S. (eds.) (1986). *Psychoeducational evaluation of children and adolescents with low-incidence handicaps.* New York: Grune & Stratton.

LEE, C., & JACKSON, R. (1992). *Faking it: A look into the mind of a creative learner.* Portsmouth, NH: Boynton/Cook.

LEE, L. (1971). *Northwestern syntax screening test.* Evanston, IL: Northwestern University Press.

LEITER, R. G. (1948). *Leiter international performance scale.* Chicago: Stoelting.

LELAND, H. W. (1978). Theoretical considerations of adaptive behavior. In W. A. Coulter & H. W. Morrow (eds.), *Adaptive behavior: Concepts and measurements.* New York: Grune & Stratton.

LENNEBERG, E. J. (1967). *Biological foundations of language.* New York: John Wiley.

LEONARD, L. B. (1976). *Meaning is child language.* New York: Grune & Stratton.

LEONARD, L., BOLDERS, J. G., & MILLER, J. A. (1976). An examination of the semantical relations reflected in the language usage of normal and language disordered children. *Journal of Speech and Hearing Research, 19,* 371–392.

LEWIS, M. (1973). Infant intelligence tests: Their use and misuse. *Human Development, 16,* 108–118.

LEWIS, R. B. (1983). Learning disabilities and reading: Instructional recommendations from current research. *Exceptional Children, 50*(3), 230–240.

LEWIS, R. B., & DOORLAG, D. H. (1987). *Teaching special students in the mainstream* (2nd ed.). Columbus, OH: Merrill.

LIDZ, C. S. (1987a). *Dynamic assessment: An interactional approach to evaluating learning potential.* New York: Guilford Press.

_____ (1987b). Historical perspectives. In C. S. Lidz (ed.), *Dynamic assessment: An interactional approach to evaluating learning potential,* 3–32. New York: Guilford Press.

LIEBERMAN, A., & MILLER, L. (1986). School improvement: Themes and variations. In A. Lieberman (ed.), *Rethinking school improvement: Research, craft and concept,* 96–111. New York: Teachers College Press.

LINDER, T. W. (1989). *Transdisciplinary play-based assessment: A functional approach to working with young children.* Baltimore, MD: P. H. Brookes.

LOBAN, W. (1963). *The language of elementary school children* (NCTE Research Report No. 1). Urbana, IL: National Council of Teachers of English.

_____ (1976). *Language development: Kindergarten through grade twelve* (Research Report No.18). Champaign, IL: National Council of Teachers of English.

LABOV, W. (1970). The logic of nonstandard English. In F. Williams (ed.), *Language and poverty,* 55–72. Chicago: Markham.

LOCKE, E. A. (1977). An empirical study of lecture notetaking among college students. *Journal of Educational Research, 71,* 93–99.

LOCUS, E. V. (1980). *Semantic and pragmatic language disorders: Assessment and remediation.* Rockville, MD: Aspen.

LONG, N. J. (1990). Comments on Ralph Gardner's "Life space interviewing: It can be effective, but don't . . . ," *Behavioral Disorders, 15,* 119–126.

LUFTIG, R. L. (1987a). The stability of children's peer social status over social situations. *Education, 103,* 49–55.

_____ (1987b). Children's loneliness, perceived ease in making friends, and estimated social adequacy. *Child Study Journal, 17,* 35–55.

_____ (1989). *Assessment of learners with special needs.* Boston, MA: Allyn & Bacon.

LUND, N. J., & DUCHAN, J. F. (1983). *Assessing children's language in naturalistic contexts.* New York: Prentice Hall.

_____ (1988). *Assessing children's language in naturalistic contexts.* Englewood Cliffs, NJ: Prentice-Hall.

LUNDELL, K., BROWN, W., & EVANS, J. (1976). *Criterion test of basic skills.* Novato, CA: Academic Therapy Publications.

LUQUET, G. H. (1913). *Les dessins d'un enfant: Etude psychologique* (Child drawings: A psychological study). Paris: Libraire Felix Alcan.

LURIA, A. R. (1961). An objective approach to the study of the abnormal child. *American Journal of Orthopsychiatry, 31,* 1–14.

_____ (1969). On the pathology of computational operations. In J. Kilpatrick and I. Wirszup (eds.), *Soviet studies in the psychology of learning and teaching mathematics, volume I,* 37–74. Chicago: University of Chicago Press.

_____ (1980). *Higher control functions in man.* New York: Basic Books.

LUSTHAUS, C. S., LUSTHAUS, E. W., & GIBBS, H. (1981). Parents' role in the decision process. *Exceptional Children, 48,* 256–257.

LUTZ, C., & LEVINE, R. A. (1982). Culture and intelligence in infancy: An ethnopsychological view. In M. Lewis (ed.), *Origins of intelligence: Infancy and early childhood.* New York: Plenum Press.

LYON, J. (1975). Deixis as the source of reference. In E. L. Keenan (ed.), *Formal semantics of natural language.* Cambridge, England: Cambridge University Press.

LYNCH, E. W., & LEWIS, R. B. (1987). Multicultural considerations. In K. A. Kavale, S. R. Forness, & M. Bender (eds.), *Handbook of learning disabilities, Vol. 1, Dimensions and diagnosis,* 399–416. Boston, MA: College Hill.

LYTLE, S. (1982). *Exploring comprehension style: A study of twelfth-grade readers' transactions with text.* Unpublished doctoral dissertation, University of Pennsylvania, Philadelphia.

MACDONALD, T. (1978). *Oliver: Parent-administered communication inventory.* Columbus, OH: Merrill.

MACGINITIE, W. (1978). *Gates–MacGinitie reading tests* (2nd ed.). Chicago: Riverside.

MAGER, R. (1975). *Preparing instructional objectives.* Belmont, CA: Fearon.

MARGOLIS, H., & MCGETTIGAN, J. (1988). Managing resistance to instructional modifications in mainstreamed environments. *Remedial and Special Education, 9,* 15–21.

MARKWARDT, F. C. (1989). *Peabody individual achievement tests–revised.* Circle Pines, MN: American Guidance Service.

MARSH, H. (1988). *Self-description questionnaire I, II and III*. San Antonio, TX: Psychological Corporation.

MARSHALL V. STATE OF GEORGIA, 282 S. E. 2d. 301, 248 Ga. 227 (1984).

MARTIN, N. (1971). What are they up to? In A. Jones & J. Mulford (eds.), *Children using language*, 79–86. London: Oxford University Press.

MARTIN, R. P. (1985). Ethics column. *The School Psychologist, 39*, 9.

MARYLAND ASSOC. FOR RETARDED CHILDREN (MARC) V. STATE OF MARYLAND, Equity No. 100/182/77676 (Cir. Ct., Baltimore Cty., 1974).

MATHINAS, D. A. (1988). Communicative competence of children with learning disabilities. *Journal of Learning Disabilities, 21*, 437–443.

MATTES, L. J., & OMARK, D. R. (1984). *Speech and language assessment for bilingual handicapped*. San Diego: College Hill Press.

MATTIE T. V. HOLLADAY, 522 F. Supp. 72 (1975).

MATTISON, R. E., & HOOPER, S. R. (1992). The history of modern classification of child and adolescent psychiatric disorders: An overview. In S. R. Hooper, G. W. Hynd, & R. E. Mattison (eds.), *Child psychopathology: Diagnostic criteria and clinical assessment*, 1–21. Hillsdale, NJ: Erlbaum.

MAZE, M. (1984). How to select a computerized guidance system. *Journal of Counseling and Development, 63*, 158–161.

MCARTHUR, D. S., & ROBERTS, G. E. (1982). *Roberts apperception test for children*. Los Angeles, CA: Western Psychological Services.

MCCARNEY, S. B., & LEIGH, J. E. (1990). *Behavior evaluation scale* (2nd ed.). Austin, TX: PRO-ED.

MCCARTHY, D. (1954). Language development in children. In A. Mussen (ed.), *Carmichael's manual of child psychology*, 352–370. New York: John Wiley.

MCCULLOUGH, C. M. (1963). *McCullough word analysis test*. Boston, MA: Ginn.

MCGAIG, R. (1981). A district-wide plan for the evaluation of student writing. In S. Haley–James (ed.), *Perspective on writing in grades 1–8*, 79–96. Urbana, IL: National Council of Teachers of English.

MCGARRY, J., & FINAN, P. L. (1982). *Implementing Massachusetts' special education law: A statewide assessment. Final report*. Boston, MA: Massachusetts State Department of Education. (ERIC Document Reproduction Service No. ED 226 542).

MCGHEE, P. E. (1979). *Humor: Its origin and development*. San Francisco: Freeman.

MCGINNIS, E., & GOLDSTEIN, A. P. (1984). *Skillstreaming the elementary school child*. Champaign, IL: Research Press.

MCLOUGHLIN, J. A. (1985). Training educational diagnosticians. *Diagnostic, 10*, 176–196.

MCLOUGHLIN, J. A., & LEWIS, R. B. (1981). *Assessing special students*. Columbus, OH: Merrill.

———— (1990). *Assessing special students* (3rd ed.). Columbus, OH: Merrill.

MCNEIL, M. R., & PRESCOTT, T. E. (1978). *Revised token test for adults*. Austin, TX: PRO-ED.

MDC STAFF (1974). *MDC behavior identification format*. Stout, WI: Material Development Center, University of Wisconsin Press.

MECHAM, M. J. (1989). *Utah test of language development*. Chicago: Riverside.

MEHAW, H., HERTWECK, A., & MEIHLS, J. L. (1986). *Handicapping the handicapped: Decision making in student's educational careers*. Palo Alto, CA: Stanford University Press.

MELLON, J. C. (1969). *Transformational sentence combining: A method for enhancing the development of syntactic fluency in English composition* (Research Report, No. 10). Urbana, IL: National Council of Teachers of English.

MERCER, C. D. (1983). *Students with learning disabilities* (2nd ed.). Columbus, OH: Merrill.

MERCER, C. D., & MERCER, A. (1985). *Teaching students with learning problems* (2nd ed.). Columbus, OH: Merrill.

MERCER, J. R. (1979). *System of multicultural pluralistic assessment technical manual*. New York: The Psychological Corporation.

MERCER, J. R., & LEWIS, J. F. (1977). *Adaptive behavior inventory for children*. San Antonio, TX: Psychological Corporation.

MERINO, B. J., & SPENCER, M. (1983). The comparability of English and Spanish versions of oral language proficiency instruments. *National Association for Bilingual Education Journal, 7*, 1–31.

MEYEN, E. (1981). *Developing instructional units for the regular and special teacher* (3rd ed.). Dubuque, IA: Wm. C. Brown.

MEYERS, J. (1987). The training of dynamic assessors. In C. S. Lidz (ed.), *Dynamic assessment: An interactional approach to evaluating learning potential*, 403–425. New York: Guilford Press.

MEYERS, J., & LYTLE, S. (1986). Assessment of the learning process. *Exceptional Children, 53* (2), 138–144.

MEYERS, J., PFEFFER, J., & ERLBAUM, V. (1985). Process assessment: A model for broadening assessment. *Journal of Special Education, 19*, 73–89.

MICHAEL, W. B., SMITH, R. A., & MICHAEL, J. J. (1984). *Dimensions of self-concept*. San Diego, CA: EDITS.

MILLER, G. A., & GILDEA, P. M. (1987). How children learn words. *Scientific American, 257*, 94–99.

MILLER, J. F., & YODER, D. (1984). *Miller–Yoder test of grammatical comprehension*. Austin, TX: PRO-ED.

MILLS V. BOARD OF EDUC. OF THE DISTRICT OF COLUMBIA, 348 F. Supp. 866 (1972).

MINICK, B. A., & SCHOOL, B. A. (1982). The IEP process: Can computers help? *Academic Therapy, 18*, 41–48.

MITCHELL, J. V., JR. (ED.) 1983). *Tests in print III*. Lincoln, NE: University of Nebraska Press.

MODGIL, C., & MODGIL, S. (1976). *Piagetian Research*, Vol. 4, London: NFER Publishing.

MOERK, E. L. (1975). Verbal interactions between children and their mothers during the preschool years. *Developmental Psychology, 11*, 788–794.

MOFFETT, J. M., & WAGNER, B. J. (1983). *Student-centered language arts and reading, K–13: A handbook for teachers*. Boston: Houghton Mifflin.

MORRISSEY, P. A., & SAFER, N. (1977). The individualized education program: Implications for special education. *Viewpoints, 53,* 31–38.

MOSES, N., KLEIN, H., & ALTMAN, E. (1990). An approach to assessing and facilitating casual language in adults with learning disabilities based on Piagetian theory. *Journal of Learning Disabilities, 23,* 220–228.

MOSES, N., & PAPISH, M. A. (1984). Mainstreaming from a cognitive perspective. *Learning Disabilities Quarterly, 7,* 212–220.

MULLIKEN, R. K., & BUCKLEY, J. J. (1983). *Assessment of multihandicapped and developmentally disabled children.* Rockville, MD: Aspen.

MURRAY, H. A., & BELLAK, L. (1973). *Thematic apperception test.* San Antonio, TX: Psychological Corporation.

MYKLEBUST, H. R. (1954). *Auditory disorders in children.* New York: Grune & Stratton.

_____ (1960). *Psychology of deafness.* New York: Grune & Stratton.

_____ (1965). *Development and disorders of written language: Picture story language test.* New York: Grune & Stratton.

_____ (ed.) (1968). *Progress in learning disabilities, volume 1.* Orlando, FL: Grune & Stratton.

_____ (1973a). *Development and disorders of written language: Studies of normal and exceptional children.* New York: Grune & Stratton.

_____ (1973b). *Picture story language test.* Orlando, FL: Grune & Stratton.

_____ (1975). *Nonverbal learning disabilities.* New York: Grune & Stratton.

_____ (1978). Toward a science of dyslexiology. In J. R. Myklebust (ed.), *Progress in learning disabilities, 4,* 1–40. New York: Grune & Stratton.

NADLER, B., & SHORE, K. (1980). Individualized education programs: A look at realities. *Education Unlimited, 2,* 30–34.

NASLUND, R. A., THORPE, L. P., & LEFEVER, D. W. (1985). *SRA achievement series.* Chicago: Science Research Associates.

NAY, N. R. (1979). *Multimethod Clinical Assessment.* New York: Gardner Press.

NEEPER, R., LAHEY, B. B., & FRICK, P. J. (1990). *Comprehensive behavior rating scale for children.* San Antonio, TX: Psychological Corporation.

NEFF, W. S. (1968). *Work and human behavior.* New York: Alberton Press.

NELSON, K. (1973). Structure and strategy in learning to talk. *Monographs of the Society for Research in Child Development, 69,* 409–415.

_____ (1974). Concept, word, and sentence: Interrelationship in acquisition and development. *Psychological Review, 81,* 267–285.

_____ (1985). *Making sense: The acquisition of shared meaning.* New York: Academic Press.

NEVIN, A., SEMMEL, M. I., & MCCANN, S. (1983). What administrators can do to facilitate the regular classroom teacher's role in implementing individualized educational plans: An empirical analysis. *Planning and Changing, 14,* 150–169.

NEWBORG, J., STOCK, J., WNEK, L., GUIDUBALDI, J., & SVINICKI, J. (1984). *Battelle developmental inventory.* Allen, TX: DLM Teaching Resources.

NEWCOMER, P. L. (1980). *Understanding and teaching emotionally disturbed children.* Boston, MA: Allyn & Bacon.

_____ (1986). *Standardized reading inventory.* Austin, TX: PRO-ED.

NEWCOMER, P. L., & HAMMILL, D. D. (1988). *Test of language development–2, primary.* Austin, TX: PRO-ED.

NEWLAND, T. E. (1971). *Blind learning aptitude test.* Champaign, IL: University of Illinois Press.

NEWPORT, E. (1977). Motherese: The speech of mothers to young children. In N. J. Castellan, D. Pisoni, & G. Potts (eds.), *Cognitive theory (Vol. 2),* 96–120. Hillsdale, NJ: Erlbaum.

NIHIRA, K. (1969). Factorial dimensions of adaptive behavior in adult retardates. *American Journal of Mental Deficiency, 73,* 868–878.

_____ (1976). Dimensions of adaptive behavior in institutionalized mentally retarded children and adults. *American Journal of Mental Deficiency, 81,* 215–226.

NIHIRA, K., LAMBERT, N., & LELAND, H. (1993a). *AAMR adaptive behavior scales–school, second edition.* Austin, TX: PRO-ED.

_____ (1993b). *AAMR adaptive behavior scales–residential and community, second edition.* Austin, TX: PRO-ED.

NIPPOLD, M. A. (1988). *Later language development: Ages nine through nineteen.* Austin, TX: PRO-ED.

NIPPOLD, M. A., CUYLER, T. S., & BRAUNBECK-PRICE, R. (1988). Explanation of ambiguous advertisements: A developmental study with children and adolescents. *Journal of Speech and Hearing Research, 23,* 49–60.

NOELL, E. A. (1983). Reading. In C. T. Wren (ed.), *Language learning disabilities: Diagnosis and remediation,* 243–296. Rockville, MD: Aspen.

N. Y. ASSOCIATION FOR THE BLIND (1966). *The flashcard vision test for children.* New York: Low Vision Lens Service.

NYE, C., & SEAMAN, D. (1985). *The effectiveness of language intervention for the language/learning disabled: A meta-analysis.* Paper presented at the Symposium on Research in Child Language Disorders, Madison, WI.

OAKLAND, J. (1983). Concurrent and predictive validity estimates for the WISC–R IQs and ELPs by racial-ethnic and SES groups. *School Psychology Review, 12,* 57–61.

OBLER, L. K. (1985). Language through the life-span. In J. Berko–Gleason (ed.), *The development of language,* 277–305. Columbus, OH: Merrill.

O'DONNELL, R. C. (1976). A critique of some indices of syntactic maturity. *Research in the Teaching of English, 16,* 31–38.

O'DONNELL, R. C., & HUNT, K. (1975). Syntactic maturity test. In W. J. Fagan, C. R. Cooper, & J. M. Jensen (eds.), *Measures for research and evaluation in the English language arts.* Urbana, IL: National Council of Teachers of English.

O'HARE, F. (1973). *Sentence combining: Improving student writing without formal grammar instruction*

(Research Report, No. 15). Urbana, IL: National Council of Teachers of English.

OLLER, D. K. (1974). Simplification as the goal of phonological processes in child speech. *Language Learning, 24*, 299–303.

——— (1978). Discussion summary: Origins of syntax, semantics, and pragmatics. In F. D. Minifie & L. L. Lloyd (eds.), *Communicative and cognitive abilities—Early behavioral assessment,* 475–480. Baltimore: University Park Press.

OLSHAVSKY, J. (1976/77). Reading as problem solving: An investigation of strategies. *Reading Research Quarterly, 12*, 654–674.

ORTIZ, A. A. (1984). Choosing the language of instruction for exceptional bilingual children. *Teaching Exceptional Children, 16*, 208–212.

ORTIZ, A. A., & MALDONANDO–COLON, E. (1986). Reducing inappropriate referrals of language minority students to special education. In A. C. Willig & H. F. Greenberg (eds.), *Bilingualism and learning disabilities,* 37–52. New York: American Library.

ORTIZ, A. A., & POLYZOI, E. (1989). Language assessment of Hispanic learning disabled and speech and language handicapped students: Research in progress. In A. A. Ortiz & B. A. Ramirec (eds.), *Schools and the culturally diverse exceptional student: Promising practices and future decisions,* 32–34. Reston, VA: The Council for Exceptional Children.

ORTIZ, A. A., & YATES, J. R. (1983). Incidence of exceptionality among Hispanics: Implications for manpower planning. *Journal of the National Association for Bilingual Education, 7*, 41–53.

——— (1984). Linguistically and culturally diverse handicapped students. In R. Podemski, B. Price, T. Smith, & G. March II (eds.), *Comprehensive administration of special education,* 114–141. Rockville, MD: Aspen.

ORTONY, A., TURNER, T. J., & LARSON–SHAPIRO, N. (1985). Cultural and instructional influences on figurative language comprehension by inner city children. *Research in the Teaching of English, 19*, 25–36.

OSBORN, W. J. (1925). Ten reasons why pupils fail in mathematics. *The Mathematics Teacher, 18*, 234–238.

OSMAN, B. B. (1979). *Learning disabilities: A family affair.* New York: Random House.

OTIS, A., & LENNON, R. (1979). *Otis-Lennon school ability test.* New York: Psychological Corporation.

OWENS, R. E. (1984). *Language development: An introduction.* Columbus, OH: Merrill.

——— (1988). *Language development: An introduction.* Columbus, OH: Merrill.

PADELFORD, W. B. (1969). The influence of socioeconomic level, sex and ethnic background and the relationship between reading achievement and self-concept. Unpublished doctoral dissertation, University of California, Los Angeles.

PALINESAR, A. S., & BROWN, A. L. (1984). Reciprocal teaching of comprehension—fostering and monitoring activities. *Cognition and Instruction, 1*, 117–175.

PARENTS IN ACTION ON SPECIAL EDUCATION V. JOSEPH P. HANNON, 506 F. Supp. 831 (1980).

PAULSON, F. L., PAULSON, P. R., & MEYER, C. A. (1991). What makes a portfolio a portfolio? *Educational Leadership, 48*(5), 60–63.

PAVLIDIS, G. (1987). The rote of eye movements in the diagnosis of dyslexia. In G. Pavlidis & D. F. Fisher (eds.), *Dyslexia: Its neuropsychology and treatment,* 97–110. New York: John Wiley.

PAYAN, R. M. (1989). Language assessment for the bilingual exceptional child. In L. M. Baca & H. T. Cervantes (eds.), *The bilingual special education interface,* 125–152. Columbus, OH: Merrill.

PEABODY CHILD STUDY CENTER (1974). *Peabody intellectual performance scale–experimental edition.* Nashville, TN: Author.

PELLEGRINI, T., & GALDA, L. (1990). Children's play, language, and early literacy. *Topics in Language Disorders, 10*, 76–88.

PELLEGRINO, J. W., & GOLDMAN, S. R. (1990). Cognitive science perspective on intelligence and learning disabilities. In H. L. Swanson & B. Keogh (eds.), *Learning disabilities: Theoretical and research issues,* 41–58. Hillsdale, NJ: Erlbaum.

PENALOSA, F. (1975). Chicano lingualism and multiglossa. In C. Eilterwandez–Chavez, A. D. Cohen, & A. F. Beltramo (eds.), *El-Lenguaje de los chicanos,* 164–170. Arlington, VA: Center for Applied Linguistics.

PENNSYLVANIA ASSOCIATION FOR RETARDED CHILDREN (PARC) V. COMMONWEALTH OF PENNSYLVANIA, 343 F. Supp. 279 (1971).

PERKINS SCHOOL FOR THE BLIND (1980). *Perkins–Binet.* Boston, MA: Author.

PETERS, A. (1983). *The units of language acquisition.* New York: Cambridge University Press.

PETERSON, C., & MCCABE, A. (1983). *Developmental psycholinguistics: Three ways of looking at a child's narrative.* New York: Plenum Press.

PETERSON, D. R. (1968). *The clinical study of social behavior.* Englewood Cliffs, NJ: Prentice-Hall.

PHADEBAS RAST IN FOOD ALLERGY (1982). Piscataway, NJ: Pharmacy Diagnostics.

PHELPS, J., STEMPEL, L., & SPECK, G. (1982). *Children's handwriting evaluation scale—a new diagnostic tool.* Unpublished manuscript, University of Houston.

PHILLIPS, E. L. (1978). *The social skills basis of psychopathology: Alternative to abnormal psychology and psychiatry.* New York: Grune & Stratton.

PIAGET, J. (1952). *The origins of intelligence in children.* New York: Norton.

——— (1962). *Play, dreams and imitation in childhood.* New York: Norton.

——— (1965). *The moral judgment of the child.* New York: Free Press.

——— (1971). *Insights and illusions of philosphy.* New York: Thomas J. Crowell.

PIAGET, J., & INHELDER, B. (1985). *The growth of logical thinking from childhood to adolescence.* New York: Basic Books.

PIERS, E. V., & HARRIS, D. B. (1984). *The Piers–Harris children's self-concept scale: Revised manual.* Los Angeles: Western Psychological Services.

PINARD, A., & LAURENDEAU, M. A. (1964). A scale of mental development based on the theory of Piaget:

Description of a project. *Journal of Research in Science Teaching, 2,* 253–260.

PLATA, M. (1982). *Assessment, placement, and programming of bilingual exceptional pupils: A practical approach.* Reston, VA: ERIC Clearinghouse on Handicapped & Gifted Children, The Council for Exceptional Children.

POOR, C. (1975). Vocational assessment potential. *Archives of Physical Medicine and Rehabilitation, 56,* 33–36.

POPLIN, M. (1985). Reductionism from the medical model to the classroom: The past, present, and future of learning disabilities. *Research Communications in Psychology, Psychiatry, and Behavior, 10*(122), 37–70.

PORCH, B. E. (1971). *Porch index of communicative ability in children.* New York: Consulting Psychologists Press.

PORTER, R. B., & CATTELL, R. B. (1982). *Children's personality questionnaire.* San Antonio, TX: Psychological Corporation.

POWER, P. W. (1991). *A guide to vocational assessment* (2nd ed.). Austin, TX: PRO-ED.

PRESCOTT, G. A., BALON, I. H., HOGAN, T. P., & FARR, R. C. (1987). *Metropolitan Achievement Tests* (6th ed.). San Antonio, TX: Psychological Corporation.

PRESIDENT'S COMMITTEE ON MENTAL RETARDATION (1970). *The six-hour retarded child.* Washington, DC: U.S. Government Printing Office.

PUGACH, M. C. (1982). Regular classroom teacher involvement in the development and utilization of IEPs. *Exceptional Children, 48,* 371–374.

QUALITY EDUCATION FOR MINORITIES PROJECT (1990). *Education that works: An action place for the education of minorities.* Cambridge, MA: The M.I.T. Press.

QUAY, H. C., & PETERSON, D. R. (1987). *Revised behavior problem checklist.* Coral Gables, FL: University of Miami.

RABINOVITCH, R. D. (1968). Reading problems in children: Definitions and classifications. In A. H. Keeney & V. T. Kenney (eds.), *Dyslexia: Diagnosis and treatment of reading disorders,* 1–10. St. Louis, MO: C. V. Mosby.

RAPP, B. C., & CARAMAZZA, A. (1989). Letter processing in reading and spelling: Some dissociations. *Reading and Writing: An Interdisciplinary Journal, 1,* 3–23.

RAPPLEYEA, S., & CHOPPA, A. J. (1989). Planning for transitions into the adult world. *LDA Newsbriefs, 24*(6), 6–7.

RAVEN, J. C. (1960). *Guide to using the standard progressive matrices.* London: H. K. Lewis.

RAVEN, J. C., COURT, J. H., & RAVEN, J. (1977). *Raven's progressive matrices.* London: H. K. Lewis.

READ, C. (1971). Preschool children's knowledge of English orthography. *Harvard Educational Review, 17,* 241–243.

REDL, F. (1959). The concept of the life space interview. *American Journal of Orthopsychiatry, 29,* 1–18.

REED, C. E. (1981). Teaching teachers about teaching writing to students from varied linguistic social and cultural groups. In M. F. Whiteman (ed.), *Writing: The nature, development, and teaching of written communication,* 139–152. New York: LEA.

REES, N. (speaker) (1988). *Pragmatics: A retrospective analysis.* (cassett recording H 8118-110). Rockville, MD: American Speech Language Hearing Association.

REID, D. K. (1988). *Teaching the learning disabled: A cognitive developmental approach.* Boston, MA: Allyn & Bacon.

REID, D. K., & HRESKO, W. P. (1981). *A cognitive approach to learning disabilities.* Toronto: McGraw–Hill.

REID, D. K., HRESKO, W. P., & HAMMILL, D. D. (1989). *Test of early reading ability–2.* Austin, TX: PRO-ED.

REID, J. B., KAVANAGH, K., & BALDWIN, D. V. (1987). Abusive parents' perceptions of child problem behaviors: An example of parental bias. *Journal of Abnormal Child Psychology, 15,* 457–466.

REISMAN, F. (1978). *A guide to the diagnostic teaching of arithmetic* (2nd ed.). Columbus, OH: Merrill.

———— (1985). *Sequential assessment of mathematics inventories–standardized inventory.* San Antonio, TX: Psychological Corporation.

REISMAN, F., & KAUFFMAN, S. H. (1980). *Teaching mathematics to children with special needs.* Columbus, OH: Merrill.

RESCHLY, D. J. (1979). Nonbiased assessment. In G. D. Phye & D. J. Reschly (eds.), *School psychology: Perspectives and issues,* 165–215. New York: Academic Press.

REYNOLDS, C. R., & RICHMOND, B. O. (1985). *Revised children's manifest anxiety scale.* Los Angeles, CA: Western Psychological Services.

REYNOLDS, W. M. (1987a). *Wepman's auditory discrimination test manual* (2nd ed.). Los Angeles, CA: Western Psychological Services.

———— (1987b). *Reynolds adolescent depression scale.* San Antonio, TX: Psychological Corporation.

REYNOLDS, W. M., ANDERSON, G., & BARTELL, N. (1985). Measuring depression in children: A multimethod assessment investigation. *Journal of Abnormal Child Psychology, 13,* 513–526.

RICHARD, G., & HAMMER, M. A. (1985). *Language processing test.* Moline, IL: Lingui System.

RICHEK, M. A., LIST, L. K., & LERNER, J. W. (1983). *Reading diagnosis: Diagnosis and remediation.* Englewood Cliffs, NJ: Prentice–Hall.

RICHMOND, B. O., & KICKLIGHTER, R. H. (1980). *Children's adaptive behavior scale.* Atlanta, GA: Humanics.

RIPICH, D., & SPENELLI, F. (eds.) (1985). *School discourse problems.* San Diego, CA: College Hill Press.

RISKO, V. J. (1981). Reading. In D. D. Smith (ed.), *Teaching the learning disabled.* Englewood Cliffs, NJ: Prentice–Hall.

RITTER, E. M. (1979). Social perspective taking ability, cognitive complexity and listener adapted communication in early and late adolescence. *Communication Monographs, 46,* 40–51.

RIZZO, J. V., & ZABEL, R. H. (1988). *Educating children and adolescents with behavioral disorders: An integrative approach.* Boston, MA: Allyn & Bacon.

ROACH, E. F., & KEPHART, N. C. (1966). *The Purdue perceptual motor survey.* Columbus, OH: Merrill.

ROBERTS, G. H. (1968). The failure strategies of third

grade arithmetic pupils. *The Arithmetic Teacher, 15,* 442–446.

ROBERTS, J. E., & CRAIS, E. R. (1989). Assessing communication skills. In D. B. Baily & M. Wolery (eds.), *Assessing infants and preschoolers with handicaps,* 339–389. Columbus, OH: Merrill.

ROELTGEN, D. (1985). Agraphia. In K. M. Heilman & E. Valenstein (eds.), *Clinical Neuropsychology,* 85–110. New York: Oxford University Press.

ROGOFF, B. (1990). *Apprenticeship in thinking: Cognitive development in social context.* New York: Oxford University Press.

RONDAL, J. (1980). Father's and mother's speech in early language development. *Journal of Child Language, 7,* 353–371.

RORSCHACH, H. (1921). *Psychodiagnostics: A diagnostic test based on perception.* New York: Grune & Stratton.

ROSE, M. (1989). *Lives on the boundary: The struggles and achievement of America's underprepared.* New York: Free Press.

ROSENZWEIG, S. (1978). *Aggressive behavior and the Rosenzweig picture-frustration study.* New York: Praeger.

ROTH, F., & SPEKMAN, N. (1986). Narrative discourse: Spontaneously generated stories of learning disabled and normally achieving students. *Journal of Speech and Hearing Disorders, 51,* 8–23.

ROTTER, J., & RAFFERTY, J. (1950). *Manual: The Rotter incomplete sentence blank.* New York: Psychological Corporation.

ROURKE, B. P. (1985). *Neuropsychology of learning disabilities: Essentials of subgroup analysis.* New York: Guildford Press.

RUBIN, D. L. (1982). Adapting syntax in writing to varying audiences as a function of age and social cognitive ability. *Journal of Child Language, 9,* 497–510.

———— (1984). Social cognition and written communication. *Written Communication, 1,* 211–243.

RUMMELHART, D., LINDSAY, P., & NORMAN, D. (1972). A process model for long-term memory. In E. Tulvining & R. Donaldson (eds.), *Organization of memory,* 67–89. New York: Academic Press.

SABIA, J., & YSSELDYKE, J. (1988). *Assessment in special and remedial education* (4th ed.). Boston, MA: Houghton Mifflin.

SACHS, J., & DEVIN, J. (1976). Young children's use of age-appropriate speech styles in social interaction and role playing. *Journal of Child Language, 3,* 81–98.

SAILOR, W., & GUESS, D. (1983). *Severely handicapped students: An instructional design.* Boston, MA: Houghton Mifflin.

SAILOR, W., & MIX, B. (1975). TARC assessment system. Lawrence, KA: H & H Enterprises.

SALVIA, J., & HUGHES, C. (1990). *Curriculum-based assessment: Testing what is taught.* New York: Macmillan.

SALVIA, J., & YSSELDYKE, J. (1988). *Assessment in special and remedial education* (4th ed.). Boston, MA: Houghton Mifflin.

SATTLER, J. M. (1988). *Assessment of children* (3rd ed.). San Diego, CA: J. M. Sattler.

SAVIN, H. B., & PERCHONOCK, E. (1965). Grammatical structure and the immediate recall of English sentences. *Journal of Verbal Learning and Verbal Behavior, 4,* 348–353.

SCARDAMALIA, M., BEREITER, C., & GOELMAN, H. (1982). The role of production factors in writing ability. In M. Nystrand (ed.), *What writers know: The language process, and structure of written language,* 173–210. New York: Academic Press.

SCARDAMALIA, M., BEREITER, C., & MCDONALD, T. D. S. (1977, April). *Role-taking in written communication investigated by manipulating anticipatory knowledge.* Paper read at the annual meeting of the American Educational Research Association.

SCARPAH, S. (1992). Vocational assessment. In H. L. Swanson & B. L. Watson (eds.), *Educational and psychological assessment of exceptional children: Theories, strategies, and applications,* 309–338. St. Louis, MO: C. V. Mosby.

SCHANK, R., & ABELSON, R. (1977). *Scripts, plans, goals, and understanding.* Hillsdale, NJ: Erlbaum.

SCHEFLIN, A. E. (1967). On the structuring of human communication. *American Behavior Scientist, 10,* 8–12.

SCHEIBE, C., & COPNDRY, J. (1987). *Learning to distinguish fantasy from reality: Children's beliefs about Santa Claus and other fantasy figures.* Poster session presented at the biannual meeting of the Society for Research in Child Development, Baltimore, MD.

SCHENCK, S. J. (1980). The diagnostic/instructional link in individualized education programs. *Journal of Special Education, 14,* 337–345.

———— (1981). An analysis of IEPs for LD youngsters. *Journal of Learning Disabilities, 14,* 221–223.

SCHNEIDER, M. F. (1989). *Children's apperceptive storytelling test.* Austin, TX: PRO-ED.

SCHUCKITT, M. A. (1984). *Drug and alcohol abuse: A clinical guide to diagnosis and treatment* (2nd ed.). New York: Plenum Press.

SCHUMAKER, J. B., DESHLER, D. D., ALLEY, G. R., & WARNER, M. M. (1983). Toward the development of an intervention model for learning disabled adolescents: The University of Kansas Institute. *Exceptional Education Quarterly, 4*(1), 45–74.

SCHUMAKER, J. B., DESHLER, D. D., & ELLIS, E. (1986). Intervention issues related to the education of LD adolescents. In J. K. Torgesen & B. Wong (eds.), *Psychological and educational perspectives on learning disabilities,* 329–360. New York: Academic Press.

SCHWARTZ, L., & MCKINLEY, N. L. (1984). *Daily communication: Strategies for the language disordered adolescent.* Eau Claire, WI: Thinking Publications.

SCOTT, C. M. (1984). Adverbial connectives in conversations of children 6 to 12. *Journal of Child Language, 11,* 423–452.

SCOVILLE, R. P., & GORDON, A. M. (1980). Children's understanding of factive presuppositions: An experiment and a review. *Journal of Child Language, 7,* 381–399.

SCRIBNER, S., & COLE, M. (1973). Cognitive consequences of formal and informal education. *Science, 82,* 552–559.

SEARLE, J. (1960). *Speech acts.* New York: Cambridge University Press.

SEARLE, J. (1969). *Speech acts.* Cambridge, MA: Harvard University Press.

SEAY, T. A., & ALTEVKRUSE, M. K. (1979). Verbal and nonverbal behavior in judgments of cafilitative conditions. *Journal of Counseling Psychology, 26,* 18–119.

SEMEL, E., & WIIG, E. (1982). *Clinical language intervention program.* Columbus, OH: Merrill.

SEMEL, E., WIIG, E., & SECORD, J. (1987). *Clinical evaluation of language fundamentals–revised.* San Antonio, TX: Psychological Corporation.

SEWELL, T. E. (1987). Dynamic assessment as a nondiscriminatory procedure. In C. S. Lidz (ed.), *Dynamic assessment: An interactional approach to evaluating learning potential,* 426–443. New York: Guilford Press.

SHANKWEILER, D., LIBERMAN, I. Y., MARK, L. S., FOWLER, C. A., & FISHER, F. W. (1979). The speed code and learning to read. *Journal of Experimental Psychology, Human Learning and Memory, 5,* 531–545.

SHAPIRO, E. S., & LENTZ, K. E. (1991). Vocational technical programs: Follow-up studies of students with learning disabilities. *Exceptional Children, 6,* 47–59.

SHAUGNESSY, M. P. (1977). *Errors and expectations: A guide for the teacher of basic writing.* New York: Oxford University Press.

SHUB, A. N., CARLIN, J. A., FRIEDMAN, R. L., KAPLAN, J. M., & KATIEN, J. C. (1973). *Diagnosis: An instructional reading aid.* Chicago: Science Research Associates.

SHULTZ, J. J., FLORIO, S., & ERICKSON, F. (1982). Where's the floor? Aspects of the cultural organization of social relationships in communication at home and in school. In P. Gilmore and A. A. Glatthorn (eds.), *Children in and out of school,* 27–39. Washington, DC: Center for Applied Linguistics.

SILVAROLI, N. J. (1986). *Classroom reading inventory* (5th ed.). Dubuque, IA: Brown.

SILVER, L., & CONNERS, C. K. (1989, February). *The ritalin controversy.* Paper presented at the meeting of the Association for Children & Adults with Learning Disabilities, Miami, Florida.

SIMON, C. S. (1985a). The language learning disabled student: Description and therapy implications. In C. S. Simon (ed.), *Communication skills and classroom success: Therapy methodologies for language learning disabled students.* San Diego, CA: College Hill Press.

——— (1985b). *Communication skills and classroom success.* San Diego, CA: College Hill Press.

SIMPSON, R. L. (1990). *Conferencing parents of exceptional children* (2nd ed.). Austin, TX: PRO-ED.

SIPERSTEIN, G. N. (1988). Students with learning disabilities in college: The need for a programmatic approach to critical transitions. *Journal of Learning Disabilities, 21,* 431–436.

SITLINGTON, P. L. (1979). The assessment process as a component of career education. In G. M. Clark & W. J. White (eds.), *Career education for the handicapped: Current perspective for teachers.* Boothwyn, PA: Educational Resources.

SKRTIC, T. M. (1987). An organizational analysis of special education reform. *Counterpoint, 8,*(2), 15–19.

SLINGERLAND, B. (1970). *Slingerland screening tests for identifying children with specific language disabilities.* Cambridge, MA: Educators Publishing Service.

SLOAN, W., & BIRCH, J. W. (1955). A rationale for degrees of retardation. *American Journal of Mental Deficiency, 60,* 258–264.

SLOBAN, D. (1967). *A field manual for cross-cultural study of the acquisition of communicative competence.* Berkeley, CA: University of California.

SLOSSEN R. L. (1963). *Slossen oral reading test.* East Aurora, NY: Slossen Educational Publications.

SMITH, D. D. (1981). *Teaching the learning disabled.* Englewood Cliffs, NJ: Prentice–Hall.

SMITH, F. (1988). Professional judgment in the diagnosis of specific learning disability. In GLRS (ed.), *SLD Eligibility Conference Handbook,* 88–95. Atlanta, GA: Metro East and West Georgia Learning Resources System.

SMITH, J. W. A. (1976). Children's emphasis of metaphor: A Piagetion interpretation. *Language and Speech, 19,* 236–243.

SMITH, M. E. (1926). An investigation of the development of the sentence and the extent of vocabulary in young children. *Studies in Child Welfare, 3*(5). Iowa City, IA: University of Iowa Press.

——— (1933). The influence of age, sex, and situation on the frequency, form and function of questions asked by preschool children. *Child Development, 4,* 201–213.

——— (1941). Measurement of size of general English vocabulary. *Genet Psychological Monograpgh, 24,* 311–345.

SMITH, P. J. (1980). Linguistic information in spelling. In U. Frith (ed.), *Cognitive processing in spelling,* 67–82. London: Academic Press.

SMITH, S. W. (1990). Individualized education programs (IEPs) in special education—from intent to acquiescence. *Exceptional Children, 57,* 6–14.

SMITH, S. W., & SIMPSON, R. L. (1989). An analysis of individualized education programs (IEPs) for students with behavior disorders. *Behavioral Disorders, 14,* 107–116.

SNOW, C. (1972). Mother's speech to children learning language. *Child Development, 43,* 549–565.

SONTE, A. (1989). Improving the effectiveness of strategy training for learning disabled students: The role of communication dynamics. *Remedial and Special Education, 10,* 35–42.

SOVIK, N. (1984). The effects of a remedial tracking program on writing performance of dysgraphic children. *Scandinavian Journal of Educational Research, 28,* 129–147.

SOVIK, N., ARNTZEN, O., & THYGESEN, R. (1986). Effects of feedback training on "normal" and dysgraphic students. In H. R. S. Kao (ed.), *Graphonomics: Contemporary research in handwriting.* North Holland, Amsterdam.

SPACHE, G. D. (1981a). *Diagnostic reading scales* (rev. ed.). Monterey, CA: CTB/McGraw–Hill.

——— (1981b). *Diagnosing and correcting reading disabilities.* Boston, MA: Allyn & Bacon.

SPACHE, G. D., & SPACHE, E. B. (1977). *Reading in the elementary school* (4th ed.). Boston, MA: Allyn & Bacon.

SPANGLER V. PASADENA BOARD OF EDUCATION, 311 F. Suppl. 501 (1970).

SPEARMAN, C. E. (1923). *The nature of intelligence and the principles of cognition.* London: Macmillan.

—— (1927). *The abilities of man.* New York: Macmillan.

SPARROW, S. S., BALLA, D. A., & CICCHETTI, D. V. (1984). *Vineland adaptive behavior scales.* Circle Pines, MN: American Guidance Service.

SPIELBERGER, C. D., EDWARDS, C. D., LUSHENE, R. E., MONTUORI, J., & PLATZEK, D. (1973). *State-trait anxiety inventory for children.* Palo Alto, CA: Consulting Psychological Press.

SPIVACK, G., HAINES, P. E., & SPOTTS, J. (1967). *Devereux adolescent behavior rating scale.* Devon, PA: Devereux Foundation.

SPIVACK, G., & SPOTTS, J. (1966). *Devereux child behavior rating scale manual.* Devon, PA: Devereux Foundation.

STAUFFER, R. G. (1976). Reading as cognitive functioning. In H. Singer & R. B. Ruddell (eds.), *Theoretical models and processes of reading,* 156–193. Newark, DE: International Reading Association.

STEIN, N. L. (1979). How children understand stories: A developmental analysis. In L. Resnick & P. Weaver (eds.), *Theory and practice of early reading* (Vol. 2), 36–150. Hillsdale, NJ: Erlbaum.

STEIN, N. L., & GLENN, C. G. (1979). An analysis of story comprehension in elementary school children. In R. O. Fredle (ed.), *Advances in discourse processing, (vol. 2), new directions,* 53–120. Norwood, NJ: Ablex.

STEPHENS, T. M. (1982a). *Criterion-referenced curriculum–mathematics.* San Antonio, TX: Psychological Corporation.

—— (1982b). *Criterion-referenced curriculum–reading.* San Antonio, TX: Psychological Corporation.

STEPHENS, T. (1978). *Social skills in the classroom.* Columbus, OH: Cedars Press.

STERNBERG, R. J. (1986). *Intelligence applied: Understanding and increasing your intellectual skills.* San Diego, CA: Harcourt Brace Jovanovich.

STERNBERG, R. J., & WAGNER, R. K. (1982). Automatization failure in learning disabilities. *Topics in Learning and Learning Disabilities, 2*(2), 1–11.

STEWART ET AL. V. PHILLIPS ET AL., Civil Action No. 70-1199F, October, 1970.

STILLMAN, R. (ed.) (1978). *Callier–Azusa scale.* Dallas, TX: University of Texas.

STONE, A., & WERSTCH, J. (1984). A social interaction analysis of learning disabilities remediation. *Journal of Learning Disabilities, 17,* 194–199.

STONE, C. A. (1989). Improving the effectiveness of strategy training for learning disabled students: The role of communicated dynamics. *Remedial and Special Education, 10*(1), 35–42.

STRAUSS, A. A., & LEHTINEN, L. E. (1947). *Psychopathology and education of the brain-injured child* (Vol. 1). New York: Grune & Stratton.

STRAYHORN, J. M., & STRAIN, P. S. (1986). Social and language skills for preventive mental health: What, how, who, and when. In P. S. Strain, M. J. Guralnick, & H. M. Walker (eds.), *Children's social behavior: Development,* assessment, and modification, 287–330. Orlando, FL: Academic Press.

STRICKLAND, D. S., & MORROW, L. M. (1990). Emerging readers and writers: Sharing big books. *The Reading Teacher, 43,* 342–343.

STRICKLAND, R. (1969). *The language arts in the elementary school.* Lexington, MA: D.C. Heath.

STRONG, E. K., CAMPBELL, D. P., & HANSEN, J. (1985). *The Strong–Campbell interest inventory.* Minneapolis, MN: National Computer Systems.

STRONG, W. (1973). *Sentence combining: A composing book.* New York: Random House.

SUCHER, F., & ALLRED, R. A. (1981). *New Sucher–Allred reading placement inventory.* Oklahoma City: Economy.

SULZER-AZAROFF, B., & MAYER, G. R. (1977). *Applying behavior analysis procedures with children and youth.* New York: Holt, Rinehart & Winston.

SURITSKY, S. K., & HUGHES, C. A. (1990). Benefits of notetaking: Implications for secondary and postsecondary students with learning disabilities. *Learning Disabilities Quarterly, 14,* 7–18.

SWABY, B. E. R. (1984). *Teaching and learning reading: A pragmatic approach.* Boston: Little, Brown & Company.

SWAN, G. E., & MCDONALD, M. L. (1978). Behavior therapy in practice: A national survey of behavior therapists. *Behavior Therapy, 9,* 799–807.

SWANSON, H. L. (1978). Verbal encoding effects on the visual short-term memory of learning disabled and normal readers. *Journal of Educational Psychology, 70,* 539–544.

—— (1986). Verbal coding deficits in learning disabled readers. In S. Ceci (ed.), *Handbook of cognitive, social and neuropsychological aspects of learning disabilities (vol. 1),* 203–228. Hillsdale, NJ: Erlbaum.

SWANSON, H. L., & WATSON, B. L. (1989). *Educational and psychological assessment of exceptional children* (2nd ed.). Columbus, OH: Merrill.

SWIFT, M. (1982). *Devereux elementary school behavior rating scale–II manual* (2nd ed.). Devon, PA: Devereux Foundation.

TALBOTT, G. D., & COONEY, M. (1982). *Today's disease: Alcohol and drug dependence.* Springfield, IL: Charles C Thomas.

TARC (1975). *Topeka association for retarded children (TARC) assessment system.* Lawrence, KS: H & H Enterprises.

TARVER, S. G., HALLAHAN, D. P., KAUFFMAN, J. M., & BALL, D. W. (1976). Verbal rehearsal and selective attention in children with learning disabilities: A developmental lag. *Journal of Experimental Child Psychology, 22,* 375–385.

TAYLOR, E. (1980). Development of attention. In M. Rutter (ed.), *Scientific foundations of development psychiatry,* 348–368. London: Heinemann Medical Books.

TERMAN, L. M., & MERRILL, M. A. (1960). *Stanford–Binet intelligence scale.* Boston, MA: Houghton Mifflin.

THARP, R. G., & GILLMORE, R. (1988). Rousing minds to life. *Teaching, learning and schooling in social context.* New York: Cambridge University Press.

THORNDIKE, R. L. (1927). *The measurement of intelli-*

gence. New York: Bureau of Publications, Teachers College, Columbia University.

THORNDIKE, R. L., & HAGEN, E. (1986). *Cognitive abilities test.* Chicago: Riverside.

THORNDIKE, R. L., HAGEN, E. P., & SATTLER, J. M. (1986). *Technical manual, Stanford–Binet intelligence scale* (4th ed.). Chicago: Riverside.

THORUM, A. R. (1986). *Fullerton language test for adolescents* (2nd ed.). Chicago: Riverside.

THURSTONE, L. L. (1938). Primary mental abilities. *Psychometric Monographs,* No. 1.

TIEGS, B., & CLARK, L. (1978). *California achievement tests.* New York: McGraw–Hill.

TIFFIN, R. (1948). *Examiner manual for the Purdue pegboard.* Chicago: Science Research Associates.

TISHER, M., & LANG, M. (1983). The children's depression scale: Review and further developments. In D. P. Cantwell & G. A. Carlson (eds.), *Affective disorder in childhood and adolescence: An update,* 375–415. New York: Spectrum.

TORGESEN, J. K. (1977). The role of nonspecific factors in the task performance of learning disabled children: A theoretical assessment. *Journal of Learning Disabilities, 10,* 5–17.

———— (1979). What shall we do with psychological processes? *Journal of Learning Disabilities, 12,* 514–521.

———— (1980). The use of efficient task strategies by learning disabled children: Conceptual and educational implications. *Journal of Learning Disabilities, 13,* 364–371.

TORGESEN, J. K., & GREENSTEIN, J. J. (1982). Why do some learning disabled children have problems remembering? Does it make a difference? *Topics in Learning and Learning Disabilities, 2*(2), 54–61.

TORGESEN, J. K., & HOUCK, G. (1980). Processing deficiencies in learning disabled children who perform poorly on the digit span task. *Journal of Educational Psychology, 72,* 142–160.

TORRANCE, P., & MYERS, P. (1970). *Creative learning and teaching.* Dodd: Mead.

TOUGH, J. (1977). *Talking and learning.* London: Wod Lock Educational.

TUCKER, B. P., & GOLDSTEIN, B. A. (1990). *Legal rights of persons with disabilities: An analysis of federal law.* Horshum, PA: LRD Publishers.

TUCKER, J. A. (1980). Ethnic proportion in classes for the learning disabled: Issues in nonbiased assessment. *Journal of Special Education, 14,* 93–105.

TUDDENHAM, R. D. (1970). A "Piagetian" test of cognitive development. In B. Dockrell (ed.), *On intelligence,* 32–51. London: Methuen.

TURNBELL, H. R. (1986). *Free appropriate public education: The law and children with disabilities.* Denver, CO: Love.

ULIBARI, D. M., SPENCER, M. L., & RIVAS, G. A. (1980). *Comparability of three oral language proficiency instruments and their relationship to achievement variables.* San Francisco, CA: AMERICAS Behavioral Research Corporation.

UNDERHILL, R. (1988). Mathematics learners' beliefs: A review. *Focus on Learning Problems in Mathematics, 10*(1), 55–69.

UNDERHILL, R. G., UPRICHARD, A. E., & HEDDENS, J.

W. (1980). *Diagnosing mathematical difficulties.* Columbus, OH: Merrill.

URIS, T. (1970). *The executive deskbook.* New York: Van Reinold.

U.S. DEPARTMENT OF LABOR (1970). *Manual of the USES general aptitude test battery, section 1.* Washington, DC: U.S. Government Printing Office.

———— (1981). The interest checklist. In R. Aero & E. Weiner (eds.), *The mind test,* 137–141. New York: Morrow.

UZGIRIS, I. C., & HUNT, J. M. (1975). *Assessment in infancy: Ordinal scales of psychological development.* Urbana, IL: University of Illinois Press.

VALADEZ, C. M. (1981). Identity, power, and writing skills: The case of the Hispanic bilingual student. In M. F. Whitman (ed.), *Writing: The nature, development, and teaching of written communication* (Vol. 1), 167–178. New York: LEA.

VALENCIA, S. (1990). A portfolio approach to classroom reading assessment: The whys, whats, and hows. *Reading Teacher, 43,* 338–340.

VALPAR INTERNATIONAL (1982). *MESA Program.* Tucson, AZ: Author.

VAN KLEECH, A. (1983). Metalinguistic skills: Cutting across spoken and written language and problem-solving abilities. In G. Wallach & K. Butler (eds.), *Language learning disabilities in school-aged children,* 128–153. Baltimore, MD: Williams & Wilkins.

VOCATIONAL EVALUATION AND WORK ADJUSTMENT ASSOCIATION (1975). The tool of vocational evaluation. *Vocational Evaluation and Work Adjustment Bulletin, 8,* 49–64.

VOCATIONAL RESEARCH INSTITUTE (1989). *The APTICOM Aptitude test battery.* Philadelphia, PA: Author.

VOGEL, S. A. (1974). Syntactic abilities in normal and dyslexic children. *Journal of Learning Disabilities, 7,* 103–109.

———— (1975). *Syntactic abilities in normal and dyslexic children.* Baltimore, MD: University Park Press.

VYE, N. J., BURNS, S., DELDOS, V. R., & BRANSFORD, J. D. (1987). A comprehesive approach to assessing intellectually handicapped children. In C. S. Lidz (ed.), *Dynamic assessment: An interactional approach to evaluating learning potential.* New York: Guilford Press.

VYGOTSKY, L. S. (1956). *Izbrannie psibhlogischeskie issledovania* (Selected psychological research). Moscow: Izdatel'stvo Akademii Pedagogicheskikh Nauk.

———— (1962). *Thought and language,* E. Hanfmann & G. Vakar (trans.). Cambridge, MA: The M.I.T. Press. (Original work published 1934).

———— (1978a). Interaction between learning and development. In L. S. Vytogsky, *Mind in society: The development of higher psychological processes,* M. Cole, V. Jon-Steiner, S. Scribner, & E. Souberman, (eds. & trans.), 79–91. Cambridge, MA: Harvard University Press. (Original work published 1935).

———— (1978b). *Mind and society: The development of higher psychological processes.* Cambridge, MA: Harvard University Press.

———— (1987). Thinking and speech. In R. W. Rieber & A. S. Carton (eds.), *The collected works of L. S. Vygotsky,* N. Minich (trans.), 375–383. New York: Plenum Press.

WADE, J., & KASS, C. (1987). Component deficit and academic remediation of learning disabilities. *Journal of Learning Disabilities, 20,* 441–447.

WAGMAN, R. (ed.) (1982). *The new complete medical and health encyclopedia* (Vols. 1–4). New York: Lexicon.

WALKER, B. J. (1988). *Diagnostic teaching of reading.* Columbus, OH: Merrill.

WALKER, H. M. (1983). *Walker problem behavior identification checklist* (rev.). Los Angeles, CA: Western Psychological Services.

WALKER, H. M., & FABRE, R. (1987). Assessment of behavior disorders in the school setting: Issues, problems, and strategies revised. In N. Hering (ed.), *Assessing and managing behavior disorders,* 198–234. Seattle, WA: University of Washington Press.

WALKER, H. M., & MCCONNELL, S. R. (1988). *Walker–McConnell scale of social competence and school adjustment.* Austin, TX: PRO-ED.

WALKER, H. M., MCCONNELL, S. R., HOLMES, P., TODIS, B., WALKER, B. J., & GOLDEN, N. (1983). *The Walker social skills curriculum.* Austin, TX: PRO-ED.

WALLACE, G., & KAUFFMAN, J. (1986). *Teaching students with learning and behavior problems* (3rd ed.). Columbus, OH: Merrill.

WALLACH, G. P., & LIEBERGOTT, J. W. (1984). Who shall be called "learning disabled"? Some new directions. In G. P. Wallach & K. G. Butler (eds.), *Language learning disabilities in school-aged children,* 1–14. Baltimore, MD: Williams & Wilkins.

WECHSLER, D. (1958). *The measurement and appraisal of adult intelligence.* (4th ed.). Baltimore: Williams & Wilkins.

———— (1974). *Manual for the Wechsler Intelligence Scale for Children-Revised.* San Antonio: The Psychological Corporation.

———— (1981a). *Manual for the Wechsler Adult Intelligence Scale-Revised.* San Antonio: The Psychological Corporation.

———— (1981b). *Wechsler adult intelligence scale of intelligence–revised.* San Antonio, TX: Psychological Corporation.

———— (1982). *Manual para la Escala de Inteligencia Wechsler–Revisada.* New York: The Psychological Corporation.

———— (1989). *Wechsler preschool and primary scale of intelligence–revised.* San Antonio, TX: Psychological Corporation.

———— (1991). *Wechsler intelligence scale for children* (3rd ed.). San Antonio, TX: Psychological Corporation.

WEHMAN, P., MOON, M. S., EVERSON, J. M., WOOD, W., & BARCUS, J. M. (1988). *Transition from school to work: New challenges for youth with severe disabilities.* Baltimore, MD: P. H. Brookes.

WEIDERHOLT, L. J. (1986). *Formal reading inventory.* Austin, TX: PRO-ED.

WEINBERG, W. A., & MCLEAN, A. (1986). A diagnostic approach to developmental specific learning disorders. *Journal of Child Neurology, 2,* 158–172.

WEISS, C., LILLYWHITE, H., & GORDON, M. (1980). *Clinical management of articulation disorders.* St. Louis, MO: C. V. Mosby.

WELLER, C., & STRAWSER, S. (1981). *Weller–Strawser scales of adaptive behavior for the learning disabled.* Novato, CA: Academic Therapy Publication.

WEPMAN, J. M. (1975). *Auditory discrimination test* (rev. 1973). Palm Springs, CA: Research Associates.

WERNER, E. O'H., & KRESHECK, J. (1974). *Structured photographic expressive language test–II.* Sandwich, IL: Janelle.

WERTSCH, J. V., & STONE, C. A. (1985). The concept of internalization in Vygotsky's account of the genesis of higher mental functions. In J. V. Wertsch (ed.), *Culture, communication, and cognition: Vygotskian perspectives,* 162–179. New York: Cambridge University Press.

WESTENDORF, D. K., CAPE, E. L., & SKRTIC, T. M. (1982). *A naturalistic study of postsecondary setting demands.* Unpublished manuscript, The University of Kansas.

WESTMAN, J. C. (1990). *Handbook of learning disabilities: A multisystem approach.* New York: Alllyn & Bacon.

WESTBY, C. (1984). Development of narrative language abilities. In G. Wallach & K. Butler (eds.), *Language learning disabilities in school-aged children,* 103–270. Baltimore, MD: Williams & Wilkins.

WHITE, B., KABON, B. J., & ATTANUCCI, J. S. (1979). *The origins of human competence—the final report of the Harvard preschool report.* Lexington, MA: D. C. Heath.

WHITE, O. R., & HARING, N. G. (eds.) (1980). *Exceptional teaching* (2nd ed.). Columbus, OH: Merrill.

WHITEMAN, M. F. (1976). *Dialect influence and the writing of black and white working class Americans.* Unpublished dissertation, Georgetown University.

WIEDERHOLT, J. L., & BRYANT, B. R. (1986). *Gray oral reading tests revised.* Austin, TX: PRO-ED.

WIIG, G. H. (1982a). Language disabilities in the school-age child. In J. H. Shames & E. H. Wiig (eds.), *Human communication disorders: An introduction,* 2–27. Columbus, OH: Merrill.

———— (1982b). *Let's talk: Developing prosocial communication skills.* Columbus, OH: Merrill.

———— (1982c). *Let's talk inventory for adolescents.* Columbus, OH: Merrill.

———— (1985). *Words, expressions, and contexts: A figurative language program.* San Antonio, TX: Psychological Corporation.

———— (1989). *Steps to language competence: Developing metalinguistic strategies.* New York: Psychological Corporation.

———— (1990). Linguistic transitions and learning disabilities: A strategic learning perspective. *Learning Disability Quarterly, 13,* 128–140.

WIIG, E. H., & BRAY, C. M. (1983). *Let's talk for children.* Columbus, OH: Merrill.

WIIG, E. H., & SECORD, W. (1985). *Test of language competence.* San Antonio, TX: Psychological Corporation.

———— (1989). *Test of language competence–expanded.* San Antonio, TX: Psychological Corporation.

WIIG, E. H., & SEMEL E. (1975). Productive language abilities in learning disabled adolescents. *Journal of Learning Disabilities, 8,* 578–586.

———— (1976). *Language disabilities in children and adolescents.* Columbus, OH: Merrill.

———— (1984). *Language assessment & intervention for the learning disabled* (2nd ed.). Columbus, OH: Merrill.

WILEN, P. K., & SWEETING, C. V. (1986). Assessment of limited English proficient Hispanic students. *School Psychology Review, 15,* 59–75.

WILL, M. C. (1986). Educating children with learning problems: A shared responsibility. *Exceptional Children, 52,* 411–415.

WILLIAMS, R., & WOLFRAM, W. (1972). *Social dialects: Differences vs. disorders.* Washington, DC: American Speech and Hearing Association.

WILLIAMSON, G. G. (ed.) (1987). *Children with Spina Bifida: Early intervention and preschool programming.* Baltimore, MD: P. H. Brookes.

WILLIG, A. C., SWEDO, J. J., & ORTIZ, A. A. (1987). *Characteristics of teaching strategies which result in high task engagement for exceptional limited English proficient Hispanic students.* Austin, TX: University of Texas, Handicapped Minority Research Institute in Language Proficiency.

WIRT, R. D., LACHAR, D., KLINEDINST, J. K., & SEAT, P. D. (1977/1984). *Multidimensional description of child personality: A manual for the personality inventory for children* (1984 revision by D. Lachar). Los Angeles, CA: Western Psychological Services.

WISCONSIN TESTS OF READING SKILLS DEVELOPMENT: WORD ATTACK, STUDY SKILLS AND COMPREHENSION (1972, 1977). Developed by the Evaluation and Reading Project staffs at the Wisconsin Research and Development Center for Cognitive Learning. Madison, WI: Learning Multi-Systems.

WITT, J. C., ELLIOTT, S. N., GRESHAM, F. M., & KRAMER, J. J. (1988). *Assessment of special children: Tests and the problem-solving process.* Glenview, IL: Scott, Foresman & Company.

WITT, J. C., & MARTENS B. (1984). Adaptive behavior: Tests and assessment issues. *School Psychology Review, 13,* 478–484.

WITT, J. C., MILLER, C. D., MCINTYRE, R. M., & SMITH, D. (1984). Effects of variables on parental perceptions of staffings. *Exceptional Children, 51,* 27–32.

WOBER, M. (1972). Culture and the concept of intelligence: A case in Uganda. *Journal of Cross-Cultural Psychology, 3,* 327–328.

WOLF, D. P. (1989). Portfolio assessment: Sampling student work. *Educational Leadership, 46*(7), 35–40.

WOLF, M., & DICKINSON, D. (1985). From oral to written language: Transitions in the school years. In J. Berki-Gleason (ed.), *The development of language,* 227–276. Columbus, OH: Merrill.

WOOD, M. L. (1982). *Language disorders in school-age children.* Englewood Cliffs, NJ: Prentice–Hall.

WOOD, M. M. (ed.) (1975). *Developmental therapy: A textbook for teachers as therapists for emotionally disturbed young children.* Baltimore, MD: University Park Press.

WOODCOCK, R. W. (1980). *Woodcock language proficiency battery. English form.* Allen, TX: DLM Teaching Resources.

———— (1981). *Woodcock language proficiency battery. Spanish form.* Allen, TX: DLM Teaching Resources.

———— (1987). *Woodcock reading mastery tests–revised.* Circle Pines, MN: American Guidance Service.

WOODCOCK, R. W., & JOHNSON, M. B. (1977). *Woodcock-Johnson psychoeducational battery.* Allen, TX: DLM Teaching Resources.

———— (1989). *Woodcock–Johnson psychoeducational battery–revised.* Allen, TX: DLM Teaching Resources.

WOODS, M. L., & MOE, A. J. (1989). *Analytical reading inventory* (4th ed.). Columbus, OH: Merrill.

WOODWARD, M. (1963). The application of Piaget's theory to research in mental deficiency. In N. R. Ellis (ed.), *Handbook of mental deficiency,* 27–52. New York: McGraw-Hill.

WOOLFOLK–CARROW, E., & LYNCH, J. (1983). *An integrative approach to language disorder in children.* New York: Grune & Stratton.

WYCKOFF, L. H. (1984). *Narrative and procedural discourse following closed head injury.* Unpublished doctoral dissertation. Gainesville, FL: University of Florida.

YANDO, R., SEITZ, V., & ZIGLER, E. (1979). *Intellectual and personality characteristics: Social class and ethnic group differences.* Hillsdale, NJ: Erlbaum.

YATES, J. R. (1987). Demography as it affects special education. In A. Ortiz & B. Ramirez (eds.), *Schools and the culturally diverse exceptional student: Promising practices and future decisions,* 1–5. Reston, VA: The Council for Exceptional Children.

You and your allergy (1990). Piscataway, NJ: Pharmacia Diagnostics.

ZACHMAN, L., JORGENSEN, C., HUISINGH, R., & BARRETT, M. (1984). *Test of problem solving.* Moline, IL: LinguiSystems.

ZAH, G. L. (1973). Cognitive integration of verbal and social information in spoken sentences. *Journal of Experimental Social Psychology, 9,* 320–334.

ZIGMOND, N., VALLECORSA, A., & SILVERMAN, R. (1983). *Assessment for intructional planning in special education.* Englewood Cliffs, NJ: Prentice–Hall.

ZINTZ, M. V. (1970). *The reading process: The teacher and the learner.* Dubuque, IA: William C. Brown.

ZWEIG, R. (1971). *Fountain Valley teacher support system in reading.* Huntington Beach, CA: Richard Zweig Associates.

Name Index

Subject Index